# Accounting

## THE MANAGERIAL CHAPTERS

### NINTH EDITION

**Charles T. Horngren**
*Stanford University*

**Walter T. Harrison Jr.**
*Baylor University*

**M. Suzanne Oliver**
*University of West Florida*

**Prentice Hall**

Boston   Columbus   Indianapolis   New York   San Francisco   Upper Saddle River
Amsterdam   Cape Town   Dubai   London   Madrid   Milan   Munich   Paris   Montréal   Toronto
Delhi   Mexico City   São Paulo   Sydney   Hong Kong   Seoul   Singapore   Taipei   Tokyo

*VP/Editorial Director*: Sally Yagan
*Editor-in-Chief*: Donna Battista
*Director of Marketing*: Kate Valentine
*Director of Editorial Services*: Ashley Santora
*VP/Director of Development*: Steve Deitmer
*Editorial Project Manager*: Rebecca Knauer
*Editorial Assistant*: Jane Avery
*Development Editor*: Shannon LeMay-Finn
*Director of Product Development, Media*:
   Zara Wanlass
*Editorial Media Project Manager*: Allison Longley
*Production Media Project Manager*: John Cassar
*Marketing Manager*: Maggie Moylan
*Marketing Assistant*: Kimberly Lovato
*Senior Managing Editor, Production*:
   Cynthia Zonneveld

*Production Project Manager*: Lynne Breitfeller
*Permissions Project Manager*: Hessa Albader
*Senior Operations Specialist*: Diane Peirano
*Senior Art Director*: Jonathan Boylan
*Cover Design*: Jonathan Boylan
*Cover Photos*: Sideways Design\Shutterstock;
   iStockphoto; Bruno Ferrari\Shutterstock;
   Francesco Ridolfi\Dreamstime LLC -Royalty Free
*Composition*: GEX Publishing Services
*Full-Service Project Management*:
   GEX Publishing Services
*Printer/Binder*: Courier Kendallville
*Cover Printer*: Lehigh Phoenix
*Typeface*: 10/12 Sabon

Credits and acknowledgments borrowed from other sources and reproduced, with permission, in this textbook appear on appropriate page within text.

Sonica83\Dreamstime LLC -Royalty Free pp. 773, 813, 880, 924, 962, 1010, 1050, 1105, 1151

Library of Congress Cataloging-in-Publication Data

Horngren, Charles T.
   Accounting / Charles T. Horngren, Walter T. Harrison Jr., M. Suzanne Oliver. -- 9th ed.
      p. cm.
   Includes bibliographical references and index.
   ISBN 978-0-13-256905-7 (casebound : alk. paper) -- ISBN 978-0-13-256901-9 (pbk. : alk. paper) -- ISBN 978-0-13-256904-0 (pbk. : alk. paper)   1. Accounting.  I. Harrison, Walter T.  II. Oliver, M. Suzanne.  III. Title.
   HF5636.H667 2012
   657--dc22
                           2010053113

10 9 8 7 6 5 4 3 2 1

**Prentice Hall**
is an imprint of

www.pearsonhighered.com

ISBN-13: 978-0-13-256904-0
ISBN-10: 0-13-256904-3

# About the Authors

**Charles T. Horngren** is the Edmund W. Littlefield professor of accounting, emeritus, at Stanford University. A graduate of Marquette University, he received his MBA from Harvard University and his PhD from the University of Chicago. He is also the recipient of honorary doctorates from Marquette University and DePaul University.

A CPA, Horngren served on the Accounting Principles Board for six years, the Financial Accounting Standards Board (FASB) Advisory Council for five years, and the Council of the AICPA for three years. For six years he served as a trustee of the Financial Accounting Foundation, which oversees the FASB and the Government Accounting Standards Board.

Horngren is a member of the Accounting Hall of Fame.

A member of the AAA, Horngren has been its president and its director of research. He received its first annual Outstanding Accounting Educator Award.

The California Certified Public Accountants Foundation gave Horngren its Faculty Excellence Award and its Distinguished Professor Award. He is the first person to have received both awards.

The AICPA presented its first Outstanding Educator Award to Horngren.

Horngren was named Accountant of the Year, in Education, by the national professional accounting fraternity, Beta Alpha Psi.

Professor Horngren is also a member of the IMA, from whom he has received its Distinguished Service Award. He was a member of the institute's Board of Regents, which administers the CMA examinations.

**Walter T. Harrison, Jr.,** is professor emeritus of accounting at the Hankamer School of Business, Baylor University. He received his BBA degree from Baylor University, his MS from Oklahoma State University, and his PhD from Michigan State University.

Professor Harrison, recipient of numerous teaching awards from student groups as well as from university administrators, has also taught at Cleveland State Community College, Michigan State University, the University of Texas, and Stanford University.

A member of AAA and the AICPA, Professor Harrison has served as chairman of the Financial Accounting Standards Committee of AAA, on the Teaching/Curriculum Development Award Committee, on the Program Advisory Committee for Accounting Education and Teaching, and on the Notable Contributions to Accounting Literature Committee.

Professor Harrison has lectured in several foreign countries and published articles in numerous journals, including *Journal of Accounting Research*, *Journal of Accountancy*, *Journal of Accounting and Public Policy*, *Economic Consequences of Financial Accounting Standards*, *Accounting Horizons*, *Issues in Accounting Education*, and *Journal of Law and Commerce*.

Professor Harrison has received scholarships, fellowships, and research grants or awards from PriceWaterhouse Coopers, Deloitte & Touche, the Ernst & Young Foundation, and the KPMG Foundation.

**M. Suzanne Oliver** is an accounting instructor at the University of West Florida in Pensacola, Florida. She received her BA in accounting information systems and her MA in accountancy from the University of West Florida.

Oliver began her career in the tax department of a regional accounting firm, specializing in benefit plan administration. She has served as a software analyst for a national software development firm and as the Oracle fixed assets analyst for Spirit Energy, formerly part of Unocal. A CPA, Oliver is a member of the AAA, AICPA, FICPA, IAAER, IMA, TACTYC, and the Florida Association of Accounting Educators.

Oliver has taught accounting courses of all levels for the University of West Florida, state colleges, community colleges, and to practitioners since 1988. She has developed and instructed online courses using MyAccountingLab, WebCT, D2L, and other proprietary software.

Oliver lives in Niceville, FL, with her husband, Greg, and son, CJ. She especially thanks her husband, Greg, her son, CJ, and her uncle and aunt, Jimmy and Lida Lewis, for their unwavering support and encouragement. Oliver donates a portion of royalties to www.raffieskids.org, a charitable organization that assists children.

# Brief Contents

*ONLINE MATERIAL: located at pearsonhighered.com/horngren*

**APPENDIX C—Check Figures**

**SPECIAL JOURNALS**

**INVESTMENTS**

# Contents

CHAPTER **22**

## The Master Budget and Responsibility Accounting    1050

# Changes to This Edition

Students and Instructors will both benefit from a variety of new content and features in the ninth edition of *Accounting*:

**ADDED Ratio Coverage.** Based on reviewer demand, we added more ratio coverage to the Financial Statement Analysis, Chapter 15, and additional individual chapters.

**ADDED Excel Formulas in Chapter 21, Capital Budgeting,** to complement the blue/green formula boxes.

**REVISED Budget Coverage.** Chapter 22: The Master Budget and Responsibility Accounting was rewritten to use the variable costing approach. Also, added coverage on traceable and untraceable costs.

**ADDED more detailed coverage of overhead variances in Chapter 23.** Flexible Budgets and Standard Costs.

**UPDATED Full MyAccountingLab Coverage: Special Purpose Journals and Investments.** The two online chapters have been posted in **MyAccountingLab**. The special purpose journals chapter covers the streamlined journalizing process using the continuing company, Smart Touch. The investments chapter covers classification and treatment of stock investments, also using Smart Touch.

These two chapters contain full **MyAccountingLab** coverage and supplements for instructors who wish to have it. These decisions have been widely supported by reviewers.

**NEW and IMPROVED Chapter Openers.** All of the chapter openers have been redesigned and rewritten. The managerial chapter openers include a visual of a smartphone device, complete with decision-making tools as apps. As students progress through these chapters, the decision being discussed is highlighted on the first page of the chapter. These visuals help set the stage while providing students with direction as they navigate through the material.

**FOCUSED on Student Success.** We've made it easy for students to identify what their focal point should be in every chapter:

- **NEW Key Takeaway Feature.** At the end of each main topic throughout the book, we've included a brief takeaway feature. This marginal feature hones in on the key point of that section so students will know exactly what they should have understood before moving on.

- **NEW Translation Guides.** We've included "translation guides" throughout the text, set off by a different font style/treatment, in which accounting terminology is translated into a language students can easily understand. In doing so, we aim to make accounting more approachable (for example: **Assets are resources that provide future economic benefits to a company. An asset is something you own that has value, like your iPod.**).

- **NEW Connect To Boxes.** We've included a marginal "Connect To" box in each chapter that focuses on topics such as IFRS, Ethics, Technology, and Accounting Information Systems. Each contains a subtitle so instructors can easily see what each box features.

- **IMPROVED Stop & Think Boxes.** We've refined many of the existing Stop & Think boxes, making them less technical.

**EXTENSIVE REVISION of the End-of-Chapter Materials:**

- **NEW End-of-Chapter Student Success Section.** We've added a new half-page, end-of-chapter "Student Success" section that does the following:
  - Lists hints on some common trouble spots/mistakes students make when taking a test on the chapter.
  - Tells students exactly where to go in the chapter and **MyAccountingLab** to get help related to a particular topic covered within that chapter.

- **IMPROVED End-of-Chapter Material.** We've improved the end-of-chapter exercises, while retaining the exercises often used in **MyAccountingLab**.

- **NEW End-of-Chapter Fraud Activity.** We've added a short end-of-chapter activity that asks students to look at a fraud issue related to the chapter.

- **NEW End-of-Chapter Communication Activity.** We've added a short end-of-chapter activity that asks students to restate key chapter content in their own words, encouraging them to learn and use chapter vocabulary.

**ACCURACY.** To ensure the level of accuracy instructors expect and require, accuracy checkers verified the in-chapter content, figures, and illustrations while additional accuracy checkers worked through the end-of-chapter material.

# Students will have more "I Get It!" moments

Students understand (or "get it") right after the instructor does a problem in class. Once they leave the classroom, however, students often struggle to complete the homework on their own. This frustration can cause them to give up on the material altogether and fall behind in the course, resulting in an entire class falling behind as the instructor attempts to keep everyone on the same page.

With the *Accounting, Ninth Edition* Student Learning System, all the features of the student textbook, study resources, and online homework system are designed to work together to provide students with the consistency and repetition that will keep both the instructor and students on track by providing more "I Get It!" moments inside and outside the classroom.

## Replicating the Classroom Experience with Demo Doc Examples

The Demo Doc Examples, available at myaccountinglab.com, consist of entire problems, worked through step-by-step and narrated with the kind of comments that instructors would say in class. Demo Docs will aid students when they are trying to solve exercises and problems on their own, duplicating the classroom experience outside of class.

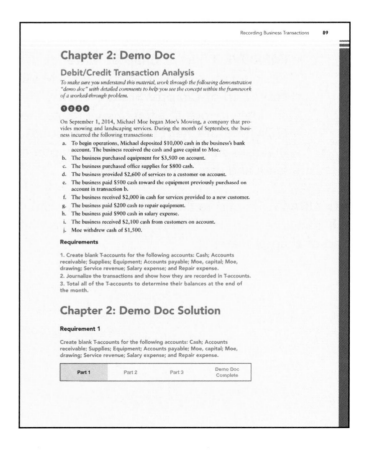

# with *Accounting* and MyAccountingLab!

## Consistency and Repetition Throughout the Learning Process

The concepts, materials, and practice problems are presented with clarity and consistency across all mediums—textbook, study resources, and online homework system. No matter which platform students use, they will continually experience the same look, feel, and language, minimizing confusion and ensuring clarity.

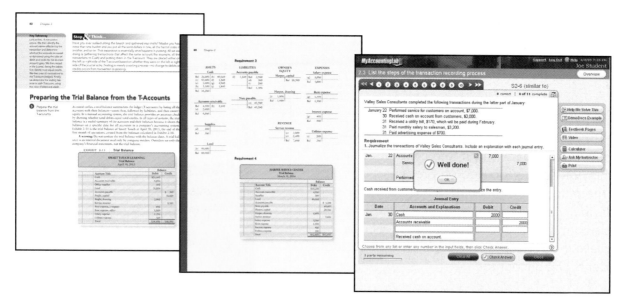

## Experiencing the Power of Practice with MyAccountingLab: myaccountinglab.com

MyAccountingLab is an online homework system that gives students more "I Get It!" moments through the power of practice. With MyAccountingLab students can:

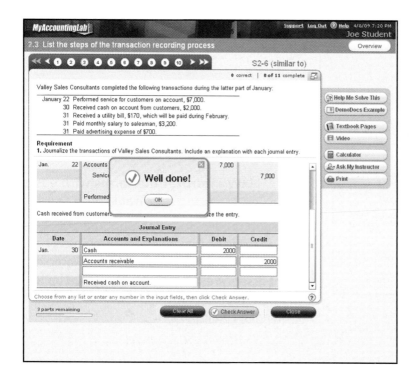

- work on the exact end-of-chapter material and/or similar problems assigned by the instructor.
- use the Study Plan for self-assessment and customized study outlines.
- use the Help Me Solve This tool for a step-by-step tutorial.
- watch a video to see additional information pertaining to the lecture.
- open the etext to the exact section of the book that will provide help on the specific problems.

# Accounting...

With its tried-and-true framework and respected author team, Horngren/Harrison/Oliver's *Accounting* is the trusted choice for instructors and students of Introductory Accounting.

The ninth edition preserves the classic, solid foundation of the previous editions, while also including a modern and fresh teaching approach that helps students understand the complexities of accounting and achieve more "I Get It" moments.

## NEW *Off to the right start:* Chapter Openers

Redesigned and rewritten, the chapter openers in this edition are focused on preparing students for the reading. The managerial chapter openers include a visual of a smartphone—complete with decision-making tools as apps—that visually displays the concepts and decision-making tools students will encounter.

### Current Assets

Current assets will be converted to cash, sold, or used up during the next 12 months, or within the business's operating cycle if the cycle is longer than a year. **Current assets are items that will be used up in a year, like your notebook paper for this class or the change in your pocket.** The operating cycle is the time span when

1. cash is used to acquire goods and services,
2. these goods and services are sold to customers, and
3. the business collects cash from customers.

## NEW *Interpret the terms with ease:* Translation Guides

Translation guides, found throughout the chapters, translate accounting terminology in a way students can understand. For example, **Current assets are items that will be used up in a year, like your notebook paper for this class or the change in your pocket.**

# The trusted choice for "I Get It" moments!

**NEW** *Link today's topics to the fundamentals:* **Connect To** _____

The Connect To marginal boxes in each chapter highlight hot topics such as IFRS, Ethics, and Accounting Information Systems as they pertain to the material being presented.

> **Connect To: Ethics**
>
> The classification of assets and liabilities as current or long-term affects many key ratios that outsiders use to evaluate the financial health of a company. Many times, the classification of a particular account is very clear—for example, a building is normally a long-term asset. But what if the company must demolish the existing building within six months due to some structural default? It would not be ethical to still show the building as a long-term asset.

**NEW** *Highlight what matters:* **Key Takeaway**

At the end of each learning objective, the authors added a new marginal feature that emphasizes the key points covered within the section so students can see what they need to understand before reading further.

**IMPROVED** *Put the concepts in context:* **Stop & Think Boxes**

Improved Stop & Think boxes relate accounting concepts to students' everyday lives by presenting them with relevant examples of the topic in practice.

*Keep it consistent:* **Consistent Examples**

Rather than learn about a new company each time an example is presented, this text provides two sets of company data that are carried through all of the in-chapter examples. As a result, students gain a sense of familiarity with the context of these examples and can focus their energy on learning the accounting principles in question.

*Illustrate the concepts:* **Decision Guidelines**

Decision Guidelines explain why the accounting concepts addressed in the chapter are important in a business setting. The left-hand side of the Decision Guidelines table explains the decision or action asked of the student in simple terms, while the right-hand side shows the accounting topics that will help facilitate those decisions.

## pearsonhighered.com/horngren

# Putting "I Get It" moments into practice!

**NEW** *Help where it's needed:* **Destination Student Success** _____

The new Destination Student Success sections at the end of each chapter list hints on some common mistakes in order to prevent students from falling into the same traps. These sections also show students exactly where to go within the chapter and in **MyAccountingLab** to get help related to a particular topic or learning objective.

---

### • Destination: Student Success

**Student Success Tips**

The following are hints on some common trouble areas for students in this chapter:

- Commit to memory the normal balance of the six main account types. The normal balance is the side of the T-account where the account INCREASES. Assets, Drawing, and Expenses have normal debit balances. Liabilities, Equity, and Revenues have normal credit balances.

- Recall that debits are listed first in every journal entry.

- Remember debits ALWAYS EQUAL credits in every journal entry.

- Keep in mind that posting is just gathering all the journal entries made to an individual T-account so that you can determine the new balance in the account. Journal debit entries are posted on the left side of the T-account. Journal credit entries are posted on the right side of the T-account.

- The accounting equation MUST ALWAYS balance after each transaction is posted.

- The trial balance lists all accounts with a balance, ordered by assets, liabilities, equity, drawing, revenues, and expenses. Total debits should equal total credits on the trial balance.

**Getting Help**

If there's a learning objective from the chapter you aren't confident about, try using one or more of the following resources:

- Review the Chapter 2 Demo Doc located on page 89 of the textbook.

- Practice additional exercises or problems at the end of Chapter 2 that cover the specific learning objective that is challenging you.

- Watch the white board videos for Chapter 2 located at myaccountinglab.com under the Chapter Resources button.

- Go to myaccountinglab.com and select the Study Plan button. Choose Chapter 2 and work the questions covering that specific learning objective until you've mastered it.

- Work the Chapter 2 pre/post tests in myaccountinglab.com.

- Visit the learning resource center on your campus for tutoring.

---

**NEW** *Examine the potential for fraud:* **End-of-Chapter Fraud Case** _____

This edition now includes a new end-of-chapter activity that asks students to look at a fraud issue related to the material. This activity helps students make the connection between the concepts and this popular accounting topic.

---

### • Fraud Case 2-1

Roy Akins was the accounting manager at Zelco, a tire manufacturer, and he played golf with Hugh Stallings, the CEO, who was something of a celebrity in the community. The CEO stood to earn a substantial bonus if Zelco increased net income by year-end. Roy was eager to get into Hugh's elite social circle; he boasted to Hugh that he knew some accounting tricks that could increase company income by simply revising a few journal entries for rental payments on storage units. At the end of the year, Roy changed the debits from "rent expense" to "prepaid rent" on several entries. Later, Hugh got his bonus, and the deviations were never discovered.

**Requirements**

1. How did the change in the journal entries affect the net income of the company at year-end?

2. Who gained and who lost as a result of these actions?

---

**NEW** *Speak accounting fluently:* **End-of-Chapter Communication Activity** _____

To help students increase their confidence, understanding, and communication of accounting terms, the end-of-chapter Communication Activity asks students to restate, in their own words, what they've learned within the chapter.

---

### • Communication Activity 2-1

In 35 words or fewer, explain the difference between a debit and a credit and explain what the normal balance of the six account types is.

*Master the material:* **Extensive Practice Opportunities**

**Five Book-Match Sets of Problems and Exercises (A, B, C, D, E):**
EXERCISES: Students will have access to exercise set A within the text. Exercise set A along with alternative static exercise sets B, C, D, and E can be assigned by the instructor and completed by students in MyAccountingLab.

PROBLEMS: Students will have access to A and B problems within the text. Problem set A and B along with alternative static problem sets C, D, and E can be assigned by the instructor and completed by students in MyAccountingLab.

**Continuing Exercise:**
The unique Continuing Exercise takes a single company and adds transactions or questions in each chapter to the existing fact pattern. As students move through the text, they complete additional steps in this comprehensive exercise. Students are able to see the big picture and learn how the accounting topics build off one another. The Continuing Exercise is also available in MyAccountingLab.

**Continuing Problem:**
For more detailed and in-depth practice, a Continuing Problem is also available. Like the Continuing Exercise, the Continuing Problem takes a single company and adds transactions or questions in each chapter to the existing fact pattern. As students move through the text, they complete additional steps in this comprehensive problem. The Continuing Problem is also available in MyAccountingLab.

**MyAccountingLab®**

**End-of-Chapter Material Integrated with MyAccountingLab**
myaccountinglab.com
Students need practice and repetition in order to successfully learn the fundamentals. All of the end-of-chapter problems and exercises in *Accounting* can be assigned and graded through MyAccountingLab. And learning goes one step further with MyAccountingLab's algorithmic versions of the questions that provide students with unlimited practice.

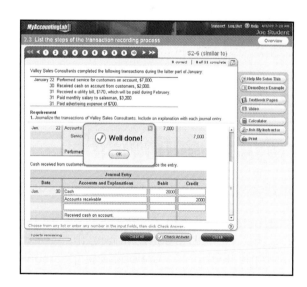

# Student and Instructor Resources

## For Students

**myaccountinglab.com Online Homework and Assessment Manager**
MyAccountingLab is Web-based tutorial and assessment software for accounting that gives students more "I Get It!" moments. MyAccountingLab provides students with a personalized interactive learning environment where they can complete their course assignments with immediate tutorial assistance, learn at their own pace, and measure their progress.

In addition to completing assignments and reviewing tutorial help, students have access to the following resources in **MyAccountingLab**:

- Pearson eText
- Data Files
- Videos
- Demo Docs
- Audio and Student PowerPoint® Presentations
- Working Papers in Both Excel and PDF
- MP3 Files with Chapter Objectives and Summaries
- Flash Cards

**Student Resource Web site: pearsonhighered.com/horngren**
The book's Web site contains the following:
- Data Files: Select end-of-chapter problems have been set up in different software applications, including Peachtree 2010, QuickBooks 2010, and Excel
- Excel Working Papers
- Online Chapter Materials (Special Purpose Journals and Investments)

## For Instructors

**MyAccountingLab**®

**myaccountinglab.com Online Homework and Assessment Manager**

**Instructor Resource Center: pearsonhighered.com/accounting**
For the instructor's convenience, the instructor resources are available on CD or can be downloaded from the textbook's catalog page (pearsonhighered.com/horngren) and **MyAccountingLab**. Available resources include the following:

- **Online Instructor's Manual:** Includes chapter summaries, teaching tips provided by reviewers, pitfalls for new students, and "best of" practices from instructors across the country. And, to effectively implement the array of resources available, a Resource Roadmap is provided, giving a description and location of each resource, along with recommendations for classroom applications. Additional resources offered in the instructor's manual include the following:

- Introduction to the Instructor's Manual with a list of resources and a roadmap to help navigate what's available in MyAccountingLab.
- Instructor tips for teaching courses in multiple formats—traditional, hybrid, or online.
- "First Day of Class" student handout that includes tips for success in the course, as well as an additional document that shows students how to register and log on to MyAccountingLab.
- Sample syllabi for 10- and 16-week courses.
- Chapter overview and teaching outline that includes a brief synopsis and overview of each chapter.
- Key topics that walk instructors through what material to cover and what examples to use when addressing certain items within the chapter.
- Student chapter summary handout.
- Assignment grid that outlines all end-of-chapter exercises and problems, the topic being covered in that particular exercise or problem, estimated completion time, level of difficulty, and availability in Excel templates.
- Ten-minute quizzes that quickly assess students' understanding of the chapter material.

- **Instructor's Solutions Manual:** Contains solutions to all end-of-chapter questions, including short exercises, exercises, and problems.
- **TestBank:** Includes more than 3,000 questions and is formatted for use with WebCT, Blackboard, and CourseCompass™. Both objective-based questions and computational problems are available.
- **PowerPoint Presentations:** These presentations help facilitate classroom discussion by demonstrating where the numbers come from and what they mean to the concept at hand.
  - Instructor PowerPoint Presentations—complete with lecture notes
  - Student PowerPoint Presentations
  - Audio Narrated PowerPoint Presentations
  - Clicker Response System (CRS) PowerPoint Presentations
- **Working Papers and Solutions in Excel and PDF Format**
- **Image Library**
- **Data and Solution Files:** Select end-of-chapter problems have been set up in different software applications, including Peachtree 2010, QuickBooks 2010, and Excel. Corresponding solution files are also provided.

# Acknowledgments

## Acknowledgments for This Edition

*The authors and editorial team thank Jodi McPherson for her vision and unwavering support over the past five years. Go SOX!*

*We would also like to extend a special thank you to the following individuals who were very helpful in the revision of this book:*

## Contributors:

Marcye Hampton, *University of Central Florida*
Brenda Mattison, *Tri-County Technical College*
Craig Reeder, *Florida Agricultural and Mechanical University*

## Advisory Panel:

Lisa Banks, *Mott Community College*
Betty Christopher, *Mission College*
Tracy Corr, *Southeast Community College*
Anthony J. Dellarte, *Luzerne County Community College*
Robert Fahnestock, *University of West Florida*
Charles Fazzi, *Saint Vincent College*
Jaclyn Felder-Strauss, *Kaplan University*
Anita Feller, *University of Illinois at Urbana–Champaign*
Marina Grau, *Houston Community College*
Geoffrey Gurka, *Mesa State College of Colorado*
Geoffrey Heriot, *Greenville Technical College*
Patty Holmes, *Des Moines Area Community College*
Emil Koren, *Saint Leo University*
Suzanne Lay, *Mesa State College of Colorado*
Maria Leach, *Auburn University–Montgomery*

Dorinda Lynn, *Pensacola State College*
Brenda Mattison, *Tri-County Technical College*
Cheryl McKay, *Monroe County Community College*
Audrey Morrison, *Pensacola State College*
Tim Murphy, *Diablo Valley College*
Ed Napravnik, *Metropolitan Community College*
Tracie Nobles, *Austin Community College*
Jamie Payton, *Gadsden State Community College*
Craig Reeder, *Florida Agricultural and Mechanical University*
Carla Rich, *Pensacola State College*
Randy Rinke, *Mercyhurst College*
Dennis Roth, *West Virginia Northern Community College*
Linda Tarrago, *Hillsborough Community College*
Melanie Torborg, *Minnesota School of Business*
Andy Williams, *Edmonds Community College*

## Accuracy Checkers:

Nabanita Bhattacharya, *Northwest Florida State College*
Ron Burris, *GEX Publishing Services*
David Doyon, *GEX Publishing Services*
Anita Hope, *Tarrant County College*
Peg Johnson, *Metropolitan Community College*

Dorinda Lynn, *Pensacola State College*
Cynthia Miller, *University of Kentucky*
Noriko Tilley, *Northwest Florida State College*
Greg Yost, *University of West Florida*

## Reviewers:

Dave Alldredge, *Salt Lake Community College*
Lee Daniel, *Troy University*
Heidi Hansel, *Kirkwood Community College*
Paige Paulson, *Salt Lake Community College*
Michelle Powell-Dancy, *Holmes Community College–Ridgeland*

Joan Ryan, *Clackamas Community College*
Beverly Strachan, *Troy University*
Rick Turpin, *Troy University*
Susan Wright, *Dekalb Technical College*

## Supplements Authors and Reviewers:

Natalie Allen, *Texas A&M University*
Helen Brubeck, *San Jose State University*
Colleen Chung, *Miami Dade College*
Wanda Edwards, *Troy State University*
Shirley Glass, *Macomb Community College*
Rob Hochschild, *Ivy Tech Community College*
Jamie McCracken, *Saint Mary-of-the-Woods College*
Brit McKay, *Georgia Southern University*
Jennie Mitchell, *Saint Mary-of-the-Woods College*

Cathy Nash, *Dekalb Technical College*
Craig Reeder, *Florida Agricultural and Mechanical University*
Rick Street, *Spokane Community College*
Allan Sheets, *International Business College*
John Stancil, *Florida Southern University College*
Noriko Tilley, *Northwest Florida State College*
Robin Turner, *Rowan-Cabarrus Community College*
Susan Wright, *Dekalb Technical College*
Greg Yost, *University of West Florida*

## Acknowledgments for Previous Editions

### Contributors:

Helen Brubeck, *San Jose State University*
Florence McGovern, *Bergen Community College*
Sherry Mills, *New Mexico State University*

### Advisory panel:

David Baglia, *Grove City College*
Joan Cezair, *Fayetteville State University*
Margaret Costello Lambert, *Oakland Community College*
Kathy Crusto-Way, *Tarrant County College*
Jim Ellis, *Bay State College–Boston*
Anita Ellzey, *Harford Community College*

Al Fagan, *University of Richmond*
Todd Jackson, *Northeastern State University*
Donnie Kristof-Nelson, *Edmonds Community College*
Cheryl McKay, *Monroe County Community College*
Mary Ann Swindlehurst, *Carroll Community College*
Andy Williams, *Edmonds Community College*

### Reviewers:

Joseph Adamo, *Cazenovia College*
Audrey Agnello, *Niagara County Community College*
William Alexander, *Indian Hills Community College–Ottumwa*
Asokan Anandarajan, *New Jersey Institute of Technology*
Susan Anders, *St. Bonaventure University*
Joe Aubert, *Bemidji State University*
Melody Ashenfelter, *Southwestern Oklahoma State University*

Charles Baird, *University of Wisconsin–Stout*
Dan Bayak, *Northampton Community College*
Richard Bedwell, *Jones County Junior College*
Judy Beebe, *Western Oregon University*
Irene Bembenista, *Davenport University*
Margaret Berezewski, *Robert Morris College*
Lecia Berven, *Iowa Lakes Community College*
Charles Betts, *Delaware Technical and Community College*
Greg Bischoff, *Houston Community College*
Margaret Black, *San Jacinto College*
William Black, *Raritan Valley Community College*
David Bland, *Cape Fear Community College*
Allen Blay, *University of California–Riverside*
Susan Blizzard, *San Antonio College*
Michael Blue, *Bloomsburg University*
Dale Bolduc, *Intercoast College*
Linda Bolduc, *Mount Wachusett Community College*
Donald Bond, *Houston Community College*
John Boyd, *Oklahoma City Community College*
Suzanne Bradford, *Angelina College*
Thomas Branton, *Alvin Community College*
Jerold Braun, *Daytona Beach Community College*
Nat Briscoe, *Northwestern State University*
Julie Browning, *California Baptist University*
Carroll Buck, *San Jose State University*

Jane Calvert, *University of Central Oklahoma*
Vickie Campbell, *Cape Fear Community College*
David Candelaria, *Mount San Jacinto College*

Lee Cannell, *El Paso Community College*
Michelle Cannon, *Ivy Tech Community College*
Greg Carlton, *Davidson County Community College*
Kay Carnes, *Gonzaga University–Spokane*
Brian Carpenter, *University of Scranton*
Thomas Carr, *International College of Naples*
Lloyd Carroll, *Borough Manhattan Community College*
Stanley Carroll, *New York City College of Technology of CUNY*
Roy Carson, *Anne Arundel Community College*
Al Case, *Southern Oregon University*
Gerald Caton, *Yavapai College*
Bea Chiang, *The College of New Jersey*
Catherine Chiang, *North Carolina Central University*
Stephen Christian, *Jackson Community College*
Shifei Chung, *Rowan University of New Jersey*
Toni Clegg, *Palm Beach Atlantic University*
Lynn Clements, *Florida Southern College*
Doug Clouse, *Lakeland Community College*
Cynthia Coleman, *Sandhills Community College*
Christie Comunale, *Long Island University*
Sally Cook, *Texas Lutheran University*
Sue Counte, *St. Louis Community College*
Chris Crosby, *York Technical College*
Ted Crosby, *Montgomery County Community College*
Barbara Crouteau, *Santa Rosa Junior College*
Chris Cusatis, *Gwynedd-Mercy College*

Julie Dailey, *Central Virginia Community College*
DeeDee Daughtry, *Johnston Community College*
Judy Daulton, *Piedmont Technical College*
David L. Davis, *Tallahassee Community College*
Elaine Dessouki, *Virginia Wesleyan College*
Ken Duffe, *Brookdale Community College*

John Eagan, *Erie Community College*
Gene Elrod, *University of Texas–Arlington*
Beth Engle, *Montgomery County Community College*

Harlan Etheridge, *University of Louisiana*
Charles Evans, *Keiser College*

Charles Fazzi, *Saint Vincent College*
Calvin Fink, *Bethune Cookman College*
Phil Fink, *University of Toledo*
Carolyn Fitzmorris, *Hutchinson Community College*
Rebecca Floor, *Greenville Technical College*
Joseph Foley, *Assumption College*
Jeannie Folk, *College of DuPage*
David Forsyth, *Palomar College*

Shelly Gardner, *Augustana College*
Harold Gellis, *York College of CUNY*
Renee Goffinet, *Spokane Community College*
Saturnino (Nino) Gonzales, *El Paso Community College*
Janet Grange, *Chicago State University*
Marina Grau, *Houston Community College*
John Graves, *PCDI*
Gloria Grayless, *Sam Houston State University*
Barbara Gregorio, *Nassau Community College*
Tim Griffin, *Hillsborough Community College*
Judy Grotrian, *Peru State College*

Amy Haas, *Kingsborough Community College*
Betty Habershon, *Prince George's Community College*
Patrick Haggerty, *Lansing Community College*
Penny Hanes, *Mercyhurst College–Erie*
Phil Harder, *Robert Morris University*
Marc Haskell, *Fresno City College*
Clair Helms, *Hinds Community College*
Kathy Heltzel, *Luzerne County Community College*
Sueann Hely, *West Kentucky Community and Technical College*
Geoffrey Heriot, *Greenville Technical College*
Humberto M. Herrera, *Laredo Community College*
Chuck Heuser, *Brookdale Community College*
Matt Hightower, *Three Rivers Community College*

Merrily Hoffman, *San Jacinto College*
Mary Hollars, *Vincennes University*
Patty Holmes, *Des Moines Area Community College–Ankeny*
Bambi Hora, *University of Central Oklahoma*
Maggie Houston, *Wright State University*
William Huffman *Missouri Southern State College*
James Hurat, *National College of Business and Technology*
Larry Huus, *University of Minnesota*
Constance Hylton, *George Mason University*

Verne Ingram, *Red Rocks Community College*

Fred Jex, *Macomb Community College*
Peg Johnson, *Metropolitan Community College*
Becky Jones, *Baylor University*
Jeffrey Jones, *Community College of Southern Nevada*
Christine Jonick, *Gainesville State College*
Paul Juriga, *Richland Community College*

Lolita Keck, *Globe College*
Christopher Kelly, *Community College of Southern Nevada*
James Kelly, *Ft. Lauderdale City College*
Ashraf Khallaf, *University of Southern Indiana*
Randy Kidd, *Longview Community College*
Chula King, *University of West Florida*
Cody King, *Georgia Southwestern State University*
Susan Koepke, *Illinois Valley Community College*
Ken Koerber, *Bucks County Community College*
Dennis Kovach, *Community College of Allegheny County–Allegheny*

Lawrence Leaman, *University of Michigan*
Denise Leggett, *Middle Tennessee State University*
Pamela Legner, *College of DuPage*
Maria Lehoczky, *American Intercontinental University*
Bruce Leung, *City College of San Francisco*
Judy Lewis, *Angelo State University*
Bruce Lindsey, *Genesee Community College*
Elizabeth Lynn Locke, *Northern Virginia Community College*

Michelle Maggio, *Westfield State College*
Bridgette Mahan, *Harold Washington College*
Lori Major, *Luzerne County Community College*
James Makofske, *Fresno City College*
Ken Mark, *Kansas City Kansas Community College*
Ariel Markelevich, *Long Island University*
Hector Martinez, *San Antonio College*
John May, *Southwestern Oklahoma State University*
Nora McCarthy, *Wharton County Junior College*
Bruce McMurrey, *Community College of Denver*

Patrick McNabb, *Ferris State University*
Pam Meyer, *University of Louisiana*
John Miller, *Metropolitan Community College*
Barry Mishra, *University of California–Riverside*
Norma Montague, *Central Carolina Community College*
Tim Murphy, *Diablo Valley College*

Lisa Nash, *Vincennes University*
Lanny Nelms, *Gwinnet Technical College*
Jennifer Niece, *Assumption College*
Deborah Niemer, *Oakland Community College*
Tom Nohl, *Community College of Southern Nevada*
Pat Novak, *Southeast Community College*

Ron O'Brien, *Fayetteville Technical Community College*
Kathleen O'Donnell, *Onondaga Community College*
John Olsavsky, *SUNY at Fredonia*
Liz Ott, *Casper College*
Glenn Owen, *Marymount College*

Carol Pace, *Grayson County College*
Susan Pallas, *Southeast Community College*
Jeffrey Patterson, *Grove City College*
Kathy Pellegrino, *Westfield State College*
Susan Pope, *University of Akron*
Robert Porter, *Cape Fear Community College*
Michelle Powell, *Holmes Community College*
Cheryl Prachyl, *University of Texas–El Paso*
Debra Prendergast, *Northwestern Business College*
Darlene Pulliam, *West Texas A&M University–Canyon*
Karl Putnam, *University of Texas–El Paso*

Margaret Quarles, *Sam Houston State University*
Behnaz Quigley, *Marymount College*

Jim Racic, *Lakeland Community College*
Paulette Ratliff-Miller, *Arkansas State University*
Carla Rich, *Pensacola State College*
Denver Riffe, *National College of Business and Technology*
Michael Robinson, *Baylor University*
Stephen Rockwell, *University of Tulsa*
Patrick Rogan, *Cosumnes River College*
Dennis Roth, *West Virginia Northern Community College*
Karen Russom, *North Harris College*
J.T. Ryan, *Onondaga Community College*

Martin Sabo, *Community College of Denver*
Phillipe Sammour, *Eastern Michigan University*
Richard Savich, *California State University–San Bernardino*
Nancy Schendel, *Iowa Lakes Community College*
Sandra Scheuermann, *University of Louisiana*

Bunney Schmidt, *Keiser College*
Debbie Schmidt, *Cerritos College*
Robert Schoener, *New Mexico State University*
Tony Scott, *Norwalk Community College*
Linda Serres Sweeny, *Sam Houston State University*
Brandi Shay, *Southwestern Community College*
Alice Sineath, *Forsyth Technical Community College*
Lois Slutsky, *Broward Community College South*
Kimberly Smith, *County College of Morris*
Chuck Smith, *Iowa Western Community College*
Ken Snow, *Kaplan Education Centers*
John Stancil, *Florida Southern College*
Lawrence Steiner, *College of Marin*
Sally Stokes, *Wilmington College*
Thomas Stolberg, *Alfred State University*
Joan Stone, *University of Central Oklahoma*
John Stone, *Potomac State College*
Thomas Szczurek, *Delaware County Community College*

Kathy Terrell, *University of Central Oklahoma*
Cynthia Thompson, *Carl Sandburg College–Carthage*

Shafi Ullah, *Broward Community College South*

Peter Van Brunt, *SUNY College of Technology at Delhi*
Kathi Villani, *Queensborough Community College*
Audrey Voyles, *San Diego Miramar College*

Patricia Walczak, *Lansing Community College*
Kay Walker-Hauser, *Beaufort County Community College–Washington*
Scott Wallace, *Blue Mountain College*
Douglas Ward, *Southwestern Community College*
Jeffrey Waybright, *Spokane Community College*
Roberta Wheeler, *Northwest Florida State College*
Bill Whitley, *Athens State University*
Randall Whitmore, *San Jacinto College*
Vicki White, *Ivy Tech Community College*
Idalene Williams, *Metropolitan Community College*
Betsy Willis, *Baylor University*
Tom Wilson, *University of Louisiana*
Joe Woods, *University of Arkansas*
Patty Worsham, *Riverside Community College*
Gloria Worthy, *Southwest Tennessee Community College*

Shi-Mu (Simon) Yang, *Adelphi University*
Lynnette Yerbuy, *Salt Lake Community College*
Laura Young, *University of Central Arkansas*

Tony Zordan, *University of St.Francis*

# 14 The Statement of Cash Flows

> How do we explain the change in the cash balance?

**SMART TOUCH LEARNING, INC.**
**Balance Sheet**
**May 31, 2013**

| Assets | | | | Liabilities | |
|---|---|---|---|---|---|
| Current assets: | | | | Current liabilities: | |
| Cash | | $4,800 | | Accounts payable | $ 48,700 |
| Accounts receivable | | 2,600 | | Salary payable | 900 |
| Inventory | | 30,500 | | Interest payable | 100 |
| Supplies | | 600 | | Unearned service revenue | 400 |
| Prepaid rent | | 2,000 | | Total current liabilities | 50,100 |
| Total current assets | | | $ 40,500 | Long-term liabilities: | |
| Plant assets: | | | | Notes payable | 20,000 |
| Furniture | $18,000 | | | Total liabilities | 70,100 |
| Less: Accumulated depreciation—furniture | 300 | 17,700 | | | |
| Building | 48,000 | | | **Stockholders' Equity** | |
| Less: Accumulated depreciation—building | 200 | 47,800 | | Common stock | 30,000 |
| Total plant assets | | | 65,500 | Retained earnings | 5,900 |
| | | | | Total stockholders' equity | 35,900 |
| Total assets | | | $106,000 | Total liabilities and stockholders' equity | $106,000 |

## Learning Objectives

1. Identify the purposes of the statement of cash flows

2. Distinguish among operating, investing, and financing cash flows

3. Prepare the statement of cash flows by the indirect method

4. Identify noncash investing and financing activities

5. Analyze cash flows

6. Prepare the statement of cash flows by the direct method (Appendix 14A)

7. Prepare the indirect statement of cash flows using a spreadsheet (Appendix 14B)

Why is cash so important? You can probably answer that question from your own experience: It takes cash to pay the bills. You have some income and you have expenses; and these events generate cash receipts and payments.

Businesses, including Smart Touch Learning, Inc., and Greg's Tunes, Inc., work the same way. Net income is a good thing, but Smart Touch and Greg's both need enough cash to pay the bills and run their operations.

This chapter covers cash flows—cash receipts and cash payments. We will see how to prepare the statement of cash flows (or cash flow statement), starting with the format used by the vast majority of non-public companies; it is called the *indirect method*. Chapter Appendix 14A covers the alternate format of the statement of cash flows, the *direct method*. The cash flow statement is required by GAAP.

Chapter Appendix 14B shows how to use a spreadsheet to prepare the statement of cash flows. This appendix presents the indirect-method spreadsheet only. The focus companies throughout the chapter once again are Smart Touch and Greg's Tunes.

# Introduction: The Statement of Cash Flows

**1** Identify the purposes of the statement of cash flows

The balance sheet reports financial position. When a comparative balance sheet for two periods is presented, it shows whether cash increased or decreased. For example, Smart Touch's comparative balance sheet reported the following:

|  | 2014 | 2013 | Increase (Decrease) |
|---|---|---|---|
| Cash.......... | $22,000 | $42,000 | $(20,000) |

Smart Touch's cash decreased by $20,000 during 2014. But the balance sheet does not show *why* cash decreased. We need the cash flow statement for that. The statement of cash flows reports **cash flows**—cash receipts and cash payments. It

- shows where cash came from (receipts) and how cash was spent (payments).
- reports why cash increased or decreased during the period.
- covers a span of time and is dated the same as the income statement—"Year Ended December 31, 2014," for example.

The statement of cash flows explains why net income as reported on the income statement does not equal the change in the cash balance. **In essence, the cash flow statement is the communicating link between the accrual based income statement and the cash reported on the balance sheet.** Exhibit 14-1 illustrates the relationships among the balance sheet, the income statement, and the statement of cash flows.

**EXHIBIT 14-1 | Timing of the Financial Statements**

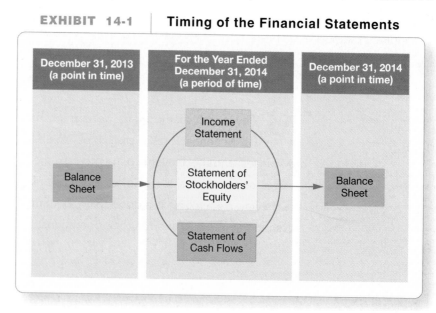

How do people use cash flow information? The statement of cash flows helps

1. **predict future cash flows.** Past cash receipts and payments help predict future cash flows.

2. **evaluate management decisions.** Wise investment decisions help the business prosper, while unwise decisions cause the business to have problems. Investors and creditors use cash flow information to evaluate managers' decisions.

3. **predict ability to pay debts and dividends.** Lenders want to know whether they will collect on their loans. Stockholders want dividends on their investments. The statement of cash flows helps make these predictions.

## Cash Equivalents

On a statement of cash flows, *Cash* means more than cash on hand and cash in the bank. *Cash* includes **cash equivalents**, which are highly liquid investments that can be converted into cash in three months or less. **As the name implies, cash equivalents are so close to cash that they are treated as "equals."** Examples of cash equivalents are money-market accounts and investments in U.S. government securities. Throughout this chapter, the term *cash* refers to both cash and cash equivalents.

> **Key Takeaway**
>
> The statement of cash flows explains why the cash balance does not equal net income (loss) from the income statement. Cash on the statement of cash flows includes cash equivalents. Cash equivalents are assets so close to being cash that they are treated like cash. The statement helps users predict future cash flows, evaluate management decisions, and predict the company's ability to pay debts and dividends.

# Operating, Investing, and Financing Activities

There are three basic types of cash flow activities, and the statement of cash flows has a section for each:

- Operating activities
- Investing activities
- Financing activities

   Each section reports cash flows coming into the company and cash flows going out of the company based on these three divisions.

**2** Distinguish among operating, investing, and financing cash flows

## Operating Activities

- Is the most important category of cash flows because it reflects the day-to-day operations that determine the future of an organization
- Generate revenues, expenses, gains, and losses
- Affect net income on the income statement
- Affect current assets and current liabilities on the balance sheet

## Investing Activities

- Increase and decrease long-term assets, such as computers, software, land, buildings, and equipment
- Include purchases and sales of these assets, plus long-term loans receivable from others (non-trade) and collections of those loans
- Include purchases and sales of long-term investments

### Financing Activities

- Increase and decrease long-term liabilities and equity
- Include issuing stock, paying dividends, and buying and selling treasury stock
- Include borrowing money and paying off loans

Exhibit 14-2 shows the relationship between operating, investing, and financing cash flows and the various parts of the balance sheet.

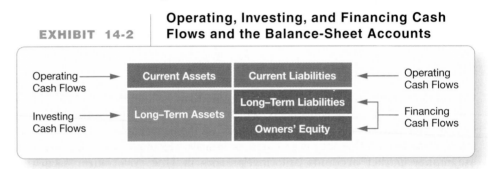

**EXHIBIT 14-2** | **Operating, Investing, and Financing Cash Flows and the Balance-Sheet Accounts**

As you can see, operating cash flows affect the current accounts. Investing cash flows affect the long-term assets. Financing cash flows affect long-term liabilities and owners' equity.

## Two Formats for Operating Activities

There are two ways to format operating activities on the statement of cash flows:

- The **indirect method** starts with net income and adjusts it to net cash provided by operating activities.
- The **direct method** restates the income statement in terms of cash. The direct method shows all the cash receipts and all the cash payments from operating activities.

    The indirect and direct methods

- use different computations but produce the same amount of cash flow from operations.
- present investing activities and financing activities in exactly the same format. Only the *operating activities* section is presented differently between the two methods.

    We will begin with the indirect method because most companies use it. To focus on the direct method, go to Appendix 14A.

# Preparing the Statement of Cash Flows by the Indirect Method

**3** Prepare the statement of cash flows by the indirect method

To prepare the statement of cash flows, you need the income statement and both the current year's and the prior year's balance sheets. Consider Smart Touch's financial statements on page 667. To prepare the statement of cash flows by the indirect method, we follow Steps 1–4:

> STEP 1:  Lay out the statement format as shown in Exhibit 14-3. Steps 2–4 will complete the statement of cash flows.

**EXHIBIT 14-3**  |  **Format of the Statement of Cash Flows: Indirect Method**

### SMART TOUCH LEARNING, INC.
### Statement of Cash Flows
### Year Ended December 31, 2014

| | | |
|---|---|---|
| ± Cash flows from operating activities: | | |
| Net income | | |
| Adjustments to reconcile net income to net cash provided by | | |
| operating activities: | | |
| + Depreciation / amortization expense | | |
| + Loss on sale of long-term assets | | |
| − Gain on sale of long-term assets | | |
| − Increases in current assets other than cash | | |
| + Decreases in current assets other than cash | | |
| + Increases in current liabilities | | |
| − Decreases in current liabilities | | |
| Net cash provided by (used for) operating activities | | |
| ± Cash flows from investing activities: | | |
| + Cash receipts from sales of long-term (plant) assets (investments, | | |
| land, building, equipment, and so on) | | |
| − Acquisition of long-term (plant) assets | | |
| Net cash provided by (used for) investing activities | | |
| ± Cash flows from financing activities: | | |
| + Cash receipts from issuance of stock | | |
| + Cash receipts from sale of treasury stock | | |
| − Purchase of treasury stock | | |
| + Cash receipts from issuance of notes or bonds payable (borrowing) | | |
| − Payment of notes or bonds payable | | |
| − Payment of dividends | | |
| Net cash provided by (used for) financing activities | | |
| = Net increase (decrease) in cash during the year | | |
| + Cash at December 31, 2013 | | |
| = Cash at December 31, 2014 | | |

**STEP 2:** Compute the change in cash from the comparative balance sheet. The change in cash is the "key reconciling figure" for the statement of cash flows. Exhibit 14-5 is the comparative balance sheet of Smart Touch, where the top line shows that cash decreased by $20,000 during 2014.

**STEP 3:** Take net income, depreciation, and any gains or losses from the income statement. Exhibit 14-6 gives the 2014 income statement of Smart Touch, with the relevant items highlighted.

**STEP 4:** Complete the statement of cash flows using data from the income statement and the comparative balance sheet. The statement is complete only after you have explained all the year-to-year changes in all the accounts on the balance sheet.

Let's apply these steps to show the operating activities of Smart Touch. Exhibit 14-4 depicts the statement of cash flows. All lettered items are tied to either a balance sheet or income statement item. That makes it easy to trace the data from one statement to the other.

**EXHIBIT 14-4** | **Indirect Method Statement of Cash Flows**

**SMART TOUCH LEARNING, INC.**
**Statement of Cash Flows**
**Year Ended December 31, 2014**

|   |   |   |   |
|---|---|---|---|
| | Cash flows from operating activities: | | |
| A | Net income | | $ 40,000 |
| | Adjustments to reconcile net income to net cash provided by operating activities: | | |
| B | Depreciation | $ 20,000 | |
| C | Gain on sale of plant assets | (10,000) | |
| | Increase in accounts receivable | (17,000) | |
| | Decrease in inventory | 2,000 | |
| D | Increase in accounts payable | 40,000 | |
| | Decrease in accrued liabilities | (5,000) | 30,000 |
| | Net cash provided by operating activities | | $ 70,000 |
| | Cash flows from investing activities: | | |
| E | Acquisition of plant assets | $(310,000) | |
| F | Cash receipt from sale of plant asset | 50,000 | |
| | Net cash used for investing activities | | (260,000) |
| | Cash flows from financing activities: | | |
| I | Cash receipt from issuance of common stock | $ 120,000 | |
| G | Cash receipt from issuance of notes payable | 90,000 | |
| H | Payment of notes payable | (10,000) | |
| J | Purchase of treasury stock | (20,000) | |
| K | Payment of dividends | (10,000) | |
| | Net cash provided by financing activities | | 170,000 |
| L | Net decrease in cash | | $ (20,000) |
| L | Cash balance, December 31, 2013 | | 42,000 |
| L | Cash balance, December 31, 2014 | | $ 22,000 |

# Cash Flows from Operating Activities

Operating cash flows begin with net income, taken from the income statement.

## A Net Income

The statement of cash flows—indirect method—begins with net income (or net loss) because revenues and expenses, which affect net income, produce cash receipts and cash payments. Revenues bring in cash receipts, and expenses must be paid. But net income as shown on the income statement is accrual based and the cash flows (cash basis net income) do not always equal the accrual basis revenues and expenses. For example, sales *on account* generate revenues that increase net income, but the company has not yet collected cash from those sales. Accrued expenses decrease net income, but the company has not paid cash *if the expenses are accrued*.

To go from net income to cash flow from operations, we must make some adjustments to net income on the statement of cash flows. These additions and subtractions follow net income and are labeled *Adjustments to reconcile net income to net cash provided by operating activities*.

**EXHIBIT 14-5** | **Comparative Balance Sheet**

### SMART TOUCH LEARNING, INC.
### Comparative Balance Sheet
### December 31, 2014 and 2013

| | 2014 | 2013 | Increase (Decrease) | |
|---|---|---|---|---|
| **Assets** | | | | |
| Current: | | | | |
| Cash | $ 22,000 | $ 42,000 | $ (20,000) | **L** |
| Accounts receivable | 90,000 | 73,000 | 17,000 | **D** |
| Inventory | 143,000 | 145,000 | (2,000) | |
| Plant assets, net | 460,000 | 210,000 | 250,000 | **E/F** |
| Total assets | $715,000 | $470,000 | $245,000 | |
| **Liabilities** | | | | |
| Current: | | | — | |
| Accounts payable | $ 90,000 | $ 50,000 | $ 40,000 | **D** |
| Accrued liabilities | 5,000 | 10,000 | (5,000) | |
| Long-term notes payable | 160,000 | 80,000 | 80,000 | **G/H** |
| **Stockholders' Equity** | | | | |
| Common stock | 370,000 | 250,000 | 120,000 | **I** |
| Retained earnings | 110,000 | 80,000 | 30,000 | **A/K** |
| Treasury stock | (20,000) | 0 | (20,000) | **J** |
| Total liabilities and stockholders' equity | $715,000 | $470,000 | $245,000 | |

**EXHIBIT 14-6** | **Income Statement**

### SMART TOUCH LEARNING, INC.
### Income Statement
### Year Ended December 31, 2014

| | | | |
|---|---|---|---|
| Revenues and gains: | | | |
| | Sales revenue | $286,000 | |
| | Interest revenue | 12,000 | |
| | Dividend revenue | 9,000 | |
| **C** | Gain on sale of plant assets | 10,000 | |
| | Total revenues and gains | | $317,000 |
| Expenses: | | | |
| | Cost of goods sold | $156,000 | |
| | Salary and wage expense | 56,000 | |
| **B** | Depreciation expense | 20,000 | |
| | Other operating expense | 16,000 | |
| | Interest expense | 15,000 | |
| | Income tax expense | 14,000 | |
| | Total expenses | | 277,000 |
| **A** | Net income | | $ 40,000 |

### B Depreciation, Depletion, and Amortization Expenses

These expenses are added back to net income to reconcile from net income to cash flow from operations. Let's see why this occurs. Depreciation is recorded as follows:

| | | | |
|---|---|---:|---:|
| Depreciation expense (E+) | | 20,000 | |
| Accumulated depreciation (CA+) | | | 20,000 |

You can see that depreciation does not affect cash because there is no Cash account in the journal entry. **Depreciation is a noncash expense.** However, depreciation, like all the other expenses, decreases net income. Therefore, to go from net income to cash flows, we must remove depreciation by adding it back to net income.

*Example:* Suppose you had only two transactions during the period:

- $40,000 cash sale
- Depreciation expense of $20,000

Accrual basis net income is $20,000 ($40,000 – $20,000), but cash flow from operations is $40,000. To reconcile from net income, $20,000, to cash flow from operations, $40,000, add back depreciation, $20,000. We would also add back any depletion and amortization expenses because they are noncash expenses, similar to depreciation.

### C Gains and Losses on the Sale of Assets

Sales of long-term assets such as land and buildings are investing activities, and these sales usually create a gain or a loss. The gain or loss is included in net income, which is already in the operating section of the cash flow statement. The gain or loss must be removed from net income on the statement of cash flows so the total cash from the sale of the asset can be shown in the investing section.

Exhibit 14-4 includes an adjustment for a gain. During 2014, Smart Touch sold equipment, and there was a gain of $10,000 on the sale. The gain was included in the calculation of net income on the income statement, so the gain must be removed from operating cash flows. The gain made net income bigger, so it is subtracted in the operating section. On the other hand, a loss on the sale of plant assets would make net income smaller, so it would be added back to net income.

### D Changes in the Current Assets and the Current Liabilities

Most current assets and current liabilities result from operating activities. For example,

- accounts receivable result from sales,
- inventory relates to cost of goods sold, and so on.

Changes in the current accounts create adjustments to net income on the cash flow statement, as follows:

↑ **Current assets**   ↓ **Cash**

1. **An increase in a current asset other than cash causes a decrease in cash.** If Accounts receivable, Inventory, or Prepaid expenses increased, then cash decreased. Therefore, we subtract the increase in the current asset from net income to get cash flow from operations. For example, Smart Touch's Accounts receivable went up by $17,000. That increase in the current asset shows as a decrease in cash on the cash flow statement (Exhibit 14-4).

↓ **Current assets**   ↑ **Cash**

2. **A decrease in a current asset other than cash causes an increase in cash.** Smart Touch's Inventory decreased by $2,000. What caused the decrease? Smart Touch must have sold some inventory and collected cash. Therefore, we add the decrease in Inventory of $2,000 in the cash flow statement (Exhibit 14-4).

3. **A decrease in a current liability causes a decrease in cash.** The payment of a current liability decreases cash. Therefore, we subtract decreases in current liabilities from net income to get cash flow from operations. Smart Touch's Accrued liabilities went down $5,000. That change shows up as a $5,000 decrease in cash flows in Exhibit 14-4.

4. **An increase in a current liability causes an increase in cash.** Smart Touch's Accounts payable increased by $40,000. This means that cash was not spent at the time the expense was incurred, but rather it will be paid at a later time—resulting in a liability. Accordingly, even though net income was reduced by the expense, cash was not reduced. However, cash will be reduced later when Smart Touch pays off its liability. Therefore, an increase in a current liability is *added* to net income in the statement of cash flows in Exhibit 14-4.

> ↓ Current liabilities    ↓ Cash

> ↑ Current liabilities    ↑ Cash

### Evaluating Cash Flows from Operating Activities

During 2014, Smart Touch's operations provided net cash flow of $70,000. This amount exceeds net income (due to the adjustments discussed in sections **B**, **C**, and **D**). However, to fully evaluate a company's cash flows, we must also examine its investing and financing activities. Exhibit 14-4 shows the completed operating activities section.

## Stop & Think...

The operating activities represent the core of the day-to-day results of any business. Remember when we learned the difference between accrual and cash basis accounting? All the operating activities section represents is a cash basis income statement. With the indirect method, we indirectly back into cash basis—that is, we start with accrual basis net income from the income statement and adjust it back to cash basis "operating" cash flows (cash basis net income).

## Cash Flows from Investing Activities

Investing activities affect long-term assets, such as Plant assets and Investments. These are shown for Smart Touch in Exhibit 14-5. Now, let's see how to compute the investing cash flows. A summary table follows in Exhibit 14-7.

**EXHIBIT 14-7** | **Computing Cash Flows from Investing Activities**

**Cash Receipts**

| | | | | | |
|---|---|---|---|---|---|
| From sale of plant assets | Beginning plant assets (net) | + Acquisition | − Depreciation expense | − Book value of assets sold | = Ending plant assets (net) |
| | Cash receipt | = Book value of assets sold | { + Gain on sale or − Loss on sale } | | |

**Cash Payments**

| | | | | | |
|---|---|---|---|---|---|
| For acquisition of plant assets | Beginning plant assets (net) | + Acquisition | − Depreciation expense | − Book value of assets sold | = Ending plant assets (net) |

## Computing Acquisitions and Sales of Plant Assets

Companies keep a separate account for each asset, but for computing investing cash flows, it is helpful to combine all the plant assets into a single Plant assets account. We subtract accumulated depreciation from the assets' cost in order to work with a single net figure for plant assets, such as Plant assets, net—$460,000. This simplifies the computations. Recall that Asset cost minus accumulated depreciation equals the book value of the asset. **So the Plant assets, net account holds the book value of plant assets.**

To illustrate, observe that Smart Touch's

- balance sheet reports plant assets, net of depreciation, of $460,000 at the end of 2014 and $210,000 at the end of 2013 (Exhibit 14-5).
- income statement shows depreciation expense of $20,000 and a $10,000 gain on sale of plant assets (Exhibit 14-6).

Also, assume that Smart Touch's acquisitions of plant assets during 2014 totaled $310,000. **E**

This gives us an incomplete T-account as follows:

**Plant assets, net**

| | | | | |
|---|---|---|---|---|
| 12/31/13 Bal | 210,000 | | | |
| | | Depreciation (from Inc Stmt) | 20,000 | **B** |
| **E** Acquisitions | 310,000 | Cost of sold assets (COSA) | ? | |
| 12/31/14 Bal | 460,000 | | | |

We also know that Smart Touch sold some older plant assets because there was a gain on sale of assets reported on the income statement. We don't care about the gain itself, we need to know the amount of cash received from the sale. Remember, we are looking for cash movement. How much cash did the business receive from the sale of plant assets? First, let's look at the cost of the sold assets. This will be the missing value in our Plant assets, net T-account.

$$12/31/13 \text{ Bal} + \text{Acquisitions} - \text{Depreciation} - \text{COSA?} = 12/31/14 \text{ Bal}$$
$$210,000 + 310,000 - 20,000 - \text{COSA?} = 460,000$$
$$500,000 - \text{COSA?} = 460,000$$
$$\text{COSA} = 40,000$$

So our completed T-account is as follows:

**Plant assets, net**

| | | | | |
|---|---|---|---|---|
| 12/31/13 Bal | 210,000 | | | |
| | | Depreciation (from Inc Stmt) | 20,000 | **B** |
| **E** Acquisitions | 310,000 | Cost of sold assets (COSA) | 40,000 | |
| 12/31/14 Bal | 460,000 | | | |

Cash received from selling plant assets can be computed by using the journal entry approach:

| | | | | |
|---|---|---|---|---|
| Cash (A+) | | **F** | ????? | |
| Gain on sale of plant assets (from the income statement) (R+) | **C** | | | 10,000 |
| Plant assets, net (from the T-account—COSA) (A–) | | | | 40,000 |

The $40,000 book-value comes from the Plant assets (Net) account on the balance sheet. The gain or loss comes from the income statement. The missing amount must be the cash received from the sale.

So, we compute the cash receipt from the sale as follows:

> Cash = $10,000 Gain + $40,000 COSA (Plant assets, net)
> Cash = $50,000 **F**

    The cash receipt from the sale of plant assets of $50,000 is shown as item **F** in the investing activities section of the statement of cash flows (see Exhibit 14-4). Exhibit 14-7 (shown previously on page 669) summarizes the computation of the investing cash flows. Items we computed are shown in color.

## Cash Flows from Financing Activities

Financing activities affect the liability and owners' equity accounts, such as Long-term notes payable, Bonds payable, Common stock, and Retained earnings. These are shown for Smart Touch in Exhibit 14-5. A summary follows in Exhibit 14-8.

**EXHIBIT 14-8** | **Computing Cash Flows from Financing Activities**

**Cash Receipts**

| | | | | | | | | |
|---|---|---|---|---|---|---|---|---|
| From issuance of notes payable | Beginning notes payable | + | Cash receipt from issuance of notes payable | − | Cash payment of notes payable | = | Ending notes payable |
| From issuance of stock | Beginning stock | + | Cash receipt from issuance of new stock | | | = | Ending stock |

**Cash Payments**

| | | | | | | | | |
|---|---|---|---|---|---|---|---|---|
| Of notes payable | Beginning notes payable | + | Cash receipt from issuance of notes payable | − | Cash payment of notes payable | = | Ending notes payable |
| To purchase treasury stock | Beginning treasury stock | + | Cost of treasury stock purchased | | | = | Ending treasury stock |
| Of dividends | Beginning retained earnings | + | Net income | − | Dividends declared | = | Ending retained earnings |

## Computing Issuances and Payments of Long-Term Notes Payable

The beginning and ending balances of Notes payable or Bonds payable are taken from the balance sheet. If either the amount of new issuances or payments is known, the other amount can be computed. For Smart Touch, new issuances of notes payable is known to be $90,000 (shown as item **G** in Exhibit 14-4). The computation of note payments uses the balance sheet amounts from the Long-term notes payable account in Exhibit 14-5 to create the following incomplete T-account:

**Long-term notes payable**

| | | | |
|---|---|---|---|
| Note payments | ? | 12/31/13 Bal | 80,000 |
| | | New notes issued | 90,000 **G** |
| | | 12/31/14 Bal | 160,000 |

Then, solve for the missing payments value:

> 12/31/13 Bal + New Notes Issued − Payments? = 12/31/14 Bal
> 80,000 + 90,000 − Payments? = 160,000
> 170,000 − Payments? = 160,000
> Payments = 10,000

Complete the T-account:

**Long-term notes payable**

|  |  |  |  |  |
|---|---|---|---|---|
| **H** Note payments | 10,000 | 12/31/13 Bal | 80,000 | |
|  |  | New notes issued | 90,000 | **G** |
|  |  | 12/31/14 Bal | 160,000 | |

The payment of $10,000 is an outflow of cash, as shown on the statement of cash flows. (See item **H** in Exhibit 14-4).

## Computing Issuances of Stock and Purchases of Treasury Stock

Cash flows for these financing activities can be determined by analyzing the stock accounts. For example, the amount of a new issuance of common stock is determined by analyzing the Common stock account. Using data from Exhibit 14-5, the incomplete Common stock T-account is as follows:

**Common stock**

|  |  |  |  |
|---|---|---|---|
|  |  | 12/31/13 Bal | 250,000 |
| Retirements | ? | Issuance | ? |
|  |  | 12/31/14 Bal | 370,000 |

We would have to be told if there were any stock retirements. Since there were no retirements, we know the balance change must be represented by new stock issuances.

Solving for the missing value is completed as follows:

$$\text{12/31/13 Bal} + \text{Issuance of Stock?} - \text{Retirements?} = \text{12/31/14 Bal}$$
$$250,000 + \text{Issuance of Stock?} - 0 = 370,000$$
$$\text{Issuance of Stock} = 120,000$$

The completed T-account for Common stock is as follows:

**Common stock**

|  |  |  |  |  |
|---|---|---|---|---|
|  |  | 12/31/13 Bal | 250,000 | |
| Retirements | 0 | Issuance | 120,000 | **I** |
|  |  | 12/31/14 Bal | 370,000 | |

Therefore, the new stock issuance shows as $120,000 positive cash flows in the financing activities section of the statement (item **I** in Exhibit 14-4).

The last item that changed on Smart Touch's balance sheet was Treasury stock. The incomplete T-account balances from the Treasury stock account on the balance sheet show the following:

**Treasury stock**

|  |  |  |  |
|---|---|---|---|
| 12/31/13 Bal | 0 |  |  |
| Purchases | ? | Sales | ? |
| 12/31/14 Bal | 20,000 |  |  |

Since we were not told that any treasury stock was sold, we must assume that 100% of the account change represents new acquisitions of treasury stock. Solving for the amount, the equation follows:

$$12/31/13 \text{ Bal} + \text{Purchases?} - \text{Sales?} = 12/31/14 \text{ Bal}$$
$$0 + \text{Purchases?} - 0 = 20,000$$
$$\text{Purchases} = 20,000$$

Completing the T-account, we have the following:

**Treasury stock**

| | | | |
|---|---|---|---|
| 12/31/13 Bal | 0 | | |
| **J** Purchases | 20,000 | Sales | 0 |
| 12/31/14 Bal | 20,000 | | |

So, $20,000 is shown as a cash outflow in the financing section of the cash flow statement for purchase of treasury stock (item **J** in Exhibit 14-4).

## Computing Dividend Payments

The amount of dividend payments can be computed by analyzing the Retained earnings account. First we input the balances from the balance sheet:

**Retained earnings**

| | | | |
|---|---|---|---|
| | | 12/31/13 Bal | 80,000 |
| Net loss | ? | Net income | ? |
| Dividend declarations | ? | | |
| | | 12/31/14 Bal | 110,000 |

Retained earnings increases when companies earn net income. Retained earnings decreases when companies have a net loss and when they declare dividends. We know that Smart Touch earned net income of $40,000 from the income statement in Exhibit 14-6.

**Retained earnings**

| | | | | |
|---|---|---|---|---|
| | | 12/31/13 Bal | 80,000 | |
| Net loss | ? | Net income | 40,000 | **A** |
| Dividend declarations | ? | | | |
| | | 12/31/14 Bal | 110,000 | |

Smart Touch can't have both net income and net loss for the same period; therefore, the missing value must be the amount of dividends Smart Touch declared. Solving for the dividends follows:

$$12/31/13 \text{ Bal} + \text{Net income} - \text{Dividends declared} = 12/31/14 \text{ Bal}$$
$$80,000 + 40,000 - \text{Dividends declared} = 110,000$$
$$120,000 - \text{Dividends declared} = 110,000$$
$$\text{Dividends declared} = 10,000$$

So our final Retained earnings T-account shows the following:

**Retained earnings**

| | | | | |
|---|---|---|---|---|
| | | 12/31/13 Bal | 80,000 | |
| | | Net income | 40,000 | **A** |
| **K** Dividend declarations | 10,000 | | | |
| | | 12/31/14 Bal | 110,000 | |

> **Connect To: IFRS**
>
> Under GAAP, interest or dividends received and interest paid are all reported as operating activities. Dividends paid are reported as a financing activity under GAAP. Under IFRS rules, interest and dividends received and paid may be classified as either operating, investing, or financing cash flows, provided that they are classified consistently from period to period.

A stock dividend has *no* effect on Cash and is *not* reported on the financing section of the cash flow statement. If there were stock dividends, they would be reported in the noncash transactions section, discussed later in the chapter. Smart Touch had no stock dividends—only cash dividends. Exhibit 14-8 (shown previously on page 671) summarizes the computation of cash flows from financing activities, highlighted in color.

## Net Change in Cash and Cash Balances  L

The next line of the cash flow statement (underneath Net cash provided by financing activities in Exhibit 14-4) represents the total change in cash for the period. In the case of Smart Touch, it is the net decrease in cash balances of $20,000 for the year. The decrease in cash of $20,000 is also represented by the following:

| Net cash provided by Operating activities | | Net cash used for Investing activities | | Net cash provided by Financing activities | | Net decrease in Cash |
|---|---|---|---|---|---|---|
| 70,000 | − | 260,000 | + | 170,000 | = | (20,000) |

Next, the beginning cash from December 31, 2013, is listed at $42,000. The net decrease of $20,000 is subtracted from beginning cash of $42,000, which equals the ending cash balance on December 31, 2014, of $22,000. **This is the key to the statement of cash flows—it explains why the cash balance for Smart Touch decreased by $20,000, even though the company reported net income for the year.**

### Stop & Think...

Most of you probably have a checking or savings account. Think about how the balance changes from month to month. It does not always change because you have earned revenues or incurred expenses (operating). Sometimes it changes because you buy a long-lasting asset, such as a computer (investing). Sometimes it changes because you make a principal payment on your car loan (financing). It is the same with business; business bank accounts do not change only because they earn revenue or incur expenses (operating). The cash flow statement explains all the reasons that cash changed (operating, investing, and financing).

# Noncash Investing and Financing Activities

**4** Identify noncash investing and financing activities

Companies make investments that do not require cash. They also obtain financing other than cash. Such transactions are called noncash investing and financing activities and appear in a separate part of the cash flow statement. Our Smart Touch example did not include transactions of this type because the company did not have any noncash transactions during the year. So, to illustrate them, let's consider the three noncash transactions for Greg's Tunes. How would they be reported? First, we gather the noncash activities for the company:

| | |
|---|---|
| 1 | Acquired $300,000 building by issuing stock |
| 2 | Acquired $70,000 land by issuing note payable |
| 3 | Paid $100,000 note payable by issuing common stock |

Now, we consider each transaction individually.

1. Greg's Tunes issued common stock of $300,000 to acquire a building. The journal entry to record the purchase would be as follows:

| | | | | |
|---|---|---|---|---|
| Building | (A+) | | 300,000 | |
| | Common stock | (Q+) | | 300,000 |

This transaction would not be reported on the cash flow statement because no cash was paid. But the building and the common stock are important. The purchase of the building is an investing activity. The issuance of common stock is a financing activity. Taken together, this transaction is a *noncash investing and financing activity*.

2. The second transaction listed indicates that Greg's Tunes acquired $70,000 of land by issuing a note. The journal entry to record the purchase would be as follows:

| | | | | |
|---|---|---|---|---|
| Land | (A+) | | 70,000 | |
| | Notes payable | (L+) | | 70,000 |

This transaction would not be reported on the cash flow statement because no cash was paid. But the land and the notes payable are important. The purchase of the land is an investing activity. The issuance of the note is a financing activity. Taken together, this transaction is a *noncash investing and financing activity*.

3. The third transaction listed indicates that Greg's Tunes exchanged $100,000 of debt by issuing common stock. The journal entry to record the transaction would be as follows:

| | | | | |
|---|---|---|---|---|
| Notes payable | (L–) | | 100,000 | |
| | Common stock | (Q+) | | 100,000 |

This transaction would not be reported on the cash flow statement because no cash was paid. But the notes payable and the stock issuance are important. The payment on the note and the issuance of the common stock are both financing activities. Taken together, this transaction, even though it is two financing transactions, is reported in the *noncash investing and financing activities*.

*Noncash investing and financing activities* are reported in a separate part of the statement of cash flows. Exhibit 14-9 illustrates noncash investing and financing activities for Greg's Tunes. This information either follows the cash flow statement or can be disclosed in a note.

**Key Takeaway**

Companies make investments that do not require cash. They also obtain financing other than cash. Such transactions are called noncash investing and financing activities and appear in a separate part of the cash flow statement.

**EXHIBIT 14-9** | **Noncash Investing and Financing Activities**

**GREG'S TUNES**
**Statement of Cash Flows—partial**
Year Ended December 31, 2014

| | | |
|---|---|---|
| Noncash investing and financing activities: | | |
| Acquisition of building by issuing common stock | | $300,000 |
| Acquisition of land by issuing note payable | | 70,000 |
| Payment of note payable by issuing common stock | | 100,000 |
| Total noncash investing and financing activities | | $470,000 |

# Measuring Cash Adequacy: Free Cash Flow

 **5** Analyze cash flows

Throughout this chapter we have focused on cash flows from operating, investing, and financing activities. Some investors want to know how much cash a company can "free up" for new opportunities. **Free cash flow** is the amount of cash available from operations after paying for planned investments in long-term assets and after paying cash dividends to shareholders. Free cash flow can be computed as follows:

$$\text{Free cash flow} = \begin{array}{c} \text{Net cash provided} \\ \text{by operating} \\ \text{activities} \end{array} - \begin{array}{c} \text{Cash payments planned} \\ \text{for investments in} \\ \text{long-term assets} \end{array} - \text{Cash dividends}$$

**Key Takeaway**

Free cash flow measures the amount of cash available from normal operations after paying for planned investments in long-term assets and after paying cash dividends to shareholders.

Many companies use free cash flow to manage their operations. Suppose Greg's Tunes expects net cash provided by operations of $200,000. Assume Greg's Tunes plans to spend $160,000 to modernize its production facilities and pays $15,000 in cash dividends. In this case, Greg's Tunes' free cash flow would be $25,000 ($200,000 − $160,000 − $15,000). If a good investment opportunity comes along, Greg's Tunes should have $25,000 cash available to invest.

The Decision Guidelines on the next page will put into practice what you have learned about the statement of cash flows prepared by the indirect method.

# Decision Guidelines 14-1

## USING CASH FLOW AND RELATED INFORMATION TO EVALUATE INVESTMENTS

Ann Browning is a private investor. Through the years, she has devised some guidelines for evaluating investments. Here are some of her guidelines.

| Question | Financial Statement | What to Look For |
|---|---|---|
| • Where is most of the company's cash coming from? | Statement of cash flows | Operating activities → Good sign<br>Investing activities → Bad sign<br>Financing activities → Okay sign |
| • Do high sales and profits translate into more cash? | Statement of cash flows | Usually, but cash flows from *operating* activities must be the main source of cash for long-term success. |
| • If sales and profits are low, how is the company generating cash? | Statement of cash flows | If *investing* activities are generating the cash, the business may be in trouble because it is selling off its long-term assets.<br><br>If *financing* activities are generating the cash, that cannot go on forever. Sooner or later, investors will demand cash flow from operating activities. |
| • Is the cash balance large enough to provide for expansion? | Balance sheet | The cash balance should be growing over time. If not, the company may be in trouble. |
| • Can the business pay its debts? | Income statement | Does the trend indicate increasing net income? |
| | Statement of cash flows | Are cash flows from operating activities the main source of cash? |
| | Balance sheet | Are the current ratio and debt ratio adequate? |

# Summary Problem 14-1

The Adams Corporation reported the following income statement and comparative balance sheet for 2014 and 2013, along with transaction data for 2014:

## ADAMS CORPORATION
### Income Statement
### Year Ended December 31, 2014

| | | |
|---|---:|---:|
| Sales revenue | | $662,000 |
| Cost of goods sold | | 560,000 |
| Gross profit | | $102,000 |
| Operating expenses: | | |
|     Salary expense | $46,000 | |
|     Depreciation expense | 10,000 | |
|     Rent expense | 2,000 | |
|     Total operating expenses | | 58,000 |
| Income from operations | | $ 44,000 |
| Other items: | | |
|     Loss on sale of equipment | | (2,000) |
| Income before income tax | | $ 42,000 |
| Income tax expense | | 16,000 |
| Net income | | $ 26,000 |

## ADAMS CORPORATION
### Balance Sheet
### December 31, 2014 and 2013

| Assets | 2014 | 2013 | Liabilities | 2014 | 2013 |
|---|---:|---:|---|---:|---:|
| Current: | | | Current: | | |
|   Cash and cash equivalents | $ 22,000 | $ 3,000 |   Accounts payable | $ 35,000 | $ 26,000 |
|   Accounts receivable | 22,000 | 23,000 |   Accrued liabilities | 7,000 | 9,000 |
|   Inventory | 35,000 | 34,000 |   Income tax payable | 10,000 | 10,000 |
|     Total current assets | $ 79,000 | $ 60,000 |     Total current liabilities | $ 52,000 | $ 45,000 |
| Equipment, net | 126,000 | 72,000 | Bonds payable | 84,000 | 53,000 |
| | | | **Stockholders' Equity** | | |
| | | | Common stock | 52,000 | 20,000 |
| | | | Retained earnings | 27,000 | 19,000 |
| | | | Treasury stock | (10,000) | (5,000) |
| Total assets | $205,000 | $132,000 | Total liabilities and stockholders' equity | $205,000 | $132,000 |

Transaction Data for 2014:

| | |
|---|---:|
| Purchase of equipment......................................................................... | $140,000 |
| Payment of dividends........................................................................... | 18,000 |
| Issuance of common stock to retire bonds payable ........................... | 13,000 |
| Issuance of bonds payable to borrow cash........................................ | 44,000 |
| Cash receipt from issuance of common stock ................................... | 19,000 |
| Cash receipt from sale of equipment (book value, $76,000) .............. | 74,000 |
| Purchase of treasury stock ................................................................. | 5,000 |

## Requirement

1. Prepare Adams Corporation's statement of cash flows for the year ended December 31, 2014. Format operating cash flows by the indirect method. Follow the four steps outlined below.

   **STEP 1.** Lay out the format of the statement of cash flows.

   **STEP 2.** From the comparative balance sheet, compute the change in cash during the year.

   **STEP 3.** From the income statement, take net income, depreciation, and the loss on sale of equipment to the statement of cash flows.

   **STEP 4.** Complete the statement of cash flows. Account for the year-to-year change in each balance sheet account. Prepare a T-account to show the transaction activity in each long-term balance-sheet account.

# Solution

| ADAMS CORPORATION Statement of Cash Flows Year Ended December 31, 2014 | | |
|---|---:|---:|
| **Cash flows from operating activities:** | | |
| Net income | | $26,000 |
| Adjustments to reconcile net income to net cash | | |
| provided by operating activities: | | |
| Depreciation | $ 10,000 | |
| Loss on sale of equipment | 2,000 | |
| Decrease in accounts receivable | 1,000 | |
| Increase in inventory | (1,000) | |
| Increase in accounts payable | 9,000 | |
| Decrease in accrued liabilities | (2,000) | 19,000 |
| Net cash provided by operating activities | | $45,000 |
| | | |
| **Cash flows from investing activities:** | | |
| Purchase of equipment | $(140,000) | |
| Sale of equipment | 74,000 | |
| Net cash used for investing activities | | (66,000) |
| | | |
| **Cash flows from financing activities:** | | |
| Issuance of common stock | $ 19,000 | |
| Payment of dividends | (18,000) | |
| Issuance of bonds payable | 44,000 | |
| Purchase of treasury stock | (5,000) | |
| Net cash provided by financing activities | | 40,000 |
| | | |
| **Net increase in cash** | | $19,000 |
| Cash balance, December 31, 2013 | | 3,000 |
| Cash balance, December 31, 2014 | | $22,000 |
| | | |
| **Noncash investing and financing activities:** | | |
| Issuance of common stock to retire bonds payable | | $13,000 |
| Total noncash investing and financing activities | | $13,000 |

Relevant T-accounts:

| Equipment, net | | |
|---|---|---|
| 12/31/13 Bal 72,000 | | |
| 140,000 | 10,000 | |
| | 76,000 | |
| 12/31/14 Bal 126,000 | | |

| Bonds payable | | |
|---|---|---|
| | 12/31/13 Bal | 53,000 |
| 13,000 | | 44,000 |
| | 12/31/14 Bal | 84,000 |

| Common stock | | |
|---|---|---|
| | 12/31/13 Bal | 20,000 |
| | | 13,000 |
| | | 19,000 |
| | 12/31/14 Bal | 52,000 |

| Retained earnings | | |
|---|---|---|
| | 12/31/13 Bal | 19,000 |
| 18,000 | | 26,000 |
| | 12/31/14 Bal | 27,000 |

| Treasury stock | |
|---|---|
| 12/31/13 Bal | 5,000 |
| | 5,000 |
| 12/31/14 Bal | 10,000 |

# Review *The Statement of Cash Flows*

## ● Accounting Vocabulary

**Cash Equivalents (p. 663)**
Highly liquid short-term investments that can be readily converted into cash in three months or less.

**Cash Flows (p. 662)**
Cash receipts and cash payments.

**Direct Method (p. 664)**
Format of the operating activities section of the statement of cash flows; lists the major categories of operating cash receipts and cash payments.

**Financing Activities (p. 664)**
Activities that obtain the cash needed to launch and sustain the business; a section of the statement of cash flows.

**Free Cash Flow (p. 676)**
The amount of cash available from operations after paying for planned investments in long-term assets and after paying dividends to shareholders.

**Indirect Method (p. 664)**
Format of the operating activities section of the statement of cash flows; starts with net income and reconciles to net cash provided by operating activities.

**Investing Activities (p. 663)**
Activities that increase or decrease long-term assets; a section of the statement of cash flows.

**Operating Activities (p. 663)**
Activities that create revenue or expense in the entity's major line of business; a section of the statement of cash flows. Operating activities affect the income statement.

## ● Destination: Student Success

### Student Success Tips

The following are hints on some common trouble areas for students in this chapter:

- Keep in mind the cash flow statement explains why the change in the cash balance is not the same as the net income or net loss for the period.

- Recall that the cash flow statement has four sections: operating, investing, financing, and noncash transactions.

- Keep in mind the cash flow statement may be prepared using the indirect method or the direct method. The indirect method is the most commonly used method.

- Remember that Cash is an asset, so changes in other asset accounts have the opposite effect on cash (when other asset account increases, cash decreases). Changes in liability and equity accounts have the same effect on cash (when liability or equity account increases, cash increases).

### Getting Help

If there's a learning objective from the chapter you aren't confident about, try using one or more of the following resources:

- Review the indirect method statement template in Exhibit 14-3.

- Review the Decision Guidelines in the chapter.

- Review Summary Problem 14-1 in the chapter to reinforce your understanding of the indirect cash flow statement.

- Practice additional exercises or problems at the end of Chapter 14 that cover the specific learning objective that is challenging you.

- Watch the white board videos for Chapter 14, located at myaccountinglab.com under the Chapter Resources button.

- Go to myaccountinglab.com and select the Study Plan button. Choose Chapter 14 and work the questions covering that specific learning objective until you've mastered it.

- Work the Chapter 14 pre/post tests in myaccountinglab.com.

- Visit the learning resource center on your campus for tutoring.

# Quick Check

1. The purposes of the cash flow statement are to
   a. evaluate management decisions.
   b. determine ability to pay liabilities and dividends.
   c. predict future cash flows.
   d. All of the above

2. The main categories of cash flow activities are
   a. direct and indirect.
   b. current and long-term.
   c. noncash investing and financing.
   d. operating, investing, and financing.

3. Operating activities are most closely related to
   a. long-term assets.
   b. current assets and current liabilities.
   c. long-term liabilities and owners' equity.
   d. dividends and treasury stock.

4. Which item does *not* appear on a statement of cash flows prepared by the indirect method?
   a. Collections from customers
   b. Depreciation
   c. Net income
   d. Gain on sale of land

5. Leather Shop earned net income of $57,000 after deducting depreciation of $5,000 and all other expenses. Current assets decreased by $4,000, and current liabilities increased by $8,000. How much was Leather Shop's cash provided by operating activities (indirect method)?
   a. $40,000
   b. $66,000
   c. $48,000
   d. $74,000

6. The Plant assets account of Star Media shows the following:

**Plant assets, net**

| | | | |
|---|---|---|---|
| Beg | 80,000 | Depr | 34,000 |
| Purchase | 428,000 | Sale | 42,000 |
| End | 432,000 | | |

Star Media sold plant assets at an $11,000 loss. Where on the statement of cash flows should Star Media report the sale of plant assets? How much should the business report for the sale?
   a. Financing cash flows—cash receipt of $42,000
   b. Investing cash flows—cash receipt of $53,000
   c. Investing cash flows—cash receipt of $31,000
   d. Investing cash flows—cash receipt of $42,000

7. Mountain Water, Corp., issued common stock of $28,000 to pay off long-term notes payable of $28,000. In what section(s) would these transaction be recorded?

   a. Financing activities payment of note ($28,000)

   b. Financing activities cash receipt $28,000

   c. Noncash investing and financing activities $28,000

   d. Both a and b are correct

8. Holmes, Inc., expects cash flow from operating activities to be $160,000, and the company plans purchases of equipment of $83,000 and repurchases of stock of $24,000. What is Holmes' free cash flow?

   a. $53,000

   b. $160,000

   c. $77,000

   d. $83,000

9. (**Appendix 14A: Direct Method**) Maxwell Furniture Center had accounts receivable of $20,000 at the beginning of the year and $54,000 at year-end. Revenue for the year totaled $116,000. How much cash did the business collect from customers?

   a. $150,000

   b. $62,000

   c. $116,000

   d. $82,000

10. (**Appendix 14A: Direct Method**) Magic Toys Company had operating expense of $48,000. At the beginning of the year, Magic Toys owed $10,000 on accrued liabilities. At year-end, accrued liabilities were $5,000. How much cash did Magic Toys pay for operating expenses?

    a. $38,000

    b. $53,000

    c. $48,000

    d. $43,000

Answers are given after Apply Your Knowledge (p. 700).

# Assess Your Progress

● Short Exercises

**S14-1**    ❶ **Purposes of the statement of cash flows [10 min]**                    MyAccountingLab
             Financial statements all have a goal. The cash flow statement does as well.

**Requirement**

   1. Describe how the statement of cash flows helps investors and creditors perform each of the following functions:
      a. Predict future cash flows.
      b. Evaluate management decisions.
      c. Predict the ability to make debt payments to lenders and to pay dividends to stockholders.

**S14-2** ❷ **Classifying cash flow items [10 min]**

Cash flow items must be categorized into one of four categories: financing, investing, noncash, or operating.

### Requirement

1. Answer the following questions about the statement of cash flows:
   a. List the categories of cash flows in the order they appear in the statement of cash flows.
   b. What is the "key reconciling figure" for the statement of cash flows? Where do you get this figure?
   c. What is the first dollar amount reported on the indirect method statement of cash flows?

**S14-3** ❸ **Classifying items on the indirect statement of cash flows [10 min]**

Destiny Corporation is preparing its statement of cash flows by the *indirect* method. Destiny has the following items for you to consider in preparing the statement:

_____ a. Increase in accounts payable    _____ g. Depreciation expense

_____ b. Payment of dividends    _____ h. Increase in inventory

_____ c. Decrease in accrued liabilities    _____ i. Decrease in accounts receivable

_____ d. Issuance of common stock    _____ j. Purchase of equipment

_____ e. Gain on sale of building

_____ f. Loss on sale of land

### Requirement

1. Identify each item as a(n)
   - Operating activity—addition to net income (O+), or subtraction from net income (O–)
   - Investing activity—addition to cash flow (I+), or subtraction from cash flow (I–)
   - Financing activity—addition to cash flow (F+), or subtraction from cash flow (F–)
   - Activity that is not used to prepare the indirect cash flow statement (N)

**S14-4** ❸ **Computing cash flows from operating activities—indirect method [10 min]**

OMD Equipment, Inc., reported the following data for 2012:

| | |
|---|---|
| **Income statement** | |
| Net income | $ 44,000 |
| Depreciation | 8,000 |
| **Balance sheet** | |
| Increase in Accounts receivable | 7,000 |
| Decrease in Accounts payable | 4,000 |

### Requirement

1. Compute OMD's net cash provided by operating activities—indirect method.

**S14-5** ❸ **Computing cash flows from operating activities—indirect method [10 min]**

One Way Cellular accountants have assembled the following data for the year ended September 30, 2012:

| | | | |
|---|---|---|---|
| Cash receipt from sale of land | $ 34,000 | Net income | $ 55,000 |
| Depreciation expense | 20,000 | Purchase of equipment | 39,000 |
| Payment of dividends | 6,100 | Decrease in current liabilities | 19,000 |
| Cash receipt from issuance of | | Increase in current assets | |
| common stock | 30,000 | other than cash | 14,000 |

## Requirement

1. Prepare the *operating* activities section using the indirect method for One Way Cellular's statement of cash flows for the year ended September 30, 2012.

*Note: Short Exercise 14-6 should be used only after completing Short Exercise 14-5.*

**S14-6** ❸ **Computing cash flows—indirect method [15 min]**

Use the data in Short Exercise 14-5 to complete this exercise.

## Requirement

1. Prepare One Way Cellular's statement of cash flows using the indirect method for the year ended September 30, 2012. Stop after determining the net increase (or decrease) in cash.

**S14-7** ❸ **Computing investing and financing cash flows [10 min]**

Kyler Media Corporation had the following income statement and balance sheet for 2012:

| KYLER MEDIA CORPORATION | |
|---|---|
| Income Statement | |
| Year Ended December 31, 2012 | |
| Service revenue | $ 80,000 |
| Depreciation expense | 5,600 |
| Other expenses | 49,000 |
| Net income | $ 25,400 |

| KYLER MEDIA CORPORATION | | | | | | |
|---|---|---|---|---|---|---|
| Comparative Balance Sheet | | | | | | |
| December 31, 2012 and 2011 | | | | | | |
| Assets | 2012 | 2011 | Liabilities | 2012 | 2011 |
| Current: | | | Current: | | |
| Cash | $ 4,800 | $ 3,800 | Accounts payable | $ 9,000 | $ 4,000 |
| Accounts receivable | 9,600 | 4,100 | Long-term notes payable | 9,000 | 15,000 |
| Equipment, net | 78,000 | 67,000 | Stockholders' Equity | | |
| | | | Common stock | 22,000 | 17,000 |
| | | | Retained earnings | 52,400 | 38,900 |
| Total assets | $ 92,400 | $ 74,900 | Total liabilities and stockholders' equity | $ 92,400 | $ 74,900 |

## Requirement

1. Compute for Kyler Media Corporation during 2012 the
   a. acquisition of equipment. The business sold no equipment during the year.
   b. payment of a long-term note payable. During the year, the business issued a $5,300 note payable.

*Note: Short Exercise 14-8 should be used only after completing Short Exercise 14-7.*

**S14-8** ❸ **Preparing the statement of cash flows—indirect method [15–20 min]**

Use the Kyler Media Corporation data in Short Exercise 14-7 and the results you calculated from the requirements.

## Requirement

1. Prepare Kyler Media's statement of cash flows—indirect method—for the year ended December 31, 2012.

**S14-9** ❸❹ **Computing the change in cash; identifying noncash transactions [5 min]**
Judy's Makeup Shops earned net income of $22,000, which included depreciation of $14,000. Judy's acquired a $119,000 building by borrowing $119,000 on a long-term note payable.

## Requirements

1. How much did Judy's cash balance increase or decrease during the year?
2. Were there any noncash transactions for the company? If so, show how they would be reported in the statement of cash flows.

**S14-10** ❺ **Computing free cash flow [5 min]**
Cooper Lopez Company expects the following for 2012:

- Net cash provided by operating activities of $158,000.
- Net cash provided by financing activities of $60,000.
- Net cash used for investing activities of $80,000 (no sales of long-term assets).
- Cash dividends paid to shareholders was $10,000.

## Requirement

1. How much free cash flow does Lopez expect for 2012?

# ● Exercises

*MyAccountingLab* **E14-11** ❶ **Predicting future cash flows [10 min]**
Anderson's Armoires reported net loss for the year of $25,000; however, it reported an increase in cash balance of $50,000. The CFO states, "Anderson's Armoires would have shown a profit were it not for the depreciation expense recorded this year."

## Requirements

1. Can the CFO be right? Why?
2. Based on the information provided, what would you predict future cash flows to be?

**E14-12** ❷ **Classifying cash flow items [10 min]**
Consider the following transactions:

a. Purchased equipment for $130,000 cash.
b. Issued $14 par preferred stock for cash.
c. Cash received from sales to customers of $35,000.
d. Cash paid to vendors, $17,000.
e. Sold building for $19,000 gain for cash.
f. Purchased common treasury shares for $28,000.
g. Paid a notes payable with 1,250 of the company's common shares.

## Requirement

1. Identify the category of the statement of cash flows in which each transaction would be reported.

**E14-13** ❸ **Classifying items on the indirect statement of cash flows [5–10 min]**
The cash flow statement categorizes like transactions for optimal reporting.

## Requirement

1. Identify each of the following transactions as one of the following:
   - Operating activity (O)
   - Investing activity (I)
   - Financing activity (F)
   - Noncash investing and financing activity (NIF)
   - Transaction that is not reported on the statement of cash flows (N)

For each cash flow, indicate whether the item increases (+) or decreases (–) cash. The *indirect* method is used to report cash flows from operating activities.

| | |
|---|---|
| _O_ a. Loss on sale of land. | _I +_ i. Cash sale of land. |
| _NIF_ b. Acquisition of equipment by issuance of note payable. | _F+_ j. Issuance of long-term note payable to borrow cash. |
| _F–_ c. Payment of long-term debt. | _O+_ k. Depreciation. |
| _NIF_ d. Acquisition of building by issuance of common stock. | _F–_ l. Purchase of treasury stock. |
| _O+_ e. Increase in salary payable. | _F+_ m. Issuance of common stock. |
| _O+_ f. Decrease in inventory. | _O+_ n. Increase in accounts payable. |
| _O–_ g. Increase in prepaid expenses. | _O+_ o. Net income. |
| _O–_ h. Decrease in accrued liabilities. | _F–_ p. Payment of cash dividend. |

**E14-14**  ❸ **Classifying transactions on the statement of cash flows—indirect method [5–10 min]**

Consider the following transactions:

| | | | | | |
|---|---|---|---|---|---|
| a. Cash | 72,000 | | g. Land | 22,000 | |
| Common stock | | 72,000 | Cash | | 22,000 |
| b. Treasury stock | 16,500 | | h. Cash | 9,600 | |
| Cash | | 16,500 | Equipment | | 9,600 |
| c. Cash | 88,000 | | i. Bonds payable | 51,000 | |
| Sales revenue | | 88,000 | Cash | | 51,000 |
| d. Land | 103,000 | | j. Building | 137,000 | |
| Cash | | 103,000 | Note payable, long-term | | 137,000 |
| e. Depreciation expense | 6,800 | | k. Loss on disposal of equipment | 1,800 | |
| Accumulated depreciation | | 6,800 | Equipment, net | | 1,800 |
| f. Dividends payable | 19,500 | | | | |
| Cash | | 19,500 | | | |

**Requirement**

1. Indicate whether each transaction would result in an operating activity, an investing activity, or a financing activity for an indirect method statement of cash flows and the accompanying schedule of noncash investing and financing activities.

**E14-15**  ❸ **Computing operating acitivites cash flow—indirect method [10–15 min]**

The records of McKnight Color Engraving reveal the following:

| | | | |
|---|---|---|---|
| Net income | $ 38,000 | Depreciation | $ 4,000 |
| Sales revenue | 51,000 | Decrease in current liabilities | 28,000 |
| Loss on sale of land | 5,000 | Increase in current assets | |
| Acquisition of land | 39,000 | other than cash | 14,000 |

## Requirements

1. Compute cash flows from operating activities by the indirect method.
2. Evaluate the operating cash flow of McKnight Color Engraving. Give the reason for your evaluation.

**E14-16** ❸ **Computing operating activities cash flow—indirect method [15–20 min]**

The accounting records of DVD Sales, Inc., include the following accounts:

| Cash | | | | Accounts receivable | | | | Inventory | |
|---|---|---|---|---|---|---|---|---|---|
| Jul 1 | 5,500 | | | Jul 1 | 21,000 | | | Jul 1 | 22,000 |
| | ???? | | | | ???? | | | | ???? |
| Jul 31 | 3,000 | | | Jul 31 | 17,000 | | | Jul 31 | 25,500 |

| Accounts payable | | | Accumulated depr.—equipment | | | Retained earnings | | | |
|---|---|---|---|---|---|---|---|---|---|
| | Jul 1 | 14,500 | Jul 1 | 55,000 | | | | Jul 1 | 65,000 |
| | | ???? | Depr | 3,000 | Dividend | 19,000 | Net Inc | 65,000 |
| | Jul 31 | 19,500 | Jul 31 | 58,000 | | | | Jul 31 | 111,000 |

## Requirement

1. Compute DVD's net cash provided by (used for) operating activities during July. Use the indirect method.

**E14-17** ❸ **Preparing the statement of cash flows—indirect method [20–30 min]**

The income statement of Minerals Plus, Inc., follows:

| MINERALS PLUS, INC. | | |
|---|---|---|
| Income Statement | | |
| Year Ended September 30, 2012 | | |
| Revenues: | | |
| Service revenue | | $ 235,000 |
| Expenses: | | |
| Cost of goods sold | $ 97,000 | |
| Salary expense | 57,000 | |
| Depreciation expense | 26,000 | |
| Income tax expense | 4,000 | 184,000 |
| Net income | | $ 51,000 |

Additional data follow:

a. Acquisition of plant assets is $118,000. Of this amount, $100,000 is paid in cash and $18,000 by signing a note payable.

b. Cash receipt from sale of land totals $28,000. There was no gain or loss.

c. Cash receipts from issuance of common stock total $29,000.

d. Payment of note payable is $18,000.

e. Payment of dividends is $8,000.

f. From the balance sheet:

|  | September 30, | |
| --- | --- | --- |
|  | 2012 | 2011 |
| Current Assets: | | |
| Cash ......................... | $ 30,000 | $ 8,000 |
| Accounts receivable .............. | 41,000 | 59,000 |
| Inventory ..................... | 97,000 | 93,000 |
| Current Liabilities: | | |
| Accounts payable ................ | $ 30,000 | $ 17,000 |
| Accrued liabilities ................ | 11,000 | 24,000 |

## Requirement

1. Prepare Minerals Plus's statement of cash flows for the year ended September 30, 2012, using the indirect method. Include a separate section for noncash investing and financing activities.

**E14-18** ③ Computing operating activities cash flow—indirect method [10–15 min]
Consider the following facts for Espresso Place:

a. Beginning and ending Retained earnings are $44,000 and $70,000, respectively. Net income for the period is $61,000.

b. Beginning and ending Plant assets, net, are $104,000 and $109,000, respectively. Depreciation for the period is $17,000, and acquisitions of new plant assets total $28,000. Plant assets were sold at a $5,000 gain.

## Requirements

1. How much are cash dividends?

2. What was the amount of the cash receipt from the sale of plant assets?

**E14-19** ③ Computing the cash effect of acquiring assets [10 min]
McKnight Exercise Equipment, Inc., reported the following financial statements for 2012:

| MCKNIGHT EXERCISE EQUIPMENT, INC. | | |
| --- | --- | --- |
| Income Statement | | |
| Year Ended December 31, 2012 | | |
| Sales revenue | | $ 714,000 |
| Cost of goods sold | $ 347,000 | |
| Depreciation expense | 52,000 | |
| Other expenses | 205,000 | |
| Total expenses | | 604,000 |
| Net income | | $ 110,000 |

| | | MCKNIGHT EXERCISE EQUIPMENT, INC. Comparative Balance Sheet December 31, 2012 and 2011 | | | |
|---|---|---|---|---|---|

| Assets | 2012 | 2011 | Liabilities | 2012 | 2011 |
|---|---|---|---|---|---|
| Current: | | | Current: | | |
| Cash | $ 19,000 | $ 18,000 | Accounts payable | $ 73,000 | $ 72,000 |
| Accounts receivable | 54,000 | 49,000 | Salary payable | 2,000 | 5,000 |
| Inventory | 81,000 | 89,000 | Long-term notes payable | 59,000 | 66,000 |
| Long-term investments | 95,000 | 77,000 | **Stockholders' Equity** | | |
| Plant assets, net | 221,000 | 183,000 | Common stock | 47,000 | 34,000 |
| | | | Retained earnings | 289,000 | 239,000 |
| | | | Total liabilities and | | |
| Total assets | $470,000 | $416,000 | stockholders' equity | $470,000 | $416,000 |

## Requirement

1. Compute the amount of McKnight Exercise's acquisition of plant assets. McKnight Exercise sold no plant assets.

## E14-20  ③ Computing the cash effect of transactions [15 min]

Use the McKnight Exercise Equipment data in Exercise 14-19.

## Requirement

1. Compute the following:

a. New borrowing or payment of long-term notes payable, with McKnight Exercise having only one long-term note payable transaction during the year.

b. Issuance of common stock, with McKnight Exercise having only one common stock transaction during the year.

c. Payment of cash dividends.

*Note: Exercise 14-21 should be used only after completing Exercises 14-19 and 14-20.*

## E14-21  ③ Computing the cash effect of transactions [15 min]

Use the McKnight Exercise Equipment data in Exercises 14-19 and 14-20.

## Requirement

1. Prepare the company's statement of cash flows—indirect method—for the year ended December 31, 2012.

## E14-22  ④ Identifying and reporting noncash transactions [15 min]

Dirtbikes, Inc., identified the following selected transactions that occurred during 2012:

a. Issued 1,250 shares of $2 par common stock for cash of $26,000.

b. Issued 5,500 shares of $2 par common stock for a building valued at $101,000.

c. Purchased new company truck with FMV of $28,000. Financed it 100% with a long-term note.

d. Paid short-term notes of $23,000 by issuing 2,400 shares of $2 par common stock.

e. Paid long-term note of $10,500 to Bank of Tallahassee. Issued new long-term note of $21,000 to Bank of Trust.

## Requirement

1. Identify any noncash transactions that occurred during the year and show how they would be reported in the noncash section of the cash flow statement.

**E14-23**  **⑤** **Analyzing free cash flow [15 min]**

Use the McKnight Exercise Equipment data in Exercises 14-19 and 14-20. McKnight plans to purchase a truck for $29,000 and a forklift for $121,000 next year.

**Requirement**

1. Calculate the amount of free cash flow McKnight has for 2012.

● Problems **(Group A)**

**P14-24A** **① ② ③** **Purpose of the statement and preparing the statement of cash flows—indirect method [40–50 min]**    *MyAccountingLab*

Classic Reserve Rare Coins (CRRC) was formed on January 1, 2012. Additional data for the year follows:

a. On January 1, 2012, CRRC issued common stock for $425,000.

b. Early in January, CRRC made the following cash payments:

   1. For store fixtures, $54,000.

   2. For inventory, $270,000.

   3. For rent expense on a store building, $10,000.

c. Later in the year, CRRC purchased inventory on account for $243,000. Before year-end, CRRC paid $163,000 of this account payable.

d. During 2012, CRRC sold 2,100 units of inventory for $350 each. Before year-end, the company collected 80% of this amount. Cost of goods sold for the year was $260,000, and ending inventory totaled $253,000.

e. The store employs three people. The combined annual payroll is $94,000, of which CRRC still owes $4,000 at year-end.

f. At the end of the year, CRRC paid income tax of $23,000.

g. Late in 2012, CRRC paid cash dividends of $41,000.

h. For equipment, CRRC uses the straight-line depreciation method, over five years, with zero residual value.

**Requirements**

1. What is the purpose of the cash flow statement?

2. Prepare CRRC's income statement for the year ended December 31, 2012. Use the single-step format, with all revenues listed together and all expenses listed together.

3. Prepare CRRC's balance sheet at December 31, 2012.

4. Prepare CRRC's statement of cash flows using the indirect method for the year ended December 31, 2012.

**P14-25A** **③** **Preparing the statement of cash flows—indirect method [35–45 min]**

Accountants for Johnson, Inc., have assembled the following data for the year ended December 31, 2012:

| | December 31, | |
| --- | --- | --- |
| | 2012 | 2011 |
| Current Accounts: | | |
| Current assets: | | |
| Cash and cash equivalents ......... | $ 92,100 | $ 17,000 |
| Accounts receivable .............. | 64,500 | 69,200 |
| Inventories .................... | 87,000 | 80,000 |
| Current liabilities: | | |
| Accounts payable ............... | 57,900 | 56,200 |
| Income tax payable ............. | 14,400 | 17,100 |

Transaction Data for 2012:

| | | | |
|---|---|---|---|
| Issuance of common stock | | Payment of note payable . . . . . . | $48,100 |
|     for cash . . . . . . . . . . . . . . . | $ 40,000 | Payment of cash dividends . . . . . | 54,000 |
| Depreciation expense . . . . . . . . | 25,000 | Issuance of note payable | |
| Purchase of equipment . . . . . . . . | 75,000 |     to borrow cash . . . . . . . . . | 67,000 |
| Acquisition of land by issuing | | Gain on sale of building . . . . . . . | 5,500 |
|     long-term note payable . . . | 122,000 | Net income . . . . . . . . . . . . . . . . | 70,500 |
| Cost basis of building sold . . . . . | 53,000 | | |

## Requirement

1. Prepare Johnson's statement of cash flows using the *indirect* method. Include an accompanying schedule of noncash investing and financing activities.

**P14-26A ③ ⑤ Preparing the statement of cash flows—indirect method, evaluating cash flows, and measuring free cash flows [35–45 min]**

The comparative balance sheet of Jackson Educational Supply at December 31, 2012, reported the following:

| | December 31, | |
|---|---|---|
| | **2012** | **2011** |
| Current assets: | | |
|     Cash and cash equivalents . . . . . . . . . . | $ 88,200 | $ 22,500 |
|     Accounts receivable . . . . . . . . . . . . . . | 14,400 | 21,700 |
|     Inventories . . . . . . . . . . . . . . . . . . . . | 63,600 | 60,400 |
| Current liabilities: | | |
|     Accounts payable . . . . . . . . . . . . . . . . | 28,600 | 27,100 |
|     Accrued liabilities . . . . . . . . . . . . . . . . | 10,600 | 11,200 |

Jackson's transactions during 2012 included the following:

| | | | |
|---|---|---|---|
| Payment of cash dividend | $ 17,200 | Depreciation expense | $ 16,700 |
| Purchase of equipment | 54,400 | Purchase of building | 100,000 |
| Issuance of long-term note payable | | Net income | 59,600 |
|     to borrow cash | 50,000 | Issuance of common stock for cash | 106,000 |

## Requirements

1. Prepare the statement of cash flows of Jackson Educational Supply for the year ended December 31, 2012. Use the *indirect* method to report cash flows from operating activities.
2. Evaluate Jackson's cash flows for the year. Mention all three categories of cash flows and give the reason for your evaluation.
3. If Jackson plans similar activity for 2013, what is its expected free cash flow?

**P14-27A ③ ④ Preparing the statement of cash flows—indirect method with noncash transactions [35-45 min]**

The 2012 comparative balance sheet and income statement of Rolling Hills, Inc., follow:

<table>
<tr><th colspan="4">ROLLING HILLS, INC.<br>Comparative Balance Sheet<br>December 31, 2012 and 2011</th></tr>
<tr><th></th><th>2012</th><th>2011</th><th>Increase (Decrease)</th></tr>
<tr><td>Current assets:</td><td></td><td></td><td></td></tr>
<tr><td>Cash and cash equivalents</td><td>$ 26,400</td><td>$ 15,900</td><td>$ 10,500</td></tr>
<tr><td>Accounts receivable</td><td>26,700</td><td>25,500</td><td>1,200</td></tr>
<tr><td>Inventories</td><td>79,800</td><td>91,700</td><td>(11,900)</td></tr>
<tr><td>Plant assets:</td><td></td><td></td><td></td></tr>
<tr><td>Land</td><td>34,600</td><td>11,000</td><td>23,600</td></tr>
<tr><td>Equipment, net</td><td>103,900</td><td>89,700</td><td>14,200</td></tr>
<tr><td>Total assets</td><td>$ 271,400</td><td>$ 233,800</td><td>$ 37,600</td></tr>
<tr><td>Current liabilities:</td><td></td><td></td><td></td></tr>
<tr><td>Accounts payable</td><td>$ 35,500</td><td>$ 30,600</td><td>$ 4,900</td></tr>
<tr><td>Accrued liabilities</td><td>28,600</td><td>30,700</td><td>(2,100)</td></tr>
<tr><td>Long-term liabilities:</td><td></td><td></td><td></td></tr>
<tr><td>Notes payable</td><td>78,000</td><td>101,000</td><td>(23,000)</td></tr>
<tr><td>Stockholders' equity:</td><td></td><td></td><td></td></tr>
<tr><td>Common stock</td><td>88,800</td><td>64,900</td><td>23,900</td></tr>
<tr><td>Retained earnings</td><td>40,500</td><td>6,600</td><td>33,900</td></tr>
<tr><td>Total liabilities and stockholders' equity</td><td>$ 271,400</td><td>$ 233,800</td><td>$ 37,600</td></tr>
</table>

<table>
<tr><th colspan="3">ROLLING HILLS, INC.<br>Income Statement<br>Year Ended December 31, 2012</th></tr>
<tr><td>Revenues:</td><td></td><td></td></tr>
<tr><td>Sales revenue</td><td></td><td>$ 436,000</td></tr>
<tr><td>Interest revenue</td><td></td><td>8,000</td></tr>
<tr><td>Total revenues</td><td></td><td>444,000</td></tr>
<tr><td>Expenses:</td><td></td><td></td></tr>
<tr><td>Cost of goods sold</td><td>$ 202,200</td><td></td></tr>
<tr><td>Salary expense</td><td>78,400</td><td></td></tr>
<tr><td>Depreciation expense</td><td>14,400</td><td></td></tr>
<tr><td>Other operating expense</td><td>10,200</td><td></td></tr>
<tr><td>Interest expense</td><td>21,900</td><td></td></tr>
<tr><td>Income tax expense</td><td>19,100</td><td></td></tr>
<tr><td>Total expenses</td><td></td><td>346,200</td></tr>
<tr><td>Net income</td><td></td><td>$ 97,800</td></tr>
</table>

Additionally, Rolling Hills purchased land of $23,600 by financing it 100% with long-term notes payable during 2012. During the year, there were no sales of land or equipment, no additional issuances of notes payable, no retirements of stock, and no treasury stock transactions.

## Requirements

1. Prepare the 2012 statement of cash flows, formatting operating activities by the *indirect* method.
2. How will what you learned in this problem help you evaluate an investment?

● Problems **(Group B)**

**P14-28B** **①②③** Purpose of the statement and preparing the statement of cash flows—indirect method [40–50 min]

National Reserve Rare Coins (NRRC) was formed on January 1, 2012. Additional data for the year follows:

---

a. On January 1, 2012, NRRC issued common stock for $525,000.
b. Early in January, NRRC made the following cash payments:
   1. For store fixtures, $55,000.
   2. For inventory, $320,000.
   3. For rent expense on a store building, $17,000.
c. Later in the year, NRRC purchased inventory on account for $244,000. Before year-end, NRRC paid $164,000 of this account payable.
d. During 2012, NRRC sold 2,500 units of inventory for $400 each. Before year end, the company collected 85% of this amount. Cost of goods sold for the year was $320,000, and ending inventory totaled $244,000.
e. The store employs three people. The combined annual payroll is $80,000, of which NRRC still owes $3,000 at year-end.
f. At the end of the year, NRRC paid income tax of $20,000.
g. Late in 2012, NRRC paid cash dividends of $39,000.
h. For equipment, NRRC uses the straight-line depreciation method, over five years, with zero residual value.

---

### Requirements

1. What is the purpose of the cash flow statement?
2. Prepare NRRC's income statement for the year ended December 31, 2012. Use the single-step format, with all revenues listed together and all expenses listed together.
3. Prepare NRRC's balance sheet at December 31, 2012.
4. Prepare NRRC's statement of cash flows using the *indirect* method for the year ended December 31, 2012.

**P14-29B** **③** Preparing the statement of cash flows—indirect method [35–45 min]

Accountants for Smithson, Inc., have assembled the following data for the year ended December 31, 2012:

| | December 31, | |
| --- | --- | --- |
| | 2012 | 2011 |
| **Current Accounts:** | | |
| Current assets: | | |
| Cash and cash equivalents .......... | $ 106,100 | $ 26,000 |
| Accounts receivable .............. | 64,300 | 68,900 |
| Inventories .................... | 80,000 | 75,000 |
| Current liabilities: | | |
| Accounts payable ................ | 57,700 | 56,100 |
| Income tax payable .............. | 14,500 | 17,000 |

| Transaction Data for 2012: | | | |
| --- | --- | --- | --- |
| Issuance of common stock | | Payment of note payable ...... | $46,100 |
| for cash .............. | $ 45,000 | Payment of cash dividends ..... | 52,000 |
| Depreciation expense ........ | 18,000 | Issuance of note payable | |
| Purchase of equipment ....... | 70,000 | to borrow cash ......... | 68,000 |
| Acquisition of land by issuing | | Gain on sale of building ....... | 3,500 |
| long-term note payable ... | 113,000 | Net income ................ | 68,500 |
| | | Cost basis of building sold ..... | $50,000 |

### Requirement

1. Prepare Smithson's statement of cash flows using the *indirect* method. Include an accompanying schedule of noncash investing and financing activities.

**P14-30B** ❸ ❺ **Preparing the statement of cash flows—indirect method, evaluating cash flows, and measuring free cash flows [35–45 min]**

The comparative balance sheet of Morgensen Educational Supply at December 31, 2012, reported the following:

| | December 31, | |
|---|---|---|
| | 2012 | 2011 |
| Current assets: | | |
| Cash and cash equivalents .......... | $ 89,600 | $ 24,500 |
| Accounts receivable ............... | 14,500 | 21,900 |
| Inventories ..................... | 62,800 | 60,000 |
| Current liabilities: | | |
| Accounts payable ................ | 30,100 | 27,600 |
| Accrued liabilities ................ | 11,100 | 11,600 |

Morgensen's transactions during 2012 included the following:

| | | | |
|---|---|---|---|
| Payment of cash dividend | $ 14,200 | Depreciation expense | $ 17,300 |
| Purchase of equipment | 55,200 | Purchase of building | 103,000 |
| Issuance of long-term note payable | | Net income | 57,600 |
| to borrow cash | 45,000 | Issuance of common stock for cash | 111,000 |

**Requirements**

1. Prepare the statement of cash flows of Morgensen Educational Supply for the year ended December 31, 2012. Use the *indirect* method to report cash flows from operating activities.

2. Evaluate Morgensen's cash flows for the year. Mention all three categories of cash flows and give the reason for your evaluation.

3. If Morgensen plans similar activity for 2013, what is its expected free cash flow?

**P14-31B** ❸ ❹ **Preparing the statement of cash flows—indirect method with noncash transactions [35–45 min]**

The 2012 comparative balance sheet and income statement of All Wired, Inc., follow:

| ALL WIRED, INC. Comparative Balance Sheet December 31, 2012 and 2011 | | | |
|---|---|---|---|
| | 2012 | 2011 | Increase (Decrease) |
| Current assets: | | | |
| Cash and cash equivalents | $ 26,700 | $ 15,600 | $ 11,100 |
| Accounts receivable | 26,500 | 25,300 | 1,200 |
| Inventories | 79,900 | 91,900 | (12,000) |
| Plant assets: | | | |
| Land | 35,500 | 11,000 | 24,500 |
| Equipment, net | 102,900 | 90,700 | 12,200 |
| Total assets | $ 271,500 | $ 234,500 | $ 37,000 |
| Current liabilities: | | | |
| Accounts payable | $ 35,600 | $ 30,500 | $ 5,100 |
| Accrued liabilities | 28,900 | 30,600 | (1,700) |
| Long-term liabilities: | | | |
| Notes payable | 77,000 | 103,000 | (26,000) |
| Stockholders' equity: | | | |
| Common stock | 88,200 | 64,300 | 23,900 |
| Retained earnings | 41,800 | 6,100 | 35,700 |
| Total liabilities and stockholders' equity | $ 271,500 | $ 234,500 | $ 37,000 |

**ALL WIRED, INC.**

**Income Statement**

Year Ended December 31, 2012

| Revenues: | | |
|---|---|---|
| Sales revenue | | $ 438,000 |
| Interest revenue | | 8,500 |
| Total revenues | | 446,500 |
| Expenses: | | |
| Cost of goods sold | $ 209,200 | |
| Salary expense | 72,400 | |
| Depreciation expense | 14,500 | |
| Other operating expense | 10,000 | |
| Interest expense | 21,500 | |
| Income tax expense | 19,400 | |
| Total expenses | | 347,000 |
| Net income | | $  99,500 |

Additionally, All Wired purchased land of $24,500 by financing it 100% with long-term notes payable during 2012. During the year, there were no sales of land or equipment, no additional issuances of notes payable, no retirements of stock, and no treasury stock transactions.

**Requirements**

1. Prepare the 2012 statement of cash flows, formatting operating activities by the *indirect* method.
2. How will what you learned in this problem help you evaluate an investment?

## ● Continuing Exercise

MyAccountingLab    **E14-32**    ❸ **Preparing the statement of cash flows—indirect method [25–35 min]**
This exercise continues the Lawlor Lawn Service, Inc., situation from Exercise 13-36 of Chapter 13. Refer to the comparative balance sheet for Lawlor Lawn Service.

**LAWLOR LAWN SERVICE, INC.**

**Comparative Balance Sheet**

May 31, 2013 and 2012

| Assets | 2013 | 2012 |
|---|---|---|
| Cash | $ 17,420 | $  2,420 |
| Accounts receivable | 2,550 | 50 |
| Lawn supplies | 150 | 40 |
| Equipment | 1,440 | 1,440 |
| Accumulated depreciation | (360) | (30) |
| Building | 120,000 | 0 |
| Accumulated depreciation | (2,500) | — |
| Total Assets | $138,700 | $  3,920 |
| **Liabilities** | | |
| Accounts payable | $      440 | $  1,440 |
| Interest payable | 555 | 0 |
| Current portion of mortgage payable | 12,000 | 0 |
| Mortgage payable | 99,000 | 0 |
| Total liabilities | $111,995 | $  1,440 |
| **Stockholders' Equity** | | |
| Common stock | 2,700 | 1,700 |
| Retained earnings | 24,005 | 780 |
| Total liabilities and stockholders' equity | $138,700 | $  3,920 |

## Requirement

1.  Prepare the statement of cash flows using the *indirect* method. Assume no dividends were declared or paid during the year.

# ● Continuing Problem

**P14-33**  ❸ **Preparing the statement of cash flows—indirect method [25–35 min]**     *MyAccountingLab*

This problem continues the Draper Consulting, Inc., situation from Problem 13-37 of Chapter 13. Refer to the comparative balance sheet for Draper Consulting.

**DRAPER CONSULTING, INC.**
**Comparative Balance Sheet**
**December 31, 2013 and 2012**

| Assets | 2013 | 2012 |
|---|---|---|
| Cash | $ 514,936 | $ 16,350 |
| Accounts receivable | 37,500 | 1,750 |
| Supplies | 2,200 | 200 |
| Equipment | 16,000 | 1,800 |
| Furniture | 5,700 | 4,200 |
| Building | 125,000 | 0 |
| Accumulated depreciation | (2,753) | (100) |
| Total assets | $ 698,583 | $ 24,200 |
| **Liabilities** | | |
| Accounts payable | $ 10,000 | $ 4,650 |
| Salary payable | 4,100 | 685 |
| Unearned service revenue | 0 | 700 |
| Interest payable | 10,667 | 0 |
| Notes payable | 40,000 | 0 |
| Bonds payable | 400,000 | 0 |
| Discount on bonds payable | (36,184) | 0 |
| **Stockholders' Equity** | | |
| Common stock | 130,000 | 18,000 |
| Retained earnings | 140,000 | 165 |
| Total liabilities and stockholders' equity | $ 698,583 | $ 24,200 |

## Requirement

1.  Prepare the statement of cash flows using the indirect method.

# Apply Your Knowledge

# ● Decision Cases

**Decision Case 14-1** The 2014 comparative income statement and the 2014 comparative balance sheet of Golf America, Inc., have just been distributed at a meeting of the company's board of directors. The members of the board of directors raise a fundamental question: Why is the cash balance so low? This question is especially hard to understand because 2014 showed record profits. As the controller of the company, you must answer the question.

**GOLF AMERICA, INC.**
**Comparative Income Statement**
Years Ended December 31, 2014 and 2013

|  | 2014 | 2013 |
|---|---|---|
| Revenues and gains: |  |  |
| Sales revenue | $444 | $310 |
| Gain on sale of equipment (sale price, $33) | 0 | 18 |
| Total revenues and gains | $444 | $328 |
| Expenses and losses: |  |  |
| Cost of goods sold | $221 | $162 |
| Salary expense | 48 | 28 |
| Depreciation expense | 46 | 22 |
| Interest expense | 13 | 20 |
| Amortization expense on patent | 11 | 11 |
| Loss on sale of land (sale price, $61) | 0 | 35 |
| Total expenses and losses | $339 | $278 |
| Net income | $105 | $ 50 |

**GOLF AMERICA, INC.**
**Comparative Balance Sheet**
December 31, 2014 and 2013

|  | 2014 | 2013 |
|---|---|---|
| **Assets** |  |  |
| Cash | $ 25 | $ 63 |
| Accounts receivable, net | 72 | 61 |
| Inventories | 194 | 181 |
| Long-term investments | 31 | 0 |
| Property, plant, and equipment, net | 125 | 61 |
| Patents | 177 | 188 |
| Totals | $624 | $554 |
| **Liabilities and Stockholders' Equity** |  |  |
| Accounts payable | $ 63 | $ 56 |
| Accrued liabilities | 12 | 17 |
| Notes payable, long-term | 179 | 264 |
| Total liabilities | $254 | $337 |
| Common stock | $149 | $ 61 |
| Retained earnings | 221 | 156 |
| Total stockholders' equity | $370 | $217 |
| Total liabilities and stockholders' equity | $624 | $554 |

## Requirements

1. Prepare a statement of cash flows for 2014 in the format that best shows the relationship between net income and operating cash flow. The company sold no plant assets or long-term investments and issued no notes payable during 2014. There were *no* noncash investing and financing transactions during the year. Show all amounts in thousands.

2. Considering net income and the company's cash flows during 2014, was it a good year or a bad year? Give your reasons.

**Decision Case 14-2** Theater by Design and **Showcase Cinemas** are asking you to recommend their stock to your clients. Because Theater by Design and **Showcase** earn about the same net income and have similar financial positions, your decision depends on their cash flow statements, summarized as follows:

| | Theater by Design | | Showcase Cinemas | |
|---|---|---|---|---|
| Net cash provided by operating activities | | $ 30,000 | | $ 70,000 |
| Cash provided by (used for) investing activities: | | | | |
| Purchase of plant assets | $(20,000) | | $(100,000) | |
| Sale of plant assets | 40,000 | 20,000 | 10,000 | (90,000) |
| Cash provided by (used for) financing activities: | | | | |
| Issuance of common stock | | — | | 30,000 |
| Paying off long-term debt | | (40,000) | | — |
| Net increase in cash | | $ 10,000 | | $ 10,000 |

**Requirement**

1.  Based on their cash flows, which company looks better? Give your reasons.

## ● Ethical Issue 14-1

Moss Exports is having a bad year. Net income is only $60,000. Also, two important overseas customers are falling behind in their payments to Moss, and Moss's accounts receivable are ballooning. The company desperately needs a loan. The Moss Exports board of directors is considering ways to put the best face on the company's financial statements. Moss's bank closely examines cash flow from operations. Daniel Peavey, Moss's controller, suggests reclassifying the receivables from the slow-paying clients as long-term. He explains to the board that removing the $80,000 rise in accounts receivable from current assets will increase net cash provided by operations. This approach may help Moss get the loan.

**Requirements**

1.  Using only the amounts given, compute net cash provided by operations, both without and with the reclassification of the receivables. Which reporting makes Moss look better?
2.  Under what condition would the reclassification of the receivables be ethical? Unethical?

## ● Fraud Case 14-1

Frank Lou had recently been promoted to construction manager at a development firm. He was responsible for dealing with contractors who were bidding on a multi-million dollar excavation job for the new high-rise. Times were tough, several contractors had gone under recently, and the ones left standing were viciously competitive. That morning, four bids were sitting on Frank's desk. The deadline was midnight, and the bids would be opened the next morning. The first bidder, Bo Freely, was a tough but personable character that Frank had known for years. Frank had lunch with him today, and after a few beers, Bo hinted that if Frank "inadvertently" mentioned the amount of the lowest bid, he'd receive a "birthday card" with a gift of cash. After lunch, Frank carefully unsealed the bids and noticed that another firm had underbid Bo's company by a small margin. Frank took Bo's bid envelope, wrote the low bid amount in pencil on it, and carried it downstairs where Bo's son William was waiting. Later that afternoon, a new bid came in from Bo's company. The next day, Bo's company got the job, and Frank got a birthday card in his mailbox.

**Requirements**

1.  Was Frank's company hurt in any way by this fraudulent action?
2.  How could this action hurt Frank?
3.  How can a business protect against this kind of fraud?

## Financial Statement Case 14-1

Use the **Amazon.com** statement of cash flows, along with the company's other financial statements at the end of this book, to answer the following questions.

### Requirements

1. Which method does **Amazon** use to report net cash flows from *operating* activities? How can you tell?
2. **Amazon** earned net income during 2009. Did operations *provide* cash or *use* cash during 2009? Give the amount. How did operating cash during 2009 compare with 2008?
3. Evaluate 2009 in terms of net income, cash flows, balance sheet position, and overall results. Be specific.

## Team Projects

**Team Project 14-1** Each member of the team should obtain the annual report of a different company. Select companies in different industries. Evaluate each company's trend of cash flows for the most recent two years. In your evaluation of the companies' cash flows, you may use any other information that is publicly available: for example, the other financial statements (income statement, balance sheet, statement of stockholders' equity, and the related notes) and news stories from magazines and newspapers. Rank the companies' cash flows from best to worst and write a two-page report on your findings.

**Team Project 14-2** Select a company and obtain its annual report, including all the financial statements. Focus on the statement of cash flows and, in particular, the cash flows from operating activities. Specify whether the company uses the *direct* method or the *indirect* method to report operating cash flows.

## Communication Activity 14-1

In 60 words or fewer, explain the difference between operating, investing, and financing activities.

---

### Quick Check Answers

1. *d* 2. *d* 3. *b* 4. *a* 5. *d* 6. *c* 7. *c* 8. *c* 9. *d* 10. *b*

**For online homework, exercises, and problems that provide you immediate feedback, please visit myaccountinglab.com.**

# Preparing the Statement of Cash Flows by the Direct Method

The Financial Accounting Standards Board (FASB) prefers the direct method of reporting cash flows from operating activities. The direct method provides clearer information about the sources and uses of cash than does the indirect method. However, very few non-public companies use the direct method because it takes more computations than the indirect method. Investing and financing cash flows are exactly the same presentation under both direct and indirect methods. Since only the preparation of the operating section differs, it is all we discuss in this appendix.

To illustrate how the operating section of the statement of cash flows differs for the direct method, we will be using the Smart Touch Learning data we used within the main chapter. The steps to prepare the statement of cash flows by the direct method are as follows:

**6** Prepare the statement of cash flows by the direct method

**STEP 1:** Lay out the operating section format of the statement of cash flows by the direct method, as shown in Exhibit 14A-1.

**EXHIBIT 14A-1** | **Format of the Statement of Cash Flows: Direct Method**

**SMART TOUCH LEARNING, INC.**
**Statement of Cash Flows**
**Year Ended December 31, 2014**

± Cash flows from operating activities:
　Receipts:
　　Collections from customers
　　Interest received
　　Dividends received on investments
　　　Total cash receipts
　Payments:
　　To suppliers
　　To employees
　　For interest and income tax
　　　Total cash payments
　Net cash provided by (used for) operating activities
± Cash flows from investing activities:
　+ Cash receipts from sales of long-term (plant) assets (investments, land, building, equipment, and so on)
　– Acquisitions of long-term (plant) assets
　Net cash provided by (used for) investing activities
± Cash flows from financing activities:
　+ Cash receipts from issuance of stock
　+ Cash receipts from sale of treasury stock
　– Purchase of treasury stock
　+ Cash receipts from issuance of notes or bonds payable (borrowing)
　– Payment of notes or bonds payable
　– Payment of dividends
　Net cash provided by (used for) financing activities
= Net increase (decrease) in cash during the year
　+ Cash at December 31, 2013
　= Cash at December 31, 2014

**STEP 2:** Use the comparative balance sheet to determine the increase or decrease in cash during the period. The change in cash is the "reconciling key figure" for the statement of cash flows. Smart Touch's comparative balance sheet shows that cash decreased by $20,000 during 2014. (See Exhibit 14A-2.)

**EXHIBIT 14A-2** | **Comparative Balance Sheet**

**SMART TOUCH LEARNING, INC.**
**Comparative Balance Sheet**
**December 31, 2014 and 2013**

| | 2014 | 2013 | Increase (Decrease) |
|---|---|---|---|
| **Assets** | | | |
| Current: | | | |
| Cash | $ 22,000 | $ 42,000 | $ (20,000) |
| Accounts receivable | 90,000 | 73,000 | 17,000 |
| Inventory | 143,000 | 145,000 | (2,000) |
| Plant assets, net | 460,000 | 210,000 | 250,000 |
| Total assets | $715,000 | $470,000 | $245,000 |
| **Liabilities** | | | |
| Current: | | | |
| Accounts payable | $ 90,000 | $ 50,000 | $ 40,000 |
| Accrued liabilities | 5,000 | 10,000 | (5,000) |
| Long-term notes payable | 160,000 | 80,000 | 80,000 |
| **Stockholders' Equity** | | | |
| Common stock | 370,000 | 250,000 | 120,000 |
| Retained earnings | 110,000 | 80,000 | 30,000 |
| Treasury stock | (20,000) | 0 | (20,000) |
| Total liabilities and stockholders' equity | $715,000 | $470,000 | $245,000 |

Operating, Investing, Financing, Net income—Operating, Dividends—Financing

**EXHIBIT 14A-3** | **Income Statement**

**SMART TOUCH LEARNING, INC.**
**Income Statement**
**Year Ended December 31, 2014**

| | | |
|---|---|---|
| Revenues and gains: | | |
| Sales revenue | $ 286,000 | |
| Interest revenue | 12,000 | |
| Dividend revenue | 9,000 | |
| Gain on sale of plant assets | 10,000 | |
| Total revenues and gains | | $317,000 |
| Expenses: | | |
| Cost of goods sold | $156,000 | |
| Salary and wage expense | 56,000 | |
| Depreciation expense | 20,000 | |
| Other operating expense | 16,000 | |
| Interest expense | 15,000 | |
| Income tax expense | 14,000 | |
| Total expenses | | 277,000 |
| Net income | | $ 40,000 |

STEP 3: Use the available data to prepare the statement of cash flows. In the case of Smart Touch, there was no additional data outside of the balance sheet and income statement data in Exhibit 14A-3 that affected the operating activities section.

*The statement of cash flows reports only transactions with cash effects.* Exhibit 14A-4 shows Smart Touch's completed direct method statement of cash flows for 2014.

**EXHIBIT 14A-4**  |  **Statement of Cash Flows—Direct Method**

**SMART TOUCH LEARNING, INC.**
**Statement of Cash Flows**
**Year Ended December 31, 2014**

| | | | |
|---|---|---:|---:|
| | Cash flows from operating activities: | | |
| | Receipts: | | |
| | Collections from customers | $ 269,000 | |
| | Interest received | 12,000 | |
| | Dividends received | 9,000 | |
| | Total cash receipts | | $ 290,000 |
| | Payments: | | |
| | To suppliers | $(135,000) | |
| | To employees | (56,000) | |
| | For interest | (15,000) | |
| | For income tax | (14,000) | |
| | Total cash payments | | (220,000) |
| | Net cash provided by operating activities | | 70,000 |
| | Cash flows from investing activities: | | |
| E | Acquisition of plant assets | $(310,000) | |
| F | Cash receipts from sale of plant assets | 50,000 | |
| | Net cash used for investing activities | | (260,000) |
| | Cash flows from financing activities: | | |
| I | Cash receipts from issuance of common stock | $ 120,000 | |
| G | Cash receipts from issuance of notes payable | 90,000 | |
| H | Payment of notes payable | (10,000) | |
| J | Purchase of treasury stock | (20,000) | |
| K | Payment of dividends | (10,000) | |
| | Net cash provided by financing activities | | 170,000 |
| L | Net decrease in cash | | $ (20,000) |
| L | Cash balance, December 31, 2013 | | 42,000 |
| L | Cash balance, December 31, 2014 | | $  22,000 |

*Letters denote same values as in Exhibit 14-4

Next, we will explain how we calculated each number.

## Cash Flows from Operating Activities

In the indirect method, we start with net income and then adjust it to "cash-basis" through a series of adjusting items. When calculating the direct method, we take each line item of the income statement and convert it from accrual to cash basis. So, in essence, the operating activities section of the direct-method cash flows statement is really just a cash-basis income statement. We can do this using the T-account method or we can modify the account change chart used earlier in the chapter as seen in Exhibit 14A-5 on the following page.

| EXHIBIT 14A-5 | Direct Method: How Changes in Account Balances Affect Cash Receipts and Cash Payments |
|---|---|

Asset ↑ Cash Flow ↓ Cash Receipts ↓ or Cash Payments ↑
Asset ↓ Cash Flow ↑ Cash Receipts ↑ or Cash Payments ↓
Liability ↑ Cash Flow ↑ Cash Receipts ↑ or Cash Payments ↓
Liability ↓ Cash Flow ↓ Cash Receipts ↓ or Cash Payments ↑
Equity ↑ Cash Flow ↑ Cash Receipts ↑ or Cash Payments ↓
Equity ↓ Cash Flow ↓ Cash Receipts ↓ or Cash Payments ↑

Notice that we have added the Cash Receipts and Cash Payments to the charts shown on page 668 and 669. An increase in Cash (indicated by ↑) is either going to arise from increasing cash receipts or decreasing cash payments (indicated by ↓). Now let's apply this information to Smart Touch.

## Cash Collections from Customers

The first item on the income statement is Sales revenue. Sales revenue represents the total of all sales, whether for cash or on account. The balance sheet account related to Sales revenue is Accounts receivable. Accounts receivable went from $73,000 at 12/31/13 to $90,000 at 12/31/14, an increase of $17,000. Applying our chart appears as follows:

Sales revenue – Increase in Accounts receivable = Cash collections from customers
$286,000 – $17,000 = $269,000
Asset ↑ Cash Flow ↓ Cash Receipts ↓ or Cash Payments ↑

So, the cash Smart Touch received from customers is $269,000. This is the first item in the operating activities section of the direct-method cash flow statement. You can verify this by looking at Exhibit 14A-4 on page 703.

## Cash Receipts of Interest

The second item on the income statement is interest revenue. The balance sheet account related to Interest revenue is Interest receivable. Since there is no Interest receivable account on the balance sheet, the interest revenue must have all been received in cash. So, the cash flow statement shows interest received of $12,000 in Exhibit 14A-4 on page 703.

## Cash Receipts of Dividends

Dividend revenue is the third item reported on the income statement. The balance sheet account related to Dividend revenue is Dividends receivable. As with the interest, there is no Dividends receivable account on the balance sheet. Therefore, the dividend revenue must have all been received in cash. So, the cash flow statement shows cash received from dividends of $9,000 in Exhibit 14A-4 on page 703.

## Gain on Sale of Plant Assets

The next item on the income statement is the gain on sale of plant assets. However, the cash received from the sale of the assets is reported in the investing section, not the operating section. As noted earlier, there is no difference in the investing section between the indirect method and direct method of the statement of cash flows.

## Payments to Suppliers

Payments to suppliers include all payments for

- inventory and
- operating expenses except employee compensation, interest, and income taxes.

*Suppliers* are those entities that provide the business with its inventory and essential services. The accounts related to supplier payments for inventory are Cost of goods sold, Inventory, and Accounts payable. Cost of goods sold on the income statement was $156,000. Inventory decreased from $145,000 at 12/31/13 to $143,000 at 12/31/14. Accounts payable increased from $50,000 at 12/31/13 to $90,000 at 12/31/14. Applying our formula, we can calculate cash paid for inventory as follows:

Cost of goods sold – Decrease in Inventory – Increase in Accounts payable = Cash paid for Inventory

| $156,000 | – | $2,000 | – | $40,000 | = | $114,000 |
|---|---|---|---|---|---|---|

Asset ↓ Cash Flow ↑ **Cash Receipts** ↑ or Cash Payments ↓ Liability ↑ Cash Flow ↑ **Cash Receipts** ↑ or Cash Payments ↓

The accounts related to supplier payments for operating expenses are Other operating expenses and Accrued liabilities. Other operating expenses on the income statement were $16,000. Accrued liabilities decreased from $10,000 at 12/31/13 to $5,000 at 12/31/14. Applying our formula, we can calculate cash paid for operating expenses as follows:

Other operating expenses + Decrease in Accrued liabilities = Cash paid for operating expenses

| $16,000 | + | $5,000 | = | $21,000 |
|---|---|---|---|---|

Liability ↓ Cash Flow ↓ **Cash Receipts** ↓ or Cash Payments ↑

Adding them together, we get total cash paid to suppliers of $135,000. (Confirm in Exhibit 14A-4 on page 703.)

Cash paid for Inventory + Cash paid for operating expenses = Cash paid to suppliers

| $114,000 | + | $21,000 | = | $135,000 |
|---|---|---|---|---|

## Payments to Employees

This category includes payments for salaries, wages, and other forms of employee compensation. Accrued amounts are not cash flows because they have not yet been paid. The accounts related to employee payments are salary and wage expense from the income statement and Salary and wage payable from the balance sheet. Since there is not a Salary payable account on the balance sheet, the Salary and wage expense account must represent all amounts paid in cash to employees. So, the cash flow statement shows cash payments to employees of $56,000 in Exhibit 14A-4 on page 703.

## Depreciation, Depletion, and Amortization Expense

These expenses are *not* reported on the direct method statement of cash flows because they do not affect cash.

## Payments for Interest Expense

These cash payments are reported separately from the other expenses. The accounts related to interest payments are Interest expense from the income statement and Interest payable from the balance sheet. Since there is no Interest payable account on the balance sheet, the Interest expense account from the income statement must represent all amounts paid in cash for interest. So, the cash flow statement shows cash payments for interest of $15,000 in Exhibit 14A-4 on page 703.

## Payments for Income Tax Expense

Like interest expense, these cash payments are reported separately from the other expenses. The accounts related to income tax payments are Income tax expense from the income statement and Income tax payable from the balance sheet. Since there is no Income tax payable account on the balance sheet, the Income tax expense account from the income statement must represent all amounts paid in cash for income tax. So, the cash flow statement shows cash payments for income tax of $14,000 in Exhibit 14A-4 on page 703.

## Net Cash Provided by Operating Activities

To calculate net cash provided by operating activities using the direct method, we add all the cash receipts and cash payments described previously and find the difference. For Smart Touch, total Cash receipts were $290,000. Total Cash payments were $220,000. So, net cash provided by operating activities is $70,000. If you refer back to the indirect-method cash flow statement shown in Exhibit 14-4 on page 666, you will find that it showed the same $70,000 for net cash provided by operating activities—only the method by which it was calculated was different.

The remainder of Smart Touch's cash flow statement is exactly the same as what we calculated using the indirect method. (See Exhibit 14-4 on page 666.)

# Summary Problem 14A-1

Assume that **Berkshire Hathaway** is considering buying Granite Shoals Corporation. Granite Shoals reported the following comparative balance sheet and income statement for 2014:

**GRANITE SHOALS CORPORATION**
**Balance Sheet**
**December 31, 2014 and 2013**

|  | 2014 | 2013 | Increase (Decrease) |
|---|---|---|---|
| Cash | $ 19,000 | $ 3,000 | $16,000 |
| Accounts receivable | 22,000 | 23,000 | (1,000) |
| Inventory | 34,000 | 31,000 | 3,000 |
| Prepaid expenses | 1,000 | 3,000 | (2,000) |
| Equipment (net) | 90,000 | 79,000 | 11,000 |
| Intangible assets | 9,000 | 9,000 | — |
| Total assets | $175,000 | $148,000 | $27,000 |
| Accounts payable | $ 14,000 | $ 9,000 | $ 5,000 |
| Accrued liabilities | 16,000 | 19,000 | (3,000) |
| Income tax payable | 14,000 | 12,000 | 2,000 |
| Long-term note payable | 45,000 | 50,000 | (5,000) |
| Common stock | 31,000 | 20,000 | 11,000 |
| Retained earnings | 64,000 | 40,000 | 24,000 |
| Treasury stock | (9,000) | (2,000) | (7,000) |
| Total liabilities and stockholders' equity | $175,000 | $148,000 | $27,000 |

**GRANITE SHOALS CORPORATION**
**Income Statement**
Year Ended December 31, 2014

| | |
|---|---|
| Sales revenue | $190,000 |
| Gain on sale of equipment | 6,000 |
| Total revenue and gains | $196,000 |
| Cost of goods sold | $ 85,000 |
| Depreciation expense | 19,000 |
| Other operating expenses | 36,000 |
| Total expenses | $140,000 |
| Income before income tax | $ 56,000 |
| Income tax expense | 18,000 |
| Net income | $ 38,000 |

## Requirements

1. Compute the following cash flow amounts for 2014:
   a. Collections from customers
   b. Payments for inventory
   c. Payments for other operating expenses
   d. Payment of income tax
   e. Acquisition of equipment. Granite Shoals sold equipment that had book value of $15,000.
   f. Cash receipt from sale of plant assets
   g. Issuance of long-term note payable. Granite Shoals paid off $10,000 of long-term notes payable.
   h. Issuance of common stock
   i. Payment of dividends
   j. Purchase of treasury stock
2. Prepare Granite Shoals Corporation's statement of cash flows (*direct* method) for the year ended December 31, 2014. There were no noncash investing and financing activities.

# Solution

**1.** Cash flow amounts:

a.

| Collections from customers | = | Sales revenue | + | Decrease in accounts receivables |
|---|---|---|---|---|
| $191,000 | = | $190,000 | + | $1,000 |

b.

| Payments for inventory | = | Cost of goods sold | + | Increase in inventory | − | Increase in accounts payable |
|---|---|---|---|---|---|---|
| $83,000 | = | $85,000 | + | $3,000 | − | $5,000 |

c.

| Payments for other operating expenses | = | Other operating expenses | − | Decrease in prepaid expenses | + | Decrease in accrued liabilities |
|---|---|---|---|---|---|---|
| $37,000 | = | $36,000 | − | $2,000 | + | $3,000 |

d.

| Payment of income tax | = | Income tax expense | − | Increase in income tax payable |
|---|---|---|---|---|
| $16,000 | = | $18,000 | − | $2,000 |

e. Equipment, net (let X = Acquisitions)

| Beginning | + | Acquisitions | − | Depreciation expense | − | Book value sold | = | Ending |
|---|---|---|---|---|---|---|---|---|
| $79,000 | + | X | − | $19,000 | − | $15,000 | = | $90,000 |
| | | X | = | $45,000 | | | | |

f. Sale of plant assets

| Cash received | = | Book value of assets sold | + | Gain on sale |
|---|---|---|---|---|
| $21,000 | = | $15,000 | + | $6,000 |

g. Long-term note payable (let X = Issuance)

| Beginning | + | Issuance | − | Payment | = | Ending |
|---|---|---|---|---|---|---|
| $50,000 | + | X | − | $10,000 | = | $45,000 |
| | | X | = | $ 5,000 | | |

h. Common stock (let X = Issuance)

| Beginning | + | Issuance | = | Ending |
|---|---|---|---|---|
| $20,000 | + | X | = | $31,000 |
| | | X | = | $11,000 |

i. Retained earnings (let X = Dividends)

| Beginning | + | Net income | − | Dividends | = | Ending |
|---|---|---|---|---|---|---|
| $40,000 | + | $38,000 | − | X | = | $64,000 |
| | | | | X | = | $14,000 |

j. Treasury stock (let X = Purchases)

| Beginning | + | Purchases | = | Ending |
|---|---|---|---|---|
| $2,000 | + | X | = | $9,000 |
| | | X | = | $7,000 |

2.

| GRANITE SHOALS CORPORATION<br>Statement of Cash Flows<br>Year Ended December 31, 2014 | | |
|---|---|---|
| **Cash flows from operating activities:** | | |
| Receipts: | | |
| Collections from customers | $ 191,000 | |
| Payments: | | |
| To suppliers ($83,000 + $37,000) | (120,000) | |
| For income tax | (16,000) | |
| Net cash provided by operating activities | | $ 55,000 |
| | | |
| **Cash flows from investing activities:** | | |
| Acquisition of plant assets | $ (45,000) | |
| Sale of plant assets ($15,000 + $6,000) | 21,000 | |
| Net cash used for investing activities | | (24,000) |
| | | |
| **Cash flows from financing activities:** | | |
| Payment of dividends | $ (14,000) | |
| Issuance of common stock | 11,000 | |
| Payment of note payable | (10,000) | |
| Purchase of treasury stock | (7,000) | |
| Issuance of note payable | 5,000 | |
| Net cash used for financing activities | | (15,000) |
| | | |
| **Net increase in cash** | | $ 16,000 |
| Cash balance, December 31, 2013 | | 3,000 |
| Cash balance, December 31, 2014 | | $ 19,000 |

# Appendix 14A Assignments

## ● Short Exercises

**S14A-1**  ❻ **Preparing the direct method statement of cash flows [15 min]**
Jelly Bean, Inc., began 2012 with cash of $53,000. During the year Jelly Bean earned revenue of $597,000 and collected $621,000 from customers. Expenses for the year totaled $437,000, of which Jelly Bean paid $427,000 in cash to suppliers and employees. Jelly Bean also paid $145,000 to purchase equipment and a cash dividend of $54,000 to its stockholders during 2012.

**Requirement**

1. Prepare the company's statement of cash flows for the year ended December 31, 2012. Format operating activities by the direct method.

**S14A-2** ⑥ **Preparing operating activities using the direct method [5 min]**

Happy Tot's Learning Center has assembled the following data for the year ended June 30, 2012:

| | |
|---|---|
| Payments to suppliers . . . . . . . . . . . . . . . . . . | $ 117,000 |
| Purchase of equipment . . . . . . . . . . . . . . . . . | 42,000 |
| Payments to employees . . . . . . . . . . . . . . . . . | 72,000 |
| Payment of note payable . . . . . . . . . . . . . . | 25,000 |
| Payment of dividends . . . . . . . . . . . . . . . . . | 7,000 |
| Cash receipt from issuance of stock . . . . . . . . | 18,000 |
| Collections from customers . . . . . . . . . . . . . | 190,000 |
| Cash receipt from sale of land . . . . . . . . . . . | 60,000 |

## Requirement

1. Prepare the *operating* activities section of the business's statement of cash flows for the year ended June 30, 2012, using the direct method.

*Note: Short Exercise 14A-3 should be used only after completing Short Exercise 14A-2.*

**S14A-3** ⑥ **Preparing the direct method statement of cash flows [15 min]**

Use the data in Short Exercise 14A-2 and your results.

## Requirement

1. Prepare the business's complete statement of cash flows for the year ended June 30, 2012, using the *direct* method for operating activities. Stop after determining the net increase (or decrease) in cash.

**S14A-4** ⑥ **Preparing the direct method statement of cash flows [15 min]**

Rouse Toy Company reported the following comparative balance sheet:

| **ROUSE TOY COMPANY** | | | | | |
|---|---|---|---|---|---|
| **Comparative Balance Sheet** | | | | | |
| **December 31, 2012 and 2011** | | | | | |
| Assets | 2012 | 2011 | Liabilities | 2012 | 2011 |
| Current: | | | Current: | | |
|   Cash | $ 17,000 | $ 11,000 |   Accounts payable | $ 43,000 | $ 38,000 |
|   Accounts receivable | 59,000 | 49,000 |   Salary payable | 24,500 | 19,000 |
|   Inventory | 78,000 | 84,000 |   Accrued liabilities | 5,000 | 13,000 |
|   Prepaid expenses | 3,100 | 2,100 | Long-term notes payable | 60,000 | 70,000 |
| Long-term investments | 75,000 | 85,000 | **Stockholders' Equity** | | |
| Plant assets, net | 227,000 | 189,000 | Common stock | 42,000 | 39,000 |
| | | | Retained earnings | 284,600 | 241,100 |
| Total assets | $459,100 | $420,100 | Total liabilities and stockholders' equity | $459,100 | $420,100 |

## Requirement

1. Compute the following for Rouse Toy Company:
   a. Collections from customers during 2012. Sales totaled $143,000.
   b. Payments for inventory during 2012. Cost of goods sold was $80,000.

# • Exercises

**E14A-5** ⑥ **Identifying activity categories—direct method [10–15 min]**

Consider the following transactions:

| | |
|---|---|
| _____ **a.** Collection of accounts receivable. | _____ **i.** Purchase of treasury stock. |
| _____ **b.** Issuance of note payable to borrow cash. | _____ **j.** Issuance of common stock for cash. |
| _____ **c.** Depreciation. | _____ **k.** Payment of account payable. |
| _____ **d.** Issuance of preferred stock for cash. | _____ **l.** Acquisition of building by issuance of common stock. |
| _____ **e.** Payment of cash dividend. | _____ **m.** Purchase of equipment. |
| _____ **f.** Sale of land. | _____ **n.** Payment of wages to employees. |
| _____ **g.** Acquisition of equipment by issuance of note payable. | _____ **o.** Collection of cash interest. |
| _____ **h.** Payment of note payable. | _____ **p.** Sale of building |

## Requirement

1. Identify each of the transactions as a(n)
   - Operating activity (O)
   - Investing activity (I)
   - Financing activity (F)
   - Noncash investing and financing activity (NIF)
   - Transaction that is not reported on the statement of cash flows (N)

   For each cash flow, indicate whether the item increases (+) or decreases (–) cash. The _direct_ method is used for cash flows from operating activities.

**E14A-6** ⑥ **Identifying activity categories of transactions—direct method [5–10 min]**

Consider the following transactions:

| | | | | | | |
|---|---|---|---|---|---|---|
| a. Land | 17,000 | | g. Salary expense | 5,200 | |
| Cash | | 17,000 | Cash | | 5,200 |
| b. Cash | 9,800 | | h. Cash | 92,000 | |
| Equipment | | 9,800 | Common stock | | 92,000 |
| c. Bonds payable | 36,000 | | i. Treasury stock | 16,300 | |
| Cash | | 36,000 | Cash | | 16,300 |
| d. Building | 128,000 | | j. Cash | 3,200 | |
| Note payable | | 128,000 | Interest revenue | | 3,200 |
| e. Cash | 2,200 | | k. Land | 64,000 | |
| Accounts receivable | | 2,200 | Cash | | 64,000 |
| f. Dividends payable | 19,800 | | l. Accounts payable | 10,200 | |
| Cash | | 19,800 | Cash | | 10,200 |

## Requirement

1. Indicate where, if at all, each of the transactions would be reported on a statement of cash flows prepared by the _direct_ method and the accompanying schedule of noncash investing and financing activities.

**E14A-7** ⑥ **Preparing operating activities cash flow—direct method [10–15 min]**
The accounting records of Fuzzy Dice Auto Parts reveal the following:

| | | | |
|---|---:|---|---:|
| Payment of salaries and wages | $ 31,000 | Net income | $ 21,000 |
| Depreciation | 13,000 | Payment of income tax | 11,000 |
| Payment of interest | 16,000 | Collection of dividend revenue | 6,000 |
| Payment of dividends | 6,000 | Payment to suppliers | 54,000 |
| Collections from customers | 117,000 | | |

## Requirement

1. Compute cash flows from operating activities using the *direct* method.

**E14A-8** ⑥ **Identifying activity categories of transactions—direct method [5–10 min]**
Selected accounts of Printing Networks, Inc., show the following:

### Accounts receivable

| | | | |
|---|---:|---|---:|
| Beginning balance | 9,100 | | |
| Service revenue | 40,000 | Cash collections | 38,000 |
| Ending balance | 11,100 | | |

### Land

| | | | |
|---|---:|---|---:|
| Beginning balance | 87,000 | | |
| Acquisition | 14,000 | | |
| Ending balance | 101,000 | | |

### Long-term notes payable

| | | | |
|---|---:|---|---:|
| | | Beginning balance | 274,000 |
| Payments | 73,000 | Issuance for cash | 84,000 |
| | | Ending balance | 285,000 |

## Requirement

1. For each account, identify the item or items that should appear on a statement of cash flows prepared by the *direct* method. Also state each item's amount and where to report the item.

**E14A-9** ⑥ **Preparing the statement of cash flows—direct method [20–30 min]**
The income statement and additional data of Best Corporation follow:

| BEST CORPORATION | | | |
|---|---|---|---|
| **Income Statement** | | | |
| **Year Ended June 30, 2012** | | | |
| Revenues: | | | |
| Sales revenue | $ 231,000 | | |
| Dividend revenue | 8,000 | $ 239,000 | |
| Expenses: | | | |
| Cost of goods sold | $ 102,000 | | |
| Salary expense | 48,000 | | |
| Depreciation expense | 28,000 | | |
| Advertising expense | 13,000 | | |
| Income tax expense | 11,000 | | |
| Interest expense | 3,000 | 205,000 | |
| Net income | | $ 34,000 | |

Additional data follow:

a. Collections from customers are $15,500 more than sales.
b. Dividend revenue, interest expense, and income tax expense equal their cash amounts.
c. Payments to suppliers are the sum of cost of goods sold plus advertising expense.
d. Payments to employees are $1,000 more than salary expense.
e. Acquisition of plant assets is $102,000.
f. Cash receipts from sale of land total $24,000.
g. Cash receipts from issuance of common stock total $32,000.
h. Payment of long-term note payable is $17,000.
i. Payment of dividends is $10,500.
j. Cash balance, June 30, 2011, was $25,000; June 30, 2012 was $28,000.

## Requirement

1. Prepare Best Corporation's statement of cash flows for the year ended June 30, 2012. Use the *direct* method.

**E14A-10  ⑥ Computing cash flow items—direct method [10–15 min]**
Consider the following facts:

a. Beginning and ending Accounts receivable are $20,000 and $24,000, respectively. Credit sales for the period total $62,000.
b. Cost of goods sold is $76,000. Beginning Inventory balance is $27,000, and ending Inventory balance is $22,000. Beginning and ending Accounts payable are $14,000 and $9,000, respectively.

## Requirements

1. Compute cash collections from customers.
2. Compute cash payments for inventory.

**E14A-11  ⑥ Computing cash flow items—direct method [20–30 min]**
Superb Mobile Homes reported the following in its financial statements for the year ended December 31, 2012:

|  | 2012 | 2011 |
|---|---|---|
| **Income Statement** | | |
| Net sales | $ 25,118 | $ 21,115 |
| Cost of sales | 18,088 | 15,432 |
| Depreciation | 273 | 232 |
| Other operating expenses | 4,411 | 4,283 |
| Income tax expense | 536 | 481 |
| Net income | $ 1,810 | $ 687 |
| **Balance Sheet** | | |
| Cash and cash equivalents | $ 15 | $ 13 |
| Accounts receivable | 799 | 619 |
| Inventories | 3,489 | 2,839 |
| Property and equipment, net | 4,346 | 3,436 |
| Accounts payable | 1,544 | 1,364 |
| Accrued liabilities | 941 | 853 |
| Long-term liabilities | 479 | 468 |
| Common stock | 671 | 443 |
| Retained earnings | 5,014 | 3,779 |

## Requirement

1.  Determine the following for Superb Mobile Homes during 2012:

    a.  Collections from customers.
    b.  Payments for inventory.
    c.  Payments of operating expenses.
    d.  Acquisitions of property and equipment (no sales of property during 2012).
    e.  Borrowing, with Superb paying no long-term liabilities.
    f.  Cash receipt from issuance of common stock.
    g.  Payment of cash dividends.

## ● Problems (Group A)

**MyAccountingLab**

### P14A-12A  ❻ Preparing the statement of cash flows—direct method [35–45 min]

MPG, Inc., accountants have developed the following data from the company's accounting records for the year ended April 30, 2012:

a.  Purchase of plant assets, $59,400.
b.  Cash receipt from issuance of notes payable, $46,100.
c.  Payments of notes payable, $44,000.
d.  Cash receipt from sale of plant assets, $24,500.
e.  Cash receipt of dividends, $4,800.
f.  Payments to suppliers, $374,300.
g.  Interest expense and payments, $12,000.
h.  Payments of salaries, $88,000.
i.  Income tax expense and payments, $37,000.
j.  Depreciation expense, $59,900.
k.  Collections from customers, $605,500.
l.  Payment of cash dividends, $49,400.
m.  Cash receipt from issuance of common stock, $64,900.
n.  Cash balance: April 30, 2011, $40,000; April 30, 2012, $121,700.

## Requirement

1.  Prepare MPG's statement of cash flows for the year ended April 30, 2012. Use the *direct* method for cash flows from operating activities.

### P14A-13A  ❻ Preparing the statement of cash flows—direct method [40 min]

Use the Classic Reserve Rare Coins data from Problem 14-24A.

## Requirements

1.  Prepare Classic Reserve Rare Coins' income statement for the year ended December 31, 2012. Use the single-step format, with all revenues listed together and all expenses listed together.

2.  Prepare Classic Reserve's balance sheet at December 31, 2012.

3.  Prepare Classic Reserve's statement of cash flows for the year ended December 31, 2012. Format cash flows from operating activities by the *direct* method.

### P14A-14A  ❻ Preparing the statement of cash flows—direct method [30–40 min]

Use the Rolling Hills data from Problem 14-27A.

## Requirements

1.  Prepare the 2012 statement of cash flows by the *direct* method.
2.  How will what you learned in this problem help you evaluate an investment?

### P14A-15A ⑥ Preparing the statement of cash flows—direct method [45–60 min]

To prepare the statement of cash flows, accountants for E-Mobile, Inc., have summarized 2012 activity in the Cash account as follows:

Cash

| | | | |
|---|---|---|---|
| Beginning balance | 87,200 | Payments of operating expenses | 46,800 |
| Issuance of common stock | 60,200 | Payments of salaries and wages | 64,500 |
| Receipts of interest revenue | 16,100 | Payment of note payable | 79,000 |
| Collections from customers | 308,400 | Payment of income tax | 7,500 |
| | | Payments on accounts payable | 101,600 |
| | | Payments of dividends | 1,400 |
| | | Payments of interest | 21,700 |
| | | Purchase of equipment | 49,500 |
| Ending balance | 99,900 | | |

### Requirement

1. Prepare E-Mobile's statement of cash flows for the year ended December 31, 2012, using the *direct* method to report operating activities.

## ● Problems (Group B)

### P14A-16B ⑥ Preparing the statement of cash flows—direct method [35–45 min]

KSG, Inc., accountants have developed the following data from the company's accounting records for the year ended June 30, 2012:

a. Purchase of plant assets, $57,400.
b. Cash receipt from issuance of notes payable, $48,100.
c. Payments of notes payable, $45,000.
d. Cash receipt from sale of plant assets, $23,500.
e. Cash receipt of dividends, $4,300.
f. Payments to suppliers, $371,300.
g. Interest expense and payments, $13,500.
h. Payments of salaries, $92,000.
i. Income tax expense and payments, $38,000.
j. Depreciation expense, $56,000.
k. Collections from customers, $607,000.
l. Payment of cash dividends, $45,400.
m. Cash receipt from issuance of common stock, $65,900.
n. Cash balance: June 30, 2011, $39,300; June 30, 2012, $125,500.

### Requirement

1. Prepare KSG's statement of cash flows for the year ended June 30, 2012. Use the *direct* method for cash flows from operating activities.

### P14A-17B ⑥ Preparing the statement of cash flows—direct method [40 min]

Use the National Reserve Rare Coins data from Problem 14-28B.

### Requirements

1. Prepare National Reserve Rare Coins' income statement for the year ended December 31, 2012. Use the single-step format, with all revenues listed together and all expenses listed together.
2. Prepare National Reserve's balance sheet at December 31, 2012.
3. Prepare National Reserve's statement of cash flows for the year ended December 31, 2012. Format cash flows from operating activities by the *direct* method.

**P14A-18B** ⑥ **Preparing the statement of cash flows—direct method [30–40 min]**

Use the All Wired data from Problem 14-31B.

### Requirements

1. Prepare the 2012 statement of cash flows by the *direct* method.
2. How will what you learned in this problem help you evaluate an investment?

**P14A-19B** ⑥ **Preparing the statement of cash flows—direct method [45–60 min]**

To prepare the statement of cash flows, accountants for I-M-Mobile, Inc., have summarized 2012 activity in the Cash account as follows:

### Cash

| | | | |
|---|---|---|---|
| Beginning balance | 87,900 | Payments of operating expenses | 46,200 |
| Issuance of common stock | 60,700 | Payments of salaries and wages | 64,500 |
| Receipts of interest revenue | 15,600 | Payment of note payable | 78,000 |
| Collections from customers | 308,700 | Payment of income tax | 8,000 |
| | | Payments on accounts payable | 101,200 |
| | | Payments of dividends | 1,200 |
| | | Payments of interest | 21,400 |
| | | Purchase of equipment | 56,500 |
| Ending balance | 95,900 | | |

### Requirement

1. Prepare I-M-Mobile's statement of cash flows for the year ended December 31, 2012, using the *direct* method to report operating activities.

# Preparing the Indirect Statement of Cash Flows Using a Spreadsheet

The body of Chapter 14 discussed the uses of the statement of cash flows in decision making and showed how to prepare the statement using T-accounts. The T-account approach works well as a learning device. In practice, however, most companies face complex situations. In these cases, a spreadsheet can help in preparing the statement of cash flows.

The spreadsheet starts with the beginning balance sheet and concludes with the ending balance sheet. Two middle columns—one for debit amounts and the other for credit amounts—complete the spreadsheet. These columns, labeled "Transaction Analysis," hold the data for the statement of cash flows. Accountants can prepare the statement directly from the lower part of the spreadsheet. This appendix is based on the Smart Touch Learning data used in Chapter 14. We illustrate this approach only with the indirect method for operating activities. This method could be used for the direct method as well.

The *indirect* method reconciles net income to net cash provided by operating activities. Exhibit 14B-1 on the following page is the spreadsheet for preparing the statement of cash flows by the *indirect* method. Panel A shows the transaction analysis, and Panel B gives the statement of cash flows.

 **7** Prepare the indirect statement of cash flows using a spreadsheet

## Transaction Analysis on the Spreadsheet—Indirect Method

a. Net income of $40,000 is the first operating cash inflow. Net income is entered on the spreadsheet (Panel B) as a debit to Net income under Cash flows from operating activities and as a credit to Retained earnings on the balance sheet (Panel A).

b. Next come the adjustments to net income, starting with depreciation of $20,000—transaction (b)—which is debited to Depreciation and credited to Plant assets, net.

c. This transaction is the sale of plant assets. The $10,000 gain on the sale is entered as a credit to Gain on sale of plant assets—a subtraction from net income—under operating cash flows. This credit removes the $10,000 gain from operations because the cash proceeds from the sale were $50,000, not $10,000. The $50,000 sale amount is then entered on the spreadsheet under investing activities. Entry (c) is completed by crediting the plant assets' book value of $40,000 to the Plant assets, net account.

d. Entry (d) debits Accounts receivable for its $17,000 increase during the year. This amount is credited to Increase in accounts receivable under operating cash flows.

e. This entry credits Inventory for its $2,000 decrease during the year. This amount is debited to Decrease in inventory under operating cash flows.

f. This entry credits Accounts payable for its $40,000 increase during the year. Then, it is debited to show as Increase in accounts payable under operating cash flows.

g. This entry debits Accrued liabilities for its $5,000 decrease during the year. Then, it is credited to show as Decrease in accrued liabilities under operating cash flows.

h. This entry debits Plant assets, net for their purchase of $310,000 and credits Acquisition of plant assets under investing cash flows.

i. This entry debits Cash receipts from issuance of common stock of $120,000 under financing cash flows. The offsetting credit is to Common stock.

j. This entry is represented by a credit to Long-term notes payable and a debit under cash flows from financing activities of $90,000 (Cash receipt from issuance of notes payable).

**EXHIBIT 14B-1** | **Spreadsheet for Statement of Cash Flows—Indirect Method**

| | SMART TOUCH LEARNING, INC.<br>Spreadsheet for Statement of Cash Flows<br>Year Ended December 31, 2014 | | | | |
|---|---|---|---|---|---|
| 4 | | Balance | Transaction | | Balance |
| 5 | Panel A—Balance Sheet | 12/31/2013 | Analysis | | 12/31/2014 |
| 6 | Cash | $ 42,000 | | $ 20,000 (n) | $ 22,000 |
| 7 | Accounts receivable | 73,000 | (d) $ 17,000 | | 90,000 |
| 8 | Inventory | 145,000 | | 2,000 (e) | 143,000 |
| 9 | Plant assets, net | 210,000 | (h)  310,000 | 20,000 (b) | |
| 10 | | | | 40,000 (c) | 460,000 |
| 11 | Total assets | $470,000 | | | $715,000 |
| 12 | | | | | |
| 13 | Accounts payable | $ 50,000 | | 40,000 (f) | $ 90,000 |
| 14 | Accrued liabilities | 10,000 | (g)  5,000 | | 5,000 |
| 15 | Long-term notes payable | 80,000 | (k)  10,000 | 90,000 (j) | 160,000 |
| 16 | Common stock | 250,000 | | 120,000 (i) | 370,000 |
| 17 | Retained earnings | 80,000 | (m)  10,000 | 40,000 (a) | 110,000 |
| 18 | Treasury stock | 0 | (l)  20,000 | | (20,000) |
| 19 | Total liabilities and stockholders' equity | $470,000 | $372,000 | $372,000 | $715,000 |
| 20 | | | | | |
| 21 | | | | | |
| 22 | Panel B—Statement of Cash Flows | | | | |
| 23 | Cash flows from operating activities: | | | | |
| 24 | Net income | | (a) $ 40,000 | | |
| 25 | Adjustments to reconcile net income to net<br>cash provided by operating activities: | | | | |
| 26 | Depreciation | | (b)  20,000 | | |
| 27 | Gain on sale of plant assets | | | $ 10,000 (c) | |
| 28 | Increase in accounts receivable | | | 17,000 (d) | |
| 29 | Decrease in inventory | | (e)  2,000 | | |
| 30 | Increase in accounts payable | | (f)  40,000 | | |
| 31 | Decrease in accrued liabilities | | | 5,000 (g) | |
| 32 | Net cash provided by operating activities | | | | |
| 33 | Cash flows from investing activities: | | | | |
| 34 | Acquisition of plant assets | | | 310,000 (h) | |
| 35 | Cash receipt from sale of plant asset | | (c)  50,000 | | |
| 36 | Net cash used for investing activities | | | | |
| 37 | Cash flows from financing activities: | | | | |
| 38 | Cash receipt from issuance of common stock | | (i)  120,000 | | |
| 39 | Cash receipt from issuance of notes payable | | (j)  90,000 | | |
| 40 | Payment of notes payable | | | 10,000 (k) | |
| 41 | Purchase of treasury stock | | | 20,000 (l) | |
| 42 | Payment of dividends | | | 10,000 (m) | |
| 43 | Net cash provided by financing activities | | | | |
| 44 | | | $362,000 | $382,000 | |
| 45 | Net decrease in cash | | (n)  20,000 | | |
| 46 | | | $382,000 | $382,000 | |

k.  This entry is the opposite of (j). It is represented by a debit (reduction) of $10,000 to Long-term notes payable and a credit under cash flows from financial activities for Payment of notes payable.

l.  The purchase of treasury stock debited the Treasury stock account on the balance sheet $20,000. The corresponding cash flow entry "Purchase of treasury stock" credits $20,000 to reduce cash flow.

m.  The $10,000 reduction (debit) to the Retained earnings account is the result of dividends declared and paid by the company. So, we show "Payment of dividends" as a credit in the financing section.

n.  The final item in Exhibit 14B-1 on page 718 is the Net decrease in cash. It is shown as a credit to Cash and a debit to Net decrease in cash of $20,000.

# Appendix 14B Assignments

## ● Problems (Group A)

### P14B-1A  ③  Preparing the statement of cash flows—indirect method [45–60 min]

The 2012 comparative balance sheet and income statement of Appleton Group, Inc., follow. Appleton had no noncash investing and financing transactions during 2012.

| APPLETON GROUP, INC. Comparative Balance Sheet December 31, 2012 and 2011 | | | |
|---|---|---|---|
| | 2012 | 2011 | Increase (Decrease) |
| **Current assets:** | | | |
| Cash and cash equivalents | $ 9,300 | $ 15,300 | $ (6,000) |
| Accounts receivable | 42,000 | 43,200 | (1,200) |
| Inventories | 97,100 | 93,700 | 3,400 |
| **Plant assets:** | | | |
| Land | 41,100 | 16,000 | 25,100 |
| Equipment, net | 101,200 | 94,300 | 6,900 |
| Total assets | $ 290,700 | $ 262,500 | $ 28,200 |
| **Current liabilities:** | | | |
| Accounts payable | $ 25,600 | $ 26,600 | $ (1,000) |
| Accrued liabilities | 24,000 | 22,800 | 1,200 |
| **Long-term liabilities:** | | | |
| Notes payable | 46,000 | 62,000 | (16,000) |
| **Stockholders' equity:** | | | |
| Common stock | 140,300 | 131,400 | 8,900 |
| Retained earnings | 54,800 | 19,700 | 35,100 |
| Total liabilities and stockholders' equity | $ 290,700 | $ 262,500 | $ 28,200 |

**Experience the Power of Practice!**

As denoted by the logo, all of these questions, as well as additional practice materials, can be found in *MyAccountingLab*.

Please visit myaccountinglab.com

| APPLETON GROUP, INC. | | |
|---|---|---|
| **Income Statement** | | |
| Year Ended December 31, 2012 | | |
| Revenues: | | |
| Sales revenue | | $ 439,000 |
| Interest revenue | | 11,800 |
| Total revenues | | $ 450,800 |
| Expenses: | | |
| Cost of goods sold | $ 205,500 | |
| Salary expense | 76,500 | |
| Depreciation expense | 15,500 | |
| Other operating expense | 49,500 | |
| Interest expense | 24,300 | |
| Income tax expense | 16,300 | |
| Total expenses | | 387,600 |
| Net income | | $ 63,200 |

## Requirement

1. Prepare the spreadsheet for the 2012 statement of cash flows. Format cash flows from operating activities by the *indirect* method.

**P14B-2A** ③ **Preparing the statement of cash flows—indirect method [45–60 min]**
Review the data from P14-27A.

## Requirement

1. Prepare the spreadsheet for Rolling Hills' 2012 statement of cash flows. Format cash flows from operating activities by the *indirect* method.

## ● Problems (Group B)

*MyAccountingLab*

**P14B-3B** ③ **Preparing the statement of cash flows—indirect method [45–60 min]**
The 2012 comparative balance sheet and income statement of Attleboro Group, Inc. follow. Attleboro had no noncash investing and financing transactions during 2012.

| ATTLEBORO GROUP, INC. Comparative Balance Sheet December 31, 2012 and 2011 | | | |
| --- | --- | --- | --- |
| | 2012 | 2011 | Increase (Decrease) |
| Current assets: | | | |
| Cash and cash equivalents | $ 11,800 | $ 15,200 | $ (3,400) |
| Accounts receivable | 42,200 | 43,900 | (1,700) |
| Inventories | 96,800 | 93,500 | 3,300 |
| Plant assets: | | | |
| Land | 39,800 | 14,000 | 25,800 |
| Equipment, net | 101,100 | 93,800 | 7,300 |
| Total assets | $ 291,700 | $ 260,400 | $ 31,300 |
| Current liabilities: | | | |
| Accounts payable | $ 25,100 | $ 26,300 | $ (1,200) |
| Accrued liabilities | 24,200 | 22,500 | 1,700 |
| Long-term liabilities: | | | |
| Notes payable | 51,000 | 64,000 | (13,000) |
| Stockholders' equity: | | | |
| Common stock | 136,600 | 128,300 | 8,300 |
| Retained earnings | 54,800 | 19,300 | 35,500 |
| Total liabilities and stockholders' equity | $ 291,700 | $ 260,400 | $ 31,300 |

| ATTLEBORO GROUP, INC. Income Statement Year Ended December 31, 2012 | | |
| --- | --- | --- |
| Revenues: | | |
| Sales revenue | | $ 441,000 |
| Interest revenue | | 11,300 |
| Total revenues | | $ 452,300 |
| Expenses: | | |
| Cost of goods sold | $ 205,300 | |
| Salary expense | 76,500 | |
| Depreciation expense | 15,100 | |
| Other operating expense | 49,600 | |
| Interest expense | 24,700 | |
| Income tax expense | 16,700 | |
| Total expenses | | 387,900 |
| Net income | | $ 64,400 |

## Requirement

1. Prepare the spreadsheet for the 2012 statement of cash flows. Format cash flows from operating activities by the *indirect* method.

**P14B-4B** ③ **Preparing the statement of cash flows—indirect method [45–60 min]**
Review the data from P14-31B.

## Requirement

1. Prepare the spreadsheet for All Wired's 2012 statement of cash flows. Format cash flows from operating activities by the *indirect* method.

# 15 Financial Statement Analysis

How can we use the financial statement results to analyze a company?

**SMART TOUCH LEARNING, INC.**
**Balance Sheet**
May 31, 2013

| Assets | | | | Liabilities | |
|---|---|---|---|---|---|
| Current assets: | | | | Current liabilities: | |
| Cash | | $ 4,800 | | Accounts payable | $ 48,700 |
| Accounts receivable | | 2,600 | | Salary payable | 900 |
| Inventory | | 30,500 | | Interest payable | 100 |
| Supplies | | 600 | | Unearned service revenue | 400 |
| Prepaid rent | | 2,000 | | Total current liabilities | 50,100 |
| Total current assets | | | $ 40,500 | Long-term liabilities: | |
| Plant assets: | | | | Notes payable | 20,000 |
| Furniture | $18,000 | | | Total liabilities | 70,100 |
| Less: Accumulated depreciation—furniture | 300 | 17,700 | | | |
| Building | 48,000 | | | **Stockholders' Equity** | |
| Less: Accumulated depreciation—building | 200 | 47,800 | | Common stock | 30,000 |
| Total plant assets | | | 65,500 | Retained earnings | 5,900 |
| | | | | Total stockholders' equity | 35,900 |
| Total assets | | | $106,000 | Total liabilities and stockholders' equity | $106,000 |

## Learning Objectives

1. Perform a horizontal analysis of financial statements

2. Perform a vertical analysis of financial statements

3. Prepare and use common-size financial statements

4. Compute and evaluate the standard financial ratios

Now that you have learned some of the "how-tos" of financial statement preparation, you may be asking, "How can I use financial statements in a meaningful way to help me manage my company better? How can I compare my company's results with companies that do what I do?"

In this chapter, you'll learn tools that allow users to see beyond the pure "numbers" on the financial statements and translate them into meaningful analysis. We'll start by analyzing the statements of Smart Touch Learning and finish the chapter by analyzing Greg's Tunes.

•   •   •

Investors and creditors cannot evaluate a company by examining only one year's data. This is why most financial statements cover at least two periods. In fact, most financial analysis covers trends of three to five years. This chapter shows you how to use some of the analytical tools for charting a company's progress through time. These tools can be used by small business owners to measure performance, by financial analysts to analyze stock investments, by auditors to obtain an overall sense of a company's financial health, by creditors to determine credit risk, or by any other person wanting to compare financial data in relevant terms.

To accurately determine a company's performance, such as for Smart Touch, we need to compare its performance

**A.** from year to year.

**B.** with a competing company, like **Learning Tree**.

**C.** with the education and training industry as a whole.

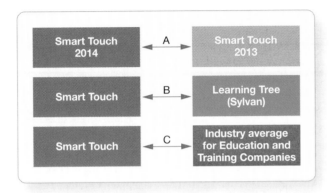

Then we will have a better idea of how to judge Smart Touch's present situation and predict what might happen in the near future.

There are three main ways to analyze financial statements:

- Horizontal analysis provides a year-to-year comparison of a company's performance in different periods.

- Another technique, vertical analysis, is a way to compare different companies.

- Comparing to the industry average provides a comparison of a company's performance in relationship to the industry in which the company operates.

We'll start with horizontal analysis.

# Horizontal Analysis

Many decisions hinge on whether the numbers—sales, expenses, and net income— are increasing or decreasing. Have sales and other revenues risen from last year? By how much?

 Perform a horizontal analysis of financial statements

Sales may have increased by $1,723 million ($3,189 – $1,466 from Exhibit 15-1 on the next page), but considered alone, this fact is not very helpful. The *percentage change* in sales over time is more relative and, therefore, more helpful. It is better to know that sales increased by 117.5% than to know that sales increased by $1,723 million.

The study of percentage changes in comparative statements is called **horizontal analysis. Horizontal analysis compares one year to the next.** Computing a percentage change in comparative statements requires two steps:

1. Compute the dollar amount of the change from the earlier period to the later period.

2. Divide the dollar amount of change by the earlier period amount. We call the earlier period the base period.

| EXHIBIT 15-1 | Comparative Income Statement, Smart Touch Learning, Inc. |
|---|---|

**SMART TOUCH LEARNING, INC.***
Income Statement (Adapted)
Year Ended December 31, 2014 and 2013

| (In millions) | 2014 | 2013 |
|---|---|---|
| **Revenues** (same as Net sales) | $3,189 | $1,466 |
| **Expenses:** | | |
| Cost of revenues (same as Cost of goods sold) | 1,458 | 626 |
| Sales and marketing expense | 246 | 120 |
| General and administrative expense | 140 | 57 |
| Research and development expense | 225 | 91 |
| Other expense | 470 | 225 |
| **Income before income tax** | 650 | 347 |
| Income tax expense | 251 | 241 |
| **Net income** | $ 399 | $ 106 |

*All values are assumed.

## Illustration: Smart Touch Learning, Inc.

Horizontal analysis is illustrated for Smart Touch as follows (dollar amounts in millions):

| | | | Increase (Decrease) | |
|---|---|---|---|---|
| | 2014 | 2013 | Amount | Percentage |
| Revenues (same as Net sales)......... | $3,189 | $1,466 | $1,723 | 117.5% |

Smart Touch sales increased by an incredible 117.5% during 2014, computed as follows:

STEP 1: Compute the dollar amount of change in sales from 2014 to 2013:

$$\begin{array}{ccc} 2014 & 2013 & \text{Increase} \\ \$3,189 - & \$1,466 = & \$1,723 \end{array}$$

STEP 2: Divide the dollar amount of change by the base-period amount. This computes the percentage change for the period:

$$\text{Percentage change} = \frac{\text{Dollar amount of change}}{\text{Base-period amount}}$$

$$= \frac{\$1,723}{\$1,466} = 1.175 = 117.5\%$$

Completed horizontal analyses for Smart Touch's financial statements are shown in the following exhibits:

- Exhibit 15-2 Income Statement
- Exhibit 15-3 Balance Sheet

**EXHIBIT 15-2** | **Comparative Income Statement—Horizontal Analysis**

SMART TOUCH LEARNING, INC.*
Income Statement (Adapted)
Year Ended December 31, 2014 and 2013

| (Dollar amounts in millions) | 2014 | 2013 | Increase (Decrease) Amount | Percentage |
|---|---|---|---|---|
| Revenues | $3,189 | $1,466 | $1,723 | 117.5% |
| Cost of revenues | 1,458 | 626 | 832 | 132.9 |
| Gross profit | $1,731 | $ 840 | $ 891 | 106.1 |
| Operating expenses: | | | | |
| Sales and marketing expense | $ 246 | $ 120 | $ 126 | 105.0 |
| General and administrative expense | 140 | 57 | 83 | 145.6 |
| Research and development expense | 225 | 91 | 134 | 147.3 |
| Other expense | 470 | 225 | 245 | 108.9 |
| Total operating expenses | $1,081 | $ 493 | $ 588 | 119.3 |
| Income before income tax | $ 650 | $ 347 | $ 303 | 87.3 |
| Income tax expense | 251 | 241 | 10 | 4.1 |
| Net income | $ 399 | $ 106 | $ 293 | 276.4 |

*All values are assumed.

**EXHIBIT 15-3** | **Comparative Balance Sheet—Horizontal Analysis**

SMART TOUCH LEARNING, INC.*
Balance Sheet (Adapted)
December 31, 2014 and 2013

| (Dollar amounts in millions) | 2014 | 2013 | Increase (Decrease) Amount | Percentage |
|---|---|---|---|---|
| **Assets** | | | | |
| Current assets: | | | | |
| Cash and cash equivalents | $ 427 | $149 | $ 278 | 186.6% |
| Other current assets | 2,266 | 411 | 1,855 | 451.3 |
| Total current assets | $2,693 | $560 | $ 2,133 | 380.9 |
| Property, plant, and equipment, net | 379 | 188 | 191 | 101.6 |
| Intangible assets, net | 194 | 106 | 88 | 83.0 |
| Other assets | 47 | 17 | 30 | 176.5 |
| Total assets | $3,313 | $871 | $ 2,442 | 280.4 |
| **Liabilities** | | | | |
| Current liabilities: | | | | |
| Accounts payable | $ 33 | $ 46 | $ (13) | (28.3)% |
| Other current liabilities | 307 | 189 | 118 | 62.4 |
| Total current liabilities | $ 340 | $235 | $ 105 | 44.7 |
| Long-term liabilities | 44 | 47 | (3) | (6.4) |
| Total liabilities | $ 384 | $282 | $ 102 | 36.2 |
| **Stockholders' Equity** | | | | |
| Common stock | $ 1 | $ 45 | $ (44) | (97.8) |
| Retained earnings and other equity | 2,928 | 544 | 2,384 | 438.2 |
| Total stockholders' equity | $2,929 | $589 | $ 2,340 | 397.3 |
| Total liabilities and stockholders' equity | $3,313 | $871 | $ 2,442 | 280.4 |

*All values are assumed.

## Horizontal Analysis of the Income Statement

Smart Touch's comparative income statement reveals exceptional growth during 2014. An increase of 100% occurs when an item doubles, so Smart Touch's 117.5% increase in revenues means that revenues more than doubled.

The item on Smart Touch's income statement with the slowest growth rate is income tax expense. Income taxes increased by only 4.1%. On the bottom line, net income grew by an incredible 276.4%. That is real progress!

## Horizontal Analysis of the Balance Sheet

Smart Touch's comparative balance sheet also shows rapid growth in assets, with total assets increasing by 280.4%. That means total assets almost quadrupled in one year. Very few companies grow that fast.

Smart Touch's liabilities grew more slowly. Total liabilities increased by 36.2%, and Accounts payable and long-term liabilities actually decreased, as indicated by the liability figures in parentheses. This is another indicator of positive growth for Smart Touch.

## Trend Analysis

**Trend analysis** is a form of horizontal analysis. **Trend precentages indicate the direction a business is taking.** How have sales changed over a five-year period? What trend does net income show? These questions can be answered by trend analysis over a period, such as three to five years.

Trend analysis percentages are computed by selecting a base year (the earliest year). The base year amounts are set equal to 100%. The amounts for each subsequent year are expressed as a percentage of the base amount. To compute trend analysis percentages, we divide each item for the following years by the base year amount.

$$\text{Trend \%} = \frac{\text{Any year \$}}{\text{Base year \$}} \times 100$$

Assume Smart Touch's total revenues were $1,000 million in 2010 and rose to $3,189 million in 2014. To illustrate trend analysis, review the trend of net sales during 2010–2014, with dollars in millions. The base year is 2010, so that year's percentage is set equal to 100.

| (In millions) | 2014 | 2013 | 2012 | 2011 | 2010 |
|---|---|---|---|---|---|
| Net sales.................. | $3,189 | 1,466 | 1,280 | 976 | 1,000 |
| Trend percentages ..... | 318.9% | 146.6% | 128% | 97.6% | 100% |

We want percentages for the five-year period 2010–2014. We compute these by dividing each year's amount by the 2010 net sales amount. Net sales decreased slightly in 2011 and then the rate of growth increased from 2012–2014.

You can perform a trend analysis on any one or multiple item(s) you consider important. Trend analysis is widely used to predict the future health of a company.

# Vertical Analysis

As we have seen, horizontal analysis and trend analysis percentages highlight changes in an item from year to year, or over *time*. But no single technique gives a complete picture of a business, so we also need vertical analysis.

**2** Perform a vertical analysis of financial statements

**Vertical analysis** of a financial statement shows the relationship of each item to its base amount, which is the 100% figure. Every other item on the statement is then reported as a percentage of that base. For the income statement, net sales is the base.

$$\text{Vertical analysis \%} = \frac{\text{Each income statement item}}{\text{Revenues (net sales)}} \times 100$$

Exhibit 15-4 shows the completed vertical analysis of Smart Touch's 2014 and 2013 comparative income statement.

The vertical analysis percentage for Smart Touch's cost of revenues is 45.7% of net sales ($1,458/$3,189 = 0.457 or 45.7%) in 2014 and 42.7% ($626/$1,466 = 0.427 or 42.7%) in 2013. This means that for every $1 in net sales, almost $0.46 in 2014 and almost $0.43 in 2013 is spent on cost of revenue.

On the bottom line, Smart Touch's net income is 12.5% of revenues in 2014 and 7.2% of revenues in 2013. That improvement from 2013 to 2014 is extremely good. Suppose under normal conditions a company's net income is 10% of revenues. A drop to 4% may cause the investors to be alarmed and sell their stock.

**EXHIBIT 15-4** | **Comparative Income Statement—Vertical Analysis**

| | 2014 | | 2013 | |
|---|---|---|---|---|
| **SMART TOUCH LEARNING, INC.*** **Comparative Income Statement (Adapted)** **Years Ended December 31, 2014 and 2013** | | | | |
| *(Dollar amounts in millions)* | Amount | Percent of Total | Amount | Percent of Total |
| Revenues | $3,189 | 100.0% | $1,466 | 100.0% |
| Cost of revenues | 1,458 | 45.7 | 626 | 42.7 |
| **Gross profit** | $1,731 | 54.3 | $ 840 | 57.3 |
| Operating expenses: | | | | |
|     Sales and marketing expense | $ 246 | 7.7 | $ 120 | 8.2 |
|     General and administrative expense | 140 | 4.4 | 57 | 3.9 |
|     Research and development expense | 225 | 7.1 | 91 | 6.2 |
|     Other expense | 470 | 14.7 | 225 | 15.3 |
|     Total operating expenses | $1,081 | 33.9 | $ 493 | 33.6 |
| Income before income tax | $ 650 | 20.4 | $ 347 | 23.7 |
| Income tax expense | 251 | 7.9 | 241 | 16.5^ |
| **Net income** | $ 399 | 12.5% | $ 106 | 7.2% |

*All values are assumed. ^The calculated percentage of 16.4 was adjusted for rounding to 16.5.

Exhibit 15-5 on the following page depicts the vertical analysis of Smart Touch's balance sheet. The base amount (100%) is total assets. The base amount is also total liabilities and equity, because they are exactly the same number, in 2014 that's $3,313. (Recall that they should always be the same number because of the accounting equation.)

**EXHIBIT 15-5** | **Comparative Balance Sheet—Vertical Analysis**

**SMART TOUCH LEARNING, INC.***
Balance Sheet (Adapted)
December 31, 2014 and 2013

| (Dollar amount in millions) | 2014 Amount | 2014 Percent of Total | 2013 Amount | 2013 Percent of Total |
|---|---|---|---|---|
| **Assets** | | | | |
| **Current Assets:** | | | | |
| Cash and cash equivalents | $ 427 | 12.9% | $149 | 17.1% |
| Other current assets | 2,266 | 68.4 | 411 | 47.2 |
| Total current assets | $2,693 | 81.3 | $560 | 64.3 |
| Property, plant, and equipment, net | 379 | 11.4 | 188 | 21.6 |
| Intangible assets, net | 194 | 5.9 | 106 | 12.1^ |
| Other assets | 47 | 1.4 | 17 | 2.0 |
| Total assets | $3,313 | 100.0% | $871 | 100.0% |
| **Liabilities** | | | | |
| **Current Liabilities:** | | | | |
| Accounts payable | $ 33 | 1.0% | $ 46 | 5.3% |
| Other current liabilities | 307 | 9.3 | 189 | 21.7 |
| Total current liabilities | $ 340 | 10.3 | $235 | 27.0 |
| Long-term liabilities | 44 | 1.3 | 47 | 5.4 |
| **Total liabilities** | $ 384 | 11.6 | $282 | 32.4 |
| **Stockholders' Equity** | | | | |
| Common stock | $ 1 | 0.0 | $ 45 | 5.2 |
| Retained earnings and other equity | 2,928 | 88.4 | 544 | 62.4 |
| Total stockholders' equity | $2,929 | 88.4 | $589 | 67.6 |
| Total liabilities and stockholders' equity | $3,313 | 100.0% | $871 | 100.0% |

*All values are assumed. ^percents rounded to balance.

The vertical analysis of Smart Touch's balance sheet reveals several interesting things:

- Current assets make up 81.3% of total assets in 2014 and 64.3% of total assets in 2013. For most companies this percentage is closer to 30%. The 81.3% of current assets represents a great deal of liquidity and a significant increase in liquidity from 2013 to 2014.

- Property, plant, and equipment make up only 11.4% of total assets in 2014 but 21.6% of total assets in 2013. This percentage is low because of the nature of Smart Touch's business. Smart Touch's Web-based operations do not require many buildings or equipment.

- Total liabilities are only 11.6% of total assets in 2014, but were 32.4% of total assets in 2013. This improvement is positive for Smart Touch. Stockholders' equity makes up 88.4% of total assets in 2014 and 67.6% of total assets in 2013. Most of Smart Touch's equity is retained earnings and other equity—signs of a strong company because most of the equity is internally generated rather than externally generated (through stock share sales).

**Key Takeaway**

Vertical analysis shows the relationship of each item on the statement to a base amount. The base amount is net sales on the income statement and total assets on the balance sheet. All other items are reported as a percentage of the 100% net sales line on the income statement or the 100% total assets line on the balance sheet.

# How Do We Compare One Company with Another?

 Prepare and use common-size financial statements

Horizontal analysis and vertical analysis provide much useful data about a company. As we have seen, Smart Touch's percentages depict a very successful company. But the data apply only to one business.

To compare Smart Touch to another company we can use a common-size statement. A **common-size statement** reports only percentages—the same percentages that appear in a vertical analysis. By only reporting percentages, it removes dollar value bias when comparing one company to another company. **Dollar value bias** is the bias one sees from comparing numbers in absolute (dollars) rather than relative (percentage) terms. For us, $1 million seems like a large number. For some large companies, it is immaterial. Smart Touch's common-size income statement is an example of removing dollar value bias. This statement comes directly from the percentages in Exhibit 15-4.

We could prepare common size statements for Smart Touch from year to year; however, we will start by preparing common size income statements for Smart Touch and **Learning Tree**, both of which compete in the service-learning industry. Which company earns a higher percentage of revenues as profits for its shareholders? Exhibit 15-6 gives both companies' common-size income statements for 2014 so that we may compare them on a relative, not absolute, basis.

| EXHIBIT 15-6 | Common-Size Income Statement Smart Touch vs. Learning Tree |
| --- | --- |

| SMART TOUCH vs. LEARNING TREE* Common-Size Income Statement Year Ended December 31, 2014 | | |
| --- | --- | --- |
| | Smart Touch | Learning Tree |
| Revenues | 100.0% | 100.0% |
| Cost of revenues | 45.7 | 36.3 |
| Gross profit | 54.3 | 63.7 |
| Sales and marketing expense | 7.7 | 21.8 |
| General and administrative expense | 4.4 | 7.3 |
| Research and development expense | 7.1 | 10.3 |
| Other expense (income) | 14.7 | (11.5) |
| Income before income tax | 20.4 | 35.8 |
| Income tax expense | 7.9 | 12.3 |
| Net income | 12.5% | 23.5% |

*All values are assumed.

Exhibit 15-6 shows that **Learning Tree** was more profitable than Smart Touch in 2014. **Learning Tree**'s gross profit percentage is 63.7%, compared to Smart Touch's 54.3%. This means that **Learning Tree** is earning more profit from every dollar of revenue than Smart Touch is earning. And, most importantly, **Learning Tree**'s percentage of net income to revenues is 23.5%. That means almost one-fourth of **Learning Tree**'s revenues result in profits for the company's stockholders. Smart Touch's percentage of net income to revenues, on the other hand, is 12.5%. Both are excellent percentages; however, the common-size statement highlights **Learning Tree**'s advantages over Smart Touch.

# Benchmarking

**Benchmarking** is the practice of comparing a company with other leading companies. It often uses the common size percentages in a graphical manner to highlight differences. There are two main types of benchmarks in financial statement analysis: benchmarking against a key competitor and benchmarking against the industry average.

## Benchmarking Against a Key Competitor

Exhibit 15-6 uses a key competitor, **Learning Tree**, to compare Smart Touch's profitability. The two companies compete in the same industry, so **Learning Tree** serves as an ideal benchmark for Smart Touch. The graphs in Exhibit 15-7

EXHIBIT 15-7

## Graphical Analysis of Common-Size Income Statement
## Smart Touch Learning vs. Learning Tree

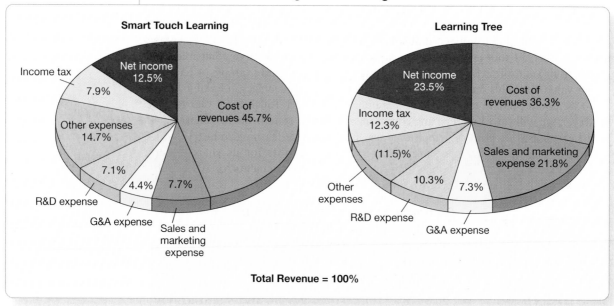

**Total Revenue = 100%**

highlight the profitability difference between the companies. Focus on the segment of the graphs showing net income. **Learning Tree** is clearly more profitable than Smart Touch.

## Benchmarking Against the Industry Average

The industry average can also serve as a very useful benchmark for evaluating a company. An industry comparison would show how Smart Touch is performing alongside the average for the e-learning industry. *Annual Statement Studies*, published by the Risk Management Association, provides common-size statements for most industries. To compare Smart Touch to the industry average, we would simply insert the industry-average common-size income statement in place of **Learning Tree** in Exhibit 15-6.

### Stop & Think...

As you are taking classes toward your degree, how do you know how quickly you can complete your studies? If you knew the average credit hours taken each semester was 12 credit hours, the 12 hours would be your benchmark. Comparing the number of classes you take to the average of 12 hours a semester is the same concept as benchmarking. Maybe you are taking 15 hours a semester. Then you'd be completing your degree faster than the average student. Maybe you take only 3 credit hours in the Spring so you can work a part-time job. Then, you'd be completing classes at a slower pace than average.

Now let's put your learning to practice. Work the summary problem on the following page, which reviews the concepts from the first half of this chapter.

**Key Takeaway**

Vertical analysis can be used to prepare common-size statements to compare companies against each other. We can benchmark (measure) a company against a key competitor or measure a company against the industry average.

# Summary Problem 15-1

## Requirements

Perform a horizontal analysis and a vertical analysis of the comparative income statement of Kimball Corporation, which makes iPod covers. State whether 2014 was a good year or a bad year, and give your reasons.

**KIMBALL CORPORATION**
**Comparative Income Statement**
Years Ended December 31, 2014 and 2013

|  | 2014 | 2013 |
|---|---|---|
| Net sales | $300,000 | $250,000 |
| Expenses: |  |  |
|    Cost of goods sold | $214,200 | $170,000 |
|    Engineering, selling, and administrative expenses | 54,000 | 48,000 |
|    Interest expense | 6,000 | 5,000 |
|    Income tax expense | 9,000 | 3,000 |
|    Other expense (income) | 2,700 | (1,000) |
|     Total expenses | 285,900 | 225,000 |
| Net income | $ 14,100 | $ 25,000 |

## Solution

**KIMBALL CORPORATION**
**Horizontal Analysis of Comparative Income Statement**
Years Ended December 31, 2014 and 2013

|  | 2014 | 2013 | Increase (Decrease) Amount | Increase (Decrease) Percent |
|---|---|---|---|---|
| Net sales | $300,000 | $250,000 | $ 50,000 | 20.0% |
| Expenses: |  |  |  |  |
|    Cost of goods sold | $214,200 | $170,000 | $ 44,200 | 26.0 |
|    Engineering, selling, and administrative expenses | 54,000 | 48,000 | 6,000 | 12.5 |
|    Interest expense | 6,000 | 5,000 | 1,000 | 20.0 |
|    Income tax expense | 9,000 | 3,000 | 6,000 | 200.0 |
|    Other expense (income) | 2,700 | (1,000) | 3,700 | —* |
|     Total expenses | 285,900 | 225,000 | 60,900 | 27.1 |
| Net income | $ 14,100 | $ 25,000 | $ (10,900) | (43.6%) |

*Percentage changes are typically not computed for shifts from a negative to a positive amount, and vice versa.

The horizontal analysis shows that net sales increased 20.0%. Total expenses increased by 27.1%, and net income decreased 43.6%. So, even though Kimball's net sales increased, the company's expenses increased by a larger percentage, netting an overall 43.6% reduction in net income between the years. This analysis identifies areas where management should review more data. For example, Cost of goods sold increased 26.0%. Managers would want to know why this increase occurred to determine if the company can implement cost saving strategies (such as purchasing from other, lower cost vendors).

| | 2014 | | 2013 | |
|---|---|---|---|---|
| KIMBALL CORPORATION<br>Vertical Analysis of Comparative Income Statement<br>Years Ended December 31, 2014 and 2013 | | | | |
| | **Amount** | **Percent** | **Amount** | **Percent** |
| Net sales | $300,000 | 100.0% | $250,000 | 100.0% |
| Expenses: | | | | |
| Cost of goods sold | $214,200 | 71.4 | $170,000 | 68.0 |
| Engineering, selling, and administrative expenses | 54,000 | 18.0 | 48,000 | 19.2 |
| Interest expense | 6,000 | 2.0 | 5,000 | 2.0 |
| Income tax expense | 9,000 | 3.0 | 3,000 | 1.2 |
| Other expense (income) | 2,700 | 0.9 | (1,000) | (0.4) |
| Total expenses | 285,900 | 95.3 | 225,000 | 90.0 |
| Net income | $ 14,100 | 4.7% | $ 25,000 | 10.0% |

The vertical analysis shows changes in the percentages of net sales. A few notable items are

- cost of goods sold—increased from 68.0% to 71.4%;
- engineering, selling, and administrative expenses—decreased from 19.2% to 18.0%.

These two items are Kimball's largest dollar expenses, so their percentage changes are important. This indicates that cost controls need to be improved, especially for COGS.

The 2014 net income declined to 4.7% of sales, compared with 10.0% the preceding year. Kimball's increase in cost of goods sold is the biggest factor in the overall decrease in net income as a percentage of sales. The horizontal analysis showed that although Net sales increased 20% from 2013 to 2014, the amount of each of those sales dollars resulting in net income decreased.

# Using Ratios to Make Decisions

 Compute and evaluate the standard financial ratios

Online financial databases, such as **Lexis/Nexis** and the **Dow Jones News Retrieval Service**, provide data on thousands of companies. Suppose you want to compare some companies' recent earnings histories. You might want to compare companies' returns on stockholders' equity. The computer could then search the databases and give you the names of the 20 companies with the highest return on equity. You can use any ratio to search for information that is relevant to a particular decision.

Remember, however, that no single ratio tells the whole picture of any company's performance. Different ratios explain different aspects of a company. The ratios we discuss in this chapter may be classified as follows:

1. Evaluating the ability to pay current liabilities
2. Evaluating the ability to sell inventory and collect receivables
3. Evaluating the ability to pay long-term debt
4. Evaluating profitability
5. Evaluating stock as an investment

# Evaluating the Ability to Pay Current Liabilities

**Working capital** is defined as follows:

> **Working capital = Current assets – Current liabilities**

Working capital measures the ability to meet short-term obligations with current assets. Two decision tools based on working-capital data are the *current ratio* and the *acid-test ratio*.

## Current Ratio

The most widely used ratio is the *current ratio*, which is current assets divided by current liabilities. **The current ratio measures a company's ability to pay current liabilities with its current assets.**

Exhibit 15-8 on the following page shows the comparative income statement and balance sheet of Greg's Tunes, which we will be using in the remainder of this chapter.

The current ratios of Greg's Tunes, at December 31, 2014 and 2013, follow, along with the average for the entertainment industry:

| Formula | Greg's Tunes' Current Ratio | | Industry Average |
|---|---|---|---|
| | 2014 | 2013 | |
| Current ratio = $\dfrac{\text{Current assets}}{\text{Current liabilities}}$ | $\dfrac{\$262,000}{\$142,000} = 1.85$ | $\dfrac{\$236,000}{\$126,000} = 1.87$ | 0.60 |

A high current ratio indicates that the business has sufficient current assets to maintain normal business operations. Compare Greg's Tunes' current ratio of 1.85 for 2014 with the industry average of 0.60.

What is an acceptable current ratio? The answer depends on the industry. The norm for companies in most industries is around 1.50, as reported by the Risk Management Association. Greg's Tunes' current ratio of 1.85 is strong. Keep in mind that we would not want to see a current ratio that is too high, say 25.0. This would indicate that the company is too liquid and, therefore, is not using its assets effectively. For example, the company may need to reduce inventory levels so as not to tie up available resources.

**EXHIBIT 15-8** | **Comparative Financial Statements**

### GREG'S TUNES, INC.
### Comparative Income Statement
Years Ended December 31, 2014 and 2013

|  | 2014 | 2013 |
|---|---|---|
| Net sales | $858,000 | $803,000 |
| Cost of goods sold | 513,000 | 509,000 |
| Gross profit | $345,000 | $294,000 |
| Operating expenses: |  |  |
|     Selling expenses | $126,000 | $114,000 |
|     General expenses | 118,000 | 123,000 |
|     Total operating expenses | $244,000 | $237,000 |
| Income from operations | $101,000 | $ 57,000 |
|     Interest revenue | 4,000 | — |
|     Interest (expense) | (24,000) | (14,000) |
| Income before income taxes | $ 81,000 | $ 43,000 |
|     Income tax expense | 33,000 | 17,000 |
| Net income | $ 48,000 | $ 26,000 |

### GREG'S TUNES, INC.
### Comparative Balance Sheet
December 31, 2014 and 2013

|  | 2014 | 2013 |
|---|---|---|
| **Assets** |  |  |
| **Current assets:** |  |  |
|     Cash | $ 29,000 | $ 32,000 |
|     Accounts receivable, net | 114,000 | 85,000 |
|     Inventories | 113,000 | 111,000 |
|     Prepaid expenses | 6,000 | 8,000 |
|     Total current assets | $262,000 | $236,000 |
| Long-term investments | 18,000 | 9,000 |
| Property, plant, and equipment, net | 507,000 | 399,000 |
|     Total assets | $787,000 | $644,000 |
| **Liabilities** |  |  |
| **Current liabilities:** |  |  |
|     Accounts payable | $ 73,000 | $ 68,000 |
|     Accrued liabilities | 27,000 | 31,000 |
|     Notes payable | 42,000 | 27,000 |
|     Total current liabilities | $142,000 | $126,000 |
| Long-term notes payable | 289,000 | 198,000 |
|     Total liabilities | $431,000 | $324,000 |
| **Stockholders' Equity** |  |  |
| Common stock, no par | $186,000 | $186,000 |
| Retained earnings | 170,000 | 134,000 |
|     Total stockholders' equity | $356,000 | $320,000 |
|     Total liabilities and stockholders' equity | $787,000 | $644,000 |

## Acid-Test Ratio

The *acid-test* (or *quick*) *ratio* tells us whether the entity could pay all its current liabilities if they came due immediately. That is, could the company pass the *acid test*?

To compute the acid-test ratio, we add cash, short-term investments (those that may be sold in the lesser of 12 months or the business operating cycle), and net current receivables (accounts and notes receivable, net of allowances) and divide this sum by current liabilities. Inventory and prepaid expenses are *not* included in the acid test because they are the least-liquid current assets. Greg's Tunes' acid-test ratios for 2014 and 2013 follow:

| | | Greg's Tunes' Acid-Test Ratio | | Industry |
| Formula | | 2014 | 2013 | Average |
|---|---|---|---|---|
| Acid-test ratio $=$ | $\dfrac{\text{Cash} + \text{Short-term investments} + \text{Net current receivables}}{\text{Current liabilities}}$ | $\dfrac{\$29,000 + \$0 + \$114,000}{\$142,000} = 1.01$ | $\dfrac{\$32,000 + \$0 + \$85,000}{\$126,000} = 0.93$ | 0.46 |

The company's acid-test ratio improved during 2014 and is significantly better than the industry average. The norm for the acid-test ratio ranges from 0.20 for shoe retailers to 1.00 for manufacturers of equipment, as reported by the Risk Management Association. An acid-test ratio of 0.90 to 1.00 is acceptable in most industries.

# Evaluating the Ability to Sell Inventory and Collect Receivables

In this section, we discuss five ratios that measure the company's ability to sell inventory and collect receivables.

## Inventory Turnover

The inventory turnover ratio measures the number of times a company sells its average level of inventory during a year. A high rate of turnover indicates ease in selling inventory; a low rate indicates difficulty. A value of 4 means that the company sold its average level of inventory four times—once every three months—during the year. If the company were a seasonal company, this would be a good ratio because it would mean it turned its inventory over each season, on average.

To compute inventory turnover, we divide cost of goods sold by the average inventory for the period. We use the cost of goods sold—not sales—because both cost of goods sold and inventory are stated *at cost*. Sales at *retail* are not comparable with inventory at *cost*.

Greg's Tunes' inventory turnover for 2014 is as follows:

| | Formula | Greg's Tunes' Inventory Turnover | Industry Average |
|---|---|---|---|
| Inventory turnover $=$ | $\dfrac{\text{Cost of goods sold}}{\text{Average inventory}}$ | $\dfrac{\$513,000}{\$112,000} = 4.6$ | 27.7 |

Cost of goods sold comes from the income statement (Exhibit 15-8). Average inventory is figured by adding the beginning inventory of $111,000 to the ending inventory of $113,000 and dividing by 2. (See the balance sheet, Exhibit 15-8.)

Inventory turnover varies widely with the nature of the business. For example, most manufacturers of farm machinery have an inventory turnover close to three times a year. In contrast, companies that remove natural gas from the ground hold their inventory for a very short period of time and have an average turnover of 30. Greg's Tunes' turnover of 4.6 times a year means on average the company has enough inventory to handle sales for over 79 days (365/4.6 times). This is very low for its industry, which has an average turnover of 27.7 times per year. This ratio has identified an area that Greg's Tunes needs to improve.

## Days in Inventory

Another key measure is the number of **days in inventory ratio**. This measures the average number of days inventory is held by the company. Greg's Tunes' days in inventory for 2014 is as follows:

| Formula | Greg's Tunes' Days in Inventory | Industry Average |
|---|---|---|
| Days in inventory $= \dfrac{365 \text{ days}}{\text{Inventory turnover ratio}}$ | $\dfrac{365 \text{ days}}{4.6} = 79$ days | 13 days |

Days in inventory varies widely, depending on the business. Greg's Tunes' days in inventory is 79 days—too high for its industry, which has a days in inventory ratio of only 13 days. This ratio has identified an area that Greg's Tunes needs to improve. Greg's Tunes should focus on reducing average inventory held. By decreasing average inventory, the company can increase inventory turnover and lower the average days in inventory. Greg's will also be able to reduce its inventory storage and insurance costs, as well as reduce the risk of holding obsolete inventory.

## Gross Profit Percentage

Gross profit (gross margin) is net sales minus the cost of goods sold. Merchandisers strive to increase the *gross profit percentage* (also called the *gross margin percentage*). This measures the profitability of each net sales dollar.

Greg's Tunes' gross profit percentage for 2014 is as follows:

| Formula | Greg's Tunes' Gross Profit Percentage | Industry Average |
|---|---|---|
| Gross profit percentage $= \dfrac{\text{Gross profit}}{\text{Net sales}}$ | $\dfrac{\$345,000}{\$858,000} = 0.402$ or 40.2% | 43% |

Gross profit percentage varies widely, depending on the business. Greg's Tunes' gross profit percentage is 40.2%, which is slightly lower than the industry, which has a gross profit percentage of 43%. This ratio has identified an area that Greg's Tunes needs to improve. To increase gross profit percentage, Greg's Tunes needs to decrease the cost of the merchandise and/or increase revenue (selling price). Additionally, addressing Greg's inventory turnover issues will probably help Greg's to increase its gross profit percentage.

## Accounts Receivable Turnover

The **accounts receivable turnover ratio** measures the ability to collect cash from credit customers. The higher the ratio, the faster the cash collections. But a receivable turnover that is too high may indicate that credit is too tight, causing the loss of sales to good customers.

To compute accounts receivable turnover, we divide net credit sales (assuming all Greg's sales from Exhibit 15-8 are on account) by average net accounts receivable.

Greg's Tunes' accounts receivable turnover ratio for 2014 is computed as follows:

| Formula | | Greg's Tunes' Accounts Receivable Turnover | Industry Average |
|---|---|---|---|
| Accounts receivable turnover | $= \dfrac{\text{Net credit sales}}{\text{Average net accounts receivable}}$ | $\dfrac{\$858,000}{\$99,500} = 8.6$ | 29.1 |

Net credit sales comes from the income statement (Exhibit 15-8). Average net accounts receivable is figured by adding the beginning Accounts receivable of $85,000 to the ending Accounts receivable of $114,000 and dividing by 2. (See the balance sheet, Exhibit 15-8.)

Greg's receivable turnover of 8.6 times per year is much slower than the industry average of 29.1. Why the difference? Greg's is a fairly new business that sells to established people who pay their accounts over time. Further, this turnover coincides with the lower than average inventory turnover. So, Greg's may achieve a higher receivable turnover by increasing its inventory turnover ratio.

## Days' Sales in Receivables

The *days' sales in receivables* ratio also measures the ability to collect receivables. **Days' sales in receivables tell us how many days' sales remain in Accounts receivable.**

To compute this ratio for Greg's Tunes for 2014, we divide 365 days by the accounts receivable turnover ratio we previously calculated:

| Formula | | Greg's Tunes' Days' Sales in Accounts Receivable | Industry Average |
|---|---|---|---|
| Days' sales in average accounts receivable | $= \dfrac{365 \text{ days}}{\text{Accounts receivable turnover ratio}}$ | $\dfrac{365}{8.6} = 42 \text{ days}$ | 25 days |

Greg's Tunes' ratio tells us that 42 average days' sales remain in Accounts receivable and need to be collected. The company's days' sales in receivables ratio is much higher (worse) than the industry average of 25 days. Greg's might give its customers a longer time to pay, such as 45 days versus 30 days. Alternatively, Greg's credit department may need to review the criteria it uses to evaluate individual customer's credit. Without the customers' good paying habits, the company's cash flow would suffer.

# Evaluating the Ability to Pay Long-Term Debt

The ratios discussed so far yield insight into current assets and current liabilities. They help us measure ability to sell inventory, collect receivables, and pay current liabilities. Most businesses also have long-term debt. Three key indicators of a business's ability to pay long-term liabilities are the *debt ratio*, the *debt to equity ratio*, and the *times-interest-earned ratio*.

## Debt Ratio

A loan officer at Metro Bank is evaluating loan applications from two companies. Both companies have asked to borrow $500,000 and have agreed to repay the loan over a five-year period. The first firm already owes $600,000 to another bank. The second company owes only $100,000. If all else is equal, the bank is more likely to lend money to Company 2 because that company owes less than Company 1.

The relationship between total liabilities and total assets—called the *debt ratio*—shows the proportion of assets financed with debt. **If the debt ratio is 1, then all the assets are financed with debt.** A debt ratio of 50% means that half the assets are financed with debt and the other half are financed by the owners of the business. The higher the debt ratio, the higher the company's financial risk.

The debt ratios for Greg's Tunes at the end of 2014 and 2013 follow:

| Formula | Greg's Tunes' Debt Ratio | | Industry Average |
|---|---|---|---|
| | 2014 | 2013 | |
| Debt ratio = $\dfrac{\text{Total liabilities}}{\text{Total assets}}$ | $\dfrac{\$431,000}{\$787,000}$ = 0.548 (54.8%) | $\dfrac{\$324,000}{\$644,000}$ = 0.503 (50.3%) | 0.69 (69%) |

Both total liabilities and total asset amounts are from the balance sheet, presented in Exhibit 15-8. Greg's debt ratio in 2014 of 54.8% is not very high. The Risk Management Association reports that the average debt ratio for most companies ranges from 57% to 67%, with relatively little variation from company to company. Greg's debt ratio indicates a fairly low-risk position compared with the industry average debt ratio of 69%.

## Debt to Equity Ratio

The relationship between total liabilities and total equity—called the **debt to equity ratio**—shows the proportion of total liabilities relative to the proportion of total equity that is financing the company's assets. Thus, this ratio measures financial leverage. If the debt to equity ratio is greater than 1, then the company is financing more assets with debt than with equity. If the ratio is less than 1, then the company is financing more assets with equity than with debt. The higher the debt to equity ratio, the higher the company's financial risk.

The debt to equity ratios for Greg's Tunes at the end of 2014 and 2013 follow:

| Formula | Greg's Tunes' Debt to Equity Ratio | | Industry Average |
|---|---|---|---|
| | 2014 | 2013 | |
| Debt to equity = $\dfrac{\text{Total liabilities}}{\text{Total equity}}$ | $\dfrac{\$431,000}{\$356,000}$ = 1.21 | $\dfrac{\$324,000}{\$320,000}$ = 1.01 | 2.23 |

Greg's debt to equity ratio in 2014 of 1.21 is not very high. Greg's debt to equity ratio indicates a fairly low-risk position compared with the industry average debt to equity ratio of 2.23.

## Times-Interest-Earned Ratio

The debt ratio and debt to equity ratio say nothing about the ability to pay interest expense. Analysts use the **times-interest-earned ratio** to relate Earnings before interest and taxes (EBIT) to interest expense. This ratio is also called the **interest-coverage ratio**. It measures the number of times EBIT can cover (pay) interest expense. A high interest-coverage ratio indicates ease in paying interest expense; a low ratio suggests difficulty.

To compute this ratio, we divide EBIT (Net income + Income tax expense + Interest expense) by interest expense. Calculation of Greg's times-interest-earned ratio follows:

| Formula | Greg's Tunes' Times-Interest-Earned Ratio | | Industry Average |
|---|---|---|---|
| | 2014 | 2013 | |
| Times-interest-earned ratio = $\dfrac{\text{EBIT}}{\text{Interest expense}}$ | $\dfrac{\$48,000 + \$33,000 + \$24,000}{\$24,000}$ = 4.38 | $\dfrac{\$26,000 + \$17,000 + \$14,000}{\$14,000}$ = 4.07 | 7.80 |

The company's times-interest-earned ratios 4.38 for 2014 and 4.07 for 2013 are significantly lower than the average for the industry of 7.80 times but is slightly better than the average U.S. business. The norm for U.S. business, as reported by the Risk Management Association, falls in the range of 2.0 to 3.0. When you consider Greg's debt ratio and its times-interest-earned ratio, Greg's Tunes appears to have little difficulty *servicing its debt*, that is, paying liabilities.

## Evaluating Profitability

The fundamental goal of business is to earn a profit. Ratios that measure profitability often are reported in the business press. Let's examine five profitability measures.

### Rate of Return on Net Sales

In business, the term *return* is used broadly as a measure of profitability. Consider a ratio called the **rate of return on net sales**, or simply **return on sales**. (The word *net* is usually omitted for convenience, even though net sales is used to compute the ratio.) **The rate of return on net sales ratio shows the percentage of each net sales dollar earned as net income.** Greg's Tunes' rate of return on sales follows:

> **Connect To: Ethics**
>
> Ratios are carefully watched by lenders, investors, and analysts. Recall that we classify assets and liabilities as current if they will be used/settled within one year or the operating cycle, whichever is longer. The classification between current and long-term is clear, and, as you have seen, it affects many ratios. A company on the border of exceeding debt ratio levels stated in its loan agreements must carefully watch these classifications, as well as the timing of decisions it makes, in order to legally protect its status with the lender.

|  | | Greg's Tunes' Rate of Return on Net Sales | | Industry |
|---|---|---|---|---|
| Formula | | 2014 | 2013 | Average |
| Rate of return on net sales $= \dfrac{\text{Net income}}{\text{Net sales}}$ | | $\dfrac{\$48{,}000}{\$858{,}000} = 0.056\ (5.6\%)$ | $\dfrac{\$26{,}000}{\$803{,}000} = 0.032\ (3.2\%)$ | $0.017\ (1.7\%)$ |

Both net income and net sales amounts are from the income statement presented in Exhibit 15-8. Companies strive for a high rate of return on net sales. The higher the rate of return, the more sales dollars end up as profit. The increase in Greg's rate of return on net sales from 2013 to 2014 is significant and identifies the company as more successful than the average CD sales and music service provider, whose rate of return on net sales is 1.7%.

### Rate of Return on Total Assets

The *rate of return on total assets*, or simply *return on assets*, measures a company's success in using assets to earn a profit. Two groups finance a company's assets:

- Creditors have loaned money to the company, and they earn interest.
- Shareholders have invested in stock, and their return is net income.

The sum of interest expense and net income divided by average total assets is the return to the two groups that have financed the company's assets. Computation of the rate of return on total assets ratio for Greg's Tunes follows:

| Formula | Greg's Tunes' 2014 Rate of Return on Total Assets | Industry Average |
|---|---|---|
| Rate of return on total assets $= \dfrac{\text{Net income} + \text{Interest expense}}{\text{Average total assets}}$ | $\dfrac{\$48{,}000 + \$24{,}000}{\$715{,}500} = 0.101\ (10.1\%)$ | $0.060\ (6.0\%)$ |

Net income and interest expense come from the income statement (Exhibit 15-8). Average total assets is figured by adding the beginning Total assets of $644,000 to the ending Total assets of $787,000 and dividing by 2. (See the balance sheet, Exhibit 15-8.) Greg's Tunes' rate of return on total assets ratio of 10.1% is much better than the industry average of 6.0%.

## Asset Turnover Ratio

The **asset turnover ratio** measures the amount of net sales generated for each average dollar of total assets invested. This ratio measures how well a company is using its assets to generate sales revenues. To compute this ratio, we divide net sales by average total assets. Greg's Tunes' 2014 asset turnover ratio is as follows:

| Formula | Greg's Tunes' 2014 Asset Turnover Ratio | Industry Average |
|---|---|---|
| Asset turnover ratio $= \dfrac{\text{Net sales}}{\text{Average total assets}}$ | $\dfrac{\$858,000}{\$715,500} = 1.20$ times | 3.52 times |

Greg's asset turnover ratio of 1.20 is much lower than the industry average of 3.52 times. Recall that Greg's gross profit percentage was lower than the industry's also. Normally, companies with high gross profit percentages will have low asset turnover. Companies with low gross profit percentages will have high asset turnover ratios. This is another area where Greg's management must consider options to increase sales and decrease its average total assets to improve this ratio.

## Rate of Return on Common Stockholders' Equity

A popular measure of profitability is *rate of return on common stockholders' equity*, often shortened to *return on equity*. This ratio shows the relationship between net income and common stockholders' equity. **The rate of return on common stockholders' equity shows how much income is earned for each $1 invested by the common shareholders.**

To compute this ratio, we first subtract preferred dividends from net income to get net income available to the common stockholders. (Greg's does not have any preferred stocks issued, so preferred dividends are zero.) Then we divide net income available to common stockholders by average common stockholders' equity during the year. Common equity is total stockholders' equity minus preferred equity. Average common stockholders' equity is the average of the beginning and ending common stockholders' equity balances [($356,000 + $320,000)/2 or $338,000].

The 2014 rate of return on common stockholders' equity for Greg's Tunes follows:

| Formula | Greg's Tunes' 2014 Rate of Return on Common Stockholders' Equity | Industry Average |
|---|---|---|
| Rate of return on common stockholders' equity $= \dfrac{\text{Net income} - \text{Preferred dividends}}{\text{Average common stockholders' equity}}$ | $\dfrac{\$48,000 - \$0}{\$338,000} = 0.142\ (14.2\%)$ | 0.105 (10.5%) |

Greg's rate of return on common stockholders' equity of 14.2% is higher than its rate of return on total assets of 10.1%. This difference results from borrowing at one rate—say, 8%—and investing the money to earn a higher rate, such as the firm's 14.2% return on equity. This practice is called **trading on the equity**, or using *leverage*. It is directly related to the debt ratio. The higher the debt ratio, the higher the leverage. Companies that finance operations with debt are said to *leverage* their positions.

During good times, leverage increases profitability. But, leverage can have a negative impact on profitability as well. Therefore, leverage is a double-edged sword, increasing profits during good times but compounding losses during bad times. Compare Greg's Tunes' rate of return on common stockholders' equity with the industry average of 10.5%. Once again, Greg's Tunes is performing much better than the average company in its industry. A rate of return on common stockholders' equity of 15%–20% year after year is considered good in most industries. At 14.2%, Greg's is doing well.

## Earnings per Share of Common Stock

*Earnings per share of common stock*, or simply *earnings per share (EPS)*, is perhaps the most widely quoted of all financial statistics. EPS is the only ratio that must appear on the face of the income statement. EPS is the amount of net income earned for each share of the company's outstanding *common* stock. Recall that

> **Outstanding stock = Issued stock – Treasury stock**

Earnings per share is computed by dividing net income available to common stockholders by the number of common shares outstanding during the year. Preferred dividends are subtracted from net income because the preferred stockholders have the first claim to dividends. Greg's Tunes has no preferred stock outstanding and, therefore, paid no preferred dividends.

The firm's EPS for 2014 and 2013 follow. (Note that Greg's had 10,000 shares of common stock outstanding throughout both years.)

| Formula | Greg's Tunes' Earnings per Share | | Industry Average |
|---|---|---|---|
| | 2014 | 2013 | |
| Earnings per share of common stock $= \dfrac{\text{Net income} - \text{Preferred dividends}}{\text{Number of shares of common stock outstanding}}$ | $\dfrac{\$48,000 - \$0}{10,000} = \$4.80$ | $\dfrac{\$26,000 - \$0}{10,000} = \$2.60$ | \$9.76 |

Greg's Tunes' EPS increased significantly in 2014 (by almost 85%). Its stockholders should not expect this big a boost in EPS every year. Most companies strive to increase EPS by 10%–15% annually, and leading companies do so. But even the most successful companies have an occasional bad year. EPS for the industry at \$9.76 is a little over twice Greg's Tunes' 2014 EPS. Therefore, Greg's Tunes needs to work on continuing to increase EPS so that it is more competitive with other companies in its industry.

# Evaluating Stock Investments

Investors purchase stock to earn a return on their investment. This return consists of two parts: (1) gains (or losses) from selling the stock at a price above (or below) purchase price and (2) dividends. The ratios we examine in this section help analysts evaluate stock investments.

## Price/Earnings Ratio

The **price/earnings ratio** is the ratio of the market price of a share of common stock to the company's earnings per share. **The price/earnings ratio shows the market price of \$1 of earnings.** This ratio, abbreviated P/E, appears in the *Wall Street Journal* stock listings.

Calculations for the P/E ratios of Greg's Tunes follow. The market price of its common stock was $60 at the end of 2014 and $35 at the end of 2013. These prices for real companies can be obtained from a financial publication, a stockbroker, or the company's Web site.

| Formula | Greg's Tunes' Price/Earnings Ratio | | Industry Average |
| | 2014 | 2013 | |
| --- | --- | --- | --- |
| P/E ratio = $\dfrac{\text{Market price per share of common stock}}{\text{Earnings per share}}$ | $\dfrac{\$60.00}{\$4.80} = 12.50$ | $\dfrac{\$35.00}{\$2.60} = 13.46$ | 17.79 |

The market price for Greg's common stock was stated in the previous paragraph. The earnings per share values were calculated immediately before the P/E ratio. Greg's P/E ratio for 2014 of 12.50 means that the company's stock is selling at 12.5 times one year's earnings. Net income is more controllable, and net income increased during 2014. Greg's would like to see this ratio increase in future years in order to be more in line with the industry average P/E of 17.79.

## Dividend Yield

**Dividend yield** is the ratio of annual dividends per share to the stock's market price per share. This ratio measures the percentage of a stock's market value that is returned annually as dividends to shareholders. *Preferred* stockholders, who invest primarily to receive dividends, pay special attention to dividend yield.

Greg's paid annual cash dividends of $1.20 per share of common stock in 2014 and $1.00 in 2013. As noted previously, market prices of the company's common stock were $60 in 2014 and $35 in 2013. The firm's dividend yields on common stock follow:

| Formula | Dividend Yield on Greg's Tunes' Common Stock | | Industry Average |
| | 2014 | 2013 | |
| --- | --- | --- | --- |
| Dividend yield on common stock* = $\dfrac{\text{Annual dividends per share of common stock}}{\text{Market price per share of common stock}}$ | $\dfrac{\$1.20}{\$60.00} = 0.020\ (2\%)$ | $\dfrac{\$1.00}{\$35.00} = 0.029\ (2.9\%)$ | 0.036 (3.6%) |

*Dividend yields may also be calculated for preferred stock.

Both the annual dividends and the market price for this calculation were given in the previous paragraph. An investor who buys Greg's Tunes' common stock for $60 can expect to receive 2% of the investment annually in the form of cash dividends. The industry, however, is paying out 3.6% annually. An investor might be willing to accept lower dividends (cash now) if the stock's market price is growing (cash later when the stock is sold).

## Dividend Payout

**Dividend payout** is the ratio of annual dividends declared per common share relative to the earnings per share of the company. This ratio measures the percentage of earnings paid annually to common shareholders as cash dividends. Recall that Greg's paid annual cash dividends of $1.20 per share of common stock in 2014 and $1.00 in 2013. Earnings per share were calculated on the previous page as $4.80 per share for 2014 and $2.60 for 2013. So, Greg's dividend payout yields are as follows:

| | | Greg's Tunes' Dividend Payout on Common Stock | | Industry |
| | Formula | 2014 | 2013 | Average |
| --- | --- | --- | --- | --- |
| Dividend Payout = | $\dfrac{\text{Annual dividends per share}}{\text{Earnings per share}}$ | $\dfrac{\$1.20}{\$4.80}$ = 0.25 or 25% | $\dfrac{\$1.00}{\$2.60}$ = 0.38 or 38% | 0.63 or 63% |

Greg's Tunes' dividend payout ratio of 25% in 2014 and 38% in 2013 is less than the industry average of 63%. Greg's, being a fairly new company, might be retaining more of its earnings for growth and expansion. An investor who buys Greg's Tunes' common stock may predict annual cash dividends to be about 25% of earnings, based on the 2014 dividend payout ratio. This investor would want to see higher market prices and higher asset turnover for Greg's Tunes' in the future for Greg's to stay competitive.

## Book Value per Share of Common Stock

*Book value per share of common stock* is common equity divided by the number of common shares outstanding. Common equity equals total stockholders' equity less preferred equity. Greg's has no preferred stock outstanding. Its book value per share of common stock ratios follow. (Note that 10,000 shares of common stock were outstanding.)

| | | Greg's Tunes' Book Value per Share of Common Stock | |
| | Formula | 2014 | 2013 |
| --- | --- | --- | --- |
| Book value per share of common stock = | $\dfrac{\text{Total stockholders' equity} - \text{Preferred equity}}{\text{Number of shares of common stock outstanding}}$ | $\dfrac{\$356,000 - \$0}{10,000}$ = $35.60 | $\dfrac{\$320,000 - \$0}{10,000}$ = $32.00 |

The industry averages are not presented for book value per share of common stock as many experts argue that book value is not useful for investment analysis. It bears no relationship to market value and provides little information beyond stockholders' equity reported on the balance sheet. But some investors base their investment decisions on book value. For example, some investors rank stocks on the basis of the ratio of market price to book value. To these investors, the lower the ratio, the more attractive the stock.

# Red Flags in Financial Statement Analyses

Analysts look for *red flags* in financial statements that may signal financial trouble. Recent accounting scandals highlight the importance of these red flags. The following conditions may reveal that the company is too risky.

- **Movement of Sales, Inventory, and Receivables.** Sales, inventory, and receivables generally move together. Increased sales lead to higher receivables and may require more inventory (or higher inventory turnover) to meet demand. Unexpected or inconsistent movements among sales, inventory, and receivables make the financial statements look suspect.

- **Earnings Problems.** Has net income decreased significantly for several years in a row? Did the company report net income in previous years but now is reporting net loss? Most companies cannot survive consecutive losses year after year.

- **Decreased Cash Flow.** Cash flow validates net income. Is cash flow from operations consistently lower than net income? If so, the company is in trouble. Are the sales of plant assets a major source of cash? If so, the company may face a cash shortage.

- **Too Much Debt.** How does the company's debt ratio compare to that of major competitors? If the debt ratio is too high, the company may be unable to pay its debts.

- **Inability to Collect Receivables.** Are days' sales in receivables growing faster than for competitors? If so, a cash shortage may be looming.

- **Buildup of Inventories.** Is inventory turnover too slow? If so, the company may be unable to sell goods, or it may be overstating inventory.

Do any of these red flags apply to either Smart Touch or Greg's Tunes from the analyses we did in the chapter? No, the financial statements of both companies depict strong and growing companies. Will both Smart Touch and Greg's Tunes continue to grow? Time will tell.

The Decision Guidelines on the following page summarize the most widely used ratios.

**Key Takeaway**

Ratio analysis is used to analyze financial statement data for many reasons. Ratios provide information about a company's performance and are best used to measure a company against other firms in the same industry and to denote trends within the company. Ratios tell users about a company's liquidity, solvency, profitability, and asset management. No one ratio can provide the whole picture a decision maker needs.

# Decision Guidelines 15-1

## USING RATIOS IN FINANCIAL STATEMENT ANALYSIS

Mike and Roberta Robinson want to begin investing for retirement. Their 401(k) retirement plan allows them to choose from six different investments. How will they determine which investments to choose? They use the standard ratios discussed in this chapter.

| Ratio | Computation | Information Provided |
|---|---|---|
| *Evaluating the ability to pay current liabilities:* | | |
| 1. Current ratio | $\dfrac{\text{Current assets}}{\text{Current liabilities}}$ | Measures ability to pay current liabilities with current assets |
| 2. Acid-test (quick) ratio | $\dfrac{\text{Cash} + \text{Short-term investments} + \text{Net current receivables}}{\text{Current liabilities}}$ | Shows ability to pay all current liabilities if they came due immediately |
| *Evaluating the ability to sell inventory and collect receivables:* | | |
| 3. Inventory turnover | $\dfrac{\text{Cost of goods sold}}{\text{Average inventory}}$ | Indicates salability of inventory—the number of times a company sells its average level of inventory during a year |
| 4. Days in inventory | $\dfrac{365 \text{ days}}{\text{Inventory turnover ratio}}$ | Measures the average number of days inventory is held by the company |
| 5. Gross profit percentage | $\dfrac{\text{Gross profit}}{\text{Net sales}}$ | Measures the profitability of each sales dollar above cost of goods sold |
| 6. Accounts receivable turnover | $\dfrac{\text{Net credit sales}}{\text{Average net accounts receivable}}$ | Measures ability to collect cash from customers |
| 7. Days' sales in receivables | $\dfrac{365}{\text{Accounts receivable turnover ratio}}$ | Shows how many days' sales remain in Accounts receivable—how many days it takes to collect the average level of receivables |
| *Evaluating the ability to pay long-term debt:* | | |
| 8. Debt ratio | $\dfrac{\text{Total liabilities}}{\text{Total assets}}$ | Indicates percentage of assets financed with debt |
| 9. Debt to equity ratio | $\dfrac{\text{Total liabilities}}{\text{Total equity}}$ | Indicates ratio of debt financing relative to equity financing |

| Ratio | Computation | Information Provided |
|---|---|---|
| 10. Times-interest-earned ratio | $\dfrac{\text{EBIT}}{\text{Interest expense}}$ | Measures the number of times EBIT can cover (pay) interest expense |

*Evaluating profitability:*

| Ratio | Computation | Information Provided |
|---|---|---|
| 11. Rate of return on net sales | $\dfrac{\text{Net income}}{\text{Net sales}}$ | Shows the percentage of each net sales dollar earned as net income |
| 12. Rate of return on total assets | $\dfrac{\text{Net income} + \text{Interest expense}}{\text{Average total assets}}$ | Measures how profitably a company uses its assets |
| 13. Asset turnover ratio | $\dfrac{\text{Net sales}}{\text{Average total assets}}$ | Measures the amount of net sales generated for each average dollar of total assets invested |
| 14. Rate of return on common stock-holders' equity | $\dfrac{\text{Net income} - \text{Preferred dividends}}{\text{Average common stockholders' equity}}$ | Gauges how much income is earned for each dollar invested by the common shareholders |
| 15. Earnings per share of common stock | $\dfrac{\text{Net income} - \text{Preferred dividends}}{\text{Number of shares of common stock outstanding}}$ | Gives the amount of net income earned for each share of the company's outstanding common stock |

*Evaluating stock investments:*

| Ratio | Computation | Information Provided |
|---|---|---|
| 16. Price/earnings ratio | $\dfrac{\text{Market price per share of common stock}}{\text{Earnings per share}}$ | Indicates the market price of \$1 of earnings |
| 17. Dividend yield | $\dfrac{\text{Annual dividends per share of common (or preferred) stock}}{\text{Market price per share of common (or preferred) stock}}$ | Measures the percentage of a stock's market value that is returned annually as dividends to stockholders |
| 18. Dividend payout | $\dfrac{\text{Annual dividends per share}}{\text{Earnings per share}}$ | Measures the percentage of earnings paid to the common shareholders as cash dividends. |
| 19. Book value per share of common stock | $\dfrac{\text{Total stockholders' equity} - \text{Preferred equity}}{\text{Number of shares of common stock outstanding}}$ | Indicates the recorded net equity amount from the balance sheet for each share of common stock outstanding |

# Summary Problem 15-2

| JAVA, INC.<br>Four-Year Selected Financial Data (adapted)<br>Years Ended January 31, 2013–2010 | | | | |
|---|---|---|---|---|
| Operating Results* | 2013 | 2012 | 2011 | 2010 |
| Net sales | $13,848 | $13,673 | $11,635 | $ 9,054 |
| Cost of goods sold | 9,704 | 8,599 | 6,775 | 5,318 |
| Interest expense | 109 | 75 | 45 | 46 |
| Income from operations | 338 | 1,455 | 1,817 | 1,333 |
| Income tax expense | 100 | 263 | 338 | 247 |
| Net income (net loss) | (8) | 877 | 1,127 | 824 |
| Cash dividends | 76 | 75 | 76 | 77 |
| **Financial Position** | | | | |
| Merchandise inventory | 1,677 | 1,904 | 1,462 | 1,056 |
| Total assets | 7,591 | 7,012 | 5,189 | 3,963 |
| Current ratio | 1.48:1 | 0.95:1 | 1.25:1 | 1.20:1 |
| Stockholders' equity | 3,010 | 2,928 | 2,630 | 1,574 |
| Average number of shares of common stock<br>   outstanding (in thousands) | 860 | 879 | 895 | 576 |

*Dollar amounts are in thousands.

## Requirement

Using the financial data presented above, compute the following ratios and evaluate
Java's results for 2011–2013:

1. Rate of return on net sales
2. Earnings per share
3. Inventory turnover
4. Times-interest-earned ratio
5. Rate of return on common stockholders' equity
6. Gross profit percentage

## Solution

| | 2013 | 2012 | 2011 |
|---|---|---|---|
| 1. Rate of return on net sales | $\dfrac{\$(8)}{\$13,848} = (0.06\%)$ | $\dfrac{\$877}{\$13,673} = 6.4\%$ | $\dfrac{\$1,127}{\$11,635} = 9.7\%$ |
| 2. Earnings per share | $\dfrac{\$(8)}{860} = \$(0.01)$ | $\dfrac{\$877}{879} = \$1.00$ | $\dfrac{\$1,127}{895} = \$1.26$ |
| 3. Inventory turnover | $\dfrac{\$9,704}{(\$1,904 + \$1,677)/2} = 5.4$ times | $\dfrac{\$8,599}{(\$1,462 + \$1,904)/2} = 5.1$ times | $\dfrac{\$6,775}{(\$1,056 + \$1,462)/2} = 5.4$ times |
| 4. Times-interest-earned ratio | $\dfrac{[\$(8) + \$100 + \$109]}{\$109} = 1.8$ times | $\dfrac{(\$75 + \$263 + \$75)}{\$75} = 5.5$ times | $\dfrac{(\$76 + \$338 + \$45)}{\$45} = 10.2$ times |
| 5. Rate of return on common stockholders' equity | $\dfrac{\$(8)}{(\$2,929 + \$3,010)/2} = (0.3\%)$ | $\dfrac{\$877}{(\$2,630 + \$2,928)/2} = 31.6\%$ | $\dfrac{\$1,127}{(\$1,574 + \$2,630)/2} = 53.6\%$ |
| 6. Gross profit percentage | $\dfrac{(\$13,848 - \$9,704)}{\$13,848} = 29.9\%$ | $\dfrac{(\$13,673 - \$8,599)}{\$13,673} = 37.1\%$ | $\dfrac{(\$11,635 - \$6,775)}{\$11,635} = 41.8\%$ |

*Evaluation:* During this period, Java's operating results deteriorated on all these measures except inventory turnover. The times-interest-earned ratio and rate of return on common stockholders' equity percentages are down sharply. From these data, it is clear that Java could sell its coffee, but not at the markups the company enjoyed in the past. The final result, in 2013, was a net loss for the year.

# Review *Financial Statement Analysis*

## ● Accounting Vocabulary

**Accounts Receivable Turnover Ratio (p. 736)**
Measures a company's ability to collect cash from credit customers. To compute accounts receivable turnover, divide net credit sales by average net accounts receivable.

**Asset Turnover Ratio (p. 740)**
Ratio that measures the amount of net sales generated for each average dollar of assets invested.

**Benchmarking (p. 729)**
The practice of comparing a company with other companies that are leaders.

**Common-Size Statement (p. 728)**
A financial statement that reports only percentages (no dollar amounts).

**Days in Inventory Ratio (p. 736)**
Ratio that measures the average number of days inventory is held by the company.

**Debt to Equity Ratio (p. 738)**
Ratio that measures the proportion of total liabilities relative to the proportion of total equity that is financing the company's assets.

**Dividend Payout (p. 743)**
The ratio of dividends declared per common share relative to the earnings per share of the company.

**Dividend Yield (p. 742)**
Ratio of annual dividends per share of stock to the stock's market price per share. Measures the percentage of a stock's market value that is returned annually as dividends to stockholders.

**Dollar Value Bias (p. 729)**
The bias one sees from comparing numbers in absolute (dollars) rather than relative (percentage) terms.

**Horizontal Analysis (p. 723)**
Study of percentage changes in comparative financial statements.

**Interest-Coverage Ratio (p. 738)**
Ratio of EBIT to interest expense. Measures the number of times that EBIT can cover (pay) interest expense. Also called the **times-interest-earned ratio**.

**Price/Earnings Ratio (p. 741)**
Ratio of the market price of a share of common stock to the company's earnings per share. Measures the value that the stock market places on $1 of a company's earnings.

**Rate of Return on Net Sales (p. 739)**
Ratio of net income to net sales. A measure of profitability. Also called **return on sales**.

**Return on Sales (p. 739)**
Ratio of net income to net sales. A measure of profitability. Also called **rate of return on net sales**.

**Times-Interest-Earned Ratio (p. 738)**
Ratio of EBIT to interest expense. Measures the number of times that EBIT can cover (pay) interest expense. Also called the **interest-coverage ratio**.

**Trading on the Equity (p. 740)**
Earning more income on borrowed money than the related interest expense, thereby increasing the earnings for the owners of the business. Also called *leverage*.

**Trend Analysis (p. 726)**
A form of horizontal analysis in which percentages are computed by selecting a base year as 100% and expressing amounts for following years as a percentage of the base amount.

**Vertical Analysis (p. 727)**
Analysis of a financial statement that reveals the relationship of each statement item to its base amount, which is the 100% figure.

**Working Capital (p. 733)**
Current assets minus current liabilities. Measures a business's ability to meet its short-term obligations with its current assets.

## ● Destination: Student Success

### Student Success Tips

The following are hints on some common trouble areas for students in this chapter:

● Remember the word "horizon" is in horizontal analysis, so it compares percentage changes from year to year (row to row)—work across the comparative statement.

● Recall that vertical analysis translates all financial statement values to percentages, with net sales being 100% on the income statement and total assets being 100% on the balance sheet. All other items are expressed as a percentage of either net sales or total assets.

● Keep in mind that common-size statements are similar to vertical analysis statements except the dollars are removed. Common-size statements allow us to compare companies that operate in the same industry.

● There are many ratios in this chapter. Remember that one ratio can't tell the whole story any more than one financial statement can. Each ratio paints a picture about the company's asset management, liquidity, solvency, or profitability.

### Getting Help

If there's a learning objective from the chapter you aren't confident about, try using one or more of the following resources:

● Review Summary Problem 15-1 in the chapter to reinforce your understanding of horizontal and vertical analysis.

● Review Summary Problem 15-2 in the chapter to reinforce your understanding of ratio analysis.

● Practice additional exercises or problems at the end of Chapter 15 that cover the specific learning objective that is challenging you.

● Watch the white board videos for Chapter 15 located at myaccountinglab.com under the Chapter Resources button.

● Go to myaccountinglab.com and select the Study Plan button. Choose Chapter 15 and work the questions covering that specific learning objective until you've mastered it.

● Work the Chapter 15 pre/post tests in myaccountinglab.com.

● Visit the learning resource center on your campus for tutoring.

Liberty Corporation reported the following figures:

| Account | 2012 | 2011 |
|---|---|---|
| Cash and cash equivalents | $ 2,450 | $ 2,094 |
| Receivables | 1,813 | 1,611 |
| Inventory | 1,324 | 1,060 |
| Prepaid expenses | 1,709 | 2,120 |
| Total current assets | $ 7,296 | $ 6,885 |
| Other assets | 18,500 | 15,737 |
| Total assets | $ 25,796 | $ 22,622 |
| Total current liabilities | $ 7,230 | $ 8,467 |
| Long-term liabilities | 4,798 | 3,792 |
| Common stock | 6,568 | 4,363 |
| Retained earnings | 7,200 | 6,000 |
| Total liabilities and equity | $ 25,796 | $ 22,622 |

| | 2012 |
|---|---|
| Sales | $ 20,941 |
| Cost of sales | 7,055 |
| Operating expenses | 7,065 |
| Operating income | $ 6,821 |
| Interest expense | 210 |
| Income tax expense | 2,563 |
| Net income | $ 4,048 |

1. Horizontal analysis of Liberty's balance sheet for 2012 would report
   a. Cash as 9.50% of total assets.
   b. 17% increase in Cash.
   c. Current ratio of 1.01.
   d. Inventory turnover of 6 times.

2. Vertical analysis of Liberty's balance sheet for 2012 would report
   a. Cash as 9.50% of total assets.
   b. Inventory turnover of 6 times.
   c. Current ratio of 1.01.
   d. 17% increase in Cash.

3. A common-size income statement for Liberty would report (amounts rounded)
   a. Net income of 19%.
   b. Sales of 100%.
   c. Cost of sales at 34%.
   d. All of the above

4. Which statement best describes Liberty's acid-test ratio?
   a. Greater than 1
   b. Equal to 1
   c. Less than 1
   d. None of the above

5. Liberty's inventory turnover during 2012 was (amounts rounded)
   a. 6 times.
   b. 7 times.
   c. 8 times.
   d. Not determinable from the data given.

6. During 2012, Liberty's days' sales in receivables ratio was (amounts rounded)
   a. 34 days.
   b. 30 days.
   c. 32 days.
   d. 28 days.

7. Which measure expresses Liberty's times-interest-earned ratio? (amounts rounded)
   a. 54.7%
   b. 19 times
   c. 34 times
   d. 32 times

8. Liberty's rate of return on common stockholders' equity can be described as
   a. weak.
   b. normal.
   c. strong.
   d. average.

9. The company has 2,500 shares of common stock outstanding. What is Liberty's earnings per share?
   a. $1.62
   b. $1.75
   c. $2.73
   d. 2.63 times

10. Liberty's stock has traded recently around $48 per share. Use your answer to question 9 to measure the company's price/earnings ratio. (Round to the nearest whole number.)
    a. 1.01
    b. 30
    c. 48
    d. 78

Answers are given after Apply Your Knowledge (p. 771).

# Assess Your Progress

## ● Short Exercises

**S15-1**   **①** **Horizontal analysis [5–10 min]**
McCormick, Corp., reported the following on its comparative income statement:

| (In millions) | 2012 | 2011 | 2010 |
|---|---|---|---|
| Revenue | $9,575 | $9,300 | $8,975 |
| Cost of sales | 6,000 | 5,975 | 5,900 |

*MyAccountingLab*

**Requirement**

    1.  Prepare a horizontal analysis of revenues and gross profit—both in dollar amounts and in percentages—for 2012 and 2011.

**S15-2** ① **Trend analysis [5–10 min]**

Mariner, Corp., reported the following revenues and net income amounts:

| (In millions) | 2013 | 2012 | 2011 | 2010 |
|---|---|---|---|---|
| Revenue ............................. | $9,910 | $9,700 | $9,210 | $9,110 |
| Net income......................... | 7,475 | 7,400 | 5,495 | 4,690 |

## Requirements

1. Calculate Mariner's trend analysis for revenues and net income. Use 2010 as the base year, and round to the nearest percent.
2. Which measure increased faster during 2011–2013?

**S15-3** ② **Vertical analysis [10–15 min]**

Tri-State Optical Company reported the following amounts on its balance sheet at December 31, 2012 and 2011:

|  | 2012 | 2011 |
|---|---|---|
| Cash and receivables ................ | $   54,530 | $   46,860 |
| Inventory ......................... | 42,435 | 32,670 |
| Property, plant, and equipment, net ..... | 108,035 | 85,470 |
| Total assets ....................... | $ 205,000 | $ 165,000 |

## Requirement

1. Prepare a vertical analysis of Tri-State assets for 2012 and 2011.

**S15-4** ③ **Common-size income statement [10 min]**

Data for Martinez, Inc., and Rosado, Corp., follow:

|  | Martinez | Rosado |
|---|---|---|
| Net sales ......................... | $   10,600 | $   18,600 |
| Cost of goods sold ................. | 6,455 | 13,522 |
| Other expenses .................... | 3,541 | 4,185 |
| Net income ....................... | $       604 | $       893 |

## Requirements

1. Prepare common-size income statements.
2. Which company earns more net income?
3. Which company's net income is a higher percentage of its net sales?

**S15-5** ④ **Evaluating current ratio [5–10 min]**

Win's Companies, a home improvement store chain, reported the following summarized figures:

| WIN'S COMPANIES | | |
|---|---|---|
| Income Statement | | |
| Years Ended May 31, 2012 and 2011 | | |
|  | 2012 | 2011 |
| Net sales | $   50,200,000 | $   43,800,000 |
| Cost of goods sold | 28,400,000 | 29,300,000 |
| Interest expense | 500,000 | 140,000 |
| All other expenses | 5,800,000 | 8,400,000 |
| Net income | $   15,500,000 | $     5,960,000 |

| Assets | 2012 | 2011 | Liabilities | 2012 | 2011 |
|--------|------|------|-------------|------|------|
| | | WIN'S COMPANIES | | | |
| | | Balance Sheet | | | |
| | | May 31, 2012 and 2011 | | | |
| Cash | $ 2,000,000 | $ 900,000 | Total current liabilities | $ 33,000,000 | $ 13,100,000 |
| Short-term investments | 28,000,000 | 9,000,000 | Long-term liabilities | 12,300,000 | 10,600,000 |
| Accounts receivable | 7,400,000 | 5,300,000 | Total liabilities | $ 45,300,000 | $ 23,700,000 |
| Inventory | 6,900,000 | 8,200,000 | **Stockholders' Equity** | | |
| Other current assets | 10,000,000 | 1,800,000 | Common stock | $ 11,000,000 | $ 11,000,000 |
| Total current assets | $ 54,300,000 | $ 25,200,000 | Retained earnings | 32,000,000 | 16,500,000 |
| All other assets | 34,000,000 | 26,000,000 | Total equity | $ 43,000,000 | $ 27,500,000 |
| Total assets | $ 88,300,000 | $ 51,200,000 | Total liabilities and equity | $ 88,300,000 | $ 51,200,000 |

## Requirements

1. Compute Win's Companies' current ratio at May 31, 2012 and 2011.
2. Did Win's Companies' current ratio improve, deteriorate, or hold steady during 2012?

**S15-6** ❹ **Computing inventory, gross profit, and receivables ratios [10–15 min]**
Use the Win's Companies data in Short Exercise 15-5 to complete the following requirements.

## Requirements

1. Compute the rate of inventory turnover, days in inventory, and gross profit percentage for 2012.
2. Compute days' sales in average receivables during 2012. Round dollar amounts to three decimal places.

**S15-7** ❹ **Measuring ability to pay liabilities [5 min]**
Use the financial statements of Win's Companies in Short Exercise 15-5.

## Requirements

1. Compute the debt ratio and the debt to equity ratio at May 31, 2012.
2. Is Win's ability to pay its liabilities strong or weak? Explain your reasoning.

**S15-8** ❹ **Measuring profitability [10 min]**
Use the financial statements of Win's Companies in Short Exercise 15-5 to complete the following profitability measures for 2012.

## Requirements

1. Compute the rate of return on net sales.
2. Compute the rate of return on total assets.
3. Compute the asset turnover ratio.
4. Compute the rate of return on common stockholders' equity.
5. Are these rates of return strong or weak? Explain your reasoning.

**S15-9** ④ **Computing EPS and P/E ratio [5–10 min]**

Use the financial statements of Win's Companies in Short Exercise 15-5. Win's has 500,000 common shares outstanding during 2012.

**Requirements**

1. Compute earnings per share (EPS) for Win's. Round to the nearest cent.
2. Compute Win's Companies' price/earnings ratio. The market price per share of Win's stock is $68.50.

**S15-10** ④ **Using ratios to reconstruct an income statement [10 min]**

A skeleton of Landmark Mills' income statement appears as follows (amounts in thousands):

| Income Statement | |
|---|---|
| Net sales | $ 7,200 |
| Cost of goods sold | (a) |
| Selling and admin expenses | 1,830 |
| Interest expense | (b) |
| Other expenses | 150 |
| Income before taxes | $ 1,325 |
| Income tax expense | (c) |
| Net income | (d) |

**Requirement**

1. Use the following ratio data to complete Landmark Mills' income statement:
   a. Inventory turnover was 3.50 (beginning inventory was $850; ending inventory was $810).
   b. Rate of return on net sales is 0.11.

**S15-11** ④ **Using ratios to reconstruct a balance sheet [15–20 min]**

A skeleton of Vintage Mills' balance sheet appears as follows (amounts in thousands):

| Balance Sheet | | | | |
|---|---|---|---|---|
| Cash | $ 75 | Total current liabilities | $ | 1,900 |
| Receivables | (a) | Long-term note payable | | (e) |
| Inventories | 725 | Other long-term | | |
| Prepaid expenses | (b) | liabilities | | 980 |
| Total current assets | $ (c) | Stockholder's equity | | 2,325 |
| Plant assets, net | (d) | | | |
| Other assets | 2,000 | Total liabilities and | | |
| Total assets | $ 6,800 | stockholders' equity | $ | (f) |

**Requirement**

1. Use the following ratio data to complete Vintage Mills' balance sheet.
   a. Current ratio is 0.80.
   b. Acid-test ratio is 0.40.

# ● Exercises

**E15-12**  ❶ **Computing working capital changes [5–15 min]**

Data for Beverage Enterprises follows:

|  | 2012 | 2011 | 2010 |
|---|---|---|---|
| Total current assets ...... | $510,000 | $ 350,000 | $240,000 |
| Total current liabilities .... | 245,000 | 175,000 | 120,000 |

## Requirement

1.  Compute the dollar amount of change and the percentage of change in Beverage Enterprises' working capital each year during 2011 and 2012. What do the calculated changes indicate?

**E15-13**  ❶ **Horizontal analysis—income statement [10–15 min]**

Data for Mariner Designs, Inc., follow:

| MARINER DESIGNS, INC. Comparative Income Statement Years Ended December 31, 2012 and 2011 | | | |
|---|---|---|---|
|  | **2012** | **2011** |  |
| Net sales revenue | $ 431,000 | $ 372,350 | 15.7% |
| Expenses: | | | |
| Cost of goods sold | $ 200,000 | $ 187,550 | 6.6% |
| Selling and general expenses | 99,000 | 91,050 | 8.73% |
| Other expense | 8,350 | 6,850 | 21.9% |
| Total expenses | $ 307,350 | $ 285,450 | 7.7% |
| Net income | $ 123,650 | $  86,900 | 42.3% |

## Requirements

1.  Prepare a horizontal analysis of the comparative income statement of Mariner Designs, Inc. Round percentage changes to one decimal place.
2.  Why did 2012 net income increase by a higher percentage than net sales revenue?

**E15-14**  ❶ **Computing trend analysis [5–10 min]**

Magic Oaks Realty's net revenue and net income for the following five-year period, using 2010 as the base year, follow:

|  | 2014 | 2013 | 2012 | 2011 | 2010 |
|---|---|---|---|---|---|
| Net revenue ....... | $1,310,000 | $1,187,000 | $1,110,000 | $1,011,000 | $1,045,000 |
| Net income ........ | 122,000 | 113,000 | 84,000 | 72,000 | 83,000 |

## Requirements

1.  Compute trend analysis for net revenue and net income. Round to the nearest full percent.
2.  Which grew faster during the period, net revenue or net income?

**E15-15** ❷ **Vertical analysis of a balance sheet [10–15 min]**

Beta Graphics, Inc., has the following data:

| BETA GRAPHICS, INC.<br>Comparative Balance Sheet<br>December 31, 2012 and 2011 | | |
| --- | --- | --- |
| | **2012** | **2011** |
| **Assets** | | |
| Total current assets | $ 42,750 | $ 59,000 |
| Property, plant, and equipment, net | 208,335 | 215,000 |
| Other assets | 33,915 | 35,500 |
| Total assets | $ 285,000 | $ 309,500 |
| **Liabilities** | | |
| Total current liabilities | $ 49,020 | $ 50,100 |
| Long-term debt | 109,155 | 102,300 |
| Total liabilities | $ 158,175 | $ 152,400 |
| **Stockholders' Equity** | | |
| Total stockholders' equity | 126,825 | 157,100 |
| Total liabilities and stockholders' equity | $ 285,000 | $ 309,500 |

### Requirement

1. Perform a vertical analysis of Beta's balance sheet for each year.

**E15-16** ❸ **Preparing common-size income statements [10–15 min]**

Consider the data presented in Exercise 15-13.

### Requirements

1. Prepare a comparative common-size income statement for Mariner Designs, Inc., using the 2012 and 2011 data. Round percentages to one-tenth percent (three decimal places).

2. To an investor, how does 2012 compare with 2011? Explain your reasoning.

**E15-17** ❹ **Computing six key ratios [10–15 min]**

The financial statements of Victor's Natural Foods include the following items:

| | Current Year | Preceding Year |
| --- | --- | --- |
| **Balance sheet:** | | |
| Cash . . . . . . . . . . . . . . . . . . . . . | $ 15,000 | $ 20,000 |
| Short-term investments . . . . . . | 11,000 | 27,000 |
| Net receivables . . . . . . . . . . . . | 54,000 | 73,000 |
| Inventory . . . . . . . . . . . . . . . . | 77,000 | 69,000 |
| Prepaid expenses . . . . . . . . . . | 15,000 | 9,000 |
| Total current assets . . . . . . . . . | $ 172,000 | $ 198,000 |
| Total current liabilities . . . . . . . | $ 133,000 | $ 93,000 |
| **Income statement:** | | |
| Net credit sales . . . . . . . . . . . . | $ 462,000 | |
| Cost of goods sold . . . . . . . . . | 315,000 | |

# Requirement

1. Compute the following ratios for the current year:

    a. Current ratio
    b. Acid-test ratio
    c. Inventory turnover
    d. Days in inventory
    e. Days' sales in receivables
    f. Gross profit percentage

**E15-18** ❹ **Analyzing the ability to pay liabilities [15–20 min]**

Large Land Photo Shop has asked you to determine whether the company's ability to pay current liabilities and total liabilities improved or deteriorated during 2012. To answer this question, you gather the following data:

|  | 2012 | 2011 |
|---|---|---|
| Cash | $ 58,000 | $ 57,000 |
| Short-term investments | 31,000 | — |
| Net receivables | 110,000 | 132,000 |
| Inventory | 247,000 | 297,000 |
| Total assets | 585,000 | 535,000 |
| Total current liabilities | 255,000 | 222,000 |
| Long-term note payable | 46,000 | 48,000 |
| Income from operations | 180,000 | 153,000 |
| Interest expense | 52,000 | 39,000 |

# Requirement

1. Compute the following ratios for 2012 and 2011:

    a. Current ratio
    b. Acid-test ratio
    c. Debt ratio
    d. Debt to equity ratio

**E15-19** ❹ **Analyzing profitability [10–15 min]**

The CJ, Inc., comparative income statement follows. The 2010 data are given as needed.

| CJ, INC. Comparative Income Statement Years Ended December 31, 2012 and 2011 | | | |
|---|---|---|---|
| (Dollars in thousands) | 2012 | 2011 | 2010 |
| Net sales | $176,000 | $160,000 | |
| Cost of goods sold | 93,400 | 86,500 | |
| Selling and general expenses | 46,000 | 41,000 | |
| Interest expense | 9,000 | 10,300 | |
| Income tax expense | 10,200 | 9,600 | |
| Net income | $ 17,400 | $ 12,600 | |
| Additional data: | | | |
| Total assets | $203,000 | $190,000 | $175,000 |
| Common stockholders' equity | $ 96,600 | $ 90,100 | $ 79,400 |
| Preferred dividends | $ 3,500 | $ 3,500 | $ 0 |
| Common shares outstanding during the year | 20,500 | 20,500 | 18,000 |

## Requirements

1. Calculate the rate of return on net sales.
2. Calculate the rate of return on total assets.
3. Calculate the asset turnover ratio.
4. Calculate the rate of return on common stockholders' equity.
5. Calculate the EPS.
6. Calculate the 2012 dividend payout on common stock.
7. Did the company's operating performance improve or deteriorate during 2012?

**E15-20** ❹ **Evaluating a stock as an investment [10–15 min]**
Data for Shamrock State Bank follows:

|  | 2012 | 2011 |
|---|---|---|
| Net income | $ 61,000 | $ 52,000 |
| Dividends—common | 26,000 | 26,000 |
| Dividends—preferred | 12,600 | 12,600 |
| Total stockholders' equity at year-end | | |
| (includes 80,000 shares of common stock) | 760,000 | 610,000 |
| Preferred stock, 6% | 210,000 | 210,000 |
| Market price per share of common stock | $ 19.50 | $ 14 |

## Requirement

1. Evaluate the common stock of Shamrock State Bank as an investment. Specifically, use the four stock ratios to determine whether the common stock has increased or decreased in attractiveness during the past year.

**E15-21** ❹ **Using ratios to reconstruct a balance sheet [20–30 min]**
The following data are adapted from the financial statements of Betty's Shops, Inc.:

| | |
|---|---|
| Total current assets | $ 1,200,000 |
| Accumulated depreciation | $ 2,400,000 |
| Total liabilities | $ 1,400,000 |
| Preferred stock | $ 0 |
| Debt ratio | 64% |
| Current ratio | 1.50 |

## Requirement

1. Complete Betty's condensed balance sheet.

| | | |
|---|---|---|
| Current assets | | |
| Property, plant, and equipment | | |
| Less: Accumulated depreciation | | |
| Total assets | | |
| Current liabilities | | |
| Long-term liabilities | | |
| Stockholders' equity | | |
| Total liabilities and stockholders' equity | | |

• Problems (Group A)

**P15-22A** ❶ Trend analysis and return on common equity [20–30 min]

Net sales revenue, net income, and common stockholders' equity for Azbel Mission Corporation, a manufacturer of contact lenses, follow for a four-year period.

|  | 2013 | 2012 | 2011 | 2010 |
|---|---|---|---|---|
| Net sales revenue . . . . . . . | $ 762,000 | $ 706,000 | $ 637,000 | $ 665,000 |
| Net income . . . . . . . . . . . . | 58,000 | 44,000 | 37,000 | 43,000 |
| Ending common stockholders' equity . . . | 376,000 | 358,000 | 330,000 | 304,000 |

### Requirements

1. Compute trend analyses for each item for 2011–2013. Use 2010 as the base year, and round to the nearest whole percent.
2. Compute the rate of return on common stockholders' equity for 2011–2013, rounding to three decimal places.

**P15-23A** ❷ Vertical analysis [20–30 min]

The McConnell Department Stores, Inc., chief executive officer (CEO) has asked you to compare the company's profit performance and financial position with the average for the industry. The CEO has given you the company's income statement and balance sheet, as well as the industry average data for retailers.

| MCCONNELL DEPARTMENT STORES, INC. Income Statement Compared with Industry Average Year Ended December 31, 2012 | | |
|---|---|---|
|  | McConnell | Industry Average |
| Net sales | $ 778,000 | 100.0% |
| Cost of goods sold | 522,816 | 65.8 |
| Gross profit | $ 255,184 | 34.2 |
| Operating expenses | 161,046 | 19.7 |
| Operating income | $ 94,138 | 14.5 |
| Other expenses | 4,668 | 0.4 |
| Net income | $ 89,470 | 14.1% |

| MCCONNELL DEPARTMENT STORES, INC. Balance Sheet Compared with Industry Average December 31, 2012 | | |
|---|---|---|
| | McConnell | Industry Average |
| Current assets | $ 325,440 | 70.9% |
| Fixed assets, net | 120,960 | 23.6 |
| Intangible assets, net | 8,640 | 0.8 |
| Other assets | 24,960 | 4.7 |
| Total assets | $ 480,000 | 100.0% |
| Current liabilities | $ 222,720 | 48.1% |
| Long-term liabilities | 107,520 | 16.6 |
| Stockholders' equity | 149,760 | 35.3 |
| Total liabilities and stockholders' equity | $ 480,000 | 100.0% |

## Requirement

1. Prepare a vertical analysis for McConnell for both its income statement and balance sheet.

*Note: Problem 15-24A should be used only after completing Problem 15-23A.*

**P15-24A** ❸ ❹ **Common-size statements, analysis of profitability and financial position, comparison with the industry, and using ratios to evaluate a company [20–30 min]**

Consider the data for McConnell Department Stores presented in P15-23A.

## Requirements

1. Prepare a common-size income statement and balance sheet for McConnell. The first column of each statement should present McConnell's common-size statement, and the second column, the industry averages.
2. For the profitability analysis, compute McConnell's (a) gross profit percentage and (b) rate of return on net sales. Compare these figures with the industry averages. Is McConnell's profit performance better or worse than the industry average?
3. For the analysis of financial position, compute McConnell's (a) current ratio and (b) debt to equity ratio. Compare these ratios with the industry averages. Is McConnell's financial position better or worse than the industry averages?

**P15-25A** ❹ **Effects of business transactions on selected ratios [30–40 min]**

Financial statement data of *American Traveler Magazine* include the following items:

| | |
|---|---|
| Cash | $ 23,000 |
| Accounts receivable, net | 79,000 |
| Inventories | 184,000 |
| Total assets | 634,000 |
| Accounts payable | 104,000 |
| Accrued liabilities | 40,000 |
| Short-term notes payable | 47,000 |
| Long-term liabilities | 221,000 |
| Net income | 74,000 |
| Common shares outstanding | 60,000 |

## Requirements

1. Compute *American Traveler*'s current ratio, debt ratio, and earnings per share. Round all ratios to two decimal places, and use the following format for your answer:

| Current Ratio | Debt Ratio | Earnings per Share |
|---|---|---|
|  |  |  |

2. Compute the three ratios after evaluating the effect of each transaction that follows. Consider each transaction *separately*.

    a. Purchased inventory of $49,000 on account.

    b. Borrowed $122,000 on a long-term note payable.

    c. Issued 6,000 shares of common stock, receiving cash of $103,000.

    d. Received cash on account, $3,000.

**P15-26A** ❹ **Using ratios to evaluate a stock investment [40–50 min]**
Comparative financial statement data of Danfield, Inc., follow:

| DANFIELD, INC. | | |
|---|---|---|
| **Comparative Income Statement** | | |
| Years Ended December 31, 2012 and 2011 | | |
|  | 2012 | 2011 |
| Net sales | $ 467,000 | $ 428,000 |
| Cost of goods sold | 237,000 | 218,000 |
| Gross profit | $ 230,000 | $ 210,000 |
| Operating expenses | 136,000 | 134,000 |
| Income from operations | $ 94,000 | $ 76,000 |
| Interest expense | 9,000 | 10,000 |
| Income before income tax | $ 85,000 | $ 66,000 |
| Income tax expense | 24,000 | 27,000 |
| Net income | $ 61,000 | $ 39,000 |

| | DANFIELD, INC. Comparative Balance Sheet December 31, 2012 and 2011 | | |
|---|---|---|---|
| | **2012** | **2011** | **2010*** |
| Current assets: | | | |
| Cash | $ 97,000 | $ 95,000 | |
| Current receivables, net | 112,000 | 118,000 | $ 102,000 |
| Inventories | 145,000 | 163,000 | 203,000 |
| Prepaid expenses | 12,000 | 5,000 | |
| Total current assets | $ 366,000 | $ 381,000 | |
| Property, plant, and equipment, net | 211,000 | 179,000 | |
| Total assets | $ 577,000 | $ 560,000 | 598,000 |
| Total current liabilities | $ 225,000 | $ 246,000 | |
| Long-term liabilities | 114,000 | 97,000 | |
| Total liabilities | $ 339,000 | $ 343,000 | |
| Preferred stock, 3% | 108,000 | 108,000 | |
| Common stockholders' equity, no par | 130,000 | 109,000 | 85,000 |
| Total liabilities and stockholders' equity | $ 577,000 | $ 560,000 | |

* Selected 2010 amounts

1. Market price of Danfield's common stock: $86.58 at December 31, 2012, and $46.54 at December 31, 2011.
2. Common shares outstanding: 12,000 during 2012 and 10,000 during 2011 and 2010.
3. All sales on credit.

## Requirements

1. Compute the following ratios for 2012 and 2011:

    a. Current ratio
    b. Times-interest-earned ratio
    c. Inventory turnover
    d. Gross profit percentage
    e. Debt to equity ratio
    f. Rate of return on common stockholders' equity
    g. Earnings per share of common stock
    h. Price/earnings ratio

2. Decide (a) whether Danfield's ability to pay debts and to sell inventory improved or deteriorated during 2012 and (b) whether the investment attractiveness of its common stock appears to have increased or decreased.

**P15-27A** ❹ **Using ratios to decide between two stock investments [45–60 min]**
Assume that you are purchasing an investment and have decided to invest in a company in the digital phone business. You have narrowed the choice to Digitalized, Corp., and Zone Network, Inc., and have assembled the following data:

Selected income statement data for the current year:

|  | Digitalized | Zone Network |
|---|---|---|
| Net sales (all on credit) . . . . . . . . . . $ | 423,035 $ | 493,115 |
| Cost of goods sold . . . . . . . . . . . . . | 206,000 | 258,000 |
| Interest expense . . . . . . . . . . . . . . | —— | 19,000 |
| Net income . . . . . . . . . . . . . . . . . | 54,000 | 66,000 |

Selected balance sheet and market price data at the *end* of the current year:

|  | Digitalized | Zone Network |
|---|---|---|
| Current assets: |  |  |
| Cash . . . . . . . . . . . . . . . . . . . . . . . $ | 23,000 $ | 21,000 |
| Short-term investments . . . . . . . . . . . . | 38,000 | 19,000 |
| Current receivables, net . . . . . . . . . . . . | 38,000 | 43,000 |
| Inventories . . . . . . . . . . . . . . . . . . . | 64,000 | 96,000 |
| Prepaid expenses . . . . . . . . . . . . . . . . | 21,000 | 13,000 |
| Total current assets . . . . . . . . . . . . . . $ | 184,000 $ | 192,000 |
| Total assets . . . . . . . . . . . . . . . . . . . $ | 266,000 $ | 326,000 |
| Total current liabilities . . . . . . . . . . . . | 102,000 | 96,000 |
| Total liabilities . . . . . . . . . . . . . . . . . | 102,000 | 131,000 |
| Common stock, $1 par (12,000 shares) | 12,000 |  |
| $2 par (16,000 shares) |  | 32,000 |
| Total stockholders' equity . . . . . . . . . . . $ | 164,000 $ | 195,000 |
| Market price per share of common stock . . $ | 76.50 $ | 94.99 |
| Dividends paid per common share . . . . . . . $ | 0.50 $ | 0.40 |

Selected balance sheet data at the *beginning* of the current year:

|  | Digitalized | Zone Network |
|---|---|---|
| Balance sheet: |  |  |
| Current receivables, net . . . . . . . . . . . . $ | 44,000 $ | 53,000 |
| Inventories . . . . . . . . . . . . . . . . . . . | 80,000 | 86,000 |
| Total assets . . . . . . . . . . . . . . . . . . . | 262,000 | 276,000 |
| Common stock, $1 par (12,000 shares) | 12,000 |  |
| $2 par (16,000 shares) |  | 32,000 |

Your strategy is to invest in companies that have low price/earnings ratios but appear to be in good shape financially. Assume that you have analyzed all other factors and that your decision depends on the results of ratio analysis.

## Requirement

1.  Compute the following ratios for both companies for the current year, and decide which company's stock better fits your investment strategy.

    a.  Acid-test ratio
    b.  Inventory turnover
    c.  Days' sales in receivables
    d.  Debt ratio
    e.  Earnings per share of common stock
    f.  Price/earnings ratio
    g.  Dividend payout

## ● Problems (Group B)

*MyAccountingLab* **P15-28B** ❶ **Trend analyses and return on common equity [20–30 min]**
Net sales revenue, net income, and common stockholders' equity for Shawnee Mission Corporation, a manufacturer of contact lenses, follow for a four-year period.

|  | 2013 | 2012 | 2011 | 2010 |
|---|---|---|---|---|
| Net sales revenue ....... | $ 759,000 | $ 701,000 | $ 639,000 | $ 659,000 |
| Net income ........... | 56,000 | 43,000 | 38,000 | 48,000 |
| Ending common stockholders' equity ... | 364,000 | 356,000 | 328,000 | 300,000 |

## Requirements

1.  Compute trend analyses for each item for 2011–2013. Use 2010 as the base year, and round to the nearest whole percent.
2.  Compute the rate of return on common stockholders' equity for 2011–2013, rounding to three decimal places.

**P15-29B** ❷ **Vertical analysis [20–30 min]**
The Specialty Department Stores, Inc., chief executive officer (CEO) has asked you to compare the company's profit performance and financial position with the average for the industry. The CEO has given you the company's income statement and balance sheet, as well as the industry average data for retailers.

| SPECIALTY DEPARTMENT STORES, INC. | | |
|---|---|---|
| Income Statement Compared with Industry Average | | |
| Year Ended December 31, 2012 | | |
|  | Specialty | Industry Average |
| Net sales | $ 782,000 | 100.0% |
| Cost of goods sold | 528,632 | 65.8 |
| Gross profit | $ 253,368 | 34.2 |
| Operating expenses | 163,438 | 19.7 |
| Operating income | $ 89,930 | 14.5 |
| Other expenses | 4,692 | 0.4 |
| Net income | $ 85,238 | 14.1% |

| SPECIALTY DEPARTMENT STORES, INC. Balance Sheet Compared with Industry Average December 31, 2012 | | |
|---|---|---|
| | Specialty | Industry Average |
| Current assets | $ 303,750 | 70.9% |
| Fixed assets, net | 117,000 | 23.6 |
| Intangible assets, net | 5,850 | 0.8 |
| Other assets | 23,400 | 4.7 |
| Total assets | $ 450,000 | 100.0% |
| Current liabilities | $ 208,800 | 48.1% |
| Long-term liabilities | 102,600 | 16.6 |
| Stockholders' equity | 138,600 | 35.3 |
| Total liabilities and stockholders' equity | $ 450,000 | 100.0% |

### Requirement

1. Prepare a vertical analysis for Specialty for both its income statement and balance sheet.

*Note: Problem 15-30B should be used only after completing Problem 15-29B.*

**P15-30B** ❸ ❹ **Common-size statements, analysis of profitability and financial position, comparison with the industry, and using ratios to evaluate a company [20–30 min]**

Consider the data for Specialty Department Stores presented in P15-29B.

### Requirements

1. Prepare a common-size income statement and balance sheet for Specialty. The first column of each statement should present Specialty's common-size statement, and the second column, the industry averages.

2. For the profitability analysis, compute Specialty's (a) gross profit percentage and (b) rate of return on net sales. Compare these figures with the industry averages. Is Specialty's profit performance better or worse than the industry average?

3. For the analysis of financial position, compute Specialty's (a) current ratio and (b) debt to equity. Compare these ratios with the industry averages. Is Specialty's financial position better or worse than the industry averages?

**P15-31B** ❹ **Effects of business transactions on selected ratios [30–40 min]**

Financial statement data of *Road Trip Magazine* include the following items:

| | |
|---|---|
| Cash | $ 24,000 |
| Accounts receivable, net | 82,000 |
| Inventories | 188,000 |
| Total assets | 638,000 |
| Accounts payable | 99,000 |
| Accrued liabilities | 39,000 |
| Short-term notes payable | 51,000 |
| Long-term liabilities | 223,000 |
| Net income | 72,000 |
| Common shares outstanding | 20,000 |

## Requirements

1. Compute *Road Trip*'s current ratio, debt ratio, and earnings per share. Round all ratios to two decimal places, and use the following format for your answer:

| Current Ratio | Debt Ratio | Earnings per Share |
|---|---|---|
| | | |

2. Compute the three ratios after evaluating the effect of each transaction that follows. Consider each transaction *separately*.

   a. Purchased inventory of $45,000 on account.
   b. Borrowed $127,000 on a long-term note payable.
   c. Issued 2,000 shares of common stock, receiving cash of $105,000.
   d. Received cash on account, $7,000.

**P15-32B** ❹ **Using ratios to evaluate a stock investment [40–50 min]**
Comparative financial statement data of Tanfield, Inc., follow:

| TANFIELD, INC. | | |
|---|---|---|
| Comparative Income Statement | | |
| Years Ended December 31, 2012 and 2011 | | |
| | 2012 | 2011 |
| Net sales | $ 460,000 | $ 422,000 |
| Cost of goods sold | 239,000 | 212,000 |
| Gross profit | $ 221,000 | $ 210,000 |
| Operating expenses | 138,000 | 136,000 |
| Income from operations | $ 83,000 | $ 74,000 |
| Interest expense | 13,000 | 16,000 |
| Income before income tax | $ 70,000 | $ 58,000 |
| Income tax expense | 19,000 | 21,000 |
| Net income | $ 51,000 | $ 37,000 |

| TANFIELD, INC.<br>Comparative Balance Sheet<br>December 31, 2012 and 2011 | 2012 | 2011 | 2010* |
|---|---|---|---|
| **Current assets:** | | | |
| Cash | $ 91,000 | $ 88,000 | |
| Current receivables, net | 113,000 | 121,000 | $ 106,000 |
| Inventories | 144,000 | 158,000 | 204,000 |
| Prepaid expenses | 16,000 | 3,000 | |
| Total current assets | $ 364,000 | $ 370,000 | |
| Property, plant, and equipment, net | 217,000 | 176,000 | |
| Total assets | $ 581,000 | $ 546,000 | 602,000 |
| Total current liabilities | $ 227,000 | $ 240,000 | |
| Long-term liabilities | 117,000 | 96,000 | |
| Total liabilities | $ 344,000 | $ 336,000 | |
| Preferred stock, 3% | 92,000 | 92,000 | |
| Common stockholders' equity, no par | 145,000 | 118,000 | 89,000 |
| Total liabilities and stockholders' equity | $ 581,000 | $ 546,000 | |

\* Selected 2010 amounts

1. Market price of Tanfield's common stock: $59.36 at December 31, 2012, and $46.65 at December 31, 2011.
2. Common shares outstanding: 13,000 during 2012 and 11,000 during 2011 and 2010.
3. All sales on credit.

**Requirements**

1. Compute the following ratios for 2012 and 2011:

   a. Current ratio
   b. Times-interest-earned ratio
   c. Inventory turnover
   d. Gross profit percentage
   e. Debt to equity ratio
   f. Rate of return on common stockholders' equity
   g. Earnings per share of common stock
   h. Price/earnings ratio

2. Decide (a) whether Tanfield's ability to pay debts and to sell inventory improved or deteriorated during 2012 and (b) whether the investment attractiveness of its common stock appears to have increased or decreased.

**P15-33B** ❹ **Using ratios to decide between two stock investments [45–60 min]**
Assume that you are purchasing an investment and have decided to invest in a company in the digital phone business. You have narrowed the choice to Best Digital, Corp., and Every Zone, Inc., and have assembled the following data.

Selected income statement data for the current year:

| | Best Digital | Every Zone |
|---|---|---|
| Net sales (all on credit) . . . . . . . . . . . $ | 420,115 $ | 498,955 |
| Cost of goods sold . . . . . . . . . . . . . . | 210,000 | 256,000 |
| Interest expense . . . . . . . . . . . . . . . | — | 16,000 |
| Net income . . . . . . . . . . . . . . . . . . | 48,000 | 74,000 |

Selected balance sheet and market price data at the *end* of the current year:

| | Best Digital | Every Zone |
|---|---|---|
| **Current assets:** | | |
| Cash | $ 25,000 $ | 23,000 |
| Short-term investments . . . . . . . . . . . . | 42,000 | 21,000 |
| Current receivables, net. . . . . . . . . . . . | 42,000 | 52,000 |
| Inventories | 69,000 | 105,000 |
| Prepaid expenses . . . . . . . . . . . . . . . . | 19,000 | 14,000 |
| Total current assets . . . . . . . . . . . . . . | $ 197,000 $ | 215,000 |
| Total assets | $ 268,000 $ | 331,000 |
| Total current liabilities . . . . . . . . . . . . | 102,000 | 100,000 |
| Total liabilities . . . . . . . . . . . . . . . . | 102,000 | 128,000 |
| Common stock, $1 par (15,000 shares) | 15,000 | |
| $1 par (16,000 shares) | | 16,000 |
| Total stockholders' equity . . . . . . . . . . | $ 166,000 $ | 203,000 |
| Market price per share of common stock ..... | $ 48.00 $ | 115.75 |
| Dividends paid per common share . . . . . . | $ 2.00 $ | 1.80 |

Selected balance sheet data at the *beginning* of the current year:

| | Best Digital | Every Zone |
|---|---|---|
| **Balance sheet:** | | |
| Current receivables, net . . . . . . . . . . . . $ | 47,000 $ | 56,000 |
| Inventories . . . . . . . . . . . . . . . . . . | 83,000 | 92,000 |
| Total assets . . . . . . . . . . . . . . . . . . | 261,000 | 274,000 |
| Common stock, $1 par (15,000 shares) | 15,000 | |
| $1 par (16,000 shares) | | 16,000 |

Your strategy is to invest in companies that have low price/earnings ratios but appear to be in good shape financially. Assume that you have analyzed all other factors and that your decision depends on the results of ratio analysis.

## Requirement

1. Compute the following ratios for both companies for the current year, and decide which company's stock better fits your investment strategy.

     a. Acid-test ratio
     b. Inventory turnover
     c. Days' sales in receivables
     d. Debt ratio
     e. Earnings per share of common stock
     f. Price/earnings ratio
     g. Dividend payout

# ● Continuing Exercise

**E15-34**  ❷ **Vertical analysis of a balance sheet [10–15 min]**

This exercise continues the Lawlor Lawn Service, Inc., situation from Exercise 14-32 of Chapter 14.

**Requirement**

1. Prepare a vertical analysis from the income statement you prepared in Chapter 4.

# ● Continuing Problem

**P15-35**  ❹ **Using ratios to evaluate a stock investment [20–25 min]**

This problem continues the Draper Consulting, Inc., situation from Problem 14-33 of Chapter 14.

**Requirement**

1. Using the results from Chapter 4, and knowing that the current market price of Draper's stock is $200 per share, calculate the following ratios for the company:

   a. Current ratio
   b. Debt ratio
   c. Debt to equity ratio
   d. Earnings per share
   e. P/E ratio
   f. Rate of return on total assets
   g. Rate of return on common stockholders' equity

# Apply Your Knowledge

# ● Decision Cases

**Decision Case 15-1**  ABC and XYZ companies both had a bad year in 2010; the companies' suffered net losses. Due to the losses, some of the measures of return deteriorated for both companies. Assume top management of ABC and XYZ are pondering ways to improve their ratios for the following year. In particular, management is considering the following transactions:

1. Borrow $100 million on long-term debt.
2. Purchase treasury stock for $500 million cash.
3. Expense one-fourth of the goodwill carried on the books.
4. Create a new design division at a cash cost of $300 million.
5. Purchase patents from Johnson, Co., paying $20 million cash.

**Requirement**

1. Top management wants to know the effects of these transactions (increase, decrease, or no effect) on the following ratios:
   a. Current ratio
   b. Debt ratio
   c. Rate of return on common stockholders' equity

**Decision Case 15-2** Lance Berkman is the controller of Saturn, a dance club whose year-end is December 31. Berkman prepares checks for suppliers in December makes the proper journal entries, and posts them to the appropriate accounts in that month. However, he holds on to the checks and mails them to the suppliers in January.

### Requirements

1. What financial ratio(s) is(are) most affected by the action?
2. What is Berkman's purpose in undertaking this activity?

## ● Ethical Issue 15-1

Ross's Ripstick Company's long-term debt agreements make certain demands on the business. For example, Ross may not purchase treasury stock in excess of the balance of retained earnings. Also, long-term debt may not exceed stockholders' equity, and the current ratio may not fall below 1.50. If Ross fails to meet any of these requirements, the company's lenders have the authority to take over management of the company.

Changes in consumer demand have made it hard for Ross to attract customers. Current liabilities have mounted faster than current assets, causing the current ratio to fall to 1.47. Before releasing financial statements, Ross's management is scrambling to improve the current ratio. The controller points out that an investment can be classified as either long-term or short-term, depending on management's intention. By deciding to convert an investment to cash within one year, Ross can classify the investment as short-term—a current asset. On the controller's recommendation, Ross's board of directors votes to reclassify long-term investments as short-term.

### Requirements

1. What effect will reclassifying the investments have on the current ratio? Is Ross's true financial position stronger as a result of reclassifying the investments?
2. Shortly after the financial statements are released, sales improve; so, too, does the current ratio. As a result, Ross's management decides not to sell the investments it had reclassified as short-term. Accordingly, the company reclassifies the investments as long-term. Has management behaved unethically? Give the reasoning underlying your answer.

## ● Fraud Case 15-1

Allen Software was a relatively new tech company led by aggressive founder Benjamin Allen. His strategy relied not so much on producing new products as using new equity capital to buy up other software companies. To keep attracting investors, Allen had to show year-to-year revenue growth. When his normal revenue streams stalled, he resorted to the tried and true "channel stuffing" technique. First, he improperly recorded shipments to his distributors as sales revenue, shipments that far exceeded the market demand for his products. Then he offered the distributors large payments to hold the excess inventory instead of returning it for a refund. Those payments were disguised as sales promotion expenses. He was able to show a considerable growth in revenues for two years running until one savvy investor group started asking questions. That led to a complaint filed with the SEC (Securities and Exchange Commission). The company is now in bankruptcy and several criminal cases are pending.

### Requirements

1. What factor may have tipped off the investor group that something was wrong?
2. In what way would those investors have been harmed?
3. If Allen had attracted enough equity capital, do you think he would have been able to conceal the scheme?

## • Financial Statement Case 15-1

Amazon.com's financial statements in Appendix A at the end of this book reveal some interesting relationships. Answer these questions about **Amazon**:

### Requirements

1. Compute trend analyses for net sales and net income. Use 2007 as the base year. What is the most notable aspect of this data?

2. Compute inventory turnover for 2009 and 2008. The inventory balance at December 31, 2009, was $2,171 million. Do the trend of net income from 2008 to 2009 and the change in the rate of inventory turnover tell the same story or a different story? Explain your answer.

## • Team Projects

**Team Project 15-1** Select an industry you are interested in, and pick any company in that industry to use as the benchmark. Then select two other companies in the same industry. For each category of ratios in the Decision Guidelines in the chapter, compute all the ratios for the three companies. Write a two-page report that compares the two companies with the benchmark company.

**Team Project 15-2** Select a company and obtain its financial statements. Convert the income statement and the balance sheet to common size, and compare the company you selected to the industry average. The Risk Management Association's *Annual Statement Studies*, Dun & Bradstreet's *Industry Norms & Key Business Ratios*, and Prentice Hall's *Almanac of Business and Industrial Financial Ratios*, by Leo Troy, publish common-size statements for most industries.

## • Communication Activity 15-1

In 75 words or fewer, explain the difference between horizontal and vertical analysis. Be sure to include in your answer how each might be used.

### Quick Check Answers

1. *b* 2. *a* 3. *d* 4. *c* 5. *a* 6. *b* 7. *d* 8. *c* 9. *a* 10. *b*

**For online homework, exercises, and problems that provide you immediate feedback, please visit myaccountinglab.com.**

# Comprehensive Problem for Chapter 15

## Analyzing a Company for Its Investment Potential

In its annual report, WRS Athletic Supply, Inc., includes the following five-year financial summary.

**WRS ATHLETIC SUPPLY, INC.**
**Five-Year Financial Summary (Partial; adapted)**

| (Dollar amounts in thousands except per share data) | 2015 | 2014 | 2013 | 2012 | 2011 | 2010 |
|---|---|---|---|---|---|---|
| Net sales | $244,524 | $217,799 | $191,329 | $165,013 | $137,634 | |
| Net sales increase | 12% | 14% | 16% | 20% | 17% | |
| Domestic comparative store sales increase | 5% | 6% | 5% | 8% | 9% | |
| Other income—net | 2,001 | 1,873 | 1,787 | 1,615 | 1,391 | |
| Cost of sales | 191,838 | 171,562 | 150,255 | 129,664 | 108,725 | |
| Operating, selling, and general and administrative expenses | 41,236 | 36,356 | 31,679 | 27,408 | 22,516 | |
| Interest: | | | | | | |
|     Interest expense | 1,063 | 1,357 | 1,383 | 1,045 | 803 | |
|     Interest income | (138) | (171) | (188) | (204) | (189) | |
| Income tax expense | 4,487 | 3,897 | 3,692 | 3,338 | 2,740 | |
| Net income | 8,039 | 6,671 | 6,295 | 5,377 | 4,430 | |
| Per share of common stock: | | | | | | |
|     Net income | 1.81 | 1.49 | 1.41 | 1.21 | 0.99 | |
|     Dividends | 0.30 | 0.28 | 0.24 | 0.20 | 0.16 | |
| **Financial Position** | | | | | | |
| Current assets, excluding inventory | $ 30,483 | $ 27,878 | $ 26,555 | $ 24,356 | $ 21,132 | |
| Inventories at LIFO cost | 24,891 | 22,614 | 21,442 | 19,793 | 17,076 | $16,497 |
| Property, plant, and equipment, net | 51,904 | 45,750 | 40,934 | 35,969 | 25,973 | |
| Total assets | 94,685 | 83,527 | 78,130 | 70,349 | 49,996 | |
| Current liabilities | 32,617 | 27,282 | 28,949 | 25,803 | 16,762 | |
| Long-term debt | 22,731 | 21,143 | 17,838 | 18,712 | 12,122 | |
| Shareholders' equity | 39,337 | 35,102 | 31,343 | 25,834 | 21,112 | |
| **Financial Ratios** | | | | | | |
| Acid-test ratio | 0.9 | 1.0 | 0.9 | 0.9 | 1.3 | |
| Rate of return on total assets | 10.2% | 9.9% | 10.3% | 10.7% | 9.6% | |
| Rate of return on shareholders' equity | 21.6% | 20.1% | 22.0% | 22.9% | 22.4% | |

## Requirement

1. Analyze the company's financial summary for the fiscal years 2011–2015 to decide whether to invest in the common stock of WRS. Include the following sections in your analysis, and fully explain your final decision.
   a. Trend analysis for net sales and net income (use 2011 as the base year).
   b. Profitability analysis.
   c. Evaluate the ability to sell inventory (WRS uses the LIFO method).
   d. Evaluate the ability to pay debts.
   e. Evaluate the dividends.

# 16 Introduction to Managerial Accounting

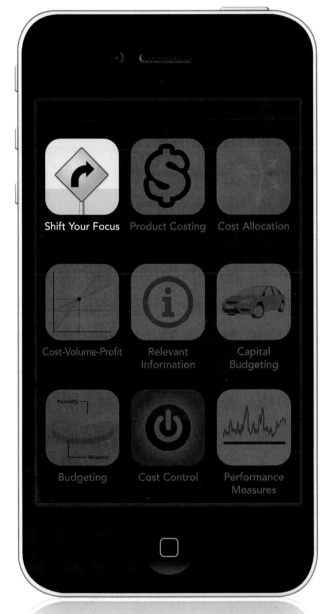

Shift Your Focus · Product Costing · Cost Allocation

Cost-Volume-Profit · Relevant Information · Capital Budgeting

Budgeting · Cost Control · Performance Measures

## Learning Objectives

1. Distinguish managerial accounting from financial accounting

2. Identify trends in the business environment and the role of management accountability

3. Apply ethical standards to decision making

4. Classify costs and prepare an income statement for a service company

5. Classify costs and prepare an income statement for a merchandising company

6. Classify costs and prepare an income statement and statement of cost of goods manufactured for a manufacturing company

After growing up in the south, you are excited about attending a prestigious college in the north. In addition to working toward your accounting degree, you are looking forward to participating in some winter sports. You soon have the opportunity to try ice skating. Since you have enjoyed inline skating for years, you think the transition from wheels to blades will be easy. Unfortunately, the transition is not smooth. By the end of the evening, you have sore ankles and several bruises from some embarrassing falls. While the basic concept of skating is the same, you soon discovered you have to learn some new techniques.

• • •

Just as you had to shift your focus from wheels to blades, from pavement to ice, we will also shift our focus in this chapter from financial accounting to managerial accounting. *Financial accounting* focuses on preparing financial statements. *Managerial* (or *management*) *accounting* focuses on the accounting tools managers use to run a business. So while the basic accounting concepts learned in financial accounting still apply, we will need to learn how to use these new tools. Anyone with an interest in owning or managing a business will find managerial accounting tools helpful in providing the information needed to make decisions. We'll explain these concepts using Smart Touch Learning and Greg's Tunes.

# Management Accountability: Financial vs. Managerial Accounting

**1** Distinguish managerial accounting from financial accounting

Before we launch into how managers use accounting, let's think about some of the groups to whom managers must answer. We call these groups the **stakeholders** of the company because each group has an interest of some sort in the business. **Management accountability** is the manager's *responsibility* to the various stakeholders of the company. Many different stakeholders have an interest in an organization, including customers, creditors, suppliers, and owners. Exhibit 16-1 shows the links between management and the various stakeholders of a company. The exhibit is organized by the three main categories of cash-flow activities: operating, investing, and financing. It also includes actions that affect society. For each activity, we list the stakeholders and what they provide to the organization. The far-right column shows how managers are accountable to the stakeholders.

**EXHIBIT 16-1** | **Management Accountability to Stakeholders**

| Stakeholders | Provide | and Management is accountable for |
|---|---|---|
| *Operating activities* | | |
| Suppliers | Products and services | Making timely payments to suppliers |
| Employees | Time and expertise | Providing a safe and productive work environment |
| Customers | Cash | Providing products and services that are safe and defect free; backing up the products and services they provide |
| *Investing activities* | | |
| Asset vendors | Long-term assets | Making timely payments to asset vendors |
| *Financing activities* | | |
| Owners | Cash or other assets | Providing a return on the owners' investment |
| Creditors | Cash | Repaying principal and interest |
| *Actions that affect society* | | |
| Governments | Permission to operate | Obeying laws and paying taxes |
| Communities | Human and physical resources | Operating in an ethical manner to support the community; ensuring the company's environmental impact does not harm the community |

To earn the stakeholders' trust, managers provide information about their decisions and the results of those decisions. Thus, management accountability requires two forms of accounting:

• Financial accounting for *external* reporting
• Managerial (or management) accounting for *internal* planning and control

*Financial accounting* provides financial statements that report results of operations, financial position, and cash flows both to managers and to external stakeholders: owners, creditors, suppliers, customers, the government, and society. Financial accounting satisfies management's accountability (responsibility) to

• owners and creditors for their investment decisions.
• regulatory agencies, such as the Securities Exchange Commission, the Federal Trade Commission, and the Internal Revenue Service.
• customers and society to ensure that the company acts responsibly.

The financial statements that you studied in Chapters 1–15 focused on financial accounting and reporting on the company as a whole.

*Managerial accounting*, on the other hand, provides information to help managers plan and control operations as they lead the business. This includes managing the company's plant, equipment, and human resources. Managerial accounting often requires forward-looking information because of the futuristic nature of business decisions. Additionally, managerial accounting reports may contain proprietary (company specific, non-public) information, whereas financial reports do not.

## Stop & Think...

You speak differently when you are speaking to your friends than when you are speaking to your boss or parents. This is the essence of managerial and financial accounting—the accounting data is formatted differently and contains more detailed information so that it "speaks" to the correct audience of users (stakeholders).

Managers are responsible to many stakeholders, so they must plan and control operations carefully.

- **Planning** means choosing goals and deciding how to achieve them. For example, a common goal is to increase operating income (profits). To achieve this goal, managers may raise selling prices or advertise more in the hope of increasing sales. The **budget** is a mathematical expression of the plan that managers use to coordinate the business's activities. **The budget shows the expected financial impact of decisions and helps identify the resources needed to achieve goals.**

- **Controlling** means implementing the plans and evaluating operations by comparing actual results to the budget. For example, managers can compare actual costs to budgeted costs to evaluate their performance. If actual costs fall below budgeted costs, that is usually good news. But if actual costs exceed the budget, managers may need to make changes. Cost data help managers make decisions.

Exhibit 16-2 on the following page highlights the differences between managerial accounting and financial accounting. Both managerial accounting and financial accounting use the accrual basis of accounting. Many managerial accounting reports also focus on cash and the timing of cash receipts and disbursements. But managerial accounting is not required to meet external reporting requirements, such as generally accepted accounting principles. Therefore, managers have more leeway in preparing management accounting reports, as you can see in points 1–4 of the exhibit.

Managers tailor their managerial accounting system to help them make wise decisions. Managers weigh the *benefits* of the system (better information leads to more informed decisions, which hopefully create higher profits) against the *costs* to develop and run the system. Weighing the costs against the benefits is called **cost/benefit analysis**. To remain in service, a managerial accounting system's benefits must exceed its costs.

Point 5 of Exhibit 16-2 indicates that managerial accounting provides more detailed and timely information than does financial accounting. On a day-to-day basis, managers identify ways to cut costs, set prices, and evaluate employee performance. Company intranets and handheld computers provide this information with the click of a mouse. While detailed information is important to managers, summary information is more valuable to external users of financial data.

Point 6 of Exhibit 16-2 reminds us that managerial accounting reports affect people's behavior. Accountability is created through measuring results. Therefore, employees try to perform well on the parts of their jobs that the accounting system measures. For example, if a manufacturing company evaluates a plant manager based only on costs, the manager may focus on cutting costs by using cheaper materials or hiring less experienced workers. These actions will cut costs, but they can hurt profits if product quality drops and sales fall as a result. Therefore, managers must consider how their decisions will motivate company employees and if that motivation will achieve the overall results the company desires.

**Key Takeaway**

Managerial accounting focuses on the information needs of internal users. Generally, managerial accounting reports provide more details so that managers have the information they need to plan and control costs. The benefits of the managerial accounting system must outweigh its cost.

**EXHIBIT 16-2** | **Financial Accounting Versus Managerial Accounting**

| | Financial Accounting | Managerial Accounting |
|---|---|---|
| 1. Primary users | External—investors, creditors, and government authorities | Internal—the company's managers |
| 2. Purpose of information | Help investors and creditors make investment and credit decisions | Help managers plan and control operations |
| 3. Focus and time dimension of the information | Relevance and reliability of the information and focus on the past—example: 2013 actual performance reported in 2014 | Relevance of the information and focus on the future—example: 2014 budget prepared in 2013 |
| 4. Rules and restrictions | Required to follow GAAP. Public companies are required to be audited by an independent CPA | Not required to follow GAAP |
| 5. Scope of information | Summary reports primarily on the company as a whole, usually on a quarterly or annual basis | Detailed reports on parts of the company (products, departments, territories), often on a daily or weekly basis |
| 6. Behavioral | Concern about adequacy of disclosures; behavioral implications are secondary | Concern about how reports will affect employee behavior |

# Today's Business Environment

**2** Identify trends in the business environment and the role of management accountability

**Connect To: Accounting Information Systems: ERP**

Enterprise resource planning (ERP) software has made huge advances in the past decade that streamline formerly time-consuming processes and provide a level of reporting not known in accounting information systems of the past. ERP systems such as those designed by Oracle and SAP allow managers to see transactions affecting costs as they are happening. This allows managers to make decisions in a timely manner. The heart of ERP systems includes virtual connectivity to vendors and customers alike.

In order to be successful, managers of both large corporations and small, privately owned businesses must consider recent business trends, such as the following:

- **Shift Toward a Service Economy. Service companies** provide health care, communication, banking, and other important benefits to society. **Google** and **DirecTV** do not sell products; they sell their services. In the last century, many developed economies shifted their focus from manufacturing to service, and now service companies employ more than half of the workforce. The U.S. Census Bureau expects services, such as technology and health care, to grow especially fast.

- **Global Competition.** To be competitive, many companies are moving operations to other countries to be closer to new markets. Other companies are partnering with foreign companies to meet local needs. For example, **Toyota**, a Japanese company, has five major assembly plants located in the U.S. in Huntsville, AL; Georgetown, KY; Princeton, IN: San Antonio, TX; and Buffalo, WV.

- **Time-Based Competition.** The Internet, electronic commerce (e-commerce), and express delivery speed the pace of business. Customers who instant message around the world will not want to wait two weeks to receive DVDs they purchased online. Time is the new competitive turf for world-class business. To compete, companies have developed the following time-saving responses:

  1. **Advanced Information Systems.** Many companies use **enterprise resource planning (ERP)** systems to integrate all their worldwide functions, departments, and data. ERP systems help to streamline operations and enable companies to respond quickly to changes in the marketplace.

2. **E-Commerce.** The Internet allows companies to sell to thousands of customers around the world by providing every product the company offers 24/7.

3. **Just-in-Time Management.** Inventory held too long becomes obsolete. Storing goods takes space and must be insured—that costs money. The just-in-time philosophy helps managers cut costs by speeding the transformation of raw materials into finished products. **Just-in-time (JIT)** means producing *just in time* to satisfy needs. Ideally, suppliers deliver materials for today's production in exactly the right quantities *just in time* to begin production, and finished units are completed *just in time* for delivery to customers.

- **Total Quality Management.** Companies must deliver high-quality goods and services in order to be successful. **Total quality management (TQM)** is a philosophy designed to integrate all organizational areas in order to provide customers with superior products and services while meeting organizational goals throughout the value chain. The **value chain** includes all the activities that add value to a company's products and services. Companies achieve this goal by continuously improving quality and reducing or eliminating defects and waste. **In TQM, each business function sets higher and higher goals to continuously improve quality.** Mark Tiffee, CEO of **A Cut Above Exteriors**, says that one example of how TQM changed his business is in the sales department. "The initial analysis showed that 78% of sales orders had errors. We saw this was a problem with our process, not our people. By working on the process, we were able to cut sales order errors down. Within eight months we had eliminated virtually all errors without any disciplinary tactics."[1]

> **Key Takeaway**
>
> Developed economies have shifted from a manufacturing focus to a service focus. Global competition, e-commerce, and the Internet have expedited both the need and the speed with which information must be available to decision makers. JIT production and TQM mean producing just in time to satisfy customer demand, while constantly improving the quality of goods and services offered to customers.

# Ethical Standards

The Bernie Madoff and **Bank of America/Merrill Lynch** scandals underscore what happens when ethics are violated. The ethical path is clear and requires ethical behavior without regard to personal consequences. Consider the following examples:

**3** Apply ethical standards to decision making

- Sarah Baker is examining the ending inventory records for the December 31 year end financial statements at Top-Flight's warehouses in Arizona. She discovers an inventory purchase of $1,000 that was counted as part of the ending inventory, but the inventory was shipped F.O.B. destination and arrived January 3. When asked about the invoice, Mike Flinders, purchasing manager, admits that he included the inventory in his ending count, though the goods were not yet in the warehouse. After all, the company would have the inventory in just a few days.

- As the accountant of Casey Computer, Co., you are aware of Casey's weak financial condition. Casey is close to signing a lucrative contract that should ensure its future. The controller states that the company *must* report a profit this year. He suggests: "Two customers have placed orders that are scheduled to be shipped January 3, when production of those orders is completed. Let's record the goods as finished and bill the customer on December 31 so we can show the profit from those orders in the current year."

---

[1]http://www.price-associates.com/solutions/performance/total-quality-management/a-cut-above-exteriors-case-study.aspx, 06/08/2010

Although the ethical path is clear in the two preceding examples, some situations pose ethical challenges for a manager. The Institute of Management Accountants (IMA) has developed standards to help managerial accountants meet ethical challenges. The IMA standards remind us that society expects professional accountants to exhibit the highest level of ethical behavior. An excerpt from the IMA's Statement of Ethical Professional Practice appears in Exhibit 16-3. These standards require management accountants to

- maintain their professional competence,
- preserve the confidentiality of the information they handle, and
- act with integrity and credibility.

**EXHIBIT 16-3** | **IMA Statement of Ethical Professional Practice (excerpt)**

Management accountants have a commitment to ethical professional practice which includes principles of Honesty, Fairness, Objectivity, and Responsibility. The standards of ethical practice include the following:

**I. COMPETENCE**
1. Maintain an appropriate level of professional expertise by continually developing knowledge and skills.
2. Perform professional duties in accordance with relevant laws, regulations, and technical standards.
3. Provide decision support information and recommendations that are accurate, clear, concise, and timely.
4. Recognize and communicate professional limitations or other constraints that would preclude responsible judgment or successful performance of an activity.

**II. CONFIDENTIALITY**
1. Keep information confidential except when disclosure is authorized or legally required.
2. Inform all relevant parties regarding appropriate use of confidential information. Monitor subordinates' activities to ensure compliance.
3. Refrain from using confidential information for unethical or illegal advantage.

**III. INTEGRITY**
1. Mitigate actual conflicts of interest, regularly communicate with business associates to avoid apparent conflicts of interest. Advise all parties of any potential conflicts.
2. Refrain from engaging in any conduct that would prejudice carrying out duties ethically.
3. Abstain from engaging in or supporting any activity that might discredit the profession.

**IV. CREDIBILITY**
1. Communicate information fairly and objectively.
2. Disclose all relevant information that could reasonably be expected to influence an intended user's understanding of the reports, analyses, or recommendations.
3. Disclose delays or deficiencies in information, timeliness, processing, or internal controls in conformance with organization policy and/or applicable law.

Adapted with permission from IMA, www.imanet.org

**Key Takeaway**

Issues where professional judgments must be made arise often. Determining the ethical action is usually easy. Acting ethically is where integrity and credibility prevail. The excerpt from the IMA's Statement of Ethical Professional Practice guides managerial accountants in ethical matters.

To resolve ethical dilemmas, the IMA also suggests discussing ethical situations with your immediate supervisor, or with an objective adviser.

Let's return to the two ethical dilemmas. By including inventory that wasn't owned by the company in the ending inventory count, Mike Flinders violated the IMA's integrity standards (overstating the company's assets). Because Sarah Baker discovered the inflated inventory report, she would not be fulfilling her ethical responsibilities (integrity and credibility) if she allowed the inventory to be overstated and did not report Flinder's actions.

The second dilemma, in which the controller asked Sarah Baker to record goods still owned by the company as a sale, also poses problems. Clearly these acts are a violation of GAAP, so you should discuss the available alternatives and their consequences with others. Following the controller's suggestion to manipulate the company's income would violate the standards of competence, integrity, and credibility. If you refuse to make the entries in December and you simply resign without attempting to find an alternative solution, you might only hurt yourself and your family. Ideally, you could convince the controller that the income manipulation is not ethical and violates the revenue recognition principle. Therefore, no entries for these transactions would be made in December.

# Service Companies

Service companies, such as **eBay** (online auction), **Verizon** (cell phone service), and your local car wash (cleaning services), sell services. **Basically, service companies sell their time, skills, and knowledge.** As with other types of businesses, service companies seek to provide services with the following three characteristics:

**4** Classify costs and prepare an income statement for a service company

- High quality
- Reasonable prices
- Timely delivery

We focused on financial statements for service companies in Chapters 1–4 using Smart Touch Learning, Inc.

Service companies have the simplest accounting since they carry no inventories of products for sale. All of their costs are **period costs**, those costs that are incurred and expensed in the same accounting *period*.

Let's look first at Smart Touch as it originally started out in early 2013 as a service company. Recall that this business sold e-learning. Smart Touch's income statement for the month ended May 31, 2013, reproduced from Chapter 3 with ratio analysis added, follows:

**EXHIBIT 16-4** | **Income Statement—Service Company**

### SMART TOUCH LEARNING, INC.
#### Income Statement
#### Month Ended May 31, 2013

| | | | |
|---|---:|---:|---:|
| Revenue: | | | |
| Service revenue | | $7,600 | 100% |
| Expenses: | | | |
| Salary expense | $1,800 | | 24% |
| Rent expense | 1,000 | | 13% |
| Utilities expense | 400 | | 5% |
| Depreciation expense—furniture | 300 | | 4% |
| Depreciation expense—building | 200 | | 3% |
| Interest expense | 100 | | 1% |
| Supplies expense | 100 | | 1% |
| Total expenses | | 3,900 | 51% |
| Net income | | $3,700 | 49% |

Smart Touch had no inventory in May, so the company's income statement has no Cost of goods sold. The largest expense is for the salaries of personnel who work for the company. Salary expense was 24% of Smart Touch's revenue in May and the company earned a 49% net income.

Service companies need to know which services are most profitable, and that means evaluating both revenues and costs. Knowing the cost per service helps managers set the price of each and then calculate operating income. Service companies often consider *all* operating expenses (period costs) as part of their cost of service. In larger, more advanced service companies, the period costs may be split between service costs (part of the cost per unit of service) and non-service costs (expenses unrelated to the service). In May 2013, Smart Touch provided 1,950 e-learning services. What is the cost per service? Use the following formula to calculate the unit cost:

**Key Takeaway**

Service companies sell their time, skills, or knowledge. All of their operating expenses are normally considered period costs and are considered part of the cost of providing each service unit. In larger, more advanced service companies, the operating expenses (period costs) may be split between service costs (part of the cost per unit of service) and non-service costs (expenses unrelated to the service).

$$\text{Unit cost per service} = \text{Total service costs} \div \text{Total number of services provided}$$
$$= \$3,900 \div 1,950$$
$$= \$2 \text{ per e-learning service}$$

# Merchandising Companies

**⑤** Classify costs and prepare an income statement for a merchandising company

**Merchandising companies,** such as **Amazon.com, Target,** and **Best Buy,** resell products they buy from suppliers. Merchandisers keep an inventory of products, and managers are accountable for the purchasing, storage, and sale of the products. You learned about merchandising companies in Chapters 5 and 6 of this textbook.

In contrast with service companies, merchandisers' income statements report Cost of goods sold as the major expense. The cost of goods sold section of the income statement is not shown in most external financial reports, but is simply listed as one item, Cost of goods sold. This section is often detailed on internal management reports to show the flow of product costs through the inventory. These product costs are **inventoriable product costs** because the products are held in inventory, an asset, until sold. For *external reporting*, GAAP require companies to treat inventoriable product costs as an asset until the product is sold or consumed, at which time the costs are expensed.

Merchandising companies' inventoriable product costs include *only* the cost to purchase the goods plus freight in—the cost to get the goods *in* the warehouse. The activity in the Inventory account provides the information for the cost of goods sold section of the income statement as shown in the following formula:

Beginning Inventory + Net Purchases + Freight In – Ending Inventory = Cost of Goods Sold

To highlight the roles of beginning inventory, purchases, and ending inventory, we use the periodic inventory system. However, the concepts in this chapter apply equally to companies that use perpetual inventory systems.

In managerial accounting, we distinguish inventoriable product costs from period costs. As noted previously, *period costs* are those operating costs that are expensed in the period in which they are incurred. Therefore, period costs are the expenses that are not part of inventoriable product cost.

Recall Greg's Tunes' December 31, 2014, results as presented in Chapter 5 as our merchandising example. Remember that Greg's Tunes first started as a service company selling musical services. Then, the company began selling music CDs and DVDs produced by other companies. At that point the company became a merchandiser. Exhibit 16-5 shows the income statement of Greg's Tunes for the year ended December 31, 2014, using the periodic inventory method and including ratio analysis.

**EXHIBIT 16-5** | **Income Statement—Merchandising Company**

### GREG'S TUNES
### Income Statement
### Year Ended December 31, 2014

| | | | |
|---|---|---|---|
| Sales revenue | | $169,300 | 102.0% |
| Less: Sales returns and allowances | $ 2,000 | | 1.2% |
| Sales discounts | 1,400 | | 0.8% |
| | | 3,400 | 2.0% |
| Net sales revenue | | $165,900 | 100.0% |
| Cost of goods sold: | | | |
| Beginning inventory | $ 0 | | |
| Purchases and freight in | 131,000 | | |
| Cost of goods available for sale | $131,000 | | |
| Ending inventory | 40,200 | | |
| Cost of goods sold | | 90,800 | 54.7% |
| Gross profit | | $ 75,100 | 45.3% |
| Operating expenses | | | |
| Selling expenses: | | | |
| Wage expense | $ 10,200 | | 6.1% |
| General expenses: | | | |
| Rent expense | 8,400 | | 5.1% |
| Insurance expense | 1,000 | | 0.6% |
| Depreciation expense | 600 | | 0.4% |
| Supplies expense | 500 | | 0.3% |
| Total operating expenses | | 20,700 | 12.5% |
| Operating income | | $ 54,400 | 32.8% |
| Other income and (expense): | | | |
| Interest expense | | (1,300) | (0.8%) |
| Net income | | $ 53,100 | 32.0% |

Greg's was not selling DVDs and CDs in 2013, so the beginning inventory at December 31, 2013, was $0. During 2014, Greg's purchased DVDs and CDs at a total cost of $131,000. At the end of 2014, Greg's ending inventory was $40,200. (You can confirm this by reviewing the balance sheet in Exhibit 5-8.) Of the $131,000 available for sale, the cost of DVDs and CDs sold in 2014 was $90,800. Notice that cost of goods sold is 54.7% of net sales revenue (cost of goods sold divided by net sales revenue of $165,900). Managers watch the gross profit percentage (45.3% for Greg's) to make sure it does not change too much. A large decrease in the gross profit percentage may indicate that the company has a problem with inventory theft or shrinkage (waste). It may also indicate a problem with retail pricing of the products. The company's profit margin (net income divided by net sales revenue) is 32% for the year ended December 31, 2014.

Merchandising companies need to know which products are most profitable. Knowing the unit cost per product helps managers set appropriate selling prices. During the year, Greg's sold 10,000 CDs and DVDs. What is the average cost of each item sold? Use the following formula to calculate the average unit cost per item:

Unit cost per item = Total cost of goods sold ÷ Total number of items sold

= $90,800 ÷ 10,000

= $9.08 per item

Now practice what you have learned by solving Summary Problem 16-1.

**Key Takeaway**

Merchandising companies resell products they buy from suppliers. Merchandisers keep an inventory of products, and managers are accountable for the purchase, storage, and sale of the products. Inventory is an asset until it is sold. Cost of goods sold is the total cost of merchandise inventory sold during the period, and includes the freight to get the goods into the warehouse. COGS divided by total units sold equals the cost per unit for the merchandiser.

# Summary Problem 16-1

Jackson, Inc., a retail distributor of futons, provided the following information for 2013:

| | |
|---|---:|
| Merchandise inventory, January 1................ | $ 20,000 |
| Merchandise inventory, December 31 ........... | 30,000 |
| Selling expense .............................................. | 50,000 |
| Delivery expense (freight out)....................... | 18,000 |
| Net purchases of futons............................... | 265,000 |
| Rent expense................................................. | 15,000 |
| Utilities expense ........................................... | 3,000 |
| Freight in...................................................... | 15,000 |
| Administrative expense ................................. | 64,000 |
| Sales revenue................................................ | 500,000 |
| | |
| Units sold during the year ............................ | 2,500 futons |

## Requirements

1. Calculate the cost of goods sold. What is the cost per futon sold?
2. Calculate the total period costs.
3. Prepare Jackson's income statement for the year ended December 31, 2013. Do not categorize operating expenses between selling and general. What is the gross profit percentage? What is the profit margin percentage?

## Solution

1.

Cost of goods sold = Beginning inventory + Net purchases + Freight in − Ending inventory

$270,000 = $20,000 + $265,000 + $15,000 − $30,000

The cost per futon sold = Cost of goods sold ÷ Number of futons sold

$108 per futon = $270,000 ÷ 2,500 futons

2. Total period costs include all expenses not included in inventory:

| | |
|---|---:|
| Selling expense ......................... | $ 50,000 |
| Delivery expense (freight out)... | 18,000 |
| Rent expense............................. | 15,000 |
| Utilities expense ....................... | 3,000 |
| Administrative expense ............ | 64,000 |
| Total period costs..................... | $150,000 |

3. The income statement follows:

**JACKSON, INC.**
**Income Statement**
Year Ended December 31, 2013

| | | | |
|---|---|---|---|
| Sales revenue | | $500,000 | 100% |
| Cost of goods sold: | | | |
| Merchandise inventory, January 1 | $ 20,000 | | |
| Net purchases and freight in ($265,000 + $15,000) | 280,000 | | |
| Cost of goods available for sale | $300,000 | | |
| Merchandise inventory, December 31 | 30,000 | | |
| Cost of goods sold | | 270,000 | 54% |
| Gross profit | | $230,000 | 46% |
| Operating expenses: | | | |
| Administrative expense | $ 64,000 | | |
| Selling expense | 50,000 | | |
| Delivery expense | 18,000 | | |
| Rent expense | 15,000 | | |
| Utilities expense | 3,000 | 150,000 | 30% |
| Operating income | | $ 80,000 | 16% |

Gross profit % = $230,000 / $500,000 × 100 = 46%
Profit margin % = $80,000 / $500,000 × 100 = 16%

# Manufacturing Companies

**6** Classify costs and prepare an income statement and statement of cost of goods manufactured for a manufacturing company

**Manufacturing companies** use labor, equipment, supplies, and facilities to convert raw materials into finished products. Managers in manufacturing companies must use these resources to create a product that customers want at a price customers are willing to pay. Managers are responsible for generating profits and maintaining positive cash flows.

In contrast with service and merchandising companies, manufacturing companies have a broad range of production activities that require tracking costs on three kinds of inventory:

1. **Materials inventory** includes raw materials used to make a product. For example, a baker's raw materials include flour, sugar, and eggs. Materials to manufacture a DVD include casings, colored insert label, blank DVD, and software program licensed to each DVD.

2. **Work in process inventory** includes goods that are in the manufacturing process but are not yet complete. Some production activities have transformed the raw materials, but the product is not yet finished or ready for sale. A baker's work in process inventory includes dough ready for cooking. A DVD manufacturer's work in process could include the DVD and software program, but not the casing and labeling.

3. **Finished goods inventory** includes completed goods that have not yet been sold. Finished goods are the products that the manufacturer sells, such as a finished cake or boxed DVD, to a merchandiser (or directly to customers).

## Types of Costs

A **direct cost** is a cost that can be directly traced to a cost object, such as a product. Direct materials and direct labor are examples of direct costs. A **cost object** is anything for which managers need a separate breakdown of its component costs. Smart Touch's DVDs are an example of a cost object. Managers may want to know the cost of a product, a department, a sales territory, or an activity. Costs that cannot be traced directly to a cost object, such as manufacturing overhead, are **indirect costs.** Indirect costs are required to make the finished product but are not as easy or cost effective to track to ONE specific finished product. In manufacturing companies, product costs include both direct and indirect costs.

### Inventoriable Product Costs

The completed product in finished goods inventory represents the *inventoriable product cost*. The inventoriable product cost includes three components of manufacturing costs:

- **Direct materials** become a physical part of the finished product. **The cost of direct materials (purchase cost plus freight in) can be traced directly to the finished product.**
- **Direct labor** is the labor of employees who convert materials into the company's products. **The cost of direct labor can be traced *directly* to the finished products.**
- **Manufacturing overhead** refers to indirect manufacturing costs. So, it includes all manufacturing costs other than direct materials and direct labor. These costs are created by all of the supporting production activities, including storing materials, setting up machines, and cleaning the work areas. These activities incur costs of indirect materials, indirect labor, repair and maintenance, utilities, rent, insurance, property taxes, manufacturing plant managers' salaries, and depreciation on manufacturing plant buildings and equipment. Manufacturing overhead is also called **factory overhead** or **indirect manufacturing cost.**

Direct labor and manufacturing overhead combined are called **conversion cost** because the direct labor and manufacturing overhead CONVERT raw materials into a finished product.

Exhibit 16-6 on the following page summarizes a manufacturer's inventoriable product costs.

### A Closer Look at Manufacturing Overhead

- Manufacturing overhead includes only those indirect costs that are related to the manufacturing operation. Insurance and depreciation on the *manufacturing plant's* building and equipment are indirect manufacturing costs, so they are part of manufacturing overhead. In contrast, depreciation on *delivery trucks* is not part of manufacturing overhead. Instead, depreciation on delivery trucks is a cost of moving the product to the customer. Its cost is delivery expense (a period cost), not an inventoriable product cost. Similarly, the cost of auto insurance for the sales force vehicles is a marketing expense (a period cost), not manufacturing overhead.
- *Manufacturing overhead includes indirect materials and indirect labor.* The spices used in cakes become physical parts of the finished product. But these costs are minor compared with the flour and sugar for the cakes. Similarly, the label is necessary but minor in relation to the DVD, case, and software. Since these low-priced materials' costs cannot conveniently be traced to a particular cake or DVD or these costs are so minor that we don't want to trace them to a specific cake or DVD,

**EXHIBIT 16-6** | **Manufacturer's Inventoriable Product Costs**

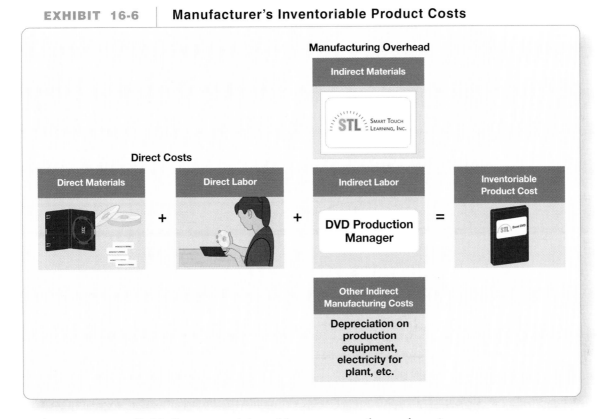

these costs are called indirect materials and become part of manufacturing overhead. Thus, **indirect materials** are materials used in making a product but whose costs either cannot conveniently be directly traced to specific finished products or whose costs are not large enough to justify tracing to the specific product.

Like indirect materials, **indirect labor** is difficult to trace to specific products so it is part of manufacturing overhead. Indirect labor is labor incurred that is necessary to make a product but whose costs either cannot conveniently be directly traced to specific finished products or whose costs are not large enough to justify tracing to the specific product. Examples include the pay of forklift operators, janitors, and plant managers. Keep in mind that with indirect costs there is often professional judgment involved as to whether a specific cost is part of the product manufacturing overhead cost (inventoriable product cost) or if the particular cost is not related to the manufacturing of the product (period cost).

Now let's assume that Smart Touch has decided in 2014 to manufacture its own brand of learning DVDs. The company's first year of operations as a manufacturer of learning DVDs is presented on the next page in the income statement in Exhibit 16-7 for the year ended December 31, 2014.

Smart Touch's cost of goods sold represents 60% of the net sales revenue. This is the inventoriable product cost of the DVDs that Smart Touch sold in 2014. Smart Touch's balance sheet at December 31, 2014, reports the inventoriable product costs of the finished DVDs that are still on hand at the end of that year. The cost of the ending inventory, $50,000, will become the beginning inventory of next year and will then be included as part of the Cost of goods sold on next year's income statement as the DVDs are sold. The operating expenses that represent 24.1% of net sales revenue are period costs.

Exhibit 16-8 summarizes the differences between inventoriable product costs and period costs for service, merchandising, and manufacturing companies. This is a reference tool that will help you determine how to categorize costs.

**EXHIBIT 16-7** | **Income Statement—Manufacturing Company**

**SMART TOUCH LEARNING, INC.**
**Income Statement**
**Year Ended December 31, 2014**

| | | | |
|---|---|---:|---:|
| Sales revenue | | $1,200,000 | 120.0% |
| Less: Sales returns and allowances | $ 120,000 | | 12.0% |
| Sales discounts | 80,000 | | 8.0% |
| | | 200,000 | 20.0% |
| Net sales revenue | | $1,000,000 | 100.0% |
| Cost of goods sold: | | | |
| Beginning finished goods inventory | $ 0 | | |
| Cost of goods manufactured* | 650,000 | | |
| Cost of goods available for sale | $ 650,000 | | |
| Ending finished goods inventory | 50,000 | | |
| Cost of goods sold | | 600,000 | 60.0% |
| Gross profit | | $ 400,000 | 40.0% |
| Operating expenses | | | |
| Wage expense | $ 120,000 | | 12.0% |
| Rent expense | 100,000 | | 10.0% |
| Insurance expense | 10,000 | | 1.0% |
| Depreciation expense | 6,000 | | 0.6% |
| Supplies expense | 5,000 | | 0.5% |
| Total operating expenses | | 241,000 | 24.1% |
| Operating income | | $ 159,000 | 15.9% |
| Other income and (expense): | | | |
| Interest expense | | (7,600) | (0.8%) |
| Net income | | $ 151,400 | 15.1% |

\* Calculation explained later in Exhibit 16-10

**EXHIBIT 16-8** | **Inventoriable Product Costs and Period Costs for Service, Merchandising, and Manufacturing Companies**

| Type of Company | Inventoriable Product Costs—Initially an asset (Inventory), and expensed (Cost of goods sold) when the inventory is sold | Period Costs—Expensed in the period incurred; never considered an asset |
|---|---|---|
| Service company | None | Salaries, depreciation, utilities, insurance, property taxes, advertising expenses |
| Merchandising company | Purchases plus freight in | Salaries, depreciation, utilities, insurance, property taxes on storage building, advertising, delivery expenses |
| Manufacturing company | Direct materials, direct labor, and manufacturing overhead (including indirect materials; indirect labor; depreciation on the manufacturing plant and equipment; plant insurance, utilities, and property taxes) | Delivery expense; depreciation expense, utilities, insurance, and property taxes on executive headquarters (separate from the manufacturing plant); advertising; CEO's salary |

Let's compare Smart Touch's manufacturing income statement in Exhibit 16-7 with Greg's Tunes' merchandising income statement in Exhibit 16-5. The only difference is that the merchandiser (Greg's) uses *purchases* in computing cost of goods sold, while the manufacturer (Smart Touch) uses the *cost of goods manufactured*. Notice that the term **cost of goods manufactured** is in the past tense. It is the manufacturing cost of the goods that Smart Touch *completed during 2014*. The following is the difference between a manufacturer and a merchandiser:

- The manufacturer *made* the product that it later sold.
- The merchandiser *purchased* a product that was already complete and ready to be sold.

**Calculating the Cost of Goods Manufactured**   The cost of goods manufactured summarizes the activities and the costs that take place in a manufacturing plant over the period. Let's begin by reviewing these activities. Exhibit 16-9 reminds us that the manufacturer starts by buying materials. Then the manufacturer uses direct labor and manufacturing plant and equipment (overhead) to transform (convert) these materials into work in process inventory. When inventory is completed, it becomes finished goods inventory. These are all inventoriable product costs because they are required for the inventory production process.

**EXHIBIT 16-9**   **Manufacturing Company: Inventoriable Product Costs and Period Costs**

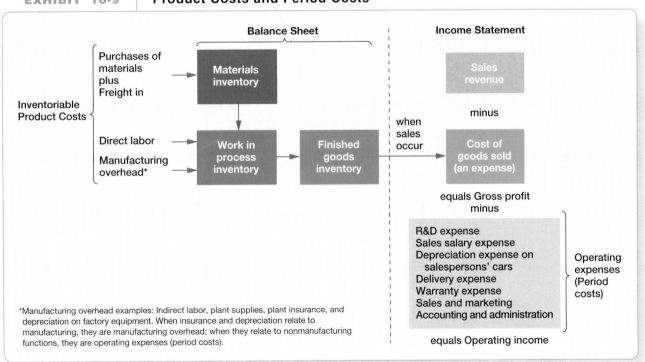

Finished goods are the only category of inventory that is ready to sell. The cost of the finished goods that the manufacturer sells becomes its cost of goods sold on the income statement. Costs the manufacturer incurs in nonmanufacturing activities, such as sales salaries, are operating expenses—period costs—and are expensed in the period incurred. Exhibit 16-9 shows that these operating costs are deducted from gross profit to compute operating income.

You now have a clear understanding of the flow of activities and costs in the plant, and you are ready to calculate the cost of goods manufactured. Exhibit 16-10 shows how Smart Touch computed its cost of goods manufactured for 2014 of $650,000. This is the cost of making 15,000 custom DVDs that Smart Touch *finished* during 2014.

**EXHIBIT 16-10** | **Schedule of Cost of Goods Manufactured**

### SMART TOUCH LEARNING, INC.
### Schedule of Cost of Goods Manufactured
Year Ended December 31, 2014

| | | | | |
|---|---|---|---|---|
| A | Beginning work in process inventory | | | $ 80,000 |
| | Direct materials used: | | | |
| B | Beginning direct materials inventory | $ 70,000 | | |
| C | Purchases of direct materials (including freight in) | 350,000 | | |
| D | Available for use | $420,000 | | |
| E | Ending direct materials inventory | (65,000) | | |
| F | Direct materials used | | $355,000 | |
| G | Direct labor | | 169,000 | |
| | Manufacturing overhead: | | | |
| H | Indirect materials | $ 17,000 | | |
| I | Indirect labor | 28,000 | | |
| J | Depreciation—plant and equipment | 10,000 | | |
| K | Plant utilities, insurance, and property taxes | 18,000 | | |
| L | Total manufacturing overhead | | 73,000 | |
| M | Total manufacturing costs incurred during the year | | | 597,000 |
| N | Total manufacturing costs to account for | | | $677,000 |
| O | Ending work in process inventory | | | (27,000) |
| P | Cost of goods manufactured | | | $650,000* |

B + C = D
D − E = F
H + I + J + K = L
F + G + L = M
A + M = N
N − O = P

The letters are provided as a means to aid students in determining which lines are used in the calculations.

\* refer to Exhibit 16-7 income statement

Cost of goods manufactured summarizes the activities and related costs incurred to produce inventory during the year. As of December 31, 2013, Smart Touch had just started manufacturing and had not completed the first custom learning DVD yet. However, the company had begun production and had spent a total of $80,000 **A** to partially complete them. This 2013 ending work in process inventory became the beginning work in process inventory for 2014.

Exhibit 16-10 shows that during the year, Smart Touch used $355,000 **F** of direct materials, $169,000 **G** of direct labor, and $73,000 **L** of manufacturing overhead.

Total manufacturing costs incurred during the year are the sum of the following three amounts:

| Total Manufacturing Costs | |
|---|---|
| Direct materials used......................................................... $355,000 **F** |
| Direct labor.................................................................. 169,000 **G** |
| Manufacturing overhead.................................................. 73,000 **L** |
| Total manufacturing costs incurred during the year ............ $597,000 **M** |

Adding total manufacturing cost for the year, $597,000 **M**, to the beginning Work in Process (WIP) Inventory of $80,000 **A** gives the total manufacturing cost to account for, $677,000 **N**. At December 31, 2014, unfinished DVDs costing only $27,000 **O** remained in WIP Inventory. The company finished 130,000 DVDs and sent them to Finished Goods (FG) Inventory. Cost of goods manufactured for the year was $650,000 **P**. The following is the computation of the cost of goods manufactured:

| Beginning + WIP **A** | Direct materials + used **F** | Direct labor + **G** | Manufacturing – overhead **L** | Ending = WIP **O** | Cost of goods manufactured **P** |
|---|---|---|---|---|---|
| $80,000 + | 355,000 + | 169,000 + | 73,000 | – 27,000 = | $650,000 |

If you refer back to Smart Touch's December, 2014, income statement in Exhibit 16-7, you will find the $650,000 **P** listed as the cost of goods manufactured.

**Flow of Costs Through the Inventory Accounts**    Exhibit 16-11 diagrams the flow of costs through Smart Touch's inventory accounts. The format—what is on hand at the beginning of the period plus what is added during the period less what is on hand at the end of the period equals what has been used/sold—is the same for all three stages:

- Direct materials
- Work in process
- Finished goods

**EXHIBIT 16-11** | **Flow of Costs Through a Manufacturer's Inventory Accounts**

| Direct Materials Inventory | | Work in Process Inventory | | Finished Goods Inventory | |
|---|---|---|---|---|---|
| Beginning inventory | $ 70,000 | Beginning inventory | $ 80,000 | Beginning inventory | $ 0 |
| + Purchases and freight in | 350,000 | + Direct materials used | $355,000 | + Cost of goods | |
| | | + Direct labor | 169,000 | manufactured | 650,000 |
| | | + Manufacturing overhead | 73,000 | | |
| | | Total manufacturing costs incurred during the year | $597,000 | | |
| = Direct materials available for use | $420,000 | = Total manufacturing costs to account for | $677,000 | = Cost of goods available for sale | $650,000 |
| – Ending inventory | (65,000) | – Ending inventory | (27,000) | – Ending inventory | (50,000) |
| = Direct materials used | $355,000 | = Cost of goods manufactured | $650,000 | = Cost of goods sold | $600,000 |

*Source:* The authors are indebted to Judith Cassidy for this presentation.

The final amount at each stage is the beginning of the next stage. Take time to see how the schedule of cost of goods manufactured in Exhibit 16-11 uses the flows of the direct materials and work in process stages for Smart Touch's year ended December 31, 2014. Then review the income statement for Greg's Tunes in Exhibit 16-5 on page 781. Because Greg's is a merchandising company, it uses only a single Inventory account.

## Calculating Unit Product Cost

Knowing the unit product cost helps managers decide on the prices to charge for each product to ensure that each product is profitable. They can then measure operating income and determine the cost of finished goods inventory. Smart Touch produced 130,000 DVDs during 2014. What did it cost to make each DVD?

| Cost of goods manufactured ÷ Total units produced = Unit product cost | | | |
|---|---|---|---|
| $650,000 | ÷ | 130,000 | = $5 per DVD |

During 2014, Smart Touch sold 120,000 DVDs, and the company knows each DVD cost $5 to produce. With this information, Smart Touch can compute its cost of goods sold as follows:

$$\underset{\text{units sold}}{\text{Number of}} \times \underset{\text{cost}}{\text{Unit product}} = \underset{\text{goods sold}}{\text{Cost of}}$$

$$120{,}000 \times \$5 \text{ per DVD} = \$600{,}000$$

Keep in mind that the manufacturer still has period costs unrelated to the product cost that it must pay, like selling costs and administrative costs. These expenses are reported on the company's income statement because they are a necessary expense in running the business (period cost) but are not part of the product cost (inventory).

## Stop & Think...

It seems lately that every time we go to the gas pump to fill up our cars, the price per gallon has changed. This change causes us to rethink our expected fuel expense each month. Similarly, the unit cost to make a product will change over time because the costs of the inputs to the production process change over time. With readily available data from computerized ERP systems, the cost of goods manufactured statement is prepared more than once (daily, monthly, yearly, or some other time interval depending on the business)—to update management's cost data about the products the company is producing and selling. By having current cost information, management can adjust the sales price to the customer, if necessary, to maintain product profitability. So back to your gas pump—this is why the price per gallon changes. Your local gas store updates the price per gallon that you pay based on updates to the cost your gas store pays per gallon.

---

**Key Takeaway**

The manufacturer creates a product from raw materials by adding direct labor and manufacturing overhead. Because at any point in time products are at various stages of completion, manufacturers have three inventory accounts: Raw materials, Work in process, and Finished goods. The schedule of cost of goods manufactured captures these production costs to determine the cost of goods manufactured for a period. Product cost per unit is calculated by dividing cost of goods manufactured by the total number of units produced.

# Decision Guidelines 16-1

## BUILDING BLOCKS OF MANAGERIAL ACCOUNTING

Let's review some of the building blocks of managerial accounting.

| Decision | Guidelines |
|---|---|
| • What information should managerial accountants provide? What is the primary focus of managerial accounting? | Managerial accounting provides information that helps managers make better decisions; it has a<br>• focus on *relevance* to business decisions, and<br>• *future* orientation. |
| • How do you decide on a company's managerial accounting system, which is not regulated by GAAP? | Use cost/benefit analysis: Design the managerial accounting system so that benefits (from helping managers make wise decisions) outweigh the costs of the system. |
| • How do you distinguish among service, merchandising, and manufacturing companies? How do their balance sheets differ? | *Service companies:*<br>• Provide customers with intangible services<br>• Have no inventories on the balance sheet<br>*Merchandising companies:*<br>• Resell tangible products purchased ready-made from suppliers<br>• Have only one category of inventory<br>*Manufacturing companies:*<br>• Use labor, plant, and equipment to transform raw materials into new finished products<br>• Have three categories of inventory:<br>  • Materials inventory<br>  • Work in process inventory<br>  • Finished goods inventory |
| • How do you compute the cost of goods sold? | • *Service companies:* No cost of goods sold, because they do not sell tangible goods<br>• *Merchandising companies:*<br><br>Beginning *merchandise* inventory<br>+ Purchases and freight in<br>− Ending *merchandise* inventory<br>= Cost of goods sold<br><br>• *Manufacturing companies:*<br><br>Beginning *finished goods* inventory<br>+ Cost of goods manufactured<br>− Ending *finished goods* inventory<br>= Cost of goods sold |

| Decision | Guidelines |
|---|---|
| • How do you compute the cost of goods manufactured for a manufacturer? | Beginning *work in process* inventory<br>+ Current period manufacturing costs (direct materials used + direct labor + manufacturing overhead)<br>– Ending *work in process* inventory<br>= Cost of goods manufactured |
| • How do you compute the cost per unit? | Cost of goods manufactured ÷ Total units produced<br>= Unit product cost |
| • Which costs are initially treated as assets for external reporting? When are these costs expensed? | *Inventoriable product costs* are initially treated as assets (Inventory); these costs are expensed (as Cost of goods sold) when the products are sold. |
| • What costs are inventoriable under GAAP? | • *Service companies:* No inventoriable product costs<br>• *Merchandising companies:* Purchases and freight in<br>• *Manufacturing companies:* Direct materials used, direct labor, and manufacturing overhead |
| • Which costs are never inventoriable product costs? | Period costs. These are always expensed as incurred. |

# Summary Problem 16-2

## Requirements

1. For a manufacturing company, identify the following as either an inventoriable product cost or a period cost:
   a. Depreciation on plant equipment
   b. Depreciation on salespersons' automobiles
   c. Insurance on plant building
   d. Marketing manager's salary
   e. Raw materials
   f. Manufacturing overhead
   g. Electricity bill for home office
   h. Production employee wages
2. Show how to compute cost of goods manufactured. Use the following amounts: direct materials used $24,000, direct labor $9,000, manufacturing overhead $17,000, beginning work in process inventory $5,000, and ending work in process inventory $4,000.
3. Using the results from Requirement 2, calculate the per unit cost for goods manufactured assuming 1,000 units were manufactured.
4. Beginning inventory had 100 units that had a unit cost of $50 each. Ending inventory has 200 units left. Calculate COGS assuming FIFO inventory costing is used.

## Solution

### Requirement 1

Inventoriable product cost: a, c, e, f, h
Period cost: b, d, g

### Requirement 2

Cost of goods manufactured:

| | | |
|---|---:|---:|
| Beginning work in process inventory | | $ 5,000 |
|     Direct materials used | $24,000 | |
|     Direct labor | 9,000 | |
|     Manufacturing overhead | 17,000 | |
|     Total manufacturing costs incurred during the period | | 50,000 |
| Total manufacturing costs to account for | | $55,000 |
| Ending work in process inventory | | (4,000) |
| Cost of goods manufactured | | $51,000 |

### Requirement 3

| Cost of goods manufactured | ÷ | Total units produced | = | Unit product cost |
|---|---|---|---|---|
| $51,000 | ÷ | 1,000 units | = | $51 per unit |

### Requirement 4

| | |
|---|---:|
| Beginning finished goods inventory (100 @ $50 per unit) | $ 5,000 |
| Cost of goods manufactured | 51,000 |
| Cost of goods available for sale | $ 56,000 |
| Ending finished goods inventory (200 @ $51 per unit) | (10,200) |
| Cost of goods sold [(100 @ $50 per unit) + (800 @ $51 per unit)] | $ 45,800 |

# Review *Introduction to Managerial Accounting*

## ● Accounting Vocabulary

**Budget (p. 775)**
A mathematical expression of the plan that managers use to coordinate the business's activities.

**Controlling (p. 775)**
Implementing plans and evaluating the results of business operations by comparing the actual results to the budget.

**Conversion Costs (p. 784)**
Direct labor plus manufacturing overhead.

**Cost/Benefit Analysis (p. 775)**
Weighing costs against benefits to help make decisions.

**Cost Object (p. 784)**
Anything for which managers want a separate measurement of cost.

**Cost of Goods Manufactured (p. 787)**
The manufacturing or plant-related costs of the goods that finished the production process in a given period.

**Direct Cost (p. 784)**
A cost that can be traced to a cost object.

**Direct Labor (p. 784)**
The compensation of employees who physically convert materials into finished products.

**Direct Materials (p. 784)**
Materials that become a physical part of a finished product and whose costs are traceable to the finished product.

**Enterprise Resource Planning (ERP) (p. 776)**
Software systems that can integrate all of a company's worldwide functions, departments, and data into a single system.

**Factory Overhead (p. 784)**
All manufacturing costs other than direct materials and direct labor. Also called **manufacturing overhead** or **indirect manufacturing costs**.

**Finished Goods Inventory (p. 784)**
Completed goods that have not yet been sold.

**Indirect Costs (p. 784)**
Costs that cannot be traced to a cost object.

**Indirect Labor (p. 785)**
Labor costs that are necessary to make a product but whose costs either cannot conveniently be directly traced to specific finished products or whose costs are not large enough to justify tracing to the specific product.

**Indirect Manufacturing Cost (p. 784)**
All manufacturing costs other than direct materials and direct labor. Also called **factory overhead** or **manufacturing overhead**.

**Indirect Materials (p. 785)**
Materials used in making a product but whose costs either cannot conveniently be directly traced to specific finished products or whose costs are not large enough to justify tracing to the specific product.

**Inventoriable Product Costs (p. 780)**
All costs of a product that GAAP require companies to treat as an asset for external financial reporting. These costs are not expensed until the product is sold.

**Just-in-Time (JIT) (p. 777)**
A system in which a company produces just in time to satisfy needs. Suppliers deliver materials just in time to begin production and finished units are completed just in time for delivery to the customer.

**Management Accountability (p. 774)**
The manager's responsibility to manage the resources of an organization.

**Manufacturing Company (p. 783)**
A company that uses labor, equipment, supplies, and facilities to convert raw materials into new finished products.

**Manufacturing Overhead (p. 784)**
All manufacturing costs other than direct materials and direct labor. Also called **factory overhead** or **indirect manufacturing costs**.

**Materials Inventory (p. 783)**
Raw materials for use in manufacturing.

**Merchandising Company (p. 780)**
A company that resells products previously bought from suppliers.

**Period Costs (p. 779)**
Operating costs that are expensed in the period in which they are incurred.

**Planning (p. 775)**
Choosing goals and deciding how to achieve them.

**Service Companies (p. 776)**
Companies that sell intangible services rather than tangible products.

**Stakeholders (p. 774)**
Groups that have a stake in a business.

**Total Quality Management (TQM) (p. 777)**
A philosophy designed to integrate all organizational areas in order to provide customers with superior products and services, while meeting organizational goals throughout the value chain.

**Value Chain (p. 777)**
Includes all activities that add value to a company's products and services.

**Work in Process Inventory (p. 783)**
Goods that have been started into the manufacturing process but are not yet complete.

## ● Destination: Student Success

### Student Success Tips

The following are hints on some common trouble areas for students in this chapter:

● Remember the difference between service, merchandising, and manufacturing firms. Service firms sell services. Merchandisers sell products that other companies produce. Manufacturing firms take raw materials and convert them into a finished product that is sold.

### Getting Help

If there's a learning objective from the chapter you aren't confident about, try using one or more of the following resources:

● Review Exhibit 16-10, the schedule of cost of goods manufactured.

● Review the Decision Guidelines in the chapter.

● Review Summary Problem 16-1 in the chapter to reinforce your understanding of merchandising companies.

## ● Destination: Student Success (Continued)

### Student Success Tips

- Recall that cost per unit is cost of goods manufactured divided by the number of units produced.

- Remember the difference between direct costs and indirect costs. For example, direct labor includes the compensation of employees who physically worked on making the products. Indirect labor includes employees that are necessary but not directly involved in physically making the products.

- Keep in mind that manufacturers have three types of Inventory assets: Raw materials, Work in process, and Finished goods.

- Remember that the schedule of cost of goods manufactured is the tool a manufacturer uses to calculate the cost of goods it produced for a period. Since the cost of direct materials, direct labor, and manufacturing overhead vary, this schedule must be produced often so a company has the most current cost of production information. This schedule contains the company's inventoriable product costs.

- Keep in mind that manufacturers still have other operating expenses, like selling and administrative expenses, that are NOT part of the cost of making the product. These operating expenses are reported on the income statement.

### Getting Help

- Review Summary Problem 16-2 in the chapter to reinforce your understanding of manufacturing companies.

- Practice additional exercises or problems at the end of Chapter 16 that cover the specific learning objective that is challenging you.

- Watch the white board videos for Chapter 16 located at myaccountinglab.com under the Chapter Resources button.

- Go to myaccountinglab.com and select the Study Plan button. Choose Chapter 16 and work the questions covering that specific learning objective until you've mastered it.

- Work the Chapter 16 pre/post tests in myaccountinglab.com.

- Visit the learning resource center on your campus for tutoring.

## ● Quick Check

1. Which is *not* a characteristic of managerial accounting information?
   - a. Emphasizes the external financial statements
   - b. Provides detailed information about individual parts of the company
   - c. Emphasizes relevance
   - d. Focuses on the future

2. World-class businesses use which of these systems to integrate all of a company's world-wide functions, departments, and data into a single system?
   - a. Cost standards
   - b. Enterprise resource planning
   - c. Just-in-time management
   - d. Items a, b, and c are correct

3. Today's business environment is characterized by
   - a. global competition.
   - b. time-based competition.
   - c. a shift toward a service economy.
   - d. Items a, b, and c are correct

4. Which of the following accounts does a manufacturing company, but not a service company, have?
   - a. Advertising expense
   - b. Salary payable
   - c. Cost of goods sold
   - d. Retained earnings

5. In computing cost of goods sold, which of the following is the manufacturer's equivalent to the merchandiser's purchases?
   - a. Total manufacturing costs to account for
   - b. Direct materials used
   - c. Total manufacturing costs incurred during the period
   - d. Cost of goods manufactured

6. Which of the following is a direct cost of manufacturing a sportboat?

   a. Salary of engineer who rearranges plant layout

   b. Depreciation on plant and equipment

   c. Cost of boat engine

   d. Cost of customer hotline

7. Which of the following is *not* part of manufacturing overhead for producing a computer?

   a. Manufacturing plant property taxes     c. Depreciation on delivery trucks

   b. Manufacturing plant utilities           d. Insurance on plant and equipment

*Questions 8 and 9 use the data that follow. Suppose a bakery reports this information:*

| | |
|---|---:|
| Beginning materials inventory . . . . . . . | $  8,000 |
| Ending materials inventory . . . . . . . . . | 7,000 |
| Beginning work in process inventory . . . | 4,000 |
| Ending work in process inventory  . . . . | 3,000 |
| Beginning finished goods inventory  . . . | 3,000 |
| Ending finished goods inventory  . . . . . | 5,000 |
| Direct labor  . . . . . . . . . . . . . . . . . . . . | 30,000 |
| Purchases of direct materials  . . . . . . . . | 95,000 |
| Manufacturing overhead  . . . . . . . . . . . | 21,000 |

8. What is cost of direct materials used?

   a. $95,000                        c. $103,000

   b. $96,000                        d. $94,000

9. What is the cost of goods manufactured?

   a. $146,000                       c. $144,000

   b. $148,000                       d. $147,000

10. A management accountant who avoids conflicts of interest meets the ethical standard of

    a. confidentiality.               c. credibility.

    b. competence.                    d. integrity.

Answers are given after Apply Your Knowledge (p. 812).

# Assess Your Progress

## ● Short Exercises

**MyAccountingLab**    **S16-1**    ❶ **Managerial accounting vs. financial accounting [5–10 min]**
Managerial and financial accounting differ in many aspects.

**Requirement**

1. For each of the following, indicate whether the statement relates to managerial accounting (MA) or financial accounting (FA):

   ___F___ a. Helps investors make investment decisions.

   ___M___ b. Provides detailed reports on parts of the company.

   ___M___ c. Helps in planning and controlling operations.

   ___F___ d. Reports must follow generally accepted accounting principles (GAAP).

   ___F___ e. Reports audited annually by independent certified public accountants.

**S16-2**    **①** **Management accountability and the stakeholders [10 min]**
Management has the responsibility to manage the resources of an organization in a responsible manner.

## Requirement

1. For each of the following management responsibilities, indicate the primary stakeholder group to whom management is responsible. In the space provided, write the letter corresponding to the appropriate stakeholder group.

_____ e____ 1. Providing high-quality, reliable products/services for a reasonable price in a

timely manner.

_____ f____ 2. Paying taxes in a timely manner.

_____ a____ 3. Providing a safe, productive work environment.

_____ 4. Generating a profit.

_____ 5. Repaying principal plus interest in a timely manner.

a. Owners
b. Creditors
c. Suppliers
d. Employees
e. Customers
f. Government
g. Community

**S16-3**    **②** **Business trends terminology [10 min]**
Consider the terms and definitions that follow:

_____ 1. A philosophy designed to integrate all organizational areas in order to provide customers with superior products and services, while meeting organizational objectives. Requires improving quality and eliminating defects and waste.

_____ 2. Use of the Internet for such business functions as sales and customer service. Enables companies to reach thousands of customers around the world.

_____ 3. Software systems that integrate all of a company's worldwide functions, departments, and data into a single system.

_____ 4. A system in which a company produces just in time to satisfy needs. Suppliers deliver materials just in time to begin production, and finished units are completed just in time for delivery to customers.

a. ERP
b. Just-in-time (JIT)
c. E-commerce
d. Total quality management

## Requirement

1. Match the term with the correct definition.

**S16-4**    **③** **Ethical decisions [5 min]**
The Institute of Management Accountants' Statement of Ethical Professional Practice (Exhibit 16-3) requires managerial accountants to meet standards regarding the following:
- Competence
- Confidentiality
- Integrity
- Credibility

## Requirement

1. Consider the following situations. Which guidelines are violated in each situation?

a. You tell your brother that your company will report earnings significantly above financial analysts' estimates.
b. You see that others take home office supplies for personal use. As an intern, you do the same thing, assuming that this is a "perk."
c. At a conference on e-commerce, you skip the afternoon session and go sightseeing.
d. You failed to read the detailed specifications of a new general ledger package that you asked your company to purchase. After it is installed, you are surprised that it is incompatible with some of your company's older accounting software.
e. You do not provide top management with the detailed job descriptions they requested because you fear they may use this information to cut a position from your department.

**S16-5**  ④ **Calculating income and unit cost for a service organization [5–10 min]**

Duncan and Oates provides hair cutting services in the local community. In February, the business incurred the following operating costs to cut the hair of 230 clients:

| | |
|---|---:|
| Hair supplies expense............................ | $ 805 |
| Building rent expense ............................ | 1,150 |
| Utilities................................................. | 184 |
| Depreciation on equipment ................... | 46 |

Duncan and Oates earned $5,200 in revenues from haircuts for the month of February.

**Requirements**

1. What is the net operating income for the month?
2. What is the cost of one haircut?

**S16-6**  ⑤ **Computing cost of goods sold [5 min]**

The Tinted View, a retail merchandiser of auto windshields, has the following information:

| | |
|---|---:|
| Web site maintenance ....... | $ 7,100 |
| Delivery expense .......... | 900 |
| Freight in ............... | 2,900 |
| Purchases ............... | 39,000 |
| Ending inventory .......... | 4,900 |
| Revenues ............... | 57,000 |
| Marketing expenses ........ | 9,900 |
| Beginning inventory ........ | 7,900 |

**Requirement**

1. Compute The Tinted View's cost of goods sold.

**S16-7**  ⑤ **Computing cost of goods sold [5–10 min]**

Consider the following partially completed income statements:

| | Fit Apparel | Jones, Inc. |
|---|---:|---:|
| Sales ......................... $ | 101,000 | (d) |
| Cost of goods sold | | |
| Beginning inventory ............. | (a) $ | 29,000 |
| Purchases and freight in .......... | 48,000 | (e) |
| Cost of goods available for sale .... | (b) | 88,000 |
| Ending inventory .............. | 1,900 | 1,900 |
| Cost of goods sold ............. | 59,000 | (f) |
| Gross margin ................... $ | 42,000 | $ 113,000 |
| Selling and administrative expenses ... | (c) | 84,000 |
| Operating income ................ $ | 13,000 | (g) |

**Requirement**

1. Compute the missing amounts.

**S16-8**    ④ ⑤ ⑥ **Match type of company with product and period costs [5 min]**
Consider the following costs:

| Type of cost: | Type of company that reports this cost on its income statment | | |
|---|---|---|---|
| Advertising costs | Manuf | Merch | Serv |
| 1. Cost of goods manufactured | | | |
| 2. The CEO's salary | | | |
| 3. Cost of goods sold | | | |
| 4. Building rent expense | | | |
| 5. Customer service expense | | | |

## Requirement

1.  For each of the costs, indicate if the cost would be found on the income statement of a service company (Serv), a merchandising company (Merch), and/or a manufacturing company (Manuf). Some costs can be found on the income statements of more than one type of company.

**S16-9**    ⑥ **Computing direct materials used [5 min]**
You are a new accounting intern at Cookie Messages. Your boss gives you the following information:

| | |
|---|---|
| Purchases of direct materials | $ 6,400 |
| Freight in | 200 |
| Property taxes | 900 |
| Ending inventory of direct materials | 1,500 |
| Beginning inventory of direct materials | 4,000 |

## Requirement

1.  Compute direct materials used.

**S16-10**    ⑥ **Distinguishing between direct and indirect costs [5–10 min]**
Consider Granger Cards' manufacturing plant.

## Requirement

1.  Match one of the following terms with each example of a manufacturing cost given below:

    1. Direct materials
    2. Direct labor
    3. Indirect materials
    4. Indirect labor
    5. Other manufacturing overhead

    ____4____ a. Artists' wages.
    ____4____ b. Wages of warehouse workers.
    ____3____ c. Paper
    ____3____ d. Depreciation on equipment.
    ____4____ e. Manufacturing plant manager's salary.
    _____ f. Property taxes on manufacturing plant.
    _____ g. Glue for envelopes.

**S16-11**    ⑥ **Computing manufacturing overhead [5–10 min]**
Glass Doctor Company manufactures sunglasses. Suppose the company's May records include the following items:

| | | | |
|---|---|---|---|
| Glue for frames | $ 350 | Company president's salary | $ 24,500 |
| Depreciation expense on company | | Plant foreman's salary | 5,000 |
| cars used by sales force | 3,000 | Plant janitor's wages | 1,000 |
| Plant depreciation expense | 9,000 | Oil for manufacturing equipment | 200 |
| Interest expense | 1,500 | Lenses | 50,000 |

## Requirements

1.  List the items and amounts that are manufacturing overhead costs.
2.  Calculate Glass Doctor's total manufacturing overhead cost in May.

**S16-12**  ⑥ **Compute cost of goods manufactured [5 min]**

All Pro Golf Company had the following inventory data for the year ended January 31, 2012:

| | |
|---|---|
| Direct materials used . . . . . . . . | $ 12,000 |
| Manufacturing overhead . . . . . | 20,000 |
| Work in process inventory: | |
|     Beginning . . . . . . . . . . . . | 7,000 |
|     Ending . . . . . . . . . . . . . . | 5,000 |
| Direct labor . . . . . . . . . . . . . . | 11,000 |
| Finished goods inventory . . . . . | 9,000 |

## Requirement

1.  Compute All Pro's cost of goods manufactured for 2012.

**S16-13**  ⑥ **Inventoriable product costs vs. period costs [5–10 min]**

Manufacturer's costs are either inventoriable product costs or period costs.

## Requirement

1.  Classify each of a paper manufacturer's costs as either an inventoriable product cost or a period cost:

    a.  Salaries of scientists studying ways to speed forest growth.
    b.  Cost of computer software to track WIP inventory.
    c.  Cost of electricity at a paper mill.
    d.  Salaries of the company's top executives.
    e.  Cost of chemicals to treat paper.
    f.  Cost of TV ads.
    g.  Depreciation on the gypsum board plant.
    h.  Cost of lumber to be cut into boards.
    i.  Life insurance on CEO.

# ● Exercises

*MyAccountingLab*  **E16-14**  ① **Management vs. financial accounting and managers' use of information [5 min]**

The following statements consider how managers use information.

a.  Companies must follow GAAP in their ____ accounting systems.
b.  Financial accounting develops reports for external parties, such as ____ and ____.
c.  When managers compare the company's actual results to the plan, they are performing the ____ role of management.
d.  ____ are decision makers inside a company.
e.  ____ accounting provides information on a company's past performance.
f.  ____ accounting systems are not restricted by GAAP but are chosen by comparing the costs versus the benefits of the system.
g.  Choosing goals and the means to achieve them is the ____ function of management.

## Requirement

1.  Complete each blank with one of the terms listed here. You may use a term more than once, and some terms may not be used at all.

| | | | |
|---|---|---|---|
| Budget | Creditors | Managers | Planning |
| Controlling | Financial | Managerial | Shareholders |

**E16-15** **2** **Understanding today's business environment [5 min]**

The following statements relate to understanding today's business environment.

a. _____ is a management philosophy that focuses on maintaining lean inventories while producing products as needed by the customer.

b. _____ is a philosophy designed to integrate all organizational areas in order to provide customers with superior products and services, while meeting organizational objectives. It requires improving quality and eliminating defects and waste throughout the value chain.

c. _____ can integrate all of a company's worldwide functions, departments, and data into a single system.

d. Firms adopt _____ to conduct business on the Internet.

## Requirement

1. Complete the statements with one of the terms listed here. You may use a term more than once, and some terms may not be used at all.

| | |
|---|---|
| E-commerce | Just-in-time (JIT) manufacturing |
| Enterprise Resource Planning (ERP) | Total quality management (TQM) |

**E16-16** **3** **Ethical decisions [15 min]**

Sue Peters is the controller at Vroom, a car dealership. Dale Miller recently has been hired as bookkeeper. Dale wanted to attend a class on Excel spreadsheets, so Sue temporarily took over Dale's duties, including overseeing a fund for filling a car's gas tank before a test drive. Sue found a shortage in this fund and confronted Dale when he returned to work. Dale admitted that he occasionally uses this fund to pay for his own gas. Sue estimated that the amount involved is close to $450.

## Requirements

1. What should Sue Peters do?

2. Would you change your answer to the previous question if Sue Peters was the one recently hired as controller and Dale Miller was a well-liked, longtime employee who indicated that he always eventually repaid the fund?

**E16-17** **4** **Calculating income and cost per unit for a service company [5–10 min]**

Fido Grooming provides grooming services in the local community. In April, Kevin Oliver, the owner, incurred the following operating costs to groom 650 dogs:

| | |
|---|---:|
| Wages . . . . . . . . . . . . . . . . . . . | $ 3,900 |
| Grooming supplies expense . . . | 1,625 |
| Building rent expense . . . . . . . . | 1,300 |
| Utilities . . . . . . . . . . . . . . . . . . | 325 |
| Depreciation on equipment . . . | 130 |

Fido Grooming earned $16,300 in revenues from grooming for the month of April.

## Requirements

1. What is Fido's net operating income for April?

2. What is the cost to groom one dog?

**E16-18** **5** **Preparing an income statement and computing the unit cost for a merchandising company [15 min]**

Snyder Brush Company sells standard hair brushes. The following information summarizes Snyder's operating activities for 2012:

| | |
|---|---:|
| Selling and administrative expenses . . . . . . . . . . | $ 49,680 |
| Purchases . . . . . . . . . . . . . . . . . . . . . . . . . . . | 78,000 |
| Sales revenue . . . . . . . . . . . . . . . . . . . . . . . | 138,000 |
| Merchandise inventory, January 1, 2012 . . . . . . | 7,500 |
| Merchandise inventory, December 31, 2012 . . . . | 12,360 |

## Requirements

1. Prepare an income statement for 2012. Compute the ratio of operating expense to total revenue and operating income to total revenue.
2. Snyder sold 6,000 brushes in 2012. Compute the unit cost for one brush.

**E16-19**  ⑥ **Computing cost of goods manufactured [15–20 min]**
Consider the following partially completed cost of goods manufactured statements.

|  | Boswell, Inc. | Laura's Bakery | Rustic Gear |
|---|---|---|---|
| Beginning work in process inventory ........... | (a) | $ 40,500 | $ 2,200 |
| Direct materials used ..................... | $ 14,200 | $ 35,200 | (g) |
| Direct labor ........................... | 10,800 | 20,700 | 1,400 |
| Manufacturing overhead ................... | (b) | 10,500 | 300 |
| Total manufacturing costs incurred during year ... | 45,300 | (d) | (h) |
| Total manufacturing costs to account for ........ | $ 55,800 | (e) | $ 7,400 |
| Ending work in process inventory ............. | (c) | (25,900) | (2,500) |
| Cost of goods manufactured ................. | $ 51,200 | (f) | (i) |

## Requirement

1. Complete the missing amounts.

**E16-20**  ⑥ **Preparing a statement of cost of goods manufactured [15–20 min]**
Knight, Corp., a lamp manufacturer, provided the following information for the year ended December 31, 2012:

| Inventories: | Beginning | Ending |
|---|---|---|
| Materials | $ 56,000 | $ 23,000 |
| Work in process | 103,000 | 63,000 |
| Finished goods | 41,000 | 48,000 |

Other information:

| | | | |
|---|---|---|---|
| Depreciation: plant building and equipment | $ 16,000 | Repairs and maintenance–plant | $ 8,000 |
| Materials purchases | 159,000 | Indirect labor | 32,000 |
| Insurance on plant | 22,000 | Direct labor | 122,000 |
| Sales salaries expense | 46,000 | Administrative expenses | 59,000 |

## Requirements

1. Prepare a schedule of cost of goods manufactured.
2. What is the unit product cost if Knight manufactured 2,160 lamps for the year?

**E16-21**  ⑥ **Flow of costs through a manufacturer's inventory accounts [15–20 min]**
Consider the following data for a manufacturer:

| | Beginning of Year | End of Year |
|---|---|---|
| Direct materials inventory .... | $ 29,000 | $ 32,000 |
| Work in process inventory .... | 44,000 | 37,000 |
| Finished goods inventory ..... | 19,000 | 24,000 |
| Purchases of direct materials ... | | 77,000 |
| Direct labor ............... | | 87,000 |
| Manufacturing overhead ..... | | 45,000 |

## Requirement

1. Compute cost of goods manufactured and cost of goods sold.

● Problems **(Group A)**

**P16-22A** ❶ ❷ ❹ **Calculating income and unit cost for a service company [15–20 min]**   *MyAccountingLab*

The Windshield People repair chips in car windshields in the company's home county. Rocky Chip, the owner, incurred the following operating costs for the month of February 2012:

| | |
|---|---:|
| Salaries and wages . . . . . . . . . . . . . . . . . . . . . | $  9,000 |
| Windshield repair materials . . . . . . . . . . . . . . | 4,900 |
| Depreciation on truck  . . . . . . . . . . . . . . . . . . | 250 |
| Depreciation on building and equipment  . . . . | 800 |
| Supplies expense . . . . . . . . . . . . . . . . . . . . . . . | 600 |
| Gasoline and utilities  . . . . . . . . . . . . . . . . . . | 2,130 |

The Windshield People earned $26,000 in revenues for the month of February by repairing 500 windshields. All costs shown are considered to be directly related to the repair service.

**Requirements**

1. Prepare an income statement for the month of February. Compute the ratio of total operating expense to total revenue and operating income to total revenue.
2. Compute the per unit cost of repairing one windshield.
3. The manager of The Windshield People must keep unit operating cost below $50 per windshield in order to get his bonus. Did he meet the goal?
4. What kind of system could The Windshield People use to integrate all its data?

**P16-23A** ❸ **Apply ethical standards to decision making [20–25 min]**

Natalia Wallace is the new controller for Smart Software, Inc., which develops and sells education software. Shortly before the December 31 fiscal year-end, James Cauvet, the company president, asks Wallace how things look for the year-end numbers. He is not happy to learn that earnings growth may be below 13% for the first time in the company's five-year history. Cauvet explains that financial analysts have again predicted a 13% earnings growth for the company and that he does not intend to disappoint them. He suggests that Wallace talk to the assistant controller, who can explain how the previous controller dealt with such situations. The assistant controller suggests the following strategies:

a. Persuade suppliers to postpone billing $13,000 in invoices until January 1.
b. Record as sales $115,000 in certain software awaiting sale that is held in a public warehouse.
c. Delay the year-end closing a few days into January of the next year, so that some of next year's sales are included as this year's sales.
d. Reduce the estimated Bad debt expense from 5% of Sales revenue to 3%, given the company's continued strong performance.
e. Postpone routine monthly maintenance expenditures from December to January.

**Requirements**

1. Which of these suggested strategies are inconsistent with IMA standards?
2. What should Wallace do if Cauvet insists that she follow all of these suggestions?

**P16-24A** ⑤ **Preparing an income statement for a merchandising company [45–55 min]**

In 2012 Charlie Snyder opened Charlie's Pets, a small retail shop selling pet supplies. On December 31, 2012, Charlie's accounting records showed the following:

| | | |
|---|---|---|
| Inventory on December 31, 2012 | $ | 10,200 |
| Inventory on January 1, 2012 | | 15,100 |
| Sales revenue | | 57,000 |
| Utilities for shop | | 3,900 |
| Rent for shop | | 4,100 |
| Sales commissions | | 2,150 |
| Purchases of merchandise | | 27,000 |

## Requirement

1. Prepare an income statement for Charlie's Pets, a merchandiser, for the year ended December 31, 2012.

**P16-25A** ⑥ **Preparing cost of goods manufactured schedule and income statement for a manufacturing company [30–45 min]**

Charlie's Pets succeeded so well that Charlie decided to manufacture his own brand of chewing bone—Fido Treats. At the end of December 2012, his accounting records showed the following:

| Inventories: | Beginning | Ending |
|---|---|---|
| Materials | $  13,400 | $   9,500 |
| Work in process | 0 | 2,000 |
| Finished goods | 0 | 5,300 |

| Other information: | | | |
|---|---|---|---|
| Direct material purchases | $  33,000 | Utilities for plant | $   1,600 |
| Plant janitorial services | 800 | Rent of plant | 13,000 |
| Sales salaries expense | 5,000 | Customer service hotline expense | 1,400 |
| Delivery expense | 1,700 | Direct labor | 22,000 |
| Sales revenue | 109,000 | | |

## Requirements

1. Prepare a schedule of cost of goods manufactured for Fido Treats for the year ended December 31, 2012.
2. Prepare an income statement for Fido Treats for the year ended December 31, 2012.
3. How does the format of the income statement for Fido Treats differ from the income statement of a merchandiser?
4. Fido Treats manufactured 18,075 units of its product in 2012. Compute the company's unit product cost for the year.

**P16-26A** ⑥ **Preparing financial statements for a manufacturer [25–35 min]**

Certain item descriptions and amounts are missing from the monthly schedule of cost of goods manufactured and the income statement of Tioga Manufacturing Company.

| TIOGA MANUFACTURING COMPANY | | | |
|---|---|---|---|
| _____ June 30, 2012 | | | |
| Beginning _____ | | | $ 22,000 |
| Direct _____: | | | |
|   Beginning direct materials inventory | $     X | | |
|   Purchase of materials | 54,000 | | |
|   _____ | $  80,000 | | |
|   Ending direct materials inventory | (23,000) | | |
|   Direct _____ | | $     X | |
|   Direct _____ | | X | |
|   Manufacturing overhead | | 43,000 | |
| Total _____ costs _____ | | | 175,000 |
| Total _____ costs _____ | | | $     X |
| Ending _____ | | | (29,000) |
| _____ | | | $     X |

| TIOGA MANUFACTURING COMPANY | | |
|---|---|---|
| _____ June 30, 2012 | | |
| Sales revenue | | $     X |
| Cost of goods sold: | | |
|   Beginning _____ | $ 112,000 | |
|   _____ | X | |
|   Cost of goods _____ | $     X | |
|   Ending _____ | X | |
| Cost of goods sold | | 217,000 |
| Gross profit | | $ 283,000 |
| _____ expenses: | | |
|   Marketing expenses | $  94,000 | |
|   Administrative expenses | X | 159,000 |
| _____ income | | $     X |

**Requirement**

1. Fill in the missing words (___) and amounts (X).

**P16-27A** ⑥ **Flow of costs through a manufacturer's inventory accounts [20–25 min]**

Root Shoe Company makes loafers. During the most recent year, Root incurred total manufacturing costs of $26,400,000. Of this amount, $2,100,000 was direct materials used and $19,800,000 was direct labor. Beginning balances for the year were Direct materials inventory, $600,000; Work in process inventory, $800,000; and Finished goods inventory, $700,000. At the end of the year, inventory accounts showed these amounts:

| | Materials | Direct Labor | Manufacturing Overhead |
|---|---|---|---|
| Direct materials inventory | $  900,000 | $         0 | $         0 |
| Work in process inventory | 400,000 | 600,000 | 400,000 |
| Finished goods inventory | 800,000 | 150,000 | 40,000 |

### Requirements

1. Compute Root Shoe Company's cost of goods manufactured for the year.
2. Compute Root's cost of goods sold for the year.
3. Compute the cost of materials purchased during the year.

## ● Problems (Group B)

MyAccountingLab

**P16-28B** ① ② ④ **Calculating income and unit cost for a service company [15–20 min]**

Total Glass Company repairs chips in car windshields in the company's home county. Gary White, the owner, incurred the following operating costs for the month of July 2012:

| | |
|---|---|
| Salaries and wages ..................... | $  11,000 |
| Windshield repair materials .............. | 4,800 |
| Depreciation on truck .................. | 550 |
| Depreciation on building and equipment .... | 1,200 |
| Supplies expense...................... | 300 |
| Gasoline and utilities .................. | 2,620 |

Total Glass Company earned $23,000 in revenues for the month of July by repairing 200 windshields. All costs shown are considered to be directly related to the repair service.

### Requirements

1. Prepare an income statement for the month of July. Compute the ratio of total operating expense to total revenue and operating income to total revenue.
2. Compute the per unit cost of repairing one windshield.
3. The manager of Total Glass Company must keep unit operating cost below $70 per windshield in order to get his bonus. Did he meet the goal?
4. What kind of system could Total Glass Company use to integrate all its data?

**P16-29B** ③ **Apply ethical standards to decision making [20–25 min]**

Ava Borzi is the new controller for Halo Software, Inc., which develops and sells education software. Shortly before the December 31 fiscal year-end, Jeremy Busch, the company president, asks Borzi how things look for the year-end numbers. He is not happy to learn that earnings growth may be below 9% for the first time in the company's five-year history. Busch explains that financial analysts have again predicted a 9% earnings growth for the company and that he does not intend to disappoint them. He suggests that Borzi talk to the assistant controller, who can explain how the previous controller dealt with such situations. The assistant controller suggests the following strategies:

a. Persuade suppliers to postpone billing $18,000 in invoices until January 1.

b. Record as sales $120,000 in certain software awaiting sale that is held in a public warehouse.

c. Delay the year-end closing a few days into January of the next year so that some of next year's sales are included as this year's sales.

d. Reduce the estimated Bad debt expense from 3% of Sales revenue to 2%, given the company's continued strong performance.

e. Postpone routine monthly maintenance expenditures from December to January.

## Requirements

1. Which of these suggested strategies are inconsistent with IMA standards?

2. What should Borzi do if Busch insists that she follow all of these suggestions?

**P16-30B ⑤ Preparing an income statement for a merchandising company [45–55 min]**

In 2012 Craig Gonzales opened Craig's Pets, a small retail shop selling pet supplies. On December 31, 2012, Craig's accounting records showed the following:

| | |
|---|---|
| Inventory on December 31, 2012 | $ 10,100 |
| Inventory on January 1, 2012 | 15,400 |
| Sales revenue | 58,000 |
| Utilities for shop | 3,300 |
| Rent for shop | 4,500 |
| Sales commissions | 2,850 |
| Purchases of merchandise | 26,000 |

## Requirement

1. Prepare an income statement for Craig's Pets, a merchandiser, for the year ended December 31, 2012.

**P16-31B ⑥ Preparing cost of goods manufactured schedule and income statement for a manufacturing company [30–45 min]**

Craig's Pets succeeded so well that Craig decided to manufacture his own brand of chewing bone—Organic Bones. At the end of December 2012, his accounting records showed the following:

| Inventories: | Beginning | Ending |
|---|---|---|
| Materials | $ 13,200 | $ 7,000 |
| Work in process | 0 | 4,000 |
| Finished goods | 0 | 5,800 |

| Other information: | | | |
|---|---|---|---|
| Direct material purchases | $ 31,000 | Utilities for plant | $ 1,900 |
| Plant janitorial services | 200 | Rent on plant | 11,000 |
| Sales salaries expense | 5,400 | Customer service hotline expense | 1,200 |
| Delivery expense | 1,400 | Direct labor | 23,000 |
| Sales revenue | 110,000 | | |

## Requirements

1. Prepare a schedule of cost of goods manufactured for Organic Bones for the year ended December 31, 2012.

2. Prepare an income statement for Organic Bones for the year ended December 31, 2012.

3. How does the format of the income statement for Organic Bones differ from the income statement of a merchandiser?

4. Organic Bones manufactured 15,400 units of its product in 2012. Compute the company's unit product cost for the year.

**P16-32B** ⑥ **Preparing financial statements for a manufacturer [25–35 min]**

Certain item descriptions and amounts are missing from the monthly schedule of cost of goods manufactured and the income statement of Pinta Manufacturing Company.

| PINTA MANUFACTURING COMPANY | | | |
|---|---|---|---|
| _____ June 30, 2012 | | | |
| Beginning _____ | | | $ 25,000 |
| Direct _____: | | | |
|     Beginning direct materials inventory | $ X | | |
|     Purchase of materials | 57,000 | | |
|     _____ | $ 85,000 | | |
|     Ending direct materials inventory | (22,000) | | |
|   Direct _____ | | $ X | |
|   Direct _____ | | X | |
|   Manufacturing overhead | | 45,000 | |
| Total _____ costs _____ | | | 182,000 |
| Total _____ costs _____ | | | $ X |
| Ending _____ | | | (21,000) |
| _____ | | | $ X |

| PINTA MANUFACTURING COMPANY | | |
|---|---|---|
| _____ June 30, 2012 | | |
| Sales revenue | | $ X |
| Cost of goods sold: | | |
|     Beginning _____ | $ 113,000 | |
|     _____ | X | |
|     Cost of goods _____ | $ X | |
|     Ending _____ | X | |
| Cost of goods sold | | 231,000 |
| Gross profit | | $ 209,000 |
| _____ expenses: | | |
|     Marketing expenses | $ 93,000 | |
|     Administrative expenses | X | 154,000 |
| _____ income | | $ X |

**Requirement**

1. Fill in the missing words (___) and amounts (X).

**P16-33B** ⑥ **Flow of costs through a manufacturer's inventory accounts [20–25 min]**

Renka Shoe Company makes loafers. During the most recent year, Renka incurred total manufacturing costs of $22,900,000. Of this amount, $2,800,000 was direct materials used and $15,800,000 was direct labor. Beginning balances for the year were Direct materials inventory, $900,000; Work in process inventory, $1,500,000; and Finished goods inventory, $900,000. At the end of the year, inventory accounts showed these amounts:

| | Materials | Direct Labor | Manufacturing Overhead |
|---|---|---|---|
| Direct materials inventory | $ 800,000 | $ 0 | $ 0 |
| Work in process inventory | 700,000 | 500,000 | 300,000 |
| Finished goods inventory | 200,000 | 550,000 | 60,000 |

## Requirements

1. Compute Renka Shoe Company's cost of goods manufactured for the year.
2. Compute Renka's cost of goods sold for the year.
3. Compute the cost of materials purchased during the year.

# ● Continuing Exercise

**E16-34** ⑥ **Classifying costs of a manufacturer [10–15 min]**

*MyAccountingLab*

This exercise continues the Lawlor Lawn Service, Inc., situation from Exercise 15-34 of Chapter 15. Lawlor is considering manufacturing a weed eater. Lawlor expects to incur the following manufacturing costs:

Shaft and handle of weed eater.

Motor of weed eater.

Factory labor for workers assembling weed eaters.

Nylon thread used by the weed eater (not traced to the job by Lawlor).

Glue to hold housing together.

Plant janitorial wages.

Depreciation on factory equipment.

Rent on plant.

Sales commission expense.

Administrative salaries

Plant utilities.

Shipping costs to deliver finished weed eaters to customers.

## Requirement

1. Classify each cost as either direct materials, direct labor, factory overhead, or period costs.

# ● Continuing Problem

**P16-35** ⑥ **Classifying costs of a manufacturer [20–25 min]**

*MyAccountingLab*

This problem continues the Draper Consulting, Inc., situation from Problem 15-35 of Chapter 15. Draper is going to manufacture billing software. During its first month of manufacturing, Draper incurred the following manufacturing costs:

| Inventories: | Beginning | | Ending |
|---|---|---|---|
| Materials | $ 10,800 | | $ 10,300 |
| Work in process | 0 | | 21,000 |
| Finished goods | 0 | | 31,500 |

| Other information: | | | |
|---|---|---|---|
| Direct material purchases | $ 19,000 | Utilities for plant | $ 10,000 |
| Plant janitorial services | 700 | Rent of plant | 13,000 |
| Sales salaries expense | 5,000 | Customer service hotline expense | 18,000 |
| Delivery expense | 1,700 | Direct labor | 190,000 |
| Sales revenue | 750,000 | | |

## Requirement

1. Prepare a schedule of cost of goods manufactured for Draper for the month ended January 31, 2014.

# Apply Your Knowledge

## ● Decision Cases

**Decision Case 16-1** PowerSwitch, Inc., designs and manufactures switches used in telecommunications. Serious flooding throughout North Carolina affected PowerSwitch's facilities. Inventory was completely ruined, and the company's computer system, including all accounting records, was destroyed.

Before the disaster recovery specialists clean the buildings, Stephen Plum, the company controller, is anxious to salvage whatever records he can to support an insurance claim for the destroyed inventory. He is standing in what is left of the accounting department with Paul Lopez, the cost accountant.

"I didn't know mud could smell so bad," Paul says. "What should I be looking for?"

"Don't worry about beginning inventory numbers," responds Stephen, "we'll get them from last year's annual report. We need first-quarter cost data."

"I was working on the first-quarter results just before the storm hit," Paul says. "Look, my report's still in my desk drawer. All I can make out is that for the first quarter, material purchases were $476,000 and direct labor, manufacturing overhead, and total manufacturing costs to account for were $505,000; $245,000; and $1,425,000; respectively. Wait! Cost of goods available for sale was $1,340,000."

"Great," says Stephen. "I remember that sales for the period were approximately $1,700,000. Given our gross profit of 30%, that's all you should need."

Paul is not sure about that, but decides to see what he can do with this information. The beginning inventory numbers are

- Direct materials, $113,000
- Work in process, $229,000
- Finished goods, $154,000

He remembers a schedule he learned in college that may help him get started.

### Requirements
1. Exhibit 16-11 resembles the schedule Paul has in mind. Use it to determine the ending inventories of direct materials, work in process, and finished goods.
2. Itemize a list of the book value of inventory lost.

**Decision Case 16-2** The IMA's Statement of Ethical Professional Practice can be applied to more than just managerial accounting. They are also relevant to college students.

### Requirement
1. Explain at least one situation that shows how each IMA standard in Exhibit 16-3 is relevant to your experiences as a student. For example, the ethical standard of competence would suggest not cutting classes!

## ● Ethical Issue 16-1

Becky Knauer recently resigned from her position as controller for Shamalay Automotive, a small, struggling foreign car dealer in Upper Saddle River, New Jersey. Becky has just started a new job as controller for Mueller Imports, a much larger dealer for the same car manufacturer. Demand for this particular make of car is exploding, and the manufacturer cannot produce enough to satisfy demand. The manufacturer's regional sales managers are each given a certain number of cars. Each sales manager then decides how to divide the cars among the independently owned dealerships in the region. Because of high demand for these cars, dealerships all want to receive as many cars as they can from the regional sales manager.

Becky's former employer, Shamalay Automotive, receives only about 25 cars a month. Consequently, Shamalay was not very profitable.

Becky is surprised to learn that her new employer, Mueller Imports, receives over 200 cars a month. Becky soon gets another surprise. Every couple of months, a local jeweler bills the dealer $5,000 for "miscellaneous services." Franz Mueller, the owner of the dealership, personally approves payment of these invoices, noting that each invoice is a "selling expense." From casual conversations with a salesperson, Becky learns that Mueller frequently gives Rolex watches to the manufacturer's regional sales manager and other sales executives. Before talking to anyone about this, Becky decides to work through her ethical dilemma.

### Requirement

1.  Put yourself in Becky's place.
    a.  What is the ethical issue?
    b.  What are your options?
    c.  What are the possible consequences?
    d.  What should you do?

## ● Fraud Case 16-1

Juan Gomez was the fastest rising star of a small CPA firm in West Palm Beach. Most of his clients traveled in stratospheric circles of wealth, and Juan knew that fitting in with this crowd was essential to his career. Although he made good money, it wasn't enough to live that kind of lifestyle. Meanwhile, Juan had become friends with one of his clients, Tony Russo. Knowing Russo's books inside and out, and being on close terms with him, Juan asked Tony for a personal loan. Juan was sure he'd be able to pay it back when he got his next bonus, but things stretched out, and additional loans were made. Two years later, Tony's company hit some losses, and the numbers were looking grim. Tony reminded Juan that it would not look good for his career if his CPA firm knew Juan had borrowed from a client, and so Juan changed a few numbers and signed off on clean financials for Tony's firm. This went on for three years, until one morning when Juan got a call. Russo had died; his sons had gone through the books, and the whole scheme came out. Juan did some prison time and lost his license, but he was repentant, and made an instructional video for accounting students to warn them of the temptations they may encounter in the real world of business.

### Requirements

1.  Although the protagonist of this story worked in public accounting, please refer to the Statement of Ethical Professional Practice in Exhibit 16-3 and discuss which of those issues are reflected in this case.
2.  Could Juan have extricated himself from his situation? How?

## ● Team Project 16-1

Search the Internet for a nearby company that also has a Web page. Arrange an interview for your team with a managerial accountant, a controller, or other accounting/finance officer of the company.

### Requirements

Before your team conducts the interview, answer the following questions:

1.  Is this a service, merchandising, or manufacturing company? What is its primary product or service?
2.  Is the primary purpose of the company's Web site to provide information about the company and its products, to sell online, or to provide financial information for investors?
3.  Are parts of the company's Web site restricted so that you need password authorization to enter? What appears to be the purpose of limiting access?
4.  Does the Web site provide an e-mail link for contacting the company?

At the interview, begin by clarifying your team's answers to questions 1 through 4, and ask the following additional questions:

5.  If the company sells over the Web, what benefits has the company derived? Did the company perform a cost-benefit analysis before deciding to begin Web sales?

    Or

    If the company does not sell over the Web, why not? Has the company performed a cost-benefit analysis and decided not to sell over the Web?

6.  What is the biggest cost of operating the Web site?

7.  Does the company make any purchases over the Internet? What percentage?

8.  How has e-commerce affected the company's managerial accounting system? Have the managerial accountant's responsibilities become more or less complex? More or less interesting?

9.  Does the company use Web-based accounting applications, such as accounts receivable or accounts payable?

10. Does the company use an ERP system? If so, do managers view the system as a success? What have been the benefits? The costs?

Your team should summarize your findings in a short paper. Provide any exhibits that enhance your explanation of key items. Provide proper references and a works cited page.

## • Communication Activity 16-1

In 100 words or fewer, explain the difference between inventoriable product costs and period costs. In your explanation, explain the inventory accounts of a manufacturer.

---

### Quick Check Answers

1. *a* 2. *b* 3. *d* 4. *c* 5. *d* 6. *c* 7. *c* 8. *b* 9. *b* 10. *d*

**For online homework, exercises, and problems that provide you immediate feedback, please visit myaccountinglab.com.**

# 17 Job Order and Process Costing

## Learning Objectives

1. Distinguish between job order costing and process costing

2. Record materials and labor in a job order costing system

3. Record overhead in a job order costing system

4. Record completion and sales of finished goods and the adjustment for under- or overallocated overhead

5. Calculate unit costs for a service company

6. Allocate costs using a process costing system—weighted-average method (see Appendix 17A)

You're a music major completing some coursework by working at a local elementary school. You enjoy being with the children, but some of the school's musical equipment desperately needs to be replaced. However, due to budget constraints, there are no immediate plans to replace the equipment. You therefore decide to work with your college service organization to raise funds for the school's music program. You suggest a spaghetti dinner for the fund raiser, but you're concerned the members of your service organization will invest a lot of time and money into a project that will not be profitable. You need to determine how much it will cost the group to prepare each dinner and the price to charge for each spaghetti plate. The price needs to be low enough to draw a crowd but high enough to cover the cost and provide a profit. How do you do it?

●    ●    ●

This chapter shows how to measure cost in situations similar to the spaghetti dinner. This type of cost accounting system is called *job order costing* because production is arranged by the job. The appendix to this chapter then covers the other main type of costing system—called *process costing*.

Businesses face the same situation. They must draw a crowd and sell enough goods and services to earn a profit. So, regardless of the type of business you own or manage, you need to know how much it costs to produce your product or service.

For example, marketing managers must consider their unit product cost in order to set the selling price high enough to cover costs. Engineers study the materials, labor, and overhead that go into a product to pinpoint ways to cut costs. Production managers then decide whether it is more profitable to make the product or to *outsource* it (buy from an outside supplier). The Finance Department arranges financing for the venture. The Accounting Department collects all the cost data from the purchasing, design, and production departments for making these decisions.

You can see that it is important for managers in all areas to know how much it costs to make a product. This chapter shows you how to figure these costs for Smart Touch Learning.

# How Much Does It Cost to Make a Product? Two Approaches

 Distinguish between job order costing and process costing

Cost accounting systems accumulate cost information so that managers can measure how much it costs to produce each unit of merchandise. For example, **Intel** must know how much each processor costs to produce. **FedEx** knows its cost of flying each pound of freight one mile. These unit costs help managers

- set selling prices that will lead to profits.
- compute cost of goods sold for the income statement.
- compute the cost of inventory for the balance sheet.

If a manager knows the cost to produce each product, then the manager can plan and control the cost of resources needed to create the product and deliver it to the customer. A cost accounting system assigns these costs to the company's product or service.

## Job Order Costing

Some companies manufacture batches of unique products or provide specialized services. A **job order costing** system accumulates costs for each batch, or job. Accounting firms, music studios, health-care providers, building contractors, and furniture manufacturers are examples of companies that use job order costing systems. For example, **Dell** makes personal computers based on customer orders (see the "Customize" button on **Dell's** Web site). As we move to a more service-based economy and with the advent of ERP systems, job order costing has become more prevalent.

## Process Costing

Other companies, such as **Procter & Gamble** and **Coca-Cola** produce identical units through a series of production steps or processes. A **process costing** system accumulates the costs of each *process* needed to complete the product. So, for example, **Coca-Cola's** process steps may include mixing, bottling, and packaging. A surfboard manufacturing company's process steps may include sanding, painting, waxing, and packaging. A medical equipment manufacturer of a blood glucose meter's process steps may include soldering, assembly, and testing. Process costing is used primarily by large producers of similar goods.

Both job order and process costing systems

- accumulate the costs incurred to make the product.
- assign costs to the products.

Accountants use **cost tracing** to assign directly traceable costs, such as direct materials and direct labor, to the product. They use a less precise technique—**cost allocation**—to assign manufacturing overhead and other indirect costs to the product. Let's see how a job order costing system works for a manufacturing company.

# How Job Costs Flow Through the Accounts: An Overview

A job order costing system tracks costs as raw materials move from the storeroom, to the production floor, to finished products. Exhibit 17-1 diagrams the flow of costs through the accounts in a job order costing system. Let's consider how a manufacturer, Smart Touch, uses job order costing. For Smart Touch, each customer order is a separate job. Smart Touch uses a job cost record to accumulate the following costs for each job:

 Record materials and labor in a job order costing system

- direct materials.
- direct labor.
- manufacturing overhead.

The company starts the job cost record when work begins on the job. As Smart Touch incurs costs, the company adds costs to the job cost record. For jobs started but not yet finished, the job cost records show costs that accumulate as costs are added to the Work in process (WIP) inventory. When Smart Touch finishes a job, the company totals the costs and transfers costs from Work in process inventory to Finished goods inventory.

When the job's units are sold, the costing system moves the costs from Finished goods inventory, an asset, to Cost of goods sold (COGS), an expense. Exhibit 17-1 summarizes this sequence.

**EXHIBIT 17-1** | **Flow of Costs Through the Accounts in a Job Order Costing System**

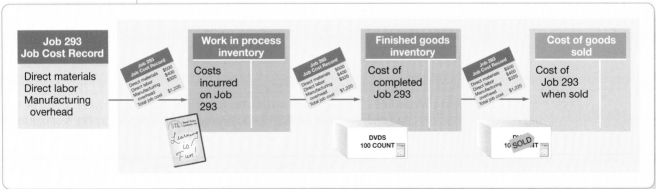

**Purchasing Materials**  On December 31, 2013, Smart Touch had the following inventory balances:

| Materials inventory | Work in process inventory | Finished goods inventory |
|---|---|---|
| Bal 12/31/13   70,000 | Bal 12/31/13   80,000 | Bal 12/31/13   0 |

During 2014, Smart Touch purchased direct materials of $350,000 and indirect materials of $17,000 on account. We record the purchase of materials as follows:

| (1) | Materials inventory (direct) (A+) | 350,000 | |
|---|---|---|---|
| | Materials inventory (indirect) (A+) | 17,000 | |
| | Accounts payable (L+) | | 367,000 |

**Materials inventory**

| | | |
|---|---|---|
| Bal 12/31/13 | 70,000 | |
| (1) Purchased | 350,000 | |
| (1) Purchased | 17,000 | |

Note that journal entry (1) shows two separate debits to Materials inventory to illustrate the source (direct and indirect materials) and to account for the materials subsidiary ledgers; however, one debit to Materials inventory for $367,000 would also be correct for the general ledger.

Materials inventory is a general ledger account. Smart Touch also uses a subsidiary ledger for materials. The subsidiary materials ledger includes a separate record for each type of material, so there is a subsidiary ledger for the blank DVDs, the paper inserts, and the casings. Exhibit 17-2 shows the subsidiary ledger of one type of casing that Smart Touch uses. The balance of the Materials inventory account in the general ledger should always equal the sum of the balances in the subsidiary materials ledger.

**EXHIBIT 17-2** | **Example Subsidiary Materials Ledger Record**

**SUBSIDIARY MATERIALS LEDGER RECORD**

STL — SMART TOUCH LEARNING, INC.

Item No. C–101            Description     5 × 6 Casings

| | Received | | | Issued | | | | Balance | | |
|---|---|---|---|---|---|---|---|---|---|---|
| Date | Units | Cost | Total Cost | Mat. Req. No. | Units | Cost | Total Cost | Units | Cost | Total Cost |
| 2014 | | | | | | | | | | |
| 1–20 | | | | | | | | 20 | $14 | $280 |
| 1–23 | 20 | $14 | $280 | | | | | 40 | 14 | 560 |
| 7–24 | | | | 334 | 10 | $14 | $140 | 30 | 14 | 420 |

**Using Materials** Smart Touch works on many jobs during the year. In 2014 the company used materials costing $355,000, including $80,000 of DVDs, $200,000 of software, and $75,000 of casings. The DVDs, software, and casings can be traced to a specific job(s), so these are all *direct materials*. Direct material costs go from the Materials inventory account directly into the Work in process inventory account.

By contrast, the $17,000 cost of printer cartridges to print the labels on the paper inserts is difficult to trace to a specific job, so the printer cartridges are *indirect materials*. The cost of indirect materials goes from the Materials inventory account into the Manufacturing overhead account. The following journal entry then records the issuance of materials into production:

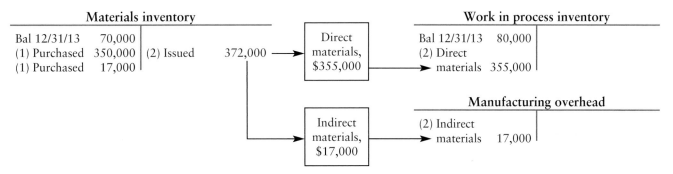

| | | | | |
|---|---|---|---|---|
| (2) | Work in process inventory (for direct materials) | (A+) | 355,000 | |
| | Manufacturing overhead (for indirect materials) | (E+) | 17,000 | |
| | Materials inventory (A–) | | | 372,000 |

We can summarize the flow of materials costs through the T-accounts as follows:

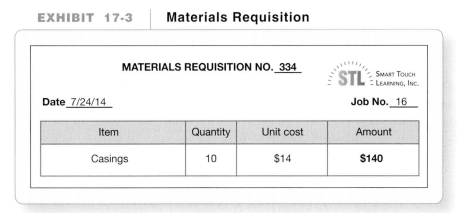

For both direct materials and indirect materials, the production team completes a document called a **materials requisition** to request the transfer of materials to the production floor. **A materials requisition sends the signal to the warehouse to bring materials into production.** These requisitions are often in electronic form rather than paper. For Job 16, Exhibit 17-3 shows Smart Touch's materials requisition for the 10 casings needed to make 10 Excel DVDs.

**EXHIBIT 17-3  |  Materials Requisition**

**MATERIALS REQUISITION NO. 334**

**STL** SMART TOUCH LEARNING, INC.

Date _7/24/14_     Job No. _16_

| Item | Quantity | Unit cost | Amount |
|---|---|---|---|
| Casings | 10 | $14 | **$140** |

Exhibit 17-4 is a **job cost record**. It assigns the cost of the direct material (casings) to Job 16. Follow the $140 cost of the casings from the materials inventory subsidiary ledger record (Exhibit 17-2), through the electronic materials requisition (Exhibit 17-3), and to the job cost record in Exhibit 17-4. Notice that all the dollar amounts in these exhibits show Smart Touch's *costs*—not the prices at which Smart Touch sells its products.

**EXHIBIT 17-4** | **Direct Materials on Job Cost Record**

**JOB COST RECORD**

STL SMART TOUCH LEARNING, INC.

Job No. _16_
Customer Name and Address _Macy's New York City_
Job Description _10 Excel DVDs_

| Date Promised | | 7–31 | Date Started | 7–24 | Date Completed | | |
|---|---|---|---|---|---|---|---|
| Date | Direct Materials | | Direct Labor | | Manufacturing Overhead Allocated | | |
| | Requisition Numbers | Amount | Labor Time Record Numbers | Amount | Date | Rate | Amount |
| 7–24 | 334 | $140 | | | | | |
| | | | | | Overall Cost Summary | | |
| | | | | | Direct Materials.......$ | | |
| | | | | | Direct Labor............. | | |
| | | | | | Manufacturing Overhead Allocated ........ | | |
| Totals | | | | | Total Job Cost.......$ | | |

Now we'll demonstrate how to account for labor costs.

## Accounting for Labor

Most companies use electronic labor/time records to streamline the labor tracking costs. Each employee completes an entry, called a labor time record, for each job he or she works on. The **labor time record** shows the employee (Ryan Oliver), the amount of time he spent on Job 16 (5 hours), and the labor cost charged to the job ($60 = 5 hours $\times$ $12 per hour).

Smart Touch totals the labor time records for each job. Exhibit 17-5 shows how Smart Touch adds the direct labor cost to the job cost record. The "Labor Time Record Numbers" show that on July 24, three employees worked on Job 16. Labor time record 251 is Ryan Oliver's ($60). Labor time records 236 and 258 indicate that two other employees also worked on Job 16. The job cost record shows that Smart Touch assigned Job 16 a total of $200 of direct labor costs for the three employees' work.

During 2014, Smart Touch incurred total labor costs of $197,000, of which $169,000 was direct labor and $28,000 was indirect labor (overhead). These amounts include the labor costs for Job 16 that we have been working with plus all the company's other jobs worked on during the year.

Smart Touch's accounting for labor cost requires the company to

- assign labor cost to individual jobs, as we saw for Ryan Oliver's work on Job 16.
- transfer labor cost incurred (Wages payable) into Work in process inventory (for direct labor) and into Manufacturing overhead (for indirect labor).

**EXHIBIT 17-5** | **Direct Labor on Job Cost Record**

### JOB COST RECORD

STL SMART TOUCH LEARNING, INC.

**Job No.** 16
**Customer Name and Address** Macy's New York City
**Job Description** 10 Excel DVDs

| Date Promised | | 7–31 | Date Started | | 7–24 | Date Completed | | |
|---|---|---|---|---|---|---|---|---|
| Date | Direct Materials | | Direct Labor | | | Manufacturing Overhead Allocated | | |
| | Requisition Numbers | Amount | Labor Time Record Numbers | Amount | | Date | Rate | Amount |
| 7–24 | 334 | $140 | 236, 251, 258 | $200 | | | | |
| | | | | | | Overall Cost Summary | | |
| | | | | | | Direct Materials..........$ | | |
| | | | | | | Direct Labor................. | | |
| | | | | | | Manufacturing Overhead Allocated............ | | |
| Totals | | | | | | Total Job Cost..........$ | | |

The following journal entry records the incurrence of manufacturing wages and the amount of labor cost applied to Work in process inventory and to the Manufacturing overhead accounts.

| (3) | Work in process inventory (for direct labor) | (A+) | 169,000 | |
|---|---|---|---|---|
| | Manufacturing overhead (for indirect labor) | (E+) | 28,000 | |
| | Wages payable    (L+) | | | 197,000 |

This entry divides total manufacturing wages between Work in process inventory ($169,000 of direct labor) and Manufacturing overhead ($28,000 of indirect labor), as shown in the following T-accounts:

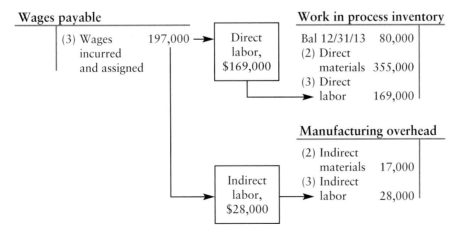

**Key Takeaway**

Direct materials and direct labor associated with a specific job are tracked to a job costing record based on a job number. When direct materials costs are incurred for a job, Work in process inventory is debited and Materials inventory is credited. When direct labor costs are incurred on a job, Work in process inventory is debited and Wages payable is credited. Indirect materials and indirect labor utilized are debited to the Manufacturing overhead account to be allocated to jobs later.

Many companies have automated these accounting procedures. The addition of labor and manufacturing overhead to materials is called **conversion costs** because the labor and overhead costs *convert* materials into a finished product.

Study the Decision Guidelines on the following page, which summarize the first half of the chapter. Then work Summary Problem 17-1 that follows.

# Decision Guidelines 17-1

## JOB ORDER COSTING: TRACING DIRECT MATERIALS AND DIRECT LABOR

Smart Touch uses a job order costing system that assigns manufacturing costs to each individual job for DVDs. These guidelines explain some of the decisions Smart Touch made in designing its system.

| Decision | Guidelines |
|---|---|
| • Should we use job costing or process costing? | Use *job order costing* when the company produces unique products (DVDs) in small batches (usually a "batch" contains a specific learning program).<br>Use *process costing* when the company produces identical products in large batches, often in a continuous flow. |

• How to record:
  • Purchase and issuance (use) of materials?

*Purchase of materials:*

| | | |
|---|---|---|
| Materials inventory | XX | |
| Accounts payable (or Cash) | | XX |

*Issuance of materials:*

| | | |
|---|---|---|
| Work in process inventory (direct materials) | XX | |
| Manufacturing overhead (indirect materials) | XX | |
| Materials inventory | | XX |

  • Incurrence and assignment of labor to jobs?

*Incurrence and assignment of labor cost to jobs:*

| | | |
|---|---|---|
| Work in process inventory (direct labor) | XX | |
| Manufacturing overhead (indirect labor) | XX | |
| Wages payable | | XX |

# Summary Problem 17-1

Tom Baker manufactures custom teakwood patio furniture. Suppose Baker has the following transactions:

a. Purchased raw materials on account, $135,000.
b. Materials costing $130,000 were requisitioned (issued) for use in production. Of this total, $30,000 were indirect materials.
c. Labor time records show that direct labor of $22,000 and indirect labor of $5,000 were incurred (but not yet paid) and assigned.

## Requirement

1. Prepare journal entries for each transaction. Then explain each journal entry in terms of what got increased and what got decreased.

## Solution

| a. | | | | |
|---|---|---|---|---|
| | Materials inventory | (A+) | 135,000 | |
| | Accounts payable | (L+) | | 135,000 |

When materials are purchased on account,

- debit (increase) Materials inventory for the *cost* of the materials purchased.
- credit (increase) Accounts payable to record the liability for the materials.

| b. | | | | |
|---|---|---|---|---|
| | Work in process inventory | (A+) | 100,000 | |
| | Manufacturing overhead | (E+) | 30,000 | |
| | Materials inventory | (A−) | | 130,000 |

When materials are requisitioned (issued) for use in production, we record the movement of materials out of materials inventory and into production, as follows:

- Debit (increase) Work in process inventory for the cost of the *direct* materials (in this case, $100,000—the $130,000 total materials requisitioned minus the $30,000 indirect materials).
- Debit (increase) Manufacturing overhead for the *indirect* materials cost.
- Credit (decrease) Materials inventory for the cost of both direct and indirect materials moved into production from the materials storage area.

| c. | | | | |
|---|---|---|---|---|
| | Work in process inventory | (A+) | 22,000 | |
| | Manufacturing overhead | (E+) | 5,000 | |
| | Wages payable | (L+) | | 27,000 |

To record the incurrence and assignment of labor costs,

- debit (increase) Work in process inventory for the cost of the *direct* labor.
- debit (increase) Manufacturing overhead for the cost of the *indirect* labor.
- credit (increase) Wages payable to record the liability for wages not paid.

# Job Order Costing: Allocating Manufacturing Overhead

**3** Record overhead in a job order costing system

All manufacturing overhead costs are *accumulated* as debits to a single general ledger account—Manufacturing overhead. We have already assigned the costs of indirect materials (entry 2, $17,000) and indirect labor (entry 3, $28,000) to Manufacturing overhead. In addition to indirect materials and indirect labor, Smart Touch incurred the following overhead costs:

- Depreciation on manufacturing plant and manufacturing equipment, $10,000
- Plant utilities, $7,000
- Plant insurance, $6,000 (previously paid)
- Property taxes incurred, but not yet paid, on the plant, $5,000

Entries 4 through 7 record these manufacturing overhead costs. The account titles in parentheses indicate the specific records that were debited in the overhead subsidiary ledger.

| | | | |
|---|---|---|---|
| (4) | Manufacturing overhead (Depreciation—plant and equipment)    (E+) | 10,000 | |
| | Accumulated depreciation—plant and equipment    (CA+) | | 10,000 |
| (5) | Manufacturing overhead (Plant utilities)    (E+) | 7,000 | |
| | Cash    (A–) | | 7,000 |
| (6) | Manufacturing overhead (Plant insurance)    (E+) | 6,000 | |
| | Prepaid insurance—plant    (A–) | | 6,000 |
| (7) | Manufacturing overhead (Property taxes—plant)    (E+) | 5,000 | |
| | Property taxes payable    (L+) | | 5,000 |

The actual manufacturing overhead costs (such as indirect materials and indirect labor, plus depreciation, utilities, insurance, and property taxes on the plant) are debited to Manufacturing overhead as they occur throughout the year. By the end of the year, the Manufacturing overhead account has accumulated all the actual overhead costs as debits:

**Manufacturing overhead**

| | |
|---|---|
| (2) Indirect materials | 17,000 |
| (3) Indirect labor | 28,000 |
| (4) Depreciation—plant and equipment | 10,000 |
| (5) Plant utilities | 7,000 |
| (6) Plant insurance | 6,000 |
| (7) Property taxes—plant | 5,000 |
| Total overhead cost | 73,000 |

Now you have seen how Smart Touch *accumulates* (debits) actual overhead costs in the accounting records. But how does Smart Touch allocate (assign) overhead costs to individual jobs? As you can see, overhead includes a variety of costs that the company cannot trace to individual jobs. For example, it is impossible to say how much of the cost of plant utilities is related to Job 16. Yet manufacturing overhead costs are as essential as direct materials and direct labor, so Smart Touch must find some way to allocate (assign) overhead costs to specific jobs. Otherwise, each job would not bear its fair share of the total cost. Smart Touch may then set unrealistic prices for some of its DVDs and wind up losing money on some of its hard-earned sales.

1. **Compute the predetermined manufacturing overhead rate.** The predetermined manufacturing overhead rate is computed as follows:

$$\text{Predetermined manufacturing overhead rate} = \frac{\text{Total estimated manufacturing overhead costs}}{\text{Total estimated quantity of the manufacturing overhead allocation base}}$$

The most accurate allocation can be made only when total overhead cost is known—and that is not until the end of the period. But managers cannot wait that long for product cost information. So the predetermined manufacturing overhead rate is calculated before the period begins. Companies use this predetermined rate to allocate estimated overhead cost to individual jobs. The predetermined manufacturing overhead rate is based on two factors:

- Total *estimated* manufacturing overhead costs for the period (in Smart Touch's case, one year)
- Total *estimated* quantity of the manufacturing overhead allocation base

The key to allocating (assigning) indirect manufacturing costs to jobs is to identify a workable manufacturing overhead allocation base. The **allocation base** is a common denominator that links overhead costs to the products. Ideally, the allocation base is the primary cost driver of manufacturing overhead—that is, the more "allocation base," the more overhead costs and vice-versa. As the phrase implies, a **cost driver** is the primary factor that causes (drives) a cost. Traditionally, manufacturing companies have used the following as cost drivers (allocation bases):

- Direct labor hours (for labor-intensive production environments)
- Direct labor cost (for labor-intensive production environments)
- Machine hours (for machine-intensive production environments)

Smart Touch uses only one allocation base, direct labor cost, to assign manufacturing overhead to jobs. Later in the textbook, we will look at other ways to assign overhead to jobs.

2. **Allocate manufacturing overhead costs to jobs as the company makes its products.** Allocate manufacturing overhead cost to jobs as follows:

$$\text{Allocated manufacturing overhead cost} = \text{Predetermined manufacturing overhead rate (from Step 1)} \times \text{Actual quantity of the allocation base used by each job}$$

As we have seen, Smart Touch traces direct costs directly to each job. But how does Smart Touch allocate overhead cost to jobs? Recall that indirect manufacturing costs include plant depreciation, utilities, insurance, and property taxes, plus indirect materials and indirect labor.

1. Smart Touch uses direct labor cost as the allocation base. In 2013, Smart Touch estimated that total overhead costs for 2014 would be $68,000 and direct labor cost would total $170,000. Using this information, we can compute the predetermined manufacturing overhead rate as follows:

$$\text{Predetermined manufacturing overhead rate} = \frac{\text{Total estimated manufacturing overhead costs}}{\text{Total estimated quantity of the manufacturing overhead allocation base}}$$

$$= \frac{\text{Total estimated manufacturing overhead costs}}{\text{Total estimated direct labor cost}}$$

$$= \frac{\$68,000}{\$170,000} = 0.40 \text{ or } 40\%$$

As jobs are completed in 2014, Smart Touch will allocate overhead costs by assigning 40% of each direct labor dollar incurred for the job as manufacturing overhead cost. Smart Touch uses the same predetermined overhead rate (40% of direct labor cost) to allocate manufacturing overhead to all jobs worked on throughout the year. Now back to Job 16.

2. The total direct labor cost for Job 16 is $200 and the predetermined manufacturing overhead rate is 40% of direct labor cost. Therefore, Smart Touch allocates $80 ($200 × 0.40) of manufacturing overhead to Job 16 (the journal entry would debit Work in progress inventory $200 and credit Manufacturing overhead $200).

The completed job cost record for the Macy's order (Exhibit 17-6) shows that Job 16 cost Smart Touch a total of $420, comprised of $140 for direct materials, $200 for direct labor, and $80 of allocated manufacturing overhead. Job 16 produced 10 DVDs, so Smart Touch's cost per DVD is $42 ($420 ÷ 10).

**EXHIBIT 17-6 | Manufacturing Overhead on Job Cost Record**

**JOB COST RECORD**

STL SMART TOUCH LEARNING, INC.

Job No.  16
Customer Name and Address  Macy's New York City
Job Description  10 Excel DVDs

| Date Promised | 7-31 | Date Started | 7-24 | Date Completed | 7-29 |
|---|---|---|---|---|---|

| Date | Direct Materials | | Direct Labor | | Manufacturing Overhead Allocated | | |
|---|---|---|---|---|---|---|---|
| | Requisition Numbers | Amount | Labor Time Record Numbers | Amount | Date | Rate | Amount |
| 7-24 | 334 | $140 | 236, 251, 258 | $200 | 7-29 | 40% of Direct Labor Cost | $80 |
| | | | | | Overall Cost Summary | | |
| | | | | | Direct Materials ............$140 | | |
| | | | | | Direct Labor....................200 | | |
| | | | | | Manufacturing Overhead Allocated .................80 | | |
| Totals | | $140 | | $200 | Total Job Cost.............$420 | | |
| | | | | | Cost per DVD..............$ 42 | | |

Smart Touch worked on many jobs, including Job 16, during 2014. The company allocated manufacturing overhead to each of these jobs. Smart Touch's direct labor cost for 2014 was $169,000, so total overhead allocated to all jobs is 40% of the $169,000 direct labor cost, or $67,600. The journal entry to allocate manufacturing overhead cost to Work in process inventory is as follows:

| (8) | Work in process inventory     (A+) | 67,600 | |
| | Manufacturing overhead     (E–) | | 67,600 |

After allocating manufacturing overhead to jobs for 2014, a $5,400 debit balance remains in the Manufacturing overhead account. This means that Smart Touch's actual overhead costs of $73,000 were greater than the overhead allocated to jobs in Work in process inventory of $67,600. We say that Smart Touch's Manufacturing overhead is *underallocated* because the company allocated only $67,600 to jobs but actually incurred $73,000 of manufacturing overhead. We will show how to correct this problem later in the chapter.

The flow of manufacturing overhead through the T-accounts follows:

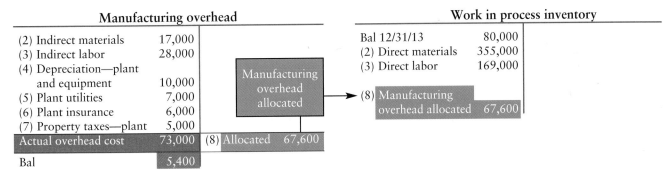

# Accounting for Completion and Sale of Finished Goods and Adjusting Manufacturing Overhead

Now you know how to accumulate and assign the cost of direct materials, direct labor, and overhead to jobs. To complete the process, we must do the following:

- Account for the completion and sale of finished goods
- Adjust manufacturing overhead at the end of the period

**4** Record completion and sales of finished goods and the adjustment for under- or overallocated overhead

## Accounting for the Completion and Sale of Finished Goods

Study Exhibit 17-1 to review the flow of costs as a job goes from work in process to finished goods to cost of goods sold. Smart Touch reported the following inventory balances one year ago, back on December 31, 2013:

| | |
|---|---|
| Materials inventory | $70,000 |
| Work in process inventory | 80,000 |
| Finished goods inventory | 0 |

The following transactions occurred in 2014:

| | |
|---|---|
| Cost of goods manufactured ......... | $ 644,600 |
| Sales on account............................ | 1,200,000 |
| Cost of goods sold......................... | 594,600 |

The $644,600 cost of goods manufactured is the cost of all jobs Smart Touch completed during 2014. (Normally, this entry would be made as each individual job is completed.) The cost of goods manufactured goes from Work in process inventory to Finished goods inventory as jobs are completed and moved into the finished goods storage area. Smart Touch records goods completed in 2014 as follows:

| (9) | Finished goods inventory (A+) | 644,600 | |
|---|---|---|---|
| | Work in process inventory (A–) | | 644,600 |

As the DVDs are sold on account, Smart Touch records sales revenue and accounts receivable, as follows:

| (10) | Accounts receivable (A+) | 1,200,000 | |
|---|---|---|---|
| | Sales revenue (R+) | | 1,200,000 |

The goods have been shipped to customers, so Smart Touch must also decrease the Finished goods inventory account and increase Cost of goods sold (perpetual inventory) with the following journal entry:

| (10b) | Cost of goods sold (E+) | 594,600 | |
|---|---|---|---|
| | Finished goods inventory (A–) | | 594,600 |

The key T-accounts for Smart Touch's manufacturing costs now show:

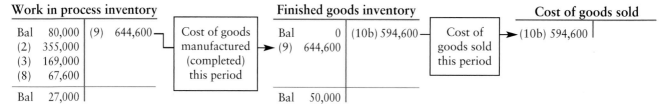

Some jobs are completed, and their costs are transferred out to Finished goods inventory, $644,600. We end the period with other jobs started but not finished ($27,000 ending balance of Work in process inventory) and jobs completed and not sold ($50,000 ending balance of Finished goods inventory).

## Adjusting Manufacturing Overhead at the End of the Period

During 2014, Smart Touch

- debits Manufacturing overhead for actual overhead costs.
- credits Manufacturing overhead for amounts allocated to Work in process inventory.

The total debits to the Manufacturing overhead account rarely equal the total credits. Why? Because Smart Touch allocates overhead to jobs using a *predetermined* manufacturing overhead rate that is based on *estimates*. The predetermined manufacturing overhead rate represents the *expected* relationship between overhead costs and the allocation base. In our example, the $5,400 debit balance of Manufacturing overhead is called **underallocated overhead** because the manufacturing overhead allocated to Work in process inventory was *less* than the actual overhead cost. (If it had been **overallocated** instead, the Manufacturing overhead account would have had a credit balance.)

Accountants adjust underallocated and overallocated overhead at the end of the period when closing the Manufacturing overhead account. Closing the account means zeroing it out, so when overhead is underallocated, as in our example, a credit to Manufacturing overhead of $5,400 is needed to bring the account balance to zero. What account should we debit? Because Smart Touch *undercosted* jobs by $5,400 during the year, the adjustment should increase (debit) the Cost of goods sold:

| (11) | Cost of goods sold    (E+) | 5,400 | |
|---|---|---|---|
| | Manufacturing overhead    (E–) | | 5,400 |

The Manufacturing overhead balance is now zero and the Cost of goods sold is up to date.

| Manufacturing overhead | | | Cost of goods sold | | |
|---|---|---|---|---|---|
| Actual | 73,000 | Allocated (8)  67,600 | (10b) | 594,600 | |
| | | Closed (11)  5,400 | (11) | 5,400 | |
| | 0 | | | 600,000 | |

Exhibit 17-7 summarizes the accounting for manufacturing overhead:

**EXHIBIT 17-7    Summary of Accounting for Manufacturing Overhead**

**Before the Period**

$$\text{Compute predetermined manufacturing overhead rate} = \frac{\text{Total estimated manufacturing overhead costs}}{\text{Total estimated quantity of the manufacturing overhead allocation base}}$$

**During the Period**

$$\text{Allocated manufacturing overhead cost} = \text{Actual quantity of the allocation base used by each job} \times \text{Predetermined manufacturing overhead rate}$$

**At the End of the Period**

Close the Manufacturing overhead account:

**Jobs are undercosted**    If actual > allocated → *Underallocated* manufacturing overhead
Need to *increase* Cost of goods sold, as follows:

| Cost of goods sold    (E+) | XXX | |
|---|---|---|
| Manufacturing overhead    (E–) | | XXX |

**Jobs are overcosted**    If allocated > actual → *Overallocated* manufacturing overhead
Need to *reduce* Cost of goods sold, as follows:

| Manufacturing overhead    (E+) | XXX | |
|---|---|---|
| Cost of goods sold    (E–) | | XXX |

# Job Order Costing in a Service Company

 Calculate unit costs for a service company

As we have seen, service firms have no inventory. These firms incur only noninventoriable costs. But their managers still need to know the costs of different jobs in order to set prices for their services as follows (amounts assumed):

| | |
|---|---|
| Cost of Job 19..................................................... | $6,000 |
| Add standard markup of 50% ($6,000 × 0.50)...... | 3,000 |
| Sale price of Job 19 ............................................. | $9,000 |

A merchandising company can set the selling price of its products this same way.

We now illustrate how service firms assign costs to jobs. The law firm of Walsh Associates considers each client a separate job. Walsh's most significant cost is direct labor—attorney time spent on clients' cases. How do service firms trace direct labor to individual jobs?

Suppose Walsh's accounting system is not automated. Walsh's employees can fill out a weekly electronic labor time record. Software totals the amount of time spent on each job. For example, attorney Lois Fox's electronic time record shows that she devoted 14 hours to client 367 and 26 hours to other clients during the week of June 10, 2014.

Fox's salary and benefits total $100,000 per year. Assuming a 40-hour workweek and 50 workweeks in each year, Fox has 2,000 available work hours per year (50 weeks × 40 hours per week). Fox's hourly pay rate is as follows:

$$\text{Hourly rate to the employer} = \frac{\$100,000 \text{ per year}}{2,000 \text{ hours per year}} = \$50 \text{ per hour}$$

Fox worked 14 hours for client 367, so the direct labor cost traced to client 367 is 14 hours × $50 per hour = $700.

Walsh's employees enter the client number into the time tracking software when they start on the client's job. The software records the time elapsed until the employee signs off on that job.

Founding partner Jacob Walsh wants to know the total cost of serving each client, not just the direct labor cost. Walsh Associates also allocates indirect costs to individual jobs (clients). The law firm develops a predetermined indirect cost allocation rate, following the same approach that Smart Touch used. In December 2013, Walsh estimates that the following indirect costs will be incurred in 2014:

| | |
|---|---|
| Office rent......................................................................... | $200,000 |
| Office support staff.......................................................... | 70,000 |
| Maintaining and updating law library for case research....... | 25,000 |
| Advertisements in the yellow pages .................................... | 3,000 |
| Sponsorship of the symphony............................................. | 2,000 |
| Total indirect costs........................................................... | $300,000 |

Walsh uses direct labor hours as the allocation base, because direct labor hours are the main driver of indirect costs. He estimates that Walsh attorneys will work 10,000 direct labor hours in 2014.

STEP 1: Compute the predetermined indirect cost allocation rate.

$$\text{Predetermined indirect cost allocation rate} = \frac{\$300,000 \text{ expected indirect costs}}{10,000 \text{ expected direct labor hours}}$$

$$= \$30 \text{ per direct labor hour}$$

STEP 2:  **Allocate indirect costs to jobs by multiplying the predetermined indirect cost allocation rate (Step 1) by the actual quantity of the allocation base used by each job.** Client 367, for example, required 14 direct labor hours of Fox's time, so the indirect costs are allocated as follows:

14 direct labor hours × $30/hour = $420

To summarize, the total costs assigned to client 367 are as follows:

| | |
|---|---|
| Direct labor: 14 hours × $50/hour .......... | $ 700 |
| Indirect costs: 14 hours × $30/hour........ | 420 |
| Total costs............................................. | $1,120 |

You have now learned how to use a job order cost system for a service company and assign costs to jobs.

## Stop & Think...

When you have car trouble, you probably go to your mechanic and ask him or her to give you an estimate of what it will cost to fix it. That estimated cost is based on the time the mechanic thinks it will take to fix your car. The mechanic's repair shop has overhead, such as tools, equipment, and building. When you receive the final bill for fixing your car, that bill will be based on both the time it actually took the mechanic to fix your car and an hourly rate that includes the mechanic repair shop's overhead. This is an example of service job costing. Your car problem is the job for the mechanic.

Review the Decision Guidelines on the following page to solidify your understanding.

**Key Takeaway**

Service firms must also allocate overhead to jobs to determine each job's real cost. Just like with manufacturing firms, a predetermined indirect cost allocation rate must be determined. The rate is then used to allocate overhead costs to service jobs.

# Decision Guidelines 17-2

## JOB ORDER COSTING

Companies using a job order costing system treat each job separately. The following are some of the decisions that a company makes when designing its job order costing system.

| Decision | Guidelines |
|---|---|
| • Are utilities, insurance, property taxes, and depreciation • manufacturing overhead or • operating expenses? | These costs are part of manufacturing overhead *only* if they are incurred in the manufacturing plant. If unrelated to manufacturing, they are operating expenses. For example, if related to the research lab, they are R&D expenses. If related to executive headquarters, they are administrative expenses. If related to distribution centers, they are selling expenses. These are all operating expenses, not manufacturing overhead. |

**• How do we record *actual* manufacturing overhead costs?**

| | | |
|---|---|---|
| Manufacturing overhead | XX | |
| Accumulated depreciation—plant and equipment | | XX |
| Prepaid insurance—plant and equipment | | XX |
| Utilities payable (or Cash) and so on | | XX |

**• How do we compute a predetermined manufacturing overhead rate?**

$$\frac{\text{Total estimated manufacturing overhead costs}}{\text{Total estimated quantity of the manufacturing overhead allocation base}}$$

**• How do we record allocation of manufacturing overhead?**

| | | |
|---|---|---|
| Work in process inventory | XX | |
| Manufacturing overhead | | XX |

**• What is the *amount* of the allocated manufacturing overhead?**

Actual quantity of the manufacturing overhead allocation base used by each job × Predetermined manufacturing overhead rate

**• How do we close Manufacturing overhead at the end of the period?**

Close directly to Cost of goods sold, as follows:
For *underallocated* overhead:

| | | |
|---|---|---|
| Cost of goods sold | XX | |
| Manufacturing overhead | | XX |

For *overallocated* overhead:

| | | |
|---|---|---|
| Manufacturing overhead | XX | |
| Cost of goods sold | | XX |

| Decision | Guidelines |
|---|---|
| • When providing services, how do we trace employees' direct labor to individual jobs? | Either use automated software that directly captures the amount of time employees spend on a client's job, or have employees fill out a time record. |

# Summary Problem 17-2

Skippy Scooters manufactures motor scooters. The company has automated production, so it allocates manufacturing overhead based on machine hours. Skippy expects to incur $240,000 of manufacturing overhead costs and to use 4,000 machine hours during 2011. At the end of 2010, Skippy reported the following inventories:

| | |
|---|---|
| Materials inventory........................ | $20,000 |
| Work in process inventory ............ | 17,000 |
| Finished goods inventory............... | 11,000 |

During January 2011, Skippy actually used 300 machine hours and recorded the following transactions:

    a. Purchased materials on account, $31,000
    b. Used direct materials, $39,000
    c. Manufacturing wages incurred totaled $40,000, of which 90% was direct labor and 10% was indirect labor
    d. Used indirect materials, $3,000
    e. Incurred other manufacturing overhead, $13,000 on account
    f. Allocated manufacturing overhead for January 2011
    g. Cost of completed motor scooters, $100,000
    h. Sold scooters on account, $175,000; cost of scooters sold, $95,000

## Requirements

1. Compute Skippy's predetermined manufacturing overhead rate for 2011.
2. Journalize the transactions in the general journal.
3. Enter the beginning balances and then post the transactions to the following accounts: Materials inventory, Work in process inventory, Finished goods inventory, Wages payable, Manufacturing overhead, and Cost of goods sold.
4. Close the ending balance of Manufacturing overhead. Post your entry to the T-accounts.
5. What are the ending balances in the three inventory accounts and in Cost of goods sold?

## Solution

### Requirement 1

$$\text{Predetermined manufacturing overhead rate} = \frac{\text{Total estimated manufacturing overhead costs}}{\text{Total estimated quantity of the manufacturing overhead allocation base}}$$

$$= \frac{\$240,000}{4,000 \text{ machine hours}}$$

$$= \$60/\text{machine hour}$$

## Requirement 2

| a. | Materials inventory (A+) | 31,000 | |
|---|---|---|---|
| | Accounts payable (L+) | | 31,000 |

| b. | Work in process inventory (A+) | 39,000 | |
|---|---|---|---|
| | Materials inventory (A–) | | 39,000 |

| c. | Work in process inventory ($40,000 × 0.90) (A+) | 36,000 | |
|---|---|---|---|
| | Manufacturing overhead ($40,000 × 0.10) (E+) | 4,000 | |
| | Wages payable (L+) | | 40,000 |

| d. | Manufacturing overhead (E+) | 3,000 | |
|---|---|---|---|
| | Materials inventory (A–) | | 3,000 |

| e. | Manufacturing overhead (E+) | 13,000 | |
|---|---|---|---|
| | Accounts payable (L+) | | 13,000 |

| f. | Work in process inventory (300 × $60) (A+) | 18,000 | |
|---|---|---|---|
| | Manufacturing overhead (E–) | | 18,000 |

| g. | Finished goods inventory (A+) | 100,000 | |
|---|---|---|---|
| | Work in process inventory (A–) | | 100,000 |

| h. | Accounts receivable (A+) | 175,000 | |
|---|---|---|---|
| | Sales revenue (R+) | | 175,000 |
| | Cost of goods sold (E+) | 95,000 | |
| | Finished goods inventory (A–) | | 95,000 |

## Requirement 3

Post the transactions:

| Materials inventory | | | |
|---|---|---|---|
| Bal | 20,000 | (b) | 39,000 |
| (a) | 31,000 | (d) | 3,000 |
| Bal | 9,000 | | |

| Work in process inventory | | | |
|---|---|---|---|
| Bal | 17,000 | (g) | 100,000 |
| (b) | 39,000 | | |
| (c) | 36,000 | | |
| (f) | 18,000 | | |
| Bal | 10,000 | | |

| Finished goods inventory | | | |
|---|---|---|---|
| Bal | 11,000 | (h) | 95,000 |
| (g) | 100,000 | | |
| Bal | 16,000 | | |

| Wages payable | | | |
|---|---|---|---|
| | | (c) | 40,000 |

| Manufacturing overhead | | | |
|---|---|---|---|
| (c) | 4,000 | (f) | 18,000 |
| (d) | 3,000 | | |
| (e) | 13,000 | | |
| Bal | 2,000 | | |

| Cost of goods sold | | |
|---|---|---|
| (h) | 95,000 | |

## Requirement 4

Close Manufacturing overhead:

| i. | | Cost of goods sold    (E+) | 2,000 | |
|---|---|---|---|---|
| | | Manufacturing overhead    (E–) | | 2,000 |

| Manufacturing overhead | | | | Cost of goods sold | | |
|---|---|---|---|---|---|---|
| (c) | 4,000 | (f) | 18,000 | (h) | 95,000 | |
| (d) | 3,000 | (i) | 2,000 | (i) | 2,000 | |
| (e) | 13,000 | | | | | |
| | | | | Bal | 97,000 | |

## Requirement 5

Ending balances:

| | |
|---|---|
| Materials inventory (from Requirement 3)...................... | $ 9,000 |
| Work in process inventory (from Requirement 3) ........... | 10,000 |
| Finished goods inventory (from Requirement 3).............. | 16,000 |
| Cost of goods sold (from Requirement 4)........................ | 97,000 |

# Review *Job Order and Process Costing*

## • Accounting Vocabulary

**Allocation Base (p. 823)**
A common denominator that links indirect costs to cost objects. Ideally, the allocation base is the primary cost driver of the indirect costs.

**Conversion Costs (p. 819)**
Direct labor plus manufacturing overhead.

**Cost Allocation (p. 815)**
Assigning indirect costs (such as manufacturing overhead) to cost objects (such as jobs or production processes).

**Cost Driver (p. 823)**
The primary factor that causes a cost to increase or decrease based on the cost driver factor's usage. (Example: more machine hours = more total machine costs.)

**Cost Tracing (p. 815)**
Assigning direct costs (such as direct materials and direct labor) to cost objects (such as jobs or production processes) that used those costs.

**Equivalent Units (p. 859)**
Allows us to measure the amount of work done on a partially finished group of units during a period and to express it in terms of fully complete units of output.

**Job Cost Record (p. 817)**
Document that accumulates the direct materials, direct labor, and manufacturing overhead costs assigned to an individual job.

**Job Order Costing (p. 814)**
A system that accumulates costs for each job. Law firms, music studios, health-care providers, mail-order catalog companies, building contractors, and custom furniture manufacturers are examples of companies that use job order costing systems.

**Labor Time Record (p. 818)**
Identifies the employee, the amount of time spent on a particular job, and the labor cost charged to the job; a record used to assign direct labor cost to specific jobs.

**Materials Requisition (p. 817)**
Request for the transfer of materials to the production floor, prepared by the production team.

**Overallocated (Manufacturing) Overhead (p. 827)**
Occurs when the manufacturing overhead allocated to Work in process inventory is more than the amount of manufacturing overhead costs actually incurred.

**Predetermined Manufacturing Overhead Rate (p. 823)**
Estimated manufacturing overhead cost per unit of the allocation base, computed at the beginning of the period.

**Process Costing (p. 814)**
System for assigning costs to large numbers of identical units that usually proceed in a continuous fashion through a series of uniform production steps or processes.

**Production Cost Report (p. 870)**
Summarizes operations for one department for a month. Combines the costs to account for and the cost per equivalent unit and shows how those costs were assigned to the goods completed and transferred out.

**Transferred-In Costs (p. 868)**
Costs that were incurred in a previous process and brought into a later process as part of the product's cost.

**Underallocated (Manufacturing) Overhead (p. 827)**
Occurs when the manufacturing overhead allocated to Work in process inventory is less than the amount of manufacturing overhead costs actually incurred.

**Weighted-Average Process Costing Method (p. 866)**
Determines the average cost of all of a specific department's equivalent units of work.

## • Destination: Student Success

### Student Success Tips

The following are hints on some common trouble areas for students in this chapter:

● Remember the difference between job order costing and process costing: Job order costing accumulates costs for each batch or job. Process costing accumulates costs of each process needed to complete the product.

● Recall that direct materials, direct labor, and manufacturing overhead costs are the costs that make up a product, whether we cost that product using job order, process, or some other costing method.

● Recall that as costs are added while making the product, we debit Work in process. When products are finished, we move the costs from Work in process (credit) to Finished goods (debit).

● Keep in mind that the formula for calculating a predetermined manufacturing overhead rate is an estimate. Actual costs will rarely exactly equal the costs allocated based on the rate.

### Getting Help

If there's a learning objective from the chapter you aren't confident about, try using one or more of the following resources:

● Review Exhibit 17-6, accounting for manufacturing overhead.

● Review Summary Problem 17-2 in the chapter to reinforce your understanding of job order costing system journal entries.

● Practice additional exercises or problems at the end of Chapter 17 that cover the specific learning objective that is challenging you.

● Watch the white board videos for Chapter 17 located at myaccountinglab.com under the Chapter Resources button.

● Go to myaccountinglab.com and select the Study Plan button. Choose Chapter 17 and work the questions covering that specific learning objective until you've mastered it.

● Work the Chapter 17 pre/post tests in myaccountinglab.com.

● Visit the learning resource center on your campus for tutoring.

# ● Quick Check

1. Would an advertising agency use job or process costing? What about a cell phone manufacturer?

   a. Advertising agency—process costing; Cell phone manufacturer—process costing

   b. Advertising agency—job order costing; Cell phone manufacturer—job order costing

   c. Advertising agency—process costing; Cell phone manufacturer—job order costing

   d. Advertising agency—job order costing; Cell phone manufacturer—process costing

2. When a manufacturing company *uses* direct materials, it *assigns* the cost by debiting

   a. Direct materials.               c. Manufacturing overhead.

   b. Work in process inventory.      d. Materials inventory.

3. When a manufacturing company *uses* indirect materials, it *assigns* the cost by debiting

   a. Work in process inventory.      c. Materials inventory.

   b. Indirect materials.             d. Manufacturing overhead.

4. When a manufacturing company *uses* direct labor, it *assigns* the cost by debiting

   a. Work in process inventory.      c. Direct labor.

   b. Manufacturing overhead.         d. Wages payable.

*Questions 5, 6, 7, and 8 are based on the following information about Gell Corporation's manufacturing of computers. Assume that Gell*

- allocates manufacturing overhead based on machine hours.
- estimated 12,000,000 machine hours and $93,000,000 of manufacturing overhead costs.
- Actually used 16,000,000 machine hours and incurred the following actual costs:

| | |
|---|---:|
| Indirect labor | $ 11,000,000 |
| Depreciation on plant | 48,000,000 |
| Machinery repair | 11,000,000 |
| Direct labor | 75,000,000 |
| Plant supplies | 6,000,000 |
| Plant utilities | 7,000,000 |
| Advertising | 35,000,000 |
| Sales commissions | 27,000,000 |

5. What is Gell's predetermined manufacturing overhead rate?

   a. $7.75/machine hour          c. $6.92/machine hour

   b. $5.81/machine hour          d. $5.19/machine hour

6. What is Gell's actual manufacturing overhead cost?

   a. $158,000,000               c. $145,000,000

   b. $83,000,000                d. $220,000,000

7. How much manufacturing overhead would Gell allocate?

   a. $83,000,000                c. $124,000,000

   b. $93,000,000                d. $220,000,000

8. What entry would Gell make to close the manufacturing overhead account?

a.

| Manufacturing overhead | 10,000,000 | |
|---|---|---|
| Cost of goods sold | | 10,000,000 |

b.

| Manufacturing overhead | 41,000,000 | |
|---|---|---|
| Cost of goods sold | | 41,000,000 |

c.

| Cost of goods sold | 41,000,000 | |
|---|---|---|
| Manufacturing overhead | | 41,000,000 |

d.

| Cost of goods sold | 10,000,000 | |
|---|---|---|
| Manufacturing overhead | | 10,000,000 |

9. A manufacturing company's management can use product cost information to

a. set prices of its products.      c. identify ways to cut production costs.

b. decide which products to emphasize.      d. a, b, and c are correct

10. For which of the following reasons would David Laugherty, owner of the Laughtery Associates law firm, want to know the total costs of a job (serving a particular client)?

a. For inventory valuation      c. For external reporting

b. To determine the fees to charge clients      d. a, b, and c are correct

Answers are given after Apply Your Knowledge (p. 855).

# Assess Your Progress

## ● Short Exercises

**MyAccountingLab**   **S17-1**   **①** **Distinguishing between job costing and process costing [5 min]**
Job costing and process costing track costs differently.

**Requirement**

1. Would the following companies use job order costing or process costing?
   a. A manufacturer of refrigerators
   b. A manufacturer of specialty wakeboards
   c. A manufacturer of luxury yachts
   d. A professional services firm
   e. A landscape contractor
   f. A custom home builder
   g. A cell phone manufacturer
   h. A manufacturer of frozen pizzas
   i. A manufacturer of multivitamins
   j. A manufacturer of tennis shoes

**S17-2**   **②** **Flow of costs in job order costing [10 min]**
For a manufacturer that uses job order costing, there is a correct order that the costs flow through the accounts.

**Requirement**

1. Order the following from 1–4. Item 1 has been completed for you.

   __1__ a. Materials inventory

   _____ b. Finished goods inventory

   _____ c. Cost of goods sold

   _____ d. Work in process inventory

**S17-3**    **②** **Accounting for materials [5–10 min]**

Rite Packs manufactures backpacks. Its plant records include the following materials-related transactions:

| | |
|---|---:|
| Purchases of canvas (on account) . . . . . . . . . . . . . . . . . . . . . | $ 71,000 |
| Purchases of sewing machine lubricating oil (on account) . . . | 1,100 |
| Materials requisitions: | |
| Canvas . . . . . . . . . . . . . . . . . . . . . . . . . . . . . . . . . . . . . . . | 64,000 |
| Sewing machine lubricating oil . . . . . . . . . . . . . . . . . . . . | 250 |

### Requirements

1. Journalize the entries to record these transactions.

2. Post these transactions to the Materials inventory account.

3. If the company had $34,000 of Materials inventory at the beginning of the period, what is the ending balance of Materials inventory?

**S17-4**    **②** **Accounting for materials [10 min]**

Consider the following T-accounts:

| Materials inventory | | |
|---|---:|---|
| Bal | 50 | |
| Purchases | 205 | Used |
| Bal | 35 | |

| Work in process inventory | | | |
|---|---:|---|---:|
| Bal | 15 | | |
| Direct materials | | Cost of goods | 550 |
| Direct labor | 285 | manufactured | |
| Manufacturing overhead | 135 | | |
| Bal | 45 | | |

### Requirement

1. Use the T-accounts to determine direct materials used and indirect materials used.

**S17-5**    **②** **Accounting for labor [5 min]**

Creative Crystal, Ltd., reports the following labor-related transactions at its plant in Portland, Oregon.

| | | |
|---|---|---:|
| Plant janitor's wages . . . . . . . . . . . . . . | $ | 570 |
| Plant furnace operator's wages . . . . . | | 880 |
| Glass blower's wages . . . . . . . . . . . . | | 78,000 |

### Requirement

1. Journalize the entry for the incurrence and assignment of these wages.

**S17-6**    **②** **Accounting for materials and labor [5 min]**

Seattle Enterprises produces LCD touch screen products. The company reports the following information at December 31, 2012:

| Materials inventory | | Work in process inventory | | Finished goods inventory | |
|---|---:|---|---:|---|---:|
| 47,000 | 31,400 | 28,000 | 123,000 | 123,000 | 109,000 |
| | | 62,000 | | | |
| | | 53,900 | | | |

| Wages payable | | Manufacturing overhead | |
|---|---:|---|---:|
| | 74,000 | 3,400 | 53,900 |
| | | 12,000 | |
| | | 36,500 | |

Seattle began operations on January 30, 2012.

### Requirements

1. What is the cost of direct materials used? The cost of indirect materials used?

2. What is the cost of direct labor? The cost of indirect labor?

**S17-7**  ❸ **Accounting for overhead [5 min]**

Teak Outdoor Furniture manufactures wood patio furniture. The company reports the following costs for June 2012:

| | |
|---|---:|
| Wood ......................... | $ 250,000 |
| Nails, glue, and stain ............ | 26,000 |
| Depreciation on saws ............ | 5,500 |
| Indirect manufacturing labor ...... | 38,000 |
| Depreciation on delivery truck ..... | 2,300 |
| Assembly-line workers' wages ..... | 57,000 |

### Requirement

1.  What is the balance in the Manufacturing overhead account before overhead is applied to jobs?

**S17-8**  ❸ **Allocating overhead [5 min]**

Job 303 includes direct materials costs of $500 and direct labor costs of $430.

### Requirement

1.  If the manufacturing overhead allocation rate is 80% of direct labor cost, what is the total cost assigned to Job 303?

*Note: Short Exercise 17-6 must be completed before attempting Short Exercise 17-9.*

**S17-9**  ❹ **Comparing actual to allocated overhead [10 min]**

Refer to the data in S17-6.

### Requirements

1.  What is the actual manufacturing overhead of Seattle Enterprises?
2.  What is the allocated manufacturing overhead?
3.  Is manufacturing overhead underallocated or overallocated? By how much?

**S17-10**  ❹ **Under/overallocated overhead [10 min]**

The T-account showing the manufacturing overhead activity for Jackson, Corp., for 2012 is as follows:

Manufacturing overhead

| | |
|---:|:---|
| 197,000 | 207,000 |

### Requirements

1.  What is the actual manufacturing overhead?
2.  What is the allocated manufacturing overhead?
3.  What is the predetermined manufacturing overhead rate as a percentage of direct labor cost, if actual direct labor costs were $165,600?
4.  Is manufacturing overhead underallocated or overallocated? By how much?
5.  Is Cost of goods sold too high or too low?

*Note: Short Exercise 17-10 must be completed before attempting Short Exercise 17-11.*

**S17-11**  ❹ **Closing out under/overallocated overhead [5 min]**

Refer to the data in S17-10.

### Requirement

1.  Journalize the entry to close out the company's Manufacturing overhead account.

**S17-12**  ⑤ **Job order costing in a service company [5 min]**
Roth Accounting pays Jaclyn Sawyer $104,400 per year. Sawyer works 1,800 hours per year.

## Requirements

1. What is the hourly cost to Roth Accounting of employing Sawyer?
2. What direct labor cost would be traced to client 507 if Sawyer works 12 hours to prepare client 507's financial statements?

*Note: Short Exercise 17-12 must be completed before attempting Short Exercise 17-13.*

**S17-13**  ⑤ **Job order costing in a service company [5 min]**
Refer to the data in S17-12. Assume that Roth's accountants are expected to work a total of 8,000 direct labor hours in 2012. Roth's estimated total indirect costs are $240,000.

## Requirements

1. What is Roth's indirect cost allocation rate?
2. What indirect costs will be allocated to client 507 if Sawyer works 12 hours to prepare the financial statements?
3. Calculate the total cost to prepare client 507's financial statements.

# ● Exercises

**E17-14**  ① **Distinguishing between job order costing and process costing [5–10 min]**     *MyAccountingLab*
Consider the following incomplete statements.

   a. _____ is used by companies that produce small quantities of many different products.
   b. **Georgia-Pacific** pulverizes wood into pulp to manufacture cardboard. The company uses a _____ system.
   c. To record costs of manufacturing thousands of identical files, the file manufacturer will use a _____ system.
   d. Companies that produce large numbers of identical products use _____ systems for product costing.
   e. The computer repair service that visits your home and repairs your computer uses a _____ system.
   f. **Apple** assembles electronic parts and software to manufacture millions of iPods. **Apple** uses a _____ system.
   g. Textbook publishers produce titles of a particular book in batches. Textbook publishers use a _____ system.
   h. A company that bottles milk into one-gallon containers uses a _____ system.
   i. A company that makes large quantities of one type of tankless hot water heater uses a _____ system.
   j. A particular governmental agency takes bids for specific items it utilizes. Each item requires a separate bid. The agency uses a _____ system.

## Requirement

1. Complete each of the statements with the term job order costing or the term process costing.

**E17-15**  ②③④ **Accounting for job costs [15 min]**
Sloan Trailers' job cost records yielded the following information:

| Job | Date | | | Total Cost of Job |
| No. | Started | Finished | Sold | at September 30 |
| --- | --- | --- | --- | --- |
| 1 | August 21 | September 16 | September 17 | $  3,100 |
| 2 | August 29 | September 21 | September 26 | 13,000 |
| 3 | September 3 | October 11 | October 13 | 6,900 |
| 4 | September 7 | September 29 | October 1 | 4,400 |

## Requirement

1. Use the dates in the table to identify the status of each job. Compute Sloan's cost of (a) Work in process inventory at September 30, (b) Finished goods inventory at September 30, and (c) Cost of goods sold for September.

**E17-16** ❷❸❹ **Job order costing journal entries [20–25 min]**

Consider the following transactions for Judy's Sofas:

a. Incurred and paid Web site expenses, $2,900.
b. Incurred manufacturing wages of $15,000, 60% of which was direct labor and 40% of which was indirect labor.
c. Purchased materials on account, $24,000.
d. Used in production: direct materials, $9,500; indirect materials, $4,500.
e. Recorded manufacturing overhead: depreciation on plant, $10,000; plant insurance, $1,300; plant property tax, $4,200 (credit Property tax payable).
f. Allocated manufacturing overhead to jobs, 250% of direct labor costs.
g. Completed production, $38,000.
h. Sold inventory on account, $20,000; cost of goods sold, $10,000.
i. Journalized the closing of the manufacturing overhead account.

## Requirement

1. Journalize the transactions in Judy's general journal.

**E17-17** ❷❸❹ **Identifying job order costing journal entries [15 min]**

Consider the following:

| Materials inventory | | Work in process inventory | | Finished goods inventory | | Accounts payable | |
|---|---|---|---|---|---|---|---|
| (a) | (b) | (b) | (f) | (f) | (g) | | (a) |
| | | (c) | | | | | |
| | | (e) | | | | | |

| Wages payable | | Manufacturing overhead | | Cost of goods sold | | Prepaid insurance | |
|---|---|---|---|---|---|---|---|
| | (c) | (b) | (e) | (g) | | | (d) |
| | | (c) | (h) | (h) | | | |
| | | (d) | | | | | |

## Requirement

1. Describe the letter transactions in the above accounts.

**E17-18** ❸❹ **Allocating manufacturing overhead [15–20 min]**

Selected cost data for Antique Print, Co., are as follows:

| | |
|---|---|
| Estimated manufacturing overhead cost for the year . . . . . | $ 115,000 |
| Estimated direct labor cost for the year . . . . . . . . . . . . . . | 71,875 |
| Actual manufacturing overhead cost for the year . . . . . . . . | 119,000 |
| Actual direct labor cost for the year . . . . . . . . . . . . . . . . | 73,000 |

## Requirements

1. Compute the predetermined manufacturing overhead rate per direct labor dollar.
2. Prepare the journal entry to allocate overhead cost for the year.
3. Use a T-account to determine the amount of underallocated or overallocated manufacturing overhead.
4. Prepare the journal entry to close the balance of the Manufacturing overhead account.

**E17-19**  ③④ **Allocating manufacturing overhead  [15–20 min]**

Brooks Foundry uses a predetermined manufacturing overhead rate to allocate over-head to individual jobs, based on the machine hours required. At the beginning of 2012, the company expected to incur the following:

| | |
|---|---|
| Manufacturing overhead costs ...... | $    840,000 |
| Direct labor costs ............... | 1,550,000 |
| Machine hours ................. | 70,000 hours |

At the end of 2012, the company had actually incurred:

| | |
|---|---|
| Direct labor cost ......................... | $    1,160,000 |
| Depreciation on manufacturing property, plant, | |
| and equipment ...................... | 600,000 |
| Property taxes on plant .................... | 40,000 |
| Sales salaries ........................... | 26,500 |
| Delivery drivers' wages .................... | 23,500 |
| Plant janitor's wages ...................... | 17,000 |
| Machine hours .......................... | 67,000 hours |

## Requirements

1. Compute Brooks' predetermined manufacturing overhead rate.
2. Prepare the journal entry to allocate manufacturing overhead.
3. Post the manufacturing overhead transactions to the Manufacturing overhead T-account. Is manufacturing overhead underallocated or overallocated? By how much?
4. Close the Manufacturing overhead account to Cost of goods sold. Does your entry increase or decrease cost of goods sold?

**E17-20**  ③④ **Allocating manufacturing overhead [10–15 min]**

Refer to the data in E17-19. Brooks' accountant found an error in her 2012 cost records. Depreciation on manufacturing property, plant, and equipment was actually $550,000, not the $600,000 she originally reported. Unadjusted balances at the end of 2012 include:

| | |
|---|---|
| Finished goods inventory ....... | $  131,000 |
| Cost of goods sold ............ | 580,000 |

## Requirements

1. Use a T-account to determine whether manufacturing overhead is underallocated or overallocated, and by how much.
2. Prepare the journal entry to close out the underallocated or overallocated manufacturing overhead.
3. What is the adjusted ending balance of Cost of goods sold?

**E17-21**  ④ **Allocating manufacturing overhead [15–20 min]**

The manufacturing records for Krazy Kayaks at the end of the 2012 fiscal year show the following information about manufacturing overhead:

| | |
|---|---|
| Overhead allocated to production ........ | $  405,900 |
| Actual manufacturing overhead costs ...... | $  428,000 |
| Overhead allocation rate for the year ...... | $        41 per machine hour |

## Requirements

1. How many machine hours did Krazy Kayaks use in 2012?

2. Was manufacturing overhead over- or underallocated for the year and by how much?

3. Prepare the journal entry to close out the over- or underallocated overhead.

**E17-22** ❹ **Using the Work in process inventory account [15–20 min]**
June production generated the following activity in Auto Chassis Company's Work in process inventory account:

**Work in process inventory**

| | |
|---|---|
| Jun 1 Bal | 20,000 |
| Direct materials used | 31,000 |
| Direct labor assigned to jobs | 33,000 |
| Manufacturing overhead allocated to jobs | 13,000 |

Additionally, Auto has completed Jobs 142 and 143, with total costs of $38,000 and $36,000, respectively.

## Requirements

1. Prepare the journal entry for production completed in June.

2. Post the journal entry made in Requirement 1. Compute the ending balance in the Work in process account on June 30.

3. Prepare the journal entry to record the sale (on credit) of Job 143 for $46,000. Also, prepare the journal entry to record Cost of goods sold for Job 143.

4. What is the gross profit on Job 143? What other costs must gross profit cover?

**E17-23** ❺ **Job order costing in a service company [15–20 min]**
Martin Realtors, a real estate consulting firm, specializes in advising companies on potential new plant sites. The company uses a job order costing system with a predetermined indirect cost allocation rate, computed as a percentage of direct labor costs. At the beginning of 2012, managing partner Andrew Martin prepared the following budget for the year:

| | |
|---|---|
| Direct labor hours (professionals) ..... | 19,600 hours |
| Direct labor costs (professionals) ...... | $ 2,450,000 |
| Office rent ..................... | 370,000 |
| Support staff salaries ............. | 1,282,500 |
| Utilities ....................... | 430,000 |

Peters Manufacturing, Inc., is inviting several consultants to bid for work. Andrew Martin estimates that this job will require about 240 direct labor hours.

## Requirements

1. Compute Martin Realtors' (a) hourly direct labor cost rate and (b) indirect cost allocation rate.

2. Compute the predicted cost of the Peters Manufacturing job.

3. If Martin wants to earn a profit that equals 45% of the job's cost, how much should he bid for the Peters Manufacturing job?

## • Problems (Group A)

**P17-24A** ❶❷❸❹ **Analyzing cost data [25–35 min]**

Bluebird Manufacturing makes carrying cases for portable electronic devices. Its costing records yield the following information:

| Job No. | Date Started | Date Finished | Sold | Total Cost of Job at October 31 | Total Manufacturing Costs Added in November |
|---|---|---|---|---|---|
| 1 | 10/3 | 10/12 | 10/13 | $ 1,900 | |
| 2 | 10/3 | 10/30 | 11/1 | 1,800 | |
| 3 | 10/17 | 11/24 | 11/27 | 400 | $ 1,500 |
| 4 | 10/29 | 11/29 | 12/3 | 800 | 1,200 |
| 5 | 11/8 | 11/12 | 11/14 | | 550 |
| 6 | 11/23 | 12/6 | 12/9 | | 700 |

### Requirements

1. Which type of costing system is Bluebird using? What piece of data did you base your answer on?

2. Use the dates in the table to identify the status of each job. Compute Bluebird's account balances at October 31 for Work in process inventory, Finished goods inventory, and Cost of goods sold. Compute, by job, account balances at November 30 for Work in process inventory, Finished goods inventory, and Cost of goods sold.

3. Prepare journal entries to record the transfer of completed units from Work in process to Finished goods for October and November.

4. Record the sale of Job 3 for $2,100.

5. What is the gross profit for Job 3? What other costs must this gross profit cover?

**P17-25A** ❷❸❹ **Accounting for construction transactions [30–45 min]**

Quaint Construction, Inc., is a home builder in Arizona. Quaint uses a job order costing system in which each house is a job. Because it constructs houses, the company uses an account titled Construction overhead. The company applies overhead based on estimated direct labor costs. For the year, it estimated construction overhead of $1,100,000 and total direct labor cost of $2,750,000. The following events occurred during August:

a. Purchased materials on account, $400,000.

b. Requisitioned direct materials and used direct labor in construction. Record the materials requisitioned.

| | Direct materials | Direct labor |
|---|---|---|
| House 402 | $ 54,000 | $ 42,000 |
| House 403 | 68,000 | 35,000 |
| House 404 | 63,000 | 57,000 |
| House 405 | 85,000 | 53,000 |

c. The company incurred total wages of $200,000. Use the data from item b to assign the wages.

d. Depreciation of construction equipment, $6,200.

e. Other overhead costs incurred on houses 402 through 405:

| | |
|---|---|
| Indirect labor . . . . . . . . . . . . . . . . . | $ 13,000 |
| Equipment rentals paid in cash . . . . . | 37,000 |
| Worker liability insurance expired . . | 3,000 |

f. Allocated overhead to jobs.

g. Houses completed: 402, 404.

h. House sold: 404 for $250,000.

**Requirements**

1. Calculate Quaint's construction overhead application rate for the year.
2. Prepare journal entries to record the events in the general journal.
3. Open T-accounts for Work in process inventory and Finished goods inventory. Post the appropriate entries to these accounts, identifying each entry by letter. Determine the ending account balances, assuming that the beginning balances were zero.
4. Add the costs of the unfinished houses, and show that this total amount equals the ending balance in the Work in process inventory account.
5. Add the cost of the completed house that has not yet been sold, and show that this equals the ending balance in Finished goods inventory.
6. Compute gross profit on the house that was sold. What costs must gross profit cover for Quaint Construction?

**P17-26A** ② ③ ④ **Preparing and using a job cost record [30–35 min]**

Lu Technology, Co., manufactures CDs and DVDs for computer software and entertainment companies. Lu uses job order costing and has a perpetual inventory system.

On April 2, Lu began production of 5,900 DVDs, Job 423, for Stick People Pictures for $1.30 sales price per DVD. Lu promised to deliver the DVDs to Stick People by April 5. Lu incurred the following costs:

| Date | Labor Time Record No. | Description | Amount |
|------|------|------|------|
| 4/2 | 655 | 10 hours @ $14 | $ 140 |
| 4/3 | 656 | 20 hours @ $13 | 260 |

| Date | Materials Requisition No. | Description | Amount |
|------|------|------|------|
| 4/2 | 63 | 31 lbs. polycarbonate plastic @ $11 | $ 341 |
| 4/2 | 64 | 25 lbs. acrylic plastic @ $27 | 675 |
| 4/3 | 74 | 3 lbs. refined aluminum @ $42 | 126 |

Stick People provides the movie file for Lu to burn onto the DVDs at a cost of $0.50 per DVD. Lu Technology allocates manufacturing overhead to jobs based on the relation between estimated overhead of $540,000 and estimated direct labor costs of $432,000. Job 423 was completed and shipped on April 3.

**Requirements**

1. Prepare a job cost record similar to Exhibit 17-6 for Job 423. Calculate the predetermined overhead rate; then allocate manufacturing overhead to the job.
2. Journalize in summary form the requisition of direct materials (including the movie files) and the assignment of direct labor and manufacturing overhead to Job 423.
3. Journalize completion of the job and the sale of the 5,900 DVDs.

**P17-27A** ❷❸❹ **Comprehensive accounting for manufacturing transactions [90–120 min]**

Howie Stars produces stars for elementary teachers to reward their students. Howie Stars' trial balance on June 1 follows:

**HOWIE STARS**
**Trial Balance**
**June 1, 2012**

| Account Title | Debit | Credit |
|---|---|---|
| Cash | $ 14,000 | |
| Accounts receivable | 155,000 | |
| Inventories: | | |
|     Materials | 5,700 | |
|     Work in process | 39,400 | |
|     Finished goods | 20,400 | |
| Plant assets | 200,000 | |
| Accumulated depreciation | | $ 72,000 |
| Accounts payable | | 127,000 |
| Wages payable | | 1,700 |
| Common stock | | 142,000 |
| Retained earnings | | 91,800 |
| Sales revenue | — | — |
| Cost of goods sold | — | |
| Manufacturing overhead | — | |
| Marketing and general expenses | — | |
| Total | $434,500 | $434,500 |

June 1 balances in the subsidiary ledgers were as follows:

- Materials subledger: Paper, $4,700; indirect materials, $1,000
- Work in process subledger: Job 120, $39,400; $0 for Job 121
- Finished goods subledger: Large Stars, $9,400; Small Stars, $11,000

June transactions are summarized as follows:

a. Collections on account, $152,000.
b. Marketing and general expenses incurred and paid, $28,000.
c. Payments on account, $36,000.
d. Materials purchases on credit: Paper, $22,900; indirect materials, $3,800.
e. Materials used in production (requisitioned):
- Job 120: paper, $850
- Job 121: paper, $7,650
- Indirect materials, $1,000
f. Wages incurred and assigned during June, $35,000. Labor time records for the month: Job 120, $3,500; Job 121, $16,600; indirect labor, $14,900.
g. Wages paid in June include the balance in the Wages payable account at May 31 and $32,200 of wages incurred during June.
h. Depreciation on plant and equipment, $2,600.
i. Manufacturing overhead was allocated at the predetermined rate of 50% of direct labor cost.
j. Jobs completed during the month: Job 120, 300,000 Large Stars at total cost of $45,500.
k. Credit sales on account: all of Job 120 for $111,000.
l. Closed the Manufacturing overhead account to Cost of goods sold.

## Requirements

1. Journalize the transactions for the company. Howie uses a perpetual inventory system.

2. Open T-accounts for the general ledger, the Materials ledger, the Work in process ledger, and the Finished goods ledger. Insert each account balance as given, and use the reference Bal. Post the journal entries to the T-accounts using the transaction letters as a reference.

3. Prepare a trial balance at June 30, 2012.

4. Use the Work in process inventory T-account to prepare a schedule of cost of goods manufactured for the month of June. (You may want to review Exhibit 16-10.)

5. Prepare an income statement for the month of June. To calculate cost of goods sold, you may want to review Exhibit 16-7. (*Hint*: In transaction l, you closed any under/overallocated manufacturing overhead to Cost of goods sold. In the income statement, show this correction as an adjustment to Cost of goods sold. If manufacturing overhead is underallocated, the adjustment will increase Cost of goods sold. If overhead is overallocated, the adjustment will decrease Cost of goods sold.)

**P17-28A** ③ ④ **Accounting manufacturing overhead [25–35 min]**
White Woods manufactures jewelry boxes. The primary materials (wood, brass, and glass) and direct labor are traced directly to the products. Manufacturing overhead costs are allocated based on machine hours. Data for 2012 follow:

|  | Estimated (Budget) | Actual |
|---|---|---|
| Machine hours . . . . . . . . . . . . . . . . . . . . . . . . . . . | 25,000 hours | 32,100 hours |
| Maintenance labor (repairs to equipment) . . . . . . | $12,000 | $28,500 |
| Plant supervisor's salary . . . . . . . . . . . . . . . . . . . . | 47,000 | 48,000 |
| Screws, nails, and glue . . . . . . . . . . . . . . . . . . . . | 24,000 | 45,000 |
| Plant utilities . . . . . . . . . . . . . . . . . . . . . . . . . . . | 41,000 | 96,850 |
| Freight out . . . . . . . . . . . . . . . . . . . . . . . . . . . | 37,000 | 46,500 |
| Depreciation on plant and | | |
| equipment . . . . . . . . . . . . . . . . . . . . . . . . . . . | 87,000 | 83,000 |
| Advertising expense . . . . . . . . . . . . . . . . . . . . . . | 43,000 | 54,000 |

## Requirements

1. Compute the predetermined manufacturing overhead rate.

2. Post actual and allocated manufacturing overhead to the Manufacturing overhead T-account.

3. Close the under- or overallocated overhead to Cost of goods sold.

4. The predetermined manufacturing overhead rate usually turns out to be inaccurate. Why don't accountants just use the actual manufacturing overhead rate?

**P17-29A** ⑤ **Job order costing in a service company [20–25 min]**
Crow Design, Inc., is a Web site design and consulting firm. The firm uses a job order costing system in which each client is a different job. Crow Design traces direct labor, licensing costs, and travel costs directly to each job. It allocates indirect costs to jobs based on a predetermined indirect cost allocation rate, computed as a percentage of direct labor costs.

At the beginning of 2012, managing partner Sally Simone prepared the following budget estimates:

| | |
|---|---|
| Direct labor hours (professional) . . . . . . | 6,250 hours |
| Direct labor costs (professional) . . . . . . . | $1,800,000 |
| Support staff salaries . . . . . . . . . . . . . . . | 765,000 |
| Computer leases . . . . . . . . . . . . . . . . . . | 46,000 |
| Office supplies . . . . . . . . . . . . . . . . . . . | 27,000 |
| Office rent . . . . . . . . . . . . . . . . . . . . . . | 62,000 |

In November 2012, Crow Design served several clients. Records for two clients appear here:

|  | Delicious Treats | Mesilla Chocolates |
|---|---|---|
| Direct labor hours ........ | 700  hours | 100  hours |
| Software licensing costs .... | $    4,000 | $    400 |
| Travel costs ............. | 8,000 | — |

## Requirements

1. Compute Crow Design's direct labor rate and its predetermined indirect cost allocation rate for 2012.
2. Compute the total cost of each job.
3. If Simone wants to earn profits equal to 50% of service revenue, how much (what fee) should she charge each of these two clients?
4. Why does Crow Design assign costs to jobs?

# ● Problems (Group B)

**P17-30B** ❶ ❷ ❸ ❹ **Analyzing cost data [25–35 min]**

Stratton Manufacturing makes carrying cases for portable electronic devices. Its costing records yield the following information:

| Job No. | Date Started | Date Finished | Sold | Total Cost of Job at October 31 | Total Manufacturing Costs Added in November |
|---|---|---|---|---|---|
| 1 | 10/3 | 10/12 | 10/13 | $     1,000 |  |
| 2 | 10/3 | 10/30 | 11/1 | 1,100 |  |
| 3 | 10/17 | 11/24 | 11/27 | 700 | $     1,400 |
| 4 | 10/29 | 11/29 | 12/3 | 300 | 1,500 |
| 5 | 11/8 | 11/12 | 11/14 |  | 650 |
| 6 | 11/23 | 12/6 | 12/9 |  | 500 |

## Requirements

1. Which type of costing system is Stratton using? What piece of data did you base your answer on?
2. Use the dates in the table to identify the status of each job. Compute Stratton's account balances at October 31 for Work in process inventory, Finished goods inventory, and Cost of goods sold. Compute, by job, account balances at November 30 for Work in process inventory, Finished goods inventory, and Cost of goods sold.
3. Prepare journal entries to record the transfer of completed units from work in process to finished goods for October and November.
4. Record the sale of Job 3 for $2,200.
5. What is the gross profit for Job 3? What other costs must this gross profit cover?

**P17-31B** ❷ ❸ ❹ **Accounting for construction transactions [30–45 min]**

Cottage Construction, Inc., is a home builder in Arizona. Cottage uses a job order costing system in which each house is a job. Because it constructs houses, the company uses an account titled Construction overhead. The company applies overhead based on estimated direct labor costs. For the year, it estimated construction overhead of $1,050,000 and total direct labor cost of $3,500,000. The following events occurred during August:

a. Purchased materials on account, $460,000.

b. Requisitioned direct materials and used direct labor in construction. Record the materials requisitioned.

|  | Direct materials | Direct labor |
|---|---|---|
| House 402 | $   50,000 | $   45,000 |
| House 403 | 69,000 | 30,000 |
| House 404 | 66,000 | 56,000 |
| House 405 | 88,000 | 55,000 |

c. The company incurred total wages of $210,000. Use the data from item b to assign the wages.

d. Depreciation of construction equipment, $6,000.

e. Other overhead costs incurred on houses 402 through 405:

| Indirect labor . . . . . . . . . . . . . . . . . | $   24,000 |
|---|---|
| Equipment rentals paid in cash . . . . . | 36,000 |
| Worker liability insurance expired  . . | 8,000 |

f. Allocated overhead to jobs.

g. Houses completed: 402, 404.

h. House sold: 404 for $200,000.

## Requirements

1. Calculate Cottage's construction overhead application rate for the year.

2. Record the events in the general journal.

3. Open T-accounts for Work in process inventory and Finished goods inventory. Post the appropriate entries to these accounts, identifying each entry by letter. Determine the ending account balances, assuming that the beginning balances were zero.

4. Add the costs of the unfinished houses, and show that this total amount equals the ending balance in the Work in process inventory account.

5. Add the cost of the completed house that has not yet been sold, and show that this equals the ending balance in Finished goods inventory.

6. Compute gross profit on the house that was sold. What costs must gross profit cover for Cottage Construction?

**P17-32B** ② ③ ④ **Preparing and using a job cost record [30–35 min]**
True Technology, Co., manufactures CDs and DVDs for computer software and entertainment companies. True uses job order costing and has a perpetual inventory system.

On November 2, True began production of 5,500 DVDs, Job 423, for Leopard Pictures for $1.60 sales price per DVD. True promised to deliver the DVDs to Leopard by November 5. True incurred the following costs:

| Date | Labor Time Record No. | Description | Amount |
|---|---|---|---|
| 11/2 | 655 | 10 hours @ $18 | $  180 |
| 11/3 | 656 | 20 hours @ $14 | 280 |

| Date | Materials Requisition No. | Description | Amount |
|---|---|---|---|
| 11/2 | 63 | 31 lbs. polycarbonate plastic @ $12 | $  372 |
| 11/2 | 64 | 25 lbs. acrylic plastic @ $29 | 725 |
| 11/3 | 74 | 3 lbs. refined aluminum @ $48 | 144 |

Leopard Pictures provides the movie file for True to burn onto the DVDs at a cost of $0.45 per DVD. True Technology allocates manufacturing overhead to jobs based on the relation between estimated overhead of $550,000 and estimated direct labor costs of $500,000. Job 423 was completed and shipped on November 3.

### Requirements

1. Prepare a job cost record similar to Exhibit 17-6 for Job 423. Calculate the predetermined overhead rate, then allocate manufacturing overhead to the job.

2. Journalize in summary form the requisition of direct materials (including the movie files) and the assignment of direct labor and manufacturing overhead to Job 423.

3. Journalize completion of the job and the sale of the 5,500 DVDs.

**P17-33B** ❷ ❸ ❹ **Comprehensive accounting for manufacturing transactions [90–120 min]**
School Stars produces stars for elementary teachers to reward their students. School Stars' trial balance on June 1 follows:

| SCHOOL STARS Trial Balance June 1, 2012 | | |
|---|---|---|
| | Balance | |
| Account Title | Debit | Credit |
| Cash | $ 17,000 | |
| Accounts receivable | 170,000 | |
| Inventories: | | |
| Materials | 6,200 | |
| Work in process | 43,000 | |
| Finished goods | 21,300 | |
| Plant assets | 250,000 | |
| Accumulated depreciation | | $ 71,000 |
| Accounts payable | | 133,000 |
| Wages payable | | 3,300 |
| Common stock | | 144,000 |
| Retained earnings | | 156,200 |
| Sales revenue | — | — |
| Cost of goods sold | — | |
| Manufacturing overhead | — | |
| Marketing and general expenses | — | |
| Total | $507,500 | $507,500 |

June 1 balances in the subsidiary ledgers were as follows:

- Materials subledger: $4,300 paper and $1,900 indirect materials
- Work in process subledger: Job 120 $43,000; $0 for Job 121
- Finished goods subledger: $9,300 Large Stars and $12,000 Small Stars

June transactions are summarized as follows:

a. Collections on account, $155,000.
b. Marketing and general expenses incurred and paid, $22,000.
c. Payments on account, $37,000.
d. Materials purchases on credit: Paper, $26,600; indirect materials, $4,200.
e. Materials used in production (requisitioned):
   - Job 120: Paper, $900
   - Job 121: Paper, $7,850
   - Indirect materials, $1,600
f. Wages incurred and assigned during June, $43,000. Labor time records for the month: Job 120, $4,800; Job 121, $18,500; indirect labor, $19,700.
g. Wages paid in June include the balance in the Wages payable account at May 31 and $39,900 of wages incurred during June.
h. Depreciation on plant and equipment, $2,700.
i. Manufacturing overhead was allocated at the predetermined rate of 90% of direct labor cost.
j. Jobs completed during the month: Job 120, 600,000 Large Stars at total cost of $53,020.
k. Credit sales on account: all of Job 120 for $133,000.
l. Closed the Manufacturing overhead account to Cost of goods sold.

## Requirements

1. Journalize the transactions for the company. School uses a perpetual inventory system.
2. Open T-accounts for the general ledger, the Materials ledger, the Work in process ledger, and the Finished goods ledger. Insert each account balance as given, and use the reference Bal. Post the journal entries to the T-accounts using the transaction letters as a reference.
3. Prepare a trial balance at June 30, 2012.
4. Use the Work in process inventory T-account to prepare a schedule of cost of goods manufactured for the month of June. (You may want to review Exhibit 16-10.)
5. Prepare an income statement for the month of June. To calculate cost of goods sold, you may want to review Exhibit 16-7. (*Hint*: In transaction l, you closed any under/overallocated manufacturing overhead to Cost of goods sold. In the income statement, show this correction as an adjustment to Cost of goods sold. If manufacturing overhead is underallocated, the adjustment will increase Cost of goods sold. If overhead is overallocated, the adjustment will decrease Cost of goods sold.)

**P17-34B** ❸ ❹ **Accounting for manufacturing overhead [25–35 min]**
Superior Woods manufactures jewelry boxes. The primary materials (wood, brass, and glass) and direct labor are traced directly to the products. Manufacturing overhead costs are allocated based on machine hours. Data for 2012 follow:

|  | Estimated (Budget) | Actual |
|---|---|---|
| Machine hours ........................... | 28,000 hours | 32,400 hours |
| Maintenance labor (repairs to equipment) ...... | $16,000 | $26,500 |
| Plant supervisor's salary .................... | 46,000 | 47,000 |
| Screws, nails, and glue .................... | 23,000 | 46,000 |
| Plant utilities ........................... | 42,000 | 93,850 |
| Freight out ............................. | 35,000 | 47,500 |
| Depreciation on plant and | | |
|    equipment ........................... | 83,000 | 82,000 |
| Advertising expense ...................... | 46,000 | 59,000 |

## Requirements

1. Compute the predetermined manufacturing overhead rate.
2. Post actual and allocated manufacturing overhead to the Manufacturing overhead T-account.

3. Close the under- or overallocated overhead to Cost of goods sold.

4. The predetermined manufacturing overhead rate usually turns out to be inaccurate. Why don't accountants just use the actual manufacturing overhead rate?

**P17-35B** ⑤ **Job order costing in a service company [20–25 min]**

Skylark Design, Inc., is a Web site design and consulting firm. The firm uses a job order costing system in which each client is a different job. Skylark Design traces direct labor, licensing costs, and travel costs directly to each job. It allocates indirect costs to jobs based on a predetermined indirect cost allocation rate, computed as a percentage of direct labor costs.

At the beginning of 2013, managing partner Judi Jacquin prepared the following budget estimates:

| | |
|---|---:|
| Direct labor hours (professional) . . . . . . | 8,000  hours |
| Direct labor costs (professional) . . . . . . . | $2,000,000 |
| Support staff salaries . . . . . . . . . . . . . . | 664,000 |
| Computer leases . . . . . . . . . . . . . . . . . . | 47,000 |
| Office supplies . . . . . . . . . . . . . . . . . . | 23,000 |
| Office rent . . . . . . . . . . . . . . . . . . . . . | 66,000 |

In November 2013, Skylark Design served several clients. Records for two clients appear here:

| | Food Coop | Martin Chocolates |
|---|---:|---:|
| Direct labor hours . . . . . . . . | 900  hours | 100  hours |
| Software licensing costs . . . . | $   3,500 | $   100 |
| Travel costs . . . . . . . . . . . . | 11,000 | — |

**Requirements**

1. Compute Skylark Design's direct labor rate and its predetermined indirect cost allocation rate for 2012.

2. Compute the total cost of each job.

3. If Jacquin wants to earn profits equal to 50% of sales revenue, how much (what fee) should she charge each of these two clients?

4. Why does Skylark Design assign costs to jobs?

# ● Continuing Exercise

**E17-36** ③ ④ **Accounting for manufacturing overhead [25–35 min]**                    *MyAccountingLab*

This exercise continues the Lawlor Lawn Service, Inc., situation from Exercise 16-34 of Chapter 16. Lawlor completed a special landscaping job for Sheldon's Ideal Designs. Lawlor collected the following data about the job:

| Sheldon job details: | |
|---|---|
| Direct materials | $  700 |
| Direct labor | $1,200 |

**Requirements**

1. Lawlor allocates overhead costs based on 60% of direct labor cost. What is the total cost of the Sheldon job?

2. If the price Sheldon paid for the job is $3,460, what is the profit or loss on the job?

## ● Continuing Problem

MyAccountingLab **P17-37** ❸ ❹ **Accounting for manufacturing overhead [25–35 min]**
This problem continues the Draper Consulting, Inc., situation from Problem 16-35 of Chapter 16. Draper Consulting uses a job order costing system in which each client is a different job. Draper traces direct labor, daily per diem, and travel costs directly to each job. It allocates indirect costs to jobs based on a predetermined indirect cost allocation rate, computed as a percentage of direct labor costs.

At the beginning of 2013, the controller prepared the following budget:

| | |
|---|---|
| Direct labor hours (professional) . . . . . . | 5,500 hours |
| Direct labor costs (professional) . . . . . . . | $990,000 |
| Support staff salaries . . . . . . . . . . . . . . | 105,000 |
| Computer leases . . . . . . . . . . . . . . . . . . | 48,000 |
| Office supplies . . . . . . . . . . . . . . . . . . | 15,000 |
| Office rent . . . . . . . . . . . . . . . . . . . . | 30,000 |

In November 2013, Draper served several clients. Records for two clients appear here:

| | Tommy's Trains | Marcia's Cookies |
|---|---|---|
| Direct labor hours . . . . . . . . | 730 hours | 300 hours |
| Meal—per diem . . . . . . . . . . | $ 2,600 | $ 600 |
| Travel costs . . . . . . . . . . . . . | 11,000 | 0 |

### Requirements

1. Compute Draper's predetermined indirect cost allocation rate for 2013.
2. Compute the total cost of each job.
3. If Draper wants to earn profits equal to 25% of sales revenue, how much (what fee) should it charge each of these two clients?
4. Why does Draper assign costs to jobs?

# Apply Your Knowledge

## ● Decision Cases

**Decision Case 17-1** Hiebert Chocolate, Ltd., is located in Memphis. The company prepares gift boxes of chocolates for private parties and corporate promotions. Each order contains a selection of chocolates determined by the customer, and the box is designed to the customer's specifications. Accordingly, Hiebert uses a job order costing system and allocates manufacturing overhead based on direct labor cost.

One of Hiebert's largest customers is the Goforth and Leos law firm. This organization sends chocolates to its clients each Christmas and also provides them to employees at the firm's gatherings. The law firm's managing partner, Bob Goforth, placed the client gift order in September for 500 boxes of cream-filled dark chocolates. But Goforth and Leos did not place its December staff-party order until the last week of November. This order was for an additional 100 boxes of chocolates identical to the ones to be distributed to clients.

Hiebert budgeted the cost per box for the original 500-box order as follows:

| | |
|---|---|
| Chocolate, filling, wrappers, box . . . . . . . . . . . . . . . . . . . . . . . . . . . . . . . . | $14.00 |
| Employee time to fill and wrap the box (10 min.) . . . . . . . . . . . | 2.00 |
| Manufacturing overhead . . . . . . . . . . . . . . . . . . . . . . . . . . . . . . . . . . . . . . | 1.00 |
| Total manufacturing cost . . . . . . . . . . . . . . . . . . . . . . . . . . . . . . . . . . . . . | $17.00 |

Ben Hiebert, president of Hiebert Chocolate, Ltd., priced the order at $20 per box.

In the past few months, Hiebert has experienced price increases for both dark chocolate and direct labor. All other costs have remained the same. Hiebert budgeted the cost per box for the second order as follows:

| | |
|---|---:|
| Chocolate, filling, wrappers, box ..................................... | $15.00 |
| Employee time to fill and wrap the box (10 min.) ........... | 2.20 |
| Manufacturing overhead ................................................. | 1.10 |
| Total manufacturing cost ............................................... | $18.30 |

### Requirements

1.  Do you agree with the cost analysis for the second order? Explain your answer.
2.  Should the two orders be accounted for as one job or two in Hiebert's system?
3.  What sale price per box should Ben Hiebert set for the second order? What are the advantages and disadvantages of this price?

**Decision Case 17-2** Nature's Own Garden manufactures organic fruit preserves sold primarily through health food stores and on the Web. The company closes for two weeks each December to enable employees to spend time with their families over the holiday season. Nature's Own Garden's manufacturing overhead is mostly straight-line depreciation on its plant, and air-conditioning costs for keeping the berries cool during the summer months. The company uses direct labor hours as the manufacturing overhead allocation base. President Cynthia Ortega has just approved new accounting software and is telling controller Jack Strong about her decision.

"I think this new software will be great," Ortega says. "It will save you time in preparing all those reports."

"Yes, and having so much more information just a click away will help us make better decisions and help control costs," replies Strong. "We need to consider how we can use the new system to improve our business practices."

"And I know just where to start," says Ortega. "You complain each year about having to predict the weather months in advance for estimating air-conditioning costs to include in the calculation of the predetermined manufacturing overhead rate, when professional meteorologists can't even get tomorrow's forecast right! I think we should calculate the predetermined overhead rate on a monthly basis."

Controller Strong is not so sure this is a good idea.

### Requirements

1.  What are the advantages and disadvantages of Ortega's proposal?
2.  Should Nature's Own Garden compute its predetermined manufacturing overhead rate on an annual basis or monthly basis? Explain.

## ● Ethical Issue 17-1

Farley, Inc., is a manufacturer that produces customized computer components for several well-known computer-assembly companies. Farley's latest contract with CompWest.com calls for Farley to deliver sound cards that simulate surround sound from two speakers. Farley spent several hundred thousand dollars to design the sound card to meet CompWest.com's specifications.

Farley's president, Bryon Wilson, has stipulated a pricing policy that requires the bid price for a new job to be based on Farley's estimated costs to design, manufacture, distribute, and provide customer service for the job, plus a profit margin. Upon reviewing the contract figures, Farley's controller, Paul York, was startled to find that the cost estimates developed by Farley's cost accountant, Tony Hayes, for the CompWest.com bid were based on only the manufacturing costs. York is upset with Hayes. He is not sure what to do next.

### Requirements

1. How did using manufacturing cost only, instead of using all costs associated with the CompWest.com job, affect the amount of Farley's bid for the job?
2. Identify the parties involved in Paul York's dilemma. What are his alternatives? How would each party be affected by each alternative? What should York do next?

## ● Fraud Case 17-1

Jerry never imagined he'd be sitting there in Washington being grilled mercilessly by a panel of congressmen. But a young government auditor picked up on his scheme last year. His company produced hi-tech navigation devices that were sold to both military and civilian clients. The military contracts were "cost-plus," meaning that payments were calculated based on actual production costs plus a profit markup. The civilian contracts were bid out in a very competitive market, and every dollar counted. Jerry knew that because all the jobs were done in the same factory, he could manipulate the allocation of overhead costs in a way that would shift costs away from the civilian contracts and into the military "cost-plus" work. That way, the company would collect more from the government and be able to shave its bids down on civilian work. He never thought anyone would discover the alterations he had made in the factory workers' time sheets, but one of his accountants had noticed and tipped off the government auditor. Now as the congressman from Michigan rakes him over the coals, Jerry is trying to figure out his chances of dodging jail time.

### Requirements

1. Based on what you have read above, what was Jerry's company using as a cost driver to allocate overhead to the various jobs?
2. Name two ways that reducing costs on the civilian contracts would benefit the company.

## ● Team Project 17-1

Major airlines like **American**, **Delta**, and **Continental** are struggling to meet the challenges of budget carriers such as **Southwest** and **JetBlue**. Suppose the **Delta** CFO has just returned from a meeting on strategies for responding to competition from budget carriers. The vice president of operations suggested doing nothing: "We just need to wait until these new airlines run out of money. They cannot be making money with their low fares." In contrast, the vice president of marketing, not wanting to lose market share, suggests cutting **Delta's** fares to match the competition. "If **JetBlue** charges only $75 for that flight from New York, so must we!" Others, including the CFO, emphasized the potential for cutting costs. Another possibility is starting a new budget airline within **Delta**. The CEO cut the meeting short, and directed the CFO to "get some hard data."

As a start, the CFO decides to collect cost and revenue data for a typical **Delta** flight, and then compare it to the data for a competitor. Assume she prepares the following schedule:

| | Delta | JetBlue |
|---|---|---|
| Route: New York to Tampa.................. | Flight 1247 | Flight 53 |
| Distance............................... | 1,000 miles | 1,000 miles |
| Seats per plane ...................... | 142 | 162 |
| One-way ticket price............................ | $80–$621* | $75 |
| Food and beverage................................ | Meal | Snack |

*The highest price is first class airfare.

Excluding food and beverage, the CFO estimates that the cost per available seat mile is 8.4 cents for **Delta**, compared to 5.3 cents for **JetBlue**. (That is, the cost of flying a seat for one mile—whether or not the seat is occupied—is 8.4 cents for **Delta**, and 5.3 cents for **JetBlue**.) Assume the average cost of food and beverage is $5 per passenger for snacks and $10 for a meal.

Split your team into two groups. Group 1 should prepare its response to Requirement 1 and group 2 should prepare its response to Requirement 2 before the entire team meets to consider Requirements 3 and 4.

### Requirements

1. Use the data to determine the following for **Delta**:
   a. The total cost of Flight 1247, assuming a full plane (100% load factor)
   b. The revenue generated by Flight 1247, assuming a 100% load factor and average revenue per one-way ticket of $102
   c. The profit per Flight 1247, given the responses to a. and b.

2. Use the data to determine the following for **JetBlue**:
   a. The total cost of Flight 53, assuming a full plane (100% load factor)
   b. The revenue generated by Flight 53, assuming a 100% load factor
   c. The profit per Flight 53, given the responses to a. and b.

3. Based on the responses to Requirements 1 and 2, carefully evaluate each of the four alternative strategies discussed in **Delta**'s executive meeting.

4. The analysis in this project is based on several simplifying assumptions. As a team, brainstorm factors that your quantitative evaluation does not include, but that may affect a comparison of **Delta**'s operations to budget carriers.

## ● Communication Activity 17-1

In 100 words or fewer, explain why we use a predetermined overhead rate instead of waiting to use the "real" rate. In your answer, explain how the rate works with the Manufacturing overhead account.

---

## Quick Check Answers

1. *d* 2. *b* 3. *d* 4. *a* 5. *a* 6. *b* 7. *c* 8. *b* 9. *d* 10. *b*

**For online homework, exercises, and problems that provide you immediate feedback, please visit myaccountinglab.com.**

# Appendix 17A

## Process Costing—Weighted-Average Method

**6** Allocate costs using a process costing system—weighted-average method

We saw in the chapter that companies like **Dell Computer**, **Boeing**, and Smart Touch use job order costing to determine the cost of their custom goods and services. In contrast, **BP Oil**, **Crayola**, and **Sony** use a series of steps (called *processes*) to make large quantities of similar products. These systems are called *process costing* systems. There are two methods for handling process costing: weighted-average and FIFO. We focus on the weighted-average method in this appendix.

To introduce process costing, we will look at the crayon manufacturing process. Let's divide **Crayola**'s manufacturing into three processes: mixing, molding, and packaging. **Crayola** accumulates the costs of each process. The company then assigns these costs to the crayons passing through that process.

Suppose **Crayola**'s production costs incurred to make 10,000 crayons and the costs per crayon are as follows:

|  | Total Costs | Cost per Crayon |
|---|---|---|
| Mixing............................. | $200 | $0.02 |
| Molding........................... | 100 | 0.01 |
| Packaging........................ | 300 | 0.03 |
| Total cost........................ | $600 | $0.06 |

The total cost to produce 10,000 crayons is the sum of the costs incurred for the three processes. The cost per crayon is the total cost divided by the number of crayons, or

$$\$600/10{,}000 = \$0.06 \text{ per crayon}$$

**Crayola** uses the cost per unit of each process to

- control costs. The company can find ways to cut the costs where actual process costs are more than planned process costs.
- set selling prices. The company wants the selling price to cover the costs of making the crayons and it also wants to earn a profit.
- calculate the ending work in process inventory and finished goods inventory of crayons for the balance sheet and the cost of goods sold for the income statement.

At any moment, some crayons are in the mixing process, some are in the molding process, and others are in the packaging process. Computing the crayons' cost becomes more complicated when some of the units are still in process. In this appendix, you will learn how to use process costing to calculate the cost of homogeneous products, using crayons as an example.

Exhibit 17A-1 on the following page compares cost flows in

- a job order costing system for **Dell Computer**, and
- a process costing system for **Crayola**.

**EXHIBIT 17A-1** | **Comparison of Job Order Costing and Process Costing**

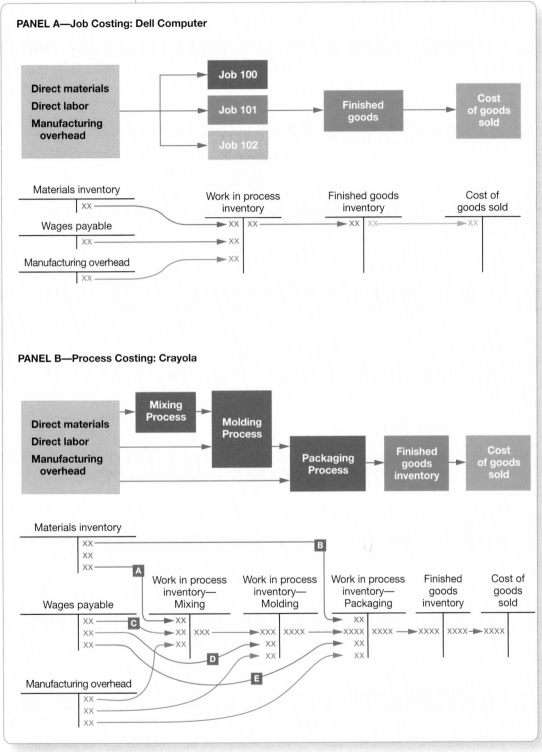

PANEL A—Job Costing: Dell Computer

PANEL B—Process Costing: Crayola

*Letters correspond to Exhibits 17A-2

Panel A shows that **Dell**'s job order costing system has a single Work in process inventory control account. The Work in process inventory account in **Dell**'s general ledger is supported by an individual subsidiary cost record for each job (for example, each custom-built computer). Panel B summarizes the flow of costs for **Crayola**. Notice the following:

1. Each process (mixing, molding, and packaging) is a separate department and each department has its own Work in process inventory account.

2. Direct materials, direct labor, and manufacturing overhead are assigned to Work in process inventory for each process that uses them.

3. When the Mixing Department's process is complete, the wax moves out of the Mixing Department and into the Molding Department. The Mixing Department's cost is also transferred out of Work in process inventory—Mixing into Work in process inventory—Molding.

4. When the Molding Department's process is complete, the finished crayons move from the Molding Department into the Packaging Department. The cost of the crayons flows out of Work in process inventory—Molding into Work in process inventory—Packaging.

5. When production is complete, the boxes of crayons go into finished goods storage. The combined costs from all departments then flow into Finished goods inventory, but only from the Work in process inventory account of the *last manufacturing process* (for **Crayola**, Packaging is the last department).

6. Note that the letters in Exhibit 17A-1 correspond to the letters in Exhibit 17A-2.

Exhibit 17A-2 illustrates this cost flow for **Crayola**.

**EXHIBIT 17A-2** | **Flow of Costs in Production of Crayons**

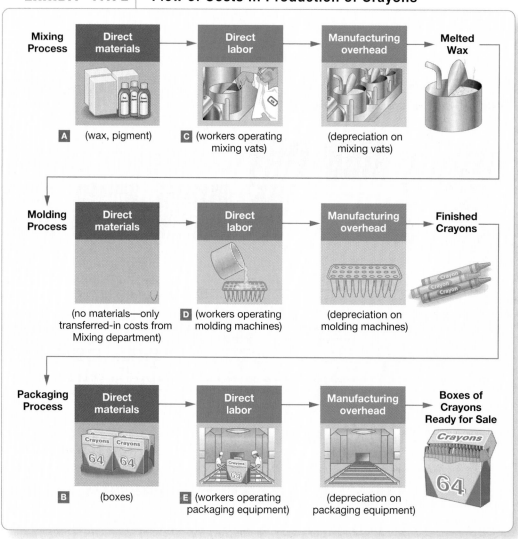

*Note letters correspond to Exhibit 17A-1

# Building Blocks of Process Costing

We use two building blocks for process costing:

- Conversion costs
- Equivalent units of production

Chapter 16 introduced three kinds of manufacturing costs: direct materials, direct labor, and manufacturing overhead. Many companies are highly automated, so direct labor is a small part of total manufacturing costs. Such companies often use only two categories:

- Direct materials
- Conversion costs (direct labor plus manufacturing overhead)

Combining direct labor and manufacturing overhead in a single category simplifies the accounting. We call this category *conversion costs* because it is the cost (direct labor plus manufacturing overhead) to *convert* raw materials into finished products.

Completing most products takes time, so **Crayola** may have work in process inventories for crayons that are only partially completed. The concept of **equivalent units** allows us to measure the amount of work done on a partially finished group of units during a period and to express it in terms of fully complete units of output. Assume **Crayola**'s production plant has 10,000 crayons in ending Work in process inventory—Packaging. Each of the 10,000 crayons is 80% complete. If conversion costs are incurred evenly throughout the process, then getting 10,000 crayons 80% of the way through production is the same amount of work as getting 8,000 crayons 100% of the way through the process (10,000 × 80%).

| Number of partially complete units | × | Percentage of process completed | = | Number of equivalent units |
|:---:|:---:|:---:|:---:|:---:|
| 10,000 | × | 80% | = | 8,000 |

So, ending Work in process inventory has 8,000 equivalent units for conversion costs.

## Stop & Think...

You've ordered three pepperoni pizzas, each cut into eight slices for a party. The pizzas cost $5 each. At the end of the party, the first pizza has two slices left and the second pizza has six slices left. The third pizza box is empty. How many equivalent WHOLE pizzas are still left? Well, you have eight slices in two boxes, so you really have one whole pizza left over that cost $5. That's the concept of equivalent units. So how much was the cost of pizza consumed? Two equivalent pizzas were consumed at $5 each, or $10.*

We use this formula when costs are incurred evenly throughout production. This is usually true for conversion costs. However, direct materials are often added at a specific point in the process. For example, **Crayola**'s wax is added at the beginning of production in the Mixing Department, and packaging materials are added at the end in the Packaging Department. How many equivalent units of wax, conversion costs, and packaging materials are in the ending work in process inventory of 10,000 crayons?

---

*The authors wish to thank Craig Reeder at FAMU for this suggestion.

Look at the timeline in Exhibit 17A-3. The 10,000 crayons in ending work in process inventory have

- 100% of their wax because wax was added at the very beginning. So, they have 10,000 equivalent units of wax. (10,000 × 100% have the wax material.)
- none of their boxes because that is the very last thing that happens in the Packaging Department. So, they have 0 equivalent units of packaging materials. (The crayons have not been packaged yet.)
- 8,000 equivalent units of conversion costs that we completed earlier.

**EXHIBIT 17A-3** | **Crayola Production Plant Timeline**

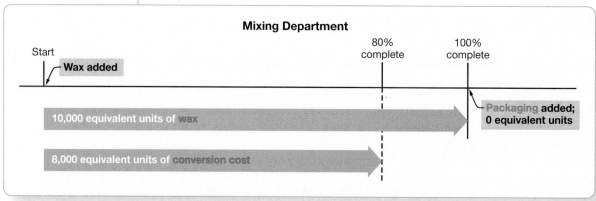

This example illustrates an important point:

> We must compute separate equivalent units for the following:
> - Direct materials
> - Conversion costs

# Process Costing in the First Department with No Beginning Work in Process Inventory

To illustrate process costing, we will use Puzzle Me, a company that recycles calendars into jigsaw puzzles. Exhibit 17A-4 illustrates the two major production processes:

- The Assembly Department applies the glue to cardboard and then presses a calendar page onto the cardboard.
- The Cutting Department cuts the calendar board into puzzle pieces and packages the puzzles in a box. The box is then moved to finished goods storage.

**EXHIBIT 17A-4** | **Flow of Costs in Producing Puzzles**

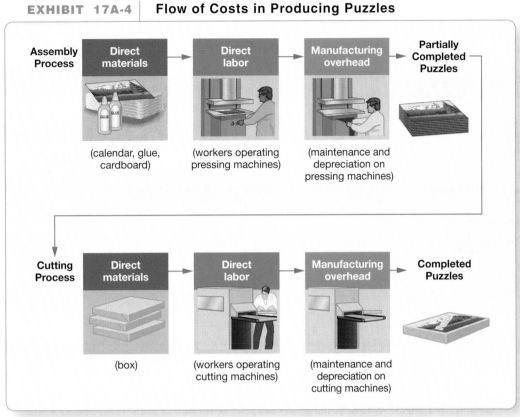

The production process uses materials, machines, and labor in both departments, and there are two Work in process inventory accounts: one for the Assembly Department and one for the Cutting Department.

During July, Puzzle Me incurred the costs shown in Exhibit 17A-5.

**EXHIBIT 17A-5** | **Puzzle Me Production Costs for July**

|  | Assembly Dept | Cutting Dept |
| --- | --- | --- |
| Units: |  |  |
| Beginning WIP—units | 0 | 5,000 |
| Started in production | 50,000 | must calculate |
| Transferred out in July | 40,000 | 38,000 |
|  |  |  |
| Beginning WIP—% complete | N/A | 60% |
| Ending WIP—% complete | 25% | 30% |
|  |  |  |
| Costs: |  |  |
| Beginning WIP—Transferred in costs | $      0 | $22,000 |
| Beginning WIP—Materials costs | $      0 | $      0 |
| Beginning WIP—Conversion costs | $      0 | $  1,200 |
| Direct materials | $140,000 | $19,000 |
| Conversion costs: |  |  |
| Direct labor | $  20,000 | $  3,840 |
| Manufacturing overhead | $  48,000 | $11,000 |
| Total conversion costs | $  68,000 | $14,840 |

The accounting period ends before all of the puzzle boards are made. Exhibit 17A-6 shows a timeline for the Assembly Department.

**EXHIBIT 17A-6 | Puzzle Me's Assembly Department Timeline**

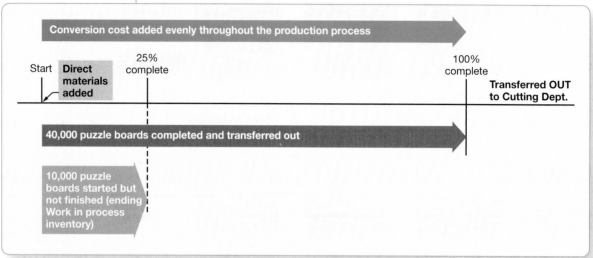

The four steps to process costing are as follows:

> - Step 1: Summarize the flow of physical units.
> - Step 2: Compute output in terms of equivalent units.
> - Step 3: Compute the cost per equivalent unit.
> - Step 4: Assign costs to units completed and to units still in ending Work in process inventory.

- "Units to account for" include the number of puzzle boards still in process at the beginning of July plus the number of puzzle boards started during July.
- "Units accounted for" shows what happened to the puzzle boards in process during July. We want to take the July costs incurred in each department and allocate them to the puzzle boards completed and to the puzzle boards still in process at the end of July.

Of the 50,000 puzzle boards started by the Assembly Department in July, 40,000 were completed and transferred out to the Cutting Department. The remaining 10,000 are only partially completed. These partially complete units are the Assembly Department's ending Work in process inventory on July 31.

The Assembly Department timeline in Exhibit 17A-6 shows that all direct materials are added at the beginning of the process. In contrast, conversion costs are incurred evenly throughout the process. This is because labor and overhead production activities occur daily. Thus, we must compute equivalent units separately for the following:

- Direct materials
- Conversion costs

The Assembly Department worked on 50,000 puzzle boards during July, as shown in Exhibit 17A-7. As Exhibit 17A-8 shows, 40,000 puzzle boards are now complete for both materials and conversion costs. Another 10,000 puzzle boards are only 25% complete. How many equivalent units did Assembly produce during July?

## Equivalent Units for Materials

Equivalent units for materials total 50,000 (**A** and **D**) because all the direct materials have been added to all 50,000 units worked on during July.

# Equivalent Units for Conversion Costs

Equivalent units for conversion costs total 42,500 (**G**). Conversion costs are complete for the 40,000 (**E**) puzzle boards completed and transferred out. But only 25% of the conversion work has been done on the 10,000 puzzle boards in ending Work in process inventory. Therefore, ending Work in process inventory represents only 2,500 (**F**) equivalent units for conversion costs.

Exhibits 17A-7 and 17A-8 summarize steps 1 and 2.

The cost per equivalent unit requires information about total costs and equivalent units. The computations are as follows:

$$\text{Cost per equivalent unit for direct materials} = \frac{\text{Total direct materials cost}}{\text{Equivalent units of materials}}$$

$$\text{Cost per equivalent unit for conversion costs} = \frac{\text{Total conversion cost}}{\text{Equivalent units for conversion}}$$

Exhibit 17A-5, presented earlier, summarizes the total costs to account for in the Assembly Department. The Assembly Department has 50,000 physical units and $208,000 of costs to account for. Our next task is to split these costs between the following:

- 40,000 puzzle boards transferred out to the Cutting Department

- 10,000 partially complete puzzle boards that remain in the Assembly Department's ending Work in process inventory

In step 2, we computed equivalent units for direct materials (50,000 (**D**)) and conversion costs (42,500 (**G**)). Because the equivalent units differ, we must compute a separate cost per unit for direct materials and for conversion costs. Exhibit 17A-5 shows that the direct materials costs are $140,000 (**H** + **I** = **J**). Conversion costs are $68,000 (**L** + **M** = **N**), which is the sum of direct labor of $20,000 and manufacturing overhead of $48,000.

The cost per equivalent unit of material is $2.80 (**J** ÷ **D** = **K**), and the cost per equivalent unit of conversion cost is $1.60 (**N** ÷ **G** = **O**), as shown in Exhibit 17A-9.

We must determine how much of the $208,000 total costs to be accounted for by the Assembly Department should be assigned to

- the 40,000 completed puzzle boards that have been transferred out to the Cutting Department.

- the 10,000 partially completed puzzle boards remaining in the Assembly Department's ending Work in process inventory.

Exhibit 17A-10 shows how to assign costs.

The total cost of completed puzzle boards for the Assembly Department is $176,000 (**P**), as shown in Exhibit 17A-10. The $176,000 is the sum of ($112,000 (**B** × **K**)) and conversion costs ($64,000 (**E** × **O**)). The cost of the 10,000 partially completed puzzle boards in ending Work in process inventory is $32,000 (**Q**), which is the sum of direct material costs ($28,000 (**C** × **K**)) and conversion costs ($4,000 (**F** × **O**)) allocated in Exhibit 17A-10.

Exhibit 17A-10 has accomplished our goal of splitting the $208,000 total cost between the following:

| | |
|---|---|
| The 40,000 puzzles completed and transferred out to the Cutting Department .................................................................................... | $176,000 **P** |
| The 10,000 puzzles remaining in the Assembly Department's ending Work in process inventory on July 31 ($28,000 + $4,000)..... | 32,000 **Q** |
| Total costs of the Assembly Department ............................................ | $208,000 |

**EXHIBIT 17A-7** | Step 1: Summarize Physical Flow of Goods

PUZZLE ME
Cost of Production—ASSEMBLY DEPT.
Month Ended July 31, 2014

| Flow of Production | Whole Units |
|---|---|
| **Step 1: PHYSICAL FLOW** | |
| Units to account for: | |
| Beginning work in process, June 30 | 0 |
| Started in production during July | 50,000 |
| Total physical units to account for | 50,000 A |

Journal entries to record July costs placed into production in the Assembly Department follow (data from Exhibit 17A-5):

| (1) Work in process inventory—Assembly | (A+) | 208,000 | |
|---|---|---|---|
| Materials inventory | (A–) | | 140,000 |
| Wages payable | (L+) | | 20,000 |
| Manufacturing overhead | (E–) | | 48,000 |
| *To assign materials, labor, and overhead cost to Assembly.* | | | |

The entry to transfer the cost of the 40,000 completed puzzles out of the Assembly Department and into the Cutting Department follows (Item **P** from Exhibit 17A-10):

| **P** Work in process inventory—Cutting | (A+) | 176,000 | |
|---|---|---|---|
| Work in process inventory—Assembly | (A–) | | 176,000 |
| *To transfer costs from Assembly to Cutting.* | | | |

After these entries are posted, the Work in process inventory—Assembly account appears as follows:

**Work in process inventory—Assembly**

| | | | | |
|---|---|---|---|---|
| Balance, June 30 | — | Transferred to Cutting | 176,000 | **P** |
| Direct materials | 140,000 | | | |
| Direct labor | 20,000 | | | |
| Manufacturing overhead | 48,000 | | | |
| **Q** Balance, July 31 | 32,000 | | | |

Note that the ending balance is the same $32,000 as item **Q** on Exhibit 17A-10's cost of production report.

# Process Costing in a Second Department

Most products require a series of processing steps. In this section, we consider a second department—Puzzle Me's Cutting Department for July—to complete the picture of process costing.

**EXHIBIT 17A-11** | **Puzzle Me's Cutting Department Timeline**

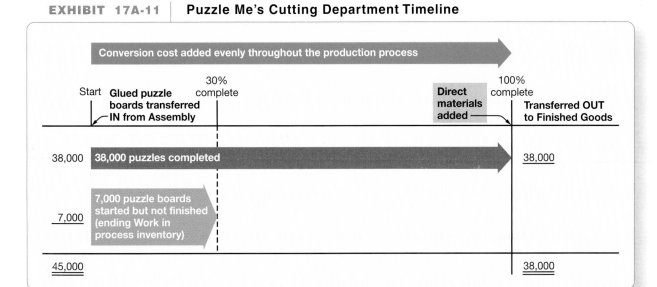

The Cutting Department receives the puzzle boards and cuts the board into puzzle pieces before inserting the pieces into the box at the end of the process. Exhibit 17A-11 shows the following:

- Glued puzzle boards are transferred in from the Assembly Department at the beginning of the Cutting Department's process.
- The Cutting Department's conversion costs are added evenly throughout the process.
- The Cutting Department's direct materials (boxes) are added at the end of the process.

Keep in mind that *direct materials* in the Cutting Department refers to the boxes added *in that department* and not to the materials (cardboard and glue) added in the Assembly Department. The materials from the Assembly Department that are *transferred into* the Cutting Department are called *transferred in costs*. Likewise, *conversion costs* in the Cutting Department refers to the direct labor and manufacturing overhead costs incurred only in the Cutting Department.

Exhibit 17A-5, presented earlier in this appendix, lists July information for both of Puzzle Me's departments. We will be referring to this data as we complete our Cutting Department allocation for July. Remember that Work in process inventory at the close of business on June 30 is both of the following:

- Ending inventory for June
- Beginning inventory for July

Exhibit 17A-5 shows that Puzzle Me's Cutting Department started the July period with 5,000 puzzle boards partially completed through work done in the Cutting Department in June. During July, the Cutting Department started work on 40,000 additional puzzle boards that were received from the Assembly Department (which we calculated earlier in Exhibits 17A-7 through 17A-10).

The weighted-average method combines the Cutting Department's

- work done last month—beginning Work in process inventory—to start the Cutting process on the 5,000 puzzle boards that were in beginning Work in process inventory.
- work done in July to complete the 5,000 puzzle boards in beginning Work in process inventory and to work on the 40,000 additional puzzle boards that were transferred in from the Assembly Department during July.

Thus, the **weighted-average process costing method** determines the average cost of all the Cutting Department's equivalent units of work on these 45,000 (**A**) puzzle boards (5,000 beginning Work in process inventory + 40,000 (**B** and **E**) transferred in from the previous department).

Just as we did for the Assembly Department, our goal is to split the total cost in the Cutting Department between the following:

- 38,000 puzzles that the Cutting Department completed and transferred out to Finished goods inventory
- 7,000 partially completed puzzles remaining in the Cutting Department's ending Work in process inventory at the end of July

We use the same four-step costing procedure that we used for the Assembly Department.

STEP 1: **Summarize the Flow of Physical Units**   Let's account for July production, using the data about physical units given in Exhibit 17A-5 and the results from Exhibit 17A-10 for the Assembly Department.

We must account for these 45,000 units (**A**) (beginning Work in process inventory of 5,000 plus 40,000 started). Exhibit 17A-12, Step 1 on the following page shows this.

Exhibit 17A-12, Step 2 shows that, of the 45,000 units to account for, Puzzle Me completed and transferred out 38,000 units. That left 7,000 units as ending Work in process inventory in the Cutting Department on July 31. Steps 2 and 3 will help us determine the costs of these units.

STEP 2: **Compute Equivalent Units**   Exhibit 17A-12, Step 2 computes the Cutting Department's equivalent units of work. Under the weighted-average method, Puzzle Me computes the equivalent units for the total work done to date. This includes all the work done in the current period (July), plus the work done last period (June) on the beginning Work in process inventory.

**EXHIBIT 17A-12** | Cost of Production—Second Department

**PUZZLE ME**
**Cost of Production—CUTTING DEPT.**
**Month Ended July 31, 2014**

**Flow of Production**

| 1 Step 1: PHYSICAL FLOW | Whole Units |
|---|---|
| Units to account for: | |
| Beginning work in process, June 30 (from Exhibit 17A-5) | 5,000 |
| Started in production during July (from Exhibit 17A-10) | 40,000 **B E** |
| Total physical units to account for | 45,000 **A** |

| 2 Step 2: EQUIVALENT UNITS | Whole Units | Transferred In | Direct Materials | Conversion Costs |
|---|---|---|---|---|
| Units accounted for: | | | | |
| Completed and transferred out during July (from Exhibit 17A-5) | 38,000 | 38,000 **B** | 38,000 **E** | 38,000 **H** |
| Ending work in process, July 31 | 7,000 | $7,000 \times 100\% = 7,000$ **C** | $7,000 \times 0\% = 0$ **F** | $7,000 \times 30\% = 2,100$ **I** |
| Total physical units to be assigned costs | 45,000 **A** | 45,000 **D** | 38,000 **G** | 40,100 **J** |

| 3 Step 3: COST PER EQUIVALENT UNIT | Transferred In | Direct Materials | Conversion Costs | Total Costs |
|---|---|---|---|---|
| Units Costs: | | | | |
| Beginning work in process, June 30 (from Exhibit 17A-5) | $ 22,000 **K** | $ 0 **N** | $ 1,200 **S** | $ 23,200 |
| Costs added during July (from Exhibit 17A-5) | $176,000 **P** | $19,000 **O** | $14,840 **T** | $209,840 |
| Total costs to account for | $198,000 **K+P=L** | $19,000 **N+O=P** | $16,040 **S+T=U** | $233,040 |
| Total equivalent units | ÷ 45,000 **D** | ÷ 38,000 **G** | ÷ 40,100 **J** | |
| Cost per equivalent unit | $ 4.40 **L÷D=M** | $ 0.50 **P÷G=R** | $ 0.40 **U÷J=W** | $ 5.30 |

| 4 Step 4: ASSIGN COSTS | Transferred In | Direct Materials | Conversion Costs | Total Costs |
|---|---|---|---|---|
| Completed and transferred out during July | $38,000 \times \$4.40 = \$167,200$ **B×M** | $38,000 \times \$0.50 = \$19,000$ **E×R** | $38,000 \times \$0.40 = \$15,200$ **H×W** | $201,400 **X** |
| Ending work in process, July 31 | $7,000 \times \$4.40 = \$ 30,800$ **C×M** | $0 \times \$0.50 = \$ 0$ **F×R** | $2,100 \times \$0.40 = \$ 840$ **I×W** | $ 31,640 **Y** |
| Total costs accounted for | | | | $233,040 |

We can see in Exhibit 17A-12, Step 2 that the total equivalent units with respect to

- transferred-in costs include all 45,000 ( **D** ) units because they are complete with respect to work done in the Assembly Department. The equivalent units for transferred-in costs will always be 100% of the units to account for, because these units must be 100% complete on previous work before coming to the Cutting Department.
- direct materials include only the 38,000 ( **E** ) finished puzzles because Cutting Department materials (boxes) are added at the end.
- conversion costs include the 38,000 ( **H** ) finished puzzles plus the 2,100 ( **I** ) puzzles (7,000 puzzle boards × 30%) that are still in process at the end of the month. Conversion work occurs evenly throughout the cutting process.

Exhibit 17A-12, Step 3 accumulates the Cutting Department's total costs to account for. In addition to direct material and conversion costs, the Cutting Department must account for transferred-in costs. **Transferred-in costs** are those costs that were incurred in a previous process (the Assembly Department, in this case) and brought into a later process (the Cutting Department) as part of the product's cost.

Exhibit 17A-12, Step 3 shows that the Cutting Department's total cost to account for ($233,040) is the sum of the following:

- The cost incurred in June to start the Cutting process on the 5,000 puzzles in Cutting's beginning Work in process inventory ($22,000 + $0 + $1,200) ( **K** + **N** + **S** )
- The costs added to Work in process inventory—Cutting during July ($209,840 = $176,000 ( **P** ) transferred in from the Assembly Department + $19,000 ( **O** ) direct materials added in the Cutting Department + $14,840 ( **T** ) conversion costs added in the Cutting Department)

Exhibit 17A-12, Step 3 also shows the cost per equivalent unit. For each cost category, we divide total cost by the number of equivalent units. Perform this computation for all cost categories: transferred-in costs, direct materials, and conversion costs. In this illustration, the total cost per equivalent unit is $5.30 ($4.40 ( **M** )+ $0.50 ( **R** ) + $0.40 ( **W** )).

Exhibit 17A-12, Step 4 shows how Puzzle Me assigns the total Cutting Department costs of $233,040 to

- units completed and transferred out to Finished goods inventory ($201,400 ( **X** )).
- units remaining in the Cutting Department's ending Work in process inventory ($31,640 ( **Y** )).

We use the same approach as we used for the Assembly Department in Exhibit 17A-10. Multiply the number of equivalent units from Step 2 by the cost per equivalent unit from Step 3.

Exhibit 17A-13 shows how Exhibit 17A-12 divided the Cutting Department's costs.

The Cutting Department's journal entries previously recorded the $176,000 in transferred-in costs of puzzle boards from the Assembly Department into the Cutting Department on page 865.

The following entry records the Cutting Department's other costs during July (data from Exhibit 17A-5):

| | | | | |
|---|---|---|---|---|
| (2) | Work in process inventory—Cutting (A+) | | 33,840 | |
| | Materials inventory (A−) | | | 19,000 |
| | Wages payable (L+) | | | 3,840 |
| | Manufacturing overhead (E−) | | | 11,000 |
| | *To assign materials and conversion costs to the Cutting Dept.* | | | |

The entry to transfer the cost of completed puzzles out of the Cutting Department and into Finished goods inventory is based on the dollar amount in Exhibit 17A-12:

| | | | | |
|---|---|---|---|---|
| **X** | Finished goods inventory (A+) | | 201,400 | |
| | Work in process inventory—Cutting (A−) | | | 201,400 |
| | *To transfer costs from the Cutting Dept. to Finished goods.* | | | |

EXHIBIT 17A-13 | **Assigning Cutting Department Costs to Units Completed and Transferred Out, and to Ending Work in Process Inventory**

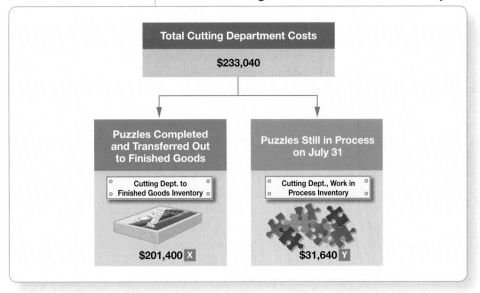

After posting, the key accounts appear as follows:

**Work in process inventory—Assembly**

| (Exhibit 17A-10) | | | |
|---|---|---|---|
| Balance, June 30 | — | Transferred to Cutting | 176,000 P |
| I Direct materials | 140,000 | | |
| M Direct labor | 20,000 | | |
| M Manufacturing overhead | 48,000 | | |
| Q Balance, July 31 | 32,000 | | |

**Work in process inventory—Cutting**

| Balance, June 30 | 23,200 | Transferred to Finished | |
|---|---|---|---|
| P Transferred in from Assembly | 176,000 | goods inventory | 201,400 X |
| O Direct materials | 19,000 | | |
| T Direct labor | 3,840 | | |
| T Manufacturing overhead | 11,000 | | |
| Y Balance, July 31 | 31,640 | | |

**Finished goods inventory**

| Balance, June 30 | 0 | | |
|---|---|---|---|
| X Transferred in from Cutting | 201,400 | | |

As we saw earlier in this chapter, accountants prepare cost reports to help production managers evaluate the efficiency of their manufacturing operations. Both job order and process costing are similar in that they

- *accumulate* costs as the product moves through production.
- *assign* costs to the units (such as gallons of gasoline or number of crayons) passing through that process.

The difference between job order costing and process costing lies in the way costs are accumulated. Job order costing uses a *job cost sheet* and process costing uses a *production cost report*. (See Exhibits 17A-10 and 17A-12 that we completed for the Assembly and Cutting Departments.)

The **production cost report** in Exhibit 17A-12 summarizes Puzzle Me's Cutting Department operations during July. The report combines the costs to account for and the cost per equivalent unit. It shows how those costs were assigned to the puzzles completed and transferred out of the Cutting Department ($201,400) and how much of the costs were assigned to ending Work in process inventory remaining in the department ($31,640).

How do managers use the production cost report?

- Controlling cost: Puzzle Me uses product cost data to reduce costs. A manager may decide that the company needs to change either suppliers or a certain component to reduce the cost of its materials. To reduce labor costs, it may need either different employee skill levels paid at different hourly rates or new production equipment.
- Evaluating performance: Managers are often rewarded based on how well they meet the budget. Puzzle Me compares the actual direct materials and conversion costs with expected amounts. If actual costs are too high, managers look for ways to cut. If actual costs are less than expected, the Cutting Department's managers may receive a bonus.
- Pricing products: Puzzle Me must set its selling price high enough to cover the manufacturing cost of each puzzle ($5.30 = $4.40 + $0.50 + $0.40 in Exhibit 17A-12) plus marketing and distribution costs.
- Identifying the most profitable products: Selling price and cost data help managers figure out which products are most profitable. They can then promote these products.
- Preparing the financial statements: Finally, the production cost report aids financial reporting. It provides inventory data for the balance sheet and cost of goods sold for the income statement.

# Appendix 17A Assignments

## ● Short Exercises

**S17A-1** ⑥ **Calculating conversion costs and unit cost [5–10 min]**

Spring Fresh produces premium bottled water. Spring Fresh purchases artesian water, stores the water in large tanks, and then runs the water through two processes: filtration and bottling.

During February, the filtration process incurred the following costs in processing 150,000 liters:

| | |
|---|---|
| Wages of workers operating the filtration equipment . . . . . . | $ 25,950 |
| Manufacturing overhead allocated to filtration . . . . . . . . . . | 20,050 |
| Water . . . . . . . . . . . . . . . . . . . . . . . . . . . . . . . . . . . . . . . . | 80,000 |

Spring Fresh had no beginning Work in process inventory in the Filtration Department in February.

### Requirements

1. Compute the February conversion costs in the Filtration Department.
2. The Filtration Department completely processed 150,000 liters in February. What was the filtration cost per liter?

*Note: Short Exercise 17A-1 must be completed before attempting Short Exercise 17A-2.*

**S17A-2** ⑥ **Drawing a timeline, and computing equivalent units [10 min]**

Refer to S17A-1. At Spring Fresh, water is added at the beginning of the filtration process. Conversion costs are added evenly throughout the process. Now assume that in February, 130,000 liters were completed and transferred out of the Filtration

Department into the Bottling Department. The 20,000 liters remaining in Filtration's ending Work in process inventory were 80% of the way through the filtration process. Recall that Spring Fresh has no beginning inventories.

## Requirements

1. Draw a timeline for the filtration process.
2. Compute the equivalent units of direct materials and conversion costs for the Filtration Department.

**S17A-3    ⑥ Computing equivalent units [5 min]**
The Mixing Department of Foods for You had 65,000 units to account for in October. Of the 65,000 units, 35,000 units were completed and transferred to the next department, and 30,000 units were 40% complete. All of the materials are added at the beginning of the process. Conversion costs are added equally throughout the mixing process.

## Requirement

1. Compute the total equivalent units of direct materials and conversion costs for October.

*Note: Short Exercise 17A-3 must be completed before attempting Short Exercise 17A-4.*

**S17A-4    ⑥ Computing the cost per equivalent unit [5 min]**
Refer to the data in S17A-3 and your results for equivalent units. The Mixing Department of Foods for You has direct materials costs of $20,800 and conversion costs of $23,500 for October.

## Requirement

1. Compute the cost per equivalent unit for direct materials and for conversion costs.

*Note: Short Exercises 17A-3 and 17A-4 must be completed before attempting Short Exercise 17A-5.*

**S17A-5    ⑥ Computing cost of units transferred out and units in ending work in process [5 min]**
Refer to S17A-3 and S17A-4. Use Food for You's costs per equivalent unit for direct materials and conversion costs that you calculated in S17A-4.

## Requirement

1. Calculate the cost of the 35,000 units completed and transferred out and the 30,000 units, 40% complete, in the ending Work in process inventory.

# • Exercises

**E17A-6**    ⑥ **Drawing a timeline, computing equivalent units, and assigning cost to completed units and ending work in process; no beginning work in process inventory or cost transferred in [20 min]**

Crafty Paint prepares and packages paint products. Crafty Paint has two departments: (1) Blending and (2) Packaging. Direct materials are added at the beginning of the blending process (dyes) and at the end of the packaging process (cans). Conversion costs are added evenly throughout each process. Data from the month of May for the Blending Department are as follows:

| Gallons: | | |
|---|---|---|
| Beginning work in process inventory | 0 | |
| Started production | 9,000 | gallons |
| Completed and transferred out to Packaging in May | 4,000 | gallons |
| Ending work in process inventory (30% of the way through | | |
| blending process) | 5,000 | gallons |
| Costs: | | |
| Beginning work in process inventory | $ 0 | |
| Costs added during May: | | |
| Direct materials | 6,750 | |
| Direct labor | 1,300 | |
| Manufacturing overhead | 2,000 | |
| Total costs added during May | $10,050 | |

## Requirements

1. Fill in the timeline for the Blending Department.
2. Use the timeline to help you compute the Blending Department's equivalent units for direct materials and for conversion costs.
3. Compute the total costs of the units (gallons)
   a. completed and transferred out to the Packaging Department.
   b. in the Blending Department ending Work in process inventory.

*Note: Exercise 17A-6 must be completed before attempting Exercise 17A-7.*

**E17A-7**    ⑥ **Preparing journal entries and posting to work in process T-accounts [15 min]**
Refer to your answers from E17A-6.

## Requirements

1. Prepare the journal entries to record the assignment of direct materials and direct labor, and the allocation of manufacturing overhead to the Blending Department. Also, prepare the journal entry to record the costs of the gallons completed and transferred out to the Packaging Department.
2. Post the journal entries to the Work in process inventory—Blending T-account. What is the ending balance?
3. What is the average cost per gallon transferred out of Blending into Packaging? Why would the company managers want to know this cost?

**E17A-8**    ⑥ **Drawing a timeline, computing equivalent units, and assigning cost to completed units and ending work in process; no beginning work in process inventory or cost transferred in [20 min]**
Samson Winery in Pleasant Valley, New York, has two departments: Fermenting and Packaging. Direct materials are added at the beginning of the fermenting process (grapes) and at the end of the packaging process (bottles). Conversion costs are

added evenly throughout each process. Data from the month of March for the Fermenting Department are as follows:

| Gallons: | |
|---|---|
| Beginning work in process inventory | 0 |
| Started production | 9,100 gallons |
| Completed and transferred out to Packaging in March | 7,900 gallons |
| Ending work in process inventory (80% of the way through fermenting process) | 1,200 gallons |
| Costs: | |
| Beginning work in process inventory | $     0 |
| Costs added during March: | |
| Direct materials | 9,828 |
| Direct labor | 3,500 |
| Manufacturing overhead | 3,588 |
| Total costs added during March | $16,916 |

## Requirements

1. Draw a timeline for the Fermenting Department.
2. Use the timeline to help you compute the equivalent units for direct materials and for conversion costs.
3. Compute the total costs of the units (gallons)
   a. completed and transferred out to the Packaging Department.
   b. in the Fermenting Department ending Work in process inventory.

*Note: Exercise 17A-8 must be completed before attempting Exercise 17A-9.*

**E17A-9**  ⑥ **Preparing journal entries and posting to work in process T-accounts [15 min]**
Refer to the data and your answers from E17A-8.

## Requirements

1. Prepare the journal entries to record the assignment of Direct materials and Direct labor and the allocation of Manufacturing overhead to the Fermenting Department. Also prepare the journal entry to record the cost of the gallons completed and transferred out to the Packaging Department.
2. Post the journal entries to the Work in process inventory—Fermenting T-account. What is the ending balance?
3. What is the average cost per gallon transferred out of Fermenting into Packaging? Why would Samson Winery's managers want to know this cost?

**E17A-10** ⑥ **Computing equivalent units, computing cost per equivalent unit; assigning costs; journalizing; second department, weighted-average method [25–30 min]**
Cool Spring Company produces premium bottled water. In the second department, the Bottling Department, conversion costs are incurred evenly throughout the bottling process, but packaging materials are not added until the end of the process. Costs in beginning Work in process inventory include transferred in costs of $1,700,

direct labor of $700, and manufacturing overhead of $330. February data for the Bottling Department follow:

| COOL SPRING COMPANY Work in process inventory—Bottling Month Ended February 28, 2013 | | | | | | |
|---|---|---|---|---|---|---|
| | Physical Units | Dollars | | | Physical Units | Dollars |
| Beginning inventory, January 31 (40% complete) | 12,000 | $ 2,730 | Transferred out | | 152,000 | $ ? |
| Production started: | | | | | | |
|    Transferred in | 163,000 | 134,800 | | | | |
|    Direct materials | | 30,400 | | | | |
|    Conversion costs: | | | | | | |
|      Direct labor | | 33,100 | | | | |
|      Manufacturing overhead | | 16,300 | | | | |
| Total to account for | 175,000 | $217,330 | | | | |
| Ending inventory, February 28 (70% complete) | 23,000 | $ ? | | | | |

### Requirements

1. Compute the Bottling Department equivalent units for the month of February. Use the weighted-average method.

2. Compute the cost per equivalent unit for February.

3. Assign the costs to units completed and transferred out and to ending Work in process inventory.

4. Prepare the journal entry to record the cost of units completed and transferred out.

5. Post all transactions to the Work in process inventory—Bottling Department T-account. What is the ending balance?

## • Problems (Group A)

**MyAccountingLab**

**P17A-11A** ⑥ **Computing equivalent units and assigning costs to completed units and ending work in process; no beginning work in process inventory or cost transferred in [30–45 min]**

Amy Electronics makes CD players in three processes: assembly, programming, and packaging. Direct materials are added at the beginning of the assembly process. Conversion costs are incurred evenly throughout the process. The Assembly Department had no Work in process inventory on October 31. In mid-November, Amy Electronics started production on 125,000 CD players. Of this number, 95,800 CD players were assembled during November and transferred out to the Programming Department. The November 30 Work in process inventory in the Assembly Department was 25% of the way through the assembly process. Direct materials costing $437,500 were placed in production in Assembly during November, and Direct labor of $200,800 and Manufacturing overhead of $134,275 were assigned to that department.

### Requirements

1. Compute the number of equivalent units and the cost per equivalent unit in the Assembly Department for November.

2. Assign total costs in the Assembly Department to (a) units completed and transferred to Programming during November and (b) units still in process at November 30.

3. Prepare a T-account for Work in process inventory—Assembly to show its activity during November, including the November 30 balance.

**P17A-12A** ⑥ **Computing equivalent units and assigning costs to completed units and ending work in process; no beginning work in process inventory or cost transferred in [30–45 min]**

Reed Paper, Co., produces the paper used by wallpaper manufacturers. Reed's four-stage process includes mixing, cooking, rolling, and cutting. During March, the Mixing Department started and completed mixing for 4,520 rolls of paper. The department started but did not finish the mixing for an additional 500 rolls, which were 20% complete with respect to both direct materials and conversion work at the end of March. Direct materials and conversion costs are incurred evenly throughout the mixing process. The Mixing Department incurred the following costs during March:

**Work in process inventory—Mixing**

| | |
|---|---|
| Bal, Mar 1 | 0 |
| Direct materials | 5,775 |
| Direct labor | 620 |
| Manufacturing overhead | 6,310 |

## Requirements

1. Compute the number of equivalent units and the cost per equivalent unit in the Mixing Department for March.

2. Show that the sum of (a) cost of goods transferred out of the Mixing Department and (b) ending Work in process inventory—Mixing equals the total cost accumulated in the department during March.

3. Journalize all transactions affecting the company's mixing process during March, including those already posted.

**P17A-13A** ⑥ **Computing equivalent units and assigning costs to completed units and ending work in process inventory; two materials, added at different points; no beginning work in process inventory or cost transferred in [30–45 min]**

Smith's Exteriors produces exterior siding for homes. The Preparation Department begins with wood, which is chopped into small bits. At the end of the process, an adhesive is added. Then the wood/adhesive mixture goes on to the Compression Department, where the wood is compressed into sheets. Conversion costs are added evenly throughout the preparation process. January data for the Preparation Department are as follows:

| Sheets | | Costs | |
|---|---|---|---|
| Beginning work in process inventory | 0 sheets | Beginning work in process inventory | $ 0 |
| Started production | 3,700 sheets | Costs adding during January: | |
| Completed and transferred out to | | Wood | 3,108 |
|    Compression in January | 2,000 sheets | Adhesives | 1,240 |
| | | Direct labor | 558 |
| Ending work in process inventory (30% | | Manufacturing overhead | 1,450 |
|    of the way through preparation process) | 1,700 sheets | Total costs | $ 6,356 |

## Requirements

1. Draw a timeline for the Preparation Department.

2. Use the timeline to help you compute the equivalent. (*Hint*: Each direct material added at a different point in the production process requires its own equivalent-unit computation.)

3. Compute the total costs of the units (sheets)
   a. completed and transferred out to the Compression Department.
   b. in the Preparation Department's ending Work in process inventory.

4. Prepare the journal entry to record the cost of the sheets completed and transferred out to the Compression Department.

5. Post the journal entries to the Work in process inventory—Preparation T-account. What is the ending balance?

**P17A-14A** ⑥ **Computing equivalent units for a second department with beginning work in process inventory; preparing a production cost report and recording transactions on the basis of the report's information; weighted-average method [45–60 min]**

Christine Carpet manufactures broadloom carpet in seven processes: spinning, dyeing, plying, spooling, tufting, latexing, and shearing. In the Dyeing Department, direct materials (dye) are added at the beginning of the process. Conversion costs are incurred evenly throughout the process. Christine uses weighted-average process costing. Information for November 2012 follows:

| Units: | |
|---|---|
| Beginning work in process inventory | 90 rolls |
| Transferred in from Spinning Department during November | 540 rolls |
| Completed during November | 510 rolls |
| Ending work in process (80% complete as to conversion work) | 120 rolls |
| Costs: | |
| Beginning work in process (transferred-in cost, $4,900; materials cost, $1,390; conversion costs, $4,900) | $ 11,190 |
| Transferred in from Spinning Department during November | 22,190 |
| Materials cost added during November | 11,210 |
| Conversion costs added during November (manufacturing wages, $8,225; manufacturing overhead, $43,839) | 52,064 |

**Requirements**

1. Prepare a timeline for Christine's Dyeing Department.

2. Use the timeline to help you compute the equivalent units, cost per equivalent unit, and total costs to account for in Christine's Dyeing Department for November.

3. Prepare the November production cost report for Christine's Dyeing Department.

4. Journalize all transactions affecting Christine's Dyeing Department during November, including the entries that have already been posted.

**P17A-15A** ⑥ **Computing equivalent units for a second department with beginning work in process inventory; assigning costs to completed units and ending work in process; weighted-average method [50–60 min]**

WaterBound uses three processes to manufacture lifts for personal watercraft: forming a lift's parts from galvanized steel, assembling the lift, and testing the completed lifts. The lifts are transferred to finished goods before shipment to marinas across the country.

WaterBound's Testing Department requires no direct materials. Conversion costs are incurred evenly throughout the testing process. Other information follows:

| Units: | |
|---|---|
| Beginning work in process | 2,000 units |
| Transferred in from the Assembling Dept. during the period | 7,000 units |
| Completed during the period | 4,000 units |
| Ending work in process (40% complete as to conversion work) | 5,000 units |
| Costs: | |
| Beginning work in process (transferred-in cost, $93,000; conversion costs, $18,000) | $ 111,000 |
| Transferred in from the Assembling Dept. during the period | 672,000 |
| Conversion costs added during the period | 54,000 |

The cost transferred into Finished goods inventory is the cost of the lifts transferred out of the Testing Department. WaterBound uses weighted-average process costing.

## Requirements

1. Draw a timeline for the Testing Department.

2. Use the timeline to compute the number of equivalent units of work performed by the Testing Department during the period.

3. Compute WaterBound's transferred-in and conversion costs per equivalent unit. Use the unit costs to assign total costs to (a) units completed and transferred out of Testing and (b) units in Testing's ending Work in process inventory.

4. Compute the cost per unit for lifts completed and transferred out to Finished goods inventory. Why would management be interested in this cost?

## ● Problems (Group B)

**P17A-16B** ⑥ **Computing equivalent units and assigning costs to completed units and ending work in process; no beginning work in process inventory or cost transferred in [30–45 min]**    *MyAccountingLab*

Beth Electronics makes CD players in three processes: assembly, programming, and packaging. Direct materials are added at the beginning of the assembly process. Conversion costs are incurred evenly throughout the process. The Assembly Department had no work in process inventory on March 31. In mid-April, Beth Electronics started production on 115,000 CD players. Of this number, 99,000 CD players were assembled during April and transferred out to the Programming Department. The April 30 work in process inventory in the Assembly Department was 45% of the way through the assembly process. Direct materials costing $345,000 were placed in production in Assembly during April, and direct labor of $150,000 and manufacturing overhead of $62,400 were assigned to that department.

## Requirements

1. Compute the number of equivalent units and the cost per equivalent unit in the Assembly Department for April.

2. Assign total costs in the Assembly Department to (a) units completed and transferred to Programming during April and (b) units still in process at April 30.

3. Prepare a T-account for Work in process inventory—Assembly to show its activity during April, including the April 30 balance.

**P17A-17B** ⑥ **Computing equivalent units and assigning costs to completed units and ending work in process; no beginning work in process inventory or cost transferred in [30–45 min]**

Smith Paper, Co., produces the paper used by wallpaper manufacturers. Smith's four-stage process includes mixing, cooking, rolling, and cutting. During September, the Mixing Department started and completed mixing for 4,405 rolls of paper. The department started but did not finish the mixing for an additional 600 rolls, which were 20% complete with respect to both direct materials and conversion work at the end of September. Direct materials and conversion costs are incurred evenly throughout the mixing process. The Mixing Department incurred the following costs during September:

### Work in process inventory–Mixing

| | |
|---|---|
| Bal, Sep 1 | 0 |
| Direct materials | 5,430 |
| Direct labor | 550 |
| Manufacturing overhead | 5,785 |

## Requirements

1. Compute the number of equivalent units and the cost per equivalent unit in the Mixing Department for September.

2. Show that the sum of (a) cost of goods transferred out of the Mixing Department and (b) ending Work in process inventory—Mixing equals the total cost accumulated in the department during September.

3. Journalize all transactions affecting the company's mixing process during September, including those already posted.

**P17A-18B** 6 **Computing equivalent units and assigning costs to completed units and ending work in process inventory; two materials, added at different points; no beginning work in process inventory or cost transferred in [30–45 min]**

Bert's Exteriors produces exterior siding for homes. The Preparation Department begins with wood, which is chopped into small bits. At the end of the process, an adhesive is added. Then the wood/adhesive mixture goes on to the Compression Department, where the wood is compressed into sheets. Conversion costs are added evenly throughout the preparation process. January data for the Preparation Department are as follows:

| Sheets | | | Costs | |
|---|---|---|---|---|
| Beginning work in process inventory | 0 | sheets | Beginning work in process inventory | $ 0 |
| Started production | 3,900 | sheets | Costs adding during January: | |
| Completed and transferred out to | | | Wood | 3,120 |
| Compression in January | 2,700 | sheets | Adhesives | 1,836 |
| | | | Direct labor | 990 |
| Ending work in process inventory (25% | | | Manufacturing overhead | 2,100 |
| of the way through the preparation process) | 1,200 | sheets | Total costs | $ 8,046 |

## Requirements

1. Draw a timeline for the Preparation Department.

2. Use the timeline to help you compute the equivalent units. (*Hint*: Each direct material added at a different point in the production process requires its own equivalent-unit computation.)

3. Compute the total costs of the units (sheets)
   a. completed and transferred out to the Compression Department.
   b. in the Preparation Department's ending Work in process inventory.

4. Prepare the journal entry to record the cost of the sheets completed and transferred out to the Compression Department.

5. Post the journal entries to the Work in process inventory—Preparation T-account. What is the ending balance?

**P17A-19B** 6 **Computing equivalent units for a second department with beginning work in process inventory; preparing a production cost report and recording transactions on the basis of the report's information; weighted-average method [45–60 min]**

Carol Carpet manufactures broadloom carpet in seven processes: spinning, dyeing, plying, spooling, tufting, latexing, and shearing. In the Dyeing Department, direct materials (dye) are added at the beginning of the process. Conversion costs are incurred evenly throughout the process. Carol uses weighted-average process costing. Information for July 2012 follows:

| Units: | |
|---|---|
| Beginning work in process inventory | 65 rolls |
| Transferred in from Spinning Department during July | 570 rolls |
| Completed during July | 520 rolls |
| Ending work in process (80% complete as to | |
| conversion work) | 115 rolls |
| Costs: | |
| Beginning work in process (transferred-in cost, $3,900; | |
| materials cost, $1,625; conversion costs, $5,555) | $ 11,080 |
| Transferred in from Spinning Department during July | 19,595 |
| Materials cost added during July | 9,805 |
| Conversion costs added during July (manufacturing | |
| wages, $9,450; manufacturing overhead, $43,135) | 52,585 |

## Requirements

1. Prepare a timeline for Carol's Dyeing Department.
2. Use the timeline to help you compute the equivalent units, cost per equivalent unit, and total costs to account for in Carol's Dyeing Department for July.
3. Prepare the July production cost report for Carol's Dyeing Department.
4. Journalize all transactions affecting Carol's Dyeing Department during July, including the entries that have already been posted.

**P17A-20B** ⑥ **Computing equivalent units for a second department with beginning work in process inventory; assigning costs to completed units and ending work in process; weighted average method [50–60 min]**

OceanBound uses three processes to manufacture lifts for personal watercrafts: forming a lift's parts from galvanized steel, assembling the lift, and testing the completed lifts. The lifts are transferred to finished goods before shipment to marinas across the country.

OceanBound's Testing Department requires no direct materials. Conversion costs are incurred evenly throughout the testing process. Other information follows:

| Units: | |
|---|---|
| Beginning work in process | 2,200 units |
| Transferred in from the Assembling Dept. during the period | 7,100 units |
| Completed during the period | 4,200 units |
| Ending work in process (40% complete as to | |
| conversion work) | 5,100 units |
| Costs: | |
| Beginning work in process (transferred in cost, $93,800; | |
| conversion costs, $18,200) | $ 112,000 |
| Transferred in from the Assembling Dept. during the period | 706,000 |
| Conversion costs added during the period | 44,200 |

The cost transferred into Finished goods inventory is the cost of the lifts transferred out of the Testing Department. OceanBound uses weighted-average process costing.

## Requirements

1. Draw a timeline for the Testing Department.
2. Use the timeline to compute the number of equivalent units of work performed by the Testing Department during the period.
3. Compute OceanBound's transferred-in and conversion costs per equivalent unit. Use the unit costs to assign total costs to (a) units completed and transferred out of Testing and (b) units in Testing's ending Work in process inventory.
4. Compute the cost per unit for lifts completed and transferred out to Finished goods inventory. Why would management be interested in this cost?

# 18 Activity-Based Costing and Other Cost Management Tools

## Learning Objectives

**1** Develop activity-based costs (ABC)

**2** Use activity-based management (ABM) to achieve target costs

**3** Describe a just-in-time (JIT) production system, and record its transactions

**4** Use the four types of quality costs to make decisions

David Larimer, Matt Sewell, and Brian Jobe are college friends who share an apartment. They split the monthly costs equally as shown below:

| Rent and utilities | $570 |
|---|---|
| Cable TV | 50 |
| High-speed Internet access | 40 |
| Groceries | 240 |
| Total monthly costs | $900 |

Each roommate's share is $300 ($900/3).

Things go smoothly the first few months. But then David calls a meeting. "Since I started having dinner at Amy's, I shouldn't have to pay a full share for the groceries." Matt then pipes in, "I'm so busy on the Internet that I never have time to watch TV. I don't want to pay for the cable TV any more. And Brian, since your friend Jennifer eats here most evenings, you should pay a double share of the grocery bill." Brian retorts, "Matt, then you should pay for the Internet access, since you're the only one around here who uses it!"

What happened? The friends originally shared the costs equally. But they are not participating equally in eating, watching TV, and using the Internet. Splitting these costs equally is not the best arrangement.

The roommates could better match their costs with the people who participate in each activity. This means splitting cable TV between David and Brian, letting Matt pay for

Internet access, and allocating the grocery bill 1/3 to Matt and 2/3 to Brian. Exhibit 18-1 compares the results of this refined system with the original system.

| EXHIBIT 18-1 | More-Refined Versus Original Cost Allocation System | | | |
|---|---|---|---|---|
| | | David | Matt | Brian |
| More-refined cost allocation system: | | | | |
| Rent and utilities | | $190 | $190 | $190 |
| Cable TV | | 25 | — | 25 |
| High-speed Internet access | | — | 40 | — |
| Groceries | | — | 80 | 160 |
| Total costs allocated | | $215 | $310 | $375 |
| Original cost allocation system | | $300 | $300 | $300 |
| Difference | | $ (85) | $ 10 | $ 75 |

No wonder David called the meeting! The original system cost him $300 a month, but under the refined system, David pays only $215.

•      •      •

Large companies such as **Microsoft** or **Sony**, as well as smaller companies like Smart Touch Learning, face situations like this every day. What is the best way to allocate our costs to the things we do? Fair allocations have high stakes: friendships for David, Matt, and Brian and profits and losses for companies. Businesses that offer multiple products and/or services use a similar approach to link the various types of production and non-manufacturing costs to their various products or services.

# Refining Cost Systems

Now we turn to a more accurate method to attach costs to products, called activity-based costing. We'll discuss how to develop an ABC system and compare it to traditional methods you learned about in the previous chapter.

**1** Develop activity-based costs (ABC)

## Sharpening the Focus: Assigning Costs Based on the Activities That Caused the Costs

Let's illustrate cost refinement by looking at Smart Touch. In today's competitive market, Smart Touch needs to know what it costs to make a DVD. The cost information helps Smart Touch set a selling price to cover costs and provide a profit. To remain competitive with other learning DVD manufacturers, Smart Touch must hold its costs down.

We have seen that direct costs (materials and labor) are easy to assign to products. But indirect costs (utilities, supervisor salaries, and plant depreciation) are another story. It is the indirect costs—and they are significant—that must be allocated somehow. One way to manage costs is to refine the way indirect costs are allocated. Exhibit 18-2 provides an example. The first column of Exhibit 18-2 starts with Smart Touch's production function—making the DVDs. Production is where most companies begin refining their cost systems.

Before business got so competitive, managers could limit their focus to a broad business function such as production, and use a single plant-wide rate to allocate manufacturing overhead cost to their inventory, as we demonstrated in Chapter 17. But today's environment calls for more refined cost accounting. Managers need better data to set prices and identify the most profitable products. They drill down to focus on the costs incurred by each activity within the production function, as shown on the right side of Exhibit 18-2. This has led to a better way to allocate indirect cost to production, called activity-based costing.

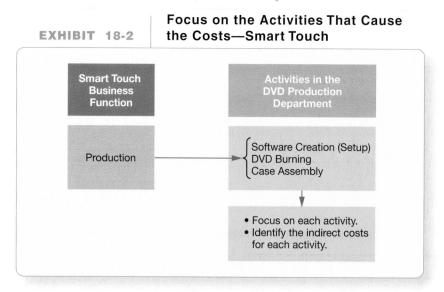

EXHIBIT 18-2 | Focus on the Activities That Cause the Costs—Smart Touch

Activity-based costing (ABC) focuses on *activities*. For example, a tire factory that produces five models of tires has a complex warehousing operation, a casting operation, a quality inspection operation, and a packaging operation, each of which is an "activity." A landscaping service company has a yard maintenance operation, a landscape design operation, a tree service operation, and a commercial turf planting operation, each of which is considered a separate activity.* Smart Touch's activities in the DVD production department are software creation, DVD burning, and case assembly. The costs of those activities become the building blocks for measuring (allocating) the costs of products and services. **Activity-based costing divides the total production process into activities and then assigns costs to products based on how much the production USES those activities to make the product.** Companies like **Dell, Coca-Cola,** and **American Express** use ABC.

Each activity has its own (usually unique) cost driver. For example, one of Smart Touch's activities is case assembly, and Smart Touch allocates indirect case assembly activity costs to DVDs based on the number of inserts a worker must put in the DVD case. DVDs that require more inserts cost more to manufacture. Exhibit 18-3 shows some representative activities and cost drivers for manufacturing companies.

EXHIBIT 18-3 | Examples of Activities and Cost Drivers

*The authors wish to thank Craig Reeder of FAMU for his suggestions.

## Stop & Think...

You go to a restaurant with three of your friends and the waiter brings one bill for $100. How do you split it up? The meal you ordered only cost $20 of the total bill. Do you pay ¼ of the bill, $25, or do you pay based on the cost of what you ordered, $20? Paying based on what you ordered is the key to activity-based costing. Production costs get allocated based on the amount of each activity of production that the products use.

## Developing an Activity-Based Costing System

The main difference between ABC and traditional systems is that ABC uses a separate allocation rate for each activity. Traditional systems, as demonstrated in Chapter 17, usually use one rate. ABC requires four steps, as outlined in Exhibit 18-4, using Smart Touch's data for the case assembly activity.

**EXHIBIT 18-4** | **Activity-Based Costing in Four Easy Steps**

| ABC Step | Application |
|---|---|
| 1. Identify each activity and estimate its total indirect cost. | Activity — Case Assembly; Estimated total indirect cost per year — $10,000 |
| 2. Identify the cost driver for each activity and estimate the total quantity of each driver's allocation base. | Cost driver for case assembly — Number of inserts; Estimated total number of inserts each year — 100,000 |
| 3. Compute the cost allocation rate for each activity. $$\text{Cost allocation rate} = \frac{\text{Estimated total indirect cost of the activity}}{\text{Estimated total quantity of the allocation base (activity)}}$$ | $$\text{Cost allocation rate} = \frac{\$10,000}{100,000 \text{ inserts}} = \$0.10 \text{ per insert}$$ |
| 4. Allocate indirect costs to the cost object—in this case, all the inserts put in DVD cases during January. $$\text{Allocated activity cost} = \text{Cost allocation rate for the activity} \times \text{Actual quantity of the allocation base used by the cost object}$$ | Cost of DVD Assembly for January $= \$0.10 \times 8,000$ inserts during January $= \underline{\$800}$ |

The first step in developing an activity-based costing system is to identify the activities. Analyzing all the activities required for a product or service forces managers to think about how each activity might be improved—or whether it is necessary at all.

## Traditional Versus Activity-Based Costing Systems: Smart Touch Learning

To illustrate an ABC system, we use Smart Touch. Smart Touch produces hundreds of different learning DVDs, including mass quantities of large audience DVDs and small quantities of "specialty" learning DVDs for specific companies.

We begin with a traditional cost system using a plant-wide manufacturing overhead allocation rate to show its weakness. You will see shortly that the ABC system that follows is clearly superior.

## A Traditional Cost System

Smart Touch's cost system allocates all manufacturing overhead the traditional way—based on a single allocation rate: 40% of direct labor cost. Smart Touch's controller, James Kolen, gathered data for two of the company's products:

- **Microsoft** Excel Training DVD (Multiple customers use this DVD)
- Specialty DVD created for a company's custom software application (A single customer uses this DVD)

Based on Smart Touch's traditional cost system, Kolen computed each product's gross profit as shown in Exhibit 18-5.

| EXHIBIT 18-5 | Smart Touch's Manufacturing Cost and Gross Profit Using Traditional Overhead Allocation | | |
|---|---|---|---|

| | | Excel DVD | Specialty DVD |
|---|---|---|---|
| Sale price per DVD | | $12.00 | $70.00 |
| Less: Manufacturing cost per DVD: | | | |
| | Direct materials | 2.40 | 2.40 |
| | Direct labor | 4.00 | 34.00 |
| | Manufacturing overhead (40% of Direct labor cost) | 1.60 | 13.60 |
| | Total manufacturing cost per DVD | 8.00 | 50.00 |
| Gross profit per DVD | | $ 4.00 | $20.00 |

The gross profit for the specialty DVD is $20 per DVD—five times as high as the $4 gross profit for the Excel DVD. Smart Touch CEO Sheena Bright is surprised that the specialty DVD appears so much more profitable. She asks Kolen to check this out. Kolen confirms that the gross profit per DVD is five times as high for the specialty DVD. Bright wonders whether Smart Touch should produce more specialty DVDs.

**Key Point:** Because direct labor cost is the single allocation base for all products, Smart Touch allocates far more total dollars of overhead cost to the Excel DVDs than to the specialty DVDs. However, total dollars of overhead are spread over more DVDs, which is why the per unit cost per DVD is less for Excel DVDs than for specialty DVDs. This costing is accurate only if direct labor really is the overhead cost driver, and only if the Excel DVD really does cause more overhead than the specialty DVD.

Noriko Kitagawa, Smart Touch's marketing manager, reviews the gross profit data and calls a meeting with production foreman Ryan Oliver and controller Kolen. At the meeting, Kitagawa suggests that the company should try expanding sales of the specialty product and reduce sales of the Excel DVD. Kolen says he is not sure that's the right answer because there may be some distortion in the way overhead is allocated. Intuitively, he feels like the specialty DVD does not really require that much more in overhead resources than the Excel product, but because it uses higher labor cost, the Excel DVD is getting more total manufacturing overhead costs allocated to the product.

Kolen fears that the problem could be Smart Touch's cost accounting system. Kolen suggests that Smart Touch break down overhead costs by activities and then look at the gross profit data again before making such an important strategic marketing decision. Exhibit 18-6 compares the traditional single-allocation-base system (Panel A) to the new ABC system that Kolen's team developed (Panel B).

## Activity-Based Cost System

Panel B of Exhibit 18-6 shows that Smart Touch's ABC team identifies three activities: setup, DVD burning, and case assembly. (*Setup* is when the company prepares the manufacturing line—sets it up—to produce a different product.) Each activity has its own cost driver. But exactly how does ABC work? The ABC team develops the new system by following the four steps described in Exhibit 18-4.

| EXHIBIT 18-6 | **Overview of Smart Touch's Traditional and ABC Systems** |
|---|---|

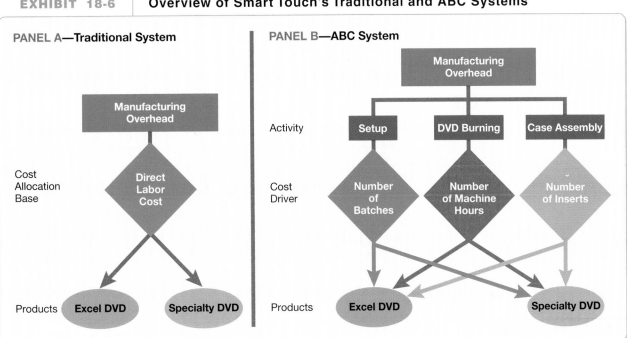

Let's see how an ABC system works, with a focus on the setup activity. Exhibit 18-7 develops Smart Touch's ABC system. Follow the details of each step. Make sure you understand exactly how each ABC step applies to Smart Touch's setup process.

| EXHIBIT 18-7 | **Smart Touch's ABC System** |
|---|---|

**Step 1: Identify activities and estimate their total indirect costs.**

Controller Kolen's team identifies all the manufacturing activities. Focus on setup.

Foreman Oliver estimates total setup costs for all production at $600,000. This cost is for all products that Smart Touch produces.

**Step 2: Identify the cost driver for each activity.**
**Then estimate the total quantity of each driver's allocation base.**

The allocation base for each activity should be its cost driver. The number of batches drives setup costs.

Kolen and Oliver estimate the setup department will have 40 batches.

**Step 3: Compute the allocation rate for each activity.**

Kolen computes the allocation rate for setup as follows:

$$\text{Cost allocation rate} = \frac{\$600,000}{40 \text{ batches}} = \$15,000 \text{ per batch}$$

**Step 4: Allocate indirect costs to the cost object—batches of DVDs in this case.***

Kolen allocates setup costs as follows:

| | | | |
|---|---|---|---|
| Excel DVD: | 3 batches | × $15,000 per batch | = $45,000 |
| Specialty DVD: | 1 batch | × $15,000 per batch | = $15,000 |

*Other Smart Touch products represent the remaining 36 batches.

Controller Kolen then uses the ABC costs allocated from Exhibit 18-7 to recompute manufacturing overhead costs, as shown in Exhibit 18-8. For each product, Kolen adds the total costs of setup, DVD burning, and assembly. He then divides each product's total manufacturing overhead cost by the number of DVDs produced to get the overhead cost per DVD product.

**EXHIBIT 18-8** | **Smart Touch's Manufacturing Overhead Costs Under ABC**

| Manufacturing Overhead Costs | Excel DVD | Specialty DVD |
|---|---|---|
| Setup (from Exhibit 18-7) | $ 45,000 | $15,000 |
| DVD Burning (amounts assumed) | 5,000 | 1,500 |
| Case Assembly (from Exhibit 18-4, based on $0.10 per insert). | | |
| Each Excel DVD has 1 insert. (100,000 Excel DVDs × 1 insert per DVD × $0.10 per insert) | 10,000 | |
| Each specialty DVD has 7 inserts. (500 specialty DVDs × 7 inserts per DVD × $0.10 per insert) | | 350 |
| Total manufacturing overhead cost | $ 60,000 | $16,850 |
| Divide by number of DVDs produced | 100,000 | 500 |
| Manufacturing overhead cost per DVD under ABC | $ 0.60 | $ 33.70 |

Activity-based costs are more accurate because ABC considers the resources (activities) each product actually uses. Focus on the bottom line of Exhibit 18-8. Manufacturing overhead costs of

- Excel DVDs are $0.60 per DVD, which is less than the $1.60 manufacturing overhead cost allocated under the old system (shown in color in Exhibit 18-5).
- specialty DVDs are $33.70 per DVD, which far exceeds the $13.60 manufacturing overhead cost under the old system (shown in color in Exhibit 18-5).

Now that we know the indirect costs of Excel and specialty DVDs under ABC, let's see how Smart Touch's managers *use* the ABC cost information to make better decisions.

# Activity-Based Management: Using ABC for Decision Making

 Use activity-based management (ABM) to achieve target costs

**Activity-based management (ABM)** uses activity-based costs to make decisions that increase profits while meeting customer needs. In this section, we show how Smart Touch can use ABC in two kinds of decisions:

1. Pricing and product mix
2. Cost cutting

## Pricing and Product Mix Decisions

Controller Kolen now knows the ABC manufacturing overhead cost per DVD (Exhibit 18-8). To determine which products are the most profitable, he recomputes each product's total manufacturing cost and gross profit. Panel A of Exhibit 18-9 shows that the total manufacturing cost per DVD for the Excel DVDs is $7.00 under the ABC system. Contrast this with the $8.00 cost per DVD under Smart Touch's traditional cost system, as shown in Panel B. More important, the ABC data in Panel A show that the specialty DVDs cost $70.10 per DVD, rather than the $50 per DVD indicated by the old system (Panel B). Smart Touch has been losing $0.10 on each specialty DVD—and this is *before* selling, administrative, and distribution expenses! It seems that specialty DVDs are not currently profitable for Smart Touch.

**EXHIBIT 18-9**

### Smart Touch's Cost Comparison— ABC vs. Traditional Allocation

**PANEL A—Manufacturing Cost per DVD and Gross Profit Under ABC**

|  | Excel DVD | Specialty DVD |
|---|---|---|
| Sale price per DVD | $12.00 | $70.00 |
| Less: Manufacturing cost per DVD: | | |
| Direct materials | 2.40 | 2.40 |
| Direct labor | 4.00 | 34.00 |
| Manufacturing overhead (from Exhibit 18-8) | 0.60 | 33.70 |
| Total manufacturing cost per DVD | 7.00 | 70.10 |
| Gross profit per DVD | $ 5.00 | $ (0.10) |

**PANEL B—Manufacturing Cost per DVD and Gross Profit Under Traditional Allocation of Costs**

|  | Excel DVD | Specialty DVD |
|---|---|---|
| Sale price per DVD | $12.00 | $70.00 |
| Less: Manufacturing cost per DVD: | | |
| Direct materials | 2.40 | 2.40 |
| Direct labor | 4.00 | 34.00 |
| Manufacturing overhead (40% of Direct labor cost) | 1.60 | 13.60 |
| Total manufacturing cost per DVD | 8.00 | 50.00 |
| Gross profit per DVD | $ 4.00 | $20.00 |

This illustration shows that ABC is the more accurate way to allocate the cost of manufacturing a product. With better cost and profitability information, Smart Touch can make better decisions that increase company profits.

Armed with a better measure of the cost of each product, Smart Touch may want to evaluate the production process to identify potential ways to reduce manufacturing overhead costs. If Smart Touch cannot cut costs enough to earn a profit on the specialty DVDs, then the company may decide to increase the sale price of the specialty DVDs. If customers will not pay more, Smart Touch may decide to drop the specialty DVDs. *This is the exact opposite of the strategy suggested by cost data from the traditional system. That system favored specialty DVDs.* This is a product mix decision. Product mix considers overall production capacity and serves to focus on producing the mix of products that is most profitable, considering limited production capabilities.

## Cutting Costs

Most companies adopt ABC to get better product costs for pricing and product-mix decisions. However, they often benefit more by cutting costs. ABC and value engineering can work together. **Value engineering** means reevaluating activities to reduce costs. It requires the following cross-functional teams:

- Marketers to identify customer needs
- Engineers to design more efficient products
- Accountants to estimate costs

Why are managers turning to value engineering? Because it gets results! Companies like **Apple** and **Carrier Corporation** are following Japanese automakers **Toyota** and **Nissan** and setting sale prices based on **target prices**—what customers

**Connect To: Business**

How do businesses create an atmosphere for implementing cost-cutting strategies? One technique is to simply ask employees for suggestions that either cut costs or create new revenues. Rewarding employees for recommendations that are implemented by offering bonuses based on a percentage of the amount of savings generated is an incentive and motivator. Who better to see ideas to help save the company money than those who work there every day?

are willing to pay for the product or service. Exhibit 18-10 compares target pricing to cost-based pricing. Study each column separately.

| EXHIBIT 18-10 | Target Pricing Versus Cost-Based Pricing |

Instead of starting with product cost and then adding a profit to determine the sale price (right column of the exhibit), target pricing (left column) does just the opposite. Target pricing starts with the price that customers are willing to pay and then subtracts the company's desired profit to determine the **target cost**. Then the company works backward to develop the product at the target cost. The company's goal is to achieve the target cost.

Let's return to our Smart Touch illustration. The ABC analysis in Exhibit 18-9, Panel A, prompts CEO Sheena Bright to push Excel DVDs because it appears that the specialty DVD is losing money. The marketing department says the selling price of the Excel DVDs is likely to fall to $10.00 per DVD. Bright wants to earn a profit equal to 20% of the sale price.

Full-product costs consider *all* production costs (direct materials, direct labor, and allocated manufacturing overhead) plus all nonmanufacturing costs (operating expenses, such as administrative and selling expenses) when determining target costs and target profits. What is Smart Touch's target full-product cost per Excel DVD? The following is the computation:

| | |
|---|---|
| Target sale price per Excel DVD | $10.00 |
| – Desired profit ($10.00 × 20%) | (2.00) |
| = Target cost per Excel DVD | $ 8.00 |

Does Smart Touch's current full-product cost meet this target? Let's see:

| | |
|---|---|
| Current total manufacturing cost per Excel DVD | $7.00 |
| + Nonmanufacturing costs (operating expenses—amount assumed) | 1.10 |
| = Current full-product cost per Excel DVD | $8.10 |

Smart Touch's current cost does not meet the target cost.

Because Smart Touch's current full-product cost, $8.10, exceeds the target cost of $8.00, Bright assembles a value engineering team to identify ways to cut costs. The team analyzes each production activity. For each activity, the team considers how to

- cut costs, given Smart Touch's current production process.
- redesign the production process to further cut costs.

Of the team's several proposals, Bright decides to *redesign setup to reduce the setup cost per batch*. Smart Touch will do this by grouping raw materials that are used together to reduce the time required to assemble the materials for each setup. Estimated total cost saving is $160,000, and the number of batches remains unchanged at 40.

Will this change allow Smart Touch to reach the target cost? Exhibit 18-11 shows how controller Kolen recomputes the cost of Setup based on the value engineering study.

**EXHIBIT 18-11** | **Recomputing Activity Costs After a Value Engineering Study—Excel DVDs**

| | | | Manufacturing Overhead | | Total Manufacturing Overhead Cost |
|---|---|---|---|---|---|
| | | Setup | DVD Burning | Assembly | |
| Estimated total indirect costs of activity: | | | | | |
| Setup ($600,000 – $160,000) | | $440,000 | | | |
| Estimated total quantity of each allocation base | | 40 batches | | | |
| Compute the cost allocation rate for each activity: | | | | | |
| (Divide estimated indirect cost by estimated | | $440,000 | Amounts | Amounts | |
| quantity of the allocation base) | ÷ | 40 batches | from | from | |
| Cost allocation rate for each activity | = | $11,000 per batch | Exhibit 18-8 | Exhibit 18-8 | |
| Actual quantity of each allocation base used | | | | | |
| by Excel DVDs: | | | | | |
| Setup (from Exhibit 18-7; Excel DVDs | | | | | |
| require three batches) | × | 3 batches | | | |
| Total Allocated Manufacturing Costs | = | $ 33,000   + | $5,000   + | $10,000   = | $48,000 |

Exhibit 18-11 shows that value engineering cuts total manufacturing overhead cost of the Excel DVDs to $48,000 from $60,000 (in Exhibit 18-8). Now Kolen totals the revised cost estimates for Excel DVDs in Exhibit 18-12.

**EXHIBIT 18-12 | ABC Manufacturing Overhead Costs After Value Engineering Study—Excel DVDs**

**PANEL A—Manufacturing Cost Under ABC** After Value Engineering Study

| | Excel DVD |
|---|---|
| Manufacturing overhead costs | |
| Setup (from Exhibit 18-11) | $ 33,000 |
| DVD Burning (from Exhibit 18-11) | 5,000 |
| Case Assembly (from Exhibit 18-11) | 10,000 |
| Total manufacturing overhead cost | $ 48,000 |
| Divide by number of DVDs produced | 100,000 |
| Manufacturing overhead cost per DVD under ABC after value engineering study | $ 0.48 |

**PANEL B—Total Manufacturing Cost and Full Product Cost Under ABC** After Value Engineering Study

| | Excel DVD |
|---|---|
| Manufacturing cost per DVD: | |
| Direct materials | $2.40 |
| Direct labor | 4.00 |
| Manufacturing overhead (from Panel A) | 0.48 |
| Total manufacturing cost per DVD after value engineering study | $6.88 |
| Non manufacturing costs per DVD (assumed) | 1.10 |
| Full product cost after value engineering study per DVD | $7.98 |

Cost of $6.88 is quite an improvement from the prior manufacturing cost of $7.00 per DVD (Exhibit 18-9, Panel A). Now Smart Touch's full cost of $7.98 is less than its target full product cost of $8.00. Value engineering worked.

Next, we'll review Decision Guidelines 18-1, which cover ABC systems and ABC management.

**Key Takeaway**

Activity-based management (ABM) uses activity-based costs to make decisions that increase profits while meeting customer needs. Most companies adopt ABC to get better product costs for pricing and product-mix decisions. However, they often benefit more by cutting costs. Target pricing takes the sales price and subtracts desired profit to determine the target cost of manufacturing. ABC and value engineering work together to reevaluate activities with the goal of reducing manufacturing overhead costs to meet the target cost. By reducing costs, companies can maintain desired profit levels.

# Decision Guidelines 18-1

## ACTIVITY-BASED COSTING

You are the manager of operations for a hi-tech electronics manufacturing company. The company's production has doubled in the last year. The company decides to adopt an ABC system. What decisions will your company face as it begins refining its cost system?

| Decision | Guidelines |
|---|---|
| • How does a company develop an ABC system? | 1. Identify each activity and estimate its total indirect costs.<br>2. Identify the cost driver for each activity. Then estimate the total quantity of each driver's allocation base.<br>3. Compute the cost allocation rate for each activity.<br>4. Allocate indirect costs to the cost object. |
| • How do we compute a cost allocation rate for an activity? | $$\frac{\text{Estimated total indirect cost of the activity}}{\text{Estimated total quantity of the allocation base (activity)}}$$ |
| • How do we allocate an activity's cost to the cost object? | $$\frac{\text{Cost allocation}}{\text{rate for the activity}} \times \frac{\text{Actual quantity of the allocation}}{\text{base used by the cost object}}$$ |
| • For what kinds of decisions do managers use ABC? | Managers use ABC data to decide on the following:<br>• Pricing and product mix<br>• Cost cutting |
| • How are target costs set? | Target sale price (based on market research) – Desired profit = Target cost |
| • How can a company achieve target costs? | Use value engineering to cut costs by improving product design and production processes. |
| • What are the main benefits of ABC? | • More accurate product cost information helps managers determine which products are most profitable to produce.<br>• More detailed information on the costs of activities and their cost drivers helps managers control costs. |

# Summary Problem 18-1

Indianapolis Auto Parts (IAP) has a Seat Manufacturing Department that uses activity-based costing. IAP's system has the following activities:

| Activity | Allocation Base | Cost Allocation Rate |
|---|---|---|
| Purchasing | Number of purchase orders | $50.00 per purchase order |
| Assembling | Number of parts | $0.50 per part |
| Packaging | Number of finished seats | $1.00 per finished seat |

Each auto seat has 20 parts. Direct materials cost per seat is $1. Direct labor cost per seat is $10. Suppose **Ford** has asked IAP for a bid on 50,000 built-in baby seats that would be installed as an option on some **Ford** SUVs. IAP will use a total of 200 purchase orders if **Ford** accepts IAP's bid.

## Requirements

1. Compute the total cost IAP will incur to (a) purchase the needed materials and then (b) assemble and (c) package 50,000 baby seats. Also, compute the average cost per seat.
2. For bidding, IAP adds a 30% markup to total cost. What total price will IAP bid for the entire **Ford** order?
3. Suppose that instead of an ABC system, IAP has a traditional product costing system that allocates indirect costs other than direct materials and direct labor at the rate of $65 per direct labor hour. The baby-seat order will require 10,000 direct labor hours. What price will IAP bid using this system's total cost?
4. Use your answers to Requirements 2 and 3 to explain how ABC can help IAP make a better decision about the bid price to offer **Ford**.

## Solution

### Requirement 1

| | |
|---|---:|
| Direct materials, 50,000 seats × $1.00 | $ 50,000 |
| Direct labor, 50,000 seats × $10.00 | 500,000 |
| Activity costs: | |
|    Purchasing, 200 purchase orders × $50.00 | 10,000 |
|    Assembling, 50,000 seats × 20 parts per seat × $0.50 | 500,000 |
|    Packaging, 50,000 seats × $1.00 | 50,000 |
| Total cost of order | $1,110,000 |
| Divide by number of seats | ÷ 50,000 |
| Average cost per seat | $ 22.20 |

### Requirement 2

| | |
|---|---:|
| Bid price (ABC system): ($1,110,000 × 130%) | $1,443,000 |

## Requirement 3

| | |
|---|---:|
| Direct materials, 50,000 seats × $1.00 ......................... | $    50,000 |
| Direct labor, 50,000 seats × $10.00 ............................. | 500,000 |
| Indirect costs, 10,000 direct labor hours × $65.00 ....... | 650,000 |
| Total cost of order................................................. | $1,200,000 |
| Bid price (traditional system): ($1,200,000 × 130%)... | $1,560,000 |

## Requirement 4

IAP's bid would be $117,000 higher using the traditional system than using ABC ($1,560,000 – $1,443,000). Assuming the ABC system more accurately captures the costs caused by the order, the traditional system over-costs the order. This leads to a higher bid price and reduces IAP's chance of winning the order. The ABC system can increase IAP's chance of winning the order by bidding a lower price.

# Just-in-Time (JIT) Systems

Competition is fierce, especially in manufacturing and technology-related services. Chinese and Indian companies are producing high-quality goods at very low costs. As we saw in the discussion of activity-based costing, there is a never-ending quest to cut costs.

**3** Describe a just-in-time (JIT) production system, and record its transactions

The cost of buying, storing, and moving inventory can be significant for companies like **Home Depot, Toyota,** and **Dell.** To lower inventory costs, many companies use a just-in-time (JIT) system.

Companies with JIT systems buy materials and complete finished goods *just in time* for delivery to customers. In traditional manufacturing, materials would be ordered in large quantities to obtain volume discounts and to have surplus materials on hand in case some of the materials turn out to be defective. Under the JIT system, the manufacturer contracts with suppliers to deliver small quantities of goods, as needed. Deliveries are small and frequent, and the suppliers must guarantee a close to zero defect rate. That way the manufacturers hold only small amounts of raw materials in the warehouse, use only materials as needed, and because of the zero defect rate and quick delivery, can be assured they won't run out of materials and have to shut down production. Because of JIT, relationships with suppliers of raw materials must be very reliable to ensure that the company has raw materials just when needed to manufacture products. Because products are made as ordered, finished goods inventories are kept to a minimal amount. This reduces the company's cost to store and insure inventory. It also allows the company to minimize the resources it has invested in raw materials and in inventory. Lastly, because the inventories are low, the risk of the inventory becoming "obsolete" or unsaleable is very small.

Production in JIT systems is completed in self-contained work cells, as shown in Exhibit 18-13. **A work cell is an area where everything needed to complete a manufacturing process is readily available.** Each work cell includes the machinery and labor resources to manufacture a product. Employees work in a team in the work cell and are empowered to complete the work without supervision. Workers complete a small batch of units and are responsible for inspecting for quality throughout the process. ` ` the completed product moves out of the work cell, the suppliers deliver more `'` to the work cell just in time to keep production moving along.

`ast`, traditional production systems separate manufacturing into various departments that focus on a single activity. Work in process must be `m` one department to another. More movements waste time, and wasted `asted` money.

**EXHIBIT 18-13** | **Production Flow Comparison: Just-in-Time Versus Traditional Production**

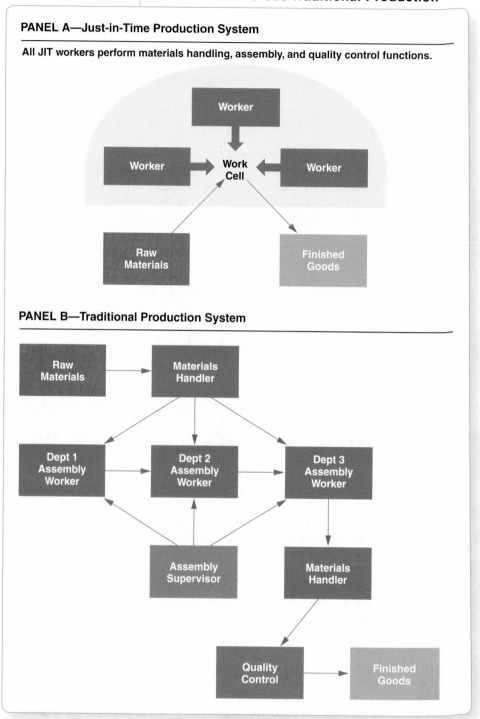

**PANEL A—Just-in-Time Production System**

All JIT workers perform materials handling, assembly, and quality control functions.

**PANEL B—Traditional Production System**

   Under JIT, a customer's order—customer demand—triggers manufacturing. The sales order "pulls" materials, labor, and overhead into production. This "demand–pull" system extends back to the suppliers of materials. As noted previously, suppliers make frequent deliveries of defect-free materials *just in time* for production. Purchasing only what customers demand reduces inventory. Less inventory frees floor space (and resources) for more productive use. Thus, JIT systems help to reduce waste. Exhibit 18-13 shows a traditional production system in Panel B. The traditional system requires more inventory, more workers, and costs more to operate than a JIT system.

Companies like **Toyota, Carrier,** and **Dell** credit JIT for saving them millions of dollars. But JIT systems are not without problems. With little or no inventory buffers, JIT users lose sales when they cannot get materials on time, or when poor-quality materials arrive just in time. There is no way to make up for lost time. As a result, as noted earlier, strong relationships with quality raw materials vendors are very important to JIT. Additionally, many JIT companies still maintain small inventories of critical materials.

## Just-in-Time Costing

JIT costing leads many companies to simplify their accounting. **Just-in-time costing,** sometimes called **backflush costing,** seems to work backwards. JIT costing starts with output that has been completed and then assigns manufacturing costs to units sold and to inventories. There are three major differences between JIT costing and traditional standard costing, as shown in Exhibit 18-14:

1. JIT costing does not track the cost of products from Materials inventory (or Raw materials inventory) to Work in process inventory to Finished goods inventory. Instead, JIT costing waits until the units are completed to record the cost of production.

2. JIT costing combines Materials inventory and Work in process inventory accounts into a single account called **Raw and in-process inventory.**

3. Under the JIT philosophy, workers perform many tasks. Most companies using JIT combine labor and manufacturing overhead costs into a single account called Conversion costs. *Conversion costs* is a temporary account that works just like the Manufacturing overhead account. Actual conversion costs accumulate as debits in the Conversion costs account and allocated conversion costs are credited to the account as units are completed. Accountants close any under- or overallocated conversion costs to Cost of goods sold at the end of the period, just like they do for under- or overallocated manufacturing overhead.

**EXHIBIT 18-14** | **Comparison of Traditional and Just-in-Time Costing**

|  | Traditional | Just-in-Time |
|---|---|---|
| **Recording production activity** | Build the costs of products as they move from materials into work in process and on to finished goods inventory | Record the costs of products when units are completed |
| **Inventory accounts** | Materials inventory<br>Work in process inventory<br>Finished goods inventory | Raw and in-process inventory<br>Finished goods inventory |
| **Manufacturing costs** | Direct materials<br>Direct labor<br>Manufacturing overhead | Direct materials<br>Conversion costs |

## JIT Costing Illustrated: Smart Touch

To illustrate JIT costing, we'll continue with our Smart Touch example. Smart Touch has only one direct material cost: blank DVDs. This cost is recorded in the Raw and in-process inventory account. All other manufacturing costs—including labor, various indirect materials, and overhead—are indirect costs of converting the "raw" DVDs into finished goods (DVD learning systems). All these indirect costs are collected in the Conversion costs account.

As noted previously, JIT does not use a separate Work in process inventory account. Instead, it uses only two inventory accounts:

- Raw and in-process inventory, which combines direct materials with work in process
- Finished goods inventory

Assume that on January 31, Smart Touch had $100,000 of beginning Raw and in-process inventory, and $200,000 of beginning Finished goods inventory. During February, Smart Touch uses JIT costing to record the following transactions:

1. Smart Touch purchased $240,000 of direct materials (blank DVDs) on account.

| 1. | Raw and in-process inventory    (A+) | 240,000 | |
|---|---|---|---|
| | Accounts payable    (L+) | | 240,000 |
| | *Purchased direct materials on account.* | | |

2. Smart Touch spent $590,000 on labor and overhead.

| 2. | Conversion costs    (E+) | 590,000 | |
|---|---|---|---|
| | Wages payable, Accumulated depreciation, etc. | | 590,000 |
| | *Incurred conversion costs.* | | |

3. Smart Touch completed 115,000 Excel DVDs that it moved to Finished goods. Recall that the standard cost of each Excel DVD in Exhibit 18-9 is $7 ($2.40 direct materials + $4.60 conversion costs). The debit (increase) to Finished goods inventory is at standard cost of $805,000 (115,000 completed Excel DVDs × $7). There is no separate Work in process inventory account in JIT costing, so Smart Touch credits the following:

| 3. | Finished goods inventory (115,000 × $7)    (A+) | 805,000 | |
|---|---|---|---|
| | Raw and in-process inventory (115,000 × $2.40)    (A–) | | 276,000 |
| | Conversion costs (115,000 × $4.60)    (E–) | | 529,000 |
| | *Completed production.* | | |

- Raw and in-process inventory is credited for the blank DVDs, $276,000 (115,000 completed Excel DVDs × $2.40 standard raw material cost per DVD).
- Conversion costs is credited for the labor and other indirect costs allocated to the finished DVDs, $529,000 (115,000 completed Excel DVDs × $4.60 standard conversion cost per DVD).

This is the key to JIT costing. The system does not track costs as the DVDs move through manufacturing. Instead, *completion* of the DVDs triggers the accounting system to go back and move costs from Raw and in-process inventory (credit) and to allocate conversion costs (credit) to attach those costs to the finished products (debit).

4. Smart Touch sold 110,000 Excel DVDs (110,000 DVDs × cost of $7 per DVD = $770,000). The cost of goods sold entry is as follows:

| 4. | Cost of goods sold    (E+) | 770,000 | |
|---|---|---|---|
| | Finished goods inventory    (A–) | | 770,000 |
| | *Cost of sales.* | | |

Exhibit 18-15 shows Smart Touch's relevant accounts. Combining the Materials inventory account with the Work in process inventory account to form the single Raw and in-process inventory account eliminates detail.

**EXHIBIT 18-15** | **Smart Touch's JIT Costing Accounts**

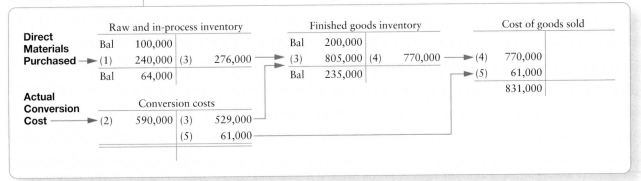

5. You can see from Exhibit 18-15 that conversion costs are underallocated by $61,000 (actual cost of $590,000 – applied cost of $529,000). Under- and overallocated conversion costs are treated just like under- and overallocated manufacturing overhead and closed to Cost of goods sold, as follows:

| 5. | | | | |
|---|---|---|---|---|
| | Cost of goods sold    (E+) | | 61,000 | |
| |    Conversion costs    (E–) | | | 61,000 |
| | *Closed conversion costs.* | | | |

In the final analysis, cost of goods sold for February is $831,000, as shown in the T-account in Exhibit 18-15.

## Stop & Think...

If you were to go to the grocery store today, you could either buy just the ingredients you need to make dinner tonight or you could purchase enough groceries to last you two weeks. If you purchase for two weeks, can you be sure you'll use all the groceries you buy or will some of it "go bad" before you eat it? Choosing to purchase just enough to get you through a short period (today) is like just-in-time costing. Companies purchase just enough raw materials for the production needs of the next day or two, rather than purchasing large amounts of raw materials that have to be stored.

**Key Takeaway**

Just-in-time (JIT) systems streamline manufacturing and accounting by developing relationships with suppliers, resulting in no need for the company to maintain large supplies of raw materials on hand. Defect-free raw materials arrive JIT to the work cell for production. Because of the more efficient production process, the accounting is streamlined to match it. Only two inventory accounts need to be kept—Raw and in-process inventory and Finished goods inventory. Labor and overhead are tracked in a temporary account, Conversion costs, where they are allocated to products as they are completed.

# Continuous Improvement and the Management of Quality

 Use the four types of quality costs to make decisions

Because just-in-time production systems have very little inventory on hand, companies are far more vulnerable to production shutdowns if they receive poor-quality or defective direct materials. For this reason, it is critical that a company's direct materials be nearly defect free.

To meet this challenge, each business function monitors its activities to improve quality and eliminate defects and waste. Continuous improvement is the goal of total quality management (TQM), and it is monitored many ways. For example, companies compare the cost of any changes they want to make against the benefits of the changes as one measure that aids decision making. Say a company is considering reorganizing a work cell to improve efficiency. The reorganization costs $40,000, but the change is expected to result in a $100,000 reduction in costs. Would the company want to implement the change considering its cost and benefits? Absolutely! Why? The change is expected to net the company an additional $60,000 in profit.

Well-designed products reduce inspections, rework, and warranty claims. Investing in research and development (R&D) can generate savings in marketing and customer service. World-class companies like **Toyota** and **Dell** *design* and *build* quality into their products rather than having to *inspect* and *repair* later.

## The Four Types of Quality Costs

The four types of quality-related costs are as follows:

1. **Prevention costs** are costs spent to *avoid* poor-quality goods or services.

2. **Appraisal costs** are costs spent to *detect* poor-quality goods or services.

3. **Internal failure costs** are costs incurred when the company detects and corrects poor-quality goods or services before delivery to customers.

4. **External failure costs** are costs spent after the company *delivers poor-quality goods or services* to customers and then has to make things right with the customer.

Exhibit 18-16 gives examples of the four types of quality costs. Most prevention costs occur in the R&D stage of the value chain. In contrast, most appraisal and internal failure costs occur while the product is being made; thus, they ultimately become part of the cost of the finished product. External failure causes an increase in customer service costs, or it could cause lost sales due to an unhappy customer. External failure costs ultimately affect warranty expense claims or worse, potential lawsuit liability exposure. Prevention is much cheaper than external failure.

**EXHIBIT 18-16** | **Four Types of Quality Costs**

| Prevention Costs | Appraisal Costs |
|---|---|
| Employee training | Inspection at various stages of production |
| Improved quality of materials | Inspection of final products or services |
| Preventive maintenance on equipment | Product testing |
| **Internal Failure Costs** | **External Failure Costs** |
| Any production problem that causes manufacturing to stop | Lost sales due to unhappy customers |
| Reworking of substandard products | Warranty costs |
| Rejected product units | Service costs at customer sites |
| | Sales returns due to product defects |

## Stop & Think...

Do you go to the dentist every six months to have your teeth cleaned? The cost of the cleaning is a prevention cost. By investing in the care of your teeth, not only do your teeth look nice, but you hope to *prevent* decay in your teeth. Preventing that decay helps you to avoid a bigger dentist bill for repairing your teeth in the future. The same is true for producing products. Monies spent ensuring consistent quality standards and screening for defective products before they ship to customers is cheaper than monies spent on returned products and warranty claims, or revenues lost from losing a customer.

# Deciding Whether to Adopt a New Quality Program

Let's revisit Smart Touch. CEO Sheena Bright is considering spending the following on a new quality program:

| | |
|---|---:|
| Inspect raw materials | $100,000 |
| Reengineer to improve product quality | 750,000 |
| Inspect finished goods | 150,000 |
| Preventive maintenance of equipment | 100,000 |

Smart Touch expects this quality program to reduce costs by the following amounts:

| | |
|---|---:|
| Avoid lost profits due to unhappy customers | $800,000 |
| Fewer sales returns | 50,000 |
| Decrease the cost of rework | 250,000 |
| Lower warranty costs | 100,000 |

**Key Takeaway**

The four types of quality-related costs are prevention, appraisal, internal failure, and external failure costs. Quality improvement programs that reduce internal and external failure costs by more than the increased cost to prevent or appraise the product are smart total quality management decisions.

Bright asks controller Kolen to

1. classify each cost into one of the four categories (prevention, appraisal, internal failure, external failure). Total the estimated cost for each category.

2. recommend whether Smart Touch should undertake the quality program. Kolen uses Exhibit 18-17 to compare the costs to

   • undertake the quality program, or

   • not undertake the quality program.

**EXHIBIT 18-17** | **Analysis of Smart Touch's Proposed Quality Program**

| Undertake the Quality Program | | | Do Not Undertake the Quality Program | | |
|---|---:|---|---|---:|---|
| **Prevention** | | | **Internal Failure** | | |
| Reengineer to improve product quality | $ 750,000 | | Cost of rework | $ 250,000 | |
| Preventive maintenance of equipment | 100,000 | | Total internal failure costs | $ 250,000 | |
| Total prevention costs | $ 850,000 | | | | |
| | | | **External Failure** | | |
| | | | Lost profits due to unhappy customers | $ 800,000 | |
| **Appraisal** | | | Sales returns | 50,000 | |
| Inspect raw materials | $ 100,000 | | Warranty costs | 100,000 | |
| Inspect finished goods | 150,000 | | Total external failure costs | $ 950,000 | |
| Total appraisal costs | $ 250,000 | | **Total costs of not undertaking the** | | |
| Total costs of the quality program | $1,100,000 | | **quality program** | $1,200,000 | |

Decision: Undertake the Quality Program and Save $100,000.

These estimates suggest that Smart Touch would save $100,000 ($1,200,000 − $1,100,000) by undertaking the quality program.

Quality costs can be hard to measure. For example, it is very hard to measure external failure costs. Lost profits due to unhappy customers do not appear in the accounting records! Therefore, TQM uses many nonfinancial measures, such as the number of customer complaints and the volume of incoming customer-service phone calls, as a means to measure success or failure.

Next, we'll review the Decision Guidelines for JIT and quality costs.

# Decision Guidelines 18-2

## JUST-IN-TIME AND QUALITY COSTS

Now, consider you are the production foreman for a soft drink manufacturer. Could implementing JIT and total quality management help you make better decisions?

| Decision | Guidelines | |
|---|---|---|
| • How do we change from traditional production to JIT? | *Traditional*<br>Similar machines grouped together<br>Larger batches<br>Higher inventories<br>Each worker does a few tasks<br><br>Many suppliers | *JIT*<br>Work cells<br>Smaller batches<br>Lower inventories<br>Each worker does a wide range of tasks<br>Fewer but well-coordinated suppliers |
| • How does costing work under JIT? | Under JIT costing,<br>1. the Materials and Work in process inventory accounts are combined into a single Raw and in-process inventory account.<br>2. labor and overhead are combined into a Conversion costs account.<br>3. summary journal entries are recorded *after* units are completed. | |
| • What are the four types of quality costs? | Prevention<br>Appraisal<br>Internal failure<br>External failure | |
| • How can we manage the four types of quality costs? | Invest up front in prevention and appraisal to reduce internal and external failure costs. | |

# Summary Problem 18-2

Flores Company manufactures cell phones and uses JIT costing. The standard unit cost is $30 is comprised of $20 direct materials and $10 conversion costs. Direct materials purchased on account during June totaled $2,500,000. Actual conversion costs totaled $1,100,000. Flores completed 100,000 cell phones in June and sold 98,000.

## Requirements

1. Journalize these transactions.
2. Were conversion costs under- or overallocated? *Hint*: You may want to prepare a T-account for the Conversion costs account. Explain your answer and then make the entry to close the Conversion costs account.
3. What is the ending balance of the Raw and in-process inventory account? How much Cost of goods sold did Flores have in June?

## Solution

### Requirement 1

| | | |
|---|---:|---:|
| Raw and in-process inventory    (A+) | 2,500,000 | |
|     Accounts payable    (L+) | | 2,500,000 |
| | | |
| Conversion costs    (E+) | 1,100,000 | |
|     Wages payable, Accumulated depreciation, etc. | | 1,100,000 |
| | | |
| Finished goods inventory    (A+) | 3,000,000 | |
|     Raw and in-process inventory (100,000 × $20)    (A–) | | 2,000,000 |
|     Conversion costs (100,000 × $10)    (E–) | | 1,000,000 |
| | | |
| Cost of goods sold (98,000 × $30)    (E+) | 2,940,000 | |
|     Finished goods inventory    (A–) | | 2,940,000 |

### Requirement 2

**Conversion costs**

| | |
|---:|---:|
| 1,100,000 | 1,000,000 |
| Bal    100,000 | |

Conversion costs were underallocated. Actual costs ($1,100,000) exceeded the cost allocated to inventory ($1,000,000).

| | | |
|---|---:|---:|
| Cost of goods sold    (E+) | 100,000 | |
|     Conversion costs    (E–) | | 100,000 |

### Requirement 3

**Raw and in-process inventory**

| | |
|---:|---:|
| 2,500,000 | 2,000,000 |
| Bal    500,000 | |

COGS = $3,040,000 ($2,940,000 + $100,000)

# Review *Activity-Based Costing and Other Cost Management Tools*

## ● Accounting Vocabulary

**Activity-Based Costing (ABC) (p. 882)**
Focuses on activities as the fundamental cost objects. The costs of those activities become the building blocks for allocating the costs of products and services.

**Activity-Based Management (ABM) (p. 886)**
Using activity-based cost information to make decisions that increase profits while satisfying customers needs.

**Appraisal Costs (p. 898)**
Costs incurred to detect poor-quality goods or services.

**Backflush Costing (p. 895)**
A costing system that starts with output completed and then assigns manufacturing costs to units sold and to inventories. Also called **just-in-time costing**.

**External Failure Costs (p. 898)**
Costs incurred when the company does not detect poor-quality goods or services until after delivery to customers.

**Internal Failure Costs (p. 898)**
Costs incurred when the company detects and corrects poor-quality goods or services before delivery to customers.

**Just-in-Time (JIT) Costing (p. 895)**
A costing system that starts with output completed and then assigns manufacturing costs to units sold and to inventories. Also called **backflush costing**.

**Prevention Costs (p. 898)**
Costs incurred to avoid poor-quality goods or services.

**Raw and In-Process Inventory (p. 895)**
Combined account for raw materials and work in process inventories under JIT systems.

**Target Cost (p. 888)**
The maximum cost to develop, produce, and deliver the product or service and earn the desired profit. Equals target price minus desired profit.

**Target Price (p. 887)**
What customers are willing to pay for the product or service.

**Value Engineering (p. 887)**
Reevaluating activities to reduce costs while satisfying customer needs.

## ● Destination: Student Success

### Student Success Tips

The following are hints on some common trouble areas for students in this chapter:

● Remember ABC costing measures manufacturing overhead by activities. By allocating costs to products based on how much they USE the activities, more accurate product costing results.

● Keep in mind that an allocation base (such as number of parts) can be used by more than one activity for ABC costing.

● Keep in mind that the goal of ABC is not only accurate costing but providing better information for Total Quality Management decision-making.

● Recall that JIT processing focuses on better vendor relationships so there is no need to maintain large raw materials inventories. Streamlined JIT production allows for streamlined accounting.

● Review the costs of quality. Keep in mind how dollars spent in preventing/appraising the process often reduce dollars spent repairing internal/external failures later.

### Getting Help

If there's a learning objective from the chapter you aren't confident about, try using one or more of the following resources:

● Review Exhibit 18-4, the four steps of ABC.

● Review Decision Guidelines 18-1 in the chapter to review ABC systems.

● Review Exhibit 18-16, the four types of quality costs.

● Review Summary Problem 18-2 in the chapter to reinforce your understanding of JIT and quality costs.

● Practice additional exercises or problems at the end of Chapter 18 that cover the specific learning objective that is challenging you.

● Watch the white board videos for Chapter 18 located at myaccountinglab.com under the Chapter Resources button.

● Go to myaccountinglab.com and select the Study Plan button. Choose Chapter 18 and work the questions covering that specific learning objective until you've mastered it.

● Work the Chapter 18 pre/post tests in myaccountinglab.com.

● Consult the Check Figures for End of Chapter starters, exercises, and problems, located at myaccountinglab.com.

● Visit the learning resource center on your campus for tutoring.

# ● Quick Check

1. Which statement is *false*?

   a. Information technology makes it feasible for most companies to adopt ABC.

   b. An ABC system is more refined than one that uses a company-wide overhead rate.

   c. ABC focuses on indirect costs.

   d. ABC is used ONLY for manufacturing companies.

**Experience the Power of Practice!**

As denoted by the logo, all of these questions, as well as additional practice materials, can be found in

**MyAccountingLab**.

Please visit myaccountinglab.com

Use the following information for questions 2–4. Two of Compute It's production activities are *kitting* (assembling the raw materials needed for each computer in one kit) and *boxing* the completed products for shipment to customers. Assume that Compute It spends $12,000,000 a month on kitting and $22,000,000 a month on boxing. Compute It allocates the following:

- Kitting costs based on the number of parts used in the computer
- Boxing costs based on the cubic feet of space the computer requires

Suppose Compute It estimates it will use 400,000,000 parts a month and ship products with a total volume of 20,000,000 cubic feet.

Assume that each desktop computer requires 125 parts and has a volume of 10 cubic feet.

2. What is the activity cost allocation rate?

|     | Kitting | Boxing |
| --- | --- | --- |
| a. | $0.03/part | $0.05/cubic foot |
| b. | $0.60/part | $0.06/cubic foot |
| c. | $0.03/part | $1.10/cubic foot |
| d. | $33.33/part | $0.91/cubic foot |

12,000,000 / 400,000,000 = 0.03    22,000,000 / 20,000,000 = 1.10

3. What are the kitting and boxing costs assigned to one desktop computer?

|     | Kitting | Boxing |
| --- | --- | --- |
| a. | $ 3.75 | $ 11.00 |
| b. | $ 0.30 | $137.50 |
| c. | $11.00 | $ 3.75 |
| d. | $ 4.05 | $148.50 |

0.03 (125) = 3.75    1.10 (10) = 11

4. Compute It contracts with its suppliers to pre-kit certain component parts before delivering them to Compute It. Assume this saves $2,000,000 of the kitting cost and reduces the total number of parts by 200,000,000 (because Compute It considers each pre-kit as one part). If a desktop now uses 90 parts, what is the new kitting cost assigned to one desktop?

   a. $4.50

   b. $1.00

   c. $2.70

   d. $3.75

5. Compute It can use ABC information for what decisions?

   a. Cost cutting

   b. Pricing

   c. Product mix

   d. Items a, b, and c are all correct

6. Which of the following would be true for a computer manufacturing company?

   a. ABC helps the company make more informed decisions about products.

   b. Manufacturing computers use only a few activities, so a companywide overhead allocation rate would work well.

   c. Most of the company's costs are for direct materials and direct labor. Indirect costs are a small proportion of total costs.

   d. All the above are true.

7. Companies enjoy many benefits from using JIT. Which is not a benefit of adopting JIT?
   a. Ability to respond quickly to changes in customer demand
   b. Lower inventory carrying costs
   c. Ability to continue production despite disruptions in deliveries of raw materials
   d. More space available for production

8. Which account is *not* used in JIT costing?
   a. Finished goods inventory
   b. Raw and in-process inventory
   c. Work in process inventory
   d. Conversion costs

9. The cost of lost future sales after a customer finds a defect in a product is which type of quality cost?
   a. Prevention cost
   b. Appraisal cost
   c. Internal failure cost
   d. External failure cost

10. Spending on testing a product before shipment to customers is which type of quality cost?
    a. External failure cost
    b. Prevention cost
    c. Appraisal cost
    d. None of the above

Answers are given after Apply Your Knowledge (p. 923).

# Assess Your Progress

## • Short Exercises

**S18-1** ❶ **Activity-based costing [5–10 min]**
Activity-based costing requires four steps.

### Requirement

1. Rank the following steps in the order in which they would be completed. Number the first step as "1" until you have ranked all four steps.
   a. Compute the cost allocation rate for each activity.
   b. Identify the cost driver for each activity and estimate the total quantity of each driver's allocation base.
   c. Allocate indirect costs to the cost object.
   d. Identify each activity and estimate its total indirect cost.

**S18-2** ❶ **Calculating costs using traditional and ABC [10 min]**
Brian and Gary are college friends planning a skiing trip to Killington before the New Year. They estimated the following costs for the trip:

| | Estimated Costs | Cost Driver | Activity Allocation Brian | Gary |
|---|---|---|---|---|
| Food | $ 550 | Pounds of food eaten | 24 | 26 |
| Skiing | 240 | # of lift tickets | 3 | 0 |
| Lodging | 320 | # of nights | 4 | 4 |
| | $ 1,110 | | | |

### Requirements

1. Brian suggests that the costs be shared equally. Calculate the amount each person would pay.
2. Gary does not like the idea because he plans to stay in the room rather than ski. Gary suggests that each type of cost be allocated to each person based on the above listed cost driver. Using the activity allocation for each person, calculate the amount that each person would pay based on his own consumption of the activity.

**S18-3**    **1** **Computing indirect manufacturing costs per unit [15 min]**

Day, Corp., is considering the use of activity-based costing. The following information is provided for the production of two product lines:

| Activity | Cost | Cost Driver |
|---|---|---|
| Setup | $    106,000 | Number of setups |
| Machine maintenance | 55,000 | Machine hours |
| Total indirect manufacturing costs | $    161,000 | |

| | Product A | Product B | Total |
|---|---|---|---|
| Direct labor hours | 6,500 | 5,500 | 12,000 |
| Number of setups | 20 | 180 | 200 |
| Number of machine hours | 1,600 | 2,400 | 4,000 |

Day plans to produce 400 units of Product A and 375 units of Product B.

## Requirement

1.  Compute the ABC indirect manufacturing cost per unit for each product.

**S18-4**    **1** **Computing indirect manufacturing costs per unit [15 min]**

The following information is provided for the Orbit Antenna, Corp., which
manufactures two products: Lo-Gain antennas, and Hi-Gain antennas for use in
remote areas.

| Activity | Cost | Cost Driver |
|---|---|---|
| Setup | $    57,000 | Number of setups |
| Machine maintenance | 27,000 | Machine hours |
| Total indirect manufacturing costs | $    84,000 | |

| | Lo-Gain | Hi-Gain | Total |
|---|---|---|---|
| Direct labor hours | 1,400 | 3,600 | 5,000 |
| Number of setups | 30 | 30 | 60 |
| Number of machine hours | 1,800 | 1,200 | 3,000 |

Orbit plans to produce 75 Lo-Gain antennas and 150 Hi-Gain antennas.

*Lo-Gain*

## Requirements

1.  Compute the ABC indirect manufacturing cost per unit for each product.
2.  Compute the indirect manufacturing cost per unit using direct labor hours from
    the single-allocation-base system.

**S18-5**    **1** **Using ABC to compute product costs per unit [15 min]**

Accel, Corp., makes two products: C and D. The following data have been summarized:

| | Product C | Product D |
|---|---|---|
| Direct materials cost per unit | $    700 | $    2,000 |
| Direct labor cost per unit | 300 | 100 |
| Indirect manufacturing cost per unit | ? | ? |

Indirect manufacturing cost information includes the following:

| Activity | Allocation Rate | Product C | Product D |
|---|---|---|---|
| Setup | $1,500/per setup | 38 setups | 75 setups |
| Machine maintenance | $    12/per hour | 1,400 hours | 4,000 hours |

The company plans to manufacture 150 units of each product.

## Requirement

1. Calculate the product cost per unit for Products C and D using activity-based costing.

**S18-6** ❶ **Using ABC to compute product costs per unit [15 min]**

Jaunkas, Corp., manufactures mid-fi and hi-fi stereo receivers. The following data have been summarized:

|  | Mid-Fi | Hi-Fi |
|---|---|---|
| Direct materials cost per unit | $ 400 | $ 1,300 |
| Direct labor cost per unit | 400 | 300 |
| Indirect manufacturing cost per unit | ? | ? |

Indirect manufacturing cost information includes the following:

| Activity | Allocation Rate | Mid–Fi | Hi–Fi |
|---|---|---|---|
| Setup | $1,700/per setup | 39 setups | 39 setups |
| Inspections | $ 400/per hour | 45 hours | 15 hours |
| Machine maintenance | $ 10/per machine hour | 1,900 machine hours | 1,200 machine hours |

The company plans to manufacture 200 units of the mid-fi receivers and 250 units of the hi-fi receivers.

## Requirement

1. Calculate the product cost per unit for both products using activity-based costing.

**S18-7** ❶ **Allocating indirect costs and computing income [10 min]**

Pacific, Inc., is a technology consulting firm focused on Web site development and integration of Internet business applications. The president of the company expects to incur $775,000 of indirect costs this year, and she expects her firm to work 5,000 direct labor hours. Pacific's systems consultants provide direct labor at a rate of $310 per hour. Clients are billed at 160% of direct labor cost. Last month Pacific's consultants spent 150 hours on Crockett's engagement.

## Requirements

1. Compute Pacific's indirect cost allocation rate per direct labor hour.
2. Compute the total cost assigned to the Crockett engagement.
3. Compute the operating income from the Crockett engagement.

*Note: Short Exercise 18-7 must be completed before attempting Short Exercise 18-8.*

**S18-8** ❶ **Computing ABC allocation rates [5 min]**

Refer to Short Exercise 18-7. The president of Pacific suspects that her allocation of indirect costs could be giving misleading results, so she decides to develop an ABC system. She identifies three activities: documentation preparation, information technology support, and training. She figures that documentation costs are driven by the number of pages, information technology support costs are driven by the number of software applications used, and training costs are driven by the number of direct labor hours worked. Estimates of the costs and quantities of the allocation bases follow:

| Activity | Estimated Cost | Allocation Base | Estimated Quantity of Allocation Base |
|---|---|---|---|
| Documentation preparation | $ 102,000 | Pages | 3,000 pages |
| Information technology support | 156,000 | Applications used | 780 applications |
| Training | 517,000 | Direct labor hours | 4,700 hours |
| Total indirect costs | $ 775,000 | | |

## Requirement

1. Compute the cost allocation rate for each activity.

*Note: Short Exercises 18-7 and 18-8 must be completed before attempting Short Exercise 18-9.*

**S18-9**  ❶ **Using ABC to allocate costs and compute profit [10–15 min]**

Refer to Short Exercises 18-7 and 18-8. Suppose Pacific's direct labor rate was $310 per hour, the documentation cost was $34 per page, the information technology support cost was $200 per application, and training costs were $110 per direct labor hour. The Crockett engagement used the following resources last month:

| Cost Driver | Crockett |
|---|---|
| Direct labor hours | 150 |
| Pages | 320 |
| Applications used | 75 |

## Requirements

1. Compute the cost assigned to the Crockett engagement, using the ABC system.
2. Compute the operating income from the Crockett engagement, using the ABC system.

*Note: Short Exercise 18-9 must be completed before attempting Short Exercise 18-10.*

**S18-10**  ❷ **Using ABC to achieve target profit [10–15 min]**

Refer to Short Exercise 18-9. Pacific desires a 25% target profit after covering all costs.

## Requirement

1. Considering the total costs assigned to the Crockett engagement in S18-9, what would Pacific have to charge the customer to achieve that profit?

*Note: Short Exercise 18-5 must be completed before attempting Short Exercise 18-11.*

**S18-11**  ❷ **Using ABC to achieve target profit [10–15 min]**

Refer to Short Exercise 18-5. Accel, Corp., desires a 25% target profit after covering all costs.

## Requirement

1. Considering the total costs assigned to the Products C and D in S18-5, what would Accel have to charge the customer to achieve that profit?

**S18-12**  ❸ **Just-in-time characteristics [5–10 min]**

Consider the following characteristics of either a JIT production system or a traditional production system.

  a. Products are produced in large batches.
  b. Large stocks of finished goods protect against lost sales if customer demand is higher than expected.
  c. Suppliers make frequent deliveries of small quantities of raw materials.
  d. Employees do a variety of jobs, including maintenance and setups as well as operating machines.
  e. Machines are grouped into self-contained production cells or production lines.
  f. Machines are grouped according to function. For example, all cutting machines are located in one area.
  g. The final operation in the production sequence "pulls" parts from the preceding operation.
  h. Each employee is responsible for inspecting his or her own work.
  i. Management works with suppliers to ensure defect-free raw materials.

## Requirement

1. Indicate whether each is characteristic of a JIT production system or a traditional production system.

**S18-13**  ❸ **Recording JIT costing journal entries [10 min]**

Quality Products uses a JIT system to manufacture trading pins for the **Hard Rock Café**. The standard cost per pin is $2 for raw materials and $3 for conversion costs. Last month Quality recorded the following data:

| | | | |
|---|---|---|---|
| Number of pins completed | 4,000 pins | Raw material purchases | $  9,500 |
| Number of pins sold | 3,300 pins | Conversion costs | $ 14,000 |

### Requirement

1.  Use JIT costing to prepare journal entries for the month, including the entry to close the Conversion costs account.

**S18-14**  ❹ **Matching cost-of-quality examples to categories [5–10 min]**

Sammy, Inc., manufactures motor scooters. Consider each of the following examples of quality costs.

_____ 1.  Preventive maintenance on machinery.

_____ 2.  Direct materials, direct labor, and manufacturing overhead costs incurred to rework a defective scooter that is detected in-house through inspection.

_____ 3.  Lost profits from lost sales if company's reputation was hurt because customers previously purchased a poor-quality scooter.

_____ 4.  Costs of inspecting raw materials, such as chassis and wheels.

_____ 5.  Working with suppliers to achieve on-time delivery of defect-free raw materials.

_____ 6.  Cost of warranty repairs on a scooter that malfunctions at customer's location.

_____ 7.  Costs of testing durability of vinyl.

_____ 8.  Cost to re-inspect reworked scooters.

### Requirement

1.  Indicate which of the following quality cost categories each example represents.
    - P    Prevention costs
    - A    Appraisal costs
    - IF   Internal failure costs
    - EF  External failure costs

## ● Exercises

**MyAccountingLab**    **E18-15**  ❶ **Product costing in an activity-based costing system [15–20 min]**

Fortunado, Inc., uses activity-based costing to account for its chrome bumper manufacturing process. Company managers have identified four manufacturing activities: materials handling, machine setup, insertion of parts, and finishing. The budgeted activity costs for 2012 and their allocation bases are as follows:

| Activity | Total Budgeted Cost | Allocation Base |
|---|---|---|
| Materials handling | $      9,000 | Number of parts |
| Machine setup | 3,900 | Number of setups |
| Insertion of parts | 42,000 | Number of parts |
| Finishing | 82,000 | Finishing direct labor hours |
| Total | $  136,900 | |

Fortunado expects to produce 500 chrome bumpers during the year. The bumpers are expected to use 4,000 parts, require 10 setups, and consume 1,000 hours of finishing time.

**Requirements**

1. Compute the cost allocation rate for each activity.
2. Compute the indirect manufacturing cost of each bumper.

**E18-16** ❶ **Product costing in an activity-based costing system [15–20 min]**
Turbo Champs, Corp., uses activity-based costing to account for its motorcycle manufacturing process. Company managers have identified three supporting manufacturing activities: inspection, machine setup, and machine maintenance. The budgeted activity costs for 2012 and their allocation bases are as follows:

| Activity | Total Budgeted Cost | Allocation Base |
|---|---|---|
| Inspection | $    6,000 | Number of inspections |
| Machine setup | 32,000 | Number of setups |
| Machine maintenance | 5,000 | Maintenance hours |
| Total | $  43,000 | |

Turbo Champs expects to produce 20 custom-built motorcycles for the year. The motorcycles are expected to require 100 inspections, 20 setups, and 100 maintenance hours.

**Requirements**

1. Compute the cost allocation rate for each activity.
2. Compute the indirect manufacturing cost of each motorcycle.

**E18-17** ❶ **Product costing in an activity-based costing system [20–30 min]**
Elton Company manufactures wheel rims. The controller budgeted the following ABC allocation rates for 2012:

| Activity | Allocation Base | Cost Allocation Rate | |
|---|---|---|---|
| Materials handling | Number of parts | $    4.00 | per part |
| Machine setup | Number of setups | 500.00 | per setup |
| Insertion of parts | Number of parts | 23.00 | per part |
| Finishing | Finishing hours | 50.00 | per hour |

The number of parts is now a feasible allocation base because Elton recently purchased bar coding technology. Elton produces two wheel rim models: standard and deluxe. Budgeted data for 2012 are as follows:

| | Standard | Deluxe |
|---|---|---|
| Parts per rim | 6.0 | 9.0 |
| Setups per 500 rims | 17.0 | 17.0 |
| Finishing hours per rim | 5.0 | 6.5 |
| Total direct labor hours per rim | 6.0 | 7.0 |

The company expects to produce 500 units of each model during the year.

## Requirements

1. Compute the total budgeted indirect manufacturing cost for 2012.

2. Compute the ABC indirect manufacturing cost per unit of each model. Carry each cost to the nearest cent.

3. Prior to 2012, Elton used a direct labor hour single-allocation-base system. Compute the (single) allocation rate based on direct labor hours for 2012. Use this rate to determine the indirect manufacturing cost per wheel rim for each model, to the nearest cent.

**E18-18**   **1  2  Using activity-based costing to make decisions [10 min]**
Dino Dog Collars uses activity-based costing. Dino's system has the following features:

| Activity | Allocation Base | Cost Allocation Rate |
|---|---|---|
| Purchasing | Number of purchase orders | $65.00 per purchase order |
| Assembling | Number of parts | $ 0.36 per part |
| Packaging | Number of finished collars | $ 0.25 per collar |

Each collar has 4 parts; direct materials cost per collar is $9. Direct labor cost is $4 per collar. Suppose Animal Hut has asked for a bid on 25,000 dog collars. Dino will issue a total of 150 purchase orders if Animal Hut accepts Dino's bid.

## Requirements

1. Compute the total cost Dino will incur to purchase the needed materials and then assemble and package 25,000 dog collars. Also compute the cost per collar.

2. For bidding, Dino adds a 40% markup to total cost. What total price will the company bid for the entire Animal Hut order?

3. Suppose that instead of an ABC system, Dino has a traditional product costing system that allocates indirect costs other than direct materials and direct labor at the rate of $9.60 per direct labor hour. The dog collar order will require 12,000 direct labor hours. What total price will Dino bid using this system's total cost?

4. Use your answers to Requirements 2 and 3 to explain how ABC can help Dino make a better decision about the bid price it will offer Animal Hut.

*Note: Exercise 18-17 must be completed before attempting Exercise 18-19.*

**E18-19**   **2  Using activity-based costing to make decisions [15–20 min]**
Refer to Exercise 18-17. For 2013, Elton's managers have decided to use the same indirect manufacturing costs per wheel rim that they computed in 2012. In addition to the unit indirect manufacturing costs, the following data are budgeted for the company's standard and deluxe models for 2013:

| | Standard | Deluxe |
|---|---|---|
| Sales price | 800.00 | 940.00 |
| Direct materials | 31.00 | 50.00 |
| Direct labor | 45.00 | 56.00 |

Because of limited machine-hour capacity, Elton can produce *either* 2,000 standard rims *or* 2,000 deluxe rims.

## Requirements

1. If Elton's managers rely on the ABC unit cost data computed in E18-17, which model will they produce? Carry each cost to the nearest cent. (Ignore operating expenses for this calculation.)

2. If the managers rely on the single-allocation-base cost data, which model will they produce?

3. Which course of action will yield more income for Elton?

*Note: Exercises 18-17 and 18-19 must be completed before attempting Exercise 18-20.*

**E18-20**    ② **Activity-based management and target cost [10 min]**

Refer to Exercises 18-17 and 18-19. Controller Michael Bender is surprised by the increase in cost of the deluxe model under ABC. Market research shows that for the deluxe rim to provide a reasonable profit, Elton will have to meet a target manufacturing cost of $656 per rim. A value engineering study by Elton's employees suggests that modifications to the finishing process could cut finishing cost from $50 to $40 per hour and reduce the finishing direct labor hours per deluxe rim from 6.5 hours to 6 hours. Direct materials would remain unchanged at $50 per rim, as would direct labor at $56 per rim. The materials handling, machine setup, and insertion of parts activity costs also would remain the same.

### Requirement

1.  Would implementing the value engineering recommendation enable Elton to achieve its target cost for the deluxe rim?

**E18-21**    ③ **Recording manufacturing costs in a JIT costing system [15–20 min]**

Lancer, Inc., produces universal remote controls. Lancer uses a JIT costing system. One of the company's products has a standard direct materials cost of $9 per unit and a standard conversion cost of $35 per unit. During January 2012, Lancer produced 600 units and sold 595. It purchased $6,300 of direct materials and incurred actual conversion costs totaling $17,500.

### Requirements

1.  Prepare summary journal entries for January.
2.  The January 1, 2012, balance of the Raw and in-process inventory account was $50. Use a T-account to find the January 31 balance.
3.  Use a T-account to determine whether conversion costs are over- or underallocated for the month. By how much? Prepare the journal entry to close the Conversion costs account.

**E18-22**    ③ **Recording manufacturing costs in a JIT costing system [10–15 min]**

Dubuc produces electronic calculators. Suppose Dubuc's standard cost per calculator is $27 for materials and $63 for conversion costs. The following data apply to August production:

| | | |
|---|---|---|
| Materials purchased | $ 6,700 | |
| Conversion costs incurred | 14,000 | |
| Number of calculators produced | | 200 calculators |
| Number of calculators sold | | 195 calculators |

### Requirements

1.  Prepare summary journal entries for August using JIT costing, including the entry to close the Conversion costs account.
2.  The beginning balance of Finished goods inventory was $1,700. Use a T-account to find the ending balance of Finished goods inventory.

**E18-23**    ④ **Classifying quality costs [5–10 min]**

Delance & Co. makes electronic components. Chris Delance, the president, recently instructed vice president Jim Bruegger to develop a total quality control program. "If we don't at least match the quality improvements our competitors are making," he told Bruegger, "we'll soon be out of business." Bruegger began by listing various "costs of quality" that Delance incurs. The first six items that came to mind were:

a. Costs incurred by Delance customer representatives traveling to customer sites to repair defective products, $15,000.
b. Lost profits from lost sales due to reputation for less-than-perfect products, $60,000.
c. Costs of inspecting components in one of Delance's production processes, $25,000.
d. Salaries of engineers who are redesigning components to withstand electrical overloads, $80,000.
e. Costs of reworking defective components after discovery by company inspectors, $40,000.
f. Costs of electronic components returned by customers, $55,000.

## Requirement

1. Classify each item as a prevention cost, an appraisal cost, an internal failure cost, or an external failure cost. Then, determine the total cost of quality by category.

**E18-24** ❹ **Classifying quality costs and using these costs to make decisions [15–20 min]**

Clarke, Inc., manufactures door panels. Suppose Clarke is considering spending the following amounts on a new total quality management (TQM) program:

| | |
|---|---|
| Strength-testing one item from each batch of panels  A | $    62,000 |
| Training employees in TQM  P | 25,000 |
| Training suppliers in TQM  E | 38,000 |
| Identifying suppliers who commit to on-time delivery of perfect-quality materials  I | 56,000 |

Clarke expects the new program would save costs through the following:

| | |
|---|---|
| Avoid lost profits from lost sales due to disappointed customers | $    94,000 |
| Avoid rework and spoilage | 60,000 |
| Avoid inspection of raw materials | 55,000 |
| Avoid warranty costs  E | 20,000 |

## Requirements

1. Classify each cost as a prevention cost, an appraisal cost, an internal failure cost, or an external failure cost.
2. Should Clarke implement the new quality program? Give your reason.

**E18-25** ❹ **Classifying quality costs and using these costs to make decisions [10–15 min]**

Kane manufactures high-quality speakers. Suppose Kane is considering spending the following amounts on a new quality program:

| | |
|---|---|
| Additional 20 minutes of testing for each speaker | $   620,000 |
| Negotiating with and training suppliers to obtain higher-quality materials and on-time delivery | 410,000 |
| Redesigning the speakers to make them easier to manufacture | 1,350,000 |

Kane expects this quality program to save costs, as follows:

| | |
|---|---|
| Reduce warranty repair costs | $   225,000 |
| Avoid inspection of raw materials | 540,000 |
| Avoid rework because of fewer defective units | 800,000 |

It also expects this program to avoid lost profits from the following:

| | |
|---|---|
| Lost sales due to disappointed customers | $   940,000 |
| Lost production time due to rework | 278,000 |

## Requirements

1. Classify each of these costs into one of the four categories of quality costs (prevention, appraisal, internal failure, external failure).
2. Should Kane implement the quality program? Give your reasons.

## • Problems (Group A)

### P18-26A ❶ Product costing in an ABC system [15–20 min]

The August Manufacturing Company in Rochester, Minnesota, assembles and tests electronic components used in handheld video phones. Consider the following data regarding component T24:

| | |
|---|---|
| Direct materials cost | $   82.00 |
| Direct labor cost | $   23.00 |
| Activity costs allocated | 66.4 ? |
| Manufacturing product cost | $ 171.4 ? |

The activities required to build the component follow:

| Activity | Allocation Base | Cost Allocated to Each Unit |
|---|---|---|
| Start station | Number of raw component chasis | 6 × $ 1.60 = $ 9.60 |
| Dip insertion | Number of dip insertions | ? × $ 0.20 = 5.20  26 |
| Manual insertion | Number of manual insertions | 10 × $ 0.40 = 4.00? |
| Wave solder | Number of components soldered | 6 × $ 1.70 = 10.20 |
| Backload | Number of backload insertions | 8 × $ 0.8 ? = 6.40 |
| Test | Testing hours | 0.43 × $ 60.00 = 25.8 ? |
| Defect analysis | Defect analysis hours | 0.13 × $ 40 ? = $ 5.20 |
| Total indirect activity costs | | $ 66.4 ? |

## Requirements

1. Complete the missing items for the two tables.
2. Why might managers favor this ABC system instead of August's older system, which allocated all conversion costs on the basis of direct labor?

### P18-27A ❶❷ Product costing in an ABC system [20–30 min]

Prescott, Inc., manufactures bookcases and uses an activity-based costing system. Prescott's activity areas and related data follow:

| Activity | Budgeted Cost of Activity | Allocation Base | Cost Allocation Rate |
|---|---|---|---|
| Materials handling | $   230,000 | Number of parts | $   0.50 |
| Assembly | 3,200,000 | Direct labor hours | 16.00 |
| Finishing | 180,000 | Number of finished units | 4.50 |

Prescott produced two styles of bookcases in October: the standard bookcase and an unfinished bookcase, which has fewer parts and requires no finishing. The totals for quantities, direct materials costs, and other data follow:

| Product | Total Units Produced | Total Direct Materials Costs | Total Direct Labor Costs | Total Number of Parts | Total Assembling Direct Labor Hours |
|---|---|---|---|---|---|
| Standard bookcase | 3,000 | $ 36,000 | $ 45,000 | 9,000 | 4,500 |
| Unfinished bookcase | 3,500 | 35,000 | 35,000 | 7,000 | 3,500 |

## Requirements

1. Compute the manufacturing product cost per unit of each type of bookcase.

2. Suppose that pre-manufacturing activities, such as product design, were assigned to the standard bookcases at $7 each, and to the unfinished bookcases at $2 each. Similar analyses were conducted of post-manufacturing activities such as distribution, marketing, and customer service. The post-manufacturing costs were $22 per standard bookcase and $14 per unfinished bookcase. Compute the full product costs per unit.

3. Which product costs are reported in the external financial statements? Which costs are used for management decision making? Explain the difference.

4. What price should Prescott's managers set for unfinished bookcases to earn $15 per bookcase?

**P18-28A** ❶ ❷ **Comparing costs from ABC and single-rate systems [30–40 min]**

Corbertt Pharmaceuticals manufactures an over-the-counter allergy medication. The company sells both large commercial containers of 1,000 capsules to health-care facilities and travel packs of 20 capsules to shops in airports, train stations, and hotels. The following information has been developed to determine if an activity-based costing system would be beneficial:

| Activity | Estimated Indirect Activity Costs | Allocation Base | Estimated Quantity of Allocation Base |
|---|---|---|---|
| Materials handling . . . . . | $    95,000 | Kilos . . . . . . . . . . | 19,000 kilos |
| Packaging . . . . . . . . . . . | 219,000 | Machine hours . . | 5,475 hours |
| Quality assurance . . . . . . | 124,500 | Samples . . . . . . . | 2,075 samples |
| Total indirect costs . . . . . | $  438,500 | | |

Other production information includes the following:

| | Commerical Containers | Travel Packs |
|---|---|---|
| Units produced . . . . . . . . | 3,500    containers | 57,000    packs |
| Weight in kilos . . . . . . . . | 14,000 | 5,700 |
| Machine hours . . . . . . . . | 2,625 | 570 |
| Number of samples   . . . . | 700 | 855 |

## Requirements

1. Compute the cost allocation rate for each activity.

2. Use the activity-based cost allocation rates to compute the activity costs per unit of the commercial containers and the travel packs. (*Hint*: First compute the total activity costs allocated to each product line, and then compute the cost per unit.)

3. Corbertt's original single-allocation-base costing system allocated indirect costs to products at $157 per machine hour. Compute the total indirect costs allocated to the commercial containers and to the travel packs under the original system. Then compute the indirect cost per unit for each product.

4. Compare the indirect activity-based costs per unit to the indirect costs per unit from the single-allocation-base system. How have the unit costs changed? Explain why the costs changed.

**P18-29A** ❸ **Recording manufacturing costs for a JIT costing system [15–25 min]**

High Point produces fleece jackets. The company uses JIT costing for its JIT production system.

High Point has two inventory accounts: Raw and in-process inventory and Finished goods inventory. On February 1, 2012, the account balances were Raw and in-process inventory, $7,000; Finished goods inventory, $2,200.

The standard cost of a jacket is $37, comprised of $13 direct materials plus $24 conversion costs. Data for February's activities follow:

| | | | |
|---|---|---|---|
| Number of jackets completed | 20,000 | Direct materials purchased | $ 257,500 |
| Number of jackets sold | 19,600 | Conversion costs incurred | $ 580,000 |

## Requirements

1. What are the major features of a JIT production system such as that of High Point?
2. Prepare summary journal entries for February. Under- or overallocated conversion costs are closed to Cost of goods sold monthly.
3. Use a T-account to determine the February 29, 2012, balance of Raw and in-process inventory.

### P18-30A  ④ Analyzing costs of quality [20–30 min]

Christi, Inc., is using a costs-of-quality approach to evaluate design engineering efforts for a new skateboard. Christi's senior managers expect the engineering work to reduce appraisal, internal failure, and external failure activities. The predicted reductions in activities over the 2-year life of the skateboards follow. Also shown are the cost allocation rates for each activity.

| Activity | Predicted Reduction in Activity Units | Activity Cost Allocation Rate Per Unit |
|---|---|---|
| Inspection of incoming materials ..... | 420 | $       37 |
| Inspection of finished goods ......... | 420 | 26 |
| Number of defective units | | |
|    discovered in-house ............ | 1,400 | 56 |
| Number of defective units | | |
|    discovered by customers .......... | 325 | 75 |
| Lost sales to dissatisfied customers .... | 150 | 103 |

## Requirements

1. Calculate the predicted quality cost savings from the design engineering work.
2. Christi spent $103,000 on design engineering for the new skateboard. What is the net benefit of this "preventive" quality activity?
3. What major difficulty would Christi's managers have in implementing this costs-of-quality approach? What alternative approach could they use to measure quality improvement?

## ● Problems  (Group B)

### P18-31B  ① Product costing in an ABC system [15–20 min]

The Abram Manufacturing Company in Rochester, Minnesota, assembles and tests electronic components used in handheld video phones. Consider the following data regarding component T24:

| | | |
|---|---|---|
| Direct materials cost | $ | 81.00 |
| Direct labor cost | $ | 21.00 |
| Activity costs allocated | | ? |
| Manufacturing product cost | $ | ? |

The activities required to build the component follow:

| Activity | Allocation Base | Cost Allocated to Each Unit | | | | |
|---|---|---|---|---|---|---|
| Start station | Number of raw component chasis | 1 | × $ | 1.20 | = $ | 1.20 |
| Dip insertion | Number of dip insertions | ? | × $ | 0.35 | = | 11.20 |
| Manual insertion | Number of manual insertions | 11 | × $ | 0.20 | = | ? |
| Wave solder | Number of components soldered | 1 | × $ | 1.60 | = | 1.60 |
| Backload | Number of backload insertions | 4 | × | ? | = | 2.80 |
| Test | Testing hours | 0.38 | × $ | 50.00 | = | ? |
| Defect analysis | Defect analysis hours | 0.14 | × | ? | = | 5.60 |
| Total indirect activity costs | | | | | $ | ? |

## Requirements

1. Complete the missing items for the two tables.
2. Why might managers favor this ABC system instead of Abram's older system, which allocated all conversion costs on the basis of direct labor?

**P18-32B** ❶ ❷ **Product costing in an ABC system [20–30 min]**

McKnight, Inc., manufactures bookcases and uses an activity-based costing system. McKnight's activity areas and related data follow:

| Activity | Budgeted Cost of Activity | Allocation Base | Cost Allocation Rate |
|---|---|---|---|
| Materials handling | $ 240,000 | Number of parts | $ 1.00 |
| Assembly | 3,300,000 | Direct labor hours | 17.00 |
| Finishing | 150,000 | Number of finished units | 2.50 |

McKnight produced two styles of bookcases in April: the standard bookcase and an unfinished bookcase, which has fewer parts and requires no finishing. The totals for quantities, direct materials costs, and other data follow:

| Product | Total Units Produced | Total Direct Materials Costs | Total Direct Labor Costs | Total Number of Parts | Total Assembling Direct Labor Hours |
|---|---|---|---|---|---|
| Standard bookcase | 2,000 | $ 24,000 | $ 30,000 | 8,000 | 3,000 |
| Unfinished bookcase | 2,600 | 26,000 | 26,000 | 7,800 | 2,600 |

## Requirements

1. Compute the manufacturing product cost per unit of each type of bookcase.
2. Suppose that pre-manufacturing activities, such as product design, were assigned to the standard bookcases at $4 each, and to the unfinished bookcases at $3 each. Similar analyses were conducted of post-manufacturing activities such as distribution, marketing, and customer service. The post-manufacturing costs were $20 per standard bookcase and $15 per unfinished bookcase. Compute the full product costs per unit.
3. Which product costs are reported in the external financial statements? Which costs are used for management decision making? Explain the difference.
4. What price should McKnight's managers set for unfinished bookcases to earn $16 per bookcase?

**P18-33B** ❶ ❷ **Comparing costs from ABC and single-rate systems [30–40 min]**

Sawyer Pharmaceuticals manufactures an over-the-counter allergy medication. The company sells both large commercial containers of 1,000 capsules to health-care facilities and travel packs of 20 capsules to shops in airports, train stations, and hotels. The following information has been developed to determine if an activity-based costing system would be beneficial:

| Activity | Estimated Indirect Activity Costs | Allocation Base | Estimated Quantity of Allocation Base |
|---|---|---|---|
| Materials handling ..... $ | 115,000 | Kilos .......... | 23,000 kilos |
| Packaging ............ | 204,000 | Machine hours .. | 4,160 hours |
| Quality assurance ...... | 114,000 | Samples ....... | 1,900 samples |
| Total indirect costs ..... $ | 433,000 | | |

Other production information includes the following:

| | Commerical Containers | Travel Packs |
|---|---|---|
| Units produced ........ | 3,400 containers | 55,000 packs |
| Weight in kilos ........ | 17,000 | 16,500 |
| Machine hours ........ | 2,720 | 550 |
| Number of samples .... | 340 | 825 |

## Requirements

1. Compute the cost allocation rate for each activity.
2. Use the activity-based cost allocation rates to compute the activity costs per unit of the commercial containers and the travel packs. (*Hint*: First compute the total activity costs allocated to each product line, and then compute the cost per unit.)
3. Sawyer's original single-allocation-base costing system allocated indirect costs to products at $150 per machine hour. Compute the total indirect costs allocated to the commercial containers and to the travel packs under the original system. Then compute the indirect cost per unit for each product.
4. Compare the indirect activity-based costs per unit to the indirect costs per unit from the single-allocation-base system. How have the unit costs changed? Explain why the costs changed as they did.

### P18-34B ③ Recording manufacturing costs for a JIT costing system [15–25 min]
Deep Freeze produces fleece jackets. The company uses JIT costing for its JIT production system.

Deep Freeze has two inventory accounts: Raw and in-process inventory and Finished goods inventory. On February 1, 2012, the account balances were Raw and in-process inventory, $10,000; Finished goods inventory, $1,600.

The standard cost of a jacket is $39, comprised of $16 direct materials plus $23 conversion costs. Data for February's activities follow:

| Number of jackets completed | 19,000 | Direct materials purchased | $ 301,500 |
|---|---|---|---|
| Number of jackets sold | 18,600 | Conversion costs incurred | $ 538,000 |

## Requirements

1. What are the major features of a JIT production system such as that of Deep Freeze?
2. Prepare summary journal entries for February. Under- or overallocated conversion costs are closed to Cost of goods sold monthly.
3. Use a T-account to determine the February 29, 2012, balance of Raw and in-process inventory.

### P18-35B ④ Analyzing costs of quality [20–30 min]
Roxi, Inc., is using a costs-of-quality approach to evaluate design engineering efforts for a new skateboard. Roxi's senior managers expect the engineering work to reduce appraisal, internal failure, and external failure activities. The predicted reductions in

activities over the 2-year life of the skateboards follow. Also shown are the cost allocation rates for each activity.

| Activity | Predicted Reduction in Activity Units | Activity Cost Allocation Rate Per Unit |
|---|---|---|
| Inspection of incoming materials ..... | 385 | $ 39 |
| Inspection of finished goods ......... | 385 | 22 |
| Number of defective units discovered in-house ............. | 1,200 | 55 |
| Number of defective units discovered by customers .......... | 300 | 73 |
| Lost sales to dissatisfied customers .... | 100 | 97 |

## Requirements

1. Calculate the predicted quality cost savings from the design engineering work.
2. Roxi spent $109,000 on design engineering for the new skateboard. What is the net benefit of this "preventive" quality activity?
3. What major difficulty would Roxi's managers have in implementing this costs-of-quality approach? What alternative approach could they use to measure quality improvement?

## ● Continuing Exercise

**MyAccountingLab** **E18-36** ❶ **Product costing in an ABC system [15–20 min]**

This exercise continues the Lawlor Lawn Service, Inc., situation from Exercise 17-34 of Chapter 17. Recall that Lawlor completed a special landscaping job for Sheldon's Ideal Designs. If Lawlor had used activity-based costing, Lawlor's data about the job, including ABC information, would be as follows:

Sheldon Job details:
Direct materials    $700
Direct labor    $1,200

ABC Costing Rates:
$275 per setup
$15 per plant

## Requirements

1. Lawlor uses one setup for the Sheldon job and installs 35 plants. What is the total cost of the Sheldon job?
2. If Sheldon paid $3,900 for the job, what is the profit or loss under ABC?

## ● Continuing Problem

**MyAccountingLab** **P18-37** ❶❷ **Comparing costs from ABC and single-rate systems [30–40 min]**

This problem continues the Draper Consulting, Inc., situation from Problem 17-35 of Chapter 17. Recall that Draper allocated indirect costs to jobs based on a predetermined indirect cost allocation rate, computed as a percentage of direct labor costs. Because Draper provides a service, there are no direct materials costs. Draper is now considering using an ABC system. Information about ABC costs follows:

| Activity | Budgeted Cost of Activity | Allocation Base | Cost Allocation Rate |
|---|---|---|---|
| Design | $ 350,000 | Number of designs | $ 7,000 |
| Programming | 550,000 | Direct labor hours | 110 |
| Testing | 288,000 | Number of tests | 3,500 |

Records for two clients appear here:

| Job | Total Direct Labor Costs | Total Number of Designs | Total Programming Direct Labor Hours | Number of Tests |
|---|---|---|---|---|
| Tommy's Trains | $  13,600 | 3 | 730 | 6 |
| Marcia's Cookies | 600 | 5 | 300 | 8 |

## Requirements

1. Compute the total cost of each job.
2. Is the job cost greater or less than that computed in Problem 17-35 for each job? Why?
3. If Draper wants to earn gross profit equal to 25% of cost, how much (what fee) should it charge each of these two clients?

# Apply Your Knowledge

## • Decision Cases

**Decision Case 18-1** Harris Systems specializes in servers for workgroup, e-commerce, and ERP applications. The company's original job costing system has two direct cost categories: direct materials and direct labor. Overhead is allocated to jobs at the single rate of $22 per direct labor hour.

A task force headed by Harris's CFO recently designed an ABC system with four activities. The ABC system retains the current system's two direct cost categories. Overhead costs are reflected in the four activities. Pertinent data follow:

| Activity | Allocation Base | Cost Allocation Rate |
|---|---|---|
| Materials handling | Number of parts | $     0.85 |
| Machine setup | Number of setups | 500.00 |
| Assembling | Assembling hours | 80.00 |
| Shipping | Number of shipments | 1,500.00 |

Harris Systems has been awarded two new contracts, which will be produced as Job A and Job B. Budget data relating to the contracts follow:

| | Job A | Job B |
|---|---|---|
| Number of parts............................. | 15,000 | 2,000 |
| Number of setups............................ | 6 | 4 |
| Number of assembling hours............ | 1,500 | 200 |
| Number of shipments....................... | 1 | 1 |
| Total direct labor hours .................. | 8,000 | 600 |
| Number of units produced .............. | 100 | 10 |
| Direct materials cost........................ | $220,000 | $30,000 |
| Direct labor cost............................. | $160,000 | $12,000 |

### Requirements

1. Compute the product cost per unit for each job, using the original costing system (with two direct cost categories and a single overhead allocation rate).

2. Suppose Harris Systems adopts the ABC system. Compute the product cost per unit for each job using ABC.

3. Which costing system more accurately assigns to jobs the costs of the resources consumed to produce them? Explain.

**Decision Case 18-2** To remain competitive, Harris Systems' management believes the company must produce Job B-type servers (from Decision Case 18-1) at a target cost of $5,400. Harris Systems has just joined a B2B e-market site that management believes will enable the firm to cut direct materials costs by 10%. Harris's management also believes that a value engineering team can reduce assembly time.

### Requirement

1. Compute the assembling cost savings per Job B-type server required to meet the $5,400 target cost. (*Hint*: Begin by calculating the direct materials, direct labor, and allocated activity costs per server.)

## ● Ethical Issue 18-1

Cassidy Manning is assistant controller at LeMar Packaging, Inc., a manufacturer of cardboard boxes and other packaging materials. Manning has just returned from a packaging industry conference on activity-based costing. She realizes that ABC may help LeMar meet its goal of reducing costs by 5% over each of the next three years.

LeMar Packaging's Order Department is a likely candidate for ABC. While orders are entered into a computer that updates the accounting records, clerks manually check customers' credit history and hand-deliver orders to shipping. This process occurs whether the sales order is for a dozen specialty boxes worth $80, or 10,000 basic boxes worth $8,000.

Manning believes that identifying the cost of processing a sales order would justify (1) further computerization of the order process and (2) changing the way the company processes small orders. However, the significant cost savings would arise from elimination of two positions in the Order Department. The company's sales order clerks have been with the company many years. Manning is uncomfortable with the prospect of proposing a change that will likely result in terminating these employees.

### Requirement

1. Use the IMA's ethical standards (see Chapter 16) to consider Manning's responsibility when cost savings come at the expense of employees' jobs.

## ● Fraud Case 18-1

Anu Ghai was a new production analyst at RHI, Inc., a large furniture factory in North Carolina. One of her first jobs was to update the activity rates for factory production costs. This was normally done once a year, by analyzing the previous year's actual data, factoring in projected changes, and calculating a new rate for the coming year. What Anu found was strange. The activity rate for "maintenance" had more than doubled in one year, and she was puzzled how that could have happened. When she spoke with Larry McAfee, the factory manager, she was told to spread the increases out over the other activity costs to "smooth out" the trends. She was a bit intimidated by Larry, an imposing and aggressive man, but she knew something wasn't quite right. Then one night she was at a restaurant and overheard a few employees who worked at RHI talking. They were joking about the work they had done fixing up Larry's home at the lake last year. Suddenly everything made sense. Larry had been using factory labor, tools, and supplies to have his lake house renovated on the weekends. Anu had a distinct feeling that if she went up against Larry on this issue, she would come out the loser. She decided to look for work elsewhere.

**Requirements**

1. Besides spotting irregularities, like the case above, what are some other ways that ABC cost data are useful for manufacturing companies?

2. What are some of the other options that Anu might have considered?

## ● Team Project 18-1

Bronson Shrimp Farms, in Brewton, Alabama, has a Processing Department that processes raw shrimp into two products:

- Headless shrimp
- Peeled and deveined shrimp

Bronson recently submitted bids for two orders: (1) headless shrimp for a cruise line and (2) peeled and deveined shrimp for a restaurant chain. Bronson won the first bid but lost the second. The production and sales managers are upset. They believe that Bronson's state-of-the-art equipment should have given the company an edge in the peeled and deveined market. Consequently, production managers are starting to keep their own sets of product cost records.

Bronson is reexamining both its production process and its costing system. The existing costing system has been in place since 1991. It allocates all indirect costs based on direct labor hours. Bronson is considering adopting activity-based costing. Controller Heather Barefield and a team of production managers performed a preliminary study. The team identified six activities, with the following (department-wide) estimated indirect costs and cost drivers for 2014:

| Activity | Estimated Total Cost of Activity | Allocation Base |
|---|---|---|
| Redesign of production process (costs of changing process and equipment) | $ 5,000 | Number of design changes |
| Production scheduling (production scheduler's salary) | 6,000 | Number of batches |
| Chilling (depreciation on refrigerators) | 1,500 | Weight (in pounds) |
| Processing (utilities and depreciation on equipment) | 19,200 | Number of cuts |
| Packaging (indirect labor and depreciation on equipment) | 1,425 | Cubic feet of surface exposed |
| Order filling (order-takers' and shipping clerks' wages) | 7,000 | Number of orders |
| Total indirect costs for the entire department | $40,125 | |

The raw shrimp are chilled and then cut. For headless shrimp, employees remove the heads, then rinse the shrimp. For peeled and deveined shrimp, the headless shrimp are further processed—the shells are removed and the backs are slit for deveining. Both headless shrimp and peeled and deveined shrimp are packaged in foam trays and covered with shrink wrap. Order-filling personnel assemble orders of headless shrimp as well as peeled and deveined shrimp.

Barefield estimates that Bronson will produce 10,000 packages of headless shrimp and 50,000 packages of peeled and deveined shrimp in 2014. The two products incur the following costs and activities per package:

| | Costs and Activities per Package | |
|---|---|---|
| | Headless Shrimp | Peeled and Deveined Shrimp |
| Shrimp ...................................... | $3.50 | $4.50 |
| Foam trays ............................. | $0.05 | $0.05 |
| Shrink wrap ........................... | $0.05 | $0.02 |
| Number of cuts ...................... | 1 cut | 3 cuts |
| Cubic feet of exposed surface ... | 1 cubic foot | 0.75 cubic foot |
| Weight (in pounds).................. | 2.5 pounds | 1 pound |
| Direct labor hours ................... | 0.01 hour | 0.05 hour |

Bronson pays direct laborers $20 per hour. Barefield estimates that each product line also will require the following *total* resources:

| | Headless Shrimp | | Peeled and Deveined Shrimp | |
|---|---|---|---|---|
| Design changes | 1 change | for all | 4 changes | for all |
| Batches | 40 batches | 10,000 | 20 batches | 50,000 |
| Sales orders | 90 orders | packages | 110 orders | packages |

## Requirements

Form groups of four students. All group members should work together to develop the group's answers to the three requirements.

1.  Using the original costing system with the single indirect cost allocation base (direct labor hours), compute the total budgeted cost per package for the headless shrimp and then for the peeled and deveined shrimp. (*Hint*: First, compute the indirect cost allocation rate—that is, the predetermined overhead rate. Then, compute the total budgeted cost per package for each product.)

2.  Use activity-based costing to recompute the total budgeted cost per package for the headless shrimp and then for the peeled and deveined shrimp. (*Hint*: First, calculate the budgeted cost allocation rate for each activity. Then, calculate the total indirect costs of (a) the entire headless shrimp product line and (b) the entire peeled and deveined shrimp product line. Next, compute the indirect cost per package of each product. Finally, calculate the total cost per package of each product.)

3.  Write a memo to Bronson CEO Gary Pololu explaining the results of the ABC study. Compare the costs reported by the ABC system with the costs reported by the original system. Point out whether the ABC system shifted costs toward headless shrimp or toward peeled and deveined shrimp, and explain why. Finally, explain whether Pololu should feel more comfortable making decisions using cost data from the original system or from the new ABC system.

## ● Communication Activity 18-1

In 75 words or fewer, explain the difference between allocating manufacturing overhead using traditional cost allocation and activity-based costing allocations.

---

### Quick Check Answers

1. *d*  2. *c*  3. *a*  4. *a*  5. *d*  6. *a*  7. *c*  8. *c*  9. *d*  10. *c*

**For online homework, exercises, and problems that provide you immediate feedback, please visit myaccountinglab.com.**

# 19 Cost-Volume-Profit Analysis

## Learning Objectives

1. Identify how changes in volume affect costs

2. Use CVP analysis to compute breakeven points

3. Use CVP analysis for profit planning, and graph the CVP relations

4. Use CVP methods to perform sensitivity analyses

5. Calculate the breakeven point for multiple products or services

6. Distinguish between variable costing and absorption costing (see Appendix 19A, located at myaccountinglab.com)

You and your friends head out to a favorite restaurant for dinner. The restaurant serves a meat dish with three side dishes for a reasonable price. The combination of good food at a good price has made this "meat and three" restaurant popular. However, when you arrive at the restaurant this time, it is not as crowded as usual. You also notice the restaurant has increased the price for a meal.

After you are seated and order, you and your friends discuss the changes. No one seems surprised by the price increase. You've all noticed that food prices have increased at the grocery store and speculate that the restaurant's supplier has also increased prices. If food costs increase, the business would have to increase the sales price per meal in order for the meals to remain profitable. Is this what is keeping some customers away? What will be the effect on profits if the restaurant charges more per meal but serves fewer meals? At what point will the business begin to operate at a loss rather than a profit? How long will the restaurant remain open if it loses a large number of customers?

These are the type of questions asked by managers in every business—what is the relationship among costs, volume, and profit? In this chapter, you'll learn about **cost-volume-profit (CVP) analysis**, a tool managers use to answer these questions. We continue this analysis using Greg's Tunes in this chapter.

# Cost Behavior

Some costs, like COGS, increase as the volume of activity increases. Other costs, like straight-line depreciation expense, are not affected by volume changes. Managers need to know how a business's costs are affected by changes in its volume of activity. Let's look at the three different types of costs:

**1** Identify how changes in volume affect costs

- Variable costs
- Fixed costs
- Mixed costs

## Variable Costs

**Variable costs** are those costs that increase or decrease in total in direct proportion to increases or decreases in the volume of activity. **Total variable costs** change in direct proportion to changes in the volume of activity. Volume is the measure or degree of an activity of a business action that affects costs—the more volume, the more cost is incurred. Those activities include selling, producing, driving, and calling. The volume of activities can be measured in many different ways, such as number of units sold, number of units produced, number of miles driven by a delivery vehicle, and the number of phone calls placed.

As you may recall, Greg's Tunes offers DJ services for parties, weddings, and other events. For each event, Greg's spends $15 for equipment rental. Greg's can perform at 15 to 30 events per month. To calculate total variable costs, Natalie Blanding, the office manager, would show the following:

| Number of Events per Month | Equipment Rental Cost per Event | Total Equipment Rental Cost per Month |
| --- | --- | --- |
| 15 | $15 | $225 |
| 20 | $15 | $300 |
| 30 | $15 | $450 |

As you can see, the total variable cost of equipment rental increases proportionately as the number of events increases. But the equipment rental cost per event does not change. Exhibit 19-1 graphs total variable cost for equipment rental as the number of events increases from 0 to 30, but the cost for each equipment rental stays at $15 per event.

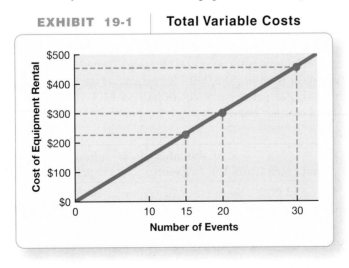

**EXHIBIT 19-1** | **Total Variable Costs**

If there are no events, Greg's incurs no equipment rental cost, so the total variable cost line begins at the bottom left corner. This point is called the *origin*, and it represents zero volume and zero cost. The *slope* of the variable cost line is the change in equipment rental cost (on the vertical axis) divided by the change in the number of events (on the horizontal axis). The slope of the graph equals the variable cost per unit. In Exhibit 19-1, the slope of the variable cost line is 15 because Greg's spends $15 on equipment rental for each event.

If Greg's Tunes performs at 15 events during the month, it will spend a total of $225 (15 events × $15 each) for equipment rental. Follow this total variable cost line to the right to see that doubling the number of events to 30 likewise doubles the total variable cost to $450 (30 × $15 = $450). Exhibit 19-1 shows how the *total variable cost* of equipment rental varies directly with the number of events. But again, note that *the per-event cost remains constant* at $15.

Remember this important fact about *variable costs*:

> **Total variable costs fluctuate with changes in volume, but the variable cost per unit remains constant.**

## Fixed Costs

In contrast, **total fixed costs** are costs that do not change over wide ranges of volume. **Fixed costs** tend to remain the same in amount, regardless of variations in level of activity. Greg's fixed costs include depreciation on the cars, as well as the part-time manager's salary. Greg's has these fixed costs regardless of the number of events—15, 20, or 30.

Suppose Greg's incurs $12,000 of fixed costs each month, and the number of monthly events is between 15 and 30. Exhibit 19-2 graphs total fixed costs as a flat line that intersects the cost axis at $12,000, because Greg's will incur the same $12,000 of fixed costs regardless of the number of events.

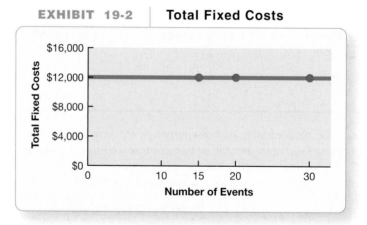

**EXHIBIT 19-2** | **Total Fixed Costs**

*Total fixed cost* does not change, as shown in Exhibit 19-2. But the *fixed cost per event* depends on the number of events. If Greg's Tunes performs at 15 events, the fixed cost per event is $800 ($12,000 ÷ 15 events). If the number of events doubles to 30, the fixed cost per event is cut in half to $400 ($12,000 ÷ 30 events). Therefore, the fixed cost per event is *inversely* proportional to the number of events, as follows:

| Total Fixed Costs | Number of Events | Fixed Cost per Event |
|---|---|---|
| $12,000 | 15 | $800 |
| $12,000 | 20 | $600 |
| $12,000 | 30 | $400 |

Remember the following important fact about *fixed costs*:

Total fixed costs remain constant, but the fixed cost per unit is inversely proportional to volume.

## Mixed Costs

Costs that have both variable and fixed components are called **mixed costs**. For example, Greg's Tunes' cell phone company charges $10 a month to provide the service and $0.15 for each minute of use. If the cell phone is used for 100 minutes, the company will bill Greg's $25 [$10 + (100 minutes × $0.15)].

Exhibit 19-3 shows how Greg's can separate its cell-phone bill into fixed and variable components. The $10 monthly charge is a fixed cost because it is the same no matter how many minutes the company uses the cell phone. The $0.15-per-minute charge is a variable cost that increases in direct proportion to the number of minutes of use. If Greg's uses the phone for 100 minutes, its total variable cost is $15 (100 minutes × $0.15). If it doubles the use to 200 minutes, total variable cost also doubles to $30 (200 minutes × $0.15), and the total bill rises to $40 ($10 + $30).

**EXHIBIT 19-3 | Mixed Costs**

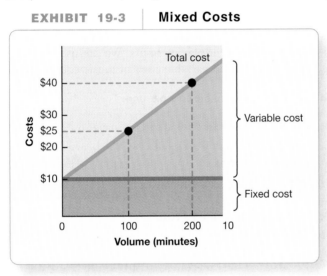

## Stop & Think...

Think about your costs related to taking this class. Which ones are fixed? Which ones are variable? The cost of your tuition and books are fixed costs, because you pay one price for the class and your books, no matter how many days you come to class. If you drive to class, the cost of gas put in your car is variable, because you only incur gas costs when you come to class. Are there any mixed costs associated with your class? Maybe your cell phone provider charges you a flat fee each month for a certain amount of minutes. If you go over that limit because you call your classmates a lot, then that would be a mixed cost associated with your class.

## High-Low Method to Separate Fixed Costs from Variable Costs

An easy method to separate mixed costs into variable and fixed components is the **high-low method**. This method requires you to identify the highest and lowest levels of activity over a period of time. Using this information, complete the following three steps:

STEP 1: Calculate the variable cost per unit.

Variable cost per unit = Change in total cost ÷ Change in volume of activity

**STEP 2:** Calculate the total fixed cost.

> Total fixed cost = Total mixed cost – Total variable cost

**STEP 3:** Create and use an equation to show the behavior of a mixed cost.

> Total mixed cost = (Variable cost per unit × number of units) + Total fixed costs

Let's revisit the Greg's Tunes illustration. A summary of Greg's Tunes' music equipment maintenance costs for the past year shows the following costs for each quarter:

|  | Event-Playing Hours | Total Maintenance Cost |  |
|---|---|---|---|
| **1st Quarter** | 360 | $1,720 | |
| **2nd Quarter** | 415 | 1,830 | |
| **3rd Quarter** | 480 | 1,960 | ← Highest Volume |
| **4th Quarter** | 240 | 1,480 | ← Lowest Volume |

The highest volume is 480 event-playing hours in the 3rd quarter of the year, and the lowest volume is 240 event-playing hours. We can use the high-low method to identify Greg's Tunes' fixed and variable costs of music equipment maintenance.

**STEP 1:** Calculate the variable cost per unit.

> Variable cost per unit = Change in total cost ÷ Change in volume of activity
> = ($1,960 – $1,480)  ÷ (480 hours – 240 hours)
> = $480  ÷ 240 hours
> = $2 per event-playing hour

**STEP 2:** Calculate the total fixed cost.

> Total fixed cost = Total mixed cost – Total variable cost
> = $1,960  – ($2 × 480)
> = $1,960  – $960
> = $1,000

This example uses the highest cost and volume to calculate the total fixed cost, but you can use any volume and calculate the same $1,000 total fixed cost.

**STEP 3:** Create and use an equation to show the behavior of a mixed cost.

> Total mixed cost                = (Variable cost per unit × number of units) + Total fixed cost
> Total equipment maintenance cost = ($2 per event-playing hour × no. of hours) +      $1,000

Using this equation, the estimated music equipment maintenance cost for 400 event-playing hours would be as follows:

> ($2 × 400 event-playing hours) + $1,000 = $1,800

This method provides a rough estimate of fixed and variable costs for cost-volume-profit analysis. The high and low volumes become the relevant range, which we discuss in the next section. Managers find the high-low method to be quick and easy, but regression analysis provides the most accurate estimates and is discussed in cost accounting textbooks.

## Relevant Range

The **relevant range** is the range of volume where total fixed costs remain constant and the variable cost *per unit* remains constant. **The relevant range is the range of events (or other activity) where total fixed costs and variable cost per unit stays the same.** To estimate costs, managers need to know the relevant range. Why? Because,

- total "fixed" costs can differ from one relevant range to another.
- the variable cost *per unit* can differ in various relevant ranges.

Exhibit 19-4 shows fixed cost for Greg's Tunes over three different relevant ranges. If the company expects to offer 15,000 event-playing hours next year, the relevant range is between 10,000 and 20,000 event-playing hours, and managers budget fixed cost of $144,000.

**EXHIBIT 19-4** | **Relevant Range**

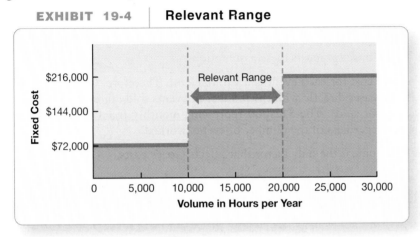

To offer 22,000 event-playing hours, Greg's will have to expand the company. This will increase total fixed costs for added rent and equipment costs. Exhibit 19-4 shows that total fixed cost increases to $216,000 as the relevant range shifts to this higher band of volume. Conversely, if Greg's expects to offer only 8,000 event-playing hours, the company will budget only $72,000 of fixed cost. Managers will have to lay off employees or take other actions to cut fixed costs.

Variable cost per unit can also change outside the relevant range. For example, Greg's Tunes may get a quantity discount for equipment maintenance if it can provide more than 20,000 event-playing hours.

Now, let's apply CVP analysis to answer some interesting management questions.

**Key Takeaway**

Variable costs are those costs that increase or decrease in total as the volume of activity increases or decreases. Fixed costs are costs that do not change over wide ranges of volume. Costs that have both variable and fixed components are called mixed costs. The high-low method is an easy way to separate mixed costs into variable and fixed components by requiring you to identify the highest and lowest levels of activity over a period of time. The relevant range is the range of activity where total fixed cost stays the same and variable cost per unit stays the same.

# Basic CVP Analysis: What Must We Sell to Break Even?

Greg's Tunes is considering expanding its events coverage to include weddings. Greg's first analyzes its existing costs, partially covered in the previous section. (For simplicity, we ignore the mixed costs.) Variable costs are $15 for equipment rental per event plus $65 in contracted labor per event. All the other monthly business expenses are fixed costs, $12,000. Average sales price per event is $200.

**2** Use CVP analysis to compute breakeven points

| | |
|---|---|
| Selling price per event.................. | $    200 |
| Variable cost per event.............. | $      80 |
| Fixed costs ............................... | $12,000 |

Greg's Tunes faces several important questions:

- How many DJ services (hereinafter, events) must the company sell to break even?
- What will profits be if sales double?
- How will changes in selling price, variable costs, or fixed costs affect profits?

Before getting started, let's review the assumptions required for CVP analysis to be accurate.

## Assumptions

CVP analysis assumes that

1. managers can classify each cost as either variable or fixed.
2. the only factor that affects total costs is change in volume, which increases variable and mixed costs. Fixed costs do not change.

Greg's Tunes' business meets these assumptions:

1. The $80 cost for each event is a variable cost. Therefore, Greg's *total variable cost* increases directly with the number of events sold (an extra $80 in cost for each event sold). The $12,000 represents monthly fixed costs and does not change regardless of the number of events worked.
2. Sales volume is the only factor that affects Greg's costs.

Most business conditions do not perfectly meet these assumptions (consider that most businesses have some mixed costs), so managers regard CVP analysis as approximate, not exact.

## How Much Must Greg Sell to Break Even? Three Approaches

Virtually all businesses want to know their breakeven point. The **breakeven point** is the sales level at which operating income is zero: Total revenues equal total costs (expenses). Sales below the breakeven point result in a loss. Sales above break even provide a profit. Greg's Tunes needs to know how many DJ events must be held to break even.

There are several ways to figure the breakeven point, including the

- income statement approach and the
- contribution margin approach.

We start with the income statement approach because it is the easiest method to remember. You are already familiar with the income statement.

### The Income Statement Approach

Let's start by expressing income in equation form and then breaking it down into its components:

$$\text{Sales revenue} - \underbrace{\text{Total costs}}_{\text{Sales revenue} - \text{Variable costs} - \text{Fixed costs}} = \text{Operating income}$$
$$\text{Sales revenue} - \text{Variable costs} - \text{Fixed costs} = \text{Operating income}$$

Sales revenue equals the unit sale price ($200 per event in this case) multiplied by the number of units (events) sold. Variable costs equal variable cost per unit ($80 in this case) times the number of units (events) sold. Greg's fixed costs total $12,000. At the breakeven point, operating income is zero. We use this information to solve the income statement equation for the number of DJ events Greg's must sell to break even.

| Sales revenue | | − | Variable costs | | − Fixed costs | = Operating income |
|---|---|---|---|---|---|---|
| $\left(\dfrac{\text{Sale price}}{\text{per unit}} \times \text{Units sold}\right)$ | | − | $\left(\dfrac{\text{Variable cost}}{\text{per unit}} \times \text{Units sold}\right)$ | | − Fixed costs | = Operating income |
| ($200 | × Units sold) − | | ($80 | × Units sold) − | $12,000 = | $0 |
| | ($200 | − | $80) | × Units sold − | $12,000 = | $0 |
| | | | $120 | × Units sold | = | $12,000 |
| | | | | Units sold | = | $12,000 ÷ $120 |
| | | | | Breakeven sales in units | = | 100 events |

Greg's Tunes must sell 100 events to break even. The breakeven sales level in dollars is $20,000 (100 events × $200).

Be sure to check your calculations. "Prove" the breakeven point by substituting the breakeven number of units into the income statement. Then check to ensure that this level of sales results in zero profit.

| Proof | Sales revenue − Variable costs − Fixed costs = Operating income |
|---|---|
| | ($200 × 100) − ($80 × 100) − $12,000 = $0 |
| | $20,000 − $8,000 − $12,000 = $0 |

## The Contribution Margin Approach: A Shortcut

This shortcut method of computing the breakeven point uses Greg's contribution margin. The **contribution margin** is sales revenue minus variable costs (expenses). **It is called the *contribution margin* because the excess of sales revenue over variable costs contributes to covering fixed costs and then to providing operating income.**

The **contribution margin income statement** shows costs by cost behavior—variable costs or fixed costs—and highlights the contribution margin. The format shows the following:

Sales revenue
− Variable costs
= Contribution margin
− Fixed costs
= Operating income

Now let's rearrange the income statement formula and use the contribution margin to develop a shortcut method for finding the number of DJ events Greg's must hold to break even.

| Sales revenue | − | Variable costs | − Fixed costs = Operating income |
|---|---|---|---|
| $\left(\dfrac{\text{Sale price}}{\text{per unit}} \times \text{Units sold}\right)$ | − | $\left(\dfrac{\text{Variable cost}}{\text{per unit}} \times \text{Units sold}\right)$ | − Fixed costs = Operating income |
| | $\left(\dfrac{\text{Sale price}}{\text{per unit}} - \dfrac{\text{Variable cost}}{\text{per unit}}\right) \times \text{Units sold}$ | | = Fixed costs + Operating income |
| | Contribution margin per unit × Units sold | | = Fixed costs + Operating income |

Dividing both sides of the equation by the contribution margin per unit yields the alternate equation:

$$\text{Units sold} = \frac{\text{Fixed costs + Operating income}}{\text{Contribution margin per unit}}$$

Greg's Tunes can use this contribution margin approach to find its breakeven point. Fixed costs total $12,000. Operating income is zero at break even. The contribution margin per event is $120 ($200 sale price − $80 variable cost). Greg's breakeven computation is as follows:

$$\text{Breakeven sales in units} = \frac{\$12,000}{\$120}$$
$$= 100 \text{ events}$$

Why does this shortcut method work? Each event Greg's Tunes sells provides $120 of contribution margin. To break even in one month, Greg's must generate enough contribution margin to cover $12,000 of monthly fixed costs. At the rate of $120 per event, Greg's must sell 100 events ($12,000/$120) to cover monthly fixed costs. You can see that the contribution margin approach just rearranges the income statement equation, so the breakeven point is the same under both methods.

To "prove" the breakeven point, you can also use the contribution margin income statement format:

| GREG'S TUNES, INC. Income Statement For one month | |
|---|---:|
| Sales revenue ($200 × 100 events) | $20,000 |
| Variable costs ($80 × 100 events) | 8,000 |
| Contribution margin ($120 × 100 events) | $12,000 |
| Fixed costs | 12,000 |
| Operating income | $    0 |

## Using the Contribution Margin Ratio to Compute the Breakeven Point in Sales Dollars

Companies can use the contribution margin ratio to compute their breakeven point in terms of *sales dollars*. The **contribution margin ratio** is the ratio of contribution margin to sales revenue. For Greg's Tunes, we have the following:

$$\text{Contribution margin ratio} = \frac{\text{Contribution margin}}{\text{Sales revenue}} = \frac{\$120}{\$200} = 0.60 \text{ or } 60\%$$

The 60% contribution margin ratio means that each dollar of sales revenue contributes $0.60 toward fixed costs and profit.

The contribution margin *ratio* approach differs from the shortcut contribution margin approach we have just seen in only one way: Here we use the contribution margin *ratio* rather than the dollar amount of the contribution margin.

$$\text{Breakeven sales in dollars} = \frac{\text{Fixed costs}}{\text{Contribution margin ratio}}$$

Using this ratio formula, Greg's breakeven point in sales dollars is as follows:

$$\text{Breakeven sales in dollars} = \frac{\$12,000}{0.60}$$
$$= \$20,000$$

This is the same $20,000 breakeven sales revenue we calculated in the contribution margin approach.

Why does the contribution margin ratio formula work? Each dollar of Greg's sales contributes $0.60 to fixed costs and profit. To break even, Greg's must generate enough contribution margin at the rate of 60% of sales to cover the $12,000 fixed costs ($12,000 ÷ 0.60 = $20,000).

Now, we have seen how companies use *contribution margin* to estimate breakeven points in CVP analysis. But managers use the contribution margin for other purposes too, such as motivating the sales force. Salespeople who know the contribution margin of each product can generate more profit by emphasizing high-margin products over low-margin products. This is why many companies base sales commissions on the contribution margins produced by sales rather than on sales revenue alone.

# Using CVP to Plan Profits

For established products and services, managers are more interested in the sales level needed to earn a target profit than in the breakeven point. **Target profit** is the operating income that results when sales revenue minus variable costs and minus fixed cost equals management's profit goal. Managers of new business ventures are also interested in the profits they can expect to earn. For example, now that Greg's Tunes knows it must sell 100 events to break even, Natalie Blanding, the controller for Greg's, wants to know how many more events must be sold to earn a monthly operating profit of $6,000.

**③ Use CVP analysis for profit planning, and graph the CVP relations**

## How Much Must Greg's Sell to Earn a Profit?

What is the only difference from our prior analysis? Here, Greg's wants to know how many events must be sold to earn a $6,000 profit. We can use the income statement approach or the shortcut contribution margin approach to find the answer. Let's start with the income statement approach.

| | Sales revenue | – | Variable costs | – Fixed costs | = Operating income |
|---|---|---|---|---|---|
| | ($200 × Units sold) – ($80 × Units sold) – | | | $12,000 = | $ 6,000 |
| | [($200 – 80) × Units sold] | | | – $12,000 = | $ 6,000 |
| | $120 × Units sold | | | = | $18,000 |
| | | | | Units sold = | $18,000 ÷ $120 |
| | | | | Units sold = | 150 events |
| **Proof** | ($200 × 150) | – | ($80 × 150) | – $12,000 | = **Operating income** |
| | $30,000 | – | $12,000 | – $12,000 = | $6,000 |

This analysis shows that Greg's must sell 150 events each month to earn an operating profit of $6,000. This is 150 – 100 = 50 more events than the breakeven sales level (100 events).

The proof shows that Greg's needs sales revenues of $30,000 to earn a profit of $6,000. Alternatively, we can compute the dollar sales necessary to earn a $6,000 profit directly, using the contribution margin ratio form of the CVP formula:

$$\text{Target sales in dollars} = \frac{\text{Fixed costs} + \text{Operating income}}{\text{Contribution margin ratio}}$$

$$= \frac{\$12,000 + \$6,000}{0.60}$$

$$= \frac{\$18,000}{0.60}$$

$$= \$30,000$$

This shows that Greg's needs $30,000 in sales revenue to earn a $6,000 profit.

## Graphing Cost-Volume-Profit Relations

Controller Natalie Blanding can graph the CVP relations for Greg's Tunes. A graph provides a picture that shows how changes in the levels of sales will affect profits. As in the variable-, fixed-, and mixed-cost graphs of Exhibits 19-1, 19-2, and 19-3, Blanding shows the volume of units (events) on the horizontal axis and dollars on the vertical axis. Then she follows four steps to graph the CVP relations for Greg's Tunes, as illustrated in Exhibit 19-5.

**EXHIBIT 19-5** | **Cost-Volume-Profit Graph**

| Events | Sales revenue | Total costs | Fixed costs | Income (Loss) |
|---|---|---|---|---|
| 0 | $0 | $12,000 | $12,000 | $(12,000) |
| 50 | 10,000 | 16,000 | 12,000 | (6,000) |
| 100 | 20,000 | 20,000 | 12,000 | 0 |
| 150 | 30,000 | 24,000 | 12,000 | 6,000 |
| 200 | 40,000 | 28,000 | 12,000 | 12,000 |

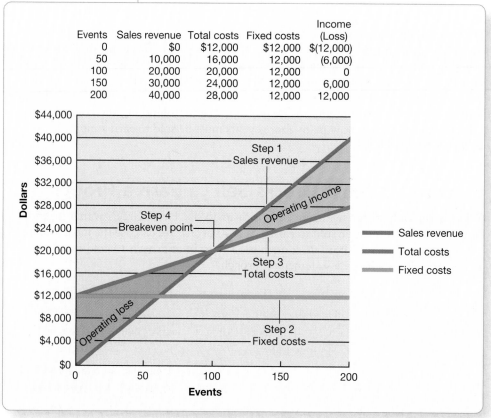

STEP 1: Choose a sales volume, such as 200 events. Plot the point for total sales revenue at that volume: 200 events × $200 per event = sales of $40,000. Draw the *sales revenue line* from the origin (0) through the $40,000 point. Why start at the origin? If Greg's sells no events, there is no revenue.

STEP 2: Draw the *fixed cost line*, a horizontal line that intersects the dollars axis at $12,000. The fixed cost line is flat because fixed costs are the same, $12,000, no matter how many events are sold.

STEP 3: Draw the *total cost line*. Total costs are the sum of variable costs plus fixed costs. Thus, total costs are *mixed*. So the total cost line follows the form of the mixed cost line in Exhibit 19-3. Begin by computing variable costs at the chosen sales volume: 200 events × $80 per event = variable costs of $16,000. Add variable costs to fixed costs: $16,000 + $12,000 = $28,000. Plot the total cost point of $28,000 for 200 events. Then draw a line through this point from the $12,000 fixed cost intercept on the dollars vertical axis. This is the *total cost line*. The total cost line starts at the fixed cost line because even if Greg's Tunes sells no events, the company still incurs the $12,000 of fixed costs.

STEP 4: Identify the *breakeven point* and the areas of operating income and loss. The breakeven point is where the sales revenue line intersects the total cost line. This is where revenue exactly equals total costs—at 100 events, or $20,000 in sales.

Mark the *operating loss* area on the graph. To the left of the breakeven point, total costs exceed sales revenue—leading to an operating loss, indicated by the orange zone.

Mark the *operating income* area on the graph. To the right of the breakeven point, the business earns a profit because sales revenue exceeds total cost, as shown by the green zone.

Why bother with a graph? Why not just use the income statement approach or the shortcut contribution margin approach? Graphs like Exhibit 19-5 help managers quickly estimate the profit or loss earned at different levels of sales. The income statement and contribution margin approaches indicate income or loss for only a single sales amount.

# Summary Problem 19-1

Happy Feet buys hiking socks for $6 a pair and sells them for $10. Management budgets monthly fixed costs of $10,000 for sales volumes between 0 and 12,000 pairs.

## Requirements

1. Use both the income statement approach and the shortcut contribution margin approach to compute the company's monthly breakeven sales in units.
2. Use the contribution margin ratio approach to compute the breakeven point in sales dollars.
3. Compute the monthly sales level (in units) required to earn a target operating income of $6,000. Use either the income statement approach or the shortcut contribution margin approach.
4. Prepare a graph of Happy Feet's CVP relationships, similar to Exhibit 19-5. Draw the sales revenue line, the fixed cost line, and the total cost line. Label the axes, the breakeven point, the operating income area, and the operating loss area.

## Solution

### Requirement 1
Income statement approach:

| Sales revenue | − | Variable costs | − Fixed costs = Operating income |
|---|---|---|---|
| $\left(\dfrac{\text{Sale price}}{\text{per unit}} \times \text{Units sold}\right)$ − | | $\left(\dfrac{\text{Variable cost}}{\text{per unit}} \times \text{Units sold}\right)$ − Fixed costs = Operating income |
| ($10 × Units sold) − | | ($6 × Units sold)    − $10,000    = $0 |
| ($10 − | | $6) × Units sold    = $10,000 |
| | | $4 × Units sold    = $10,000 |
| | | Units sold    = $10,000 ÷ $4 |
| | Breakeven sales in units | = 2,500 units |

Shortcut contribution margin approach:

$$\text{Units sold} = \frac{\text{Fixed costs} + \text{Operating income}}{\text{Contribution margin per unit}}$$

$$\text{Breakeven sales in units} = \frac{\$10{,}000 + \$0}{\$10 - \$6}$$

$$= \frac{\$10{,}000}{\$4}$$

$$= 2{,}500 \text{ units}$$

## Requirement 2

$$\text{Breakeven sales in dollars} = \frac{\text{Fixed costs} + \text{Operating income}}{\text{Contribution margin ratio}}$$

$$= \frac{\$10{,}000 + \$0}{0.40^*}$$

$$= \$25{,}000$$

$$^*\text{Contribution margin ratio} = \frac{\text{Contribution margin per unit}}{\text{Sale price per unit}} = \frac{\$4}{\$10} = 0.40$$

## Requirement 3

Income statement equation approach:

| Sales revenue | − | Variable costs | − Fixed costs | = Operating income |
|---|---|---|---|---|
| $\left(\dfrac{\text{Sale price}}{\text{per unit}} \times \text{Units sold}\right)$ | − | $\left(\dfrac{\text{Variable cost}}{\text{per unit}} \times \text{Units sold}\right)$ | − Fixed costs | = Operating income |
| ($10 × Units sold) | − | ($6 × Units sold) | − $10,000 | = $6,000 |
| ($10 | − | $6) × Units sold | | = $10,000 + $6,000 |
| | | $4 × Units sold | | = $16,000 |
| | | Units sold | | = $16,000 ÷ $4 |
| | | Units sold | | = 4,000 units |

Shortcut contribution margin approach:

$$\text{Units sold} = \frac{\text{Fixed costs} + \text{Operating income}}{\text{Contribution margin per unit}}$$

$$= \frac{\$10{,}000 + \$6{,}000}{\$10 - \$6}$$

$$= \frac{\$16{,}000}{\$4}$$

$$= 4{,}000 \text{ units}$$

**Requirement 4**

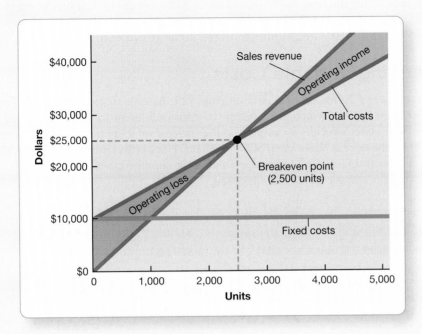

# Using CVP for Sensitivity Analysis

Managers often want to predict how changes in sale price, costs, or volume affect their profits. Managers can use CVP relationships to conduct sensitivity analysis. **Sensitivity analysis** is a "what if" technique that asks what results are likely if selling price or costs change, or if an underlying assumption changes. So sensitivity analysis allows managers to see how various business strategies will affect how much profit the company will make and thus empowers managers with better information for decision making. Let's see how Greg's Tunes can use CVP analysis to estimate the effects of some changes in its business environment.

**4** Use CVP methods to perform sensitivity analyses

## Changing the Selling Price

Competition in the DJ event services business is so fierce that Greg's Tunes believes it must cut the selling price to $180 per event to maintain market share. Suppose Greg's Tunes' variable costs remain $80 per event and fixed costs stay at $12,000. How will the lower sale price affect the breakeven point?

Using the income statement approach, the results are as follows:

| Sales revenue | – | Variable costs | – | Fixed costs | = Operating income |
|---|---|---|---|---|---|
| ($180 × Units sold) | – | ($80 × Units sold) | – | $12,000 | = $0 |
| | [($180 – $80) × Units sold] | | – | $12,000 | = $0 |
| | $100 × Units sold | | | | = $12,000 |
| | | | | Units sold | = $12,000 ÷ $100 |
| | | | | Units sold | = 120 events |

| **Proof** | ($180 × 120) | – | ($80 × 120) | – | $12,000 | = **Operating income** |
|---|---|---|---|---|---|---|
| | $21,600 | – | $9,600 | – | $12,000 | = $0 |

With the original $200 sale price, Greg's Tunes' breakeven point was 100 events. With the new lower sale price of $180 per event, the breakeven point increases to 120 events. The lower sale price means that each event contributes less toward fixed costs, so Greg's Tunes must sell 20 more events to break even.

## Changing Variable Costs

Return to Greg's Tunes' original data on page 929. Assume that one of Greg's Tunes' suppliers raises prices, which increases the cost for each event to $120 (instead of the original $80). Greg's decides it cannot pass this increase on to its customers, so the company holds the price at the original $200 per event. Fixed costs remain at $12,000. How many events must Greg's sell to break even after the supplier raises prices?

Using the income statement approach,

| Sales revenue | – | Variable costs | – | Fixed costs | = Operating income |
|---|---|---|---|---|---|
| ($200 × Units sold) | – | ($120 × Units sold) – | | $12,000 | = $0 |
| | [($200 – 120) × Units sold] | | – | $12,000 | = $0 |
| | | $80 × Units sold | | = | $12,000 |
| | | | Units sold | = | $12,000 ÷ $80 |
| | | | Units sold | = | 150 events |

| Proof | ($200 × 150) | – | ($120 × 150) | – | $12,000 | = Operating income |
|---|---|---|---|---|---|---|
| | $30,000 | – | $18,000 | – | $12,000 | = $0 |

Higher variable costs per event reduce Greg's Tunes' per-unit contribution margin from $120 per event to $80 per event. As a result, Greg's must sell more events to break even—150 rather than the original 100. This analysis shows why managers are particularly concerned with controlling costs during an economic downturn. Increases in cost raise the breakeven point, and a higher breakeven point can lead to problems if demand falls due to a recession.

Of course, a decrease in variable costs would have the opposite effect. Lower variable costs increase the contribution margin on each event and, therefore, lower the breakeven point.

## Changing Fixed Costs

Return to Greg's original data on page 929. Controller Natalie Blanding is considering spending an additional $3,000 on Web site banner ads. This would increase fixed costs from $12,000 to $15,000. If the events are sold at the original price of $200 each and variable costs remain at $80 per event, what is the new breakeven point?

Using the income statement approach,

| Sales revenue | – | Variable costs | – | Fixed costs | = Operating income |
|---|---|---|---|---|---|
| ($200 × Units sold) | – | ($80 × Units sold) – | | $15,000 | = $0 |
| | [($200 – $80) × Units sold] | | – | $15,000 | = $0 |
| | | $120 × Units sold | | = | $15,000 |
| | | | Units sold | = | $15,000 ÷ $120 |
| | | | Units sold | = | 125 events |

| Proof | ($200 × 125) | – | ($80 × 125) | – | $15,000 | = Operating income |
|---|---|---|---|---|---|---|
| | $25,000 | – | $10,000 | – | $15,000 | = $0 |

Higher fixed costs increase the total contribution margin required to break even. In this case, increasing the fixed costs from $12,000 to $15,000 increases the breakeven point to 125 events (from the original 100 events).

Managers usually prefer a lower breakeven point to a higher one. But do not overemphasize this one aspect of CVP analysis. Even though investing in the Web banner ads increases Greg's Tunes' breakeven point, the company should pay the extra $3,000 if that would increase both sales and profits.

Exhibit 19-6 shows how all of these changes affect the contribution margin per unit and the breakeven point.

**EXHIBIT 19-6**    **How Changes in Selling Price, Variable Costs, and Fixed Costs Affect the Contribution Margin per Unit and the Breakeven Point**

| Cause | Effect | Result |
|---|---|---|
| Change | Contribution Margin per Unit | Breakeven Point |
| Selling Price per Unit Increases | Increases | Decreases |
| Selling Price per Unit Decreases | Decreases | Increases |
| Variable Cost per Unit Increases | Decreases | Increases |
| Variable Cost per Unit Decreases | Increases | Decreases |
| Total Fixed Cost Increases | Is not affected | Increases |
| Total Fixed Cost Decreases | Is not affected | Decreases |

## Margin of Safety

The **margin of safety** is the excess of expected sales over breakeven sales. **The margin of safety is therefore the "cushion" or drop in sales that the company can absorb without incuring an operating loss.**

Managers use the margin of safety to evaluate the risk of both their current operations and their plans for the future. Let's apply the margin of safety to Greg's Tunes.

Greg's Tunes' original breakeven point was 100 events. Suppose the company expects to sell 170 events. The margin of safety is as follows:

**Expected sales – Breakeven sales = Margin of safety in units**

170 events  –  100 events  =  70 events

**Margin of safety in units × Sales price = Margin of safety in dollars**

70 events  ×  $200  =  $14,000

Sales can drop by 70 events, or $14,000, before Greg's incurs a loss. This margin of safety (70 events) is 41.2% of total expected sales (170 events). That is a comfortable margin of safety.

Margin of safety focuses on the sales part of the equation—that is, how many sales dollars the company is generating above breakeven sales dollars. Conversely, target profit focuses on how much operating income is left over from sales revenue after covering all variable and fixed costs.

**Stop & Think...**

If you have done really well on all your assignments in a particular course for the semester and currently have an A, you have created a sort of "margin of safety" for your grade. That is, by performing above the minimum (C, or break even), you have a cushion to help you maintain a good grade even if you happen to perform poorly on a future assignment.

**Key Takeaway**

Sensitivity analysis is a "what if" technique that asks what results are likely if selling price or costs change or if an underlying assumption changes. The income statement approach to break even is just adjusted for the new proposed values. The margin of safety is the "cushion" or drop in sales that the company can absorb before incurring a loss.

# Effect of Sales Mix on CVP Analysis

**5** Calculate the breakeven point for multiple products or services

Most companies sell more than one product. Selling price and variable costs differ for each product, so each product makes a different contribution to profits. The same CVP formulas we used earlier apply to a company with multiple products.

To calculate break even for each product, we must compute the *weighted-average contribution margin* of all the company's products. The sales mix provides the weights that make up total product sales. The weights equal 100% of total product sales. **Sales mix** (or *product mix*) is the combination of products that make up total sales. For example, Cool Cat Furniture sold 6,000 cat beds and 4,000 scratching posts during the past year. The sales mix of 6,000 beds and 4,000 posts creates a ratio of 6,000/10,000 or 60% cat beds and 4,000/10,000 or 40% scratching posts. You could also convert this to the least common ratio, as 6/10 is the same as 3/5 cat beds and 4/10 is the same as 2/5 scratching posts. So, we say the sales mix or product mix is 3:2, or for every three cat beds, Cool Cat expects to sell two scratching posts.

Cool Cat's total fixed costs are $40,000. The cat bed's unit selling price is $44 and variable cost per bed are $24. The scratching post's unit selling price is $100 and variable cost per post is $30. To compute breakeven sales in units for both products Cool Cat completes the following three steps.

STEP 1: Calculate the weighted-average contribution margin per unit, as follows:

|  | Cat Beds | Scratching Posts | Total |
|---|---|---|---|
| Sale price per unit | $ 44 | $100 | |
| Variable cost per unit | 24 | 30 | |
| Contribution margin per unit | $ 20 | $ 70 | |
| Sales mix in units | × 3 | × 2 | 5 |
| Contribution margin | $ 60 | $140 | $200 |
| Weighted-average contribution margin per unit ($200/5) | | | $ 40 |

STEP 2: Calculate the breakeven point in units for the "package" of products:

$$\text{Breakeven sales in total units} = \frac{\text{Fixed costs + Operating income}}{\text{Weighted-average contribution margin per unit}}$$

$$= \frac{\$40,000 + \$0}{\$40}$$

$$= 1,000 \text{ items}$$

STEP 3: Calculate the breakeven point in units for each product. Multiply the "package" breakeven point in units by each product's proportion of the sales mix.

Breakeven sales of cat beds (1,000 × 3/5) ...................... 600 cat beds
Breakeven sales of scratching posts (1,000 × 2/5) .......... 400 scratching posts

In this example, the calculations yield round numbers. When the calculations do not yield round numbers, round your answer up to the next whole number.

The overall breakeven point in sales dollars is $66,400:

| 600 cat beds at $44 selling price each............................. | $26,400 |
|---|---|
| 400 scratching posts at $100 selling price each .............. | 40,000 |
| Total sales revenue ..................................................... | $66,400 |

We can prove this breakeven point by preparing a contribution margin income statement:

| | Cat Beds | Scratching Posts | Total |
|---|---|---|---|
| Sales revenue: | | | |
| Cat beds (600 × $44) | $26,400 | | |
| Scratching posts (400 × $100) | | $40,000 | $ 66,400 |
| Variable costs: | | | |
| Cat beds (600 × $24) | 14,400 | | |
| Scratching posts (400 × $30) | | 12,000 | 26,400 |
| Contribution margin | $12,000 | $28,000 | $ 40,000 |
| Fixed costs | | | (40,000) |
| Operating income | | | $       0 |

If the sales mix changes, then Cool Cat can repeat this analysis using new sales mix information to find the breakeven points for each product.

In addition to finding the breakeven point, Cool Cat can also estimate the sales needed to generate a certain level of operating profit. Suppose Cool Cat would like to earn operating income of $20,000. How many units of each product must Cool Cat now sell?

$$\text{Breakeven sales in total units} = \frac{\text{Fixed costs} + \text{Operating income}}{\text{Weighted-average contribution margin per unit}}$$

$$= \frac{\$40,000 + \$20,000}{\$40}$$

$$= 1,500 \text{ items}$$

Breakeven sales of cat beds (1,500 × 3/5) ...................... 900 cat beds
Breakeven sales of scratching posts (1,500 × 2/5) ........... 600 scratching posts

We can prove this planned profit level by preparing a contribution margin income statement:

| | Cat Beds | Scratching Posts | Total |
|---|---|---|---|
| Sales revenue: | | | |
| Cat beds (900 × $44) | $39,600 | | |
| Scratching posts (600 × $100) | | $60,000 | $99,600 |
| Variable costs: | | | |
| Cat beds (900 × $24) | 21,600 | | |
| Scratching posts (600 × $30) | | 18,000 | 39,600 |
| Contribution margin | $18,000 | $42,000 | $60,000 |
| Fixed costs | | | 40,000 |
| Operating income | | | $20,000 |

You have learned how to use CVP analysis as a managerial tool. Now you can review the CVP Analysis Decision Guidelines on the next page to make sure you understand these basic concepts.

**Key Takeaway**

Most companies sell more than one product. Selling price and variable costs differ for each product, so each product makes a different contribution to profits. To calculate break even for each product, we compute the weighted-average contribution margin of all the company's products. The combination of products that make up total sales, called the sales mix (or product mix), provides the weights that make up total product sales.

# Decision Guidelines 19-1

## COST-VOLUME-PROFIT ANALYSIS

As a manager, you will find CVP very useful. Here are some questions you will ask, and guidelines for answering them.

| Decision | Guidelines |
|---|---|
| • How do changes in volume of activity affect | |
| • total costs? | Total *variable* costs → Change in proportion to changes in volume (number of products or services sold) |
| | Total *fixed* costs → No change |
| • cost per unit? | Variable cost per unit → No change |
| • fixed cost per unit? | Decreases when volume rises (fixed costs are spread over *more* units) |
| | Increases when volume drops (fixed costs are spread over *fewer* units) |

• How do I calculate the sales needed to break even or earn a target operating income

• in units?

*Income Statement Approach:*

$$\text{Sales revenue} - \text{Variable costs} - \text{Fixed costs} = \text{Operating income}$$

$$\left(\frac{\text{Sale price}}{\text{per unit}} \times \text{Units sold}\right) - \left(\frac{\text{Variable cost}}{\text{per unit}} \times \text{Units sold}\right) - \text{Fixed costs} = \text{Operating income}$$

*Shortcut Contribution Margin Approach:*

$$\left(\frac{\text{Sale price}}{\text{per unit}} - \frac{\text{Variable cost}}{\text{per unit}}\right) \times \text{Units sold} = \text{Fixed costs} + \text{Operating income}$$

$$\text{Contribution margin per unit} \times \text{Units sold} = \text{Fixed costs} + \text{Operating income}$$

$$\text{Units sold} = \frac{\text{Fixed Costs} + \text{Operating income}}{\text{Contribution margin per unit}}$$

• in dollars?

*Shortcut Contribution Margin Ratio Approach:*

$$\frac{\text{Fixed costs} + \text{Operating income}}{\text{Contribution margin ratio}}$$

| Decision | Guidelines |
|---|---|

| Cause | Effect | Result |
|---|---|---|
| Change | Contribution Margin per Unit | Breakeven Point |
| Selling price per unit increases | Increases | Decreases |
| Selling price per unit decreases | Decreases | Increases |
| Variable cost per unit increases | Decreases | Increases |
| Variable cost per unit decreases | Increases | Decreases |
| Total fixed cost increases | Is not affected | Increases |
| Total fixed cost decreases | Is not affected | Decreases |

- How will changes in sale price, variable costs, or fixed costs affect the breakeven point?

- How do I use CVP analysis to measure risk?

**Margin of safety in units = Expected sales – Breakeven sales**

- How do I calculate my breakeven point when I sell more than one product or service?

**STEP 1:** Compute the weighted-average contribution margin per unit.
**STEP 2:** Calculate the breakeven point in units for the "package" of products.
**STEP 3:** Calculate the breakeven point in units for each product. Multiply the "package" breakeven point in units by each product's proportion of the sales mix.

# Summary Problem 19-2

Happy Feet buys hiking socks for $6 a pair and sells them for $10. Management budgets monthly fixed costs of $12,000 for sales volumes between 0 and 12,000 pairs.

## Requirements

Consider each of the following questions separately by using the foregoing information each time.

1. Calculate the breakeven point in units.
2. Happy Feet reduces its selling price from $10 a pair to $8 a pair. Calculate the new breakeven point in units.
3. Happy Feet finds a new supplier for the socks. Variable costs will decrease by $1 a pair. Calculate the new breakeven point in units.
4. Happy Feet plans to advertise in hiking magazines. The advertising campaign will increase total fixed costs by $2,000 per month. Calculate the new breakeven point in units.
5. In addition to selling hiking socks, Happy Feet would like to start selling sports socks. Happy Feet expects to sell one pair of hiking socks for every three pairs of sports socks. Happy Feet will buy the sports socks for $4 a pair and sell them for $8 a pair. Total fixed costs will stay at $12,000 per month. Calculate the breakeven point in units for both hiking socks and sports socks.

## Solution

### Requirement 1

$$\text{Units sold} = \frac{\text{Fixed costs}}{\text{Contribution margin per unit}}$$

$$\text{Breakeven sales in units} = \frac{\$12,000}{\$10 - \$6}$$

$$= \frac{\$12,000}{\$4}$$

$$= 3,000 \text{ units}$$

### Requirement 2

$$\text{Units sold} = \frac{\text{Fixed costs}}{\text{Contribution margin per unit}}$$

$$\text{Breakeven sales in units} = \frac{\$12,000}{\$8 - \$6}$$

$$= \frac{\$12,000}{\$2}$$

$$= 6,000 \text{ units}$$

### Requirement 3

$$\text{Units sold} = \frac{\text{Fixed costs}}{\text{Contribution margin per unit}}$$

$$\text{Breakeven sales in units} = \frac{\$12,000}{\$10 - \$5}$$

$$= \frac{\$12,000}{\$5}$$

$$= 2,400 \text{ units}$$

## Requirement 4

$$\text{Units sold} = \frac{\text{Fixed costs}}{\text{Contribution margin per unit}}$$

$$\text{Breakeven sales in units} = \frac{\$14{,}000}{\$10 - \$6}$$

$$= \frac{\$14{,}000}{\$4}$$

$$= 3{,}500 \text{ units}$$

## Requirement 5

STEP 1: Calculate the weighted-average contribution margin:

|  | Hiking | Sports |  |
|---|---|---|---|
| Sale price per unit | $10.00 | $ 8.00 |  |
| Variable cost per unit | 6.00 | 4.00 |  |
| Contribution margin per unit | $ 4.00 | $ 4.00 |  |
| Sales mix in units | × 1 | × 3 | 4 |
| Contribution margin | $ 4.00 | $12.00 | $16.00 |
| Weighted-average CM ($16/4) |  |  | $ 4.00 |

STEP 2: Calculate breakeven point for "package" of products:

$$\text{Breakeven sales in units} = \frac{\text{Fixed costs}}{\text{Contribution margin per unit}}$$

$$= \frac{\$12{,}000}{\$4}$$

$$= 3{,}000 \text{ units}$$

STEP 3: Calculate breakeven point for each product:

Number of hiking socks (3,000 × (1/4)) ......................... 750
Number of sport socks (3,000 × (3/4)) ........................... 2,250

# Review *Cost-Volume-Profit Analysis*

## ● Accounting Vocabulary

**Breakeven Point (p. 930)**
The sales level at which operating income is zero: Total revenues equal total expenses (costs).

**Contribution Margin (p. 931)**
Sales revenue minus variable expenses (costs).

**Contribution Margin Income Statement (p. 931)**
Income statement that groups costs by cost behavior—variable costs or fixed costs—and highlights the contribution margin.

**Contribution Margin Ratio (p. 932)**
Ratio of contribution margin to sales revenue.

**Cost-Volume-Profit (CVP) Analysis (p. 924)**
Expresses the relationships among costs, volume, and profit or loss.

**Fixed Costs (p. 926)**
Costs that tend to remain the same in amount, regardless of variations in level of activity.

**High-Low Method (p. 927)**
A method used to separate mixed costs into variable and fixed components, using the highest and lowest activity levels.

**Margin of Safety (p. 939)**
Excess of expected sales over breakeven sales. A drop in sales that a company can absorb without incurring an operating loss.

**Mixed Costs (p. 927)**
Costs that have both variable and fixed components.

**Relevant Range (p. 929)**
The range of volume where total fixed costs remain constant and the variable cost per unit remains constant.

**Sales Mix (p. 940)**
Combination of products that make up total sales.

**Sensitivity Analysis (p. 937)**
A "what if" technique that asks what results are likely if selling price or costs change, or if an underlying assumption changes.

**Target Profit (p. 933)**
The operating income that results when sales revenue minus variable and minus fixed costs equals management's profit goal.

**Total Fixed Costs (p. 926)**
Costs that do not change over wide ranges in volume.

**Total Variable Costs (p. 925)**
Costs that change in total in direct proportion to changes in volume.

**Variable Costs (p. 925)**
Costs that increase or decrease in total in direct proportion to increases or decreases in the volume of activity.

## ● Destination: Student Success

### Student Success Tips

The following are hints on some common trouble areas for students in this chapter:

● Remember the difference between variable, fixed, and mixed costs.

● Keep in mind that breakeven means the company has neither net income NOR net loss.

● Recall that the income statement approach to breakeven is really just the income statement you learned in Chapter 1.

● Consider that the breakeven formula can be used to make different assumptions about sales price, variable costs, fixed costs, and target profits.

● Keep in mind when calculating breakeven values whether the calculation is asking for number of units or for a dollar amount.

● Recall that the high-low method is a way to separate mixed costs into fixed and variable portions.

● Remember the margin of safety is the amount of sales dollars above breakeven, so it's the safety net of extra profit the company has before profits go to zero or worse, a net loss.

● Remember that most companies make more than one product, so sales mix must be considered in finding a weighted-average contribution margin to determine breakeven for multiple products.

### Getting Help

If there's a learning objective from the chapter you aren't confident about, try using one or more of the following resources:

● Review the Decision Guidelines 19-1 in the chapter.

● Review Summary Problem 19-1 in the chapter to reinforce your understanding of breakeven and sensitivity analysis.

● Review Exhibit 19-6 for information about how CVP changes affect contribution margin per unit and breakeven point.

● Review Summary Problem 19-2 in the chapter to reinforce your understanding of breakeven point for multiple products.

● Practice additional exercises or problems at the end of Chapter 19 that cover the specific learning objective that is challenging you.

● Watch the white board videos for Chapter 19, located at myaccountinglab.com under the Chapter Resources button.

● Go to myaccountinglab.com and select the Study Plan button. Choose Chapter 19 and work the questions covering that specific learning objective until you've mastered it.

● Work the Chapter 19 pre/post tests in myaccountinglab.com.

● Consult the Check Figures for End of Chapter short exercises, exercises, and problems, located at myaccountinglab.com.

● Visit the learning resource center on your campus for tutoring.

## ● Quick Check

1. For Frank's Funky Sounds, units of production depreciation on the trucks is a
   - a. variable cost.
   - b. fixed cost.
   - c. mixed cost.
   - d. high-low cost.

2. Assume Intervale Railway is considering hiring a reservations agency to handle passenger reservations. The agency would charge a flat fee of $13,000 per month, plus $3 per passenger reservation. What is the total reservation cost if 200,000 passengers take the trip next month?
   - a. $613,000
   - b. $3.07
   - c. $600,000
   - d. $13,000

3. If Intervale Railway's fixed costs total $90,000 per month, the variable cost per passenger is $45, and tickets sell for $75, what is the breakeven point in units?
   - a. 1,200 passengers
   - b. 2,000 passengers
   - c. 225,000 passengers
   - d. 3,000 passengers

4. Suppose Intervale Railway's total revenues are $4,000,000, its variable costs are $2,000,000, and its fixed costs are $800,000. Compute the breakeven point in dollars.
   - a. $4,000,000
   - b. $800,000
   - c. $1,600,000
   - d. $2,000,000

5. If Intervale Railway's fixed costs total $90,000 per month, the variable cost per passenger is $45, and tickets sell for $75, how much revenue must the Railway generate to earn $120,000 in operating income per month?
   - a. $350,000
   - b. $210,000
   - c. $7,000
   - d. $525,000

6. On a CVP graph, the total cost line intersects the vertical (dollars) axis at
   - a. the origin.
   - b. the level of the fixed costs.
   - c. the breakeven point.
   - d. the level of the variable costs.

7. If a company increases its selling price per unit for Product A, then the new breakeven point will
   - a. increase.
   - b. decrease.
   - c. remain the same.

8. If a company increases its fixed costs for Product B, then the contribution margin per unit will
   - a. increase.
   - b. decrease.
   - c. remain the same.

9. The Best Appliances had the following revenue over the past five years:

| | |
|---|---|
| 2007 | $ 600,000 |
| 2008 | 700,000 |
| 2009 | 900,000 |
| 2010 | 800,000 |
| 2011 | 1,000,000 |

To predict revenues for 2012, The Best uses the average for the past five years. The company's breakeven revenue is $800,000 per year. What is The Best's predicted margin of safety for 2012?
   - a. $800,000
   - b. $0
   - c. $200,000
   - d. $100,000

10. Rocky Mountain Waterpark sells half of its tickets for the regular price of $75. The other half go to senior citizens and children for the discounted price of $35. Variable cost per passenger is $15 for both groups, and fixed costs total $60,000 per month. What is Rocky Mountain's breakeven point in total guests? Regular guests? Discount guests?

a. 2,000/1,000/1,000          c. 750/375/375

b. 800/400/400                d. 1,500/750/750

Answers are given after Apply Your Knowledge (p. 961).

# Assess Your Progress

## • Short Exercises

**MyAccountingLab**

**S19-1**  **1** **Variable, fixed, and mixed costs  [5–10 min]**
Philadelphia Acoustics builds innovative speakers for music and home theater systems. Consider the following costs:

1. Units of production depreciation on routers used to cut wood enclosures.

2. Wood for speaker enclosures.

3. Patents on crossover relays.

4. Total compensation to salesperson, who receives a salary plus a commission based on meeting sales goals.

5. Crossover relays.

6. Straight-line depreciation on manufacturing plant.

7. Grill cloth.

8. Cell phone costs of salesperson (plan includes 1,200 minutes; overseas calls are charged at an average of $0.15 per minute).

9. Glue.

10. Quality inspector's salary.

### Requirement

1. Identify the costs as variable (V), fixed (F), or mixed (M).

**S19-2**  **1** **Variable, fixed, and mixed costs [5–10 min]**
Holly's DayCare has been in operation for several years. Consider the following costs:

1. Building rent.

2. Toys.

3. Salary of office manager, who also receives a bonus based on number of students enrolled.

4. Afternoon snacks.

5. Lawn service contract at $200 a month; any extra work needed is billed at an hourly rate based on the time needed to complete the job.

6. Holly's salary.

7. Wages of afterschool employees.

8. Drawing paper for student art work.

9. Straight-line depreciation of tables, chairs, and playground equipment.

10. Fee paid to security company for monthly service (contract includes up to four responses in a month; responses over four in a month incur an additional fee per response).

### Requirement

1. Identify the costs as variable (V), fixed (F), or mixed (M).

**S19-3**  **1** **Mixed costs—high-low method [5–10 min]**
Martin owns a machine shop. In reviewing his utility bill for the last 12 months, he found that his highest bill of $2,800 occurred in August when his machines worked 1,400 machine hours. His lowest utility bill of $2,600 occurred in December when his machines worked 900 machine hours.

## Requirements

1. Calculate (a) the variable rate per machine hour and (b) Martin's total fixed utility cost.
2. Show the equation for determining the total utility cost for Martin's.
3. If Martin's anticipates using 1,200 machine hours in January, predict his total utility bill using the equation from Requirement 2.
4. Draw a graph illustrating your total cost under this plan. Label the axes, and show your costs at 900, 1,200, and 1,400 machine hours.

**S19-4**   ❷ **Computing breakeven point in sales units [5–10 min]**
Story Park competes with Splash World by providing a variety of rides. Story sells tickets at $50 per person as a one-day entrance fee. Variable costs are $10 per person, and fixed costs are $240,000 per month.

## Requirement

1. Compute the number of tickets Story must sell to break even. Perform a numerical proof to show that your answer is correct.

*Note: Short Exercise 19-4 must be completed before attempting Short Exercise 19-5.*

**S19-5**   ❷ **Computing breakeven point in sales dollars [5 min]**
Refer to Short Exercise 19-4.

## Requirements

1. Compute Story Park's contribution margin ratio. Carry your computation to two decimal places.
2. Use the contribution margin ratio CVP formula to determine the sales revenue Story Park needs to break even.

**S19-6**   ❷ ❸ **Computing contribution margin, breakeven point, and units to achieve operating income [10–15 min]**
Consider the following facts:

|  | A | B | C |
|---|---|---|---|
| Number of units | 1,300 | 3,600 | 7,500 |
| Sale price per unit | $    100 | $    40 | $    125 |
| Variable costs per unit | 40 | 10 | 100 |
| Total fixed costs | 72,000 | 60,000 | 40,000 |
| Target operating income | 180,000 | 75,000 | 100,000 |
| Calculate: |  |  |  |
| Contribution margin per unit | ———— | ———— | ———— |
| Contribution margin ratio | ———— | ———— | ———— |
| Breakeven points in units | ———— | ———— | ———— |
| Breakeven point in sales dollars | ———— | ———— | ———— |
| Units to achieve target operating income | ———— | ———— | ———— |

## Requirement

1. Compute the missing information.

*Note: Short Exercise 19-4 must be completed before attempting Short Exercise 19-7.*

**S19-7** ④ **Sensitivity analysis of changing sale price and variable costs on breakeven point [10 min]**
Refer to Short Exercise 19-4.

## Requirements

1. Suppose Story Park cuts its ticket price from $50 to $40 to increase the number of tickets sold. Compute the new breakeven point in tickets and in sales dollars.

2. Ignore the information in Requirement 1. Instead, assume that Story Park increases the variable cost from $10 to $20 per ticket. Compute the new breakeven point in tickets and in sales dollars.

*Note: Short Exercise 19-4 must be completed before attempting Short Exercise 19-8.*

**S19-8** ④ **Sensitivity analysis of changing fixed cost on breakeven point [5–10 min]**
Refer to Short Exercise 19-4. Suppose Story Park reduces fixed costs from $240,000 per month to $170,000 per month.

## Requirement

1. Compute the new breakeven point in tickets and in sales dollars.

*Note: Short Exercise 19-4 must be completed before attempting Short Exercise 19-9.*

**S19-9** ④ **Computing margin of safety [5–10 min]**
Refer to Short Exercise 19-4.

## Requirement

1. If Story Park expects to sell 6,200 tickets, compute the margin of safety in tickets and in sales dollars.

**S19-10** ⑤ **Calculating weighted-average contribution margin [5–10 min]**
Wet Weekend Swim Park sells individual and family tickets, which include a meal, three beverages, and unlimited use of the swimming pools. Wet Weekend has the following ticket prices and variable costs for 2012:

|  | Individual | Family |
|---|---|---|
| Sale price per ticket . . . . . . | $  30 | $  90 |
| Variable cost per ticket . . . | 15 | 60 |

Wet Weekend expects to sell two individual tickets for every four family tickets. Wet Weekend's total fixed costs are $75,000.

## Requirements

1. Compute the weighted-average contribution margin per ticket.
2. Calculate the total number of tickets Wet Weekend must sell to break even.
3. Calculate the number of individual tickets and the number of family tickets the company must sell to break even.

*Note: Short Exercise 19-10 must be completed before attempting Short Exercise 19-11.*

**S19-11** ⑤ **Calculating breakeven point for two products [5–10 min]**
Refer to Short Exercise 19-10. For 2013, Wet Weekend expects a sales mix of two individual tickets for every three family tickets.

## Requirements

1. Compute the new weighted-average contribution margin per ticket.
2. Calculate the total number of tickets Wet Weekend must sell to break even.
3. Calculate the number of individual tickets and the number of family tickets the company must sell to break even.

# • Exercises

**E19-12** ❶ **CVP definitions [15 min]**
Consider the following terms and definitions.

\_\_\_\_\_ 1. Costs that do not change in total despite wide changes in volume.

\_\_\_\_\_ 2. The sales level at which operating income is zero: Total revenues equal

total costs.

\_\_\_\_\_ 3. Drop in sales a company can absorb without incurring an operating loss.

\_\_\_\_\_ 4. Combination of products that make up total sales.

\_\_\_\_\_ 5. Sales revenue minus variable costs.

\_\_\_\_\_ 6. Describes how costs change as volume changes.

\_\_\_\_\_ 7. Costs that change in total in direct proportion to changes in volume.

\_\_\_\_\_ 8. The band of volume where total fixed costs remain constant and the variable

cost *per unit* remains constant.

a. Breakeven
b. Contribution margin
c. Cost behavior
d. Margin of safety
e. Relevant range
f. Sales mix
g. Fixed costs
h. Variable costs

## Requirement

1. Match the terms with the correct definitions.

**E19-13** ❶ **Mixed costs—the high-low method [10–15 min]**
The manager of Able Car Inspection reviewed his monthly operating costs for the past year. His costs ranged from $4,000 for 1,000 inspections to $3,600 for 600 inspections.

## Requirements

1. Calculate the variable cost per inspection.
2. Calculate the total fixed costs.
3. Write the equation and calculate the operating costs for 800 inspections.
4. Draw a graph illustrating your total cost under this plan. Label the axes, and show your costs at 600, 800, and 1,000 inspections.

**E19-14** ❷ **Preparing contribution margin income statements and calculating breakeven sales [15 min]**
For its top managers, Worldwide Travel formats its income statement as follows:

| WORLDWIDE TRAVEL | |
| :-- | --: |
| **Contribution Margin Income Statement** | |
| **Three Months Ended March 31, 2012** | |
| Sales revenue | $ 317,500 |
| Variable costs | 95,250 |
| Contribution margin | $ 222,250 |
| Fixed costs | 175,000 |
| Operating income | $ 47,250 |

Worldwide's relevant range is between sales of $245,000 and $364,000.

## Requirements

1. Calculate the contribution margin ratio.
2. Prepare two contribution margin income statements: one at the $245,000 level and one at the $364,000 level. (*Hint*: The proportion of each sales dollar that goes toward variable costs is constant within the relevant range.)
3. Compute breakeven sales in dollars.

**E19-15**  ❷ **Computing breakeven sales by the contribution margin approach [15 min]**
Trendy Toes, Co., produces sports socks. The company has fixed costs of $95,000 and variable costs of $0.95 per package. Each package sells for $1.90.

## Requirements

1.  Compute the contribution margin per package and the contribution margin ratio. (Round your answers to two decimal places.)
2.  Find the breakeven point in units and in dollars, using the contribution margin approach.

**E19-16**  ❸ **Computing a change in breakeven sales [10–15 min]**
Owner Yinan Song is considering franchising her Noodles restaurant concept. She believes people will pay $7.50 for a large bowl of noodles. Variable costs are $3.00 per bowl. Song estimates monthly fixed costs for a franchise at $9,000.

## Requirements

1.  Use the contribution margin ratio approach to find a franchise's breakeven sales in dollars.
2.  Song believes most locations could generate $40,000 in monthly sales. Is franchising a good idea for Song if franchisees want a minimum monthly operating income of $13,500?

**E19-17**  ❸ **Computing breakeven sales and operating income or loss under different conditions [10–15 min]**
Gary's Steel Parts produces parts for the automobile industry. The company has monthly fixed costs of $660,000 and a contribution margin of 75% of revenues.

## Requirements

1.  Compute Gary's monthly breakeven sales in dollars. Use the contribution margin ratio approach.
2.  Use contribution margin income statements to compute Gary's monthly operating income or operating loss if revenues are $530,000 and if they are $1,040,000.
3.  Do the results in Requirement 2 make sense given the breakeven sales you computed in Requirement 1? Explain.

**E19-18**  ❸ **Analyzing a cost-volume profit graph [15–20 min]**
John Kyler is considering starting a Web-based educational business, e-Prep MBA. He plans to offer a short-course review of accounting for students entering MBA programs. The materials would be available on a password-protected Web site; students would complete the course through self-study. Kyler would have to grade the course assignments, but most of the work is in developing the course materials, setting up the site, and marketing. Unfortunately, Kyler's hard drive crashed before he finished his financial analysis. However, he did recover the following partial CVP chart:

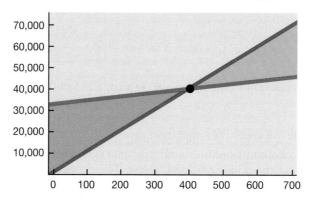

## Requirements

1. Label each axis, the sales revenue line, the total costs line, the fixed costs, the operating income area, and the breakeven point.
2. If Kyler attracts 300 students to take the course, will the venture be profitable?
3. What are the breakeven sales in students and dollars?

**E19-19** **4** **Impact on breakeven point if sale price, variable costs, and fixed costs change [15 min]**

Dependable Drivers Driving School charges $250 per student to prepare and administer written and driving tests. Variable costs of $100 per student include trainers' wages, study materials, and gasoline. Annual fixed costs of $75,000 include the training facility and fleet of cars.

## Requirements

1. For each of the following independent situations, calculate the contribution margin per unit and the breakeven point in units by first referring to the original data provided:
   a. Breakeven point with no change in information.
   b. Decrease sales price to $220 per student.
   c. Decrease variable costs to $50 per student.
   d. Decrease fixed costs to $60,000.
2. Compare the impact of changes in the sales price, variable costs, and fixed costs on the contribution margin per unit and the breakeven point in units.

**E19-20** **4** **Computing margin of safety [15 min]**

Rodney's Repair Shop has a monthly target operating income of $15,000. Variable costs are 75% of sales, and monthly fixed costs are $10,000.

## Requirements

1. Compute the monthly margin of safety in dollars if the shop achieves its income goal.
2. Express Rodney's margin of safety as a percentage of target sales.

**E19-21** **5** **Calculating breakeven point for two products [15–20 min]**

Speedy's Scooters plans to sell a standard scooter for $55 and a chrome scooter for $70. Speedy's purchases the standard scooter for $30 and the chrome scooter for $40. Speedy expects to sell one standard scooter for every three chrome scooters. His monthly fixed costs are $23,000.

## Requirements

1. How many of each type of scooter must Speedy's Scooters sell each month to break even?
2. To earn $25,300?

# ● Problem (Group A)

**P19-22A** **①②③** **Calculating cost-volume profit elements [45–60 min]**
The budgets of four companies yield the following information:

| | | Company | | |
|---|---|---|---|---|
| | Blue | Red | Green | Yellow |
| Sales revenue | $ 960,000 | $ (4) | $ 770,000 | $ (10) |
| Variable costs | (1) | 132,000 | 462,000 | 162,000 |
| Fixed costs | (2) | 145,000 | 220,000 | (11) |
| Operating income (loss) | $ 32,000 | $ (5) | $ (7) | $ 93,000 |
| Units sold | 160,000 | 11,000 | (8) | (12) |
| Contribution margin per unit | $ 2.70 | $ (6) | $ 77.00 | $ 16.00 |
| Contribution margin ratio | (3) | 0.70 | (9) | 0.40 |

## Requirements

1. Fill in the blanks for each missing value. (Round the contribution margin per unit to the nearest cent.)
2. Which company has the lowest breakeven point in sales dollars?
3. What causes the low breakeven point?

**P19-23A** **②③** **Break even sales; sales to earn a target operating income; contribution margin income statement [30–45 min]**
England Productions performs London shows. The average show sells 1,300 tickets at $60 per ticket. There are 150 shows a year. No additional shows can be held as the theater is also used by other production companies. The average show has a cast of 65, each earning a net average of $340 per show. The cast is paid after each show. The other variable cost is a program-printing cost of $8 per guest. Annual fixed costs total $728,000.

## Requirements

1. Compute revenue and variable costs for each show.
2. Use the income statement equation approach to compute the number of shows England Productions must perform each year to break even.
3. Use the contribution margin approach to compute the number of shows needed each year to earn a profit of $5,687,500. Is this profit goal realistic? Give your reasoning.
4. Prepare England Productions' contribution margin income statement for 150 shows performed in 2012. Report only two categories of costs: variable and fixed.

**P19-24A** **②③④** **Analyzing CVP relationships [30–45 min]**
Kincaid Company sells flags with team logos. Kincaid has fixed costs of $583,200 per year plus variable costs of $4.80 per flag. Each flag sells for $12.00.

## Requirements

1. Use the income statement equation approach to compute the number of flags Kincaid must sell each year to break even.
2. Use the contribution margin ratio CVP formula to compute the dollar sales Kincaid needs to earn $33,000 in operating income for 2012. (Round the contribution margin to two decimal places.)
3. Prepare Kincaid's contribution margin income statement for the year ended December 31, 2012, for sales of 72,000 flags. Cost of goods sold is 70% of variable costs. Operating costs make up the rest of variable costs and all of fixed costs. (Round your final answers to the nearest whole number.)

4. The company is considering an expansion that will increase fixed costs by 21% and variable costs by $0.60 per flag. Compute the new breakeven point in units and in dollars. Should Kincaid undertake the expansion? Give your reasoning. Round your final answers to the nearest whole number.

**P19-25A** ❷❸❹ **Computing breakeven sales and sales needed to earn a target operating income; graphing CVP relationships; sensitivity analysis [30–45 min]**
National Investor Group is opening an office in Portland. Fixed monthly costs are office rent ($8,500), depreciation on office furniture ($2,000), utilities ($2,100), special telephone lines ($1,100), a connection with an online brokerage service ($2,800), and the salary of a financial planner ($4,500). Variable costs include payments to the financial planner (8% of revenue), advertising (13% of revenue), supplies and postage (3% of revenue), and usage fees for the telephone lines and computerized brokerage service (6% of revenue).

## Requirements

1. Use the contribution margin ratio CVP formula to compute National's breakeven revenue in dollars. If the average trade leads to $1,000 in revenue for National, how many trades must be made to break even?

2. Use the income statement equation approach to compute the dollar revenues needed to earn a target monthly operating income of $12,600.

3. Graph National's CVP relationships. Assume that an average trade leads to $1,000 in revenue for National. Show the breakeven point, the sales revenue line, the fixed cost line, the total cost line, the operating loss area, the operating income area, and the sales in units (trades) and dollars when monthly operating income of $12,600 is earned.

4. Suppose that the average revenue National earns increases to $1,200 per trade. Compute the new breakeven point in trades. How does this affect the breakeven point?

**P19-26A** ❹❺ **Calculating breakeven point for two products; margin of safety [20 min]**
The contribution margin income statement of Delectable Donuts for August 2012 follows:

| DELECTABLE DONUTS | | | |
|---|---|---|---|
| **Contribution Margin Income Statement** | | | |
| For the Month of August 2012 | | | |
| Sales revenue | | | $ 150,000 |
| Variable costs: | | | |
| Cost of goods sold | | $ 41,000 | |
| Marketing costs | | 15,000 | |
| General and administrative costs | | 4,000 | 60,000 |
| Contribution margin | | | $ 90,000 |
| Fixed costs: | | | |
| Marketing costs | | 37,800 | |
| General and administrative costs | | 12,600 | 50,400 |
| Operating income | | | $ 39,600 |

Delectable sells four dozen plain donuts for every dozen custard-filled donuts. A dozen plain donuts sells for $4, with total variable cost of $1.60 per dozen. A dozen custard-filled donuts sells for $5, with total variable cost of $2 per dozen.

## Requirements

1. Calculate the weighted-average contribution margin.

2. Determine Delectable's monthly breakeven point in dozens of plain donuts and custard-filled donuts. Prove your answer by preparing a summary contribution

margin income statement at the breakeven level of sales. Show only two categories of costs: variable and fixed.

3. Compute Delectable's margin of safety in dollars for August 2012.

4. If Delectable can increase monthly sales revenue from August's level by 20%, what will operating income be? (The sales mix remains unchanged.)

## ● Problem (Group B)

**P19-27B ① ② ③ Calculating cost-volume profit elements [45–60 min]**

The budgets of four companies yield the following information:

| | Company | | | |
|---|---|---|---|---|
| | Up | Down | Left | Right |
| Sales revenue | $ 900,000 | $      (4) | $ 710,000 | $      (10) |
| Variable costs | (1) | 208,000 | 319,500 | 240,000 |
| Fixed costs | (2) | 135,000 | 235,000 | (11) |
| Operating income (loss) | $  10,000 | $      (5) | $      (7) | $  49,000 |
| Units sold | 100,000 | 16,000 | (8) | (12) |
| Contribution margin per unit | $    3.60 | $      (6) | $   78.10 | $   10.00 |
| Contribution margin ratio | (3) | 0.60 | (9) | 0.20 |

### Requirements

1. Fill in the blanks for each missing value. (Round the contribution margin to the nearest cent.)

2. Which company has the lowest breakeven point in sales dollars?

3. What causes the low breakeven point?

**P19-28B ② ③ Breakeven sales; sales to earn a target operating income; contribution margin income statement [30–45 min]**

British Productions performs London shows. The average show sells 900 tickets at $65 per ticket. There are 155 shows a year. No additional shows can be held as the theater is also used by other production companies. The average show has a cast of 55, each earning a net average of $330 per show. The cast is paid after each show. The other variable cost is program-printing cost of $9 per guest. Annual fixed costs total $580,500.

### Requirements

1. Compute revenue and variable costs for each show.

2. Use the income statement equation approach to compute the number of shows British Productions must perform each year to break even.

3. Use the contribution margin approach to compute the number of shows needed each year to earn a profit of $4,128,000. Is this profit goal realistic? Give your reasoning.

4. Prepare British Productions' contribution margin income statement for 155 shows performed in 2012. Report only two categories of costs: variable and fixed.

**P19-29B ② ③ ④ Analyzing CVP relationships [30–45 min]**

Kincaid Company sells flags with team logos. Kincaid has fixed costs of $664,000 per year plus variable costs of $4.50 per flag. Each flag sells for $12.50.

### Requirements

1. Use the income statement equation approach to compute the number of flags Kincaid must sell each year to break even.

2. Use the contribution margin ratio CVP formula to compute the dollar sales. Kincaid needs to earn $33,600 in operating income for 2012. (Round the contribution margin to two decimal places.)

3. Prepare Kincaid's contribution margin income statement for the year ended December 31, 2012, for sales of 75,000 flags. Cost of goods sold is 60% of variable costs. Operating costs make up the rest of variable costs and all of fixed costs. (Round your final answers to the nearest whole number.)

4. The company is considering an expansion that will increase fixed costs by 24% and variable costs by $0.25 per flag. Compute the new breakeven point in units and in dollars. Should Kincaid undertake the expansion? Give your reasoning. (Round your final answers to the nearest whole number.)

**P19-30B** ❷ ❸ ❹ **Computing breakeven sales and sales needed to earn a target operating income; graphing CVP relationships; sensitivity analysis [30–45 min]**
Diversified Investor Group is opening an office in Boise. Fixed monthly costs are office rent ($8,100), depreciation on office furniture ($1,600), utilities ($2,500), special telephone lines ($1,200), a connection with an online brokerage service ($2,700), and the salary of a financial planner ($4,900). Variable costs include payments to the financial planner (8% of revenue), advertising (14% of revenue), supplies and postage (1% of revenue), and usage fees for the telephone lines and computerized brokerage service (7% of revenue).

## Requirements

1. Use the contribution margin ratio CVP formula to compute Diversified's breakeven revenue in dollars. If the average trade leads to $750 in revenue for Diversified, how many trades must be made to break even?

2. Use the income statement equation approach to compute the dollar revenues needed to earn a target monthly operating income of $10,500.

3. Graph Diversified's CVP relationships. Assume that an average trade leads to $750 in revenue for Diversified. Show the breakeven point, the sales revenue line, the fixed cost line, the total cost line, the operating loss area, the operating income area, and the sales in units (trades) and dollars when monthly operating income of $10,500 is earned.

4. Suppose that the average revenue Diversified earns increases to $1,000 per trade. Compute the new breakeven point in trades. How does this affect the breakeven point?

**P19-31B** ❹ ❺ **Calculating breakeven point for two products; margin of safety [20 min]**
The contribution margin income statement of Dandy Donuts for May 2012 follows:

| DANDY DONUTS | | |
|---|---|---|
| Contribution Margin Income Statement | | |
| For the Month of May 2012 | | |
| Sales revenue | | $ 190,000 |
| Variable costs: | | |
|    Cost of goods sold | $ 56,000 | |
|    Marketing costs | 20,000 | |
|    General and administrative costs | 19,000 | 95,000 |
| Contribution margin | | $ 95,000 |
| Fixed costs: | | |
|    Marketing costs | 50,700 | |
|    General and administrative costs | 27,300 | 78,000 |
| Operating income | | $ 17,000 |

Dandy sells three dozen plain donuts for every dozen custard-filled donuts. A dozen plain donuts sells for $6, with a variable cost of $3 per dozen. A dozen custard-filled donuts sells for $8, with a variable cost of $4 per dozen.

**Requirements**

1. Calculate the weighted-average contribution margin.
2. Determine Dandy's monthly breakeven point in dozens of plain donuts and custard-filled donuts. Prove your answer by preparing a summary contribution margin income statement at the breakeven level of sales. Show only two categories of costs: variable and fixed.
3. Compute Dandy's margin of safety in dollars for May 2012.
4. If Dandy can increase the monthly sales revenue from May's level by 25%, what will operating income be? (The sales mix remains unchanged.)

## ● Continuing Exercise

*MyAccountingLab* **E19-32** ❸ **Computing contribution margin, breakeven point, and units to achieve operating income [10–15 min]**
This exercise continues the Lawlor Lawn Service, Inc., situation from Exercise 18-36 of Chapter 18. Lawlor Lawn Service currently charges $100 for a standard lawn service and incurs $60 in variable cost. Assume fixed costs are $1,400 per month.

**Requirements**

1. What is the number of lawns that must be serviced to reach break even?
2. If Lawlor desires to make a profit of $1,800, how many lawns must be serviced?

## ● Continuing Problem

*MyAccountingLab* **P19-33** ❷❸❹ **Computing breakeven sales and sales needed to earn a target operating income; sensitivity analysis [30–45 min]**
This problem continues the Draper Consulting, Inc., situation from Problem 18-37 of Chapter 18. Draper Consulting provides consulting service at an average price of $175 per hour and incurs variable cost of $100 per hour. Assume average fixed costs are $5,250 a month.

**Requirements**

1. What is the number of hours that must be billed to reach break even?
2. If Draper desires to make a profit of $3,000, how many consulting hours must be completed?
3. Draper thinks it can reduce fixed cost to $3,990 per month, but variable cost will increase to $105 per hour. What is the new break even in hours?

# Apply Your Knowledge

## ● Decision Case 19-1

Steve and Linda Hom live in Bartlesville, Oklahoma. Two years ago, they visited Thailand. Linda, a professional chef, was impressed with the cooking methods and the spices used in the Thai food. Bartlesville does not have a Thai restaurant, and the Homs are contemplating opening one. Linda would supervise the cooking, and Steve would leave his current job to be the maitre d'. The restaurant would serve dinner Tuesday–Saturday.

Steve has noticed a restaurant for lease. The restaurant has seven tables, each of which can seat four. Tables can be moved together for a large party. Linda is planning two seatings per evening, and the restaurant will be open 50 weeks per year.

The Homs have drawn up the following estimates:

| | |
|---|---|
| Average revenue, including beverages and dessert............ | $ 45 per meal |
| Average cost of food........................................................ | $ 15 per meal |
| Chef's and dishwasher's salaries...................................... | $ 5,100 per month |
| Rent (premises, equipment)............................................. | $ 4,000 per month |
| Cleaning (linen and premises).......................................... | $ 800 per month |
| Replacement of dishes, cutlery, glasses........................... | $ 300 per month |
| Utilities, advertising, telephone....................................... | $ 2,300 per month |

## Requirements

1. Compute the *annual* breakeven number of meals and sales revenue for the restaurant.
2. Also compute the number of meals and the amount of sales revenue needed to earn operating income of $75,600 for the year.
3. How many meals must the Homs serve each night to earn their target income of $75,600?
4. What factors should the Homs consider before they make their decision as to whether to open the restaurant or not?

## ● Ethical Issue 19-1

You have just begun your summer internship at Omni Instruments. The company supplies sterilized surgical instruments for physicians. To expand sales, Omni is considering paying a commission to its sales force. The controller, Matthew Barnhill, asks you to compute: (1) the new breakeven sales figure, and (2) the operating profit if sales increase 15% under the new sales commission plan. He thinks you can handle this task because you learned CVP analysis in your accounting class.

You spend the next day collecting information from the accounting records, performing the analysis, and writing a memo to explain the results. The company president is pleased with your memo. You report that the new sales commission plan will lead to a significant increase in operating income and only a small increase in breakeven sales.

The following week, you realize that you made an error in the CVP analysis. You overlooked the sales personnel's $2,800 monthly salaries and you did not include this fixed marketing cost in your computations. You are not sure what to do. If you tell Matthew Barnhill of your mistake, he will have to tell the president. In this case, you are afraid Omni might not offer you permanent employment after your internship.

## Requirements

1. How would your error affect breakeven sales and operating income under the proposed sales commission plan? Could this cause the president to reject the sales commission proposal?
2. Consider your ethical responsibilities. Is there a difference between: (a) initially making an error, and (b) subsequently failing to inform the controller?
3. Suppose you tell Matthew Barnhill of the error in your analysis. Why might the consequences not be as bad as you fear? Should Barnhill take any responsibility for your error? What could Barnhill have done differently?
4. After considering all the factors, should you inform Barnhill or simply keep quiet?

## ● Fraud Case 19-1

Amanda Jackson loved reading obituaries. She was retired, but she had worked many bookkeeping jobs in her day and had made herself an expert in creating false invoices and opening bank accounts for fake companies. The scam was easy. When someone dies, the whole family is in grief, and one of the family members must clean up the deceased person's paperwork, close out accounts, pay the last bills, etc. If the now deceased person had ordered a pricey box set of classical music CDs, or had his ventilation system cleaned out, or even gotten therapeutic massages, who would bother questioning the bill? Sometimes the families of the deceased person paid Amanda's fake bills, and sometimes they didn't, but nobody ever looked any further. Yes, Amanda Jackson loved reading obituaries.

### Requirements

1. Although this fraud pertains to individuals, how do businesses make sure they do not pay fake invoices?

2. If a person dies, is anyone liable for paying the remaining bills of the deceased?

## ● Team Project 19-1 (Based on Online Appendix 19A)

FASTPACK Manufacturing produces filament packaging tape. In 2014, FASTPACK produced and sold 15,000,000 rolls of tape. The company has recently expanded its capacity, so it now can produce up to 30,000,000 rolls per year. FASTPACK's accounting records show the following results from 2014:

| | |
|---|---|
| Sale price per roll ................................................................ | $ 3.00 |
| Variable manufacturing costs per roll................................. | $ 2.00 |
| Variable marketing and administrative costs per roll........... | $ 0.50 |
| Total fixed manufacturing overhead costs.......................... | $8,400,000 |
| Total fixed marketing and administrative costs.................... | $1,100,000 |
| Sales.................................................................................... | 15,000,000 rolls |
| Production ............................................................................ | 15,000,000 rolls |

There were no beginning or ending inventories in 2014.

In January 2015, FASTPACK hired a new president, Kevin McDaniel. McDaniel has a one-year contract that specifies he will be paid 10% of FASTPACK's 2015 absorption costing operating income, instead of a salary. In 2015, McDaniel must make two major decisions:

- Should FASTPACK undertake a major advertising campaign? This campaign would raise sales to 24,000,000 rolls. This is the maximum level of sales FASTPACK can expect to make in the near future. The ad campaign would add an additional $2,300,000 in fixed marketing and administrative costs. Without the campaign, sales will be 15,000,000 rolls.
- How many rolls of tape will FASTPACK produce?

At the end of the year, FASTPACK's Board of Directors will evaluate McDaniel's performance and decide whether to offer him a contract for the following year.

### Requirements

Within your group, form two subgroups. The first subgroup assumes the role of Kevin McDaniel, FASTPACK's new president. The second subgroup assumes the role of FASTPACK's Board of Directors. McDaniel will meet with the Board of Directors shortly after the end of 2014 to decide whether he will remain at FASTPACK. Most of your effort should be devoted to advance preparation for this meeting. Each subgroup should meet separately to prepare for the meeting between the Board and McDaniel.

*Kevin McDaniel should*

1. compute FASTPACK's 2014 operating income.

2. decide whether to adopt the advertising campaign. Prepare a memo to the Board of Directors explaining this decision. Give this memo to the Board of Directors as soon as possible (before the joint meeting).

3. assume FASTPACK adopts the advertising campaign. Decide how many rolls of tape to produce in 2015.

4. (given the response to Requirement 3) prepare an absorption costing income statement for the year ended December 31, 2015, ending with operating income before bonus. Then compute the bonus separately. The variable cost per unit and the total fixed costs (with the exception of the advertising campaign) remain the same as in 2014. Give this income statement and bonus computation to the Board of Directors as soon as possible (before the meeting with the Board).

5. decide whether he wishes to remain at FASTPACK for another year. He currently has an offer from another company. The contract with the other company is identical to the one he currently has with FASTPACK—he will be paid 10% of absorption costing operating income instead of a salary.

*The Board of Directors should*

1. compute FASTPACK's 2014 operating income.
2. determine whether FASTPACK should adopt the advertising campaign.
3. determine how many rolls of tape FASTPACK should produce in 2015.
4. evaluate McDaniel's performance, based on his decisions and the information he provided the Board. (*Hint*: You may want to prepare a variable costing income statement.)
5. evaluate the contract's bonus provision. Is the Board satisfied with this provision? If so, explain why. If not, recommend how it should be changed.

After McDaniel has given the Board his memo and income statement, and after the Board has had a chance to evaluate McDaniel's performance, McDaniel and the Board should meet. The purpose of the meeting is to decide whether it is in their mutual interest for McDaniel to remain with FASTPACK, and if so, the terms of the contract FASTPACK will offer McDaniel.

## ● Communication Activity 19-1

In 25 words or fewer, explain what it means for a company to break even.

---

## Quick Check Answers

1. *a* 2. *a* 3. *d* 4. *c* 5. *d* 6. *b* 7. *b* 8. *c* 9. *b* 10. *d*

**For online homework, exercises, and problems that provide you immediate feedback, please visit myaccountinglab.com.**

# 20 Short-Term Business Decisions

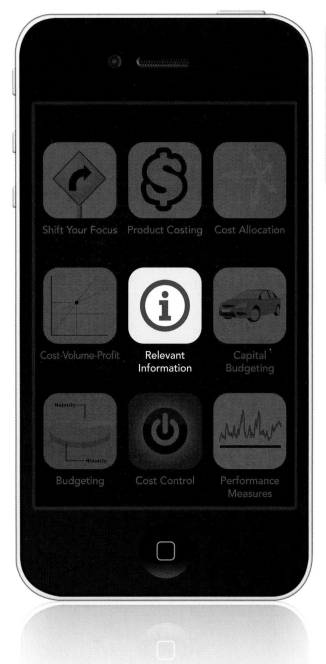

Shift Your Focus

Product Costing

Cost Allocation

Cost-Volume-Profit

Relevant Information

Capital Budgeting

Budgeting

Cost Control

Performance Measures

## Learning Objectives

1. Describe and identify information relevant to business decisions

2. Make special order and pricing decisions

3. Make dropping a product and product-mix decisions

4. Make outsourcing and sell as is or process further decisions

Most major companies receive special order requests at reduced pricing as they grow. Smart Touch Learning, Inc., is considering a special order for its Excel DVDs. But why would Smart Touch consider selling its Excel DVDs at a reduced price? What costs and other information must Smart Touch consider in making the decision to accept or reject the order?

In Chapter 19, we saw how managers use cost behavior to determine the company's breakeven point and to estimate the sales volume needed to achieve target profits. In this chapter, we will see how managers use their knowledge of cost behavior to make six special business decisions, such as whether or not to accept a special order. The decisions we will discuss in this chapter pertain to short periods of time so managers do not need to worry about the time value of money. In other words, they do not need to compute the present value of the revenues and expenses relating to the decision. In Chapter 21 we will discuss longer-term decisions (such as plant expansions) in which the time value of money becomes important. Before we look at the six business decisions in detail, let's consider a manager's decision-making process and the information managers need to evaluate their options.

# How Managers Make Decisions

Exhibit 20-1 illustrates how managers make decisions among alternative courses of action. Managerial accountants help with the third step: gathering and analyzing *relevant information* to compare alternatives.

**1** Describe and identify information relevant to business decisions

**EXHIBIT 20-1** | **How Managers Make Decisions**

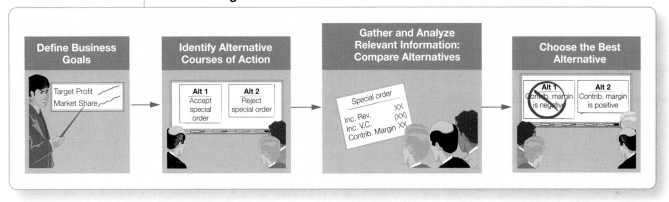

## Relevant Information

When managers make decisions, they focus on costs and revenues that are relevant to the decisions. Exhibit 20-2 shows that **relevant information** is

1. expected *future* data that
2. *differs* among alternatives.

    **Relevant costs** are those costs that are relevant to a particular decision. To illustrate, if Smart Touch were considering purchasing a Dodge or a **Toyota** delivery truck, the cost of the truck, the sales tax, and the insurance premium costs would all be relevant because these costs

- are incurred in the *future* (after Smart Touch decides which truck to buy), and
- *differ between alternatives* (each truck has a different invoice price, sales tax, and insurance premium).

    These costs are *relevant* because they can affect the decision of which truck to purchase.

**EXHIBIT 20-2** | **Relevant Information**

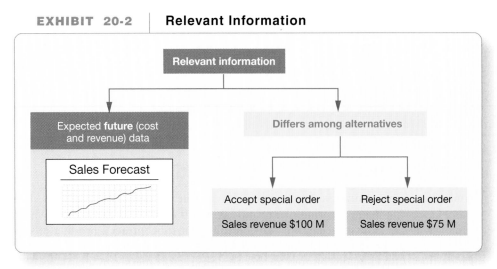

Irrelevant costs are costs that *do not* affect the decision. For example, because the Dodge and **Toyota** both have similar fuel efficiency and maintenance ratings, we do not expect the truck operating costs to differ between those two alternatives. Because these costs do not differ, they do not affect Smart Touch's decision. In other words, they are *irrelevant* to the decision. Similarly, the cost of an annual license tag is also irrelevant because the tag costs the same whether Smart Touch buys the Dodge or the **Toyota**.

Sunk costs are costs that were incurred in the *past* and cannot be changed regardless of which future action is taken. Sunk costs are always irrelevant to the decision. **Since sunk costs are already spent (sunk), they are never used in future decision making.** Perhaps Smart Touch wants to trade in its current **Ford** truck when the company buys the new truck. The amount Smart Touch paid for the **Ford** truck—which the company bought for $15,000 a year ago—is a sunk cost. No decision made *now* can alter the sunk costs spent in the past. Smart Touch already bought the **Ford** truck so *the price the company paid for it is a sunk cost.* All Smart Touch can do *now* is keep the **Ford** truck, trade it in, or sell it for the best price the company can get, even if that price is substantially less than what Smart Touch originally paid for the truck.

What *is* relevant is what Smart Touch can get if it sells the **Ford** truck in the future. Suppose that the Dodge dealership offers $8,000 for the **Ford** truck, but the **Toyota** dealership offers $10,000. Because the amounts differ and the transaction will take place in the future, the trade-in cost *is* relevant to Smart Touch's decision. Why? Because the trade-in values are different.

The same principle applies to all situations—*only relevant data affect decisions.* Let's consider another application of this principle.

Suppose Smart Touch is deciding whether to use DVDs made from new materials or DVDs made from recycled materials for its Excel Learning DVDs. Assume Smart Touch predicts the following costs under the two alternatives:

|  | New Materials | Recycled Materials | Cost Difference |
|---|---|---|---|
| Manufacturing cost per DVD: |  |  |  |
| Direct materials ...................... | $2.40 | $2.60 | $0.20 |
| Direct labor ........................... | $4.00 | $4.00 | $0.00 |

The cost of direct materials is relevant because this cost differs between alternatives (the recycled DVDs cost $0.20 more per DVD than the new material DVDs). The labor cost is irrelevant because that cost is the same for both.

## Stop & Think...

You are considering replacing your old computer with the latest model. Is the $1,200 you spent in 2005 on the computer relevant to your decision about buying the new model?

**Answer:** The $1,200 cost of your old computer is irrelevant. It is a *sunk* cost that you incurred in the past so it is the same whether or not you buy the new computer.

## Relevant Nonfinancial Information

Nonfinancial, or qualitative factors, also play a role in managers' decisions. For example, closing manufacturing plants and laying off employees can seriously hurt employee morale. **Outsourcing,** the decision to buy or subcontract a product or service rather than produce it in-house, can reduce control over delivery time or product quality. Offering discounted prices to select customers can upset regular customers and tempt them to take their business elsewhere. Managers must always consider the potential quantitative *and* qualitative effects of their decisions.

Managers who ignore qualitative factors can make serious mistakes. For example, the City of Nottingham, England, spent $1.6 million on 215 solar-powered parking meters after seeing how well the parking meters worked in countries along the Mediterranean Sea. However, they did not consider that British skies are typically overcast. The result was that the meters did not always work because of the lack of sunlight. The city *lost* money because people parked for free! Relevant qualitative information has the same characteristics as relevant financial information. The qualitative effect occurs in the *future* and it *differs* between alternatives. In the parking meter example, the amount of *future* sunshine required *differed* between alternatives. The mechanical meters did not require any sunshine, but the solar-powered meters needed a lot of sunshine.

## Keys to Making Short-Term Special Decisions

Our approach to making short-term special decisions is called the **relevant information approach,** or the **incremental analysis approach.** Instead of looking at the company's *entire* income statement under each decision alternative, we will just look at how operating income would *differ* under each alternative. Using this approach, we will leave out irrelevant information—the costs and revenues that will not differ between alternatives. We will consider six kinds of short-term special decisions in this chapter:

1. Special sales orders

2. Pricing

3. Dropping products, departments, and territories

4. Product mix

5. Outsourcing (make or buy)

6. Selling as is or processing further

As you study these decisions, keep in mind the two keys in analyzing short-term special business decisions shown in Exhibit 20-3:

1. **Focus on relevant revenues, costs, and profits.** Irrelevant information only clouds the picture and creates information overload.

2. **Use a contribution margin approach that separates variable costs from fixed costs.** Because fixed costs and variable costs behave differently, they must be analyzed separately. Traditional (absorption costing) income statements, which blend fixed and variable costs together, can mislead managers. Contribution margin income statements, which isolate costs by behavior (variable or fixed), help managers gather the cost-behavior information they need. Keep in mind that unit manufacturing costs are mixed costs, too, so they can also mislead managers. If you use unit manufacturing costs in your analysis, be sure to first separate the unit cost into its fixed and variable portions.

We will use these two keys in each decision.

**Connect To: Ethics**

Management must consider all the possible financial and non-financial factors in outsourcing. Although the outsourcing company (OC) may be able to provide a component or service at a reduced cost, is the OC acting responsibly in its production? Is it complying with all environmental standards? Does the OC meet the same green standards as the company buying from the OC? These considerations are as vital to outsourcing decisions as potential cost savings.

**Key Takeaway**

Relevant information is expected future data that differs among alternatives. Relevant costs are costs that may affect which decision you make. Irrelevant costs are costs that won't change the decision you make. Sunk costs are costs that were incurred in the past and cannot be changed regardless of which future action is taken. The two keys to making short-term decisions are to focus on relevant revenues, costs, and profits, and to use a contribution margin approach to separate variable and fixed costs.

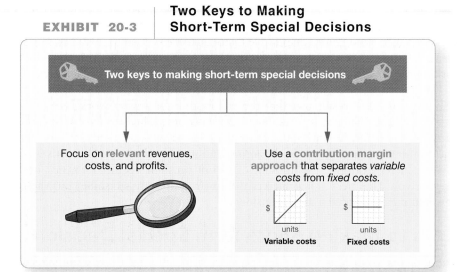

EXHIBIT 20-3 | **Two Keys to Making Short-Term Special Decisions**

# Special Sales Order and Regular Pricing Decisions

**2** Make special order and pricing decisions

We will start our discussion by looking at special sales order decisions and regular pricing decisions. In the past, managers did not consider pricing to be a short-term decision. However, product life cycles are getting shorter in most industries. Companies often sell products for only a few months before replacing them with an updated model, even if the updating is small. The clothing and technology industries have always had short life cycles. Even auto and housing styles change frequently. Pricing has become a shorter-term decision than it was in the past.

First, we'll examine a special sales order in detail. Then we'll discuss regular pricing decisions.

## When to Accept a Special Sales Order

A special order occurs when a customer requests a one-time order at a *reduced* sale price. Before agreeing to the special deal, management must consider the questions shown in Exhibit 20-4.

**EXHIBIT 20-4 | Special Order Considerations**

- Does the company have excess capacity available to fill this order?

- Will the reduced sales price be high enough to cover the *incremental* costs of filling the order (the variable costs and any additional fixed costs)?

- Will the special order affect regular sales in the long run?

First, managers must consider available manufacturing capacity. If the company is already using all its existing manufacturing capacity and selling all units made at its *regular* sales price, it would not be profitable to fill a special order at a *reduced* sales price. Therefore, available excess capacity is a necessity for accepting a special order. This is true for service firms as well as manufacturers.

Second, managers need to consider whether the special reduced sales price is high enough to cover the incremental costs of filling the special order. The special price *must* be greater than the variable costs of filling the order or the company will lose money on the deal. In other words, the special order must provide a *positive* contribution margin.

Next, the company must consider fixed costs. If the company has excess capacity, fixed costs probably will not be affected by producing more units (or delivering more service). However, in some cases, management may have to incur some other fixed cost to fill the special order, such as additional insurance premiums. If so, they will need to consider whether the special sales price is high enough to generate a positive contribution margin *and* cover the additional fixed costs.

Finally, managers need to consider whether the special order will affect regular sales in the long run. Will regular customers find out about the special order and demand a lower price? Will the special order customer come back *again and again*, asking for the same reduced price? Will the special order price start a price war with competitors? Managers should determine the answers to these questions and consider how customers will respond. Managers may decide that any profit from the special sales order is not worth these risks.

Let's consider a special sales order example. We learned in Chapter 18 that Smart Touch normally sells its Excel DVDs for $12.00 each. Assume that a company has offered Smart Touch $67,500 for 10,000 DVDs, or $6.75 per DVD. This sale

- will use manufacturing capacity that would otherwise be idle (excess capacity).
- will not change fixed costs.
- will not require any variable *nonmanufacturing* expenses (because no extra marketing costs are incurred with this special order).
- will not affect regular sales.

We have addressed every consideration except one: Is the special sales price high enough to cover the variable *manufacturing* costs associated with the order? First, we'll review the *wrong* way and then we'll review the *right* way to figure out the answer to this question.

Suppose Smart Touch made and sold 100,000 DVDs before considering the special order. Using the traditional (absorption costing) income statement on the left-hand side of Exhibit 20-5, the ABC manufacturing cost per unit is $7.00 (from Chapter 18, Exhibit 18-9). A manager who does not examine these numbers carefully may believe that Smart Touch should *not* accept the special order at a sale price of $6.75 because each DVD costs $7.00 to manufacture. But appearances can be deceiving! Recall that the unit manufacturing cost of the DVD, $7.00, is a *mixed* cost, containing both fixed and variable cost components. To correctly answer our question, we need to find only the *variable* portion of the manufacturing unit cost.

The right-hand side of Exhibit 20-5 shows the contribution margin income statement that separates variable expenses from fixed expenses. The contribution margin income statement allows us to see that the *variable* manufacturing cost per DVD is only $6.50 ($650,000 ÷ 100,000). The special sales price of $6.75 per DVD is *higher* than the variable manufacturing cost of $6.50. Therefore, the special order will provide a positive contribution margin of $0.25 per DVD ($6.75 – $6.50). Since the special order is for 10,000 DVDs, Smart Touch's total contribution margin should increase by $2,500 (10,000 DVDs × $0.25 per DVD) if it accepts this order.

| | |
|---|---|
| EXHIBIT 20-5 | **Traditional (Absorption Costing) Format and Contribution Margin Format Income Statements** |

**SMART TOUCH LEARNING, INC.**
**Income Statement (at a production and sales level of 100,000 Excel DVDs)**
**Year Ended December 31, 2013**

| Traditional (Absorption Costing) Format | | Contribution Margin Format | | |
|---|---|---|---|---|
| Sales revenue | $1,200,000 | Sales revenue | | $1,200,000 |
| Cost of goods sold | 700,000 | Variable expenses: | | |
| Gross profit | $ 500,000 | Manufacturing | $640,000 | |
| Marketing and administrative expenses | 110,000 | Marketing and administrative | 10,000 | 650,000 |
| | | Contribution margin | | $ 550,000 |
| | | Fixed expenses: | | |
| | | Manufacturing | $ 60,000 | |
| | | Marketing and administrative | 100,000 | 160,000 |
| Operating income | $ 390,000 | Operating income | | $ 390,000 |

Using an incremental analysis approach, Smart Touch compares the additional revenues from the special order with the incremental expenses to see if the special order will contribute to profits. Exhibit 20-6 shows that the special sales order will increase revenue by $67,500 (10,000 × $6.75) but will also increase variable manufacturing cost by $65,000 (10,000 × $6.50). As a result, Smart Touch's contribution margin will increase by $2,500, as previously shown. The other costs seen in Exhibit 20-5 are not relevant to the decision. Variable marketing and administrative expenses will be the same whether or not Smart Touch accepts the special order, because Smart Touch made no special efforts to get this sale. Fixed manufacturing expenses will not change because Smart Touch has enough idle capacity to produce 10,000 extra Excel DVDs without needing additional facilities. Fixed marketing and administrative expenses will not be affected by this special order either. Because there are no additional fixed costs, the total increase in contribution margin flows directly to operating income. As a result, the special sales order will increase operating income by $2,500.

| | |
|---|---|
| EXHIBIT 20-6 | **Incremental Analysis of Special Sales Order of 10,000 Excel DVDs** |

| | |
|---|---|
| Expected increase in revenues (10,000 DVDs × $6.75) | $ 67,500 |
| Expected increase in variable manufacturing costs (10,000 DVDs × $6.50) | (65,000) |
| Expected increase in operating income | $ 2,500 |

Notice that the analysis follows the two keys to making short-term special business decisions discussed earlier: (1) Focus on relevant data (revenues and costs that *will change* if Smart Touch accepts the special order) and (2) use of a contribution margin approach that separates variable costs from fixed costs.

To summarize, for special sales orders, the decision rule is as follows:

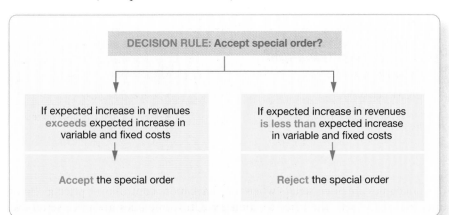

## How to Set Regular Prices

In the special order decision, Smart Touch decided to sell a limited quantity of DVDs for $6.75 each, even though the normal price was $12.00 per unit. But how did Smart Touch decide to set its regular price at $12.00 per DVD? Exhibit 20-7 shows that managers start with three basic questions when setting regular prices for their products or services.

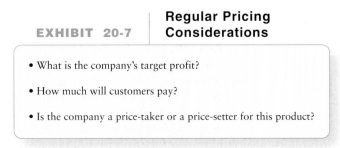

**EXHIBIT 20-7**  |  **Regular Pricing Considerations**

- What is the company's target profit?
- How much will customers pay?
- Is the company a price-taker or a price-setter for this product?

The answers to these questions are complex and ever-changing. Stockholders expect the company to achieve certain profits. Economic conditions, historical company earnings, industry risk, competition, and new business developments all affect the level of profit that stockholders expect. Stockholders usually tie their profit expectations to the amount of assets invested in the company. For example, stockholders may expect a 10% annual return on their investment. A company's stock price tends to decline if it does not meet target profits, so managers must keep costs low while generating enough revenue to meet target profits.

This leads to the second question: How much will customers pay? Managers cannot set prices above what customers are willing to pay or sales will decline. The amount customers will pay depends on the competition, the product's uniqueness, the effectiveness of marketing campaigns, general economic conditions, and so forth.

To address the third pricing question, imagine a horizontal line with price-takers at one end and price-setters at the other end. A company's products and services fall somewhere along this line, shown in Exhibit 20-8. Companies are price-takers when they have little or no control over the prices of their products or services. This occurs when their products and services are *not* unique or when competition is intense. Examples include food commodities (milk and corn), natural resources (oil and lumber), and generic consumer products and services (paper towels, dry cleaning, and banking).

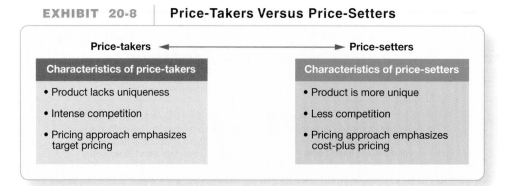

EXHIBIT 20-8 | Price-Takers Versus Price-Setters

Price-takers ←————————→ Price-setters

| Characteristics of price-takers | Characteristics of price-setters |
|---|---|
| • Product lacks uniqueness | • Product is more unique |
| • Intense competition | • Less competition |
| • Pricing approach emphasizes target pricing | • Pricing approach emphasizes cost-plus pricing |

Companies are price-setters when they have more control over pricing—in other words, they can "set" the price to some extent. Companies are price-setters when their products are unique, which results in less competition. Unique products, such as original art and jewelry, specially manufactured machinery, patented perfume scents, and the latest technological gadget (like an iPad), can command higher prices.

Obviously, managers would rather be price-setters than price-takers. To gain more control over pricing, companies try to differentiate their products. They want to make their products unique in terms of features, service, or quality, or at least make the buyer *think* their product is unique or somehow better. Companies achieve this differentiation through their advertising efforts. Consider **Nike's** tennis shoes, **Starbucks'** coffee, **Kleenex's** tissues, **Tylenol's** acetaminophen, **Capital One's** credit cards, **Shell's** gas, **Abercrombie and Fitch's** jeans—the list goes on and on. Are these products really better or significantly different from their lower-priced competitors? It is possible. If these companies can make customers *believe* that this is true, they will gain more control over their pricing because customers are willing to pay *more* for their product or service. What is the downside? These companies must charge higher prices or sell more just to cover their advertising costs.

A company's approach to pricing depends on whether its product or service is on the price-taking or price-setting side of the spectrum. Price-takers emphasize a target-pricing approach. Price-setters emphasize a cost-plus pricing approach. Keep in mind that many products fall somewhere along the horizontal line in Exhibit 20-8. Therefore, managers tend to use both approaches to some extent. We will now discuss each approach in turn.

### Stop & Think...

It is lunchtime....you want a hamburger. Where do you go—**Wendy's**, **McDonald's**, or your college's cafeteria? Why? A hamburger is the same wherever you go, right? The answer to that question is the key to changing a product (a hamburger) from a commodity to a unique product (a **Wendy's** hamburger). The advertising, conditioning of your family, etc. have possibly made you think that the three companies' hamburgers are different. The perceived uniqueness of the hamburger helps the company (say **Wendy's**) be a price-setter instead of a price-taker.

### Target Pricing

When a company is a price-taker, it emphasizes a target pricing approach to managing costs and profits. Target pricing starts with the market price of the product (the price customers are willing to pay) and then subtracts the company's desired profit to determine the maximum allowed **target full product cost**—the *full* cost to develop, produce, and deliver the product or service.

| Revenue at market price | | Revenue (at market price) |
|---|---|---|
| Less: Desired profit | O R | – COGS (Target full product cost) |
| Target full product cost | | Target net income (Desired profit) |

In this relationship, the market price is "taken." Recall from Chapter 16 that a product's *full* cost contains all elements from the value chain—both inventoriable costs and period costs. It also includes fixed and variable costs. If the product's current cost is higher than the target full cost, the company must find ways to reduce the product's cost or it will not meet its profit goals. Managers often use ABC costing along with value engineering (as discussed in Chapter 18) to find ways to cut costs.

Assume that Excel Learning DVDs are a commodity, and that the current market price is $11.00 per DVD (not the $12.00 sales price assumed in the earlier Smart Touch example). Because the DVDs are a commodity, Smart Touch will emphasize a target-pricing approach. Assume Smart Touch's stockholders expect a 10% annual return on the company's assets. If the company has $3,000,000 average assets, the desired profit is $300,000 ($3,000,000 × 10%). Exhibit 20-9 calculates the target full cost at the current sales volume of 100,000 DVDs. Once we know the target full cost, we can analyze the fixed and variable cost components separately.

**EXHIBIT 20-9** | **Calculating Target Full Cost**

| | Calculations | |
|---|---|---|
| Revenue at market price | 100,000 DVDs × $11.00 sales price | $1,100,000 |
| Less: Desired profit | 10% × $3,000,000 average assets | 300,000 |
| Target full cost | | $ 800,000 |

Can Smart Touch make and sell 100,000 Excel Learning DVDs at a full cost of $800,000? We know from Smart Touch's contribution margin income statement (Exhibit 20-5) that the company's variable costs are $6.50 per unit ($650,000 ÷ 100,000 units). This variable cost per unit includes both manufacturing costs ($6.40 per unit) and marketing and administrative costs ($0.10 per unit). We also know the company incurs $160,000 in fixed costs in its current relevant range. Again, some fixed costs stem from manufacturing and some from marketing and administrative activities. *In setting regular sales prices, companies must cover **all** of their costs—whether the costs are inventoriable or period, fixed or variable.*

Making and selling 100,000 DVDs currently costs the company $810,000 [(100,000 units × $6.50 variable cost per unit) + $160,000 of fixed costs], which is more than the target full cost ($800,000). So, what are Smart Touch's options?

1. Accept the lower operating income of $290,000, which is a 9.67% return, not the 10% target return required by stockholders.

2. Reduce fixed costs by $10,000 or more.

3. Reduce variable costs by $10,000 or more.

4. Use other strategies. For example, Smart Touch could attempt to increase sales volume. Recall that the company has excess manufacturing capacity, so making and selling more units would only affect variable costs; however, it would mean that current fixed costs are spread over more units. The company could also consider changing or adding to its product mix. Finally, it could attempt to differentiate its Excel Learning DVDs from the competition to gain more control over sales prices (be a price-setter).

Let's look at some of these options. Smart Touch may first try to cut fixed costs. As shown in Exhibit 20-10, the company would have to reduce fixed costs to $150,000 to meet its target profit level.

| EXHIBIT 20-10 | Calculating Target Fixed Cost | |
| --- | --- | --- |
| | **Calculations** | |
| Target full cost | (From Exhibit 20-9) | $ 800,000 |
| Less: Current variable costs | 100,000 DVDs × $6.50 | 650,000 |
| Target fixed cost | | $ 150,000 |

If the company cannot reduce its fixed costs by $10,000 ($160,000 current fixed costs – $150,000 target fixed costs), it would have to lower its variable cost to $6.40 per unit, as shown in Exhibit 20-11.

| EXHIBIT 20-11 | Calculating Target DVD Variable Cost | |
| --- | --- | --- |
| | **Calculations** | |
| Target full cost | (From Exhibit 20-9) | $ 800,000 |
| Less: Current fixed costs | (From Exhibit 20-5) | 160,000 |
| Target total variable costs | | $ 640,000 |
| Divided by the number of DVDs | | ÷ 100,000 |
| Target variable cost per unit | | $ 6.40 |

If Smart Touch cannot reduce variable cost per unit to $6.40, then the company could try to meet its target profit through a combination of lowering both fixed costs and variable costs.

Another strategy would be to increase sales. Smart Touch's managers can use CVP analysis, as you learned in Chapter 19, to figure out how many Excel Learning DVDs the company would have to sell to achieve its target profit. How could the company increase demand for the Excel Learning DVDs? Perhaps it could reach new markets or advertise. How much would advertising cost—and how many extra Excel Learning DVDs would the company have to sell to cover the cost of advertising? These are only some of the questions managers must ask. As you can see, managers do not have an easy task when the current cost exceeds the target full cost. Sometimes companies just cannot compete given the current market price. If that is the case, they may have no other choice than to quit making that product.

## Cost-Plus Pricing

When a company is a price-setter, it emphasizes a cost-plus approach to pricing. This pricing approach is essentially the *opposite* of the target-pricing approach. Cost-plus pricing starts with the company's full costs (as a given) and *adds* its desired profit to determine a cost-plus price.

Full product cost
Plus: Desired profit
Cost-plus price

When the product is unique, the company has more control over pricing. The company still needs to make sure that the cost-plus price is not higher than what customers are willing to pay. Now, back to our original Smart Touch example. This time, assume the Excel Learning DVDs benefit from brand recognition so the company has some control over the price it charges for its DVDs. Exhibit 20-12 takes a cost-plus pricing approach, assuming the current level of sales.

**EXHIBIT 20-12 | Calculating Cost-Plus Price**

|  | Calculations |  |
|---|---|---|
| Current variable costs | 100,000 DVDs × $6.50 | $ 650,000 |
| Plus: Current fixed costs | (From Exhibit 20-5) | 160,000 |
| Full product cost |  | $ 810,000 |
| Plus: Desired profit | 10% × $3,000,000 average assets | 300,000 |
| Target revenue |  | $1,110,000 |
| Divided by the number of DVDs |  | ÷ 100,000 |
| Cost-plus price per DVD |  | $ 11.10 |

If the current market price for generic Excel Learning DVDs is $11.00, as we assumed earlier, can Smart Touch sell its brand-name DVDs for $11.10, or more, each? The answer depends on how well the company has been able to differentiate its product or brand name. The company may use focus groups or marketing surveys to find out how customers would respond to its cost-plus price. The company may find out that its cost-plus price is too high, or it may find that it could set the price even higher without losing sales.

Notice how pricing decisions used our two keys to decision making: (1) focus on relevant information and (2) use a contribution margin approach that separates variable costs from fixed costs. In pricing decisions, all cost information is relevant because the company must cover *all* costs along the value chain before it can generate a profit. However, we still need to consider variable costs and fixed costs separately because they behave differently at different volumes.

Our pricing decision rule is as follows:

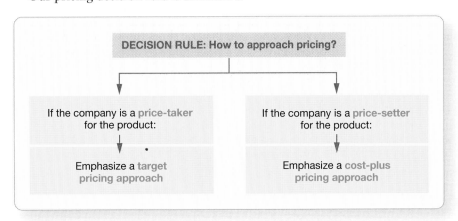

Now take some time to review the Decision Guidelines on the next page.

# Decision Guidelines 20-1

## RELEVANT INFORMATION FOR BUSINESS DECISIONS

**Nike** makes special order and regular pricing decisions. Even though it sells mass-produced tennis shoes and sport clothing, **Nike** has differentiated its products with advertising and with athlete endorsements. **Nike's** managers consider both quantitative and qualitative factors as they make pricing decisions. Here are key guidelines **Nike's** managers follow in making their decisions.

| Decision | Guidelines |
|---|---|
| • What information is relevant to a short-term special business decision? | Relevant data <br> 1. are expected *future* data. <br> 2. *differ* between alternatives. |
| • What are two key guidelines in making short-term special business decisions? | 1. Focus on *relevant* data. <br> 2. Use a *contribution margin* approach that separates variable costs from fixed costs. |
| • Should **Nike** accept a lower sale price than the regular price for a large order from a customer in Labadee, Haiti? | If the revenue from the order exceeds the extra variable and fixed costs incurred to fill the order, then accepting the order will increase operating income. |
| • What should **Nike** consider in setting its regular product prices? | **Nike** considers <br> 1. the profit stockholders expect it to make. <br> 2. the price customers will pay. <br> 3. whether it is a price-setter or a price-taker. |
| • What approach should **Nike** take to pricing? | **Nike** has differentiated its products by advertising. Thus, **Nike** tends to be a price-setter. **Nike's** managers can emphasize a cost-plus approach to pricing. |
| • What approach should discount shoe stores, such as **Payless Shoes**, take to pricing? | **Payless Shoes** sells generic shoes (no-name brands) at low prices. **Payless** is a price-taker so managers use a target-pricing approach to pricing. |

# Summary Problem 20-1

MC Alexander Industries makes tennis balls. Its only plant can produce up to 2,500,000 cans of balls per year. Current production is 2,000,000 cans. Annual manufacturing, selling, and administrative fixed costs total $700,000. The variable cost of making and selling each can of balls is $1.00. Stockholders expect a 12% annual return on the company's $3,000,000 of assets.

## Requirements

1. What is MC Alexander's current full cost of making and selling 2,000,000 cans of tennis balls? What is the current full *unit* cost of each can of tennis balls?
2. Assume MC Alexander is a price-taker, and the current market price is $1.45 per can of balls (this is the price at which manufacturers sell to retailers). What is the *target* full cost of producing and selling 2,000,000 cans of balls? Given MC Alexander's current costs, will the company reach stockholders' profit goals?
3. If MC Alexander cannot change its fixed costs, what is the target variable cost per can of balls?
4. Suppose MC Alexander could spend an extra $100,000 on advertising to differentiate its product so that it could be a price-setter. Assuming the original volume and costs, plus the $100,000 of new advertising costs, what cost-plus price will MC Alexander want to charge for a can of balls?
5. **Nike** has just asked MC Alexander to supply the company with 400,000 cans of balls at a special order price of $1.20 per can. **Nike** wants MC Alexander to package the balls under the **Nike** label (MC Alexander will imprint the **Nike** logo on each ball and can). MC Alexander will have to spend $10,000 to change the packaging machinery. Assuming the original volume and costs, should MC Alexander accept this special order? (Unlike the chapter problem, assume MC Alexander will incur variable selling costs as well as variable manufacturing costs related to this order.)

# Solution

## Requirement 1

The full unit cost is as follows:

| | |
|---|---:|
| Fixed costs ................................................................................. | $ 700,000 |
| Plus: Total variable costs (2,000,000 cans × $1.00 per unit) ... | + 2,000,000 |
| Total full product costs ........................................................... | $2,700,000 |
| Divided by the number of cans................................................. | ÷ 2,000,000 |
| Full product cost per can......................................................... | $      1.35 |

## Requirement 2

The target full cost is as follows:

| | Calculations | Total | | | |
|---|---|---:|---|---|---:|
| Revenue at market price | 2,000,000 units × $1.45 price = | $2,900,000 | O | Revenue | $2,900,000 |
| Less: Desired profit | 12% × $3,000,000 of assets | 360,000 | R | COGS | 2,540,000 |
| Target *full* product cost | | $2,540,000 | | Target net income  $  360,000 | |

MC Alexander's current total full product costs ($2,700,000 from Requirement 1) are $160,000 higher than the target full product cost ($2,540,000). If MC Alexander cannot reduce product costs, it will not be able to meet stockholders' profit expectations.

### Requirement 3

Assuming MC Alexander cannot reduce its fixed costs, the target variable cost per can is as follows:

|  | Total |
| --- | --- |
| Target *full* product cost (from Requirement 2)......................... | $2,540,000 |
| Less: Fixed costs...................................................................... | 700,000 |
| Target total variable cost......................................................... | $1,840,000 |
| Divided by the number of units................................................ | ÷2,000,000 |
| Target variable cost per unit.................................................... | $ 0.92 |

Since MC Alexander cannot reduce its fixed costs, it needs to reduce variable costs by $0.08 per can ($1.00 – $0.92) to meet its profit goals. This would require an 8% cost reduction, which may not be possible.

### Requirement 4

If MC Alexander can differentiate its tennis balls, it will gain more control over pricing. The company's new cost-plus price would be as follows:

|  |  |
| --- | --- |
| Current total costs (from Requirement 1)................................ | $2,700,000 |
| Plus: Additional cost of advertising ......................................... | + 100,000 |
| Plus: Desired profit (from Requirement 2).............................. | + 360,000 |
| Target revenue ...................................................................... | $3,160,000 |
| Divided by the number of units................................................ | ÷ 2,000,000 |
| Cost-plus price per unit........................................................... | $ 1.58 |

MC Alexander must study the market to determine whether retailers would pay $1.58 per can of balls.

### Requirement 5

**Nike's** special order price ($1.20) is less than the current full cost of each can of balls ($1.35 from Requirement 1). However, this should not influence management's decision. MC Alexander could fill **Nike's** special order using existing excess capacity. MC Alexander takes an incremental analysis approach to its decision, comparing the extra revenue with the incremental costs of accepting the order. Variable costs will increase if MC Alexander accepts the order, so the variable costs are relevant. Only the *additional* fixed costs of changing the packaging machine ($10,000) are relevant since all other fixed costs will remain unchanged.

|  |  |
| --- | --- |
| Revenue from special order (400,000 × $1.20 per unit) .......... | $ 480,000 |
| Less: Variable cost of special order (400,000 × $1.00)............ | 400,000 |
| Contribution margin from special order.................................... | $ 80,000 |
| Less: Additional fixed costs of special order............................ | 10,000 |
| Operating income provided by special order ............................ | $ 70,000 |

MC Alexander should accept the special order because it will increase operating income by $70,000. However, MC Alexander also needs to consider whether its regular customers will find out about the special price and demand lower prices too.

# When to Drop Products, Departments, or Territories

Managers must often decide whether to drop products, departments, or territories that are not as profitable as desired. How do managers make these decisions? Exhibit 20-13 lists some of the questions managers must consider when deciding whether to drop a product, department, or territory.

**3** Make dropping a product and product-mix decisions

| EXHIBIT 20-13 | Considerations for Dropping Products, Departments, or Territories |
|---|---|

- Does the product, department, or territory provide a positive contribution margin?

- Will fixed costs continue to exist, even if the company drops the product?

- Are there any direct fixed costs that can be avoided if the company drops the product, department, or territory?

- Will dropping the product, department, or territory affect sales of the company's other products?

- What could the company do with the freed manufacturing capacity?

Once again, we follow the two key guidelines for special business decisions: (1) focus on relevant data and (2) use a contribution margin approach. The relevant financial data are still the changes in revenues and expenses. But now we are considering a *decrease* in volume rather than an *increase*, as we did in the special sales order decision. In the following example, we will consider how managers decide to drop a product. Managers would use the same process in deciding whether to drop a department or territory.

Earlier, we focused on only one of Smart Touch's products—Excel Learning DVDs. Now we'll focus on both of its products—the Excel Learning DVDs and the specialty DVDs we covered in Chapter 18. Exhibit 20-14 shows the company's contribution margin income statement by product, assuming fixed costs are shared by both products. Because the specialty DVD line has an operating *loss* of $420, management is considering dropping the product.

| EXHIBIT 20-14 | Contribution Margin Income Statements by Product |
|---|---|

| SMART TOUCH LEARNING, INC. Income Statement For the Month Ended January 31, 2014 | | | |
|---|---|---|---|
| | | **Products** | |
| | | **Excel DVDs (100,000 DVDs)** | **Specialty DVDs (350 DVDs)** |
| | **Total** | **(From Exhibit 20-5)** | |
| Sales revenue | $1,224,500 | $1,200,000 | $24,500 |
| Variable expenses: | | | |
| Manufacturing | 652,740 | 640,000 | 12,740 |
| Marketing and administrative | 10,035 | 10,000 | 35 |
| Total variable expenses | 662,775 | 650,000 | 12,775 |
| Contribution margin | $ 561,725 | $ 550,000 | $11,725 |
| Fixed expenses: | | | |
| Manufacturing | 71,795 | 60,000 | 11,795 |
| Marketing and administrative | 100,350 | 100,000 | 350 |
| Total fixed expenses | 172,145 | 160,000 | 12,145 |
| Operating income (loss) | $ 389,580 | $ 390,000 | $ (420) |

The first question management should ask is "Does the product provide a positive contribution margin?" If the product has a negative contribution margin, then the product is not even covering its variable costs. Therefore, the company should drop the product. However, if the product has a positive contribution margin, then it is *helping* to cover some of the company's fixed costs. In Smart Touch's case, the specialty DVDs provide a positive contribution margin of $11,725. Smart Touch's managers now need to consider fixed costs.

Suppose Smart Touch allocates fixed costs using the ABC costs per unit calculated in Chapter 18, Exhibit 18-9 ($7.00 per unit). Smart Touch could allocate fixed costs in many different ways, and each way would allocate a different amount of fixed costs to each product. Therefore, allocated fixed costs are *irrelevant* because they are arbitrary in amount. What is relevant are the following:

1. Will the fixed costs continue to exist *even if* the product is dropped?

2. Are there any *direct* fixed costs of the specialty DVDs that can be avoided if the product is dropped?

## Dropping Products Under Various Assumptions

Now we'll consider various assumptions when dropping products.

### Fixed Costs Will Continue to Exist and Will Not Change

Fixed costs that will continue to exist even after a product is dropped are often called unavoidable fixed costs. Unavoidable fixed costs are *irrelevant* to the decision because they *will not change* if the company drops the product. Let's assume that all of Smart Touch's fixed costs of $172,145 will continue to exist even if the company drops the specialty DVDs. Assume that Smart Touch makes the specialty DVDs in the same plant using the same machinery as the Excel Learning DVDs. Thus, only the contribution margin the specialty DVDs provide is relevant. If Smart Touch drops the specialty DVDs, it will lose the $11,725 contribution margin.

The incremental analysis shown in Exhibit 20-15 verifies the loss. If Smart Touch drops the specialty DVDs, revenue will decrease by $24,500, but variable expenses will decrease by only $12,775, resulting in a net $11,725 decrease in operating income. Because fixed costs are unaffected, they are not included in the analysis. This analysis suggests that management should *not* drop specialty DVDs. It is actually more beneficial for Smart Touch to lose $420 than to drop the specialty DVDs and lose $11,725 in operating income.

| **EXHIBIT 20-15** | **Incremental Analysis for Dropping a Product When Fixed Costs Will *Not* Change** |
|---|---|

| | |
|---|---:|
| Expected decrease in revenues (350 specialty DVDs × $70.00) | $(24,500) |
| Expected decrease in variable costs (From Exhibit 20-14, $12,740 + $35) | 12,775 |
| Expected *decrease* in operating income | $(11,725) |

### Direct Fixed Costs Will Change

Since Smart Touch allocates its fixed costs using ABC costing, some of the fixed costs *belong* only to the specialty DVD product. These would be direct fixed costs of the specialty DVDs only.[1] Assume that $12,000 of the fixed costs will be avoidable

---

[1]To aid in decision-making, companies should separate direct fixed costs from indirect fixed costs on their contribution margin income statements. Companies should *trace direct fixed costs* to the appropriate product and only *allocate indirect fixed costs* among products.

if Smart Touch drops the specialty DVD product. Then, $12,000 are avoidable fixed costs and *are relevant* to the decision because they would change (go away) if the product is dropped.

Exhibit 20-16 shows that, in this situation, operating income will *increase* by $275 if Smart Touch drops the specialty DVDs. Why? Because revenues will decline by $24,500 but expenses will decline even more—by $24,775. The result is a net increase to operating income of $275. This analysis suggests that management should drop specialty DVDs.

| EXHIBIT 20-16 | **Incremental Analysis for Dropping a Product When Fixed Costs *Will* Change** |
| --- | --- |

| | | |
| --- | --- | --- |
| Expected decrease in revenues (350 specialty DVDs × $70.00) | | $(24,500) |
| Expected decrease in variable costs (From Exhibit 20-14, $12,740 + $35) | 12,775 | |
| Expected decrease in fixed costs | 12,000 | |
|     Expected decrease in total expenses | | 24,775 |
|         Expected increase in operating income | | $    275 |

## Other Considerations

Management must also consider whether dropping the product, department, or territory would hurt other product sales. In the examples given so far, we assumed that dropping the specialty DVDs would not affect Smart Touch's other product sales. However, think about a grocery store. Even if the produce department is not profitable, would managers drop it? Probably not, because if they did, they would lose customers who want one-stop shopping. In such situations, managers must also include the loss of contribution margin from *other* departments affected by the change when deciding whether to drop a department.

Management should also consider what it could do with freed manufacturing capacity. In the Smart Touch example, we assumed that the company produces both Excel Learning DVDs and specialty DVDs using the same manufacturing equipment. If Smart Touch drops the specialty DVDs, could it make and sell another product using the freed machine hours? Is product demand strong enough that Smart Touch could make and sell more of the Excel Learning DVDs? Managers should consider whether using the machinery to produce a different product or expanding existing product lines would be more profitable than using the machinery to produce specialty DVDs.

Special decisions should take into account all costs affected by the choice of action. Managers must ask the following questions: What total costs—variable and fixed—will change? Are there additional environmental costs (for example, waste water disposal) that should be considered? As Exhibits 20-15 and 20-16 show, the key to deciding whether to drop products, departments, or territories is to compare the lost revenue against the costs that can be saved and to consider what would be done with the freed capacity. The decision rule is as follows:

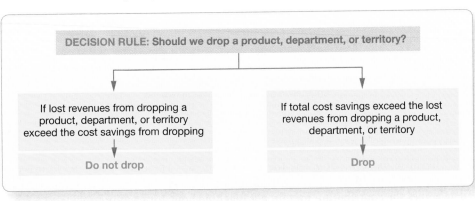

# Product Mix: Which Product to Emphasize?

Companies do not have unlimited resources. **Constraints** that restrict production or sale of a product vary from company to company. For a manufacturer like Smart Touch, the production constraint may be labor hours, machine hours, or available materials. For a merchandiser like **Walmart**, the primary constraint is cubic feet of display space. Other companies are constrained by sales demand. Competition may be stiff, and so the company may be able to sell only a limited number of units. In such cases, the company produces only as much as it can sell. However, if a company can sell all the units it can produce, which products should it emphasize? For which items should production be increased? Companies facing constraints consider the questions shown in Exhibit 20-17.

**EXHIBIT  20-17  | Product Mix Considerations**

- What constraint(s) stop(s) the company from making (or displaying) all the units the company can sell?

- Which products offer the highest contribution margin per unit of the constraint?

- Would emphasizing one product over another affect fixed costs?

Let's return to our Smart Touch example. Assume the company can sell all the Excel DVDs and all the specialty DVDs it produces, but it only has 2,000 machine hours of manufacturing capacity. The company uses the same machines to make both types of DVDs. In this case, machine hours is the constraint. Note that this is a short-term decision because in the long run, Smart Touch could expand its production facilities to meet sales demand if it made financial sense to do so. The data in Exhibit 20-18 suggest that specialty DVDs are more profitable than Excel DVDs.

**EXHIBIT  20-18  | Smart Touch's Contribution Margin per Unit**

|  | Excel DVD | Specialty DVD |
|---|---|---|
| Sale price per DVD | $12.00 | $70.00 |
| Variable cost per DVD | 6.50 | 36.50 |
| Contribution margin | 5.50 | 33.50 |
| Contribution margin ratio |  |  |
| Excel DVDs $5.50/$12.00 | 46% |  |
| Specialty DVDs $33.50/$70.00 |  | 48% |

However, an important piece of information is missing—the time it takes to make each product. Assume that Smart Touch can produce either 80 Excel DVDs *or* 10 specialty DVDs per machine hour. *The company will incur the same fixed costs either way so fixed costs are irrelevant.* Which product should it emphasize?

To maximize profits when fixed costs are irrelevant, follow the decision rule:

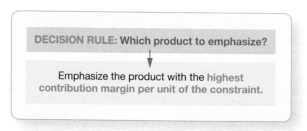

DECISION RULE: Which product to emphasize?

Emphasize the product with the highest contribution margin per unit of the constraint.

Because *machine hours* is the constraint, Smart Touch needs to figure out which product has the *highest contribution margin per machine hour*. Exhibit 20-19 determines the contribution margin per machine hour for each product.

| EXHIBIT 20-19 | Smart Touch's Contribution Margin per Machine Hour | Excel DVD | Specialty DVD |
|---|---|---|---|
| | (1) DVDs that can be produced each machine hour | 80 | 10 |
| | (2) Contribution margin per DVD from Exhibit 20-18 | $ 5.50 | $ 33.50 |
| | Contribution margin per machine hour (1) × (2) | $ 440 | $ 335 |
| | Available capacity—number of machine hours | 2,000 | 2,000 |
| | Total contribution margin at full capacity | $880,000 | $670,000 |

Excel DVDs have a higher contribution margin per machine hour, $440, than specialty DVDs, $335. Smart Touch will earn more profit by producing Excel DVDs. Why? Because even though Excel DVDs have a lower contribution margin *per unit*, Smart Touch can make eight times as many Excel DVDs as specialty DVDs in the 2,000 available machine hours. Exhibit 20-19 also proves that Smart Touch earns more total profit by making Excel DVDs. Multiplying the contribution margin per machine hour by the available number of machine hours shows that Smart Touch can earn $880,000 of contribution margin by producing only Excel DVDs, but only $670,000 by producing only specialty DVDs.

To maximize profit, Smart Touch should make 160,000 Excel DVDs (2,000 machine hours × 80 Excel DVDs per hour) and zero specialty DVDs. Why should Smart Touch make zero specialty DVDs? Because for every machine hour spent making specialty DVDs, Smart Touch would *give up* $105 of contribution margin ($440 per hour for Excel DVDs versus $335 per hour for specialty DVDs).

We made two assumptions here: (1) Smart Touch's sales of other products will not be hurt by this decision and (2) Smart Touch can sell as many Excel DVDs as it can produce. Let's challenge these assumptions. First, how could making only Excel DVDs hurt sales of other products? By producing the specialty DVDs, Smart Touch also sells many of its standard offerings like the Excel DVDs that coordinate with the specialty DVDs. Other DVD sales might fall if Smart Touch no longer offers specialty DVDs.

Let's challenge our second assumption. Suppose that a new competitor has decreased the demand for Smart Touch's Excel DVDs. Now the company can only sell 120,000 Excel DVDs. Smart Touch should only make as many Excel DVDs as it can sell and use the remaining machine hours to produce specialty DVDs. How will this constraint in sales demand change profitability?

Recall from Exhibit 20-19 that Smart Touch will make $880,000 of contribution margin by using all 2,000 machine hours to produce Excel DVDs. However, if Smart Touch only makes 120,000 Excel DVDs, it will only use 1,500 machine hours (120,000 Excel DVDs ÷ 80 Excel DVDs per machine hour). That leaves 500 machine hours available for making specialty DVDs. Smart Touch's new contribution margin will be as shown in Exhibit 20-20.

| EXHIBIT 20-20 | Smart Touch's Contribution Margin per Machine Hour—Limited Market for Product | Excel DVD | Specialty DVD | Total |
|---|---|---|---|---|
| | (1) DVDs that can be produced each machine hour | 80 | 10 | |
| | (2) Contribution margin per DVD from Exhibit 20-18 | $ 5.50 | $ 33.50 | |
| | Contribution margin per machine hour (1) × (2) | $ 440 | $ 335 | |
| | Machine hours devoted to product | 1,500 | 500 | |
| | Total contribution margin at full capacity | $660,000 | $167,500 | $827,500 |

Because of the change in product mix, Smart Touch's total contribution margin will fall from $880,000 to $827,500, a $52,500 decrease. Smart Touch had to give up $105 of contribution margin per machine hour ($440 – $335) on the 500 hours it spent producing specialty DVDs rather than Excel DVDs. However, Smart Touch had no choice—the company would have incurred an *actual loss* from producing Excel DVDs that it could not sell. If Smart Touch had produced 160,000 Excel DVDs but only sold 120,000, the company would have spent $220,000 to make the unsold DVDs (40,000 Excel DVDs × $5.50 variable cost per Excel DVD), yet received no sales revenue from them.

What about fixed costs? In most cases, changing the product mix emphasis in the short run will not affect fixed costs, so fixed costs are irrelevant. However, it is possible that fixed costs could differ by emphasizing a different product mix. What if Smart Touch had a month-to-month lease on a production camera used only for making specialty DVDs? If Smart Touch only made Excel DVDs, it could *avoid* the production camera cost. However, if Smart Touch makes any specialty DVDs, it needs the camera. In this case, the fixed costs become relevant because they differ between alternative product mixes (specialty DVDs only *versus* Excel DVDs only, or both products).

Notice that the analysis again follows the two guidelines for special business decisions: (1) focus on relevant data (only those revenues and costs that differ) and (2) use a contribution margin approach, which separates variable from fixed costs.

# Outsourcing and Sell as Is or Process Further Decisions

 Make outsourcing and sell as is or process further decisions

Now let's consider other management decisions, such as whether the company should outsource or sell a product as it is or process it further. We'll start with outsourcing decisions.

## When to Outsource

**Delta** outsources much of its reservation work and airplane maintenance. **IBM** outsources most of its desktop production of personal computers. Make-or-buy decisions are often called outsourcing decisions because managers must decide whether to buy a component product or service, or produce it in-house. The heart of these decisions is *how best to use available resources*.

How do managers make outsourcing decisions? Greg's Tunes, a manufacturer of music CDs, is deciding whether to make the paper liners for the CD cases in-house or whether to outsource them to Becky's Box Designs, a company that specializes in producing paper liners. Greg's Tunes' cost to produce 250,000 liners is as follows:

|  | Total Cost (250,000 liners) |
| --- | --- |
| Direct materials...................................................... | $ 40,000 |
| Direct labor............................................................. | 20,000 |
| Variable manufacturing overhead ......................... | 15,000 |
| Fixed manufacturing overhead.............................. | 50,000 |
| Total manufacturing cost....................................... | $125,000 |
| Number of liners.................................................... | ÷ 250,000 |
| Cost per liner ......................................................... | $    0.50 |

Becky's Box Designs offers to sell Greg's Tunes the liners for $0.37 each. Should Greg's Tunes make the liners or buy them from Becky's Box Designs? Greg's Tunes' $0.50 cost per unit to make the liner is $0.13 higher than the cost of buying it from Becky's Box Designs. Initially, it seems that Greg's Tunes should outsource the liners. But the correct answer is not so simple. Why? Because manufacturing unit costs contain both fixed and variable components. In deciding whether to outsource, managers must assess fixed and variable costs separately. Exhibit 20-21 shows some of the questions managers must consider when deciding whether to outsource.

**EXHIBIT 20-21 | Outsourcing Considerations**

- How do the company's variable costs compare to the outsourcing cost?
- Are any fixed costs avoidable if the company outsources?
- What could the company do with the freed manufacturing capacity?

How do these considerations apply to Greg's Tunes? By purchasing the liners, Greg's Tunes can avoid all variable manufacturing costs—$40,000 of direct materials, $20,000 of direct labor, and $15,000 of variable manufacturing overhead. In total, the company will save $75,000 in variable manufacturing costs, or $0.30 per liner ($75,000 ÷ 250,000 liners). However, Greg's Tunes will have to pay the variable outsourcing price of $0.37 per unit, or $92,500 for the 250,000 liners. Based only on variable costs, the lower cost alternative is to manufacture the liners in-house. However, managers must still consider fixed costs.

Assume first that Greg's Tunes cannot avoid any of the fixed costs by outsourcing. In this case, the company's fixed costs are irrelevant to the decision because Greg's Tunes would continue to incur $50,000 of fixed costs either way (the fixed costs do not differ between alternatives). Greg's Tunes should continue to make its own liners because the variable cost of outsourcing the liners, $92,500, exceeds the variable cost of making the liners, $75,000.

However, what if Greg's Tunes can avoid some fixed costs by outsourcing the liners? Assume that management can reduce fixed overhead cost by $10,000 by outsourcing the liners. Greg's Tunes will still incur $40,000 of fixed overhead ($50,000 – $10,000) if it outsources the liners. In this case, fixed costs become relevant to the decision because they differ between alternatives. Exhibit 20-22 shows the differences in costs between the make and buy alternatives under this scenario.

**EXHIBIT 20-22** | **Incremental Analysis for Outsourcing Decision**

| Liner Costs | Make Liners | Buy Liners | Difference |
|---|---|---|---|
| Variable costs: | | | |
|     Direct materials | $ 40,000 | — | $40,000 |
|     Direct labor | 20,000 | — | 20,000 |
|     Variable overhead | 15,000 | — | 15,000 |
| Purchase cost from Becky's | | | |
|     (250,000 × $0.37) | — | $ 92,500 | (92,500) |
| Fixed overhead | 50,000 | 40,000 | 10,000 |
| Total cost of liners | $125,000 | $132,500 | $ (7,500) |

Exhibit 20-22 shows that even with the $10,000 reduction in fixed costs, it would still cost Greg's Tunes less to make the liners than to buy them from Becky's Box Designs. The net savings from making 250,000 liners is $7,500. Exhibit 20-22 also shows that outsourcing decisions follow our two key guidelines for special business decisions: (1) Focus on relevant data (differences in costs in this case) and (2) use a contribution margin approach that separates variable costs from fixed costs.

Note how the unit cost—which does *not* separate costs according to behavior—can be deceiving. If Greg's Tunes' managers made their decision by comparing the total manufacturing cost per liner ($0.50) to the outsourcing unit cost per liner ($0.37), they would have incorrectly decided to outsource. Recall that the manufacturing unit cost ($0.50) contains both fixed and variable components, whereas the outsourcing cost ($0.37) is strictly variable. To make the correct decision, Greg's Tunes had to separate the two cost components and analyze them separately.

Our decision rule for outsourcing is as follows:

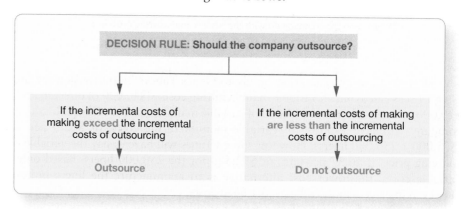

We have not considered what Greg's Tunes could do with the freed manufacturing capacity it would have if it outsourced the liners. The analysis in Exhibit 20-22 assumes there is no other use for the production facilities if Greg's Tunes buys the liners from Becky's Box Designs. But suppose Greg's Tunes has an opportunity to use its freed-up facilities to make more CDs, which have an expected profit of $18,000. Now, Greg's Tunes must consider its **opportunity cost**—the benefit given up by not choosing an alternative course of action. In this case, Greg's Tunes' opportunity cost of making the liners is the $18,000 profit it gives up if it does not free its production facilities to make the additional CDs.

How do Greg's Tunes' managers decide among three alternatives?

1. Use the facilities to make the liners.

2. Buy the liners and leave facilities idle (continue to assume $10,000 of avoidable fixed costs from outsourcing liners).

3. Buy the liners and use facilities to make more CDs (continue to assume $10,000 of avoidable fixed costs from outsourcing liners).

The alternative with the lowest *net* cost is the best use of Greg's Tunes' facilities. Exhibit 20-23 compares the three alternatives.

**EXHIBIT 20-23** | **Best Use of Facilities, Given Opportunity Costs**

|  | | Buy Liners | |
| --- | --- | --- | --- |
|  | Make Liners | Facilities Idle | Make Additional CDs |
| Expected cost of 250,000 liners (From Exhibit 20-22) | $125,000 | $132,500 | $132,500 |
| Expected *profit* from additional CDs | — | — | (18,000) |
| Expected net cost of obtaining 250,000 liners | $125,000 | $132,500 | $114,500 |

Greg's Tunes should buy the liners from Becky's Box Designs and use the freed manufacturing capacity to make more CDs. If Greg's Tunes makes the liners, or if it buys the liners from Becky's Box Designs but leaves its production facilities idle, it will give up the opportunity to earn $18,000.

Greg's Tunes' managers should consider qualitative factors as well as revenue and cost differences in making their final decision. For example, Greg's Tunes' managers may believe they can better control quality by making the liners themselves. This is an argument for Greg's to continue making the liners.

## Stop & Think...

Assume you purchase a new desk for your room. The desk requires assembly. You can choose to either put the desk together yourself or pay someone (outsource) to put the desk together for you. If you choose to pay someone to put the desk together for you, what can you do with the time you save? Maybe you can put in a few extra hours at your job and earn more than what you'll pay to have your desk put together. This is similar to the outsourcing decision—by focusing on doing what jobs you do best (your job versus putting together a desk), your overall financial position is better.

Outsourcing decisions are increasingly important in today's globally wired economy. In the past, make-or-buy decisions often ended up as "make" because coordination, information exchange, and paperwork problems made buying from suppliers too inconvenient. Now, companies can use the Internet to tap into information systems of suppliers and customers located around the world. Paperwork vanishes, and information required to satisfy the strictest JIT delivery schedule is available in real time. As a result, companies are focusing on their core competencies and are outsourcing more functions.

## Sell As Is or Process Further?

At what point in processing should a company sell its product? Many companies, especially in the food processing and natural resource industries, face this business decision. Companies in these industries process a raw material (milk, corn, livestock, crude oil, lumber, to name a few) to a point before it is saleable. For example, **Kraft** pasteurizes raw milk before it is saleable. **Kraft** must then decide whether it should sell the pasteurized milk "as is" or process it further into other dairy products (reduced-fat milk, butter, sour cream, cheese, and other dairy products). Managers consider the questions shown in Exhibit 20-24 when deciding whether to sell as is or process further.

**EXHIBIT 20-24** | **Sell As Is or Process Further Considerations**

- How much revenue will the company receive if we sell the product as is?

- How much revenue will the company receive if the company sells the product after processing it further?

- How much will it cost to process the product further?

Consider one of **Chevron**'s sell as is or process further decisions. Suppose **Chevron** spent $125,000 to process crude oil into 50,000 gallons of regular gasoline, as shown in Exhibit 20-25. After processing crude oil into regular gasoline, should **Chevron** sell the regular gas as is or should it spend more to process the gasoline into premium grade? In making the decision, **Chevron**'s managers consider the following relevant information:

**EXHIBIT 20-25** | **Sell As Is or Process Further Decision**

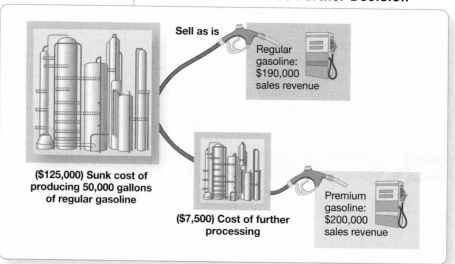

- **Chevron** could sell premium gasoline for $4.00 per gallon, for a total of $200,000 (50,000 × $4.00).

- **Chevron** could sell regular gasoline for $3.80 per gallon, for a total of $190,000 (50,000 × $3.80).

- **Chevron** would have to spend $0.15 per gallon, or $7,500 (50,000 gallons × $0.15), to further process regular gasoline into premium-grade gas.

Notice that **Chevron**'s managers do *not* consider the $125,000 spent on processing crude oil into regular gasoline. Why? It is a *sunk* cost. Recall from our previous discussion that a sunk cost is a past cost that cannot be changed regardless of which future action the company takes. **Chevron** has incurred $125,000—regardless of whether it sells the regular gasoline as is or processes it further into premium gasoline. Therefore, the cost is *not* relevant to the decision.

By analyzing only the relevant costs in Exhibit 20-26, managers see that they can increase profit by $2,500 if they convert the regular gasoline into premium gasoline. The $10,000 extra revenue ($200,000 – $190,000) outweighs the incremental $7,500 cost of the extra processing.

**EXHIBIT 20-26** | **Incremental Analysis for Sell As Is or Process Further Decision**

|  | Sell As Is | Process Further | Difference |
|---|---|---|---|
| Expected revenue from selling 50,000 gallons of regular gasoline at $3.80 per gallon | $190,000 | | |
| Expected revenue from selling 50,000 gallons of premium gasoline at $4.00 per gallon | | $200,000 | $10,000 |
| Additional costs of $0.15 per gallon to convert 50,000 gallons of regular gasoline into premium gasoline | | (7,500) | (7,500) |
| Total net revenue | $190,000 | $192,500 | $ 2,500 |

Thus, the decision rule is as follows:

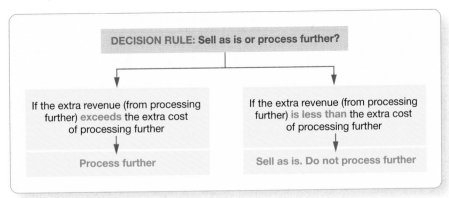

DECISION RULE: Sell as is or process further?

If the extra revenue (from processing further) **exceeds** the extra cost of processing further → **Process further**

If the extra revenue (from processing further) **is less than** the extra cost of processing further → **Sell as is. Do not process further**

Recall that our keys to decision making include (1) focusing on relevant information and (2) using a contribution margin approach that separates variable costs from fixed costs. The analysis in Exhibit 20-26 includes only those *future* costs and revenues that *differ* between alternatives. We assumed **Chevron** already has the equipment and labor necessary to convert regular gasoline into premium grade gasoline. Because fixed costs would not differ between alternatives, they were irrelevant. However, if **Chevron** has to acquire equipment or hire employees to convert the gasoline into premium grade gasoline, the extra fixed costs would be relevant. Once again, we see that fixed costs are only relevant if they *differ* between alternatives.

Next, take some time to review the Decision Guidelines for short-term business decisions on the next page.

**Key Takeaway**

When a company is considering outsourcing, if the incremental costs of making the product exceed the incremental costs of outsourcing, then the company should outsource the product. When a company is considering selling a product as is or processing it further, if the extra revenue from processing the product further exceeds the extra costs to process the product further, then the company should process the product further.

# Decision Guidelines 20-2

## SHORT-TERM SPECIAL BUSINESS DECISIONS

Amazon.com has confronted most of the special business decisions we have covered in this chapter. Here are the key guidelines Amazon.com's managers follow in making their decisions.

| Decision | Guidelines |
|---|---|
| • Should **Amazon** drop its electronics product line? | If the cost savings exceed the lost revenues from dropping the electronics product line, then dropping the product will increase operating income. |
| • Given limited warehouse space, which products should **Amazon** focus on selling? | **Amazon.com** should focus on selling the products with the highest contribution margin per unit of the constraint, which is cubic feet of warehouse space. |
| • Should **Amazon** outsource its warehousing operations? | If the incremental costs of operating its own warehouses exceed the costs of outsourcing, then outsourcing will increase operating income. |
| • How should **Amazon** decide whether to sell a product as is or process it further? | It should process products further only if the extra sales revenue (from processing further) exceeds the extra costs of additional processing. |

# Summary Problem 20-2

Shelly's Shades produces standard and deluxe sunglasses:

|  | Standard | Deluxe |
|---|---|---|
| Sale price per pair............................................ | $20 | $30 |
| Variable expenses per pair.............................. | 16 | 21 |

The company has 15,000 machine hours available. In one machine hour, Shelly's can produce 70 pairs of the standard model or 30 pairs of the deluxe model.

### Requirements

1. Which model should Shelly's emphasize?
2. Shelly's incurs the following costs for 20,000 of its hiking shades:

| | |
|---|---|
| Direct materials............................................................. | $ 20,000 |
| Direct labor.................................................................... | 80,000 |
| Variable manufacturing overhead ................................. | 40,000 |
| Fixed manufacturing overhead...................................... | 80,000 |
| Total manufacturing cost .............................................. | $220,000 |
| Cost per pair ($220,000 ÷ 20,000)............................... | $ 11 |

Another manufacturer has offered to sell similar shades to Shelly's for $10, a total purchase cost of $200,000. If Shelly's outsources *and* leaves its plant idle, it can save $50,000 of fixed overhead cost. Or, it can use the freed manufacturing facilities to make other products that will contribute $70,000 to profits. In this case, the company will not be able to avoid any fixed costs. Identify and analyze the alternatives. What is the best course of action?

## Solution

### Requirement 1

|  | Standard | Deluxe |
|---|---|---|
| Sale price per pair........................................... | $ 20 | $ 30 |
| Variable expense per pair ............................... | 16 | 21 |
| Contribution margin per pair.......................... | $ 4 | $ 9 |
| Units produced each machine hour ............... | × 70 | × 30 |
| Contribution margin per machine hour.......... | $ 280 | $ 270 |
| Capacity—number of machine hours ............ | × 15,000 | × 15,000 |
| Total contribution margin at full capacity ...... | $4,200,000 | $4,050,000 |

*Decision*: Emphasize the standard model because it has the higher contribution margin per unit of the constraint—machine hours.

**Requirement 2**

| | | Buy Shades | |
| | Make Shades | Facilities Idle | Make Other Products |
| --- | --- | --- | --- |
| Relevant costs: | | | |
| Direct materials ............................ | $ 20,000 | — | — |
| Direct labor .................................. | 80,000 | — | — |
| Variable overhead.......................... | 40,000 | — | — |
| Fixed overhead .............................. | 80,000 | $ 30,000 | $ 80,000 |
| Purchase cost (20,000 × $10)........ | — | 200,000 | 200,000 |
| Total cost of obtaining shades ........ | 220,000 | 230,000 | 280,000 |
| Profit from other products............. | — | — | (70,000) |
| Net cost of obtaining shades ...... | $220,000 | $230,000 | $210,000 |

*Decision*: Shelly's should buy the shades from the outside supplier and use the freed manufacturing facilities to make other products.

# Review *Short-Term Business Decisions*

## ● Accounting Vocabulary

**Constraint (p. 980)**
A factor that restricts production or sale of a product.

**Incremental Analysis Approach (p. 965)**
A method that looks at how operating income would *differ* under each decision alternative. Leaves out irrelevant information—the costs and revenues that will not differ between alternatives. Also called the **relevant information approach**.

**Irrelevant Costs (p. 964)**
Costs that *do not* affect a decision.

**Opportunity Cost (p. 984)**
The benefit given up by not choosing an alternative course of action.

**Outsourcing (p. 964)**
The decision to buy or subcontract a component product or service rather than produce it in-house.

**Relevant Costs (p. 963)**
Costs that *do* affect a decision.

**Relevant Information (p. 963)**
Expected *future* data that *differs* among alternatives.

**Relevant Information Approach (p. 965)**
A method that looks at how operating income would *differ* under each decision alternative. Leaves out irrelevant information—the costs and revenues that will not differ between alternatives. Also called the **incremental analysis approach**.

**Sunk Cost (p. 964)**
A past cost that cannot be changed regardless of which future action is taken.

**Target Full Product Cost (p. 970)**
The total cost in developing, producing, and delivering a product or service.

## ● Destination: Student Success

### Student Success Tips

The following are hints on some common trouble areas for students in this chapter:

- Remember the difference between relevant costs, irrelevant costs, and sunk costs.

- Keep in mind the two keys to short-term special decisions: Focus on relevant revenues, costs, and profits; and use a contribution margin approach that separates variable and fixed costs.

- Recall the special sales order considerations in Exhibit 20-4 and the incremental analysis approach used to analyze these special orders.

- Consider the difference between price-setters and price-takers. Companies are price-setters when they have more control over pricing because their product is unique—that is, they can "set" the price. Companies are price-takers when the competition is intense and the product is not unique.

- Recall the considerations for dropping product lines, departments, or territories in Exhibit 20-13.

- Remember the considerations for outsourcing a function or component: How will variable and/or fixed costs change? What can the company do with the freed manufacturing capacity? If the incremental costs of making the product exceed the incremental costs of outsourcing, then the company should outsource the product.

- Keep in mind that when a company is considering selling a product as is or processing it further, if the extra revenue from processing the product further exceeds the extra costs to process the product further, then the company should process the product further.

### Getting Help

If there's a learning objective from the chapter you aren't confident about, try using one or more of the following resources:

- Review the Decision Guidelines 20-1 in the chapter.

- Review Summary Problem 20-1 in the chapter to reinforce your understanding of make or buy decisions.

- Review Summary Problem 20-2 in the chapter to reinforce your understanding of production constraints.

- Practice additional exercises or problems at the end of Chapter 20 that cover the specific learning objective that is challenging you.

- Watch the white board videos for Chapter 20 located at myaccountinglab.com under the Chapter Resources button.

- Go to myaccountinglab.com and select the Study Plan button. Choose Chapter 20 and work the questions covering that specific learning objective until you've mastered it.

- Work the Chapter 20 pre/post tests in myaccountinglab.com.

- Consult the Check Figures for End of Chapter starters, exercises, and problems, located at myaccountinglab.com.

- Visit the learning resource center on your campus for tutoring.

## • Quick Check

1. In making short-term special decisions, you should
   a. use a traditional absorption costing approach.
   b. focus on total costs.
   c. separate variable from fixed costs.
   d. only focus on quantitative factors.

2. Which of the following is relevant to Kitchenware.com's decision to accept a special order at a lower sale price from a large customer in China?
   a. The cost of shipping the order to the customer
   b. The cost of Kitchenware.com's warehouses in the United States
   c. Founder Eric Crowley's salary
   d. Kitchenware.com's investment in its Web site

3. Which of the following costs are irrelevant to business decisions?
   a. Avoidable costs                    c. Sunk costs
   b. Costs that differ between alternatives    d. Variable costs

4. When making decisions, managers should consider
   a. revenues that differ between alternatives.
   b. costs that do not differ between alternatives.
   c. only variable costs.
   d. sunk costs in their decisions.

5. When pricing a product or service, managers must consider which of the following?
   a. Only period costs            c. Only variable costs
   b. Only manufacturing costs      d. All costs

6. When companies are price-setters, their products and services
   a. are priced by managers using a target-pricing emphasis.
   b. tend to have a lot of competitors.
   c. tend to be commodities.
   d. tend to be unique.

7. In deciding whether to drop its electronics product line, Kitchenware.com would consider
   a. how dropping the electronics product line would affect sales of its other products like CDs.
   b. the costs it could save by dropping the product line.
   c. the revenues it would lose from dropping the product line.
   d. All of the above

8. In deciding which product lines to emphasize, Kitchenware.com should focus on the product line that has the highest
   a. contribution margin per unit of product.
   b. contribution margin per unit of the constraining factor.
   c. profit per unit of product.
   d. contribution margin ratio.

9. When making outsourcing decisions
   a. expected use of the freed capacity is irrelevant.
   b. the variable cost of producing the product in-house is relevant.
   c. the total manufacturing unit cost of making the product in-house is relevant.
   d. avoidable fixed costs are irrelevant.

10. When deciding whether to sell as is or process a product further, managers should ignore which of the following?

    a. The costs of processing the product thus far

    b. The cost of processing further

    c. The revenue if the product is sold as is

    d. The revenue if the product is processed further

Answers are given after Apply Your Knowledge (p. 1009).

# Assess Your Progress

## ● Short Exercises

**S20-1**    **❶ Describing and identifying information relevant to business decisions [5 min]**    *MyAccountingLab*

You are trying to decide whether to trade in your inkjet printer for a more recent model. Your usage pattern will remain unchanged, but the old and new printers use different ink cartridges.

### Requirement

1. Indicate if the following items are relevant or irrelevant to your decision:

    a. The price of the new printer
    b. The price you paid for the old printer
    c. The trade-in value of the old printer
    d. Paper costs
    e. The difference between ink cartridges' costs

**S20-2**    **❷ Making special order and pricing decisions [10 min]**

Mount Snow operates a Rocky Mountain ski resort. The company is planning its lift ticket pricing for the coming ski season. Investors would like to earn a 16% return on the company's $109,375,000 of assets. The company primarily incurs fixed costs to groom the runs and operate the lifts. Mount Snow projects fixed costs to be $35,000,000 for the ski season. The resort serves about 700,000 skiers and snow-boarders each season. Variable costs are about $12 per guest. Currently, the resort has such a favorable reputation among skiers and snowboarders that it has some control over the lift ticket prices.

### Requirements

1. Would Mount Snow emphasize target pricing or cost-plus pricing. Why?

2. If other resorts in the area charge $83 per day, what price should Mount Snow charge?

*Note: Short Exercise 20-2 must be completed before attempting Short Exercise 20-3.*

**S20-3**    **❷ Making special order and pricing decisions [10 min]**

Consider Mount Snow from Short Exercise 20-2. Assume that Mount Snow's reputation has diminished and other resorts in the vicinity are only charging $80 per lift ticket. Mount Snow has become a price-taker and will not be able to charge more than its competitors. At the market price, Mount Snow managers believe they will still serve 700,000 skiers and snowboarders each season.

### Requirements

1. If Mount Snow cannot reduce its costs, what profit will it earn? State your answer in dollars and as a percent of assets. Will investors be happy with the profit level?

2. Assume Mount Snow has found ways to cut its fixed costs to $32,900,000. What is its new target variable cost per skier/snowboarder?

**S20-4**  ③ **Making dropping a product and product-mix decisions [5–10 min]**

Deela Fashions operates three departments: Men's, Women's, and Accessories. Departmental operating income data for the third quarter of 2012 are as follows:

| | | | **DEELA FASHIONS** | | |
| --- | --- | --- | --- | --- | --- |
| | | | **Income Statement** | | |
| | | | For the quarter ended September 30, 2012 | | |
| | | **Department** | | | |
| | | Men's | Women's | Accessories | Total |
| Sales revenue | | $      108,000 | $       55,000 | $    100,000 | $    263,000 |
| Variable expenses | | 58,000 | 30,000 | 92,000 | 180,000 |
| Fixed expenses | | 26,000 | 21,000 | 26,000 | 73,000 |
| Total expenses | | 84,000 | 51,000 | 118,000 | 253,000 |
| Operating income (loss) | | $      24,000 | $        4,000 | $     (18,000) | $      10,000 |

Assume that the fixed expenses assigned to each department include only direct fixed costs of the department:

- Salary of the department's manager
- Cost of advertising directly related to that department

If Deela Fashions drops a department, it will not incur these fixed expenses.

### Requirement

1.  Under these circumstances, should Deela Fashions drop any of the departments? Give your reasoning.

**S20-5**  ③ **Making dropping a product and product-mix decisions [15 min]**

StoreAll produces plastic storage bins for household storage needs. The company makes two sizes of bins: large (50 gallon) and regular (35 gallon). Demand for the product is so high that StoreAll can sell as many of each size as it can produce. The company uses the same machinery to produce both sizes. The machinery can only be run for 3,300 hours per period. StoreAll can produce 9 large bins every hour, whereas it can produce 15 regular bins in the same amount of time. Fixed costs amount to $110,000 per period. Sales prices and variable costs are as follows:

| | Regular | Large |
| --- | --- | --- |
| Sales price per unit...................................... | $9.00 | $10.80 |
| Variable cost per unit ............................. | $3.10 | $  4.20 |

### Requirements

1.  Which product should StoreAll emphasize? Why?
2.  To maximize profits, how many of each size bin should StoreAll produce?
3.  Given this product mix, what will the company's operating income be?

**S20-6**  ④ **Making outsourcing and sell as is or process further decisions [10 min]**

Suppose a Roasted Olive restaurant is considering whether to (1) bake bread for its restaurant in-house or (2) buy the bread from a local bakery. The chef estimates that variable costs of making each loaf include $0.52 of ingredients, $0.24 of variable overhead (electricity to run the oven), and $0.70 of direct labor for kneading and forming the loaves. Allocating fixed overhead (depreciation on the kitchen equipment and building) based on direct labor assigns $0.96 of fixed overhead per loaf. None of the fixed costs are avoidable. The local bakery would charge $1.75 per loaf.

### Requirements

1. What is the unit cost of making the bread in-house (use absorption costing)?
2. Should Roasted Olive bake the bread in-house or buy from the local bakery? Why?
3. In addition to the financial analysis, what else should Roasted Olive consider when making this decision?

**S20-7**    ❹ **Making outsourcing decisions [10–15 min]**

Priscilla Nailey manages a fleet of 375 delivery trucks for Jones Corporation. Nailey must decide if the company should outsource the fleet management function. If she outsources to Fleet Management Services (FMS), FMS will be responsible for maintenance and scheduling activities. This alternative would require Nailey to lay off her five employees. However, her own job would be secure; she would be Jones's liaison with FMS. If she continues to manage the fleet she will need fleet-management software that costs $8,250 a year to lease. FMS offers to manage this fleet for an annual fee of $285,000. Nailey performed the following analysis:

| | Retain In-House | Outsource to FMS | Difference |
|---|---|---|---|
| **JONES CORPORATION** | | | |
| **Outsourcing Decision Analysis** | | | |
| Annual leasing fee for software | $    8,250 | $    — | $    8,250 |
| Annual maintenance of trucks | 147,000 | — | 147,000 |
| Total annual salaries of five other fleet management employees | 175,000 | — | 175,000 |
| Fleet Management Services' annual fee | — | 285,000 | (285,000) |
| Total cost / cost savings | $  330,250 | $  285,000 | $  45,250 |

### Requirements

1. Which alternative will maximize Jones's short-term operating income?
2. What qualitative factors should Jones consider before making a final decision?

**S20-8**    ❹ **Sell as is or process further decisions [10 min]**

Cocoaheaven processes cocoa beans into cocoa powder at a processing cost of $9,500 per batch. Cocoaheaven can sell the cocoa powder as is or it can process the cocoa powder further into either chocolate syrup or boxed assorted chocolates. Once processed, each batch of cocoa beans would result in the following sales revenue:

| | |
|---|---|
| Cocoa powder........................................... | $ 16,500 |
| Chocolate syrup ...................................... | $102,000 |
| Boxed assorted chocolates...................... | $196,000 |

The cost of transforming the cocoa powder into chocolate syrup would be $70,000. Likewise, the company would incur a cost of $176,000 to transform the cocoa powder into boxed assorted chocolates. The company president has decided to make boxed assorted chocolates due to its high sales value and to the fact that the cocoa bean processing cost of $9,500 eats up most of the cocoa powder profits.

### Requirement

1. Has the president made the right or wrong decision? Explain your answer. Be sure to include the correct financial analysis in your response.

# • Exercises

MyAccountingLab    **E20-9** **①** **Describing and identifying information relevant to business decisions [5–10 min]**

Dan Jacobs, production manager for GreenLife, invested in computer-controlled production machinery last year. He purchased the machinery from Superior Design at a cost of $3,000,000. A representative from Superior Design has recently contacted Dan because the company has designed an even more efficient piece of machinery. The new design would double the production output of the year-old machinery but would cost GreenLife another $4,500,000. Jacobs is afraid to bring this new equipment to the company president's attention because he convinced the president to invest $3,000,000 in the machinery last year.

## Requirement

1. Explain what is relevant and irrelevant to Jacobs' dilemma. What should he do?

**E20-10** **②** **Making special order and pricing decisions [10–15 min]**

Suppose the Baseball Hall of Fame in Cooperstown, New York, has approached Hobby-Cardz with a special order. The Hall of Fame wishes to purchase 57,000 baseball card packs for a special promotional campaign and offers $0.41 per pack, a total of $23,370. Hobby-Cardz's total production cost is $0.61 per pack, as follows:

| | |
|---|---|
| Variable costs: | |
| Direct materials | $ 0.13 |
| Direct labor | 0.06 |
| Variable overhead | 0.12 |
| Fixed overhead | 0.30 |
| Total cost | $ 0.61 |

Hobby-Cardz has enough excess capacity to handle the special order.

## Requirements

1. Prepare an incremental analysis to determine whether Hobby-Cardz should accept the special sales order.

2. Now assume that the Hall of Fame wants special hologram baseball cards. Hobby-Cardz will spend $5,900 to develop this hologram, which will be useless after the special order is completed. Should Hobby-Cardz accept the special order under these circumstances?

**E20-11** **②** **Making special order and pricing decisions [20–25 min]**

San Jose Sunglasses sell for about $157 per pair. Suppose that the company incurs the following average costs per pair:

| | |
|---|---|
| Direct materials | $ 39 |
| Direct labor | 15 |
| Variable manufacturing overhead | 8 |
| Variable marketing expenses | 2 |
| Fixed manufacturing overhead | 20* |
| Total cost | $ 84 |

* $2,200,000 total fixed manufacturing overhead ÷ 110,000 pairs of sunglasses

San Jose has enough idle capacity to accept a one-time-only special order from Washington Shades for 25,000 pairs of sunglasses at $80 per pair. San Jose will not incur any variable marketing expenses for the order.

## Requirements

1. How would accepting the order affect San Jose's operating income? In addition to the special order's effect on profits, what other (longer-term qualitative) factors should San Jose's managers consider in deciding whether to accept the order?

2. San Jose's marketing manager, Peter Bing, argues against accepting the special order because the offer price of $80 is less than San Jose's $84 cost to make the sunglasses. Bing asks you, as one of San Jose's staff accountants, to explain whether his analysis is correct.

**E20-12**  **②** **Making special order and pricing decisions [10–15 min]**

Stenback Builders builds 1,500 square-foot starter tract homes in the fast-growing suburbs of Atlanta. Land and labor are cheap, and competition among developers is fierce. The homes are a standard model, with any upgrades added by the buyer after the sale. Stenback Builders' costs per developed sub-lot are as follows:

| | |
|---|---|
| Land . . . . . . . . . . . . . . . . . . . . . . . . . | $ 59,000 |
| Construction . . . . . . . . . . . . . . . . . . . | $ 124,000 |
| Landscaping . . . . . . . . . . . . . . . . . . . | $ 6,000 |
| Variable marketing costs . . . . . . . . . . . . | $ 5,000 |

Stenback Builders would like to earn a profit of 14% of the variable cost of each home sale. Similar homes offered by competing builders sell for $208,000 each.

221.

## Requirements

1. Which approach to pricing should Stenback Builders emphasize? Why?

2. Will Stenback Builders be able to achieve its target profit levels?   No

3. Bathrooms and kitchens are typically the most important selling features of a home. Stenback Builders could differentiate the homes by upgrading the bathrooms and kitchens. The upgrades would cost $22,000 per home but would enable Stenback Builders to increase the selling prices by $38,500 per home. (Kitchen and bathroom   216 upgrades typically add about 175% of their cost to the value of any home.) If   246.5 Stenback Builders makes the upgrades, what will the new cost-plus price per home be? Should the company differentiate its product in this manner?

**E20-13**  **③** **Making dropping a product and product-mix decisions [10 min]**

Top managers of Movie Street are alarmed by their operating losses. They are considering dropping the VCR-tape product line. Company accountants have prepared the following analysis to help make this decision:

| MOVIE STREET | | | |
|---|---|---|---|
| Income Statement | | | |
| For the Year Ended December 31, 2012 | | | |
| | Total | DVD Discs | VCR Tapes |
| Sales revenue | $ 432,000 | $ 305,000 | $ 127,000 |
| Variable expenses | 246,000 | 150,000 | 96,000 |
| Contribution margin | $ 186,000 | $ 155,000 | $ 31,000 |
| Fixed expenses: | | | |
| Manufacturing | 128,000 | 71,000 | 57,000 |
| Marketing and administrative | 67,000 | 52,000 | 15,000 |
| Total fixed expenses | 195,000 | 123,000 | 72,000 |
| Operating income (loss) | $ (9,000) | $ 32,000 | $ (41,000) |

Total fixed costs will not change if the company stops selling VCR tapes.

## Requirement

1. Prepare an incremental analysis to show whether Movie Street should drop the VCR-tape product line. Will dropping VCR tapes add $41,000 to operating income? Explain.

*Note: Exercise 20-13 must be completed before attempting Exercise 20-14.*

**E20-14** ❸ **Making dropping a product and product-mix decisions [10 min]**
Refer to Exercise 20-13. Assume that Movie Street can avoid $41,000 of fixed expenses by dropping the VCR-tape product line (these costs are direct fixed costs of the VCR product line).

## Requirement

1. Prepare an incremental analysis to show whether Movie Street should stop selling VCR tapes.

**E20-15** ❸ **Product mix under production constraints [15 min]**
Lifemaster produces two types of exercise treadmills: regular and deluxe. The exercise craze is such that Lifemaster could use all its available machine hours to produce either model. The two models are processed through the same production departments. Data for both models is as follows:

|  | Per Unit | |
|---|---|---|
|  | Deluxe | Regular |
| Sale price | $  1,020 | $  560 |
| Costs: |  |  |
| Direct materials | 300 | 90 |
| Direct labor | 88 | 188 |
| Variable manufacturing overhead | 264 | 88 |
| Fixed manufacturing overhead* | 138 | 46 |
| Variable operating expenses | 111 | 65 |
| Total cost | 901 | 477 |
| Operating income | $  119 | $  83 |

*Allocated on the basis of machine hours.

## Requirements

1. What is the constraint?
2. Which model should Lifemaster produce? (*Hint:* Use the allocation of fixed manufacturing overhead to determine the proportion of machine hours used by each product.)
3. If Lifemaster should produce both models, compute the mix that will maximize operating income.

**E20-16** ❸ **Making dropping a product and product-mix decisions [10–15 min]**
Klintan sells both designer and moderately priced fashion accessories. Top management is deciding which product line to emphasize. Accountants have provided the following data:

|  | Per Item | |
|---|---|---|
|  | Designer | Moderately Priced |
| Average sale price | $  210 | $  81 |
| Average variable expenses | 90 | 26 |
| Average contribution margin | $  120 | $  55 |
| Average fixed expenses (allocated) | 15 | 5 |
| Average operating income | $  105 | $  50 |

The Klintan store in Grand Junction, Colorado, has 9,000 square feet of floor space. If Klintan emphasizes moderately priced goods, it can display 630 items in the store.

If Klintan emphasizes designer wear, it can only display 270 designer items. These numbers are also the average monthly sales in units.

## Requirement

1. Prepare an analysis to show which product the company should emphasize.

**E20-17**    **③ Making dropping a product and product-mix decisions [15–20 min]**
Each morning, Ned Stenback stocks the drink case at Ned's Beach Hut in Myrtle Beach, South Carolina. The drink case has 115 linear feet of refrigerated drink space. Each linear foot can hold either six 12-ounce cans or three 20-ounce bottles.

Ned's Beach Hut sells three types of cold drinks:
1. Yummy Time in 12-oz. cans, for $1.45 per can
2. Yummy Time in 20-oz. bottles, for $1.75 per bottle
3. Pretty Pop in 20-oz. bottles, for $2.30 per bottle

Ned's Beach Hut pays its suppliers:
1. $0.15 per 12-oz. can of Yummy Time
2. $0.35 per 20-oz. bottle of Yummy Time
3. $0.65 per 20-oz. bottle of Pretty Pop

Ned's Beach Hut's monthly fixed expenses include:

| | | |
|---|---|---:|
| Hut rental | $ | 360 |
| Refrigerator rental | | 80 |
| Ned's salary | | 1,500 |
| Total fixed expenses | $ | 1,940 |

Ned's Beach Hut can sell all the drinks stocked in the display case each morning.

## Requirements

1. What is Ned's Beach Hut's constraining factor? What should Ned stock to maximize profits?
2. Suppose Ned's Beach Hut refuses to devote more than 75 linear feet to any individual product. Under this condition, how many linear feet of each drink should Ned's stock? How many units of each product will be available for sale each day?

**E20-18**    **④ Making outsourcing decisions [10–15 min]**
Fiber Systems manufactures an optical switch that it uses in its final product. The switch has the following manufacturing costs per unit:

| | |
|---|---:|
| Direct materials | $  9.00 |
| Direct labor | 1.50 |
| Variable overhead | 5.00 |
| Fixed overhead | 9.00 |
| Manufacturing product cost | $  24.50 |

Another company has offered to sell Fiber Systems the switch for $18.50 per unit. If Fiber Systems buys the switch from the outside supplier, the manufacturing facilities that will be idled cannot be used for any other purpose, yet none of the fixed costs are avoidable.

## Requirement

1. Prepare an outsourcing analysis to determine if Fiber Systems should make or buy the switch.

*Note: Exercise 20-18 must be completed before attempting Exercise 20-19.*

**E20-19**    **④ Making outsourcing decisions [10–15 min]**
Refer to Exercise 20-18. Fiber Systems needs 84,000 optical switches. By outsourcing them, Fiber Systems can use its idle facilities to manufacture another product that will contribute $253,000 to operating income.

## Requirements

1. Identify the *incremental* costs that Fiber Systems will incur to acquire 84,000 switches under three alternative plans.

2. Which plan makes the best use of Fiber System's facilities? Support your answer.

**E20-20** ④ **Making sell as is or process further decisions [10 min]**

Naturalmaid processes organic milk into plain yogurt. Naturalmaid sells plain yogurt to hospitals, nursing homes, and restaurants in bulk, one-gallon containers. Each batch, processed at a cost of $800, yields 600 gallons of plain yogurt. Naturalmaid sells the one-gallon tubs for $7 each and spends $0.16 for each plastic tub. Naturalmaid has recently begun to reconsider its strategy. Naturalmaid wonders if it would be more profitable to sell individual-size portions of fruited organic yogurt at local food stores. Naturalmaid could further process each batch of plain yogurt into 12,800 individual portions (3/4 cup each) of fruited yogurt. A recent market analysis indicates that demand for the product exists. Naturalmaid would sell each individual portion for $0.54. Packaging would cost $0.07 per portion, and fruit would cost $0.11 per portion. Fixed costs would not change.

## Requirement

1. Should Naturalmaid continue to sell only the gallon-size plain yogurt (sell as is), or convert the plain yogurt into individual-size portions of fruited yogurt (process further)? Why?

## ● Problems (Group A)

*MyAccountingLab*   **P20-21A** ① ② **Identifying which information is relevant, and making special order and pricing decisions [15–20 min]**

Buoy manufactures flotation vests in Charleston, South Carolina. Buoy's contribution margin income statement for the month ended December 31, 2012, contains the following data:

| BUOY | |
|---|---|
| **Income Statement** | |
| For the Month Ended December 31, 2012 | |
| Sales in units | 32,000 |
| Sales revenue | $ 544,000 |
| Variable expenses: | |
|     Manufacturing | 96,000 |
|     Marketing and administrative | 110,000 |
|     Total variable expenses | $ 206,000 |
| Contribution margin | $ 338,000 |
| Fixed expenses: | |
|     Manufacturing | 127,000 |
|     Marketing and administrative | 95,000 |
|     Total fixed expenses | $ 222,000 |
| Operating income | $ 116,000 |

Suppose Overboard wishes to buy 3,900 vests from Buoy. Acceptance of the order will not increase Buoy's variable marketing and administrative expenses. The Buoy plant has enough unused capacity to manufacture the additional vests. Overboard has offered $8.00 per vest, which is below the normal sale price of $17.

## Requirements

1. Identify each cost in the income statement as either relevant or irrelevant to Buoy's decision.

2. Prepare an incremental analysis to determine whether Buoy should accept this special sales order.

3. Identify long-term factors Buoy should consider in deciding whether to accept the special sales order.

**P20-22A** ❷ **Making special order and pricing decisions [15–20 min]**
Green Thumb operates a commercial plant nursery where it propagates plants for garden centers throughout the region. Green Thumb has $4,800,000 in assets. Its yearly fixed costs are $600,000, and the variable costs for the potting soil, container, label, seedling, and labor for each gallon-size plant total $1.35. Green Thumb's volume is currently 470,000 units. Competitors offer the same plants, at the same quality, to garden centers for $3.60 each. Garden centers then mark them up to sell to the public for $9 to $12, depending on the type of plant.

## Requirements

1. Green Thumb's owners want to earn a 10% return on the company's assets. What is Green Thumb's target full cost?

2. Given Green Thumb's current costs, will its owners be able to achieve their target profit?

3. Assume Green Thumb has identified ways to cut its variable costs to $1.20 per unit. What is its new target fixed cost? Will this decrease in variable costs allow the company to achieve its target profit?

4. Green Thumb started an aggressive advertising campaign strategy to differentiate its plants from those grown by other nurseries. Monrovia Plants made this strategy work so Green Thumb has decided to try it, too. Green Thumb does not expect volume to be affected, but it hopes to gain more control over pricing. If Green Thumb has to spend $115,000 this year to advertise, and its variable costs continue to be $1.20 per unit, what will its cost-plus price be? Do you think Green Thumb will be able to sell its plants to garden centers at the cost-plus price? Why or why not?

**P20-23A** ❸ **Making dropping a product and product-mix decisions [20–25 min]**
Members of the board of directors of Safe Zone have received the following operating income data for the year ended May 31, 2012:

<table>
<tr><td colspan="4" align="center">**SAFE ZONE**<br>**Income Statement**<br>For the Year Ended May 31, 2012</td></tr>
<tr><td></td><td colspan="2" align="center">Product Line</td><td></td></tr>
<tr><td></td><td align="center">Industrial<br>Systems</td><td align="center">Household<br>Systems</td><td align="center">Total</td></tr>
<tr><td>Sales revenue</td><td>$ 370,000</td><td>$ 390,000</td><td>$ 760,000</td></tr>
<tr><td>Cost of goods sold:</td><td></td><td></td><td></td></tr>
<tr><td>  Variable</td><td>36,000</td><td>42,000</td><td>78,000</td></tr>
<tr><td>  Fixed</td><td>260,000</td><td>65,000</td><td>325,000</td></tr>
<tr><td>  Total cost of goods sold</td><td>$ 296,000</td><td>$ 107,000</td><td>$ 403,000</td></tr>
<tr><td>Gross profit</td><td>$ 74,000</td><td>$ 283,000</td><td>$ 357,000</td></tr>
<tr><td>Marketing and administrative expenses:</td><td></td><td></td><td></td></tr>
<tr><td>  Variable</td><td>66,000</td><td>75,000</td><td>141,000</td></tr>
<tr><td>  Fixed</td><td>44,000</td><td>24,000</td><td>68,000</td></tr>
<tr><td>  Total marketing and administrative exp.</td><td>$ 110,000</td><td>$ 99,000</td><td>$ 209,000</td></tr>
<tr><td>Operating income (loss)</td><td>$ (36,000)</td><td>$ 184,000</td><td>$ 148,000</td></tr>
</table>

Members of the board are surprised that the industrial systems product line is losing money. They commission a study to determine whether the company should drop the line. Company accountants estimate that dropping industrial systems will decrease fixed cost of goods sold by $84,000 and decrease fixed marketing and administrative expenses by $14,000.

**Requirements**

1. Prepare an incremental analysis to show whether Safe Zone should drop the industrial systems product line.

2. Prepare contribution margin income statements to show Safe Zone's total operating income under the two alternatives: (a) with the industrial systems line and (b) without the line. Compare the *difference* between the two alternatives' income numbers to your answer to Requirement 1.

3. What have you learned from the comparison in Requirement 2?

**P20-24A** ❸ **Making dropping a product and product-mix decisions [10–15 min]**

Brik, located in Port St. Lucie, Florida, produces two lines of electric toothbrushes: deluxe and standard. Because Brik can sell all the toothbrushes it can produce, the owners are expanding the plant. They are deciding which product line to emphasize. To make this decision, they assemble the following data:

|  | Per Unit | |
|---|---|---|
|  | Deluxe Toothbrush | Standard Toothbrush |
| Sale price | $ 88 | $ 52 |
| Variable expenses | 24 | 16 |
| Contribution margin | $ 64 | $ 36 |
| Contribution margin ratio | 72.7% | 69.2% |

After expansion, the factory will have a production capacity of 4,900 machine hours per month. The plant can manufacture either 60 standard electric toothbrushes or 28 deluxe electric toothbrushes per machine hour.

**Requirements**

1. Identify the constraining factor for Brik.

2. Prepare an analysis to show which product line to emphasize.

**P20-25A** ❹ **Making outsourcing decisions [20–30 min]**

Outdoor Life manufactures snowboards. Its cost of making 2,000 bindings is as follows:

| Direct materials | $ 17,550 |
|---|---|
| Direct labor | 3,400 |
| Variable overhead | 2,040 |
| Fixed overhead | 6,300 |
| Total manufacturing costs for 2,000 bindings | $ 29,290 |

Suppose Lancaster will sell bindings to Outdoor Life for $14 each. Outdoor Life would pay $3 per unit to transport the bindings to its manufacturing plant, where it would add its own logo at a cost of $0.70 per binding.

**Requirements**

1. Outdoor Life's accountants predict that purchasing the bindings from Lancaster will enable the company to avoid $2,100 of fixed overhead. Prepare an analysis to show whether Outdoor Life should make or buy the bindings.

2.  The facilities freed by purchasing bindings from Lancaster can be used to manufacture another product that will contribute $2,700 to profit. Total fixed costs will be the same as if Outdoor Life had produced the bindings. Show which alternative makes the best use of Outdoor Life's facilities: (a) make bindings, (b) buy bindings and leave facilities idle, or (c) buy bindings and make another product.

**P20-26A** ❹ **Making sell as is or process further decisions [20–25 min]**

Smith Petroleum has spent $204,000 to refine 62,000 gallons of petroleum distillate, which can be sold for $6.40 a gallon. Alternatively, Smith can process the distillate further and produce 56,000 gallons of cleaner fluid. The additional processing will cost $1.75 per gallon of distillate. The cleaner fluid can be sold for $9.00 a gallon. To sell the cleaner fluid, Smith must pay a sales commission of $0.13 a gallon and a transportation charge of $0.18 a gallon.

## Requirements

1.  Diagram Smith's decision alternatives, using Exhibit 20-26 as a guide.
2.  Identify the sunk cost. Is the sunk cost relevant to Smith's decision?
3.  Should Smith sell the petroleum distillate or process it into cleaner fluid? Show the expected net revenue difference between the two alternatives.

# ● Problems (Group B)

**P20-27B** ❶❷ **Identifying which information is relevant, and making special order and pricing decisions [15–20 min]**                MyAccountingLab ▊

Safe Sailing manufactures flotation vests in Tampa, Florida. Safe Sailing's contribution margin income statement for the month ended December 31, 2012, contains the following data:

| SAFE SAILING | |
|---|---|
| Income Statement | |
| For the Month Ended December 31, 2012 | |
| Sales in units | 41,000 |
| Sales revenue | $  820,000 |
| Variable expenses: | |
| Manufacturing | 205,000 |
| Marketing and administrative | 105,000 |
| Total variable expenses | $  310,000 |
| Contribution margin | $  510,000 |
| Fixed expenses: | |
| Manufacturing | 126,000 |
| Marketing and administrative | 91,000 |
| Total fixed expenses | $  217,000 |
| Operating income | $  293,000 |

Suppose Overtown wishes to buy 3,800 vests from Safe Sailing. Acceptance of the order will not increase Safe Sailing's variable marketing and administrative expenses. The Safe Sailing plant has enough unused capacity to manufacture the additional vests. Overtown has offered $12.00 per vest, which is below the normal sale price of $20.00.

## Requirements

1.  Identify each cost in the income statement as either relevant or irrelevant to Safe Sailing's decision.

2. Prepare an incremental analysis to determine whether Safe Sailing should accept this special sales order.

3. Identify long-term factors Safe Sailing should consider in deciding whether to accept the special sales order.

**P20-28B ② Making special order and pricing decisions [15–20 min]**
Nature Place operates a commercial plant nursery, where it propagates plants for garden centers throughout the region. Nature Place has $5,100,000 in assets. Its yearly fixed costs are $650,000 and the variable costs for the potting soil, container, label, seedling, and labor for each gallon-size plant total $1.40. Nature Place's volume is currently 480,000 units. Competitors offer the same plants, at the same quality, to garden centers for $3.75 each. Garden centers then mark them up to sell to the public for $7 to $10, depending on the type of plant.

## Requirements

1. Nature Place's owners want to earn a 11% return on the company's assets. What is Nature Place's target full cost?

2. Given Nature Place's current costs, will its owners be able to achieve their target profit?

3. Assume Nature Place has identified ways to cut its variable costs to $1.25 per unit. What is its new target fixed cost? Will this decrease in variable costs allow the company to achieve its target profit?

4. Nature Place started an aggressive advertising campaign strategy to differentiate its plants from those grown by other nurseries. Monrovia Plants made this strategy work so Nature Place has decided to try it, too. Nature Place does not expect volume to be affected, but it hopes to gain more control over pricing. If Nature Place has to spend $125,000 this year to advertise, and its variable costs continue to be $1.25 per unit, what will its cost-plus price be? Do you think Nature Place will be able to sell its plants to garden centers at the cost-plus price? Why or why not?

**P20-29B ③ Making dropping a product and product-mix decisions [20–25 min]**
Members of the board of directors of Control One have received the following operating income data for the year ended March 31, 2012:

| CONTROL ONE | | | |
|---|---|---|---|
| Income Statement | | | |
| For the Year Ended March 31, 2012 | | | |
| | Product Line | | |
| | Industrial Systems | Household Systems | Total |
| Sales revenue | $ 330,000 | $ 370,000 | $ 700,000 |
| Cost of goods sold: | | | |
|   Variable | 33,000 | 47,000 | 80,000 |
|   Fixed | 240,000 | 69,000 | 309,000 |
|   Total cost of goods sold | $ 273,000 | $ 116,000 | $ 389,000 |
| Gross profit | $ 57,000 | $ 254,000 | $ 311,000 |
| Marketing and administrative expenses: | | | |
|   Variable | 64,000 | 73,000 | 137,000 |
|   Fixed | 39,000 | 27,000 | 66,000 |
|   Total marketing and administrative exp. | $ 103,000 | $ 100,000 | $ 203,000 |
| Operating income (loss) | $ (46,000) | $ 154,000 | $ 108,000 |

Members of the board are surprised that the industrial systems product line is losing money. They commission a study to determine whether the company should drop the line. Company accountants estimate that dropping industrial systems will decrease fixed cost of goods sold by $82,000 and decrease fixed marketing and administrative expenses by $15,000.

### Requirements

1. Prepare an incremental analysis to show whether Control One should drop the industrial systems product line.

2. Prepare contribution margin income statements to show Control One's total operating income under the two alternatives: (a) with the industrial systems line and (b) without the line. Compare the *difference* between the two alternatives' income numbers to your answer to Requirement 1.

3. What have you learned from this comparison in Requirement 2?

**P20-30B** ❸ **Making dropping a product and product-mix decisions [10–15 min]**
Breit, located in San Antonio, Texas, produces two lines of electric toothbrushes: deluxe and standard. Because Breit can sell all the toothbrushes it can produce, the owners are expanding the plant. They are deciding which product line to emphasize. To make this decision, they assemble the following data:

| | Per Unit | |
| --- | --- | --- |
| | Deluxe Toothbrush | Standard Toothbrush |
| Sale price | $ 90 | $ 50 |
| Variable expenses | 23 | 18 |
| Contribution margin | $ 67 | $ 32 |
| Contribution margin ratio | 74.4% | 64.0% |

After expansion, the factory will have a production capacity of 4,300 machine hours per month. The plant can manufacture either 65 standard electric toothbrushes or 27 deluxe electric toothbrushes per machine hour.

### Requirements

1. Identify the constraining factor for Breit.

2. Prepare an analysis to show which product line the company should emphasize.

**P20-31B** ❹ **Making outsourcing decisions [20–30 min]**
Cool Boards manufactures snowboards. Its cost of making 2,100 bindings is as follows:

| | |
| --- | --- |
| Direct materials | $ 17,580 |
| Direct labor | 2,600 |
| Variable overhead | 2,100 |
| Fixed overhead | 6,500 |
| Total manufacturing costs for 2,100 bindings | $ 28,780 |

Suppose Lewis will sell bindings to Cool Boards for $15 each. Cool Boards would pay $1 per unit to transport the bindings to its manufacturing plant, where it would add its own logo at a cost of $0.40 per binding.

### Requirements

1. Cool Boards' accountants predict that purchasing the bindings from Lewis will enable the company to avoid $2,600 of fixed overhead. Prepare an analysis to show whether Cool Boards should make or buy the bindings.

2.  The facilities freed by purchasing bindings from Lewis can be used to manufacture another product that will contribute $3,500 to profit. Total fixed costs will be the same as if Cool Boards had produced the bindings. Show which alternative makes the best use of Cool Boards' facilities: (a) make bindings, (b) buy bindings and leave facilities idle, or (c) buy bindings and make another product.

**P20-32B** ④ **Make sell as is or process further decisions [20–25 min]**
Cole Petroleum has spent $206,000 to refine 63,000 gallons of petroleum distillate, which can be sold for $6.30 a gallon. Alternatively, Cole can process the distillate further and produce 53,000 gallons of cleaner fluid. The additional processing will cost $1.80 per gallon of distillate. The cleaner fluid can be sold for $9.20 a gallon. To sell the cleaner fluid, Cole must pay a sales commission of $0.12 a gallon and a transportation charge of $0.15 a gallon.

### Requirements

1.  Diagram Cole's decision alternatives, using Exhibit 20-26 as a guide.
2.  Identify the sunk cost. Is the sunk cost relevant to Cole's decision?
3.  Should Cole sell the petroleum distillate or process it into cleaner fluid? Show the expected net revenue difference between the two alternatives.

## ● Continuing Exercise

*MyAccountingLab* **E20-33** ② **Making special order and pricing decisions [15–20 min]**
This exercise continues the Lawlor Lawn Service, Inc., situation from Exercise 19-32 of Chapter 19. Lawlor Lawn Service currently charges $100 for a standard lawn service and incurs $60 in variable cost. Assume fixed costs are $1,400 per month. Lawlor has been offered a special contract for $80 each for 20 lawns in one subdivision. This special contract will not affect Lawlor's other business.

### Requirements

1.  Should Lawlor take the special contract?
2.  What will Lawlor's incremental profit be on the special contract?

## ● Continuing Problem

*MyAccountingLab* **P20-34** ④ **Make sell as is or process further decisions [20–25 min]**
This problem continues the Draper Consulting, Inc., situation from Problem 19-33 of Chapter 19. Draper Consulting provides consulting service at an average price of $175 per hour and incurs variable costs of $100 per hour. Assume average fixed costs are $5,250 a month.

Draper has developed new software that will revolutionize billing for companies. Draper has already invested $200,000 in the software. It can market the software as is at $30,000 a client and expects to sell to eight clients. Draper can develop the software further, adding integration to **Microsoft** products at an additional development cost of $120,000. The additional development will allow Draper to sell the software for $38,000 each, but to 20 clients.

### Requirement

1.  Should Draper sell the software as is or develop it further?

# Apply Your Knowledge

## ● Decision Case 20-1

BKFin.com provides banks access to sophisticated financial information and analysis systems over the Web. The company combines these tools with benchmarking data access, including e-mail and wireless communications, so that banks can instantly evaluate individual loan applications and entire loan portfolios.

BKFin.com's CEO Jon Wise is happy with the company's growth. To better focus on client service, Wise is considering outsourcing some functions. CFO Jenny Lee suggests that the company's e-mail may be the place to start. She recently attended a conference and learned that companies like **Continental Airlines, DellNet, GTE,** and **NBC** were outsourcing their e-mail function. Wise asks Lee to identify costs related to BKFin.com's in-house Microsoft Exchange mail application, which has 2,300 mailboxes. This information follows:

Variable costs:

| | |
|---|---|
| E-mail license............................................................ | $7 per mailbox per month |
| Virus protection license ........................................... | $1 per mailbox per month |
| Other variable costs................................................. | $8 per mailbox per month |

Fixed costs:

| | |
|---|---|
| Computer hardware costs......................................... | $94,300 per month |
| $8,050 monthly salary for two information technology staff members who work only on e-mail .............................. | $16,100 per month |

### Requirements

1. Compute the *total cost* per mailbox per month of BKFin.com's current e-mail function.
2. Suppose Mail.com, a leading provider of Internet messaging outsourcing services, offers to host BKFin.com's e-mail function for $9 per mailbox per month. If BKFin.com outsources its e-mail to Mail.com, BKFin.com will still need the virus protection software, its computer hardware, and one information technology staff member, who would be responsible for maintaining virus protection, quarantining suspicious e-mail, and managing content (e.g., screening e-mail for objectionable content). Should CEO Wise accept Mail.com's offer?
3. Suppose for an additional $5 per mailbox per month, Mail.com will also provide virus protection, quarantine, and content-management services. Outsourcing these additional functions would mean that BKFin.com would not need either an e-mail information technology staff member or the separate virus protection license. Should CEO Wise outsource these extra services to Mail.com?

## ● Ethical Issue 20-1

Mary Tan is the controller for Duck Associates, a property management company in Portland, Oregon. Each year Tan and payroll clerk Toby Stock meet with the external auditors about payroll accounting. This year, the auditors suggest that Tan consider outsourcing Duck Associates' payroll accounting to a company specializing in payroll processing services. This would allow Tan and her staff to focus on their primary responsibility: accounting for the properties under management. At present, payroll requires 1.5 employee positions—payroll clerk Toby Stock and a bookkeeper who spends half her time entering payroll data in the system.

Tan considers this suggestion, and she lists the following items relating to outsourcing payroll accounting:

a. The current payroll software that was purchased for $4,000 three years ago would not be needed if payroll processing were outsourced.
b. Duck Associates' bookkeeper would spend half her time preparing the weekly payroll input form that is given to the payroll processing service. She is paid $450 a week.

c.  Duck Associates would no longer need payroll clerk Toby Stock, whose annual salary is $42,000.

d.  The payroll processing service would charge $2,000 a month.

### Requirements

1.  Would outsourcing the payroll function increase or decrease Duck Associates' operating income?

2.  Tan believes that outsourcing payroll would simplify her job, but she does not like the prospect of having to lay off Stock, who has become a close personal friend. She does not believe there is another position available for Stock at his current salary. Can you think of other factors that might support keeping Stock, rather than outsourcing payroll processing? How should each of the factors affect Tan's decision if she wants to do what is best for Duck Associates and act ethically?

## ● Fraud Case 20-1

Frank Perdue had built up a successful development company. When he became City Commissioner, everyone said it was good to have a businessman on the Commission. Businessmen know how to control costs and make sound economic decisions, they said, and Frank could help the city tighten its belt. One of his first projects was an analysis of the Human Resources Department. He claimed that if the whole function was outsourced, it would save the taxpayers money. A year later, after painful layoffs and a bumpy transition, the new contractor, NewSoft, was in place. Two years later, NewSoft's billing rates had steadily increased, and there were complaints about service. After five years, the supposed savings had vanished, and Frank had moved on to state government, his campaigns fueled by "generous" campaign contributions from companies like NewSoft.

### Requirements

1.  Although this case differs from "fraud" in the usual sense, describe the conflict of interest in this case. Who benefitted and who did not?

2.  When making business decisions of this sort, some factors are quantitative and some are not. Discuss some of the non-quantitative factors related to this case. (Challenge)

## ● Team Project 20-1

John Menard is the founder and sole owner of **Menards**. Analysts have estimated that his chain of home improvement stores scattered around nine midwestern states generate about $3 billion in annual sales. But how can **Menards** compete with giant **Home Depot**?

Suppose Menard is trying to decide whether to produce **Menards'** own line of Formica countertops, cabinets, and picnic tables.

Assume **Menards** would incur the following unit costs in producing its own product lines:

|  | Countertops | Cabinets | Picnic Tables |
|---|---|---|---|
| Direct materials per unit..................................... | $15 | $10 | $25 |
| Direct labor per unit........................................... | 10 | 5 | 15 |
| Variable manufacturing overhead per unit.......... | 5 | 2 | 6 |

Rather than making these products, assume that **Menards** could buy them from outside suppliers. Suppliers would charge **Menards** $40 per countertop, $25 per cabinet, and $65 per picnic table.

Whether Menard makes or buys these products, assume that he expects the following annual sales:

- Countertops—487,200 at $130 each
- Picnic tables—100,000 at $225 each
- Cabinets—150,000 at $75 each

Assume that **Menards** has a production facility with excess capacity that could be used to produce these products with no additional fixed costs. If "making" is sufficiently more profitable than outsourcing, Menard will start production of his new line of products. John Menard has asked your consulting group for a recommendation.

**Requirements**

1. Are the following items relevant or irrelevant in Menard's decision to build a new plant that will manufacture his own products?
   a. The unit sale prices of the countertops, cabinets, and picnic tables (the sale prices that **Menards** charges its customers)
   b. The prices outside suppliers would charge **Menards** for the three products, if **Menards** decides to outsource the products rather than make them
   c. The direct materials, direct labor, and variable overhead **Menards** would incur to manufacture the three product lines
   d. John Menard's salary

2. Determine whether **Menards** should make or outsource the countertops, cabinets, and picnic tables. In other words, what is the annual difference in cash flows if **Menards** decides to make rather than outsource each of these three products?

3. Write a memo giving your recommendation to John Menard. The memo should clearly state your recommendation, along with a brief summary of the reasons for your recommendation.

## ● Communication Activity 20-1

In 50 words or fewer, explain the difference between relevant costs, irrelevant costs, and sunk costs.

### Quick Check Answers

1. *c*  2. *a*  3. *c*  4. *a*  5. *d*  6. *d*  7. *d*  8. *b*  9. *b*  10. *a*

**For online homework, exercises, and problems that provide you immediate feedback, please visit myaccountinglab.com.**

# 21

# Capital Investment Decisions and the Time Value of Money

Shift Your Focus  Product Costing  Cost Allocation

Cost-Volume-Profit  Relevant Information  **Capital Budgeting**

Budgeting  Cost Control  Performance Measures

## Learning Objectives

**1** Describe the importance of capital investments and the capital budgeting process

**2** Use the payback period and rate of return methods to make capital investment decisions

**3** Use the time value of money to compute the present and future values of single lump sums and annuities

**4** Use discounted cash flow models to make capital investment decisions

Your car wouldn't start again this morning. Now you know you're going to be late to work for the second time this week, and your manager is not going to be happy. As you wait for the bus, you realize you have to make a decision about the car before you lose your job. You have already taken it to a repair shop and received a large estimate on the cost of repairs. Now you need to decide if you will repair the car or trade it in for a new one. This is a major decision with long-term effects, so you want to carefully consider your options. Should you invest more money in your current car? If you do, how long will the repairs last before the car needs more work? What does it cost you to operate the current car? If you buy a new, more energy-efficient car, you will make a large initial investment—more than repairing the current car—but any needed repairs in the next few years will be covered by the warranty. Also, day-to-day operating costs will be lower with the new, more efficient model. Will these cost savings be enough to make the large initial investment a wise choice? Should you repair your current car or buy a new one?

Most people have limited resources and want to make the best decision about how to use those resources. In this chapter, we'll see how companies like Smart Touch Learning and Greg's Tunes, which also have limited resources, use capital investment analysis techniques to decide which long-term capital investments to make.

# Capital Budgeting

The process of making capital investment decisions is often referred to as **capital budgeting. Capital budgeting is planning to invest in long-term assets in a way that returns the most profitability to the company.** Companies make capital investments when they acquire *capital assets*—assets used for a long period of time. Capital investments include buying new equipment, building new plants, automating production, and developing major commercial Web sites. In addition to affecting operations for many years, capital investments usually require large sums of money.

Capital investment decisions affect all businesses as they try to become more efficient by automating production and implementing new technologies. Grocers and retailers, such as **Walmart**, have invested in expensive self-scan check-out machines, while airlines, such as **Delta** and **Continental**, have invested in self check-in kiosks. These new technologies cost money. How do managers decide whether these expansions in plant and equipment will be good investments? They use capital budgeting analysis. Some companies, such as **Georgia-Pacific**, employ staff solely dedicated to capital budgeting analysis. They spend thousands of hours a year determining which capital investments to pursue.

**1** Describe the importance of capital investments and the capital budgeting process

## Four Methods of Capital Budgeting Analysis

In this chapter, we discuss four popular methods of analyzing potential capital investments:

1. Payback period

2. Rate of return (ROR)

3. Net present value (NPV)

4. Internal rate of return (IRR)

The first two methods, payback period and rate of return, are fairly quick and easy and work well for capital investments that have a relatively short life span, such as computer equipment and software that may have a useful life of only three to five years. Payback period and rate of return are also used to screen potential investments from those that are less desirable. The payback period provides management with valuable information on how fast the cash invested will be recouped. The rate of return shows the effect of the investment on the company's accrual-based income.

However, these two methods are inadequate if the capital investments have a longer life span. Why? Because these methods do not consider the time value of money. The last two methods, net present value and internal rate of return, factor in the time value of money so they are more appropriate for longer-term capital investments, such as Smart Touch's expansion to manufacturing DVDs. Management often uses a combination of methods to make final capital investment decisions.

Capital budgeting is not an exact science. Although the calculations these methods require may appear precise, remember that they are based on predictions about an uncertain future—estimates. These estimates must consider many unknown factors, such as changing consumer preferences, competition, the state of the economy, and government regulations. The further into the future the decision extends, the more likely that actual results will differ from predictions. Long-term decisions are riskier than short-term decisions.

## Focus on Cash Flows

Generally accepted accounting principles (GAAP) are based on accrual accounting, but capital budgeting focuses on cash flows. The desirability of a capital asset depends on its ability to generate net cash inflows—that is, inflows in excess of outflows—over the asset's useful life. Recall that operating income based on accrual accounting contains noncash expenses, such as depreciation expense and bad-debt expense. The capital investment's *net cash inflows*, therefore, will differ from its operating income. Of the four capital budgeting methods covered in this chapter, only the rate of return method uses accrual-based accounting income. The other three methods use the investment's projected *net cash inflows*.

What do the projected *net cash inflows* include? Cash *inflows* include future cash revenue generated from the investment, any future savings in ongoing cash operating costs resulting from the investment, and any future residual value of the asset. How are these cash inflows projected? Employees from production, marketing, materials management, accounting, and other departments provide inputs to aid managers in estimating the projected cash flows. Good estimates are a critical part of making the best decisions.

To determine the investment's *net* cash inflows, the inflows are *netted* against the investment's *future cash outflows*, such as the investment's ongoing cash operating costs and cash paid for refurbishment, repairs, and maintenance costs. The initial investment itself is also a significant cash outflow. However, in our calculations, *we will always consider the amount of the investment separately from all other cash flows related to the investment.* The projected net cash inflows are "given" in our examples and in the assignment material. In reality, much of capital investment analysis revolves around projecting these figures as accurately as possible using input from employees throughout the organization (production, marketing, and so forth, depending on the type of capital investment).

## Capital Budgeting Process

The first step in the capital budgeting process is to identify potential investments—for example, new technology and equipment that may make the company more efficient, competitive, and/or profitable. Employees, consultants, and outside sales vendors often offer capital investment proposals to management. After identifying potential capital investments, managers project the investments' net cash inflows and then analyze the investments using one or more of the four capital budgeting methods previously described. Sometimes the analysis involves a two-stage process. In the first stage, managers screen the investments using one or both of the methods that do *not* incorporate the time value of money—payback period or rate of return. These simple methods quickly weed out undesirable investments. Potential investments that "pass stage one" go on to a second stage of analysis. In the second stage, managers further analyze the potential investments using the net present value and/or internal rate of return methods. Because these methods consider the time value of money, they provide more accurate information about the potential investment's profitability.

Some companies can pursue all of the potential investments that meet or exceed their decision criteria. However, because of limited resources, other companies must engage in **capital rationing**, and choose among alternative capital investments. Based on the availability of funds, managers determine if and when to make specific capital investments. **So, capital rationing occurs when the company has limited assets available to invest in long-term assets.** For example, management may decide to wait three years to buy a certain piece of equipment because it considers other investments more important. In the intervening three years, the company will reassess whether it should still invest in the equipment. Perhaps technology has changed, and even better equipment is available. Perhaps consumer tastes have changed so the company no longer needs the equipment. Because of changing factors, long-term capital budgets are rarely set in stone.

Most companies perform **post-audits** of their capital investments. After investing in the assets, they compare the actual net cash inflows generated from the investment to the projected net cash inflows. **Post-audits help companies determine whether the investments are going as planned and deserve continued support, or whether they should abandon the project and sell the assets.** Managers also use feedback from post-audits to better estimate net cash flow projections for future projects. If managers expect routine post-audits, they will more likely submit realistic net cash flow estimates with their capital investment proposals.

# Using Payback Period and Rate of Return to Make Capital Investment Decisions

Next, we'll review two capital investment decision tools that companies use to initially screen capital investment choices—payback period and rate of return. When we review formulas, we'll also show you the Excel formulas with an "X" symbol. Note that these Excel formulas are provided as an alternate tool only.

**2** Use the payback period and rate of return methods to make capital investment decisions

## Payback Period

**Payback** is the length of time it takes to recover, in net cash inflows, the cost of the capital outlay. The payback model measures how quickly managers expect to recover their investment dollars. All else being equal, the shorter the payback period, the more attractive the asset. Computing the payback period depends on whether net cash inflows are equal each year, or whether they differ over time. We consider each in turn.

### Payback with Equal Annual Net Cash Inflows

Smart Touch is considering investing $240,000 in hardware and software to upgrade its Web site to provide a business-to-business (B2B) portal. Employees throughout the company will use the B2B portal to access company-approved suppliers. Smart Touch expects the portal to save $60,000 a year for each of the six years of its useful life. The savings will arise from reducing the number of purchasing personnel the company employs and from lower prices on the goods and services purchased. Net cash inflows arise from an increase in revenues, a decrease in expenses, or both. In Smart Touch's case, the net cash inflows result from lower expenses.

When net cash inflows are equal each year, managers compute the payback period as shown in Exhibit 21-1.

**EXHIBIT 21-1** | **Calculating Payback Period—Equal Cash Flows**

$$\text{Payback period} = \frac{\text{Amount invested}}{\text{Expected annual net cash inflow}}$$

Smart Touch computes the investment's payback period as follows:

$$\text{Payback period for B2B portal} = \frac{\$240,000}{\$60,000} = 4 \text{ years}$$

=SUM(240,000/60,000)

Exhibit 21-2 verifies that Smart Touch expects to recoup the $240,000 investment in the B2B portal by the end of year 4, when the accumulated net cash inflows total $240,000.

Smart Touch is also considering investing $240,000 to upgrade its Web site. The company expects the upgraded Web site to generate $80,000 in net cash inflows each year of its three-year life. The payback period is computed as follows:

$$\text{Payback period for Web site development} = \frac{\$240,000}{\$80,000} = 3 \text{ years}$$

=SUM(240,000/80,000)

Exhibit 21-2 verifies that Smart Touch will recoup the $240,000 investment for the Web site upgrade by the end of year 3, when the accumulated net cash inflows total $240,000.

**EXHIBIT 21-2** | **Payback—Equal Annual Net Cash Inflows**

| Net Cash Outflows | | Net Cash Inflows | | | |
|---|---|---|---|---|---|
| | | B2B Portal | | Web Site Upgrade | |
| Year | Amount Invested | Annual | Accumulated | Annual | Accumulated |
| 0 | 240,000 | — | — | — | — |
| 1 | — | $60,000 | $ 60,000 | $80,000 | $ 80,000 |
| 2 | — | 60,000 | 120,000 | 80,000 | 160,000 |
| 3 | — | 60,000 | 180,000 | 80,000 | 240,000 |
| 4 | — | 60,000 | 240,000 | | |
| 5 | — | 60,000 | 300,000 | | |
| 6 | — | 60,000 | 360,000 | | |

## Payback with Unequal Net Cash Inflows

The payback equation in Exhibit 21-1 only works when net cash inflows are the same each period. When periodic cash flows are unequal, you must total net cash inflows until the amount invested is recovered. Assume that Smart Touch is considering an alternate investment, the Z80 portal. The Z80 portal differs from the B2B portal and the Web site in two respects: (1) It has *unequal* net cash inflows during its life and (2) it has a $30,000 residual value at the end of its life. The Z80 portal will generate net cash inflows of $100,000 in year 1, $80,000 in year 2, $50,000 each year in years 3 and 4, $40,000 each in years 5 and 6, and $30,000 in residual value when it is sold at the end of its life. Exhibit 21-3 shows the payback schedule for these unequal annual net cash inflows.

| EXHIBIT 21-3 | Payback: Unequal Annual Net Cash Inflows |
|---|---|

| Net Cash Outflows Z80 Portal | | Net Cash Inflows Z80 Portal | | |
|---|---|---|---|---|
| Year | Amount Invested | Annual | | Accumulated |
| 0 | $240,000 | — | | — |
| 1 | — | 100,000 | *Useful Life* | $100,000 |
| 2 | — | 80,000 | | 180,000 |
| 3 | — | 50,000 | | 230,000 |
| 4 | — | 50,000 | | 280,000 |
| 5 | — | 40,000 | | 320,000 |
| 6 | — | 40,000 | | 360,000 |
| 6–Residual Value | | 30,000 | ↓ | 390,000 |

By the end of year 3, the company has recovered $230,000 of the $240,000 initially invested, so it is only $10,000 short of payback. Because the expected net cash inflow in year 4 is $50,000, by the end of year 4 the company will have recovered *more* than the initial investment. Therefore, the payback period is somewhere between three and four years. Assuming that the cash flow occurs evenly throughout the fourth year, the payback period is calculated as follows:

$$\text{Payback} = 3 \text{ years} + \frac{\$10,000 \text{ (amount needed to complete recovery in year 4)}}{\$50,000 \text{ (net cash inflow in year 4)}}$$

$$= 3.2 \text{ years}$$

## Criticism of the Payback Period Method

A major criticism of the payback period method is that it focuses only on time, not on profitability. The payback period considers only those cash flows that occur *during* the payback period. This method ignores any cash flows that occur *after* that period. For example, Exhibit 21-2 shows that the B2B portal will continue to generate net cash inflows for two years after its payback period. These additional net cash inflows amount to $120,000 ($60,000 × 2 years), yet the payback period method ignores this extra cash. A similar situation occurs with the Z80 portal. As shown in Exhibit 21-3, the Z80 portal will provide an additional $150,000 of net cash inflows, including residual value, after its payback period of 3.2 years ($390,000 total accumulated cash inflows – $240,000 amount invested). However, the Web site's useful life, as shown in Exhibit 21-2, is the *same* as its payback period (three years). No cash flows are ignored, yet the Web site will merely cover its cost and provide no profit. Because this is the case, the company has no financial reason to invest in the Web site.

Exhibit 21-4 compares the payback period of the three investments. As the exhibit illustrates, the payback period method does not consider the asset's profitability. The method only tells management how quickly it will recover the cash. Even though the Web site has the shortest payback period, both the B2B portal and the Z80 portal are better investments because they provide profit. The key point is that the investment with the shortest payback period is best *only if all other factors are the same*. Therefore, managers usually use the payback period method as a screening device to "weed out" investments that will take too long to recoup. They rarely use payback period as the sole method for deciding whether to invest in the asset.

When using the payback period method, managers are guided by following decision rule:

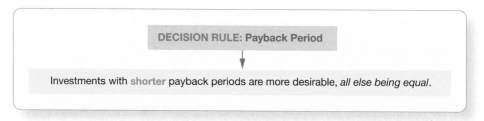

> **DECISION RULE: Payback Period**
>
> ↓
>
> Investments with shorter payback periods are more desirable, *all else being equal*.

EXHIBIT 21-4 | **Comparing Payback Periods Between Investments**

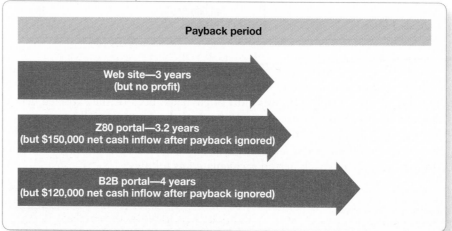

**Payback period**

Web site—3 years
(but no profit)

Z80 portal—3.2 years
(but $150,000 net cash inflow after payback ignored)

B2B portal—4 years
(but $120,000 net cash inflow after payback ignored)

## Stop & Think...

Let's say you loan $50 to a friend today (a Friday). The friend says he will pay you $25 next Friday when he gets paid and another $25 the following Friday. What is your payback period? The friend will pay you back in 2 weeks.

## Rate of Return (ROR)

Companies are in business to earn profits. One measure of profitability is the **rate of return (ROR)** on an asset. The formula for calculating ROR is shown in Exhibit 21-5.

EXHIBIT 21-5 | **Calculating Rate of Return**

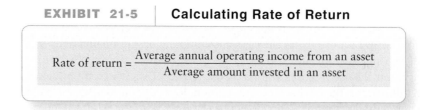

$$\text{Rate of return} = \frac{\text{Average annual operating income from an asset}}{\text{Average amount invested in an asset}}$$

The ROR focuses on the *operating income, not the net cash inflow,* an asset generates. **The ROR measures the *average* accounting rate of return over the asset's entire life.** Let's first consider investments with no residual value.

Recall the B2B portal, which costs $240,000, has equal annual net cash inflows of $60,000, a six-year useful life, and no (zero) residual value.

Let's look at the average annual operating income in the numerator first. The average annual operating income of an asset is simply the asset's total operating income over the course of its operating life divided by its lifespan (number of years).

Operating income is based on *accrual accounting*. Therefore, any noncash expenses, such as depreciation expense, must be subtracted from the asset's net cash inflows to arrive at its operating income. Exhibit 21-6 displays the formula for calculating average annual operating income.

| EXHIBIT 21-6 | Calculating Average Annual Operating Income from Asset | |
|---|---|---|
| Total net cash inflows during operating life of the asset | | A |
| Less: Total depreciation during operating life of the asset (Cost – Residual Value) | | B |
| Total operating income during operating life | | (A – B) |
| Divide by: Asset's operating life in years | | C |
| Average annual operating income from asset | | [(A – B)/C] |

The B2B portal's average annual operating income is as follows:

| | |
|---|---|
| Total net cash inflows during operating life of the asset ($60,000 × 6 years) | $ 360,000 |
| Less: Total depreciation during operating life of asset (cost – any salvage value) | 240,000 |
| Total operating income during operating life of asset | $ 120,000 |
| Divide by: Asset's operating life (in years) | ÷ 6 years |
| Average annual operating income from asset | $  20,000 |

Now let's look at the denominator of the ROR equation. The *average* amount invested in an asset is its *net book value* at the beginning of the asset's useful life plus the net book value at the end of the asset's useful life divided by 2. Another way to say that is the asset's cost plus the asset's residual value divided by 2. The net book value of the asset decreases each year because of the annual depreciation shown in Exhibit 21-6.

Because the B2B portal does not have a residual value, the *average* amount invested is $120,000 [($240,000 cost + $0 residual value) ÷ 2].

We calculate the B2B's ROR as follows:

$$\text{Rate of return} = \frac{\$20,000}{(\$240,000 + \$0)/2} = \frac{\$20,000}{\$120,000} = 0.167 = 16.70\%$$

=SUM(20000/((240000+0)/2))

Now consider the Z80 portal (data from Exhibit 21-3). Recall that the Z80 portal differed from the B2B portal only in that it had unequal net cash inflows during its life and a $30,000 residual value at the end of its life. Its average annual operating income is calculated as follows:

| | |
|---|---|
| Total net cash inflows *during* operating life of asset (does not include the residual value at end of life) (Year 1 + Year 2, etc.) | $ 360,000 |
| Less: Total depreciation during operating life of asset (cost – any salvage value) ($240,000 cost – $30,000 residual value) | 210,000 |
| Total operating income during operating life of asset | $ 150,000 |
| Divide by: Asset's operating life (in years) | ÷ 6 years |
| Average annual operating income from asset | $  25,000 |

Notice that the Z80 portal's average annual operating income of $25,000 is higher than the B2B portal's operating income of $20,000. Since the Z80 asset has a residual value at the end of its life, less depreciation is expensed each year, leading to a higher average annual operating income.

Now let's calculate the denominator of the ROR equation, the average amount invested in the asset. For the Z80, the average asset investment is as follows:

$$\text{Average amount invested} = (\text{Amount invested in asset} + \text{Residual value})/2$$
$$\$135,000 \quad = \quad (\$240,000 \quad + \quad \$30,000) \quad /2$$

We calculate the Z80's ROR as follows:

$$\text{Rate of return} = \frac{\$25,000}{(\$240,000 + \$30,000)/2} = \frac{\$25,000}{\$135,000} = 0.185 = 18.5\%$$

Companies that use the ROR model set a minimum required rate of return. If Smart Touch requires a ROR of at least 20%, then its managers would not approve an investment in the B2B portal or the Z80 portal because the ROR for both investments is less than 20%.

The decision rule is as follows:

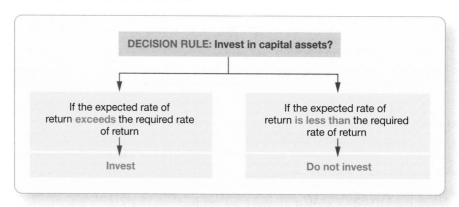

**DECISION RULE: Invest in capital assets?**

| If the expected rate of return **exceeds** the required rate of return | If the expected rate of return **is less than** the required rate of return |
| --- | --- |
| Invest | Do not invest |

Next, let's take some time to review the Decision Guidelines for capital budgeting on the following page.

---

=SUM(25000/((240000+30000)/2))

**Key Takeaway**

The payback period focuses on the time it takes for the company to recoup its cash investment but ignores all cash flows occurring after the payback period. Because it ignores any additional cash flows (including any residual value), the method does not consider the profitability of the project. The ROR, however, measures the profitability of the asset over its entire life using accrual accounting figures. It is the only method that uses accrual accounting rather than net cash inflows in its computations. The payback period and ROR methods are simple and quick to compute so managers often use them to screen out undesirable investments. However, both methods ignore the time value of money.

# Decision Guidelines 21-1

## CAPITAL BUDGETING

**Amazon.com** started as a virtual retailer. It held no inventory. Instead, it bought books and CDs only as needed to fill customer orders. As the company grew, its managers decided to invest in their own warehouse facilities. Why? Owning warehouse facilities allows **Amazon** to save money by buying in bulk. Also, shipping all items in the customer's order in one package, from one location, saves shipping costs. Here are some of the guidelines **Amazon's** managers used as they made the major capital budgeting decision to invest in building warehouses.

| Decision | Guidelines |
|---|---|
| • Why is this decision important? | Capital budgeting decisions typically require large investments and affect operations for years to come. |
| • What method shows us how soon we will recoup our cash investment? | The payback period method shows managers how quickly they will recoup their investment. This method highlights investments that are too risky due to long payback periods. However, it does not reveal any information about the investment's profitability. |
| • Does any method consider the impact of the investment on accrual accounting income? | The rate of return (ROR) is the only capital budgeting method that shows how the investment will affect accrual accounting income, which is important to financial statement users. All other methods of capital investment analysis focus on the investment's net cash inflows. |
| • How do we compute the payback period if cash flows are *equal*? | $$\text{Payback period} = \frac{\text{Amount invested}}{\text{Expected annual net cash inflow}}$$ |
| • How do we compute the payback period if cash flows are *unequal*? | Accumulate net cash inflows until the amount invested is recovered. |
| • How do we compute the ROR? | $$\frac{\text{Rate}}{\text{of return}} = \frac{\text{Average annual operating income from an asset}}{\text{Average amount invested in an asset}}$$ |

# Summary Problem 21-1

Dyno-max is considering buying a new water treatment system for its Austin, Texas, plant. The company screens its potential capital investments using the payback period and rate of return methods. If a potential investment has a payback period of less than four years and a minimum 12% rate of return, it will be considered further. The data for the water treatment system follow:

| | |
|---|---|
| Cost of water treatment system..................................................... | $48,000 |
| Estimated residual value................................................................ | $ 0 |
| Estimated annual net cash inflow (each year for 5 years) from anticipated environmental cleanup savings ............................... | $13,000 |
| Estimated useful life ..................................................................... | 5 years |

## Requirements

1. Compute the water treatment system's payback period.
2. Compute the water treatment system's ROR.
3. Should Dyno-max turn down this investment proposal or consider it further?

## Solution

### Requirement 1

$$\text{Payback period} = \frac{\text{Amount invested}}{\text{Expected annual net cash inflow}} = \frac{\$48,000}{\$13,000} = 3.7 \text{ years (rounded)}$$

### Requirement 2

$$\text{Rate of return} = \frac{\text{Average annual operating income from an asset}}{\text{Average amount invested in an asset}}$$

$$= \frac{\$3,400^*}{(\$48,000 + \$0)/2}$$

$$= \frac{\$3,400}{\$24,000}$$

$$= 0.142 \text{ (rounded)}$$

$$= 14.2\%$$

| | |
|---|---|
| *Total net cash inflows during life ($13,000 × 5 years) | $ 65,000 |
| Less: total depreciation during life ............................. | 48,000 |
| Total operating income during life ........................... | $ 17,000 |
| Divided by: life of the asset ....................................... | ÷ 5 years |
| Average annual operating income ........................... | $ 3,400 |

### Requirement 3

The water treatment system proposal passes both initial screening tests. The payback period is slightly less than four years, and the rate of return is higher than 12%. Dyno-max should further analyze the proposal using a method that incorporates the time value of money.

# A Review of the Time Value of Money

A dollar received today is worth more than a dollar to be received in the future. Why? Because you can invest today's dollar and earn extra income so you'll have more money next year. The fact that invested money earns income over time is called the *time value of money*, and this explains why we would prefer to receive cash sooner rather than later. The time value of money means that the timing of capital investments' net cash inflows is important. Two methods of capital investment analysis incorporate the time value of money: the net present value (NPV) and internal rate of return (IRR). This section reviews time value of money to make sure you have a firm foundation for discussing these two methods.

**3** Use the time value of money to compute the present and future values of single lump sums and annuities

## Factors Affecting the Time Value of Money

The time value of money depends on several key factors:

1.  The principal amount ($p$)
2.  The number of periods ($n$)
3.  The interest rate ($i$)

The principal ($p$) refers to the amount of the investment or borrowing. Because this chapter deals with capital investments, we will primarily discuss the principal in terms of investments. However, the same concepts apply to borrowings (which we covered in Chapter 8). We state the principal as either a single lump sum or an annuity. For example, if you win the lottery, you have the choice of receiving all the winnings now (a single lump sum) or receiving a series of equal payments for a period of time in the future (an annuity). An **annuity** is a stream of *equal installments* made at *equal time intervals under the same interest rate.*[1] **For example, $100 a month for 12 months at 5% is an annuity.**

The number of periods ($n$) is the length of time from the beginning of the investment until termination. All else being equal, the shorter the investment period, the lower the total amount of interest earned. If you withdraw your savings after four years rather than five years, you will earn less interest. In this chapter, the number of periods is stated in years.[2]

The interest rate ($i$) is the annual percentage earned on the investment. **Simple interest** means that interest is calculated *only* on the principal amount. **Compound interest** means that interest is calculated on the principal *and* on all previously earned interest. *Compound interest assumes that all interest earned will remain invested and earn additional interest at the same interest rate.* Exhibit 21-7 compares simple interest (6%) on a five-year, $10,000 CD with interest compounded yearly (rounded to the nearest dollar). As you can see, the amount of compound interest earned yearly grows as the base on which it is calculated (principal plus cumulative interest to date) grows. Over the life of this investment, the total amount of compound interest is more than the total amount of simple interest. Most investments yield compound interest so we assume compound interest, rather than simple interest, for the rest of this chapter.

Fortunately, time value calculations involving compound interest do not have to be as tedious as those shown in Exhibit 21-7. Formulas and tables (or proper use of business calculators programmed with these formulas, or spreadsheet software such as Microsoft Excel) simplify the calculations. In the next sections, we will discuss how to use these tools to perform time value calculations.

---

[1] An *ordinary annuity* is an annuity in which the installments occur at the *end* of each period. An *annuity due* is an annuity in which the installments occur at the beginning of each period. Throughout this chapter, we use ordinary annuities because they are better suited to capital budgeting cash flow assumptions.
[2] The number of periods can also be stated in days, months, or quarters. If so, the interest rate needs to be adjusted to reflect the number of time periods in the year.

| | | | | **Simple Versus Compound Interest for a** |
|---|---|---|---|---|
| | **EXHIBIT 21-7** | | | **Principal Amount of $10,000, at 6%, over 5 Years** |

| Year | Simple Interest Calculation | Simple Interest | Compound Interest Calculation | Compound Interest |
|---|---|---|---|---|
| 1 | $10,000 × 6% = | $ 600 | $10,000 × 6% = | $ 600 |
| 2 | $10,000 × 6% = | 600 | ($10,000 + 600) × 6% = | 636 |
| 3 | $10,000 × 6% = | 600 | ($10,000 + 600 + 636) × 6% = | 674 |
| 4 | $10,000 × 6% = | 600 | ($10,000 + 600 + 636 + 674) × 6% = | 715 |
| 5 | $10,000 × 6% = | 600 | ($10,000 + 600 + 636 + 674 + 715) × 6% = | 758 |
| | Total interest | $3,000 | Total interest | $3,383 |

# Future Values and Present Values: Points Along the Time Line

Consider the time line in Exhibit 21-8. The future value or present value of an investment simply refers to the value of an investment at different points in time.

| | **Present Value and Future Value** |
|---|---|
| **EXHIBIT 21-8** | **Along the Time Continuum** |

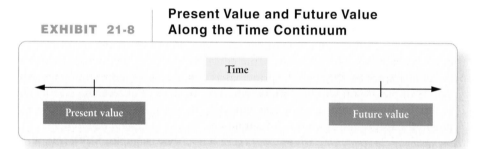

We can calculate the future value or the present value of any investment by knowing (or assuming) information about the three factors we listed earlier: (1) the principal amount, (2) the period of time, and (3) the interest rate. For example, in Exhibit 21-7, we calculated the interest that would be earned on (1) a $10,000 principal, (2) invested for five years, (3) at 6% interest. The future value of the investment is simply its worth at the end of the five-year time frame—the original principal *plus* the interest earned. In our example, the future value of the investment is as follows:

$$\text{Future value} = \text{Principal} + \text{Interest earned}$$
$$= \$10,000 + \$3,383$$
$$= \$13,383$$

If we invest $10,000 *today*, its *present value* is simply $10,000. So another way of stating the future value is as follows:

$$\text{Future value} = \text{Present value} + \text{Interest earned}$$

We can rearrange the equation as follows:

$$\text{Present value} = \text{Future value} - \text{Interest earned}$$
$$\$10,000 = \$13,383 - \$3,383$$

The only difference between present value and future value is the amount of interest that is earned in the intervening time span.

# Future Value and Present Value Factors

Calculating each period's compound interest, as we did in Exhibit 21-7, and then adding it to the present value to determine the future value (or subtracting it from the future value to determine the present value) is tedious. Fortunately, mathematical formulas have been developed that specify future values and present values for unlimited combinations of interest rates ($i$) and time periods ($n$). Separate formulas exist for single lump-sum investments and annuities.

These formulas are programmed into most business calculators so that the user only needs to correctly enter the principal amount, interest rate, and number of time periods to find present or future values. These formulas are also programmed into spreadsheet functions in Microsoft Excel. In this chapter, we will use tables and show the Excel formulas to demonstrate these calculations. Note that since the table values are rounded, your Excel results will differ slightly. These tables contain the results of the formulas for various interest rate and time period combinations.

The formulas and resulting tables are shown in Appendix B at the end of this book:

1. Present Value of $1 (Appendix B, Table B-1)—*used to calculate the value today of one future amount (a lump sum)*

2. Present Value of Annuity of $1 (Appendix B, Table B-2)—*used to calculate the value today of a series of equal future amounts (annuities)*

3. Future Value of $1 (Appendix B, Table B-3)—*used to calculate a value at a future date of one present amount (lump sum)*

4. Future Value of Annuity of $1 (Appendix B, Table B-4)—*used to calculate a value at a future date of a series of equal amounts (annuities)*

Take a moment to look at these tables because we are going to use them throughout the rest of the chapter. Note that the columns are interest rates ($i$) and the rows are periods ($n$).

The data in each table, known as future value factors (FV factors) and present value factors (PV factors), are for an investment (or loan) of $1. To find the future value of an amount other than $1, you simply multiply the FV factor by the present amount. To find the present value of an amount other than $1, you multiply the PV factor by the future amount.

The annuity tables are derived from the lump-sum tables. For example, the Annuity PV factors (in the Present Value of Annuity of $1 table) are the *sums* of the PV factors found in the Present Value of $1 tables for a given number of time periods. The annuity tables allow us to perform "one-step" calculations rather than separately computing the present value of each annual cash installment and then summing the individual present values.

## Calculating Future Values of Single Sums and Annuities Using FV Factors

Let's go back to our $10,000 lump-sum investment. If we want to know the future value of the investment five years from now at an interest rate of 6%, we determine the FV factor from the table labeled Future Value of $1 (Appendix B, Table B-3). We use this table for lump-sum amounts. We look down the 6% column, and across the 5 periods row, and find the future value factor is 1.338. We finish our calculations as follows:

=FV(.06,5,,-10000)

Future value = Principal amount × (FV factor for $i = 6\%$, $n = 5$)

             = $10,000 × (1.338)

             = $13,380

---

Excel note: Excel results will differ slightly than results calculated using the tables because all table values are rounded to three decimal places.

This figure materially agrees with our earlier calculation of the investment's future value of $13,383 in Exhibit 21-7. (The difference of $3 is due to two facts: (1) The tables round the FV and PV factors to three decimal places and (2) we rounded our earlier yearly interest calculations in Exhibit 21-7 to the nearest dollar.)

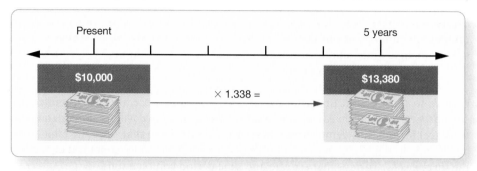

Let's also consider our alternative investment strategy, investing $2,000 at the end of each year for five years. The procedure for calculating the future value of an *annuity* is quite similar to calculating the future value of a lump-sum amount. This time, we use the Future Value of Annuity of $1 table (Appendix B, Table B-4). Assuming 6% interest, we once again look down the 6% column. Because we will be making five annual installments, we look across the row marked 5 periods. The Annuity FV factor is 5.637. We finish the calculation as follows:

=FV(.06,5,-2000)

Future value = Amount of each cash installment × (Annuity FV factor for $i$ = 6%, $n$ = 5)

= $2,000 × (5.637)

= $11,274

This is considerably less than the future value of $13,380 of the lump sum of $10,000, even though we have invested $10,000 out-of-pocket either way. The difference is that we didn't invest $10,000 for the *entire* five years—we invested $2,000 each year. So, we earned less interest.

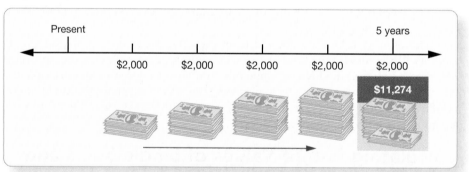

## Calculating Present Values of Single Sums and Annuities Using PV Factors

The process for calculating present values—often called discounting cash flows—is similar to the process for calculating future values. The difference is the point in time at which you are assessing the investment's worth. Rather than determining its value at a future date, you are determining its value at an earlier point in time (today). For our example, assume you have just won the lottery after purchasing one $5 lottery ticket. The state offers you the following three payout options for your after-tax prize money:

Option #1: $1,000,000 now

Option #2: $150,000 at the end of each year for the next 10 years

Option #3: $2,000,000 10 years from now

Which alternative should you take? You might be tempted to wait 10 years to "double" your winnings. You may be tempted to take the money now and spend it. However, assume you plan to prudently invest all money received—no matter when you receive it—so that you have financial flexibility in the future (for example, for buying a house, retiring early, or taking exotic vacations). How can you choose among the three payment alternatives, when the total amount of each option varies ($1,000,000 versus $1,500,000 versus $2,000,000) and the timing of the cash flows varies (now versus some each year versus later)? Comparing these three options is like comparing apples to oranges—we just cannot do it—unless we find some common basis for comparison. Our common basis for comparison will be the prize-money's worth at a certain point in time—namely, today. In other words, if we convert each payment option to its *present value*, we can compare apples to apples.

We already know the principal amount and timing of each payment option, so the only assumption we will have to make is the interest rate. The interest rate will vary, depending on the amount of risk you are willing to take with your investment. Riskier investments (such as stock investments) command higher interest rates; safer investments (such as FDIC-insured bank deposits) yield lower interest rates. Let's say that after investigating possible investment alternatives, you choose an investment contract with an 8% annual return. We already know that the present value of Option #1 is $1,000,000 because we would receive that $1,000,000 today. Let's convert the other two payment options to their present values so that we can compare them. We will need to use the Present Value of Annuity of $1 table (Appendix B, Table B-2) to convert payment Option #2 (since it is an annuity) and the Present Value of $1 table (Appendix B, Table B-1) to convert payment Option #3 (since it is a single-lump-sum). To obtain the PV factors, we will look down the 8% column and across the 10 period row. Then, we finish the calculations as follows:

**Option #2**

Present value = Amount of each cash installment × (Annuity PV factor for $i$ = 8%, $n$ = 10)
Present value = $150,000 × (6.710)
Present value = $1,006,500

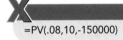

**Option #3**

Present value = Principal amount × (PV factor for $i$ = 8%, $n$ = 10)
Present value = $2,000,000 × (0.463)
Present value = $926,000

Exhibit 21-9 shows that we have converted each payout option to a common basis—its worth *today*—so we can make a valid comparison among the options. Based on this comparison, we should choose Option #2 because its worth, in today's dollars, is the highest of the three options.

**EXHIBIT 21-9** | **Present Value of Lottery Payout Options**

| Payment Options | Present Value of Lottery Payout ($i$ = 8%, $n$ = 10) |
|---|---|
| Option #1 | $1,000,000 |
| Option #2 | $1,006,500 |
| Option #3 | $ 926,000 |

Now that you have reviewed time value of money concepts, we will discuss the two capital budgeting methods that incorporate the time value of money: net present value (NPV) and internal rate of return (IRR).

**Key Takeaway**

Invested money earns income over time. This is called the time value of money, and it explains why we would prefer to receive cash sooner rather than later. The time value of money means that the timing of capital investments' net cash inflows is important. The cash inflows and outflows are either single amounts or annuities. An annuity is equal cash flows over equal time periods at the same interest rate. Time value of money tables in Appendix B help us to adjust the cash flows to the same time period (i.e., today or the present value, or a future date or the future value).

# Using Discounted Cash Flow Models to Make Capital Investment Decisions

**4** Use discounted cash flow models to make capital investment decisions

Neither the payback period nor the ROR recognizes the time value of money. That is, these models fail to consider the *timing* of the net cash inflows an asset generates. *Discounted cash flow models*—the NPV and the IRR—overcome this weakness. These models incorporate compound interest by assuming that companies will reinvest future cash flows when they are received. Over 85% of large industrial firms in the United States use discounted cash-flow methods to make capital investment decisions. Companies that provide services also use these models.

The NPV and IRR methods rely on present value calculations to *compare* the amount of the investment (the investment's initial cost) with its expected net cash inflows. Recall that an investment's *net cash inflows* includes all *future* cash flows related to the investment, such as future increased sales or cost savings netted against the investment's cash operating costs. Because the cash outflow for the investment occurs *now*, but the net cash inflows from the investment occur in the *future*, companies can only make valid "apple-to-apple" comparisons if they convert the cash flows to the *same point in time*—namely the present value. Companies use the present value to make the comparison (rather than the future value) because the investment's initial cost is already stated at its present value.[3]

If the present value of the investment's net cash inflows exceeds the initial cost of the investment, that's a good investment. In terms of our earlier lottery example, the lottery ticket turned out to be a "good investment" because the present value of its net cash inflows (the present value of the lottery payout under *any* of the three payout options) exceeded the cost of the investment (the lottery ticket cost $5 to purchase). Let's begin our discussion by taking a closer look at the NPV method.

## Net Present Value (NPV)

Greg's Tunes is considering producing CD players and digital video recorders (DVRs). The products require different specialized machines that each cost $1,000,000. Each machine has a five-year life and zero residual value. The two products have different patterns of predicted net cash inflows, as shown in Exhibit 21-10.

**EXHIBIT 21-10** | **Expected Cash Inflows for Two Projects**

| | Annual Net Cash Inflows | |
| --- | --- | --- |
| Year | CD Players | DVRs |
| 1 | $ 305,450 | $ 500,000 |
| 2 | $ 305,450 | 350,000 |
| 3 | $ 305,450 | 300,000 |
| 4 | $ 305,450 | 250,000 |
| 5 | $ 305,450 | 40,000 |
| Total | $1,527,250 | $1,440,000 |

The CD-player project generates more net cash inflows, but the DVR project brings in cash sooner. To decide how attractive each investment is, we find its **net present value (NPV)**. The NPV is the *net difference* between the present value of the investment's net cash inflows and the investment's cost (cash outflows). We *discount* the net cash inflows—just as we did in the lottery example—using Greg's minimum desired rate of

---

[3] If the investment is to be purchased through lease payments, rather than a current cash outlay, we would still use the current cash price of the investment as its initial cost. If no current cash price is available, we would discount the future lease payments back to their present value to estimate the investment's current cash price.

return. This rate is called the **discount rate** because it is the interest rate used for the present value calculations. **The discount rate is the interest rate that discounts or reduces future amounts to their lesser value in the present (today).** It is also called the **required rate of return** or **hurdle rate** because the investment must meet or exceed this rate to be acceptable. **To help you understand what a hurdle rate is, visualize a runner jumping over a hurdle at a track—the hurdle is the minimum height the runner must jump.** The discount rate depends on the riskiness of investments. The higher the risk, the higher the discount (interest) rate. Greg's discount rate for these investments is 14%.

We then compare the present value of the net cash inflows to the investment's initial cost to decide which projects meet or exceed management's minimum desired rate of return. In other words, management is deciding whether the $1,000,000 option is worth more (because the company would give it up now to invest in the project) or whether the project's future net cash inflows are worth more. Management can only make a valid comparison between the two sums of money by comparing them at the *same* point in time—namely, at their present value.

## NPV with Equal Periodic Net Cash Inflows (Annuity)

Greg's expects the CD-player project to generate $305,450 of net cash inflows each year for five years. Because these cash flows are equal in amount, and occur every year, they are an annuity. Therefore, we use the Present Value of Annuity of $1 table (Appendix B, Table B-2) to find the appropriate Annuity PV factor for $i = 14\%, n = 5$.

The present value of the net cash inflows from Greg's CD-player project is as follows:

> Present value = Amount of each cash net cash inflow × (Annuity PV factor for
> $i = 14\%, n = 5$)
> = $305,450 × (3.433)
> = $1,048,610

=NPV(.14,305450,305450,
305450,305450,305450)

or

=PV(.14,5,-305450)
Then subtract the $1,000,000
initial investment

Next, we simply subtract the investment's initial cost of $1,000,000 (cash outflows) from the present value of the net cash inflows of $1,048,610. The difference of $48,610 is the *net* present value (NPV), as shown in Exhibit 21-11.

**EXHIBIT 21-11**

### NPV of Equal Net Cash Inflows—CD-Player Project

| Time | | Annuity PV Factor (i = 14%, n = 5) | Net Cash Inflow | Present Value |
|---|---|---|---|---|
| 1–5 yrs | Present value of annuity of equal annual net cash inflows for 5 years at 14% | 3.433* × | $305,450 = | $ 1,048,610 |
| 0 | Investment | | | (1,000,000) |
| | Net present value of the CD-player project | | | $ 48,610 |

*Annuity PV Factor is found in Appendix B, Table B-2.

A *positive* NPV means that the project earns *more* than the required rate of return. A negative NPV means that the project earns less than the required rate of return. This leads to the following decision rule:

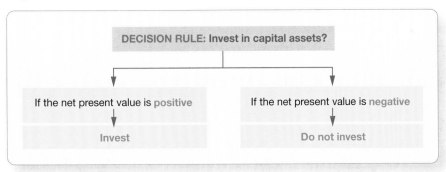

DECISION RULE: Invest in capital assets?

If the net present value is positive → Invest

If the net present value is negative → Do not invest

In Greg's Tunes' case, the CD-player project is an attractive investment. The $48,610 positive NPV means that the CD-player project earns *more than* Greg's Tunes' 14% target rate of return.

Another way managers can use present value analysis is to start the capital budgeting process by computing the total present value of the net cash inflows from the project to determine the *maximum* the company can invest in the project and still earn the target rate of return. For Greg's, the present value of the net cash inflows is $1,048,610. This means that Greg's Tunes can invest a maximum of $1,048,610 and still earn the 14% target rate of return (i.e., if Greg's invests $1,048,610, NPV will be 0 and return will be exactly 14%). Because Greg's Tunes' managers believe they can undertake the project for $1,000,000, the project is an attractive investment.

## NPV with Unequal Periodic Net Cash Inflows

In contrast to the CD-player project, the net cash inflows of the DVR project are unequal—$500,000 in year 1, $350,000 in year 2, and so on. Because these amounts vary by year, Greg's Tunes' managers *cannot* use the annuity table to compute the present value of the DVR project. They must compute the present value of each individual year's net cash inflows *separately (as separate lump sums received in different years)*, using the Present Value of $1 table (Appendix B, Table B-1). Exhibit 21-12 shows that the $500,000 net cash inflow received in year 1 is discounted using a PV factor of $i = 14\%, n = 1$, while the $350,000 net cash inflow received in year 2 is discounted using a PV factor of $i = 14\%, n = 2$, and so forth. After separately discounting each of the five year's net cash inflows, we add each result to find that the *total* present value of the DVR project's net cash inflows is $1,078,910. Finally, we subtract the investment's cost of $1,000,000 (cash outflows) to arrive at the DVR project's NPV: $78,910.

=NPV(.14,500000,350000,
300000,250000,40000)

Then subtract the $1,000,000
initial investment

**EXHIBIT 21-12** | **NPV with Unequal Net Cash Inflows—DVR Project**

| Year | | PV Factor ($i = 14\%$) | | Net Cash Inflow | | Present Value |
|---|---|---|---|---|---|---|
| | Present value of each year's net cash inflows discounted at 14% | | | | | |
| 1 | Year 1 ($n = 1$) | 0.877† | × | $500,000 | = | $ 438,500 |
| 2 | Year 2 ($n = 2$) | 0.769 | × | 350,000 | = | 269,150 |
| 3 | Year 3 ($n = 3$) | 0.675 | × | 300,000 | = | 202,500 |
| 4 | Year 4 ($n = 4$) | 0.592 | × | 250,000 | = | 148,000 |
| 5 | Year 5 ($n = 5$) | 0.519 | × | 40,000 | = | 20,760 |
| | Total present value of net cash inflows | | | | | $ 1,078,910 |
| 0 | Investment | | | | | (1,000,000) |
| | Net present value of the DVR project | | | | | $ 78,910 |

†PV Factors are found in Appendix B, Table B-1.

Because the NPV is positive, Greg's Tunes expects the DVR project to earn more than the 14% target rate of return, making this an attractive investment.

## Stop & Think...

Assume you win the lottery today and you have the choice of taking $1,000,000 today or $120,000 a year for the next 10 years. If you think that you can earn 6%, which option should you take? That is the key to NPV. We must find the NPV of the $120,000 annuity at 6% (PV factor is 7.360) to compare. The value of the $120,000 annuity today is $883,200, which is less than the $1,000,000. So, you should take the $1,000,000 payout today rather than the $120,000 annuity.

## Capital Rationing and the Profitability Index

Exhibits 21-11 and 21-12 show that both the CD player and DVR projects have positive NPVs. Therefore, both are attractive investments. Because resources are limited, companies are not always able to invest in all capital assets that meet their investment criteria. As mentioned earlier, this is called *capital rationing*. For example, Greg's may not have the funds to invest in both the DVR and CD-player projects at this time. In this case, Greg's should choose the DVR project because it yields a higher NPV. The DVR project should earn an additional $78,910 beyond the 14% required rate of return, while the CD-player project returns an additional $48,610.

This example illustrates an important point. The CD-player project promises more *total* net cash inflows. But the *timing* of the DVR cash flows—loaded near the beginning of the project—gives the DVR investment a higher NPV. The DVR project is more attractive because of the time value of money. Its dollars, which are received sooner, are worth more now than the more-distant dollars of the CD-player project.

If Greg's had to choose between the CD and DVR project, the company would choose the DVR project because it yields a higher NPV ($78,910). However, comparing the NPV of the two projects is *only* valid because both projects require the same initial cost—$1,000,000. In contrast, Exhibit 21-13 summarizes three capital investment options faced by Smart Touch. Each capital project requires a different initial investment. All three projects are attractive because each yields a positive NPV. Assuming Smart Touch can only invest in one project at this time, which one should it choose? Project B yields the highest NPV, but it also requires a larger initial investment than the alternatives.

**EXHIBIT 21-13** | **Smart Touch Capital Investment Options**

| Cash Flows | Project A | Project B | Project C |
|---|---|---|---|
| Present value of net cash inflows | $ 150,000 | $ 238,000 | $ 182,000 |
| Investment | (125,000) | (200,000) | (150,000) |
| Net present value (NPV) | $ 25,000 | $ 38,000 | $ 32,000 |

To choose among the projects, Smart Touch computes the **profitability index** (also known as the **present value index**). The profitability index is computed as follows:

> Profitability index = Present value of net cash inflows ÷ Investment

The profitability index computes the number of dollars returned for every dollar invested, *with all calculations performed in present value dollars*. It allows us to compare alternative investments in present value terms (like the NPV method), but it also considers differences in the investments' initial cost. Let's compute the profitability index for all three alternatives.

| Present value of net cash inflows | ÷ Investment | = Profitability index |
|---|---|---|
| Project A: $150,000 | ÷ $125,000 = | 1.20 |
| Project B: $238,000 | ÷ $200,000 = | 1.19 |
| Project C: $182,000 | ÷ $150,000 = | 1.21 |

The profitability index shows that Project C is the best of the three alternatives because it returns $1.21 (in present value dollars) for every $1.00 invested. Projects A and B return slightly less.

Let's also compute the profitability index for Greg's Tunes' CD-player and DVR projects:

CD-player:   $1,048,610 ÷ $1,000,000 = 1.049
DVR:    $1,078,910 ÷ $1,000,000 = 1.079

The profitability index confirms our prior conclusion that the DVR project is more profitable than the CD-player project. The DVR project returns $1.079 (in present value dollars) for every $1.00 invested (beyond the 14% return already used to discount the cash flows). We did not need the profitability index to determine that the DVR project was preferable because both projects required the same investment ($1,000,000). Because Greg's chose the DVR project over the CD-player project, the CD-player project is the opportunity cost. *Opportunity cost* is the benefit foregone by not choosing an alternative course of action.

## NPV of a Project with Residual Value

Many assets yield cash inflows at the end of their useful lives because they have residual value. Companies discount an investment's residual value to its present value when determining the *total* present value of the project's net cash inflows. The residual value is discounted as a single lump sum—not an annuity—because it will be received only once, when the asset is sold. In short, it is just another type of cash inflow of the project.

Suppose Greg's expects that the CD project equipment will be worth $100,000 at the end of its five-year life. To determine the CD-player project's NPV, we discount the residual value of $100,000 using the Present Value of $1 table ($i = 14\%$, $n = 5$). (See Appendix B, Table B-1.) We then *add* its present value of $51,900 to the present value of the CD project's other net cash inflows we calculated in Exhibit 21-11 ($1,048,610). This gives the new net present value calculation as shown in Exhibit 21-14:

**EXHIBIT 21-14** | **NPV of a Project with Residual Value**

=NPV(.14,305450,305450,
305450,305450,405450)

Then subtract the $1,000,000
initial investment

| Year | | PV Factor ($i = 14\%$, $n = 5$) | Net Cash Inflow | Present Value |
|------|---|---|---|---|
| 1–5 | Present value of annuity | 3.433 × | $305,450 = | $ 1,048,610 |
| 5 | Present value of residual value (single lump sum) | 0.519 × | $100,000 = | 51,900 |
| | Total present value of net cash inflows | | | $ 1,100,510 |
| 0 | Investment | | | (1,000,000) |
| | Net present value (NPV) | | | $    100,510 |

Because of the expected residual value, the CD-player project is now more attractive than the DVR project. If Greg's could pursue only the CD or DVR project because of capital rationing, Greg's would now choose the CD project, because its NPV of $100,510 is higher than the DVR project's NPV of $78,910, and both projects require the same investment of $1,000,000.

## Sensitivity Analysis

Capital budgeting decisions affect cash flows far into the future. Greg's managers might want to know whether their decision would be affected by any of their major assumptions, for example,

- changing the discount rate from 14% to 12% or to 16%.
- changing the net cash flows by 10%.

After reviewing the basic information for NPV analysis, managers perform sensitivity analyses to recalculate and review the results.

# Internal Rate of Return (IRR)

Another discounted cash flow model for capital budgeting is the internal rate of return. The **internal rate of return (IRR)** is the rate of return (based on discounted cash flows) a company can expect to earn by investing in a capital asset. *It is the interest rate that makes the NPV of the investment equal to zero.*

Let's look at this concept in another light by substituting in the definition of NPV:

Present value of the investment's net cash inflows – Investment's cost (Present value of cash outflows) = 0

In other words, the IRR is the *interest rate* that makes the cost of the investment equal to the present value of the investment's net cash inflows. The higher the IRR, the more desirable the project.

## IRR with Equal Periodic Net Cash Inflows (Annuity)

Let's first consider Greg's CD-player project, which would cost $1,000,000 and result in five equal yearly cash inflows of $305,450. We compute the IRR of an investment with equal periodic cash flows (annuity) by taking the following steps:

1. The IRR is the interest rate that makes the cost of the investment *equal to* the present value of the investment's net cash inflows, so we set up the following equation:

Investment's cost = Present value of investment's net cash inflows
Investment's cost = Amount of each equal net cash inflow × Annuity PV factor ($i = ?$, $n = $ given)

2. Next, we plug in the information we do know—the investment cost, $1,000,000, the equal annual net cash inflows, $305,450, but assume there is no residual value, and the number of periods (five years):

$1,000,000 = $305,450 × Annuity PV factor ($i = ?$, $n = 5$)

3. We then rearrange the equation and solve for the Annuity PV factor ($i = ?$, $n = 5$):

$1,000,000 ÷ $305,450 = Annuity PV factor ($i = ?$, $n = 5$)
3.274 = Annuity PV factor ($i = ?$, $n = 5$)

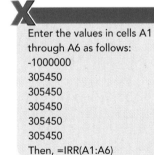

Enter the values in cells A1 through A6 as follows:
-1000000
305450
305450
305450
305450
305450
Then, =IRR(A1:A6)

4. Finally, we find the interest rate that corresponds to this Annuity PV factor. Turn to the Present Value of Annuity of $1 table (Appendix B, Table B-2). Scan the row corresponding to the project's expected life—five years, in our example. Choose the column(s) with the number closest to the Annuity PV factor you calculated in step 3. The 3.274 annuity factor is in the 16% column. Therefore, the IRR of the CD-player project is 16%. Greg's expects the project to earn an internal rate of return of 16% over its life. Exhibit 21-15 confirms this result: Using a 16% discount rate, the project's NPV is zero. In other words, 16% is the discount rate that makes the investment cost equal to the present value of the investment's net cash inflows.

**EXHIBIT 21-15** | **IRR—CD-Player Project**

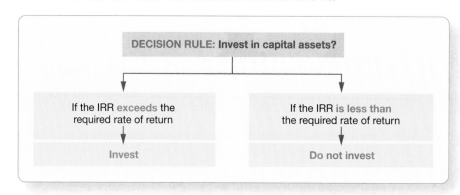

| Years | | Annuity PV Factor (i = 16%, n = 5) | Net Cash Inflow | | Total Present Value |
|---|---|---|---|---|---|
| 1–5 | Present value of annuity of equal annual net cash inflows for 5 years at 16% | 3.274 × | $305,450 | = | $1,000,000† |
| 0 | Investment | | | | (1,000,000) |
| | Net present value of the CD-player project | | | | $ 0‡ |

†Slight rounding of $43.
‡The zero difference proves that the IRR is 16%.

To decide whether the project is acceptable, compare the IRR with the minimum desired rate of return. The decision rule is as follows:

**DECISION RULE: Invest in capital assets?**

If the IRR exceeds the required rate of return → Invest

If the IRR is less than the required rate of return → Do not invest

Recall that Greg's Tunes' required rate of return or hurdle rate is 14%. Because the CD project's IRR (16%) is higher than the hurdle rate (14%), Greg's would invest in the project.

In the CD-player project, the exact Annuity PV factor (3.274) appears in the Present Value of an Annuity of $1 table (Appendix B, Table B-2). Many times, the exact factor will not appear in the table. For example, let's find the IRR of Smart Touch's B2B Web portal from Exhibit 21-2. Recall the B2B portal had a six-year life with annual net cash inflows of $60,000. The investment costs $240,000. We find its Annuity PV factor using the same steps:

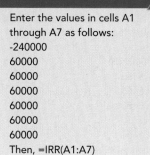

Enter the values in cells A1 through A7 as follows:
-240000
60000
60000
60000
60000
60000
60000
Then, =IRR(A1:A7)

| Investment's cost | = Present value of investment's net cash inflows |
|---|---|
| Investment's cost | = Amount of each equal net cash inflow × Annuity PV factor (i = ?, n = given) |
| $240,000 | = $60,000 × Annuity PV factor (i = ?, n = 6) |
| $240,000 ÷ $60,000 | = Annuity PV factor (i = ?, n = 6) |
| 4.00 | = Annuity PV factor (i = ?, n = 6) |

Now look in the Present Value of Annuity of $1 table in the row marked 6 periods (Appendix B, Table B-2). You will not see 4.00 under any column. The closest two factors are 3.889 (at 14%) and 4.111 (at 12%). Thus, the B2B portal's IRR must be somewhere between 12% and 14%. If we need a more precise figure, we could interpolate, or use a business calculator or Microsoft Excel to find the portal's exact IRR of 12.978% (see Excel formula in margin). If Smart Touch had a 14% required rate of return, it would *not* invest in the B2B portal because the portal's IRR is less than 14%.

## IRR with Unequal Periodic Cash Flows

Because the DVR project has unequal cash inflows, Greg's cannot use the Present Value of Annuity of $1 table to find the asset's IRR. Rather, Greg's must use a trial-and-error procedure to determine the discount rate making the project's NPV equal to zero. For example, because the company's minimum required rate of return is 14%, Greg's might start by calculating whether the DVR project earns at least 14%. Recall from Exhibit 21-12 that the DVR's NPV using a 14% discount rate is $78,910. Since the NPV is *positive*, the IRR must be *higher* than 14%. Greg's continues the trial-and-error process using *higher* discount rates until the company finds the rate that brings the net present value of the DVR project to *zero*. Exhibit 21-16 shows that at 16%, the DVR has an NPV of $40,390. Therefore, the IRR must be higher than 16%. At 18%, the NPV is $3,980, which is very close to zero. Thus, the IRR must be slightly higher than 18%. If we use a business calculator or Excel, rather than the trial-and-error procedure, we would find the IRR is 18.23%.

**EXHIBIT 21-16** | **Finding the DVR's IRR Through Trial-and-Error**

| Years | | Net Cash Inflow | PV Factor (for $i = 16\%$) | | Present Value at 16% | Net Cash Inflow | PV Factor (for $i = 18\%$) | | Present Value at 18% |
|---|---|---|---|---|---|---|---|---|---|
| 1 | Inflows | $500,000 | × | 0.862* = | $ 431,000 | $500,000 | × | 0.847* = | $ 423,500 |
| 2 | Inflows | 350,000 | × | 0.743 = | 260,050 | 350,000 | × | 0.718 = | 251,300 |
| 3 | Inflows | 300,000 | × | 0.641 = | 192,300 | 300,000 | × | 0.609 = | 182,700 |
| 4 | Inflows | 250,000 | × | 0.552 = | 138,000 | 250,000 | × | 0.516 = | 129,000 |
| 5 | Inflows | 40,000 | × | 0.476 = | 19,040 | 40,000 | × | 0.437 = | 17,480 |
| | Total present value of net cash inflows | | | | $ 1,040,390 | | | | $ 1,003,980 |
| 0 | Investment | | | | (1,000,000) | | | | (1,000,000) |
| | Net present value (NPV) | | | | $ 40,390 | | | | $ 3,980 |

*PV Factors are found in Appendix B, Table B-1.

The DVR's internal rate of return is higher than Greg's 14% required rate of return so the DVR project is attractive.

## Comparing Capital Budgeting Methods

We have discussed four capital budgeting methods commonly used by companies to make capital investment decisions. Two of these methods do not incorporate the time value of money: payback period and ROR. Exhibit 21-17 summarizes the similarities and differences between these two methods.

**EXHIBIT 21-17** | **Capital Budgeting Methods That *Ignore* the Time Value of Money**

| Payback period | Rate of return |
|---|---|
| • Simple to compute | • The only method that uses accrual accounting figures |
| • Focuses on the time it takes to recover the company's cash investment | • Shows how the investment will affect operating income, which is important to financial statement users |
| • Ignores any cash flows occurring after the payback period, including any residual value | • Measures the profitability of the asset over its entire life |
| • Highlights risks of investments with longer cash recovery periods | • Ignores the time value of money |
| • Ignores the time value of money | |

The discounted cash-flow methods are superior because they consider both the time value of money and profitability. These methods compare an investment's initial cost (cash outflow) with its future net cash inflows—all converted to the *same point in time*—the present value. Profitability is built into the discounted cash-flow methods because they consider *all* cash inflows and outflows over the project's life. Exhibit 21-18 considers the similarities and differences between the two discounted cash-flow methods.

Enter the values in cells A1 through A6 as follows:
-1000000
500000
350000
300000
250000
40000
Then, =IRR(A1:A6)

**Key Takeaway**

The NPV is the net difference between the present value of the investment's net cash inflows and the investment's cost (cash outflows), discounted at the company's required rate of return (hurdle) rate. The investment must meet or exceed the hurdle rate to be acceptable. The IRR is the interest rate that makes the cost of the investment equal to the present value of the investment's net cash inflows. Capital investment (budgeting) methods that consider the time value of money (like NPV and IRR) are best for decision making.

**EXHIBIT 21-18** | Capital Budgeting Methods That *Incorporate* the Time Value of Money

| Net present value | Internal rate of return |
|---|---|
| • Incorporates the time value of money and the asset's net cash flows over its entire life | • Incorporates the time value of money and the asset's net cash flows over its entire life |
| • Indicates whether the asset will earn the company's minimum required rate of return | • Computes the project's unique rate of return |
| • Shows the excess or deficiency of the asset's present value of net cash inflows over its initial investment cost | • No additional steps needed for capital rationing decisions |
| • The profitability index should be computed for capital rationing decisions when the assets require different initial investments | |

Managers often use more than one method to gain different perspectives on risks and returns. For example, Smart Touch could decide to pursue capital projects with positive NPVs, provided that those projects have a payback of four years or fewer.

Next, let's review the Decision Guidelines on the following page, which cover the two capital budgeting methods that consider the time value of money.

# Decision Guidelines 21-2

**CAPITAL BUDGETING**

Here are more of the guidelines **Amazon.com**'s managers used as they made the major capital budgeting decision to invest in building warehouses.

| Decision | Guideline |
|---|---|
| • Which capital budgeting methods are best? | Discounted cash-flow methods (NPV and IRR) are best because they incorporate both profitability and the time value of money. |
| • Why do the NPV and IRR models use the present value? | Because an investment's cash inflows and cash outflows occur at different points in time, they must be converted to a common point in time to make a valid comparison (that is, to determine whether inflows exceed cash outflows). These methods use the *present* value as the common point in time. |
| • How do we know whether investing in warehouse facilities will be worthwhile? | An investment in warehouse facilities may be worthwhile if the NPV is positive or the IRR exceeds the required rate of return. |
| • How do we compute the net present value with | |
| • equal annual cash flows? | Compute the present value of the investment's net cash inflows using the Present Value of an Annuity of $1 table and then subtract the investment's cost. |
| • unequal annual cash flows? | Compute the present value of each year's net cash inflows using the Present Value of $1 (lump sum) table, sum the present values of the inflows, and then subtract the investment's cost. |
| • How do we compute the internal rate of return (IRR) with | |
| • equal annual cash flows? | Find the interest rate that yields the following PV factor: $$\text{Annuity PV factor} = \frac{\text{Investment cost}}{\text{Expected annual net cash inflow}}$$ |
| • unequal annual cash flows? | Trial and error, spreadsheet software, or business calculator |

# Summary Problem 21-2

Recall from Summary Problem 21-1 that Dyno-max is considering buying a new water treatment system. The investment proposal passed the initial screening tests (payback period and rate of return) so the company now wants to analyze the proposal using the discounted cash flow methods. Recall that the water treatment system costs $48,000, has a five-year life, and no residual value. The estimated net cash inflows from environmental cleanup savings are $13,000 per year over its life. The company's required rate of return is 16%.

### Requirements

1. Compute the water treatment system's NPV.
2. Find the water treatment system's IRR (exact percentage is not required).
3. Should Dyno-max buy the water treatment system? Why?

## Solution

### Requirement 1

| | |
|---|---:|
| Present value of annuity of equal annual net cash inflows at 16% ($13,000 × 3.274*)..................................... | $ 42,562 |
| Investment............................................................................. | (48,000) |
| Net present value ................................................................. | $ (5,438) |

*Annuity PV factor (*i* = 16%, *n* = 5)

### Requirement 2

**Enter the values in cells A1 through A6 as follows:**
-48000
13000
13000
13000
13000
13000
Then, =IRR(A1:A6)

> Investment's cost = Amount of each equal net cash inflow × Annuity PV factor
> ($i$ = ?, $n$ = 5)
> $48,000 = $13,000 × Annuity PV factor ($i$ = ?, $n$ = 5)
> $48,000 ÷ $13,000 = Annuity PV factor ($i$ = ?, $n$ = 5)
> 3.692 = Annuity PV factor ($i$ = ?, $n$ = 5)

Because the cash flows occur for five years, we look for the PV factor 3.692 in the row marked $n$ = 5 on the Present Value of Annuity of $1 table (Appendix B, Table B-2). The PV factor is 3.605 at 12% and 3.791 at 10%. Therefore, the water treatment system has an IRR that falls between 10% and 12%. (*Optional:* Using a business calculator or Excel, we find an 11.03864% internal rate of return.)

### Requirement 3

*Decision:* Do not buy the water treatment system. It has a negative NPV and its IRR falls below the company's required rate of return. Both methods consider profitability and the time value of money. Since the savings came mainly from the estimated environmental cleanup savings, the company may want to study this issue further to ensure all environmental savings, both short term and long term, were considered in the initial evaluation.

# Review *Capital Investment Decisions and the Time Value of Money*

## ● Accounting Vocabulary

**Annuity (p. 1021)**
A stream of equal installments made at equal time intervals under the same interest rate.

**Capital Budgeting (p. 1011)**
The process of making capital investment decisions. Companies make capital investments when they acquire *capital assets*—assets used for a long period of time.

**Capital Rationing (p. 1012)**
Choosing among alternative capital investments due to limited funds.

**Compound Interest (p. 1021)**
Interest computed on the principal *and* all previously earned interest.

**Discount Rate (p. 1027)**
Management's minimum desired rate of return on an investment. Also called the **required rate of return** and **hurdle rate**.

**Hurdle Rate (p. 1027)**
The rate an investment must meet or exceed in order to be acceptable. Also called the **discount rate** and **required rate of return**.

**Internal Rate of Return (IRR) (p. 1031)**
The rate of return (based on discounted cash flows) that a company can expect to earn by investing in a capital asset. The interest rate that makes the NPV of the investment equal to zero.

**Net Present Value (NPV) (p. 1026)**
The net *difference* between the present value of the investment's net cash inflows and the investment's cost (cash outflows).

**Payback (p. 1013)**
The length of time it takes to recover, in net cash inflows, the cost of a capital outlay.

**Post-Audits (p. 1013)**
Comparing a capital investment's actual net cash inflows to its projected net cash inflows.

**Present Value Index (p. 1029)**
An index that computes the number of dollars returned for every dollar invested, *with all calculations performed in present value dollars*. Computed as present value of net cash inflows divided by investment. Also called the **profitability index**.

**Profitability Index (p. 1029)**
An index that computes the number of dollars returned for every dollar invested, *with all calculations performed in present value dollars*. Computed as present value of net cash inflows divided by investment. Also called the **present value index**.

**Rate of Return (ROR) (p. 1016)**
A measure of profitability computed by dividing the average annual operating income from an asset by the average amount invested in the asset.

**Required Rate of Return (p. 1027)**
The rate an investment must meet or exceed in order to be acceptable. Also called the **discount rate** and **hurdle rate**.

**Simple Interest (p. 1021)**
Interest computed *only* on the principal amount.

## ● Destination: Student Success

### Student Success Tips

The following are hints on some common trouble areas for students in this chapter:

● Remember that the payback period and rate of return don't consider the time value of money. NPV and IRR do consider the time value of money.

● Keep in mind the definition of an annuity: equal amounts, equal time periods, and a constant interest rate.

● Consider that NPV discounts the future cash inflows that come from investing in an asset to the present value today because the decision will be made today (in the present).

● Keep in mind that the discount rate where NPV equals zero is the IRR.

● Recall the discounted cash flow values can be calculated using the tables in Appendix B, a business calculator, or Excel. The results between the table values and the other methods will vary slightly due to rounding in the Appendix B tables.

● Remember that when deciding between two investments where both are positive, capital rationing may come into play. Capital rationing means the company has limited resources available for capital investments; thus, it will choose the investment that has the highest NPV.

### Getting Help

If there's a learning objective from the chapter you aren't confident about, try using one or more of the following resources:

● Consider drawing a time line to help you visualize when cash inflows and outflows are occurring.

● Review Decision Guidelines 21-1 and 21-2 in the chapter.

● Review Summary Problems 21-1 and 21-2 in the chapter to reinforce your understanding of payback period, ROR, NPV and IRR.

● Practice additional exercises or problems at the end of Chapter 21 that cover the specific learning objective that is challenging you.

● Watch the white board videos for Chapter 21, located at myaccountinglab.com under the Chapter Resources button.

● Go to myaccountinglab.com and select the Study Plan button. Choose Chapter 21 and work the questions covering that specific learning objective until you've mastered it.

● Work the Chapter 21 pre/post tests in myaccountinglab.com.

● Consult the Check Figures for End of Chapter starters, exercises, and problems, located at myaccountinglab.com.

● Visit the learning resource center on your campus for tutoring.

## ● Quick Check

1. What is the first step of capital budgeting?

   a. Gathering the money for the investment

   b. Identifying potential projects

   c. Getting the accountant involved

   d. All of the above

2. Ian, Corp., is considering two expansion projects. The first project streamlines the company's warehousing facilities. The second project automates inventory utilizing bar code scanners. Both projects generate positive NPV, yet Ian, Corp., only chooses the bar coding project. Why?

   a. The payback period is greater than the warehouse project's life.

   b. The internal rate of return of the warehousing project is less than the company's required rate of return for capital projects.

   c. The company is practicing capital rationing.

   d. All of the above are true.

3. Which of the following methods does not consider the investment's profitability?

   a. ROR                      c. NPV

   b. Payback                  d. IRR

4. Suppose Francine Dunkelberg's Sweets is considering investing in warehouse-management software that costs $550,000, has $75,000 residual value, and should lead to cost savings of $130,000 per year for its five-year life. In calculating the ROR, which of the following figures should be used as the equation's denominator (average amount invested in the asset)?

   a. $275,000                 c. $625,000

   b. $237,500                 d. $312,500

5. Your rich aunt has promised to give you $2,000 a year at the end of each of the next four years to help you pay for college. Using a discount rate of 12%, the present value of the gift can be stated as

   a. PV = $2,000 (PV factor, $i = 4\%$, $n = 12$).

   b. PV = $2,000 (Annuity PV factor, $i = 12\%$, $n = 4$).

   c. PV = $2,000 (Annuity FV factor, $i = 12\%$, $n = 4$).

   d. PV = $2,000 \times 12\% \times 4$.

6. Which of the following affects the present value of an investment?

   a. The type of investment (annuity versus single lump sum)

   b. The number of time periods (length of the investment)

   c. The interest rate

   d. All of the above

7. Which of the following is true regarding capital rationing decisions?
   a. Companies should always choose the investment with the highest NPV.
   b. Companies should always choose the investment with the highest ROR.
   c. Companies should always choose the investment with the shortest payback period.
   d. None of the above

8. In computing the IRR on an expansion at Mountain Creek Resort, Vernon Valley would consider all of the following *except?*
   a. Present value factors
   b. Depreciation on the assets built in the expansion
   c. Predicted cash inflows over the life of the expansion
   d. The cost of the expansion

9. The IRR is
   a. the interest rate at which the NPV of the investment is zero.
   b. the firm's hurdle rate.
   c. the same as the ROR.
   d. None of the above

10. Which of the following is the most reliable method for making capital budgeting decisions?
    a. ROR method
    b. Post-audit method
    c. NPV method
    d. Payback method

Answers are given after Apply Your Knowledge (p. 1049).

# Assess Your Progress

● Short Exercises

**S21-1**   ❶ **The importance of capital investments and the capital budgeting process**   *MyAccountingLab*
**[10 min]**
Review the following activities of the capital budgeting process:

   a. Budget capital investments.
   b. Project investments' cash flows.
   c. Perform post-audits.
   d. Make investments.
   e. Use feedback to reassess investments already made.
   f. Identify potential capital investments.
   g. Screen/analyze investments using one or more of the methods discussed.

**Requirement**
   1. Place the activities in sequential order as they occur in the capital budgeting process.

**S21-2**    ❷ **Using the payback period and rate of return methods to make capital investment decisions [10 min]**

Consider how Smith Valley Snow Park Lodge could use capital budgeting to decide whether the $13,500,000 Snow Park Lodge expansion would be a good investment.

Assume Smith Valley's managers developed the following estimates concerning the expansion:

| | |
|---|---:|
| Number of additional skiers per day . . . . . . . . . . . . . | 117 |
| Average number of days per year that weather conditions allow skiing at Smith Valley . . . . . . . | 142 |
| Useful life of expansion (in years) . . . . . . . . . . . . . . . | 10 |
| Average cash spent by each skier per day . . . . . . . . . $ | 236 |
| Average variable cost of serving each skier per day . . . $ | 76 |
| Cost of expansion . . . . . . . . . . . . . . . . . . . . . . . . . | $13,500,000 |
| Discount rate . . . . . . . . . . . . . . . . . . . . . . . . . . . . | 10% |

Assume that Smith Valley uses the straight-line depreciation method and expects the lodge expansion to have a residual value of $1,000,000 at the end of its 10-year life.

### Requirements

1. Compute the average annual net cash inflow from the expansion.
2. Compute the average annual operating income from the expansion.

*Note: Short Exercise 21-2 must be completed before attempting Short Exercise 21-3.*

**S21-3**    ❷ **Using the payback method to make capital investment decisions [5 min]**

Refer to the Smith Valley Snow Park Lodge expansion project in S21-2.

### Requirement

1. Compute the payback period for the expansion project.

*Note: Short Exercise 21-2 must be completed before attempting Short Exercise 21-4.*

**S21-4**    ❷ **Using the rate of return method to make capital investment decisions [5–10 min]**

Refer to the Smith Valley Snow Park Lodge expansion project in S21-2.

### Requirement

1. Calculate the ROR.

*Note: Short Exercise 21-2 must be completed before attempting Short Exercise 21-5.*

**S21-5**    ❷ **Using the payback and rate of return methods to make capital investment decisions [5–10 min]**

Refer to the Smith Valley Snow Park Lodge expansion project in S21-2. *Assume the expansion has zero residual value.*

### Requirements

1. Will the payback period change? Explain your answer and recalculate if necessary.
2. Will the project's ROR change? Explain your answer and recalculate if necessary.
3. Assume Smith Valley screens its potential capital investments using the following decision criteria:

| | |
|---|---|
| Maximum payback period . . . . . . . . . . . . . | 5.3 years |
| Minimum rate of return . . . . . . . . . . . . . . . | 16.55% |

Will Smith Valley consider this project further, or reject it?

**S21-6**    ❷ **Using the payback and rate of return methods to make capital investment decisions [5–10 min]**

Suppose Smith Valley is deciding whether to purchase new accounting software. The payback period for the $28,575 software package is three years, and the software's expected life is eight years. Smith Valley's required rate of return is 14.0%.

## Requirement

1.  Assuming equal yearly cash flows, what are the expected annual cash savings from the new software?

**S21-7**    ❸ **Using the time value of money to compute the present and future values of single lump sums and annuities [10–15 min]**

Your grandfather would like to share some of his fortune with you. He offers to give you money under one of the following scenarios (you get to choose):

1.  $8,750 a year at the end of each of the next seven years.
2.  $50,050 (lump sum) now.
3.  $100,250 (lump sum) seven years from now.

## Requirement

1.  Calculate the present value of each scenario using a 6% discount rate. Which scenario yields the highest present value? Would your preference change if you used a 12% discount rate?

**S21-8**    ❸ **Using the time value of money to compute the present and future values of single lump sums and annuities [5–10 min]**

Assume you make the following investments:

a.  You invest $8,000 for five years at 14% interest.
b.  In a different account earning 14% interest, you invest $1,750 at the end of each year for five years.

## Requirement

1.  Calculate the value of each investment at the end of five years.

**S21-9**    ❸ **Using the time value of money to compute the present and future values of single lump sums and annuities [10–15 min]**

Refer to the lottery payout options summarized in Exhibit 21-9.

## Requirement

1.  Rather than comparing the payout options at their present values (as done in the chapter), compare the payout options at their future value, 10 years from now.
    a.  Using an 8% interest rate, what is the future value of each payout option?
    b.  Rank your preference among payout options.
    c.  Does computing the future value rather than the present value of the options change your preference between payout options? Explain your reasoning.

**S21-10**    ❸ **Using the time value of money to compute the present and future values of single lump sums and annuities [10–15 min]**

Use the Present Value of $1 table (Appendix B, Table B-1) to determine the present value of $1 received one year from now. Assume an 8% interest rate. Use the same table to find the present value of $1 received two years from now. Continue this process for a total of five years.

## Requirements

1.  What is the *total* present value of the cash flows received over the five-year period?
2.  Could you characterize this stream of cash flows as an annuity? Why or why not?
3.  Use the Present Value of Annuity of $1 table (Appendix B, Table B-2) to determine the present value of the same stream of cash flows. Compare your results to your answer to Requirement 1.
4.  Explain your findings.

*Note: Short Exercise 21-2 must be completed before attempting Short Exercise 21-11.*

### S21-11 ④ Using discounted cash flow models to make capital investment decisions [10–15 min]

Refer to the Smith Valley Snow Park Lodge expansion project in S21-2.

**Requirement**

1. What is the project's NPV? Is the investment attractive? Why?

*Note: Short Exercise 21-2 must be completed before attempting Short Exercise 21-12.*

### S21-12 ④ Using discounted cash flow models to make capital investment decisions [10–15 min]

Refer to S21-2. *Assume the expansion has no residual value.*

**Requirement**

1. What is the project's NPV? Is the investment attractive? Why?

*Note: Short Exercise 21-12 must be completed before attempting Short Exercise 21-13.*

### S21-13 ④ Using discounted cash flow models to make capital investment decisions [10–15 min]

Refer to S21-12. *Continue to assume that the expansion has no residual value.*

**Requirement**

1. What is the project's IRR? Is the investment attractive? Why?

## ● Exercises

*MyAccountingLab*

### E21-14 ① The importance of capital investments and the capital budgeting process [15–20 min]

You have just started a business and want your new employees to be well informed about capital budgeting.

**Requirement**

1. Match each definition with its capital budgeting method.

METHODS
1. Rate of return.
2. Internal rate of return.
3. Net present value.
4. Payback period.

DEFINITIONS
A. Is only concerned with the time it takes to get cash outflows returned.
B. Considers operating income but not the time value of money in its analyses.
C. Compares the present value of cash out to the cash in to determine investment worthiness.
D. The true rate of return an investment earns.

### E21-15 ② Using the payback and rate of return methods to make capital investment decisions [5–10 min]

Preston, Co., is considering acquiring a manufacturing plant. The purchase price is $1,100,000. The owners believe the plant will generate net cash inflows of $297,000 annually. It will have to be replaced in six years.

**Requirement**

1. Use the payback method to determine whether Preston should purchase this plant.

**E21-16** ❷ **Using the payback and rate of return methods to make capital investment decisions [5–10 min]**

Robinson Hardware is adding a new product line that will require an investment of $1,454,000. Managers estimate that this investment will have a 10-year life and generate net cash inflows of $300,000 the first year, $270,000 the second year, and $260,000 each year thereafter for eight years.

## Requirement

1.  Compute the payback period.

*Note: Exercise 21-16 must be completed before attempting Exercise 21-17.*

**E21-17** ❷ **Using the payback and rate of return methods to make capital investment decisions [10–15 min]**

Refer to the Robinson Hardware information in E21-16. Assume the project has no residual value.

## Requirement

1.  Compute the ROR for the investment.

**E21-18** ❸ **Using the time value of money to compute the present and future values of single lump sums and annuities [15–20 min]**

Assume you want to retire early at age 52. You plan to save using one of the following two strategies: (1) save $3,000 a year in an IRA beginning when you are 22 and ending when you are 52 (30 years), or (2) wait until you are 37 to start saving and then save $6,000 per year for the next 15 years. Assume you will earn the historic stock market average of 14% per year.

## Requirements

1.  How much "out-of-pocket" cash will you invest under the two options?
2.  How much savings will you have accumulated at age 52 under the two options?
3.  Explain the results.
4.  If you were to let the savings continue to grow for 10 more years (with no further out-of-pocket investments), what would the investments be worth when you are age 62?

**E21-19** ❸ **Using the time value of money to compute the present and future values of single lump sums and annuities [15–20 min]**

Your best friend just received a gift of $7,000 from his favorite aunt. He wants to save the money to use as "starter" money after college. He can invest it (1) risk-free at 6%, (2) taking on moderate risk at 8%, or (3) taking on high risk at 14%.

## Requirement

1.  Help your friend project the investment's worth at the end of four years under each investment strategy and explain the results to him.

**E21-20** ❸ **Using the time value of money to compute the present and future values of single lump sums and annuities [5–10 min]**

Janice wants to take the next five years off work to travel around the world. She estimates her annual cash needs at $28,000 (if she needs more, she will work odd jobs). Janice believes she can invest her savings at 8% until she depletes her funds.

## Requirements

1.  How much money does Janice need now to fund her travels?
2.  After speaking with a number of banks, Janice learns she will only be able to invest her funds at 4%. How much does she need now to fund her travels?

**E21-21** ❸ **Using the time value of money to compute the present and future values of single lump sums and annuities [10–15 min]**

Congratulations! You have won a state lotto. The state lottery offers you the following (after-tax) payout options:

---
Option #1: $15,000,000 after five years.
Option #2: $2,150,000 per year for the next five years.
Option #3: $13,000,000 after three years.

---

## Requirement

1. Assuming you can earn 8% on your funds, which option would you prefer?

**E21-22** ❹ **Using discounted cash flow models to make capital investment decisions [15–20 min]**

Use the NPV method to determine whether Kyler Products should invest in the following projects:

- *Project A*: Costs $260,000 and offers seven annual net cash inflows of $57,000. Kyler Products requires an annual return of 16% on projects like A.
- *Project B*: Costs $375,000 and offers 10 annual net cash inflows of $75,000. Kyler Products demands an annual return of 14% on investments of this nature.

## Requirements

1. What is the NPV of each project?
2. What is the maximum acceptable price to pay for each project?
3. What is the profitability index of each project?

**E21-23** ❹ **Using discounted cash flow models to make capital investment decisions [15–20 min]**

Sprocket Industries is deciding whether to automate one phase of its production process. The manufacturing equipment has a six-year life and will cost $905,000. Projected net cash inflows are as follows:

| | |
|---|---|
| Year 1 | $260,000 |
| Year 2 | $254,000 |
| Year 3 | $225,000 |
| Year 4 | $215,000 |
| Year 5 | $205,000 |
| Year 6 | $173,000 |

## Requirements

1. Compute this project's NPV using Sprocket's 16% hurdle rate. Should Sprocket invest in the equipment?
2. Sprocket could refurbish the equipment at the end of six years for $103,000. The refurbished equipment could be used one more year, providing $75,000 of net cash inflows in year 7. Additionally, the refurbished equipment would have a $54,000 residual value at the end of year 7. Should Sprocket invest in the equipment and refurbishing it after six years? (*Hint*: In addition to your answer to Requirement 1, discount the additional cash outflow and inflows back to the present value.)

*Note: Exercise 21-22 must be completed before attempting Exercise 21-24.*

**E21-24** ❹ **Using discounted cash flow models to make capital investment decisions [15 min]**

Refer to the data regarding Kyler Products in E21-22.

## Requirement

1. Compute the IRR of each project and use this information to identify the better investment.

**E21-25**  ❹ **Using discounted cash flow models to make capital investment decisions [10–15 min]**

Brighton Manufacturing is considering three capital investment proposals. At this time, Brighton only has funds available to pursue one of the three investments.

|  | Equipment A | Equipment B | Equipment C |
|---|---|---|---|
| Present value of net cash inflows | $  1,735,915 | $  1,969,888 | $  2,207,765 |
| Investment | (1,563,887) | (1,669,397) | (1,886,979) |
| NPV | $     172,028 | $     300,491 | $     320,786 |

## Requirement

1. Which investment should Brighton pursue at this time? Why?

## ● Problems (Group A)

**P21-26A**  ❶ **Describing the importance of capital investments and the capital budgeting process [10–15 min]**    *MyAccountingLab*

Consider the following statements about capital budgeting.

a. _____ is (are) more appropriate for long-term investments.

b. _____ highlights risky investments.

c. _____ shows the effect of the investment on the company's accrual-based income.

d. _____ is the interest rate that makes the NPV of an investment equal to zero.

e. In capital rationing decisions, management must identify the discount rate when the _____ method is used.

f. _____ provides management with information on how fast the cash invested will be recouped.

g. _____ is the rate of return, using discounted cash flows, a company can expect to earn by investing in the asset.

h. _____ does not consider the asset's profitability.

i. _____ uses accrual accounting rather than net cash inflows in its computation.

## Requirement

1. Fill in each statement with the appropriate capital budgeting method: Payback period, ROR, NPV, or IRR.

**P21-27A**  ❷❹ **Using payback, rate of return, discounted cash flow models, and profitability index to make capital investment decisions [20–30 min]**

Water Planet is considering purchasing a water park in Atlanta, Georgia, for $1,870,000. The new facility will generate annual net cash inflows of $460,000 for eight years. Engineers estimate that the facility will remain useful for eight years and have no residual value. The company uses straight-line depreciation, and its stockholders demand an annual return of 10% on investments of this nature.

## Requirements

1. Compute the payback period, the ROR, the NPV, the IRR, and the profitability index of this investment.

2. Recommend whether the company should invest in this project.

**P21-28A** ❷ ❹ **Using payback, rate of return, discounted cash flow models, and profitability index to make capital investment decisions; Calculating IRR [30–45 min]**

Leches operates a chain of sandwich shops. The company is considering two possible expansion plans. Plan A would open eight smaller shops at a cost of $8,400,000. Expected annual net cash inflows are $1,500,000, with zero residual value at the end of 10 years. Under Plan B, Leches would open three larger shops at a cost of $8,250,000. This plan is expected to generate net cash inflows of $1,080,000 per year for 10 years, the estimated useful life of the properties. Estimated residual value for Plan B is $1,000,000. Leches uses straight-line depreciation and requires an annual return of 10%.

## Requirements

1. Compute the payback period, the ROR, the NPV, and the profitability index of these two plans. What are the strengths and weaknesses of these capital budgeting models?
2. Which expansion plan should Leches choose? Why?
3. Estimate Plan A's IRR. How does the IRR compare with the company's required rate of return?

**P21-29A** ❸ **Using the time value of money to compute the present and future values of single lump sums and annuities [15–20 min]**

You are planning for a very early retirement. You would like to retire at age 40 and have enough money saved to be able to draw $235,000 per year for the next 40 years (based on family history, you think you will live to age 80). You plan to save by making 15 equal annual installments (from age 25 to age 40) into a fairly risky investment fund that you expect will earn 12% per year. You will leave the money in this fund until it is completely depleted when you are 80 years old.

## Requirements

1. How much money must you accumulate by retirement to make your plan work? (*Hint:* Find the present value of the $235,000 withdrawals.)
2. How does this amount compare to the total amount you will draw out of the investment during retirement? How can these numbers be so different?
3. How much must you pay into the investment each year for the first 15 years? (*Hint:* Your answer from Requirement 1 becomes the future value of this annuity.)
4. How does the total "out-of-pocket" savings compare to the investment's value at the end of the 15-year savings period and the withdrawals you will make during retirement?

## ● Problems (Group B)

**P21-30B** ❶ **Describing the importance of capital investments and the capital budgeting process [10–15 min]**

Consider the following statements about capital budgeting.

a. _____ is (are) often used by management to screen potential investments from those less desired.
b. _____ does not consider the asset's profitability.
c. _____ is calculated by dividing the average amount invested by the asset's average annual operating income.
d. _____ is the rate of return, using discounted cash flows, a company can expect to earn by investing in the asset.

e.  In capital rationing decisions, the profitability index must be computed to compare investments requiring different initial investments when the _____ method is used.

f.  _____ ignores any residual value.

g.  _____ is the interest rate that makes the NPV of an investment equal to zero.

h.  _____ highlights risky investments.

i.  _____ shows the effect of the investment on the company's accrual-based income.

## Requirement

1.  Fill in each statement with the appropriate capital budgeting method: Payback period, ROR, NPV, or IRR.

**P21-31B** ② ④ **Using payback, rate of return, discounted cash flow models, and profitability index to make capital investment decisions [20–30 min]**
Splash World is considering purchasing a water park in Omaha, Nebraska, for $1,820,000. The new facility will generate annual net cash inflows of $472,000 for eight years. Engineers estimate that the facility will remain useful for eight years and have no residual value. The company uses straight-line depreciation, and its stockholders demand an annual return of 10% on investments of this nature.

## Requirements

1.  Compute the payback period, the ROR, the NPV, the IRR, and the profitability index of this investment.

2.  Recommend whether the company should invest in this project.

**P21-32B** ② ④ **Using payback, rate of return, discounted cash flow models, and profitability index to make capital investment decisions; Calculating IRR [30–45 min]**
Lulus operates a chain of sandwich shops. The company is considering two possible expansion plans. Plan A would open eight smaller shops at a cost of $8,450,000. Expected annual net cash inflows are $1,750,000, with zero residual value at the end of eight years. Under Plan B, Lulus would open three larger shops at a cost of $8,000,000. This plan is expected to generate net cash inflows of $1,020,000 per year for eight years, which is the estimated useful life of the properties. Estimated residual value for Plan B is $1,200,000. Lulus uses straight-line depreciation and requires an annual return of 6%

## Requirements

1.  Compute the payback period, the ROR, the NPV, and the profitability index of these two plans. What are the strengths and weaknesses of these capital budgeting models?

2.  Which expansion plan should Lulus choose? Why?

3.  Estimate Plan A's IRR. How does the IRR compare with the company's required rate of return?

**P21-33B** ③ **Using the time value of money to compute the present and future values of single lump sums and annuities [15–20 min]**
You are planning for an early retirement. You would like to retire at age 40 and have enough money saved to be able to draw $240,000 per year for the next 35 years (based on family history, you think you will live to age 75). You plan to save by making 10 equal annual installments (from age 30 to age 40) into a fairly risky investment fund that you expect will earn 16% per year. You will leave the money in this fund until it is completely depleted when you are 75 years old.

### Requirements

1. How much money must you accumulate by retirement to make your plan work? (*Hint:* Find the present value of the $240,000 withdrawals.)
2. How does this amount compare to the total amount you will draw out of the investment during retirement? How can these numbers be so different?
3. How much must you pay into the investment each year for the first 10 years? (*Hint:* Your answer from Requirement 1 becomes the future value of this annuity.)
4. How does the total "out-of-pocket" savings compare to the investment's value at the end of the 10-year savings period and the withdrawals you will make during retirement?

## • Continuing Exercise

**MyAccountingLab** **E21-34** **② ④ Using payback, accounting rate of return, discounted cash flow, and IRR to make capital investment decisions [30–45 min]**
This exercise continues the Lawlor Lawn Service, Inc., situation from Exercise 20-33 of Chapter 20. Lawlor Lawn Service is considering purchasing a mower that will generate cash inflows of $9,000 per year. The mower has a zero residual value and an estimated useful life of three years. The mower costs $20,000. Lawlor's required rate of return is 12%.

### Requirements

1. Calculate payback period, rate of return, net present value, and IRR for the mower investment.
2. Should Lawlor invest in the new mower?

## • Continuing Problem

**MyAccountingLab** **P21-35** **② ④ Using payback, accounting rate of return, discounted cash flow, and IRR to make capital investment decisions [30–45 min]**
This problem continues the Draper Consulting, Inc., situation from Problem 20-34 of Chapter 20. Draper Consulting is considering purchasing two different types of servers. Server A will generate cash inflows of $25,000 per year and has a zero residual value. Server A's estimated useful life is three years and it costs $40,000.

Server B will generate cash inflows of $25,000 in year 1, $11,000 in year 2, and $4,000 in year 3. Server B has a $4,000 residual value and an estimated life of three years. Server B also costs $40,000. Draper's required rate of return is 14%.

### Requirements

1. Calculate payback period, rate of return, net present value, and IRR for both server investments.
2. Assuming capital rationing applies, which server should Draper invest in?

# Apply Your Knowledge

## • Decision Case 21-1

Dominic Hunter, a second-year business student at the University of Utah, will graduate in two years with an accounting major and a Spanish minor. Hunter is trying to decide where to work this summer. He has two choices: work full-time for a bottling plant or work part-time in the accounting department of a meat-packing plant. He probably will work at the same place next summer as well. He is able to work 12 weeks during the summer.

The bottling plant will pay Hunter $380 per week this year and 7% more next summer. At the meat-packing plant, he could work 20 hours per week at $8.75 per hour. Hunter believes that the experience he gains this summer will qualify him for a full-time accounting position with the meat-packing plant next summer. That position will pay $550 per week.

Hunter sees two additional benefits of working part-time this summer. By working only part-time, he could take two accounting courses this summer (tuition is $225 per hour for each of the four-hour courses) and reduce his studying workload during the Fall and Spring semesters. Second, he would have the time to work as a grader in the university's accounting department during the 15-week fall term and make additional income. Grading pays $50 per week.

### Requirements

1. Suppose that Hunter ignores the time value of money in decisions that cover this short time period. Suppose also that his sole goal is to make as much money as possible between now and the end of next summer. What should he do? What nonquantitative factors might Hunter consider? What would *you* do if you were faced with these alternatives?

2. Now suppose that Hunter considers the time value of money for all cash flows that he expects to receive one year or more in the future. Which alternative does this consideration favor? Why?

## ● Fraud Case 21-1

John Johnson's landscape company was on its last legs, so when John got a call from Capital Funding, Ltd., offering a non-secured loan, he thought it might be his last chance to keep the business afloat. The loan officer explained that the government was promoting loans to keep small businesses from folding during the recession, and that his company qualified. John knew his credit rating was terrible, but he didn't want to lay off his staff of six and look for work himself, so he put aside his doubts and showed up at the office to fill out the paperwork. The gentleman was professional and reassuring. Two days later, John got a call assuring him that the funds would be transferred as soon as they received a "processing fee" of $900. This was a bit of shock for John, but he delivered the check. He could hardly sleep that night, and he called back first thing the next morning. There was no answer. He drove by the loan office. It was vacant. They had vanished without a trace.

### Requirements

1. Did John have reason to be suspicious? What were the warning signs?
2. What should small businesses do when they are in financial trouble?

## ● Communication Activity 21-1

In 70 words or fewer, explain the difference between NPV and IRR.

---

## Quick Check Answers

1. *b* 2. *c* 3. *b* 4. *d* 5. *b* 6. *d* 7. *d* 8. *b* 9. *a* 10. *c*

**For online homework, exercises, and problems that provide you immediate feedback, please visit myaccountinglab.com.**

# 22 The Master Budget and Responsibility Accounting

## Learning Objectives

1. Learn why managers use budgets

2. Understand the components of the master budget

3. Prepare an operating budget

4. Prepare a financial budget

5. Use sensitivity analysis in budgeting

6. Prepare performance reports for responsibility centers and account for traceable and common shared fixed costs

You're set to graduate in a few weeks and already have a great job offer. Your excitement, however, is paired with some anxiety. You'll be financially independent for the first time, not relying on your parents for financial support. You want to make sure you'll be able to live within your means. You've heard of friends who graduated and quickly created a financial mess by carelessly using credit cards, so you've decided to make a budget for your first year out of college. Your salary will be your only source of income. Your expenses will include rent, food, utilities, car operation and maintenance, insurance, and entertainment. You also need a more professional wardrobe and will have some expenses related to setting up your new apartment. Also, you have a student loan that will need to be repaid beginning six months after graduation, so you need to include your student loan payment in your budget. Some of these expenses will be the same each month, like your rent. Some will vary from month to month, like interest expense on your student loan.

Creating a budget will help you make critical decisions, such as how much rent you can afford. You'll also use the budget to plan and control your other expenses. Careful budgeting helps both individuals and businesses set goals that help plan for the future.

As you will see throughout this chapter, knowing how *costs* behave continues to be important when organizations are forming budgets. Total fixed costs will not change as volume changes within the relevant range. However, total variable costs must be adjusted when sales volume is expected to fluctuate. In this chapter, we'll continue to use Smart Touch Learning and Greg's Tunes to demonstrate budgeting.

# Why Managers Use Budgets

Let's continue our study of budgets by moving from your personal budget to see how a small service business develops a simple budget. When Smart Touch Learning, Inc., first began, it was a small online service company that provided e-learning services to customers. Assume Smart Touch wants to earn $550,000 a month and expects to sell 20,000 e-learning services per month at a price of $30 each. Over the past six months, it paid an average of $18,000 a month to its Internet service provider, and spent an additional $20,000 per month on salaries. Smart Touch expects these monthly costs to remain about the same, so these are the monthly fixed costs. Smart Touch spent 5% of its revenues for banner ads on other Web sites. Smart Touch also incurs $2.25 in server space expense for each e-learning service provided. Because advertising and server space expenses fluctuate with revenue, advertising and server space expenses are variable.

1 Learn why managers use budgets

Exhibit 22-1 shows how to compute a budgeted income statement using the variable costing approach. The **budgeted income statement** projects operating income for the period. **A budgeted income statement shows** *estimated* (budgeted) **values, whereas an income statement shows** *actual* **results.**

**EXHIBIT 22-1** | **Service Company Budget**

| SMART TOUCH LEARNING, INC. Budgeted Income Statement For the Month Ended May 31, 2014 | |
| --- | --- |
| Service revenue (20,000 × $30 each) | $600,000 |
| Variable expenses: | |
|     Server space expense (20,000 × $2.25 each) | $ 45,000 |
|     Advertising expense (5% × $600,000 revenue) | 30,000 |
|         Total variable expenses | 75,000 |
| Contribution margin | $525,000 |
| Fixed expenses: | |
|     Salary expense | $ 20,000 |
|     Internet access expense | 18,000 |
|         Total fixed expenses | 38,000 |
| Budgeted operating income | $487,000 |

As you can see from the exhibit, Smart Touch's contribution margin is strong, at $525,000. For each e-learning service sold, 87.5% ($525,000/$600,000) of revenue is contributing to the covering of fixed costs and to making a profit. Smart Touch's budgeted operating income of $487,000 will not meet its $550,000 per month operating income goal. It will have to increase revenue (perhaps through word-of-mouth advertising) or cut expenses (perhaps by reducing server space expense of $2.25 per service or by reducing the other variable and/or fixed costs).

## Using Budgets to Plan and Control

Large international for-profit companies, such as **Amazon.com**, and nonprofit organizations, such as **Habitat for Humanity**, use budgets for the same reasons as you do in your personal life or in your small business—to plan and control actions and the related revenues and expenses. Managers also use budgets to plan for technology upgrades, other capital asset replacements, improvements, or expansions. Strategic as well as operational plans are budgeted for as well. Exhibit 22-2 shows how managers use budgets in fulfilling their major responsibilities. First, they develop strategies—overall business goals like **Amazon**'s goal to expand its international operations, or **Gateway**'s goal to be a value leader in the personal computer market while diversifying into other markets. Companies then plan and budget for specific actions to achieve those goals. The next step is to act. For example, **Amazon** planned for and then added a grocery feature to its Web sites.

**EXHIBIT 22-2** | **Managers Use Budgets to Plan and Control Business Activities**

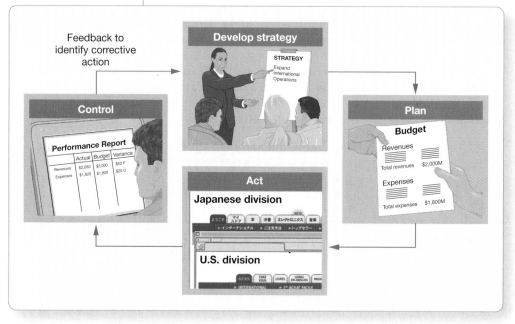

After acting, managers compare actual results with the budget. This feedback allows them to determine what, if any, corrective action to take. If, for example, **Amazon** spent more than expected to add the grocery feature to its Web sites, managers must cut other costs or increase revenues. These decisions affect the company's future strategies and plans.

**Amazon** has a number of budgets, as its managers develop budgets for their own divisions. Software then combines the division budgets to create an organization-wide budget for the whole company. Managers also prepare both long-term and short-term budgets. Some of the budgets are long-term forecasts that project demand for various business segments for the next 20 years. Keep in mind that all budgets incorporate management's strategic and operational plans.

However, most companies budget their cash flows monthly, weekly, and even daily to ensure that they have enough cash. They also budget revenues and expenses—and operating income—for months, quarters, and years. This chapter focuses on short-term budgets of one year or less. Chapter 21 explained how companies budget for major capital expenditures on property, plant, and equipment.

# Benefits of Budgeting

Exhibit 22-3 summarizes three key benefits of budgeting. Budgeting forces managers to plan, promotes coordination and communication, and provides a benchmark for evaluating actual performance. The budget really represents the plan the company has in place to achieve its goals.

**EXHIBIT 22-3** | **Benefits of Budgeting**

Budgets force managers to plan.

Budgets promote coordination and communication.

Budgets provide a benchmark that motivates employees and helps managers evaluate performance against planned goals.

## Planning

Exhibit 22-1 shows the expected income from Smart Touch's online e-learning business is $487,000. This is short of the target operating income of $550,000. The sooner Smart Touch learns of the expected shortfall, the more time it has to modify its plan and to devise strategies to increase revenues or cut expenses so the company can achieve its planned goals. The better Smart Touch's plan, and the more time it has to act on the plan, the more likely it will be to find a way to meet the target.

## Coordination and Communication

The master budget coordinates a company's activities. Creating a master budget facilitates coordination and communication by requiring managers at different levels and in different functions across the entire value chain to work together to make a single, unified, comprehensive plan for the business. For example, **Amazon** stimulates sales by offering free shipping on orders over a specified dollar amount. If sales increase, the shipping department may have to hire additional employees to handle the increase in shipments. The budget encourages communication among managers to ensure that the extra profits from increased sales outweigh the revenue lost from not charging for shipping.

## Benchmarking

Budgets provide a benchmark that motivates employees and helps managers evaluate performance. In most companies, part of the manager's performance evaluation depends on how actual results compare to the budget. So, for example, the budgeted expenses for international expansion encourage **Amazon**'s employees to increase the efficiency of international warehousing operations and to find less-expensive technology to support the Web sites.

Let's return to Smart Touch's e-learning business. Suppose that comparing actual results to the budget in Exhibit 22-1 leads to the performance report in Exhibit 22-4.

**EXHIBIT 22-4**    **Service Company Income Statement Performance Report**

| SMART TOUCH LEARNING, INC.<br>Income Statement Performance Report<br>For the Month Ended May 31, 2014 | | | |
|---|---|---|---|
| | Actual | Budget | Variance<br>(Actual–Budget) |
| Number of e-learning services: | 19,000 | 20,000 | (1,000) |
| Service revenue | $589,000 | $600,000 | $(11,000) |
| Variable expenses: | | | |
|    Server space expense | $ 38,000 | $ 45,000 | $ (7,000) |
|    Advertising expense | 29,450 | 30,000 | (550) |
|      Total variable expenses | 67,450 | 75,000 | (7,550) |
| Contribution margin | $521,550 | $525,000 | $ (3,450) |
| Fixed expenses: | | | |
|    Salary expense | $ 20,000 | $ 20,000 | $  — |
|    Internet access expense | 18,000 | 18,000 | — |
|      Total fixed expenses | 38,000 | 38,000 | — |
| Budgeted operating income | $483,550 | $487,000 | $ (3,450) |

This report identifies areas where the actual results differed from the budget. The differences are itemized below:

1. Actual service revenue was $11,000 less than budgeted service revenue. This was caused by two factors. First, Smart Touch sold 1,000 fewer services than it planned to sell (19,000 actual – 20,000 budgeted). Second, Smart Touch was able to sell at a higher average price per service $31 ($589,000/19,000 services) than the $30 per service it planned.

2. Variable expenses were less than budgeted for both server space expense and advertising expense. Actual server space expense was less than budgeted server space expense because Smart Touch sold 1,000 fewer services and because Smart Touch reduced the server space expense per service from $2.25 budgeted to $2.00 ($38,000/19,000 services) actual per service. Advertising expense remained constant at 5% of revenues, but due to the $11,000 reduction in revenues, advertising expense was $550 less ($11,000 × 5%).

3. Actual fixed expenses were exactly the same as budgeted fixed expenses. Although not common, considering Smart Touch's fixed expenses, one wouldn't expect these to change unless Smart Touch changed the pay rate or number of employees or unless Smart Touch negotiated a new contract with its Internet service provider.

After management reviews the variances, Smart Touch will want to consider how it can implement new strategies to meet its goals. Can Smart Touch increase the number of services sold at the new higher price? Should the company increase its advertising budget in hopes of increasing the number of services sold? Can Smart Touch reduce any of its fixed expenses?

Smart Touch needs to know the answers to these kinds of questions to decide how to meet its goals.

**Key Takeaway**

A budgeted income statement shows estimated amounts, whereas the income statement shows actual results. Managers use budgets to develop strategies (overall business goals) and to create plans and follow actions that enable them to achieve those goals. They also review results against the goals (control), often using a performance report that compares budgeted amounts to actual amounts.

# Understanding the Components of the Master Budget

Now that you know *why* managers go to the trouble of developing budgets, let's consider the steps managers take to prepare a budget.

**2** Understand the components of the master budget

## Components of the Master Budget

The **master budget** is the set of budgeted financial statements and supporting schedules for the entire organization. Exhibit 22-5 shows the order in which managers prepare the components of the master budget for a merchandiser such as **Amazon** or Greg's Tunes.

**EXHIBIT 22-5** | **Master Budget for a Merchandising Company**

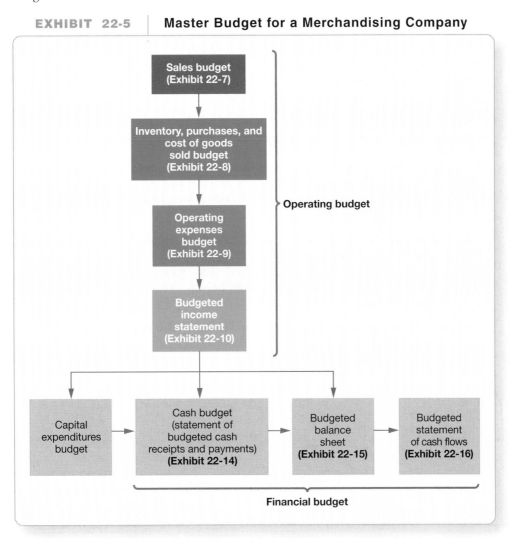

The exhibit shows that the master budget includes three types of budgets:

1. The operating budget
2. The capital expenditures budget
3. The financial budget

The **operating budget** is the set of budgets that project sales revenue, cost of goods sold, and operating expenses, leading to the budgeted income statement that projects operating income for the period. The first component of the operating budget is the sales budget, the cornerstone of the master budget. Why? Because sales affect most other components of the master budget. After projecting sales revenue, cost of goods sold, and operating expenses, management prepares the end result of the operating budget: the budgeted income statement that projects operating income for the period.

The second type of budget is the **capital expenditures budget**. This budget presents the company's plan for purchasing property, plant, equipment, and other long-term assets.

The third type of budget is the **financial budget**. Prior components of the master budget, including the budgeted income statement and the capital expenditures budget, along with plans for raising cash and paying debts, provide information for the first element of the financial budget: the cash budget. The **cash budget** details how the business expects to go from the beginning cash balance to the desired ending cash balance and feeds into the budgeted balance sheet, which, in turn, feeds into the budgeted statement of cash flows. These budgeted financial statements look exactly like ordinary statements. The only difference is that they list budgeted (projected) amounts rather than actual amounts.

## Data for Greg's Tunes

In this chapter, we will use Greg's Tunes to see how managers prepare operating and financial budgets. Chapter 21 explained the capital budgeting process. Here is the information you have. We will refer back to this information as we create the operating and financial budgets.

1. **You manage Greg's Tunes, Inc., which carries a complete line of music CDs and DVDs.** You are to prepare the store's master budget for April, May, June, and July, the main selling season. The division manager and the head of the accounting department will arrive from headquarters next week to review the budget with you.

2. **Your store's balance sheet at March 31, 2014, the beginning of the budget period, appears in Exhibit 22-6.**

**EXHIBIT 22-6** | **Balance Sheet**

GREG'S TUNES, INC.
Balance Sheet
March 31, 2014

| Assets | | | Liabilities | | |
|---|---|---|---|---|---|
| Current assets: | | | Current liabilities: | | |
| Cash | | $ 16,400 | Accounts payable | | $ 16,800 |
| Accounts receivable | | 16,000 | Salary and commissions payable | | 4,250 |
| Inventory | | 48,000 | Total liabilities | | $ 21,050 |
| Prepaid insurance | | 1,800 | | | |
| Total current assets | | $ 82,200 | **Stockholders' Equity** | | |
| Plant assets: | | | Common stock, no par | | 20,000 |
| Equipment and fixtures | 32,000 | | Retained earnings | | 60,350 |
| Less: Accumulated depreciation | 12,800 | | Total stockholders' equity | | $ 80,350 |
| Total plant assets | | $ 19,200 | Total liabilities and stockholders' | | |
| Total assets | | $101,400 | equity | | $101,400 |

3. **Sales in March were $40,000. The sales manager predicts the following monthly sales:**

| | |
|---|---:|
| April.................................................................................. | $50,000 |
| May ................................................................................. | 80,000 |
| June.................................................................................. | 60,000 |
| July .................................................................................. | 50,000 |
| August.............................................................................. | 40,000 |

   Sales are 60% cash and 40% on credit (on account). Greg's Tunes collects all credit sales the month after the sale. The $16,000 of accounts receivable at March 31, 2014, is March's credit sales ONLY (40% of $40,000). There are no other accounts receivable. Uncollectible accounts are immaterial and thus aren't included in the master budget.

4. **Greg's Tunes has a rule of thumb for maintaining enough inventory so that it does not run out of stock and potentially lose sales. It wants to have inventory at the end of each month of $20,000, plus it wants to keep an additional amount equal to 80% of what it expects to sell in the coming month.** So the rule is that ending inventory should be equal to $20,000 plus 80% of next month's cost of goods sold. Cost of goods sold averages 70% of sales. This is a variable cost.

5. **The accounts payable balance is only inventory purchases not yet paid.** Greg's pays for inventory purchases as follows: 50% during the month of purchase and 50% the month after purchase. Accounts payable consists of inventory purchases only. March purchases were $33,600, so accounts payable on Greg's March 31, 2014, balance sheet shows $16,800 ($33,600 × 0.50).

6. **Monthly payroll is salary of $2,500 plus sales commissions equal to 15% of sales.** This is a mixed cost, with both a fixed and a variable component. The company pays half this amount during the month and half early in the following month. Therefore, at the end of each month, Greg's reports salary and commissions payable equal to half the month's payroll. The $4,250 balance in Salaries and commissions payable in Exhibit 22-6 is half the March payroll of $8,500:

   March payroll = Salary of $2,500 + Sales commissions of $6,000 (0.15 × $40,000)
   = $8,500

7. **Other monthly expenses are as follows:**

| | |
|---|---|
| Rent expense (fixed cost)......................... | $2,000, paid as incurred |
| Depreciation expense, including truck (fixed cost) ............................... | 500 |
| Insurance expense (fixed cost)................. | 200 expiration of prepaid amount |
| Miscellaneous expenses (variable cost).... | 5% of sales, paid as incurred |

8. **Greg's plans to purchase a used delivery truck in April for $3,000 cash.**

9. **Greg's requires a minimum cash balance of $10,000 before financing at the end of each month.** The store can borrow money in $1,000 increments at an annual interest rate of 12%. Management borrows no more than the amount needed to maintain the $10,000 minimum cash balance before financing. Total interest expense will vary (variable cost) as the amount of borrowing varies from month to month. Notes payable require $1,000 payments of principal, plus

monthly interest on the unpaid principal balance. Borrowing and all principal and interest payments occur at the end of the month.

10. **Income taxes are ignored in order to simplify the process.**

As you prepare the master budget, remember that you are developing the store's operating and financial plan for the next four months. The steps in this process may seem mechanical, but are easily calculated with the use of Excel. (Workpapers in Excel are provided in myaccountinglab.com for every end of chapter problem.) Additionally, the template for the two Summary Problems is provided in myaccountinglab.com as a tool for you to use. In creating the master budget, you must think carefully about pricing, product lines, job assignments, needs for additional equipment, and negotiations with banks. Successful managers use this opportunity to make decisions that affect the future course of business.

# Preparing the Operating Budget

 Prepare an operating budget

The first three components of the operating budget as shown in Exhibit 22-5 are as follows:

1. Sales budget (Exhibit 22-7)
2. Inventory, purchases, and cost of goods sold budget (Exhibit 22-8)
3. Operating expenses budget (Exhibit 22-9)

The results of these three budgets feed into the fourth element of the operating budget: the budgeted income statement (Exhibit 22-10). We consider each, in turn.

## The Sales Budget

The forecast of sales revenue is the cornerstone of the master budget because the level of sales affects expenses and almost all other elements of the master budget. Budgeted total sales for each product equals the sales price multiplied by the expected number of units sold. The overall sales budget in Exhibit 22-7 is the sum of the budgets for the individual products. Trace the April through July total sales of $240,000 to the budgeted income statement in Exhibit 22-10.

**EXHIBIT 22-7** | **Sales Budget**

| | | | | | April–July |
|---|---|---|---|---|---|
| GREG'S TUNES, INC. Sales Budget April–July 2014 | | | | | |
| | April | May | June | July | April–July Total |
| Cash sales, 60% | $30,000 | $48,000 | $36,000 | $30,000 | |
| Credit collections, one month after sale, 40% | 20,000 | 32,000 | 24,000 | 20,000 | |
| Total sales, 100% | $50,000 | $80,000 | $60,000 | $50,000 | $240,000 |

## The Inventory, Purchases, and Cost of Goods Sold Budget

This budget determines cost of goods sold for the budgeted income statement, ending inventory for the budgeted balance sheet, and purchases for the cash budget. The familiar cost of goods sold computation specifies the relations among these items:

Beginning inventory + Purchases − Ending inventory = Cost of goods sold

Beginning inventory is known from last month's balance sheet, budgeted cost of goods sold averages 70% of sales, and budgeted ending inventory is a computed amount. Recall that Greg's minimum inventory rule is as follows: Ending inventory should be equal to $20,000 plus 80% of next month's cost of goods sold. You must solve for the budgeted purchases figure. To do this, rearrange the previous equation to isolate purchases on the left side:

> Purchases = Cost of goods sold + Ending inventory − Beginning inventory

This equation makes sense. How much inventory does Greg's Tunes need to purchase? Greg's should have the minimum amount of inventory to be sure the company balances providing goods to customers with turning over (selling) the inventory efficiently. Keeping inventory at the minimum level that meets these needs helps reduce inventory storage costs, insurance costs, and warehousing costs, and reduces the potential for inventory to become obsolete (not sellable). Exhibit 22-8 shows Greg's inventory, purchases, and cost of goods sold budget.

**EXHIBIT 22-8** | **Inventory, Purchases, and Cost of Goods Sold Budget**

**GREG'S TUNES, INC.**
**Inventory, Purchases, and Cost of Goods Sold Budget**
**April–July 2014**

|  | April | May | June | July | April–July Total | Source |
|---|---|---|---|---|---|---|
| Cost of goods sold (70% × sales) | $ 35,000 | $ 56,000 | $ 42,000 | $ 35,000 | $168,000 | Exhibit 22-7 |
| Desired ending inventory [$20,000 + (80% × COGS for next month)] | 64,800† | 53,600 | 48,000 | 42,400^ | | |
| Total inventory required | $ 99,800 | $109,600 | $ 90,000 | $ 77,400 | | |
| Beginning inventory | (48,000)* | (64,800) | (53,600) | (48,000) | | |
| Purchases | $ 51,800 | $ 44,800 | $ 36,400 | $ 29,400 | | |

†$20,000 + (0.80 × $56,000) = $64,800
*Balance at March 31 (Exhibit 22-6)
^$20,000 + [0.80 × (0.70 × $40,000)]

Trace the total budgeted cost of goods sold from Exhibit 22-8 of $168,000 to the budgeted income statement in Exhibit 22-10. We will use the budgeted inventory and purchases amounts later.

## The Operating Expenses Budget

Recall that Greg's operating expenses include variable and fixed expenses. One of Greg's expenses is fixed salaries of $2,500. One of Greg's variable expenses is sales commissions equal to 15% of sales (from item 6 on page 1057). Half the total salary and commission expense is paid in the month incurred and the remaining half is paid in the following month. Greg's variable operating expenses also include miscellaneous expenses of 5% of sales for the month. Greg's also has other fixed expenses of $2,000 rent, $500 depreciation, and $200 of insurance expense (from item 7 on page 1057). Exhibit 22-9 shows the operating expenses budget. Study each expense to make sure you know how it is computed. For example, sales commissions and miscellaneous expenses fluctuate with sales (variable). Salary, rent, depreciation, and insurance are the same each month (fixed).

Trace the April through July totals from the operating expenses budget in Exhibit 22-9 (commissions of $36,000, miscellaneous expenses of $12,000, and so on) to the budgeted income statement in Exhibit 22-10.

**EXHIBIT 22-9** | **Operating Expenses Budget**

GREG'S TUNES, INC.
Operating Expenses Budget
April–July 2014

| | April | May | June | July | April–July Total | Source |
|---|---|---|---|---|---|---|
| Variable operating expenses: | | | | | | |
| Commission expense, 15% of sales | $ 7,500 | $12,000 | $ 9,000 | $ 7,500 | $36,000 | Exhibit 22-7 |
| Miscellaneous expenses, 5% of sales | 2,500 | 4,000 | 3,000 | 2,500 | 12,000 | Exhibit 22-7 |
| Total variable operating expenses: | $10,000 | $16,000 | $12,000 | $10,000 | $48,000 | |
| Fixed operating expenses: | | | | | | |
| Salary expense, fixed amount | 2,500 | 2,500 | 2,500 | 2,500 | 10,000 | |
| Rent expense, fixed amount | 2,000 | 2,000 | 2,000 | 2,000 | 8,000 | |
| Depreciation expense, fixed amount | 500 | 500 | 500 | 500 | 2,000 | |
| Insurance expense, fixed amount | 200 | 200 | 200 | 200 | 800 | |
| Total fixed operating expenses | $ 5,200 | $ 5,200 | $ 5,200 | $ 5,200 | $20,800 | |
| Total operating expenses | $15,200 | $21,200 | $17,200 | $15,200 | $68,800 | |

## The Budgeted Income Statement

Use the sales budget (Exhibit 22-7); the inventory, purchases, and cost of goods sold budget (Exhibit 22-8); and the operating expenses budget (Exhibit 22-9) to prepare the budgeted income statement in Exhibit 22-10. (We explain the computation of interest expense as part of the cash budget in the next section.) Notice that the income statement highlights the contribution margin, which you learned about in Chapter 19. Recall that the contribution margin is Revenue minus Variable costs. The contribution margin should be large enough to cover fixed expenses and to make a profit for Greg's.

**EXHIBIT 22-10** | **Budgeted Income Statement**

GREG'S TUNES, INC.
Budgeted Income Statement
Four Months Ending July 31, 2014

| | | Amount | Source |
|---|---|---|---|
| Sales revenue | | $240,000 | Exhibit 22-7 |
| Cost of goods sold | | 168,000 | Exhibit 22-8 |
| Gross profit | | $ 72,000 | |
| Variable operating expenses: | | | |
| Commissions expense | $36,000 | | Exhibit 22-9 |
| Miscellaneous expenses | 12,000 | | Exhibit 22-9 |
| Total variable operating expenses | | 48,000 | |
| Contribution margin | | $ 24,000 | |
| Fixed operating expenses: | | | |
| Salary expense | $10,000 | | Exhibit 22-9 |
| Rent expense | 8,000 | | Exhibit 22-9 |
| Depreciation expense | 2,000 | | Exhibit 22-9 |
| Insurance expense | 800 | | Exhibit 22-9 |
| Total fixed operating expenses | | 20,800 | |
| Operating income | | $ 3,200 | |
| Interest expense | | (210) | *Exhibit 22-14 |
| Net income (loss) | | $ 2,990 | |

* $80 + $70 + $60

### Key Takeaway

The first three components of the operating budget include the sales budget; the inventory, purchases, and cost of goods sold budget; and the operating expenses budget. The sales budget depicts the breakdown of sales based on the terms of collection. The inventory, purchases, and cost of goods sold budget aids in planning for adequate inventory to meet sales (COGS) and for inventory purchases. The operating expenses budget captures the planned variable and fixed operating expenses necessary for normal operations. The three budgets help to form the budgeted income statement. Together these form the operational budget that depicts the company's operational strategy for a period of time.

Take this opportunity to solidify your understanding of operating budgets by carefully working out Summary Problem 22-1.

# Summary Problem 22-1

Review the Greg's Tunes example. You now think July sales might be $40,000 instead of the projected $50,000 in Exhibit 22-7. You also assume a change in sales collections as follows:

60% in the month of the sale

20% in the month after the sale

19% two months after the sale

1% never collected

You want to see how this change in sales affects the budget.

### Requirement

1. Revise the sales budget (Exhibit 22-7); the inventory, purchases, and cost of goods sold budget (Exhibit 22-8); and the operating expenses budget (Exhibit 22-9). Prepare a revised budgeted income statement for the four months ended July 31, 2014.

## Solution

### Requirement

1. Revised figures appear in color for emphasis.

**EXHIBIT 22-7R** | **Revised—Sales Budget**

GREG'S TUNES, INC.
Revised—Sales Budget
April–July 2014

|  | April | May | June | July | April–July Total |
|---|---|---|---|---|---|
| Cash sales, 60% | $30,000 | $48,000 | $36,000 | $24,000 | |
| Credit collections, one month after sale, 20% | 10,000 | 16,000 | 12,000 | 8,000 | |
| Credit collections, two months after sale, 19% | 9,500 | 15,200 | 11,400 | 7,600 | |
| Bad debts, 1% | 500 | 800 | 600 | 400 | |
| Total sales, 100% | $50,000 | $80,000 | $60,000 | $40,000 | $230,000 |

**EXHIBIT 22-8R** | **Revised—Inventory, Purchases, and Cost of Goods Sold Budget**

GREG'S TUNES, INC.
Revised—Inventory, Purchases, and Cost of Goods Sold Budget
April–July 2014

|  | April | May | June | July | April–July Total | Source |
|---|---|---|---|---|---|---|
| Cost of goods sold, (70% × sales) | $ 35,000 | $ 56,000 | $ 42,000 | $ 28,000 | $161,000 | Exhibit 22-7R |
| Desired ending inventory [$20,000 + (80% × COGS for next month)] | 64,800 | 53,600 | 42,400 | 42,400 | | |
| Total inventory required | $ 99,800 | $109,600 | $ 84,400 | $ 70,400 | | |
| Beginning inventory | (48,000) * | (64,800) | (53,600) | (42,400) | | |
| Purchases | $ 51,800 | $ 44,800 | $ 30,800 | $ 28,000 | | |

*March 31 inventory balance (Exhibit 22-6)

**EXHIBIT 22-9R** | **Revised—Operating Expenses Budget**

GREG'S TUNES, INC.
Revised—Operating Expenses Budget
April–July 2014

| | April | May | June | July | April–July Total | Source |
|---|---|---|---|---|---|---|
| Variable operating expenses: | | | | | | |
| Commission expense, 15% of sales | $ 7,500 | $12,000 | $ 9,000 | $ 6,000 | $34,500 | Exhibit 22-7R |
| Miscellaneous expenses, 5% of sales | 2,500 | 4,000 | 3,000 | 2,000 | 11,500 | Exhibit 22-7R |
| Bad debt expense, 1% of sales | 500 | 800 | 600 | 400 | 2,300 | Exhibit 22-7R |
| Total variable operating expenses: | $10,500 | $16,800 | $12,600 | $ 8,400 | $48,300 | |
| Fixed operating expenses: | | | | | | |
| Salary expense, fixed amount | 2,500 | 2,500 | 2,500 | 2,500 | 10,000 | |
| Rent expense, fixed amount | 2,000 | 2,000 | 2,000 | 2,000 | 8,000 | |
| Depreciation expense, fixed amount | 500 | 500 | 500 | 500 | 2,000 | |
| Insurance expense, fixed amount | 200 | 200 | 200 | 200 | 800 | |
| Total fixed operating expenses | $ 5,200 | $ 5,200 | $ 5,200 | $ 5,200 | $20,800 | |
| Total operating expenses | $15,700 | $22,000 | $17,800 | $13,600 | $69,100 | |

**EXHIBIT 22-10R** | **Revised—Budgeted Income Statement**

GREG'S TUNES, INC.
Revised—Budgeted Income Statement
Four Months Ending July 31, 2014

| | | | Source |
|---|---|---|---|
| Sales revenue | | $230,000 | Exhibit 22-7R |
| Cost of goods sold | | 161,000 | Exhibit 22-8R |
| Gross profit | | $ 69,000 | |
| Variable operating expenses: | | | |
| Commission expense | $34,500 | | Exhibit 22-9R |
| Miscellaneous expenses | 11,500 | | Exhibit 22-9R |
| Bad debt expense | 2,300 | | |
| Total variable operating expenses | | 48,300 | |
| Contribution margin | | $ 20,700 | |
| Fixed operating expenses: | | | |
| Salary expense | $10,000 | | Exhibit 22-9R |
| Rent expense | 8,000 | | Exhibit 22-9R |
| Depreciation expense | 2,000 | | Exhibit 22-9R |
| Insurance expense | 800 | | Exhibit 22-9R |
| Total fixed operating expenses | | 20,800 | |
| Operating income (loss) | | $ (100) | |
| Interest expense | | (450) | *Exhibit 22-14R |
| Net income (loss) | | $ (550) | |

* $160 + $150 + $140

The Master Budget and Responsibility Accounting **1063**

# Preparing the Financial Budget

Armed with a clear understanding of Greg's Tunes' operating budget, you are now ready to prepare the financial budget. Exhibit 22-5 shows that the financial budget includes the cash budget, the budgeted balance sheet, and the budgeted statement of cash flows. We start with the cash budget.

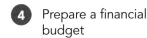 **4** Prepare a financial budget

## Preparing the Cash Budget

The *cash budget*, or statement of budgeted cash receipts and payments, details how the business expects to go from the beginning cash balance to the desired ending balance. The cash budget has four major parts:

- Budgeted cash collections from customers (Exhibit 22-11)
- Budgeted cash payments for purchases (Exhibit 22-12)
- Budgeted cash payments for operating expenses (Exhibit 22-13)
- Budgeted cash payments for capital expenditures (for example, the $3,000 capital expenditure to acquire the delivery truck). Recall that we don't cover the preparation of the capital expenditures budget in this chapter.

Cash collections and payments depend on revenues and expenses, which appear in the operating budget. This is why you cannot prepare the cash budget until you have finished the operating budget.

### Budgeted Cash Collections from Customers

Recall from item 3 on page 1057 that Greg's sales are 60% cash and 40% on credit. The 40% credit sales are collected the month after the sale is made. Exhibit 22-11 shows that April's budgeted cash collections consist of two parts: (1) April's cash sales from the sales budget in Exhibit 22-7 ($30,000) plus (2) collections of March's credit sales ($16,000 from the March 31 balance sheet, Exhibit 22-6). Trace April's $46,000 ($30,000 + $16,000) total cash collections to the cash budget in Exhibit 22-14 on page 1066.

**EXHIBIT 22-11** | **Budgeted Cash Collections**

| | April | May | June | July | April–July Total | Source |
|---|---|---|---|---|---|---|
| **GREG'S TUNES, INC.** <br> **Budgeted Cash Collections from Customers** <br> **April–July 2014** | | | | | | |
| Cash sales, 60% | $30,000 | $48,000 | $36,000 | $30,000 | | Exhibit 22-7 |
| Credit collections, one month after sale, 40% | 16,000* | 20,000 | 32,000 | 24,000 | | Exhibit 22-7 |
| Total collections | $46,000 | $68,000 | $68,000 | $54,000 | $236,000 | |

*March 31 accounts receivable (Exhibit 22-6)

### Budgeted Cash Payments for Purchases

Recall from item 5 on page 1057 that Greg's pays for inventory purchases 50% during the month of purchase and 50% the month after purchase. Exhibit 22-12 uses the inventory, purchases, and cost of goods sold budget from Exhibit 22-8 to compute budgeted cash payments for purchases of inventory. April's cash payments for purchases consist of two parts: (1) payment of 50% of March's purchases ($16,800 accounts payable balance from the March 31 balance sheet, Exhibit 22-6) plus (2) payment for 50% of April's purchases (50% × $51,800 = $25,900). Trace April's $42,700 ($16,800 + $25,900) cash payment for purchases to the cash budget in Exhibit 22-14.

**EXHIBIT 22-12** | **Budgeted Cash Payments for Purchases**

**GREG'S TUNES, INC.**
**Budgeted Cash Payments for Purchases**
April–July 2014

| | April | May | June | July | April–July Total | Source |
|---|---|---|---|---|---|---|
| 50% of last month's purchases | $16,800* | $25,900 | $22,400 | $18,200 | | Exhibit 22-8 |
| 50% of this month's purchases | 25,900 | 22,400 | 18,200 | 14,700 | | Exhibit 22-8 |
| Total payments for purchases | $42,700 | $48,300 | $40,600 | $32,900 | $164,500 | |

*March 31 accounts payable (Exhibit 22-6)

## Budgeted Cash Payments for Operating Expenses

Exhibit 22-13 uses the operating expenses budget (Exhibit 22-9) and Greg's payment information to compute cash payments for operating expenses. Greg's pays half the salary in the month incurred and half in the following month. Recall that Greg's operating expenses also include $2,000 rent, $500 depreciation, $200 of insurance expense, and miscellaneous expenses of 5% of sales for the month (from item 7 on page 1057). Greg's pays all those expenses in the month incurred except for insurance and depreciation. Recall that the insurance was prepaid insurance, so the cash payment for insurance was made before this budget period; therefore, no cash payment is made for insurance during April–July. Depreciation is a noncash expense, so it's not included in the budgeted cash payments for operating expenses. April's cash payments for operating expenses consist of four items:

| | |
|---|---|
| Payment of 50% of March's salary and commissions (from March 31 balance sheet, Exhibit 22-6) | $ 4,250 |
| Payment of 50% of April's salary and commissions (50% × $10,000, Exhibit 22-9) | 5,000 |
| Payment of rent expense (Exhibit 22-9) | 2,000 |
| Payment of miscellaneous expenses (Exhibit 22-9) | 2,500 |
| Total April cash payments for operating expenses | $13,750 |

Follow April's $13,750 cash payments for operating expenses from Exhibit 22-13 to the cash budget in Exhibit 22-14.

**EXHIBIT 22-13** | **Budgeted Cash Payments for Operating Expenses**

**GREG'S TUNES, INC**
**Budgeted Cash Payments for Operating Expenses**
**April–July 2014**

| | April | May | June | July | April–July Total | Source |
|---|---|---|---|---|---|---|
| Variable operating expenses | | | | | | |
| 50% of last month's commission expenses | $ 3,000 | $ 3,750 | $ 6,000 | $ 4,500 | | Exhibit 22-9 |
| 50% of this month's commission expenses | 3,750 | 6,000 | 4,500 | 3,750 | | Exhibit 22-9 |
| Miscellaneous expenses, 5% of sales | 2,500 | 4,000 | 3,000 | 2,500 | | Exhibit 22-9 |
| Total payments for variable operating expenses | 9,250 | 13,750 | 13,500 | 10,750 | | |
| Fixed operating expenses: | | | | | | |
| 50% of last month's salary expenses | $ 1,250 | $ 1,250 | $ 1,250 | $ 1,250 | | Exhibit 22-9 |
| 50% of this month's salary expenses | 1,250 | 1,250 | 1,250 | 1,250 | | Exhibit 22-9 |
| Rent expense | 2,000 | 2,000 | 2,000 | 2,000 | | Exhibit 22-9 |
| Total payments for fixed operating expenses | 4,500 | 4,500 | 4,500 | 4,500 | | |
| Total payments for operating expenses | $13,750 | $18,250 | $18,000 | $15,250 | $65,250 | |

## Stop & Think...

Why are depreciation expense and insurance expense from the operating expenses budget (Exhibit 22-9) *excluded* from the budgeted cash payments for operating expenses in Exhibit 22-13?

**Answer:** These expenses do not require cash outlays in the current period. Depreciation is the periodic write-off of the cost of the equipment and fixtures that Greg's Tunes acquired previously. Insurance expense is the expiration of insurance paid for in a previous period; thus, no cash payment was made to the insurance company this period.

## The Cash Budget

To prepare the cash budget in Exhibit 22-14, start with the beginning cash balance (Exhibit 22-6) and add the budgeted cash collections from Exhibit 22-11 to determine the cash available. Then, subtract cash payments for purchases (Exhibit 22-12), operating expenses (Exhibit 22-13), and any capital expenditures. This yields the ending cash balance before financing.

Item 9 on page 1057 states that Greg's Tunes requires a minimum cash balance before financing of $10,000. April's $2,950 budgeted cash balance before financing falls $7,050 short of the minimum required ($10,000 – $2,950). To be able to access short-term financing, Greg's must have secured an existing line of credit with the company's bank. Securing this credit in advance is crucial to having the credit available to draw upon when cash shortages arise. Because Greg's borrows in $1,000 increments, the company will have to borrow $8,000 to cover April's expected shortfall. The budgeted ending cash balance equals the "ending cash balance before financing," adjusted for the total effects of the financing (an $8,000 inflow in April). Exhibit 22-14 shows that Greg's expects to end April with $10,950 of cash ($2,950 + $8,000). Recall additionally that when Greg's borrows, the amount borrowed is to be paid back in $1,000 installments plus interest at 12% annually. Note that in May, Greg's begins to pay the $8,000 borrowed in April. Greg's must also pay interest at 12%. For May, the interest paid is calculated as $8,000 owed × 12% × $\frac{1}{12}$ of the year, or $80 interest. For June, Greg's interest owed will change because the principal of the note has been paid down $1,000 in May. June interest is calculated as ($8,000 – $1,000) owed × 12% × $\frac{1}{12}$ of the year, or $70 interest. For July, interest is ($8,000 – $1,000 – $1,000) owed × 12% × $\frac{1}{12}$

of the year, or $60 interest. Exhibit 22-14 also shows the cash balance at the end of May, June, and July.

**EXHIBIT 22-14** | **Cash Budget**

GREG'S TUNES, INC.
Cash Budget
Four Months Ending July 31, 2014

|  | April | May | June | July | Source |
|---|---|---|---|---|---|
| Beginning cash balance | $ 16,400* | $ 10,950 | $ 11,320 | $ 19,650 | |
| Cash collections | 46,000 | 68,000 | 68,000 | 54,000 | Exhibit 22-11 |
| Cash available | $ 62,400 | $ 78,950 | $ 79,320 | $ 73,650 | |
| Cash payments: | | | | | |
|   Purchases of inventory | 42,700 | 48,300 | 40,600 | 32,900 | Exhibit 22-12 |
|   Operating expenses | 13,750 | 18,250 | 18,000 | 15,250 | Exhibit 22-13 |
|   Purchase of delivery truck | 3,000 | | | | |
| Total cash payments | 59,450 | 66,550 | 58,600 | 48,150 | |
| (1) Ending cash balance before financing | $ 2,950 | $ 12,400 | $ 20,720 | $ 25,500 | |
| Minimum cash balance desired | (10,000) | (10,000) | (10,000) | (10,000) | |
| Cash excess (deficiency) | $ (7,050) | $ 2,400 | $ 10,720 | $ 15,500 | |
|   Financing of cash deficiency: | | | | | |
|     Borrowing (at end of month)[a] | 8,000 | — | — | — | |
|     Principal payments (at end of month, at $1,000) | | (1,000) | (1,000) | (1,000) | |
|     Interest expense (at 12% annually)[b] | | (80) | (70) | (60) | |
| (2) Total effects of financing | 8,000 | (1,080) | (1,070) | (1,060) | |
| Ending cash balance (1) + (2) | $ 10,950 | $ 11,320 | $ 19,650 | $ 24,440 | |

*March 31 cash balance (Exhibit 22-6)
[a] Borrowing occurs in multiples of $1,000 and only for the amount needed to maintain a minimum cash balance before financing of $10,000
[b] Interest expense: May: $8,000 × (0.12 × 1/12) = $80; June: ($8,000 – $1,000) × (0.12 × 1/12) = $70; July: ($8,000 – $1,000 – $1,000) × (0.12 × 1/12) = $60

The cash balance at the end of July of $24,440 is the cash balance in the July 31 budgeted balance sheet in Exhibit 22-15.

**EXHIBIT 22-15** | **Budgeted Balance Sheet**

**GREG'S TUNES, INC.**
**Budgeted Balance Sheet**
**July 31, 2014**

| Assets | | Source |
|---|---|---|
| Current assets: | | |
| Cash | $ 24,440 | Exhibit 22-14 |
| Accounts receivable | 20,000 | Exhibit 22-7 |
| Inventory | 42,400 | Exhibit 22-8 |
| Prepaid insurance | 1,000 | Beg. Bal. $1,800 – (Exhibit 22-9) ($200 per month expiration × 4 months) |
| Total current assets | $ 87,840 | |
| Plant assets: | | |
| Equipment and fixtures | $ 35,000 | Beg. Bal. $32,000 + (Item 8, p 1057) $3,000 truck acquisition |
| Less: Accumulated depreciation | 14,800 | Beg. Bal. $12,800 + (Exhibit 22-9) ($500 per month depreciation × 4 months) |
| Total plant assets | 20,200 | |
| Total assets | $108,040 | |
| **Liabilities** | | |
| Current liabilities: | | |
| Accounts payable | $ 14,700 | July purchases from Exhibit 22-8 of $29,400 × 50% paid in month after purchase |
| Salary and commissions payable | 5,000 | (July salary of $2,500 plus July commissions of $7,500 from Exhibit 22-9) × 50% paid in month after incurred |
| Short-term notes payable | 5,000 | $8,000 borrowed in April (revised cash budget) – ($1,000 principal repayments × 3 months) (Exhibit 22-14) |
| Total liabilities | $ 24,700 | |
| **Stockholders' Equity** | | |
| Common stock, no par | $ 20,000 | Exhibit 22-6 |
| Retained earnings | 63,340 | Beg. Bal. $60,350 + net income from Exhibit 22-10 income statement $2,990 |
| Total stockholders' equity | 83,340 | |
| Total liabilities and stockholders' equity | $108,040 | |

## The Budgeted Balance Sheet

To prepare the budgeted balance sheet, project each asset, liability, and stockholders' equity account based on the plans outlined in the previous exhibits.

Study the budgeted balance sheet in Exhibit 22-15 to make certain you understand the computation of each figure. For example, on the budgeted balance sheet as of July 31, 2014, budgeted cash equals the ending cash balance from the cash budget in Exhibit 22-14. Accounts receivable as of July 31 equal July's credit sales of $20,000, shown in the sales budget (Exhibit 22-7). July 31 inventory of $42,400 is July's desired ending inventory in the inventory, purchases, and cost of goods sold budget in Exhibit 22-8. Detailed computations for each of the other accounts appear in Exhibit 22-15.

## The Budgeted Statement of Cash Flows

The final step is preparing the budgeted statement of cash flows. Use the information from the schedules of cash collections and payments, the cash budget, and the beginning balance of cash to project cash flows from operating, investing, and financing activities. Take time to study Exhibit 22-16 on the next page and make sure you understand the origin of each figure.

**EXHIBIT 22-16** | **Budgeted Statement of Cash Flows**

### GREG'S TUNES, INC.
### Budgeted Statement of Cash Flows
### Four Months Ending July 31, 2014

| | | | Source |
|---|---|---|---|
| Cash flows from operating activities: | | | |
| Receipts: | | | |
| Collections from customers | $ 236,000 | | Exhibit 22-11 |
| Total cash receipts | | $ 236,000 | |
| Payments: | | | |
| To suppliers for purchases of inventory | (164,500) | | Exhibit 22-12 |
| For operating expenses | (65,250) | | Exhibit 22-13 |
| For interest | (210) | | Exhibit 22-14 |
| Total cash payments | | (229,960) | |
| Net cash provided by operating activities | | $ 6,040 | |
| Cash flows from investing activities: | | | |
| Acquisition of delivery truck | (3,000) | | |
| Net cash used by investing activities | | (3,000) | |
| Cash flows from financing activities: | | | |
| Proceeds from issuance of notes payable | 8,000 | | Exhibit 22-14 |
| Payment of notes payable | (3,000) | | Exhibit 22-14 |
| Net cash provided by financing activities | | 5,000 | |
| Net increase in cash | | $ 8,040 | |
| Cash balance, April 1, 2014 | | 16,400 | Exhibit 22-6 |
| Cash balance, July 31, 2014 | | $ 24,440 | Exhibit 22-14 |

# Getting Employees to Accept the Budget

What is the most important part of Greg's Tunes' budgeting system? Despite all the numbers we have crunched, it is not the mechanics. It is getting managers and employees to accept the budget so Greg's can reap the planning, coordination, and control benefits illustrated in Exhibit 22-3.

Few people enjoy having their work monitored and evaluated. So if managers use the budget as a benchmark to evaluate employees' performance, managers must first motivate employees to accept the budget's goals. Here is how they can do it:

- Managers must support the budget themselves, or no one else will.
- Managers must show employees how budgets can help them achieve better results.
- Managers must have employees participate in developing the budget.

But these principles alone are not enough. As the manager of Greg's, your performance is evaluated by comparing actual results to the budget. When you develop the company's budget, you may be tempted to build in *slack*. For example, you might want to budget fewer sales and higher purchases than you expect. This increases the chance that actual performance will be better than the budget and that you will receive a good evaluation. But adding slack into the budget makes it less accurate—and less useful for planning and control. When the division manager and the head of the accounting department arrive from headquarters next week, they will scour your budget to find any slack you may have inserted.

Now, we'll continue our budget example started in Summary Problem 22-1 in Summary Problem 22-2.

**Key Takeaway**

The cash budget details how the business expects to go from the beginning cash balance to the desired ending balance each period. The cash budget has four major parts: cash collections from customers, cash payments for purchases, cash payments for operating expenses, and cash payments for capital expenditures. The results of these budgets are combined to form the cash budget. After preparing the cash budget, the rest of the financial statement budgets are prepared, including the budgeted balance sheet and budgeted statement of cash flows. These budgets depict the financial plan that implements the strategic goals of the company.

# Summary Problem 22-2

Continue the revised Greg's Tunes illustration from Summary Problem 22-1. Recall that you think July sales will be $40,000 instead of $50,000, as projected in Exhibit 22-7. You also assume a change in sales collections as follows:

60% in the month of the sale

20% in the month after the sale

19% two months after the sale

1% never collected

How will this affect the financial budget?

## Requirements

1. Revise the schedule of budgeted cash collections (Exhibit 22-11), the schedule of budgeted cash payments for purchases (Exhibit 22-12), and the schedule of budgeted cash payments for operating expenses (Exhibit 22-13).

2. Prepare a revised cash budget (Exhibit 22-14), a revised budgeted balance sheet at July 31, 2014 (Exhibit 22-15), and a revised budgeted statement of cash flows for the four months ended July 31, 2014 (Exhibit 22-16). *Note: Round values to the nearest dollar.*

## Solution

### Requirement 1

1. Revised figures appear in color for emphasis.

**EXHIBIT 22-11R** | **Revised—Budgeted Cash Collections from Customers**

GREG'S TUNES, INC.
Revised—Budgeted Cash Collections from Customers
April–July 2014

|  | April | May | June | July | April–July Total | Source |
|---|---|---|---|---|---|---|
| Cash sales, 60% | $30,000 | $48,000 | $36,000 | $24,000 | | Exhibit 22-7R |
| Credit collections, one month after sale, 20% | 8,000 | 10,000 | 16,000 | 12,000 | | Exhibit 22-7R |
| Credit collections, two months after sale, 19% | ^ | 7,600 | 9,500 | 15,200 | | Exhibit 22-7R |
| Total collections | $38,000 | $65,600 | $61,500 | $51,200 | $216,300 | |

*Notice that $400 (1% × $40,000 sales) of the March 31 Accounts receivable balance (Exhibit 22-6) of $16,000 is never collected (bad debt) and thus should appear as an expense on the March 31 income statement and will reduce the March 31 balance in Retained earnings.
^There were no accounts receivable for February.

**EXHIBIT 22-12R** | **Revised—Budgeted Cash Payments for Purchases**

GREG'S TUNES, INC.
Revised—Budgeted Cash Payments for Purchases
April–July 2014

|  | April | May | June | July | April–July Total | Source |
|---|---|---|---|---|---|---|
| 50% of last month's purchases | $16,800* | $25,900 | $22,400 | $15,400 | | Exhibit 22-8R |
| 50% of this month's purchases | 25,900 | 22,400 | 15,400 | 14,000 | | Exhibit 22-8R |
| Total payments for purchases | $42,700 | $48,300 | $37,800 | $29,400 | $158,200 | |

*March 31 accounts payable (Exhibit 22-6)

**EXHIBIT 22-13R** | **Revised—Budgeted Cash Payments for Operating Expenses**

GREG'S TUNES, INC
Revised—Budgeted Cash Payments for Operating Expenses
April–July 2014

| | April | May | June | July | April–July Total | Source |
|---|---|---|---|---|---|---|
| Variable operating expenses: | | | | | | |
| 50% of last month's commission expense | $ 3,000 | $ 3,750 | $ 6,000 | $ 4,500 | | Exhibit 22-9R |
| 50% of this month's commission expense | 3,750 | 6,000 | 4,500 | 3,000 | | Exhibit 22-9R |
| Miscellaneous expenses, 5% of sales | 2,500 | 4,000 | 3,000 | 2,000 | | Exhibit 22-9R |
| Total payments for variable operating expenses | 9,250 | 13,750 | 13,500 | 9,500 | | |
| Fixed operating expenses: | | | | | | |
| 50% of last month's salary expense | $ 1,250 | $ 1,250 | $ 1,250 | $ 1,250 | | Exhibit 22-9R |
| 50% of this month's salary expense | 1,250 | 1,250 | 1,250 | 1,250 | | Exhibit 22-9R |
| Rent expense | 2,000 | 2,000 | 2,000 | 2,000 | | Exhibit 22-9R |
| Total payments for fixed operating expenses | 4,500 | 4,500 | 4,500 | 4,500 | | |
| Total payments for operating expenses | $13,750 | $18,250 | $18,000 | $14,000 | $64,000 | |

## Requirement 2

**EXHIBIT 22-14R** | **Revised—Cash Budget**

GREG'S TUNES, INC.
Revised—Cash Budget
Four Months Ending July 31, 2014

| | April | May | June | July | Source |
|---|---|---|---|---|---|
| Beginning cash balance | $ 16,400* | $ 10,950 | $ 8,840 | $ 13,390 | |
| Cash collections | 38,000 | 65,600 | 61,500 | 51,200 | Exhibit 22-11R |
| Cash available | $ 54,400 | $ 76,550 | $ 70,340 | $ 64,590 | |
| Cash payments: | | | | | |
| Purchases of inventory | 42,700 | 48,300 | 37,800 | 29,400 | Exhibit 22-12R |
| Operating expenses | 13,750 | 18,250 | 18,000 | 14,000 | Exhibit 22-13R |
| Purchase of delivery truck | 3,000 | | | | |
| Total cash payments | 59,450 | 66,550 | 55,800 | 43,400 | |
| (1)  Ending cash balance before financing | $ (5,050) | $ 10,000 | $ 14,540 | $ 21,190 | |
| Minimum cash balance desired | (10,000) | (10,000) | (10,000) | (10,000) | |
| Cash excess (deficiency) | $(15,050) | $ — | $ 4,540 | $ 11,190 | |
| Financing of cash deficiency | | | | | |
| Borrowing (at end of month)a | 16,000 | — | — | — | |
| Principal payments (at end of month, at $1,000) | | (1,000) | (1,000) | (1,000) | |
| Interest expense (at 12% annually)b | | (160) | (150) | (140) | |
| (2)  Total effects of financing | 16,000 | (1,160) | (1,150) | (1,140) | |
| Ending cash balance (1) + (2) | $ 10,950 | $ 8,840 | $ 13,390 | $ 20,050 | |

*March 31 cash balance (Exhibit 22-6)

a Borrowing occurs in multiples of $1,000 and only for the amount needed to maintain a minimum cash balance before financing of $10,000

b Interest expense: May: $16,000 × (0.12 × 1/12) = $160; June: ($16,000 – $1,000) × (0.12 × 1/12) = $150; July: ($16,000 – $1,000 – $1,000) × (0.12 × 1/12) = $140

**EXHIBIT 22-15R** | **Revised—Budgeted Balance Sheet**

| | | GREG'S TUNES, INC.<br>Revised—Budgeted Balance Sheet<br>July 31, 2014 |
|---|---|---|
| **Assets** | | **Source** |
| Current assets: | | |
|   Cash | $ 20,050 | Revised cash budget (Exhibit 22-14R) |
|   Accounts receivable | 27,000 | Revised sales budget (Exhibit 22-7R)—collections not made yet<br>(June, $11,400 + July, $8,000 + July, $7,600) |
|   Inventory | 42,400 | Revised inventory, purchases, and COGS budget (Exhibit 22-8R) |
|   Prepaid insurance | 1,000 | Beg. Bal. $1,800 – (200 per month expiration $\times$ 4 months) |
|   Total current assets | $ 90,450 | |
| Plant assets: | | |
|   Equipment and fixtures | $ 35,000 | April Beg. Bal. $32,000 (Exhibit 22-6) + $3,000 truck acquisition |
|   Less: Accumulated depreciation | 14,800 | April Beg. Bal. $12,800 (Exhibit 22-6) + ($500 per month<br>depreciation $\times$ 4 months) |
|   Total plant assets | 20,200 | |
| Total assets | $110,650 | |
| **Liabilities** | | |
| Current liabilities: | | |
|   Accounts payable | $ 14,000 | July purchases of $28,000 $\times$ 50% paid in month after purchase |
|   Salary and commissions payable | 4,250 | July salary and comissions of $8,500 $\times$ 50% paid in month<br>after incurred |
|   Short-term notes payable | 13,000 | $16,000 borrowed in April (revised cash budget Exhibit 22-14R) –<br>($1,000 principal repayments $\times$ 3 months) |
| Total liabilities | $ 31,250 | |
| **Stockholders' Equity** | | |
|   Common stock | $ 20,000 | Exhibit 22-6 |
|   Retained earnings | 59,400 | Beg. Bal. $60,350 – March accounts receivable never collected<br>$400 – loss from revised income statement $550 |
| Total stockholders' equity | 79,400 | |
| Total liabilities and stockholders' equity | $110,650 | |

**EXHIBIT 22-16R** | **Revised—Budgeted Statement of Cash Flows**

GREG'S TUNES, INC.
Revised—Budgeted Statement of Cash Flows
Four Months Ending July 31, 2014

| | | | Source |
|---|---|---|---|
| Cash flows from operating activities: | | | |
| Receipts: | | | |
| Collections from customers | $216,300 | | Revised budgeted cash collections (Exhibit 22-11R) |
| Total cash receipts | | $ 216,300 | |
| Payments: | | | |
| To suppliers for purchases of inventory | (158,200) | | Revised budgeted cash payments for purchases (Exhibit 22-12R) |
| For operating expenses | (64,000) | | Revised budgeted cash payments for operating expenses (Exhibit 22-13R) |
| For interest | (450) | | Revised cash budget (Exhibit 22-14R) |
| Total cash payments | | (222,650) | |
| Net cash provided by operating activities | | $ (6,350) | |
| Cash flows from investing activities: | | | |
| Acquisition of delivery truck | (3,000) | | |
| Net cash used by investing activities | | (3,000) | |
| Cash flows from financing activities: | | | |
| Proceeds from issuance of notes payable | 16,000 | | Revised cash budget (Exhibit 22-14R) |
| Payment of notes payable | (3,000) | | Revised cash budget (Exhibit 22-14R) |
| Net cash provided by financing activities | | 13,000 | |
| Net increase in cash | | $ 3,650 | |
| Cash balance, April 1, 2014 | | 16,400 | Exhibit 22-6 |
| Cash balance, July 31, 2014 | | $ 20,050 | Exhibit 22-14R |

# Using Information Technology for Sensitivity Analysis and Rolling Up Unit Budgets

 **5** Use sensitivity analysis in budgeting

Exhibits 22-7 through 22-16 show that managers must prepare many calculations to develop the master budget for just one of the retail stores in the Greg's Tunes merchandising chain. Technology makes it more cost-effective for managers to

- conduct sensitivity analysis on their own unit's budget, and
- combine individual unit budgets to create the companywide master budget.

## Sensitivity Analysis

The master budget models the company's *planned* activities. Top management pays special attention to ensure that the results of the budgeted income statement (Exhibit 22-10), the cash budget (Exhibit 22-14), and the budgeted balance sheet (Exhibit 22-15) support key strategies.

But actual results often differ from plans, so management wants to know how budgeted income and cash flows would change if key assumptions turned out to be incorrect. In Chapter 19, we defined *sensitivity analysis* as a *what-if* technique that asks *what* a result will be *if* a predicted amount is not achieved or *if* an underlying assumption changes. *What if* the stock market crashes? How will this affect **Amazon.com**'s sales? Will it have to postpone a planned expansion in Asia and Europe? *What* will Greg's Tunes' cash balance be on July 31 *if* the period's sales are 45% cash, not 60% cash? Will Greg's have to borrow more cash?

Most companies use computer spreadsheet programs like Excel to prepare master budget schedules and statements. Today, what-if budget questions are easily changed within Excel with a few keystrokes. (Note: All the budgets presented in the chapter material and in both Summary Problems are available online at myaccountinglab.com for your use.)

Technology makes it cost-effective to perform more comprehensive sensitivity analyses. Armed with a better understanding of how changes in sales and costs are likely to affect the company's bottom line, today's managers can react quickly if key assumptions underlying the master budget (such as sales price or quantity) turn out to be wrong. Summary Problems 22-1 and 22-2 are examples of sensitivity analysis for Greg's Tunes.

## Rolling Up Individual Unit Budgets into the Companywide Budget

Greg's Tunes operates three retail stores. As Exhibit 22-17 shows, Greg's Tunes' headquarters must roll up the budget data from each of the stores to prepare the companywide master budgeted income statement. This roll-up can be difficult for companies whose units use different spreadsheets to prepare the budgets.

**EXHIBIT 22-17** | **Rolling Up Individual Unit Budgets into the Companywide Budget**

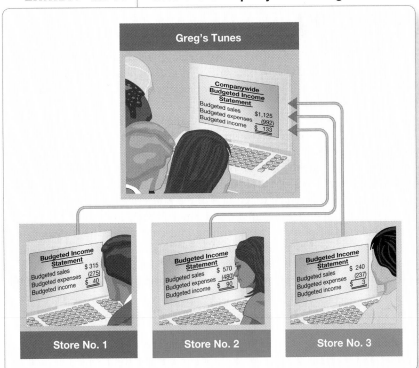

Companies like **Sunoco** turn to budget-management software to solve this problem. Often designed as a component of the company's Enterprise Resource Planning (ERP) system (or data warehouse), this software helps managers develop and analyze budgets.

Software allows managers to conduct sensitivity analyses on their own unit's data. When the manager is satisfied with his or her budget, he or she can enter it in the companywide budget easily. His or her unit's budget automatically rolls up with budgets from all other units around the world.

Whether at headquarters or on the road, top executives can log into the budget system through the Internet and conduct their own sensitivity analyses on individual units' budgets or on the companywide budget. The result: Managers spend less time compiling and summarizing data and more time analyzing and making decisions that ensure the budget leads the company to achieve its key strategic goals.

## Stop & Think...

Consider two budget situations: (1) Greg's Tunes' marketing analysts produce a forecast for four-month sales of $4,500,000 for the company's three stores. (2) Much uncertainty exists about the period's sales. The most likely amount is $4,500,000, but marketing considers any amount between $3,900,000 and $5,100,000 to be possible. How will the budgeting process differ in these two circumstances?

**Answer:** Greg's will prepare a master budget for the expected sales level of $4,500,000 in either case. Because of the uncertainty in the second situation, executives will want a set of budgets covering the entire range of volume rather than a single level. Greg's Tunes' managers may prepare budgets based on sales of, for example, $3,900,000, $4,200,000, $4,500,000, $4,800,000, and $5,100,000. These budgets will help managers plan for sales levels throughout the forecasted range.

# Responsibility Accounting

 Prepare performance reports for responsibility centers and account for traceable and common shared fixed costs.

You have now seen how managers set strategic goals and then develop plans and budget resources for activities that will help reach those goals. Let's look more closely at how managers *use* reports to control operations. We'll use Smart Touch's information for this analysis.

Each manager is responsible for planning and controlling some part of the firm's activities. A **responsibility center** is a part of the organization for which a manager has decision-making authority and accountability for the results of those decisions. **A responsibility center is the part of the organization that a particular manager is responsible for.** Lower-level managers are often responsible for budgeting and controlling costs of a single value-chain function. For example, one manager is responsible for planning and controlling the *production* of Smart Touch's DVDs at the plant, while another manager is responsible for planning and controlling the *distribution* of the product to customers. Lower-level managers report to higher-level managers, who have broader responsibilities. Managers in charge of production and distribution report to senior managers responsible for profits earned by an entire product line.

## Four Types of Responsibility Centers

**Responsibility accounting** is a system for evaluating the performance of each responsibility center and its manager. The goal of these reports is to provide relevant information to those managers empowered to make decisions.

This decentralization highlights the need for reports on individual *segments*, which are parts of the company for which managers need reports. Segments are typically defined as one of the types of responsibility centers illustrated in Exhibit 22-18. The four types of responsibility centers are as follows:

1. **In a cost center, managers are accountable for costs (expenses) only.** Manufacturing operations, such as the CD production lines, are cost centers. The line foreman

**EXHIBIT 22-18** | **Four Types of Responsibility Centers**

1. In a **cost center**, such as a production line for CDs, managers are responsible for costs.

2. In a **revenue center**, such as the Midwest sales region, managers are responsible for generating sales revenue.

3. In a **profit center**, such as a line of products, managers are responsible for both revenues and costs.

4. In an **investment center**, such as the CD, DVD, and e-learning divisions, managers are responsible for investments, revenues, and costs.

controls costs by monitoring materials costs, repairs and maintenance expenses, employee costs (wages, salaries, and benefits), and employee efficiency. The foreman is *not* responsible for generating revenues because he or she is not involved in selling the product. The plant manager evaluates the foreman on his or her ability to control *costs* by comparing actual costs to budgeted costs (covered in the next chapter).

2. **In a revenue center, managers are primarily accountable for revenues.** Examples include the Midwest and Southeast sales regions of businesses that carry Smart Touch's products, such as CDs and DVDs.

3. **In a profit center, managers are accountable for both revenues and costs (expenses) and, therefore, profits.** The (higher-level) manager responsible for the entire CD product line would be accountable for increasing sales revenue *and* controlling costs to achieve the profit goals. Profit center reports include both revenues and expenses to show the profit center's income.

4. **In an investment center, managers are accountable for investments, revenues, and costs (expenses).** Examples include the **Chevrolet** division (subsidiary) of **General Motors** and the DVD division of Smart Touch. Managers of investment centers are responsible for (1) generating sales, (2) controlling expenses, (3) managing the amount of capital required to earn the income (revenues minus expenses), and (4) planning future investments for growth and expansion of the company.

Top management often evaluates investment center managers based on return on investment (ROI), residual income (RI), or economic value added (EVA). Chapter 24 explains how these measures are calculated and used. All else being equal, the manager will receive a more favorable evaluation if the division's actual ROI, RI, or EVA exceeds the amount budgeted.

## Responsibility Accounting Performance Reports

Exhibit 22-19 shows how an organization like Smart Touch may assign responsibility.

At the top level, the CEO oversees each of the three divisions. Division managers generally have broad responsibility, including deciding how to use assets to maximize ROI. Most companies classify divisions as *investment centers*.

**EXHIBIT 22-19** | **Partial Organization Chart**

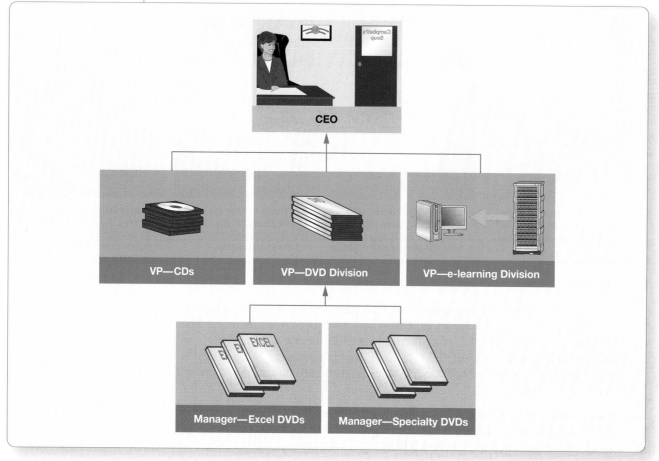

Each division manager supervises all the product lines in that division. Exhibit 22-19 shows that the VP of the DVD division oversees the Excel and Specialty DVD lines. Product lines are generally considered *profit centers*. Thus, the manager of the Excel DVD product line is responsible for evaluating lower-level managers of both

- *cost centers* (such as plants that make Excel DVD products) and
- *revenue centers* (such as managers responsible for selling Excel DVD products).

## Learn about Service Departments

In most companies, there are departments that provide services to multiple departments or divisions for the company. These shared resources are often called *service departments* because they provide *services* to other departments at the same company. Another common characteristic of service departments is that they usually do not generate revenues. This is similar to the shared production overhead we allocated in the activity-based costing chapter, only now we are talking about nonproduction related service departments. Some examples of service departments follow:

- Payroll and Human Resources
- Accounting
- Copying/Graphic Services

- Physical Plant (repairs and maintains administrative and production facilities)
- Advertising (companywide, not specific products)
- Mail and Shipping Services
- Shared Facilities (such as meeting rooms used by various departments)
- Legal Services
- Travel Booking Services

This list is not all-inclusive, but merely some common centralized functions. For example, at your college or university, there are many similar shared services that support academic departments such as the library, admissions, counseling center and information technology. The key is that a service department is a centralized, nonrevenue generating department that provides services to many departments within a company.

It is clear these service costs provide value to other parts of the company. But should we charge these costs to those divisions, products, or segments? The key to that question is to determine if the cost is *traceable* to a particular product, division, or business segment. If the costs are purely variable, tracing those costs to a specific product, division, or segment is easily identifiable. If the costs are fixed, it becomes a bit more challenging. **Traceable fixed costs** are fixed costs that can be directly associated with an individual product, division, or business segment. **A traceable fixed cost would disappear if the company discontinued making the product or discontinued operating the division or the segment.** For example, Smart Touch's DVD manager's salary is traceable to the DVD product line. **Untraceable fixed costs (or common fixed costs)** are those fixed costs that cannot be directly associated with an individual product, division, or business segment. For example, the salary of Sheena Bright, president of Smart Touch, is not traceable to a specific product line, division, or business segment. Therefore, her salary would be an untraceable fixed cost.

## Assigning Traceable Service Department Costs

So, how do companies charge various departments for their use of service departments? Let's start with an example. Suppose Smart Touch incurs $40,000 per month to operate the Centralized Ordering Department. $30,000 is considered traceable fixed costs of the three divisions: CDs, DVDs, and e-Learning. $10,000 of the total $40,000 of Centralized Ordering Department costs are considered untraceable (common). How should the company assign the $30,000 traceable fixed cost among the three divisions? Splitting the cost equally—charging each division $10,000—may not be fair, especially if the three units do not use the services equally. Smart Touch's data for assigning the payroll costs follows in Exhibit 22-20, showing not only the three divisions but also a further separation of information, for the DVD division.

Ideally, the company should assign the $30,000 traceable fixed costs based on each division's use of centralized ordering services. The company should use the primary activity that drives (increases or decreases) the cost of central ordering services as the assignment base. As you may recall from Chapter 18, companies identify cost drivers when they implement activity-based costing (ABC). Therefore, a company that has already implemented ABC should know what cost drivers would be suitable for assigning traceable service department charges. For example, order processing cost may be driven by the number of orders placed. Exhibit 22-21 provides several examples of centralized services and common assignment bases.

**EXHIBIT 22-20** | **Smart Touch Learning's Data for Traceable Cost Assignment**

| Divisions Sharing Order Processing Services | Number of Orders (assignment base) | Sales Revenue | Variable Expenses (includes variable COGS) |
|---|---|---|---|
| CD | 100,000 | $3,600,000 | $3,040,000 |
| DVD | 140,000 | 1,200,000 | 850,000 |
| e-Learning | 160,000 | 3,840,000 | 3,350,000 |
| Total | 400,000 | $8,640,000 | $7,240,000 |

| Departments in the DVD Division Sharing Order Processing Services | Number of Orders (assignment base) | Sales Revenue | Variable Expenses (includes variable COGS) |
|---|---|---|---|
| Excel DVDs | 84,000 | $ 960,000 | $680,000 |
| Specialty DVDs | 56,000 | 240,000 | 170,000 |
| Total | 140,000 | $1,200,000 | $850,000 |

**EXHIBIT 22-21** | **Common Service Departments**

| Centralized Service Departments | Examples of Departments' Cost | Typical Base Used to Assign Traceable Portion |
|---|---|---|
| Payroll and Human Resources | Payroll and human resources' salaries, depreciation on equipment and facilities, payroll software | Number of employees |
| Accounting | Accounting personnel salaries, depreciation on equipment and facilities used by accounting staff, accounting software costs | Number of reports prepared |
| Copying/Graphic Services | Copier depreciation, toner and paper, salaries of Copying/Graphic Services | Number of copies made for department |
| Physical Plant | Salaries of physical plant employees, depreciation on physical plant equipment, cost of repair and maintenance parts, plant supplies (glue, bolts, small tools) | Number of repairs made |
| Order Processing | Cost of telephone lines and employee salaries | Number of orders |
| Mail and Shipping Services | Cost of shipping/mailing, salaries of shipping personnel, depreciation on equipment and facilities used by mail personnel | Pieces of mail processed |
| Shared Facilities | Depreciation on furniture and fixtures, utilities cost | Allocation based on hours of use |
| Legal | Salaries of legal department personnel, depreciation on legal department equipment, software costs | Number of hours spent on legal matters |
| Travel | Salaries of travel department personnel, depreciation on travel department equipment, software costs | Number of business trips booked |

Based on the data in Exhibit 22-20, Smart Touch would probably chose the "number of orders" as the cost driver for assigning the $30,000 in traceable fixed ordering costs as this would closely match how much each division uses the Order Processing Department. First, Smart Touch would calculate a cost per order of $0.075 ($30,000/400,000 orders). Smart Touch's data is in Exhibit 22-20. Exhibit 22-22 shows the assignment of the $30,000 traceable costs based on the total number of orders placed for each division.

**EXHIBIT 22-22** | **Smart Touch's Assignment of Traceable Order Processing Services (Three Divisions) Using Number of Orders**

| Divisions Sharing Order Processing Services | Number of Orders (assignment base) | Cost per Order | Service Department Charge (Orders × $0.075 per order) |
|---|---|---|---|
| CD | 100,000 | $0.075 | $ 7,500 |
| DVD | 140,000 | $0.075 | 10,500 |
| e-Learning | 160,000 | $0.075 | 12,000 |
| Total | 400,000 | $0.075 | $30,000 |

The assignment of the Order Processing Department's traceable costs for Smart Touch can be further broken down by product line. We determined in Exhibit 22-22 that the DVD division was allocated $10,500 of the total $30,000 traceable Order Processing Department costs when we used number of orders as an activity base. From earlier chapters we know that Smart Touch's DVD division mainly produces two types of DVDs—Excel DVDs and Specialty DVDs. Of the $10,500 in traceable order processing costs of the DVD division, only $7,000 of those costs are traceable to the two products and $3,500 of those costs are untraceable (common). We need to assign the $7,000 in traceable order processing costs for the DVD division to the two product lines within the DVD division to determine the profit from each product line. First, Smart Touch would calculate a cost per order of $0.05 ($7,000/140,000 orders). Then, Smart Touch would assign the $7,000 traceable order processing costs between Excel and Specialty DVDs as before and as shown in Exhibit 22-23.

**EXHIBIT 22-23** | **Smart Touch's Assignment of Traceable Order Processing Services (DVD Division) Using Number of Orders**

| Divisions Sharing Order Processing Services | Number of Orders (assignment base) | Cost per Order | Service Department Charge (orders × $0.05) |
|---|---|---|---|
| Excel DVD | 84,000 | $0.05 | $4,200 |
| Specialty DVD | 56,000 | $0.05 | 2,800 |
| Total | 140,000 | $0.05 | $7,000 |

Step 3 would calculate income by division and by product line after assigning all traceable costs. To simplify the example, we assume the only traceable fixed costs are from the Order Processing Department. Exhibit 22-24 illustrates responsibility accounting reports for each of the levels of management shown in Exhibit 22-19. **Responsibility accounting reports show the results of the segment or division for which a particular manager is responsible.** This is illustrated in Exhibit 22-24 for the divisions and the whole company, and in Exhibit 22-25 for the DVD division and its products only.

Notice the headings in blue for the segment-specific income: Divisional segment margin and Product segment margin. Assume you were Smart Touch's DVD division manager. How would this information help you make better decisions? By highlighting costs in a contribution margin format and reporting results by division, it helps managers to have the best information to make decisions. As shown in previous chapters' analyses, the Excel DVD division continues to stand out as the most profitable product for the DVD division.

**EXHIBIT 22-24** | **Smart Touch Income Statement—Segments Defined as Divisions**

**SMART TOUCH LEARNING, INC.**
**Income Statement**
For the Year Ended December 31, 2014

|  | Total Company | CD | DVD | e-Learning |
|---|---|---|---|---|
| Sales revenue | $8,640,000 | $3,600,000 | $1,200,000 | $3,840,000 |
| Less: Variable expenses | 7,240,000 | 3,040,000 | 850,000 | 3,350,000 |
| Contribution margin | 1,400,000 | 560,000 | 350,000 | 490,000 |
| Less: Traceable fixed expenses (Exhibit 22-22) | 30,000 | 7,500 | 10,500 | 12,000 |
| Divisional segment margin | 1,370,000 | $ 552,500 | $ 339,500 | $ 478,000 |
| Less: Common fixed expenses not traceable to specific divisions | 10,000 | | | |
| Net operating income (loss) | $1,360,000 | | | |

**EXHIBIT 22-25** | **Smart Touch Income Statement—Segments Defined as Product Lines Within the DVD Division**

**SMART TOUCH LEARNING, INC.**
**Divisional Income Statement**
For the Year Ended December 31, 2014

|  | DVD Division | Excel DVD | Specialty DVD |
|---|---|---|---|
| Sales revenue | $1,200,000 | $960,000 | $240,000 |
| Less: Variable expenses | 850,000 | 680,000 | 170,000 |
| Contribution margin | 350,000 | 280,000 | 70,000 |
| Less: Traceable fixed expenses (Exhibit 22-23) | 7,000 | 4,200 | 2,800 |
| Product segment margin | 343,000 | $275,800 | $ 67,200 |
| Less: Common fixed expenses not traceable to specific products | 3,500 | | |
| Divisional segment margin | $ 339,500 | | |

Further, managers could compare these values to the budgeted values to determine where the actual results differed from the budget plan, which we'll review in the next chapter.

## Stop & Think...

Say you and your roommate share groceries at your apartment. The last grocery trip was $200. How do you split up the costs? There are many ways you could divide the grocery bill. You could split the total grocery cost between the two of you evenly, $100 each. You could split the bill based on the number of meals each of you eats a week. If you eat at the apartment 5 times a week, but your roommate eats at the apartment 15 times a week, then your roommate would rightfully pay a bigger part of the grocery bill ($200 × 15/20 meals, or $150). Your roommate may balk at this, arguing that your meals are larger than hers. Then how do you split the bill? This is the same logic we use in assigning shared cost. Maybe there's an item on the grocery bill, such as spices, that isn't really traceable to either roommate but is more of a common cost. No system is perfect, but you aim for the assignment that best measures the traceable costs to the correct business segment.

The Decision Guidelines on the next page review budgets and responsibility accounting. Study these guidelines before working on Summary Problem 22-3.

# Decision Guidelines 22-1

## THE MASTER BUDGET AND RESPONSIBILITY ACCOUNTING

**Amazon.com**'s initial strategy was to "get big fast." But without a budget, spending got out of control. So founder and CEO Jeff Bezos added a second strategic goal—to become the world's most cost-efficient, high-quality e-tailer. Today, **Amazon**'s managers use budgets to help reach both the growth and cost-efficiency goals. Let's consider some of the decisions **Amazon** made as it set up its budgeting process.

| Decision | Guidelines |
|---|---|
| • What benefits should **Amazon** expect to obtain from developing a budget? | • Requires managers to *plan* how to increase sales and how to cut costs<br>• Promotes *coordination and communication*, such as communicating the importance of the cost-efficiency goal<br>• Provides a *benchmark* that motivates employees and helps managers evaluate how well employees contributed to the sales growth and cost-efficiency goals |
| • In what order should **Amazon**'s managers prepare the components of the master budget? | Begin with the *operating budget*.<br>• Start with the *sales budget*, which feeds into all other budgets.<br>• The sales budget determines the *inventory, purchases, and cost of goods sold budget*.<br>• The sales, cost of goods sold, and *operating expenses budgets* determine the *budgeted income statement*.<br>Next, prepare the *capital expenditures budget*.<br>Finally, prepare the *financial budget*.<br>• Start with the *cash budget*.<br>• The cash budget provides the ending cash balance for the *budgeted balance sheet* and the details for the *budgeted statement of cash flows*. |
| • What extra steps should **Amazon** take given the uncertainty of Internet-based sales forecasts? | Prepare a *sensitivity analysis* and project budgeted results at different sales levels. |
| • How does **Amazon** compute budgeted purchases? | $$\text{Purchases} = \frac{\text{Cost of}}{\text{goods sold}} + \frac{\text{Ending}}{\text{inventory}} - \frac{\text{Beginning}}{\text{inventory}}$$ |
| • What kind of a responsibility center does each manager supervise? | • *Cost center*: The manager is responsible for costs.<br>• *Revenue center*: The manager is responsible for revenues.<br>• *Profit center*: The manager is responsible for both revenues and costs, and, therefore, profits.<br>• *Investment center*: The manager is responsible for revenues, costs, and the amount of the investment required to earn the income. |
| • What is the difference between traceable fixed costs and common fixed costs? | *Traceable fixed costs* are fixed costs that can be directly associated with an individual product, division, or business segment. A traceable fixed costs would disappear if the company discontinued making the product or discontinued operating the division or segment.<br><br>*Common fixed costs* (or *untraceable fixed costs*) are those fixed costs that cannot be directly associated with an individual product, division, or segment. |

# Summary Problem 22-3

Wilke's Tool-a-Rama manufactures small tools and tool sets. The company utilizes a shared warehouse facility that stores the inventory. The Small Tools division uses 150,000 square feet of the warehouse and the Tool Set division uses 100,000 square feet of the warehouse. The total cost of the warehouse facility was $30,000, of which $25,000 are traceable fixed costs. Further, the Small Tools division has two main products: wrenches and screwdrivers. The wrenches use 60,000 square feet of the warehouse and the screwdrivers use 75,000 square feet. The remaining 15,000 square feet is used by the Small Tools division manager, so it isn't traceable to either Small Tools division product. Additionally, income and expense data for each division for the month of August 2013 follows.

| Additional data: | Small Tools | | Tool Set |
|---|---|---|---|
| | Wrenches | Screwdrivers | |
| Sales revenue | $65,000 | $35,000 | $140,000 |
| Variable cost of goods sold | 31,200 | 16,800 | 56,000 |
| Fixed cost of goods sold | 12,000 | 8,000 | 25,000 |
| Variable selling expenses | 8,000 | 10,000 | 13,000 |

## Requirements

1. Calculate the cost per square foot for the warehouse facility and show the cost used by each division. Calculate the cost used by each product of the Small Tools division.
2. Prepare an income statement by division and by product for the month ended August 31, 2013.

## Solution

### Requirements

1. $25,000/250,000 square feet of space = $0.10 per square foot.

| Divisions Sharing Warehouse Facilities | Number of Square Feet (assignment base) | Cost per Square Foot | Traceable Warehouse Costs (number of square feet × $0.10 per square foot) |
|---|---|---|---|
| Small Tools | 150,000 | $0.10 | $15,000 |
| Tools Sets | 100,000 | $0.10 | 10,000 |
| Total | 250,000 | $0.10 | $25,000 |

| Products Sharing Warehouse Facilities | Number of Square Feet (assignment base) | Cost per Square Foot | Traceable Warehouse Costs (number of square feet × $0.10 per square foot) |
|---|---|---|---|
| Wrenches | 60,000 | $0.10 | $ 6,000 |
| Screwdrivers | 75,000 | $0.10 | 7,500 |
| Total | 135,000 | $0.10 | $13,500 |

2.

### WILKE'S TOOL-A-RAMA
### Income Statement
### For the Month Ended August 31, 2013

|  | Total Company | Small Tools | Tool Set |
|---|---|---|---|
| Sales revenue | $240,000 | $100,000 | $140,000 |
| Less: Variable COGS | 104,000 | 48,000 | 56,000 |
| Variable selling expenses | 31,000 | 18,000 | 13,000 |
| Contribution margin | $105,000 | $ 34,000 | $ 71,000 |
| Less: Fixed COGS | 45,000 | 20,000 | 25,000 |
| Traceable fixed expenses (from Requirement 1) | 25,000 | 15,000 | 10,000 |
| Divisional segment margin | $ 35,000 | $ (1,000) | $ 36,000 |
| Less: Common fixed expenses not traceable | | | |
| to specific divisions | 5,000 | | |
| Net operating income (loss) | $ 30,000 | | |

### WILKE'S TOOL-A-RAMA
### Divisional Income Statement
### For the Month Ended August 31, 2013

|  | Small Tools Division | Wrenches | Screwdrivers |
|---|---|---|---|
| Sales revenue | $100,000 | $65,000 | $35,000 |
| Less: Variable COGS | 48,000 | 31,200 | 16,800 |
| Variable selling expenses | 18,000 | 8,000 | 10,000 |
| Contribution margin | $ 34,000 | $25,800 | $ 8,200 |
| Less: Fixed COGS | 20,000 | 12,000 | 8,000 |
| Traceable fixed expenses (from Requirement 1) | 13,500 | 6,000 | 7,500 |
| Product segment margin | $ 500 | $ 7,800 | $ (7,300) |
| Less: Common fixed expenses not traceable to | | | |
| specific products | 1,500 | | |
| Divisional segment margin | $ (1,000) | | |

# Review *The Master Budget and Responsibility Accounting*

## ● Accounting Vocabulary

**Budgeted Income Statement (p. 1051)**
Statement that projects operating income for a period.

**Capital Expenditures Budget (p. 1056)**
A company's plan for purchases of property, plant, equipment, and other long-term assets.

**Cash Budget (p. 1056)**
Details how the business expects to go from the beginning cash balance to the desired ending cash balance.

**Common Fixed Costs (p 1077)**
Fixed costs that cannot be directly associated with an individual product, division, or business segment. Also called **untraceable fixed costs.**

**Financial Budget (p. 1056)**
The cash budget (cash inflows and outflows), the budgeted income statement, the budgeted balance sheet, and the budgeted statement of cash flows.

**Master Budget (p. 1055)**
The set of budgeted financial statements and supporting schedules for the entire organization. Includes the operating budget, the capital expenditures budget, and the financial budget.

**Operating Budget (p. 1056)**
Set of budgets that project sales revenue, cost of goods sold, and operating expenses, leading to the budgeted income statement that projects operating income for the period.

**Responsibility Accounting (p. 1074)**
A system for evaluating the performance of each responsibility center and its manager.

**Responsibility Center (p. 1074)**
A part of the organization for which a manager has decision-making authority and accountability for the results of those decisions.

**Traceable Fixed Costs (p. 1077)**
Fixed costs that can be directly associated with an individual product, division, or business segment. A traceable fixed cost would disappear if the company discontinued making the product or discontinued operating the division or the segment.

**Untraceable Fixed Costs (p. 1077)**
Fixed costs that cannot be directly associated with an individual product, division, or business segment. Also called **common fixed costs.**

## ● Destination: Student Success

### Student Success Tips

The following are hints on some common trouble areas for students in this chapter:

● Remember that the master budget represents the company's plan of action.

● Keep in mind the three types of budgets within the master budget: operating, capital expenditures, and financial.

● Recall that the operating budget includes the sales budget; the inventory, purchases, and COGS budget; the operating expenses budget; and the income statement. These budgets show the accrual basis planned operations.

● Keep in mind that the capital expenditures budget shows the company's plan for purchasing long-term assets.

● Recall the financial budget includes many budgets. The cash collections from customers, cash payments for purchases, and cash payments for operating expenses budgets help create the cash budget. The budgeted balance sheet and budgeted statement of cash flows round out the financial budgets.

● Keep in mind the four different types of responsibility centers: cost centers, revenue centers, profit centers, and investment centers.

● Remember that traceable fixed costs are those costs that would eventually disappear if the company ceased to sell the individual segment (such as a product). Common fixed costs (untraceable) are those costs that cannot be traced to a specific product, division, or segment.

### Getting Help

If there's a learning objective from the chapter you aren't confident about, try using one or more of the following resources:

● Review the Excel templates at myaccountinglab.com for the in-chapter problem and for Summary Problems 22-1 and 22-2.

● Review Decision Guidelines 22-1 in the chapter.

● Review Summary Problem 22-1 in the chapter to reinforce your understanding of the operating budget.

● Review Summary Problem 22-2 in the chapter to reinforce your understanding of the financial budget.

● Review Summary Problem 22-3 in the chapter to reinforce your understanding of segment performance reporting and traceable fixed costs.

● Practice additional exercises or problems at the end of Chapter 22 that cover the specific learning objective that is challenging you.

● Watch the white board videos for Chapter 22 located at myaccountinglab.com under the Chapter Resources button.

● Go to myaccountinglab.com and select the Study Plan button. Choose Chapter 22 and work the questions covering that specific learning objective until you've mastered it.

● Work the Chapter 22 pre/post tests in myaccountinglab.com.

● Consult the Check Figures for End of Chapter starters, exercises, and problems, located at myaccountinglab.com.

● Visit the learning resource center on your campus for tutoring.

## ● Quick Check

1. **Amazon.com** expected to receive which of the following benefits when it started its budgeting process?
   a. The budget provides **Amazon.com**'s managers with a benchmark against which to compare actual results for performance evaluation.
   b. The planning required to develop the budget helps managers foresee and avoid potential problems before they occur.
   c. The budget helps motivate employees to achieve **Amazon.com**'s sales growth and cost-reduction goals.
   d. All of the above

2. Which of the following is the cornerstone (or most critical element) of the master budget?
   a. The operating expenses budget
   b. The budgeted balance sheet
   c. The sales budget
   d. The inventory, purchases, and cost of goods sold budget

3. The budgeted statement of cash flows is part of which element of **Amazon.com**'s master budget?
   a. The financial budget
   b. The operating budget
   c. The capital expenditures budget
   d. None of the above

   Use the following information to answer questions 4 through 6. Suppose Mallcentral sells 1,000,000 hardcover books a day at an average price of $30. Assume that Mallcentral's purchase price for the books is 75% of the selling price it charges retail customers. Mallcentral has no beginning inventory, but it wants to have a three-day supply of ending inventory. Assume that operating expenses are $1,000,000 per day.

4. Compute Mallcentral's budgeted sales for the next (seven-day) week.
   a. $157,500,000
   b. $217,000,000
   c. $435,000,000
   d. $210,000,000

5. Determine Mallcentral's budgeted purchases for the next (seven-day) week.
   a. $300,000,000
   b. $225,000,000
   c. $157,500,000
   d. $75,000,000

6. What is Mallcentral's budgeted contribution margin for a (seven-day) week?
   a. $157,500,000
   b. $52,500,000
   c. $45,500,000
   d. $164,500,000

7. Which of the following expenses would *not* appear in Mallcentral's cash budget?
   a. Depreciation expense
   b. Marketing expense
   c. Interest expense
   d. Wages expense

8. Information technology has made it easier for **Amazon.com**'s managers to perform all of the following tasks *except*
   a. preparing responsibility center performance reports that identify variances between actual and budgeted revenues and costs.
   b. rolling up individual units' budgets into the companywide budget.
   c. sensitivity analyses.
   d. removing slack from the budget.

9. Which of the following managers is responsible for revenues and expenses but not ROI?
   a. Investment center manager
   b. Cost center manager
   c. Profit center manager
   d. Revenue center manager

10. Suppose Reeder, Corp., has three divisions, all using the warehouse: Pipes, Seals, and Flanges. The total warehousing cost is $40,000. Total warehouse space is 100,000 square feet, of which Pipes uses 30,000 square feet, Seals uses 25,000 square feet, and Flanges uses 20,000 square feet. The remaining warehouse space is used by the warehouse manager. Which of the following is true?

a. Traceable fixed costs are $30,000.　　c. Traceable fixed costs are $40,000.

b. Common fixed costs are $40,000.　　d. Common fixed costs are $30,000.

Answers are given after Apply Your Knowledge (p. 1104).

# Assess Your Progress

## • Short Exercises

**MyAccountingLab**

**S22-1**　**❶ Why managers use budgets [5 min]**
Consider the budget for any business.

**Requirement**

1. List the three key benefits companies get from preparing the budget.

**S22-2**　**❷ Understanding the components of the master budget [5–10 min]**
The following are some of the components included in the master budget.

> a. Budgeted balance sheet
> b. Sales budget
> c. Capital expenditures budget
> d. Budgeted income statement
> e. Cash budget
> f. Inventory, purchases, and cost of goods sold budget
> g. Budgeted statement of cash flows

**Requirement**

1. List in order of preparation the items of the master budget.

**S22-3**　**❸ Preparing an operating budget [5 min]**
Grippers sells its rock-climbing shoes worldwide. Grippers expects to sell 8,500 pairs of shoes for $180 each in January, and 3,500 pairs of shoes for $190 each in February. All sales are cash only.

**Requirement**

1. Prepare the sales budget for January and February.

*Note: Short Exercise 22-3 must be completed before attempting Short Exercise 22-4.*

**S22-4**　**❸ Preparing an operating budget [10 min]**
Review your results from S22-3. Grippers expects cost of goods sold to average 60% of sales revenue, and the company expects to sell 4,100 pairs of shoes in March for $260 each. Grippers' target ending inventory is $10,000 plus 50% of the next month's cost of goods sold.

**Requirement**

1. Use this information and the sales budget prepared in S22-3 to prepare Grippers' inventory, purchases, and cost of goods sold budget for January and February.

*Note: Short Exercise 22-3 must be completed before attempting Short Exercise 22-5.*

**S22-5** ❹ **Preparing a financial budget [15–20 min]**
Refer to the Grippers sales budget that you prepared in S22-3. Now assume that Grippers' sales are collected as follows:
November sales totaled $400,000 and December sales were $425,000.

| |
|---|
| 50% in the month of the sale |
| 30% in the month after the sale |
| 18% two months after the sale |
| 2% never collected |

**Requirement**

1. Prepare a schedule for the budgeted cash collections for January and February. Round answers to the nearest dollar.

*Note: Short Exercises 22-3 and 22-4 must be completed before attempting Short Exercise 22-6.*

**S22-6** ❹ **Preparing a financial budget [15–20 min]**
Refer to the Grippers inventory, purchases, and cost of goods sold budget your prepared in S22-4. Assume Grippers pays for inventory purchases 50% in the month of purchase and 50% in the month after purchase.

**Requirement**

1. Prepare a schedule for the budgeted cash payments for purchases for January and February.

*Note: Short Exercises 22-5 and 22-6 must be completed before attempting Short Exercise 22-7.*

**S22-7** ❹ **Preparing a financial budget [5–10 min]**
Grippers has $12,500 in cash on hand on January 1. Refer to S22-5 and S22-6 for cash collections and cash payment information. Assume Grippers has cash payment for operating expenses including salaries of $50,000 plus 1% of sales, all paid in the month of sale. The company requires a minimum cash balance of $10,000.

**Requirement**

1. Prepare a cash budget for January and February. Will Grippers need to borrow cash by the end of February?

*Note: Short Exercise 22-5 must be completed before attempting Short Exercise 22-8.*

**S22-8** ❺ **Using sensitivity analysis in budgeting [10–15 min]**
Refer to the Grippers cash collections from customers budget that you prepared in S22-5. Now assume that Grippers' sales are collected as follows:

**Requirement**

| |
|---|
| 60% in the month of the sale |
| 30% in the month after the sale |
| 8% two months after the sale |
| 2% never collected |

1. Prepare a revised schedule for the budgeted cash collections for January and February.

**S22-9**  **⑤ Using sensitivity analysis in budgeting [10–15 min]**

Maplehaven Sporting Goods Store has the following sales budget:

**MAPLEHAVEN SPORTING GOODS STORE**

**Sales Budget**

April–July

| | April | May | June | July | April–July Total |
|---|---|---|---|---|---|
| Cash sales, 80% | $ 40,800 | $ 64,000 | $ 51,200 | $ 40,800 | |
| Credit sales, 20% | 10,200 | 16,000 | 12,800 | 10,200 | |
| Total sales, 100% | $ 51,000 | $ 80,000 | $ 64,000 | $ 51,000 | $ 246,000 |

Suppose June sales are expected to be $80,000 rather than $64,000.

## Requirement

1.  Revise Maplehaven's sales budget.

**S22-10**  **⑥ Preparing performance reports for responsibility centers [5 min]**

Consider the following list of responsibility centers and phrases.

| | |
|---|---|
| A cost center | A revenue center |
| An investment center | Lower |
| A profit center | Higher |
| A responsibility center | |

## Requirement

1.  Fill in the blanks with the phrase that best completes the sentence.

a.  The maintenance department at the San Diego Zoo is _____.

b.  The concession stand at the San Diego Zoo is _____.

c.  The menswear department at **Bloomingdale's**, which is responsible for buying and selling merchandise, is _____.

d.  A production line at a Palm Pilot plant is _____.

e.  _____ is any segment of the business whose manager is accountable for specific activities.

f.  Gatorade, a division of **Quaker Oats**, is _____.

g.  The sales manager in charge of **Nike's** northwest sales territory oversees _____.

h.  Managers of cost and revenue centers are at _____ levels of the organization than are managers of profit and investment centers.

**S22-11**  **⑥ Preparing performance reports for responsibility centers [5–10 min]**

Wham-O is a distributor of board games and water toys manufactured by other companies. The company utilizes a shared Testing Facility where toys are safety tested. The Board Games division uses 3,000 testing hours a month. The Water Toys division uses 6,000 testing hours a month. The additional 1,000 hours are used testing R&D projects for the company. The total fixed costs of the Testing Facility were $100,000. Additionally, income and expense data for each division for the month of April 2012 follows:

| | Board Games | Water Toys |
|---|---|---|
| Sales revenue . . . . . . . . . . . . | $450,000 | $300,000 |
| Variable cost of goods sold . . . | 216,000 | 120,000 |
| Fixed cost of goods sold . . . . . | 120,000 | 140,000 |
| Variable selling expenses . . . . | 60,000 | 40,000 |

## Requirements

1. Calculate the rate per hour for Testing Facilities. Calculate the traceable fixed costs for each division.

2. Prepare an income statement for the company using the contribution margin approach. Calculate divisional segment margin for both divisions.

# ● Exercises

**E22-12   ① Why managers use budgets [15 min]**

Doug Ramirez owns a chain of travel goods stores. Last year, his sales staff sold 20,000 suitcases at an average sale price of $190. Variable expenses were 75% of sales revenue, and the total fixed expense was $250,000. This year, the chain sold more expensive product lines. Sales were 15,000 suitcases at an average price of $290. The variable expense percentage and the total fixed expenses were the same both years. Ramirez evaluates the chain manager by comparing this year's income with last year's income.

## Requirement

1. Prepare a performance report for this year, similar to Exhibit 22-4. How would you improve Ramirez's performance evaluation system to better analyze this year's results?

**E22-13   ② Understanding the components of the master budget [15–20 min]**

Sarah Edwards, division manager for Pillows Plus, is speaking to the controller, Diana Rothman, about the budgeting process. Sarah states, "I'm not an accountant, so can you explain the three main parts of the master budget to me and tell me their purpose?"

## Requirement

1. Answer Sarah's question.

**E22-14   ③ Preparing an operating budget [15–20 min]**

Tremont, Inc., sells tire rims. Its sales budget for the nine months ended September 30 follows:

|  | Quarter Ended | | | Nine-Month |
|---|---|---|---|---|
|  | March 31 | June 30 | September 30 | Total |
| Cash sales, 20% . . . . . | $    24,000 $ | 34,000 $ | 29,000 $ | 87,000 |
| Credits sales, 80% . . . | 96,000 | 136,000 | 116,000 | 348,000 |
| Total sales, 100% . . . . | $  120,000 $ | 170,000 $ | 145,000 $ | 435,000 |

In the past, cost of goods sold has been 40% of total sales. The director of marketing and the financial vice president agree that each quarter's ending inventory should not be below $20,000 plus 10% of cost of goods sold for the following quarter. The marketing director expects sales of $220,000 during the fourth quarter. The January 1 inventory was $32,000.

## Requirement

1. Prepare an inventory, purchases, and cost of goods sold budget for each of the first three quarters of the year. Compute cost of goods sold for the entire nine-month period.

*Note: Exercise 22-14 must be completed before attempting Exercise 22-15.*

**E22-15** ③ **Preparing an operating budget [15–20 min]**

Consider the facts presented in E22-14. Tremont's operating expenses include the following:

---

Rent, $2,000 a month

Salary, $3,000 a month

Commissions, 3% of sales

Depreciation, $1,000 a month

Miscellaneous expenses, 1% of sales

---

## Requirement

1. Prepare an operating expenses budget for each of the three quarters of 2012 and totals for the nine-month period.

**E22-16** ④ **Preparing a financial budget [20–30 min]**

Agua Pure is a distributor of bottled water.

## Requirement

1. For each of the Items a. through c., compute the amount of cash receipts or payments Agua Pure will budget for September. The solution to one item may depend on the answer to an earlier item.

   a. Management expects to sell equipment that cost $20,000 at a gain of $5,000. Accumulated depreciation on this equipment is $5,000.

   b. Management expects to sell 7,300 cases of water in August and 9,800 in September. Each case sells for $14. Cash sales average 10% of total sales, and credit sales make up the rest. Three-fourths of credit sales are collected in the month of sale, with the balance collected the following month.

   c. The company pays rent and property taxes of $4,300 each month. Commissions and other selling expenses average 20% of sales. Agua Pure pays one-half of commissions and other selling expenses in the month incurred, with the balance paid in the following month.

**E22-17** ④ ⑤ **Preparing a financial budget, and using sensitivity analysis in budgeting [15–20 min]**

Ling Auto Parts, a family-owned auto parts store, began January with $10,200 cash. Management forecasts that collections from credit customers will be $11,700 in January and $15,000 in February. The store is scheduled to receive $7,000 cash on a business note receivable in January. Projected cash payments include inventory purchases ($14,500 in January and $13,900 in February) and operating expenses ($2,900 each month).

Ling Auto Parts' bank requires a $10,000 minimum balance in the store's checking account. At the end of any month when the account balance dips below $10,000, the bank automatically extends credit to the store in multiples of $1,000. Ling Auto Parts borrows as little as possible and pays back loans in quarterly installments of $2,500, plus 5% interest on the entire unpaid principal. The first payment occurs three months after the loan. (*Note: We recommend you use the Excel work papers provided at myaccountinglab.com.*)

## Requirements

1. Prepare Ling Auto Parts' cash budget for January and February.

2. How much cash will Ling Auto Parts borrow in February if collections from customers that month total $14,000 instead of $15,000?

**E22-18** ④ **Preparing a financial budget [20 min]**

You recently began a job as an accounting intern at Reilly Golf Park. Your first task was to help prepare the cash budget for April and May. Unfortunately, the computer with the budget file crashed, and you did not have a backup or even a paper copy.

You ran a program to salvage bits of data from the budget file. After entering the following data in the budget, you may have just enough information to reconstruct the budget.

| REILLY GOLF PARK Cash Budget April and May | April | May |
|---|---|---|
| Beginning cash balance | $ 18,000 | $ 20 ? |
| Cash collections | 95 ? | 82,000 |
| Cash from sale of plant assets | 0 | 2,100 |
| Cash available | 113,000 | 104 ? |
| Cash payments: | | |
| Purchase of inventory | $ 51 ? | $ 44,000 |
| Operating expenses | 46,000 | 38 ? |
| Total cash payments | 97,000 | 82 ? |
| Ending cash balance before financing | 16 ? | 22,100 |
| Less: Minimum cash balance required | 20,000 | 20,000 |
| Cash excess (deficiency) | $ (4,000) ? | $ (2100) ? |
| Financing of cash deficiency: | | |
| Borrowing (at end of month) | 4000 ? | 0 ? |
| Principal repayments (at end of month) | 0 ? | ? |
| Interest expense | 0 ? | ? |
| Total effects of financing | 4000 ? | ? |
| Ending cash balance | $ 2000 ? | $ 2000 ? |

Reilly Golf Park eliminates any cash deficiency by borrowing the exact amount needed from First Street Bank, where the current interest rate is 6%. Reilly Golf Park first pays interest on its outstanding debt at the end of each month. The company then repays all borrowed amounts at the end of the month with any excess cash above the minimum required but after paying monthly interest expenses.

### Requirement

1. Complete the cash budget.

**E22-19** ④ **Preparing a financial budget [25–30 min]**
Consider the following June actual ending balances and July 31, 2012, budgeted amounts for Oleans.com:

a. June 30 inventory balance, $17,750
b. July payments for inventory, $4,300
c. July payments of accounts payable and accrued liabilities, $8,200
d. June 30 accounts payable balance, $10,600
e. June 30 furniture and fixtures balance, $34,500; accumulated depreciation balance, $29,830
f. June 30 equity, $28,360
g. July depreciation expense, $900
h. Cost of goods sold, 50% of sales
i. Other July expenses, including income tax, total $6,000, paid in cash
j. June 30 cash balance, $11,400
k. July budgeted credit sales, $12,700
l. June 30 accounts receivable balance, $5,140
m. July cash receipts, $14,200

### Requirement

1. Prepare a budgeted balance sheet.

**E22-20** ⑥ **Preparing performance reports for responsibility centers [5 min]**
Consider the following:

a. The bakery department of a **Publix** supermarket reports income for the current year.

b. **Pace Foods** is a subsidiary of **Campbell Soup Company**.

c. The personnel department of **State Farm Insurance Companies** prepares its budget and subsequent performance report on the basis of its expected expenses for the year.

d. The shopping section of **Burpee.com** reports both revenues and expenses.

e. **Burpee.com**'s investor relations Web site provides operating and financial information to investors and other interested parties.

f. The manager of a **BP** service station is evaluated based on the station's revenues and expenses.

g. A charter airline records revenues and expenses for each airplane each month.

h. The manager of the Southwest sales territory is evaluated based on a comparison of current period sales against budgeted sales.

## Requirement

1. Identify each responsibility center as a cost center, a revenue center, a profit center, or an investment center.

**E22-21** ⑥ **Preparing performance reports for responsibility centers [15–20 min]**
Love My Phone is based in Kingswood, Texas. The merchandising company has two divisions: Cell Phones and MP3 Players. The Cell Phone division has two main product lines: Basic and Advanced. The Basic product line includes phones whose primary function is storing contacts and making/receiving calls. The Advanced product line includes multi-application phones that, in addition to the Basic phones usage, contain a variety of applications. Applications include texting, surfing the Internet, interfacing to Outlook, creating documents, taking pictures, and so on. The company uses a shared order processing department. There are $25,000 in fixed order processing costs each month, of which $20,000 are traceable to the two divisions by the number of orders placed. 3,000 orders a month are processed by the MP3 Player division and 7,000 orders a month are processed by the Cell Phone division. 1,000 of the orders processed for the Cell Phone division cannot be traced to either product line. Facts related to the divisions and products for the month ended September 30, 2012, follow:

|  | Cell Phones Division | | MP3 Players Division |
|---|---|---|---|
|  | Basic | Advanced |  |
| Number of orders processed per month . . . | 2,000 | 4,000 | 3,000 |
| Sales revenue . . . . . . . . . . . . . . . . . . . . . | $75,000 | $300,000 | $150,000 |
| COGS (variable) . . . . . . . . . . . . . . . . . . . . | 52,500 | 180,000 | 60,000 |
| Fixed selling expenses . . . . . . . . . . . . . . . . | 12,000 | 9,000 | 25,000 |
| Variable selling expenses . . . . . . . . . . . . . . | 9,000 | 16,000 | 14,000 |

## Requirements

1. Calculate the rate per order for Order Processing. Calculate the traceable fixed costs for each division and for each product in the Cell Phone division.

2. Prepare an income statement for the company using the contribution margin approach. Calculate net income for the company, divisional segment margin for both divisions, and product segment margin for both products.

## ● Problems (Group A)

### P22-22A ❸ Preparing an operating budget [30 min]

Thumbtack's March 31, 2012, budgeted balance sheet follows:

| THUMBTACK OFFICE SUPPLY | | | | |
|---|---|---|---|---|
| **Budgeted Balance Sheet** | | | | |
| **March 31, 2012** | | | | |
| Assets | | Liabilities | | |
| Current assets: | | Current liabilities: | | |
| Cash | $18,000 | Accounts payable | | $12,500 |
| Accounts receivable | 12,000 | Salary and commissions payable | | 1,400 |
| Inventory | 16,000 | Total liabilities | | $13,900 |
| Prepaid insurance | 2,200 | | | |
| Total current assets | $48,200 | Stockholders' Equity | | |
| Plant assets: | | Common stock | | 16,000 |
| Equipment and fixtures | 45,000 | Retained earnings | | 33,300 |
| Less: Accumulated depreciation | 30,000 | Total stockholders' equity | | $49,300 |
| Total plant assets | $15,000 | | | |
| Total assets | $63,200 | Total liabilities and stockholders' equity | | $63,200 |

The budget committee of Thumbtack Office Supply has assembled the following data.

a. Sales in April were $40,000. You forecast that monthly sales will increase 2% over April's sales in May. June's sales will increase 4% over April's sales. July's sales will increase 20% over April's sales. Collections are 80% in the month of sale and 20% in the month following sale.

b. Thumbtack maintains inventory of $11,000 plus 25% of the COGS budgeted for the following month. COGS = 50% of sales revenue. Purchases are paid 30% in the month of purchase and 70% in the month following the purchase.

c. Monthly salaries amount to $7,000. Sales commissions equal 5% of sales for that month. Salaries and commissions are paid 30% in the month incurred and 70% in the following month.

d. Other monthly expenses are as follows:

| Rent expense | $2,400, paid as incurred |
|---|---|
| Depreciation expense | $200 |
| Insurance expense | $100, expiration of prepaid amount |
| Income tax | 20% of operating income, paid as incurred |

### Requirements

1. Prepare Thumbtack's sales budget for April and May, 2012. Round *all* amounts to the nearest $1.

2. Prepare Thumbtack's inventory, purchases, and cost of goods sold budget for April and May.

3. Prepare Thumbtack's operating expenses budget for April and May.

4. Prepare Thumbtack's budgeted income statement for April and May.

*Note: We recommend you solve this and the related problems (P22-23A and P22-24A) using Excel templates that you create.*

*Note: Problem 22-22A must be completed before attempting Problem 22-23A.*

**P22-23A** ❹ **Preparing a financial budget [30 min]**
Refer to P22-22A.

## Requirements

1. Prepare the schedule of budgeted cash collections from customers for April and May.
2. Prepare the schedule of budgeted cash payments for purchases for April and May.
3. Prepare the schedule of budgeted cash payments for operating expenses for April and May.
4. Prepare the cash budget for April and May. Assume no financing took place.

*Note: Problems 22-22A and 22-23A must be completed before attempting Problem 22-24A.*

**P22-24A** ❹ **Preparing a financial budget [30 min]**
Refer to P22-22A and P22-23A.

## Requirements

1. Prepare a budgeted balance sheet as of May 31, 2012.
2. Prepare the budgeted statement of cash flows for the two months ended May 31, 2012. (Note: You should omit sections of the cash flow statements where the company has no activity.)

**P22-25A** ❸ ❹ **Preparing an operating and a financial budget [50–60 min]**
Class Printing Supply of Baltimore has applied for a loan. **Bank of America** has requested a budgeted balance sheet at April 30, 2012, and a budgeted statement of cash flows for April. The March 31, 2012, budgeted balance sheet follows:

| CLASS PRINTING SUPPLY | | | | |
|---|---|---|---|---|
| Budgeted Balance Sheet | | | | |
| March 31, 2012 | | | | |
| **Assets** | | **Liabilities** | | |
| Current assets: | | Current liabilities: | | |
| Cash | $ 50,500 | Accounts payable | | $ 8,600 |
| Accounts receivable | 12,800 | | | |
| Inventory | 11,900 | Total liabilities | | $ 8,600 |
| Total current assets | $ 75,200 | **Stockholders' Equity** | | |
| Plant assets: | | Common stock | | 42,000 |
| Equipment and fixtures | 81,100 | Retained earnings | | 93,200 |
| Less: Accumulated depreciation | 12,500 | Total stockholders' equity | | $135,200 |
| Total plant assets | $ 68,600 | | | |
| Total assets | $143,800 | Total liabilities and stockholders' equity | | $143,800 |

As Class Printing's controller, you have assembled the following additional information:

a. April dividends of $2,500 were declared and paid.
b. April capital expenditures of $16,400 budgeted for cash purchase of equipment.
c. April depreciation expense, $700.
d. Cost of goods sold, 40% of sales.
e. April operating expenses, including salaries, total $38,000, 20% of which will be paid in cash and the remainder will be paid next month.
f. Additional April operating expenses also include miscellaneous expenses of 5% of sales, all paid in April.
g. April budgeted sales, $89,000, 60% is collected in April and 40% in May.
h. April cash payments of March 31 liabilities incurred for March purchases of inventory, $8,600.
i. April purchases of inventory, $10,900 for cash and $37,500 on credit. Half the credit purchases will be paid in April and half in May.

## Requirements

1. Prepare the sales budget for April.
2. Prepare the operating expenses budget for April.
3. Prepare the budgeted income statement for April.
4. Prepare the budgeted cash collections from customers for April.
5. Prepare the budgeted cash payments for operating expenses for April.
6. Prepare the cash budget for April.
7. Prepare the budgeted balance sheet for Class Printing at April 30, 2012.
8. Prepare the budgeted statement of cash flows for April.

*Note: Problems 22-22A through 22-24A must be completed before attempting Problem 22-26A.*

**P22-26A** ③ ⑤ **Preparing an operating budget using sensitivity analysis [30–40 min]**
Refer to your results from P22-22A, P22-23A, and P22-24A. Assume the following changes to the original facts:

a. Collections of receivables are 60% in the month of sale, 38% in the month following the sale, and 2% are never collected. Assume the March receivables balance is net of the allowance for uncollectibles.
b. Minimum required inventory levels are $8,000 plus 30% of next month's COGS.
c. Purchases of inventory will be paid 20% in the month of purchase, 80% in the month following purchase.
d. Salaries and commissions are paid 60% in the month incurred and 40% in the following month.

## Requirements

1. Prepare Thumbtack's revised sales budget for April and May. Round all calculations to the nearest dollar.
2. Prepare Thumbtack's revised inventory, purchases, and cost of goods sold budget for April and May.
3. Prepare Thumbtack's revised operating expenses budget for April and May.
4. Prepare Thumbtack's revised budgeted income statement for April and May.

*Note: Problem 22-26A must be completed before attempting Problem 22-27A.*

**P22-27A** ④ ⑤ **Preparing a financial budget using sensitivity analysis [30–40 min]**
Refer to the original data in P22-22A and the revisions presented in P22-26A.

## Requirements

1. Prepare the schedule of budgeted cash collections from customers for April and May.
2. Prepare the schedule of budgeted cash payments for purchases for April and May.
3. Prepare the schedule of budgeted cash payments for operating expenses for April and May.
4. Prepare the cash budget for April and May. Assume no financing took place.

*Note: Problems 22-26A and 22-27A must be completed before attempting Problem 22-28A.*

**P22-28A** ④ ⑤ **Preparing a financial budget using sensitivity analysis [30 min]**
Refer to P22-26A and P22-27A.

## Requirements

1. Prepare a budgeted balance sheet as of May 31, 2012.
2. Prepare the budgeted statement of cash flows for the two months ended May 31, 2012. (Note: You should omit sections of the cash flow statements where the company has no activity.)

**P22-29A** ⑥ **Preparing performance reports for responsibility centers [25–40 min]**

Jalapenos! is based in Pleasant Hill, California. The merchandising company has three divisions: Clothing, Food, and Spices. The Clothing division has two main product lines: T-shirts and Sweatshirts. The company uses a shared warehousing facility. There are $50,000 in fixed warehousing costs each month, of which $40,000 are traceable to the three divisions based on the amount of square feet used. There is 100,000 square feet of warehouse space in the facility. The clothing division uses 60,000 square feet of the space, but 5,000 of that space isn't traceable to t-shirts or sweatshirts. Facts related to the divisions and products for the month ended October 31, 2012, follow:

| | Clothing | | Food | Spices |
|---|---|---|---|---|
| | T-shirts | Sweatshirts | | |
| Square feet used . . . . . . . . . . . . . . . | 40,000 | 15,000 | 30,000 | 10,000 |
| Sales revenue . . . . . . . . . . . . . . . . . | $300,000 | $100,000 | $150,000 | $80,000 |
| COGS (variable) . . . . . . . . . . . . . . . | $210,000 | $ 60,000 | $ 60,000 | $32,000 |
| Fixed selling expenses . . . . . . . . . . . . | $ 7,000 | $ 5,000 | $ 3,000 | $ 1,000 |
| Variable selling expenses . . . . . . . . . | $ 9,000 | $ 8,500 | $ 11,000 | $ 2,500 |

## Requirements

1. Calculate the rate per square foot for Warehousing. Calculate the traceable fixed costs for each division and for each product in the Clothing division.
2. Prepare an income statement for the company using the contribution margin approach. Calculate net income for the company, divisional segment margin for both divisions, and product segment margin for both products.

● Problems (Group B)

**P22-30B** ③ **Preparing an operating budget [30 min]**

Clipboard Office Supply's March 31, 2012, budgeted balance sheet follows:

**CLIPBOARD OFFICE SUPPLY**
**Budgeted Balance Sheet**
**March 31, 2012**

| Assets | | Liabilities | |
|---|---|---|---|
| Current assets: | | Current liabilities: | |
| Cash | $28,000 | Accounts payable | $10,500 |
| Accounts receivable | 11,500 | Salary and commissions payable | 1,200 |
| Inventory | 15,000 | Total liabilities | $11,700 |
| Prepaid insurance | 1,000 | | |
| Total current assets | $55,500 | Stockholders' Equity | |
| Plant assets: | | Common stock | 25,000 |
| Equipment and fixtures | 55,000 | Retained earnings | 53,800 |
| Less: Accumulated depreciation | 20,000 | Total stockholders' equity | $78,800 |
| Total plant assets | $35,000 | | |
| Total assets | $90,500 | Total liabilities and stockholders' equity | $90,500 |

The budget committee of Clipboard Office Supply has assembled the following data.

a. Sales in April were $48,000. You forecast that monthly sales will increase 5% over April's sales in May. June's sales will increase 10% over April's sales. July's sales will increase 15% over April's sales. Collections are 80% in the month of sale and 20% in the month following sale.

b. Clipboard maintains inventory of $9,000 plus 25% of the COGS budgeted for the following month. COGS = 50% of sales revenue. Purchases are paid 40% in the month of purchase and 60% in the month following the purchase.

c. Monthly salaries amount to $6,000. Sales commissions equal 5% of sales for that month. Salaries and commissions are paid 60% in the month incurred and 40% in the following month.

d. Other monthly expenses are as follows:

| | |
|---|---|
| Rent expense | $2,800, paid as incurred |
| Depreciation expense | $300 |
| Insurance expense | $100, expiration of prepaid amount |
| Income tax | 25% of operating income, paid as incurred |

## Requirements

1. Prepare Clipboard's sales budget for April and May, 2012.
2. Prepare Clipboard's inventory, purchases, and cost of goods sold budget for April and May.
3. Prepare Clipboard's operating expenses budget for April and May.
4. Prepare Clipboard's budgeted income statement for April and May.

*Note: We recommend you solve this and the related problems (P22-31B and P22-32B) using Excel templates that you create.*

*Note: Problem 22-30B must be completed before attempting Problem 22-31B.*

## P22-31B ❹ Preparing a financial budget [30 min]
Refer to P22-30B.

## Requirements

1. Prepare the schedule of budgeted cash collections from customers for April and May.
2. Prepare the schedule of budgeted cash payments for purchases for April and May.
3. Prepare the schedule of budgeted cash payments for operating expenses for April and May.
4. Prepare the cash budget for April and May. Assume no financing took place.

*Note: Problems 22-30B and 22-31B must be completed before attempting Problem 22-32B.*

## P22-32B ❹ Preparing a financial budget [30 min]
Refer to P22-30B and P22-31B.

## Requirements

1. Prepare a budgeted balance sheet as of May 31, 2012.
2. Prepare the budgeted statement of cash flows for the two months ended May 31, 2012. (Note: You should omit sections of the cash flow statements where the company has no activity.)

## P22-33B ③ ④ Preparing an operating and a financial budget [50–60 min]

Alliance Printing of Baltimore has applied for a loan. **Bank of America** has requested a budgeted balance sheet at April 30, 2012, and a budgeted statement of cash flows for April. The March 31, 2012, budgeted balance sheet follows:

| ALLIANCE PRINTING | | | | |
|---|---|---|---|---|
| **Budgeted Balance Sheet** | | | | |
| **March 31, 2012** | | | | |
| **Assets** | | | **Liabilities** | |
| Current assets: | | | Current liabilities: | |
| Cash | $ 51,100 | | Accounts payable | $ 7,800 |
| Accounts receivable | 14,900 | | Total liabilities | $ 7,800 |
| Inventory | 12,100 | | | |
| Total current assets | $ 78,100 | | **Stockholders' Equity** | |
| Plant assets: | | | Common stock | 36,000 |
| Equipment and fixtures | 80,800 | | Retained earnings | 102,800 |
| Less: Accumulated depreciation | 12,300 | | Total stockholders' equity | $138,800 |
| Total plant assets | $ 68,500 | | | |
| Total assets | $146,600 | | Total liabilities and stockholders' equity | $146,600 |

As Alliance Printing's controller, you have assembled the following information:

a. April dividends of $8,000 were declared and paid.

b. April capital expenditures of $16,700, budgeted for cash purchase of equipment.

c. April depreciation expense, $400.

d. Cost of goods sold, 30% of sales.

e. April operating expenses, including salaries, total $35,000, 40% of which will be paid in cash and the remainder will be paid next month.

f. Additional April operating expenses also include miscellaneous expenses of 5% of sales, all paid in April.

g. April budgeted sales, $85,000, 60% is collected in April and 40% in May.

h. April cash payments of March 31 liabilities incurred for March purchases of inventory, $7,800.

i. April purchases of inventory, $11,200 for cash and $37,300 on credit. Half the credit purchases will be paid in April and half in May.

## Requirements

1. Prepare the sales budget for April.
2. Prepare the operating expenses budget for April.
3. Prepare the budgeted income statement for April.
4. Prepare the budgeted cash collections from customers for April.
5. Prepare the budgeted cash payments for operating expenses for April.
6. Prepare the cash budget for April.
7. Prepare the budgeted balance sheet for Alliance Printing at April 30, 2012.
8. Prepare the budgeted statement of cash flows for April.

*Note: Problems 22-30B through 22-32B must be completed before attempting Problem 22-34B.*

**P22-34B** ③ ⑤ **Preparing an operating budget and using sensitivity analysis [30–40 min]**
Refer to your results from P22-30B, P22-31B, and P22-32B. Assume the following changes to the original facts:

a. Collections of receivables are 60% in the month of sale, 35% in the month following the sale, and 5% are never collected. Assume the March receivables balance is net of the allowance for uncollectibles.
b. Minimum required inventory levels are $5,000 plus 40% of next month's COGS.
c. Purchases of inventory will be paid 30% in the month of purchase, 70% in the month following purchase.
d. Salaries and commissions are paid 40% in the month incurred and 60% in the following month.

### Requirements

1. Prepare Clipboard's revised sales budget for April and May. Round all calculations to the nearest dollar.
2. Prepare Clipboard's revised inventory, purchases, and cost of goods sold budget for April and May.
3. Prepare Clipboard's revised operating expenses budget for April and May.
4. Prepare Clipboard's revised budgeted income statement for April and May.

*Note: Problem 22-34B must be completed before attempting Problem 22-35B.*

**P22-35B** ④ ⑤ **Preparing a financial budget using sensitivity analysis [30-40 min]**
Refer to the original data in P22-30B and the revisions presented in P22-34B.

### Requirements

1. Prepare the schedule of budgeted cash collections from customers for April and May.
2. Prepare the schedule of budgeted cash payments for purchases for April and May.
3. Prepare the schedule of budgeted cash payments for operating expenses for April and May.
4. Prepare the cash budget for April and May. Assume no financing took place.

*Note: Problems 22-34B and 22-35B must be completed before attempting Problem 22-36B.*

**P22-36B** ④ ⑤ **Preparing a financial budget using sensitivity analysis [30 min]**
Refer to P22-34B and P22-35B.

### Requirements

1. Prepare a budgeted balance sheet as of May 31, 2012.
2. Prepare the budgeted statement of cash flows for the two months ended May 31, 2012. (Note: You should omit sections of the cash flow statements where the company has no activity.)

**P22-37B** ⑥ **Preparing performance reports for responsibility centers [25-40 min]**
Ensalada is based in Pleasant Hill, California. The merchandising company has three divisions: Clothing, Food, and Spices. The Clothing division has two main product lines: T-shirts and Sweatshirts. The company uses a shared warehousing facility. There are $65,000 in fixed warehousing costs each month, of which $30,000 are traceable to the three divisions based on the amount of square feet used. There is 100,000 square feet of warehouse space in the facility. The clothing division uses 50,000 square feet of the space, but 5,000 of that space isn't traceable to T-shirts or sweatshirts. Facts related to the divisions and products for the month ended October 31, 2012, follow:

|  | Clothing | | Food | Spices |
|---|---|---|---|---|
|  | T-shirts | Sweatshirts |  |  |
| Square feet used ............... | 30,000 | 15,000 | 10,000 | 40,000 |
| Sales revenue ................... | $440,000 | $150,000 | $ 80,000 | $180,000 |
| COGS (variable) ................ | $308,000 | $ 90,000 | $ 32,000 | $ 72,000 |
| Fixed selling expenses ............ | $ 5,000 | $ 10,000 | $ 6,000 | $ 700 |
| Variable selling expenses ......... | $ 14,000 | $ 9,000 | $ 8,500 | $ 2,100 |

### Requirements

1. Calculate the rate per square foot for Warehousing. Calculate the traceable fixed costs for each division and for each product in the Clothing division.

2. Prepare an income statement for the company using the contribution margin approach. Calculate net income for the company, divisional segment margin for both divisions, and product segment margin for both products.

## Continuing Exercise

**MyAccountingLab** **E22-38** ❸ **Preparing an operating budget [30 min]**

This exercise continues the Lawlor Lawn Service, Inc., situation from Exercise 21-34 of Chapter 21. Lawlor Lawn Service is projecting sales for July of $100,000. August's sales will be 8% higher than July's. September's sales are expected to be 10% higher than August's. October's sales are expected to be 5% higher than September's. COGS is expected to be 30% of sales. Lawlor desires to keep minimum inventory of $1,000 plus 10% of next month's COGS. Beginning inventory on June 30 is $11,000. Purchases are paid for in the month of purchase. Operating expenses are estimated to be $10,000 a month for rent, and $750 per month in depreciation.

### Requirements

1. Prepare a sales budget for the quarter ended September 30, 2013.

2. Prepare an inventory, purchases, and cost of goods sold budget for the quarter ended September 30, 2013.

3. Prepare an operating expenses budget for the quarter ended September 30, 2013.

4. Prepare a budgeted income statement for the quarter ended September 30, 2013.

## Continuing Problem

**MyAccountingLab** **P22-39** ❹ **Preparing a financial budget [30 min]**

This problem continues the Draper Consulting, Inc., situation from P21-35 of Chapter 21. Assume Draper Consulting began January with $29,000 cash. Management forecasts that collections from credit customers will be $49,000 in January and $51,500 in February. Projected cash payments include equipment purchases ($17,000 in January and $40,000 in February) and operating expenses ($6,000 each month).

Draper's bank requires a $20,000 minimum balance in the store's checking account. At the end of any month when the account balance dips below $20,000, the bank automatically extends credit to the store in multiples of $5,000. Draper borrows as little as possible and pays back loans each month in $1,000 increments, plus 5% interest on the entire unpaid principal. The first payment occurs one month after the loan.

### Requirements

1. Prepare Draper Consulting's cash budget for January and February 2013.

2. How much cash will Draper borrow in February if collections from customers that month total $21,500 instead of $51,500?

# Apply Your Knowledge

## Decision Cases

**Decision Case 22-1** Donna Tse has recently accepted the position of assistant manager at Cycle World, a bicycle store in St. Louis. She has just finished her accounting courses. Cycle

World's manager and owner, Jeff Towry, asks Tse to prepare a budgeted income statement for 2015 based on the information he has collected. Tse's budget follows:

**CYCLE WORLD**
**Budgeted Income Statement**
**For the Year Ending July 31, 2015**

| | | |
|---|---|---|
| Sales revenue | | $244,000 |
| Cost of goods sold | | 177,000 |
| Gross profit | | $ 67,000 |
| Operating expenses: | | |
| Salary and commission expense | $ 46,000 | |
| Rent expense | 8,000 | |
| Depreciation expense | 2,000 | |
| Insurance expense | 800 | |
| Miscellaneous expenses | 12,000 | 68,800 |
| Operating loss | | $ (1,800) |
| Interest expense | | (225) |
| Net loss | | $ (2,025) |

## Requirement

1. Tse does not want to give Towry this budget without making constructive suggestions for steps Towry could take to improve expected performance. Write a memo to Towry outlining your suggestions.

**Decision Case 22-2**  Each autumn, as a hobby, Anne Magnuson weaves cotton place mats to sell through a local craft shop. The mats sell for $20 per set of four. The shop charges a 10% commission and remits the net proceeds to Magnuson at the end of December. Magnuson has woven and sold 25 sets each for the last two years. She has enough cotton in inventory to make another 25 sets. She paid $7 per set for the cotton. Magnuson uses a four-harness loom that she purchased for cash exactly two years ago. It is depreciated at the rate of $10 per month. The accounts payable relate to the cotton inventory and are payable by September 30.

Magnuson is considering buying an eight-harness loom so that she can weave more intricate patterns in linen. The new loom costs $1,000; it would be depreciated at $20 per month. Her bank has agreed to lend her $1,000 at 18% interest, with $200 payment of principal, plus accrued interest payable each December 31. Magnuson believes she can weave 15 linen place mat sets in time for the Christmas rush if she does not weave any cotton mats. She predicts that each linen set will sell for $50. Linen costs $18 per set. Magnuson's supplier will sell her linen on credit, payable December 31.

Magnuson plans to keep her old loom whether or not she buys the new loom. The balance sheet for her weaving business at August 31, 2014, is as follows:

**ANNE MAGNUSON, WEAVER**
**Balance Sheet**
**August 31, 2014**

| Current assets: | | | Current liabilities: | |
|---|---|---|---|---|
| Cash | $ 25 | | Accounts payable | $ 74 |
| Inventory of cotton | 175 | | | |
| | 200 | | | |
| Fixed assets: | | | | |
| Loom | 500 | | Stockholders' equity | 386 |
| Less: Accumulated depreciation | 240 | | | |
| | 260 | | | |
| Total assets | $ 460 | | Total liabilities and owner's equity | $460 |

**Requirements**

1. Prepare a cash budget for the four months ending December 31, 2014, for two alternatives: weaving the place mats in cotton using the existing loom, and weaving the place mats in linen using the new loom. For each alternative, prepare a budgeted income statement for the four months ending December 31, 2014, and a budgeted balance sheet at December 31, 2014.

2. On the basis of financial considerations only, what should Magnuson do? Give your reason.

3. What nonfinancial factors might Magnuson consider in her decision?

## ● Ethical Issue 22-1

**Residence Suites** operates a regional hotel chain. Each hotel is operated by a manager and an assistant manager/controller. Many of the staff who run the front desk, clean the rooms, and prepare the breakfast buffet work part-time or have a second job so turnover is high.

Assistant manager/controller Terry Dunn asked the new bookkeeper to help prepare the hotel's master budget. The master budget is prepared once a year and is submitted to company headquarters for approval. Once approved, the master budget is used to evaluate the hotel's performance. These performance evaluations affect hotel managers' bonuses and they also affect company decisions on which hotels deserve extra funds for capital improvements.

When the budget was almost complete, Dunn asked the bookkeeper to increase amounts budgeted for labor and supplies by 15%. When asked why, Dunn responded that hotel manager Clay Murry told her to do this when she began working at the hotel. Murry explained that this budgetary cushion gave him flexibility in running the hotel. For example, because company headquarters tightly controls capital improvement funds, Murry can use the extra money budgeted for labor and supplies to replace broken televisions or pay "bonuses" to keep valued employees. Dunn initially accepted this explanation because she had observed similar behavior at the hotel where she worked previously.

**Requirements**

Put yourself in Dunn's position. In deciding how to deal with the situation, answer the following questions:

1. What is the ethical issue?

2. What are my options?

3. What are the possible consequences?

4. What should I do?

## ● Fraud Case 22-1

Patrick had worked in the garment business for years and had set up a small clothing outlet as a front for a scheme. At first, he placed small orders with a few carefully chosen manufacturers and made sure to pay promptly. After a few months, he used those companies as credit references, and placed progressively larger orders with bigger outfits. Then, with a good track record of payments, he started buying from FiestaWear, a trendy, upmarket apparel factory in Los Angeles. After two years, he sprung the trap. He placed a $280,000 order for garments from FiestaWear and asked them to "expedite" the delivery. The moment the merchandise arrived, his rented trucks rushed the goods to Mexico, he closed up his outlet, and vanished into the woodwork. When FiestaWear realized that something was fishy, it called the FBI. The company had been duped by a ploy known as the "overbuy." The merchandise was easy for Patrick to sell on the black market.

**Requirements**

1. What can a company do to protect against this kind of business risk?

2. Where does the expense for uncollectible accounts get reported in the financial statements?

## • Team Project 22-1

Xellnet provides e-commerce software for the pharmaceuticals industry. Xellnet is organized into several divisions. A companywide planning committee sets general strategy and goals for the company and its divisions, but each division develops its own budget.

Lonnie Draper is the new division manager of wireless communications software. His division has two departments: Development and Sales. Chad Sanchez manages the 20 or so programmers and systems specialists typically employed in the development department to create and update the division's software applications. Liz Smith manages the sales department.

Xellnet considers the divisions to be investment centers. To earn his bonus next year, Draper must achieve a 30% return on the $3 million invested in his division. Within the wireless division, development is a cost center, while sales is a revenue center.

Budgeting is in progress. Sanchez met with his staff and is now struggling with two sets of numbers. Alternative A is his best estimate of next year's costs. However, unexpected problems can arise when writing software, and finding competent programmers is an ongoing challenge. He knows that Draper was a programmer before he earned an MBA so he should be sensitive to this uncertainty. Consequently, he is thinking of increasing his budgeted costs (Alternative B). His department's bonuses largely depend on whether the department meets its budgeted costs.

**XELLNET**
**Wireless Division**
Development Budget 2013

|  | Alternative A | Alternative B |
|---|---|---|
| Salaries expense (including overtime and part time) | $2,400,000 | $2,640,000 |
| Software expense | 120,000 | 132,000 |
| Travel expense | 65,000 | 71,500 |
| Depreciation expense | 255,000 | 255,000 |
| Miscellaneous expense | 100,000 | 110,000 |
| Total expense | $2,940,000 | $3,208,500 |

Liz Smith is also struggling with her sales budget. Companies have made their initial investments in communications software so it is harder to win new customers. If things go well, she believes her sales team can maintain the level of growth achieved over the last few years. This is Alternative A in the sales budget. However, if Smith is too optimistic, sales may fall short of the budget. If this happens, her team will not receive bonuses. Therefore, Smith is considering reducing the sales numbers and submitting Alternative B.

**XELLNET**
**Wireless Division**
Sales Budget 2013

|  | Alternative A | Alternative B |
|---|---|---|
| Sales revenue | $5,000,000 | $4,500,000 |
| Salaries expense | 360,000 | 360,000 |
| Travel expense | 240,000 | 210,500 |

Split your team into three groups. Each group should meet separately before the entire team meets.

### Requirements

1. The first group plays the role of development manager Chad Sanchez. Before meeting with the entire team, determine which set of budget numbers you are going to present to Lonnie Draper. Write a memo supporting your decision. Give this memo to the third group before the team meeting.

2.   The second group plays the role of sales manager Liz Smith. Before meeting with the entire team, determine which set of budget numbers you are going to present to Lonnie Draper. Write a memo supporting your decision. Give this memo to the third group before the team meeting.

3.   The third group plays the role of division manager Lonnie Draper. Before meeting with the entire team, use the memos that Sanchez and Smith provided you to prepare a division budget based on the sales and development budgets. Your divisional overhead costs (additional costs beyond those incurred by the development and sales departments) are approximately $390,000. Determine whether the wireless division can meet its targeted 30% return on assets given the budgeted alternatives submitted by your department managers.

During the meeting of the entire team, the group playing Draper presents the division budget and considers its implications. Each group should take turns discussing its concerns with the proposed budget. The team as a whole should consider whether the division budget must be revised. The team should prepare a report that includes the division budget and a summary of the issues covered in the team meeting.

## ● Communication Activity 22-1

In 75 words or fewer, explain the difference between traceable fixed costs and common fixed costs.

### Quick Check Answers

1. *d* 2. *c* 3. *a* 4. *d* 5. *b* 6. *b* 7. *a* 8. *d* 9. *c* 10. *a*

**For online homework, exercises, and problems that provide you immediate feedback, please visit myaccountinglab.com.**

# 23 Flexible Budgets and Standard Costs

## Learning Objectives

1. Prepare a flexible budget for the income statement

2. Prepare an income statement performance report

3. Identify the benefits of standard costs and learn how to set standards

4. Compute standard cost variances for direct materials and direct labor

5. Analyze manufacturing overhead in a standard cost system

6. Record transactions at standard cost and prepare a standard cost income statement

Remember your personal budget from the previous chapter? You prepared a budget for your first year out of college to help you plan and control your spending. Now that you've been working for a few months, you need to reevaluate your situation. Have you been able to keep spending within the budget limits, or did you underestimate some expenses?

After comparing the budgeted amount for utilities with the actual amount you spent, you find you have been spending more than expected. What changes do you need to make? You have to either increase your earnings or decrease your spending. Could you use less electricity by lowering the thermostat in the winter? Should you consider getting a part-time job to supplement your salary? Should you make up the difference by taking lunch to work rather than eating out every day? Or would a combination of changes be best?

Just as we sometimes have to make hard decisions about our personal budgets, businesses have to make similar decisions. An economic downturn or increased competition may cause a decrease in sales. If that happens, spending must also decrease in order for the company to remain profitable.

This chapter builds on your knowledge of budgeting. A *budget variance* is just the difference between an actual amount and a budgeted figure. This chapter shows how managers use variances to operate a business. It is important to know *why* actual amounts differ from the budget. That will enable you to identify problems and decide what action to take.

In this chapter, you will learn how to figure out *why* actual results differ from your budget. This is the first step in correcting problems. You will also learn to use another management tool—standard costing.

# How Managers Use Flexible Budgets

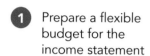 Prepare a flexible budget for the income statement

Let's consider Smart Touch Learning, Inc. At the beginning of the year, Smart Touch's managers prepared a master budget. The master budget is a **static budget**, which means that it is prepared for only *one* level of sales volume. The static budget does not change after it is developed.

Exhibit 23-1 shows that Smart Touch's actual operating income for the month of June is $16,000. This is $4,000 higher than expected from the static budget. This is a $4,000 favorable variance for June operating income. A **variance** is the difference between an actual amount and the budgeted amount. The variances in the third column of Exhibit 23-1 are as follows:

- Favorable (F) if an actual amount increases operating income (Actual revenue > Budgeted revenue; Actual cost (expense) < Budgeted cost (expense))

- Unfavorable (U) if an actual amount decreases operating income (Actual revenue < Budgeted revenue; Actual cost (expense) > Budgeted cost (expense))

**EXHIBIT 23-1** | **Actual Results Versus Static Budget**

**SMART TOUCH LEARNING, INC.**
**Comparison of Actual Results with Static Budget**
Month Ended June 30, 2014

|  |  |  | Actual Results | Static Budget | Variance |
|---|---|---|---|---|---|
| Units (DVDs) |  |  | 10,000 | 8,000 | 2,000 F |
| Sales revenue |  |  | $121,000 | $96,000 | $25,000 F |
| Variable expenses |  |  | 86,000 | 64,000 | 22,000 U |
| Contribution margin |  |  | $ 35,000 | $32,000 | $3,000 F |
| Fixed expenses |  |  | 19,000 | 20,000 | 1,000 F |
| Operating income |  |  | $ 16,000 | $12,000 | $4,000 F |

Smart Touch's variance for operating income is favorable primarily because Smart Touch sold 10,000 learning DVDs rather than the 8,000 DVDs it budgeted to sell during June. But there is more to this story. Smart Touch needs a *flexible budget* to show budgeted income at different sales levels. Let's see how to prepare and use a flexible budget.

## What Is a Flexible Budget?

The report in Exhibit 23-1 is hard to analyze because the static budget is based on 8,000 DVDs, but the actual results are for 10,000 DVDs. This report raises more questions than it answers—for example,

- why did the $22,000 unfavorable variable expense variance occur?
- did workers waste materials?

- did the cost of materials suddenly increase?
- how much of the additional expense arose because Smart Touch sold 10,000 rather than 8,000 DVDs?
- how was the company able to reduce fixed expenses by $1,000?

We need a flexible budget to help answer these questions.

A **flexible budget** summarizes costs (expenses) and revenues for several different volume levels within a relevant range. **Flexible budgets separate variable costs from fixed costs; the variable costs put the "flex" in the flexible budget.** To create a flexible budget, you need to know the following:

- Budgeted selling price per unit
- Variable cost per unit (which includes variable cost of goods sold and all variable operating expenses)
- Total fixed costs (such as fixed cost of goods sold and fixed operating expenses)
- Different volume levels within the relevant range

Exhibit 23-2 is a flexible budget for Smart Touch's revenues and costs that shows what will happen if sales reach 5,000, 8,000, or 10,000 DVDs during June. The budgeted sale price per DVD is $12. Budgeted variable costs are $8 per DVD, and budgeted fixed costs total $20,000.

**EXHIBIT 23-2** | **Flexible Budget**

| | | | Per Unit | By Units (DVDs) | | |
|---|---|---|---|---|---|---|
| | | | | 5,000 | 8,000 | 10,000 |
| | Units (DVDs) | | | | | |
| | Sales revenue | | $12 | $60,000 | $96,000 | $120,000 |
| | Variable expenses | | $ 8 | 40,000 | 64,000 | 80,000 |
| | Contribution margin | | | $20,000 | $32,000 | $ 40,000 |
| | Fixed expenses* | | | 20,000 | 20,000 | 20,000 |
| | Operating income | | | $       0 | $12,000 | $ 20,000 |

*SMART TOUCH LEARNING, INC.*
*Flexible Budget*
*Month Ended June 30, 2014*

\* Fixed expenses are usually given as a total rather than as a cost per unit

Notice in Exhibit 23-2 that sales revenue, variable costs, and contribution margin increase as more DVDs are sold. But fixed costs remain constant regardless of the number of DVDs sold within the relevant range of 5,000–10,000 DVDs. *Variable cost per unit and total fixed cost only stay constant within a specific relevant range of output.* Why? Because fixed costs and the variable cost per DVD may change outside this range. In our example, Smart Touch's relevant range is 5,000–10,000 DVDs. If the company sells 12,000 DVDs, it will have to rent additional equipment, which will increase total fixed costs above the current $20,000. Smart Touch may also have to pay workers for overtime pay, so the variable cost per DVD may be more than $8.

## Stop & Think...

Assume you are a waiter or waitress. Each night, you cannot be sure how much you will receive in tips from your customers. The more tips you receive, the more income you have to spend on gas, CDs, or possibly to save for a vacation. Informally, you probably figure in your head how much you will receive each night in tips and of that amount, how much you want to save or spend. The flexible budget is just a formalization of that same process for a business.

**Key Takeaway**

The master budget is a static budget, which means it is prepared for only one level of sales volume. A variance is the difference between an actual amount and a budgeted amount. A flexible budget summarizes costs and revenues for several different volume levels within a relevant range.

# Using the Flexible Budget: Why Do Actual Results Differ from the Static Budget?

**2** Prepare an income statement performance report

It is not enough to know that a variance occurred. That is like knowing you have a fever. The doctor needs to know *why* your temperature is above normal.

Managers must know *why* a variance occurred in order to pinpoint problems and take corrective action. As you can see in Exhibit 23-1, the static budget under-estimated both sales and variable costs. The variance in Exhibit 23-1 is called a *static budget variance* because actual activity differed from what was expected in the static budget. To develop more useful information, managers divide the static budget variance into two broad categories:

- **Flexible budget variance**—arises because the company had different revenues and/or costs than expected for the *actual* units sold. The flexible budget variance occurs because sales price per unit, variable cost per unit, and/or fixed cost was different than planned on the budget.

- **Sales volume variance**—arises because the actual number of units sold differed from the number of units on which the static budget was based. Sales volume variance is the volume difference between actual sales and budgeted sales.

Exhibit 23-3 diagrams these variances.

**EXHIBIT 23-3** | **The Static Budget Variance: The Sales Volume Variance and the Flexible Budget Variance**

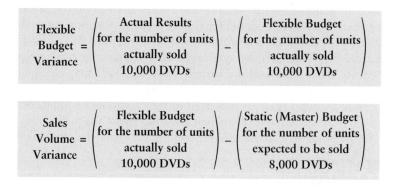

| Actual Results | | Flexible Budget<br>based on actual<br>number of units sold | | Static (Master) Budget<br>based on expected<br>number of units sold |
|---|---|---|---|---|
| | Flexible Budget Variance | | Sales Volume Variance | |
| | | Static Budget Variance | | |

Following are the formulas for computing the two variances:

$$\text{Flexible Budget Variance} = \left(\begin{array}{c}\text{Actual Results}\\\text{for the number of units}\\\text{actually sold}\\\text{10,000 DVDs}\end{array}\right) - \left(\begin{array}{c}\text{Flexible Budget}\\\text{for the number of units}\\\text{actually sold}\\\text{10,000 DVDs}\end{array}\right)$$

$$\text{Sales Volume Variance} = \left(\begin{array}{c}\text{Flexible Budget}\\\text{for the number of units}\\\text{actually sold}\\\text{10,000 DVDs}\end{array}\right) - \left(\begin{array}{c}\text{Static (Master) Budget}\\\text{for the number of units}\\\text{expected to be sold}\\\text{8,000 DVDs}\end{array}\right)$$

We have seen that Smart Touch budgeted (planned to sell) 8,000 DVDs during June. Actual sales were 10,000 DVDs. We will need to compute the flexible budget variance and the sales volume variance for Smart Touch. Exhibit 23-4 is Smart Touch's income statement performance report for June. Recall the variances in the second and fourth column of Exhibit 23-4 are

- favorable (F) if an actual amount increases operating income.

- unfavorable (U) if an actual amount decreases operating income.

**EXHIBIT 23-4** | **Income Statement Performance Report**

| | 1 | 2 (1) – (3) | 3 | 4 (3) – (5) | 5 |
|---|---|---|---|---|---|
| | Actual Results at Actual Prices* | Flexible Budget Variance | Flexible Budget for Actual Number of Units Sold~ | Sales Volume Variance | Static (Master) Budget* |
| Units (DVDs) | 10,000 | 0 | 10,000 | 2,000 F | 8,000 |
| Sales revenue | $121,000 | $1,000 F | $120,000 | $24,000 F | $96,000 |
| Variable expenses | 86,000 | 6,000 U | 80,000 | 16,000 U | 64,000 |
| Contribution margin | $ 35,000 | $5,000 U | $ 40,000 | $ 8,000 F | $32,000 |
| Fixed expenses | 19,000 | 1,000 F | 20,000 | 0 | 20,000 |
| Operating income | $ 16,000 | $4,000 U | $ 20,000 | $ 8,000 F | $12,000 |

SMART TOUCH LEARNING, INC.
Income Statement Performance Report
Month Ended June 30, 2014

Flexible budget variance, $4,000 U          Sales volume variance, $8,000 F

Static budget variance, $4,000 F

*Values from Exhibit 23-1
~Values from Exhibit 23-2

Column 1 of the performance report shows the actual results—based on the 10,000 DVDs actually sold. Operating income was $16,000 for June.

Column 3 is Smart Touch's flexible budget (shown in Exhibit 23-2) for the 10,000 DVDs actually sold. Operating income should have been $20,000.

Column 5 (originally shown in Exhibit 23-1) gives the static budget for the 8,000 DVDs expected to be sold for June. Smart Touch budgeted earnings of $12,000.

The budget variances appear in columns 2 and 4 of the exhibit. Let's begin with actual results in column 1. This data comes from Exhibit 23-1.

Column 1 of Exhibit 23-4 gives the actual results for June—10,000 DVDs and operating income of $16,000. Operating income is $4,000 less than Smart Touch would have expected for 10,000 DVDs (column 3, flexible budget for actual number of units sold). Managers want to know why operating income did not measure up to the flexible budget.

- It was not because the selling price of DVDs took a dive. Sales revenue was $1,000 more than expected for 10,000 DVDs.

- Variable costs were $6,000 too high for 10,000 DVDs.

- Fixed costs were $1,000 too low for 10,000 DVDs.

So, managers would focus on why the variable costs were higher than expected to determine whether the increase is controllable (can be reduced) or uncontrollable (due to some abnormal or isolated event). Overall, expenses rose by $5,000 ($6,000 increase in variable expenses minus $1,000 decrease in fixed expenses) above the flexible budget, while sales revenue only increased by $1,000, resulting in the overall $4,000 unfavorable flexible budget variance.

Now let's look at column 4, the sales volume variance, which is the difference between column 3 and column 5.

The flexible budget for 10,000 units from Exhibit 23-2 is in column 3. The static budget for 8,000 units from Exhibit 23-1 is in column 5. The differences between the static budget and the flexible budget—column 4—arise only because Smart Touch sold 10,000 DVDs rather than the number of DVDs it planned to sell, 8,000.

**Connect To: AIS—ERP**

Preparing flexible budgets is easy with the use of spreadsheets and/or enterprise resource planning (ERP) software. The key is getting the right information about the inputs (standard costs) and what is projected for sales, the economy, the availability of materials and labor, etc. Further, managers need timely feedback via the income statement performance report to continuously evaluate the decisions made and how those decisions affected performance. The biggest question managers ask is "Was the difference (variance) controllable?" If so, management can make decisions that will enhance future profitability based on this information. If the variance was uncontrollable, management can determine whether the variance is an isolated event or something that will affect future standards. If so, that must be reflected in the flexible budget and standard costs so management will have the most relevant and up-to-date information on which to make decisions.

Column 4 shows the sales volume variances. Sales revenue is $24,000 more than Smart Touch planned (2,000 more DVDs sold at $12 budgeted sales price). Variable expenses were $16,000 higher (unfavorable) than planned for the same reason (2,000 more DVDs sold at $8 variable cost per DVD = $16,000). Fixed expenses were the same for both budgets as the units were within the relevant range. Overall, operating income is favorable by $8,000 because Smart Touch sold more DVDs than it planned to sell (10,000 sold rather than the 8,000 budgeted). Notice this is also the planned contribution margin difference of $8,000 (2,000 more DVDs sold at $4 contributed per DVD). The static budget is developed *before* the period. The performance report in Exhibit 23-4 is prepared after the *end* of the period. Why? Because *the actual units sold are not known until the end of the period.*

Next, take some time to review the Decision Guidelines on the following page.

# Decision Guidelines 23-1

## FLEXIBLE BUDGETS

You and your roommate have started a business that prints T-shirts (for example, for school and student organizations). How can you use flexible budgets to plan and control your costs?

| Decision | Guidelines |
|---|---|
| • How do you estimate sales revenue, costs, and profits within your relevant range? | Prepare a set of flexible budgets for different sales levels, as in Exhibit 23-2. |
| • How do you use budgets to help control costs? | Prepare an income statement performance report, as in Exhibit 23-4. Review the results to determine which variances are controllable and which are uncontrollable. Managers will focus on the controllable variances. |
| • On which output level is the budget based? | Static (master) budget—*expected* number of T-shirts, estimated before the period |
| • On which output level do managers compare actual results to? | Flexible budget—*actual* number of T-shirts, not known until the end of the period |
| • Why does your actual income differ from budgeted income? | Prepare an income statement performance report comparing actual results, flexible budget for the actual number of T-shirts sold, and static (master) budget, as in Exhibit 23-4. This report will highlight differences for you to investigate further. |
| • How much of the difference occurs because revenues and costs are not what they should have been for the actual number of T-shirts sold? | Compute the flexible budget variance (FBV) by comparing actual results with the flexible budget.<br>• Favorable FBV—Actual sales revenue > Flexible budget sales revenue<br>• Favorable FBV—Actual cost (expense) < Flexible budget cost (expense)<br>• Unfavorable FBV—Actual sales revenue < Flexible budget sales revenue<br>• Unfavorable FBV—Actual cost (expense) > Flexible budget cost (expense) |
| • How much of the difference arises because the actual number of T-shirts sold does not equal budgeted sales? | Compute the sales volume variance (SVV) by comparing the flexible budget with the static budget.<br>• Favorable SVV—Actual number of T-shirts sold > Expected number of T-shirts sold<br>• Unfavorable SVV—Actual number of T-shirts sold < Expected number of T-shirts sold |
| • What actions can you take to avoid an unfavorable sales volume variance? | • Design more attractive T-shirts to increase demand.<br>• Provide marketing incentives to increase the number of T-shirts sold. |
| • What actions can you take to avoid an unfavorable flexible budget variance? | • Avoid an unfavorable flexible budget variance for *sales revenue* by maintaining (not discounting) your selling price.<br>• Avoid an unfavorable flexible budget variance for *costs* by controlling variable costs, such as the cost of the T-shirts, dye, and labor, and by controlling fixed costs. |

# Summary Problem 23-1

Exhibit 23-4 shows that Smart Touch sold 10,000 DVDs during June. Now assume that Smart Touch sold 7,000 DVDs (instead of 10,000) and that the actual sale price averaged $12.50 per DVD. Actual variable costs were $57,400, and actual fixed costs were $19,000.

### Requirements

1. Prepare a revised income statement performance report using Exhibit 23-4 as a guide. (*Hint:* You will need to calculate the flexible budget amounts for 7,000 DVDs.)
2. As the company owner, which employees would you praise or criticize after you analyze this performance report?

## Solution

### Requirement 1

**SMART TOUCH LEARNING, INC.**
**Income Statement Performance Report**
**Month Ended June 30, 2014**

| | 1 | 2<br>(1) – (3) | 3 | 4<br>(3) – (5) | 5 |
|---|---|---|---|---|---|
| | Actual Results at Actual Prices | Flexible Budget Variance | Flexible Budget for Actual Number of Units Sold | Sales Volume Variance | Static (Master) Budget~ |
| Units (DVDs) | 7,000 | 0 | 7,000 | 1,000 U | 8,000 |
| Sales revenue | $87,500 | $3,500 F | $84,000 | $12,000 U | $96,000 |
| Variable expenses | 57,400 | 1,400 U | 56,000 | 8,000 F | 64,000 |
| Contribution margin | $30,100 | $2,100 F | $28,000 | $ 4,000 U | $32,000 |
| Fixed expenses | 19,000 | 1,000 F | 20,000 | 0 | 20,000 |
| Operating income | $11,100 | $3,100 F | $ 8,000 | $ 4,000 U | $12,000 |

Flexible budget variance, $3,100 F     Sales volume variance, $4,000 U

Static budget variance, $900 U

~Values from Exhibit 23-1

### Requirement 2

As the company owner, you should determine the *causes* of the variances before praising or criticizing employees. It is especially important to determine whether the variance is due to factors the manager can control. For example

- the $1,000 favorable flexible budget variance for fixed costs could be due to a reduction in insurance premiums. The savings might have come from delaying a scheduled overhaul of equipment that decreased fixed expenses in the short term, but could increase the company's costs in the long run.
- the $4,000 unfavorable sales volume variance could be due to an ineffective sales staff or it could be due to a long period of snow that made it difficult for employees to get to work and brought work to a standstill.

Smart managers use variances to raise questions and direct attention, not to fix blame.

# Standard Costing

Most companies use **standard costs** (expenses) to develop their flexible budgets. **Think of a standard cost as a budget for a single unit.** For example, Smart Touch's standard variable cost is $8 per DVD (Exhibit 23-2). This $8 variable cost includes the standard cost of inputs like the direct materials, direct labor, and variable overhead needed for one DVD.

In a standard cost system, each input has both a price standard and a quantity standard. Smart Touch has a standard for the following:

- Price it pays per square foot of vinyl (this determines the price standard)
- Amount of vinyl for making the DVDs (this determines the quantity standard)

Let's see how managers set these price and quantity standards.

**3** Identify the benefits of standard costs and learn how to set standards

## Price Standards

The price standard for direct materials starts with the base purchase cost of each unit of inventory. Accountants help managers set a price standard for materials after considering early-pay discounts, freight in, and receiving costs.

World-class businesses demand efficient, lean production, while providing the highest quality product and excellent customer service. Lean production cost savings can be achieved several ways. A company can work with existing suppliers to cut its costs. A company could also use the Internet to solicit price quotes from suppliers around the world.

For direct labor, accountants work with human resource managers to determine standard labor rates. They must consider basic pay rates, payroll taxes, and fringe benefits. Job descriptions reveal the level of experience needed for each task. A big part of this is ensuring that employees receive training for the job and are paid fairly for the job.

Accountants work with production managers to estimate manufacturing overhead costs. Production managers identify an appropriate allocation base such as direct labor hours or direct labor cost, as you learned in Chapter 17, or allocate overhead using activity-based costing, as you learned in Chapter 18. Accountants then compute the standard overhead rates. Exhibit 23-5 summarizes the setting of standard costs.

**EXHIBIT 23-5** | **Summary of Standard Setting Issues**

|  | Price Standard | Quantity Standard |
|---|---|---|
| Direct Materials | Responsibility: Purchasing manager<br><br>Factors: Purchase price, discounts, delivery requirements, credit policy | Responsibility: Production manager and engineers<br>Factors: Product specifications, spoilage, production scheduling |
| Direct Labor | Responsibility: Human resource managers<br><br>Factors: Wage rate based on experience requirements, payroll taxes, fringe benefits | Responsibility: Production manager and engineers<br>Factors: Time requirements for the production level and employee experience needed |
| Manufacturing Overhead | Responsibility: Production managers<br><br>Factors: Nature and amount of resources needed for support activities (e.g., moving materials, maintaining equipment, and inspecting output) | |

# Application

Let's see how Smart Touch might determine its production cost standards for materials, labor, and overhead.

The manager in charge of purchasing for Smart Touch indicates that the purchase price, net of discounts, is $1.90 per square foot of vinyl. Delivery, receiving, and inspection add an average of $0.10 per square foot. Smart Touch's hourly wage for workers is $8 and payroll taxes and fringe benefits total $2.50 per direct labor hour. Variable overhead will total $6,400 based on 8,000 DVDs (static budget), fixed overhead is $9,600, and overhead is allocated based on 3,200 estimated direct-labor hours. Now let's compute Smart Touch's cost standards for direct materials, direct labor, and overhead based on the static budget of 8,000 DVDs:

Direct materials price standard for vinyl:

| | |
|---|---|
| Purchase price, net of discounts............................................. | $1.90 per square foot |
| Delivery, receiving, and inspection ...................................... | 0.10 per square foot |
| Total standard cost per square foot of vinyl......................... | $2.00 per square foot |

Direct labor price (or rate) standard:

| | |
|---|---|
| Hourly wage ......................................................... | $ 8.00 per direct labor hour |
| Payroll taxes and fringe benefits............................. | 2.50 per direct labor hour |
| Total standard cost per direct labor hour................ | $10.50 per direct labor hour |

Variable overhead price (or rate) standard:

$$= \frac{\text{Estimated variable overhead cost}}{\text{Estimated quantity of allocation base}}$$

$$= \frac{\$6,400}{3,200 \text{ direct labor hours}}$$

$$= \$2.00 \text{ per direct labor hour}$$

Fixed overhead price (or rate) standard:

$$= \frac{\text{Estimated fixed overhead cost}}{\text{Estimated quantity of allocation base}}$$

$$= \frac{\$9,600}{3,200 \text{ direct labor hours}}$$

$$= \$3.00 \text{ per direct labor hour}$$

# Quantity Standards

Production managers and engineers set direct material and direct labor *quantity standards*. To set its labor standards, **Westinghouse Air Brake**'s Chicago plant analyzed every moment in the production of the brakes.

To eliminate unnecessary work, **Westinghouse** rearranged machines in tight U-shaped work cells so that work could flow better. Workers no longer had to move parts all over the plant floor, as illustrated in the following diagram.

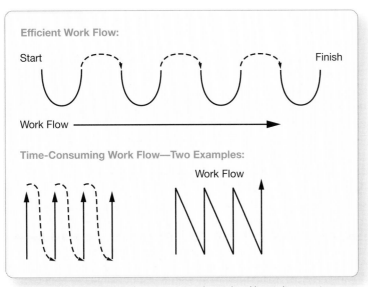

*Note: Solid lines indicate production processes whereas dotted lines indicate moving parts and/or WIP to a different location in the plant.

**Westinghouse** conducted time-and-motion studies to streamline various tasks. For example, the plant installed a conveyer at waist height to minimize bending and lifting. The result? Workers slashed one element of standard time by 90%.

Companies from the **Ritz-Carlton** to **Federal Express** develop quantity standards based on "best practices." This is often called *benchmarking*. The *best practice* may be an internal benchmark from other plants or divisions within the company or it may be an external benchmark from other companies. Internal benchmarks are easy to obtain, but managers can also purchase external benchmark data. For example, **Riverside Hospital** in Columbus, Ohio, can compare its cost of performing an appendectomy with the "best practice" cost developed by a consulting firm that compares many different hospitals' costs for the same procedure.

## Why Do Companies Use Standard Costs?

U.S. surveys show that more than 80% of responding companies use standard costing. Over half of responding companies in the United Kingdom, Ireland, Sweden, and Japan use standard costing. Why? Standard costing helps managers

- prepare the master budget,
- set target levels of performance (static budget),
- identify performance standards (standard quantities and standard costs),
- set sales prices of products and services, and
- decrease accounting costs.

Standard cost systems might appear to be expensive. Indeed, the company must invest up front to develop the standards. But standards can save accounting costs. It is cheaper to value inventories at standard rather than actual costs. With standard costs, accountants avoid the LIFO, FIFO, or average-cost computations.

## Variance Analysis

Once we establish standard costs, we can use the standards to assign costs to production. At least once a year, we will compare our actual production costs to the standard costs to locate variances. Exhibit 23-6 shows how to separate total variances for materials and labor into price and efficiency (quantity) variances. Study this exhibit carefully. It is used for the materials variances and the labor variances.

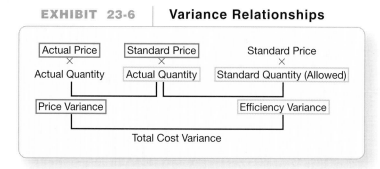

EXHIBIT 23-6 | **Variance Relationships**

A **price (rate) variance** measures how well the business keeps unit prices of material and labor inputs within standards. As the name suggests, the price variance is the *difference in prices* (actual price per unit – standard price per unit) of an input, multiplied by the *actual quantity* used of the input:

Price Variance = (Actual Price × Actual Quantity) – (Standard Price × Actual Quantity)

Or, Price Variance = (Actual Price – Standard Price) × Actual Quantity

$$= (AP - SP) \times AQ$$

An **efficiency (or quantity) variance** measures how well the business uses its materials or human resources. The efficiency variance measures the difference in quantities (actual quantity of input used – standard quantity of input allowed for the actual number of units produced), multiplied by the standard price per unit of the input:

Efficiency Variance = (Standard Price × Actual Quantity) – (Standard Price × Standard Quantity)

Or, Efficiency Variance = (Actual Quantity – Standard Quantity) × Standard Price

$$= (AQ - SQ) \times SP$$

Exhibit 23-7 illustrates these variances and emphasizes two points:

EXHIBIT 23-7 | **The Relationships Among Price, Efficiency, Flexible Budget, Sales Volume, and Static Budget Variances**

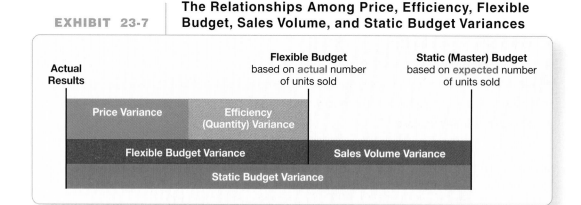

- First, the price and efficiency variances add up to the flexible budget variance.
- Second, static budgets like column 5 of Exhibit 23-4 play no role in the price and efficiency variances.

The static budget is used only to compute the sales volume variance (the variance caused because the company sold a different quantity than it thought it would sell when it created the budget)—never to compute the flexible budget variance or the price and efficiency cost variances for materials and labor.

## Stop & Think...

When you go to the gas station, do you fill up your car? How many miles per gallon does your car normally get? What is the usual price per gallon that you pay for gas? Assume you normally pay $4.00 per gallon and buy 10 gallons of gas. That is your standard cost for gas for your car. But what if the next time you need to fill up, you have to pay $4.25 per gallon, but you only have to buy 9.8 gallons of gas? The price variance is unfavorable because it is $0.25 more per gallon, but your car is using the gas more efficiently because you used .2 gallons less than normal.

> **Key Takeaway**
>
> Most companies use standard costs to develop their flexible budgets. Standard cost is a budget for a single unit of materials, labor, and overhead. Price variances measure the difference in actual and standard prices. Efficiency variances measure the difference in actual and standard quantities used.

# How Smart Touch Uses Standard Costing: Analyzing the Flexible Budget Variance

Now we'll return to our Smart Touch example. Exhibit 23-4 showed that the main cause for concern at Smart Touch is the $4,000 unfavorable flexible budget variance for operating income. The first step in identifying the causes of the cost variance is to identify the variable and fixed costs, as shown in Panel A of Exhibit 23-8.

Carefully study Exhibit 23-8 on the next page. Panel A shows the $5,000 flexible budget variance from Exhibit 23-4 for 10,000 DVDs. Panel B shows how to compute the flexible budget amounts for 10,000 DVDs. Panel C shows how to compute actual materials and labor costs for 10,000 DVDs. Trace the following:

**4** Compute standard cost variances for direct materials and direct labor

- Flexible budget amounts from Panel B to column (2) of Panel A
- Actual costs from Panel C to column (1) of Panel A

Column 3 of Panel A gives the flexible budget variances for direct materials and direct labor. For now, focus on materials and labor. We will cover overhead later.

## Direct Materials Variances

There are two types of direct materials variances. We'll cover both next.

### Direct Materials Price Variance

Let's investigate the $2,800 unfavorable variance for direct materials in Exhibit 23-8, Panel A. Recall that the direct materials standard price was $2.00 per square foot, and 10,000 square feet are needed for 10,000 DVDs (1 square foot per DVD × 10,000 DVDs). The actual price of materials was $1.90 per square foot, and 12,000 square feet were actually used to make 10,000 DVDs. Using the formula, the materials price variance is $1,200 favorable. The calculation follows:

$$
\begin{aligned}
\text{Materials Price Variance} &= (\text{AP} - \text{SP}) \times \text{AQ} \\
&= (\$1.90 \text{ per square foot} - \$2.00 \text{ per square foot}) \times 12{,}000 \text{ square feet} \\
&= -\$0.10 \text{ per square foot} \times 12{,}000 \text{ square feet} \\
&= -\$1{,}200, \text{ or } \$1{,}200 \text{ F}
\end{aligned}
$$

**EXHIBIT 23-8** | **Data for Standard Costing Example**

**PANEL A—Comparison of Actual Results with Flexible Budget for 10,000 DVDs**

SMART TOUCH LEARNING, INC.
Comparison of Actual Results with Flexible Budget
Month Ended June 30, 2014

| | Actual Results at Actual Prices | Flexible Budget for 10,000 DVDs | Flexible Budget Variance |
|---|---|---|---|
| Variable costs: | | | |
| Direct materials | $ 22,800 | $ 20,000 | $2,800 U |
| Direct labor | 41,800 | 42,000 | 200 F |
| Variable overhead | 9,000 | 8,000 | 1,000 U |
| Marketing and administrative costs | 12,400 | 10,000 | 2,400 U |
| Total variable costs | 86,000 | 80,000 | 6,000 U |
| Fixed costs: | | | |
| Fixed overhead | 12,300 | 9,600‡ | 2,700 U |
| Marketing and administrative expense | 6,700 | 10,400 | 3,700 F |
| Total fixed costs | 19,000 | 20,000 | 1,000 F |
| Total costs | $105,000 | $100,000 | $5,000 U |

‡Fixed overhead was budgeted at $9,600 per month (Application Answer on page 1114).

**PANEL B—Computation of Flexible Budget for Direct Materials, Direct Labor, and Variable Overhead for 10,000 DVDs—Based on Standard Costs**

| | (1) Standard Quantity of Inputs Allowed for 10,000 DVDs | (2) Standard Price per Unit of Input | (3) (1) × (2) Flexible Budget for 10,000 DVDs |
|---|---|---|---|
| Direct materials | 1 square foot per DVD × 10,000 DVDs = 10,000 square feet | $ 2.00 | $20,000 |
| Direct labor | .40 hours per DVD × 10,000 DVDs = 4,000 hours | $10.50 | 42,000 |
| Variable overhead | .40 hours per DVD × 10,000 DVDs = 4,000 hours | $ 2.00 | 8,000 |

**PANEL C—Computation of Actual Costs for Direct Materials and Direct Labor for 10,000 DVDs**

| | (1) Actual Quantity of Inputs Used for 10,000 DVDs | (2) Actual Price per Unit of Input | (3) (1) × (2) Actual Cost for 10,000 DVDs |
|---|---|---|---|
| Direct materials | 12,000 square feet actually used | $1.90 actual cost/square foot | $22,800 |
| Direct labor | 3,800 hours actually used | $11.00 actual cost/hour | 41,800 |

The $1,200 direct materials price variance (from page 1117) is *favorable* because the purchasing manager spent $0.10 *less* per square foot of vinyl than budgeted ($1.90 actual price – $2.00 standard price).

## Direct Materials Efficiency Variance

Now let's see what portion of the unfavorable materials variance was due to the quantity used.

The standard quantity of inputs is the *quantity that should have been used* for the actual units produced. For Smart Touch, the *standard quantity of inputs (vinyl) that workers should have used for the actual number of DVDs produced* (10,000 DVDs) is 1 square foot of vinyl per DVD, or a total of 10,000 square feet. The direct materials efficiency variance is as follows:

$$\text{Direct Materials Efficiency Variance} = (AQ - SQ) \times SP$$
$$= (12{,}000 \text{ square feet} - 10{,}000 \text{ square feet}) \times \$2.00 \text{ per square foot}$$
$$= +2{,}000 \text{ square feet} \times \$2.00 \text{ per square foot}$$
$$= +\$4{,}000, \text{ or } \$4{,}000 \text{ U}$$

The $4,000 direct materials efficiency variance is *unfavorable* because workers used 2,000 *more* square feet of vinyl than they planned (budgeted) to use for 10,000 DVDs.

## Summary of Direct Materials Variances

Exhibit 23-9 summarizes how Smart Touch splits the $2,800 unfavorable direct materials flexible budget variance into price and efficiency effects.

**EXHIBIT 23-9** | **Smart Touch Direct Materials Variance**

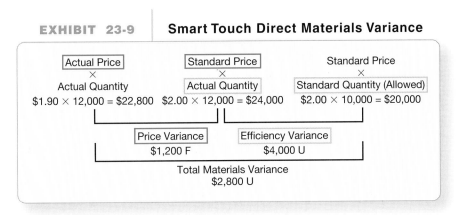

In summary, Smart Touch spent $2,800 more than it should have for vinyl because

- a good price for the vinyl increased profits by $1,200, but
- inefficient use of the vinyl reduced profits by $4,000.

Let's consider why each variance may have occurred and who may be responsible.

1. The purchasing manager is in the best position to explain the favorable price variance. Smart Touch's purchasing manager may have negotiated a good price for vinyl.

2. The manager in charge of making DVDs can explain why workers used so much vinyl to make the 10,000 DVDs. Was the vinyl of lower quality? Did workers waste materials? Did the production equipment malfunction? Smart Touch's top management needs this information to decide what corrective action to take.

These variances raise questions that can help pinpoint problems. But be careful! A favorable variance does not always mean that a manager did a good job, nor does an unfavorable variance mean that a manager did a bad job. Perhaps Smart Touch's purchasing manager got a lower price by purchasing inferior-quality materials. This could lead to wasted materials. If so, the purchasing manager's decision hurt the company. This illustrates why good managers

- use variances as a guide for investigation rather than merely to assign blame.
- investigate favorable as well as unfavorable variances.

## Direct Labor Variances

Smart Touch uses a similar approach to analyze the direct labor flexible budget variance.

Let's review Exhibit 22-8 to determine why Smart Touch spent $200 less on labor than it should have spent for 10,000 DVDs. To determine this, Smart Touch computes the labor price and efficiency variances in exactly the same way as it did for direct materials. Recall from Exhibit 22-8 the standard price for direct labor is $10.50 per hour, and 4,000 hours were budgeted for 10,000 DVDs (.40 hours per DVD × 10,000 DVDs). But actual direct labor cost was $11.00 per hour, and it took 3,800 hours to make 10,000 DVDs.

### Direct Labor Price (Rate) Variance

Using the formula, the direct labor price variance was $1,900 unfavorable. The calculation follows:

$$
\begin{aligned}
\text{Direct Labor Price Variance} &= (AP - SP) \times AH \\
&= (\$11.00 - \$10.50) \times 3{,}800 \text{ hours} \\
&= \$0.50 \times 3{,}800 \text{ hours} \\
&= +\$1{,}900, \text{ or } \$1{,}900 \text{ U}
\end{aligned}
$$

The $1,900 direct labor price variance is *unfavorable* because Smart Touch paid workers $0.50 *more* per hour than budgeted ($11.00 actual price – $10.50 standard price).

### Direct Labor Efficiency Variance

Now let's see how efficiently Smart Touch used its labor. The *standard quantity of direct labor hours that workers should have used to make 10,000 DVDs* is .40 direct labor hours each, or 4,000 total direct labor hours. The direct labor efficiency variance is as follows:

$$
\begin{aligned}
\text{Direct Labor Efficiency Variance} &= (AH - SH) \times SP \\
&= (3{,}800 \text{ hours} - 4{,}000 \text{ hours}) \times \$10.50 \text{ per hour} \\
&= -200 \text{ hours} \times \$10.50 \\
&= -\$2{,}100, \text{ or } \$2{,}100 \text{ F}
\end{aligned}
$$

The $2,100 direct labor efficiency variance is *favorable* because laborers actually worked 200 *fewer* hours than the budget called for.

### Summary of Direct Labor Variances

Exhibit 23-10 summarizes how Smart Touch computes the direct labor price and efficiency variances.

EXHIBIT 23-10 | **Smart Touch—Direct Labor Variance**

| Actual Price | Standard Price | Standard Price |
|---|---|---|
| × | × | × |
| Actual Hours | Actual Hours | Standard Hours Allowed |
| $11.00 × 3,800 = $41,800 | $10.50 × 3,800 = $39,900 | $10.50 × (10,000 × .40) = $42,000 |

Price Variance
$1,900 U

Efficiency Variance
$2,100 F

Total Labor Variance
$200 F

The $200 favorable direct labor variance suggests that total labor costs were close to expectations. But to manage Smart Touch's labor costs, we need to gain more insight:

- Smart Touch paid its employees an average of $11.00 per hour in June instead of the standard rate of $10.50—for an unfavorable price variance.
- Workers made 10,000 DVDs in 3,800 hours instead of the budgeted 4,000 hours—for a favorable efficiency variance.

This situation reveals a trade-off. Smart Touch hired more experienced (and thus more expensive) workers and had an unfavorable price variance. But the workers turned out more work than expected, and the strategy was successful. The overall effect on profits was favorable. This possibility reminds us that managers should take care in using variances to evaluate performance. Go slow, analyze the data, and then take action.

**Key Takeaway**

Standard cost variances for direct materials and direct labor are each split between the price variance and efficiency variance. The price variance measures the difference between actual and standard price for direct materials and labor used. The efficiency variance measures the difference between actual and standard usage for direct materials and labor based on standard prices. In analyzing each variance, management must consider the overall effect of each decision and how it affected overall results for the production period.

# Manufacturing Overhead Variances

In this section of the chapter, we use the terms *manufacturing overhead* and *overhead* interchangeably. The total overhead variance is the difference between

**5** Analyze manufacturing overhead in a standard cost system

Actual overhead cost    and    Standard overhead allocated to production

Exhibit 23-8 shows that Smart Touch actually incurred $21,300 of overhead: $9,000 variable and $12,300 fixed. The next step is to see how Smart Touch allocates overhead in a standard cost system.

## Allocating Overhead in a Standard Cost System

In a standard costing system, the manufacturing overhead allocated to production is as follows:

$$\begin{matrix} \text{Overhead} \\ \text{allocated to} \\ \text{production} \end{matrix} = \begin{matrix} \text{Standard} \\ \text{(predetermined)} \\ \text{overhead rate} \end{matrix} \times \begin{matrix} \text{Standard quantity} \\ \text{of the allocation} \\ \text{base allowed for} \\ \textit{actual} \text{ output} \end{matrix}$$

Let's begin by computing Smart Touch's standard variable and fixed overhead rates as follows (static budget data from page 1114 based on 3,200 direct labor hours to produce 8,000 DVDs):

$$\begin{aligned}
\text{Standard overhead rate} &= \frac{\text{Budgeted manufacturing overhead cost}}{\text{Budgeted direct labor hours}} \\[6pt]
&= \frac{\text{Variable overhead + Fixed overhead}}{\text{Budgeted direct labor hours}} \\[6pt]
&= \frac{\$6,400 + \$9,600}{3,200 \text{ direct labor hours}} \\[6pt]
&= \frac{\$6,400}{3,200} + \frac{\$9,600}{3,200} \\[6pt]
&= \$2.00 \text{ variable} + \$3.00 \text{ fixed} \\[6pt]
&= \$5.00 \text{ per direct labor hour}
\end{aligned}$$

So Smart Touch uses a $2.00 per direct labor hour rate to apply variable overhead to jobs and $3.00 per direct labor hour rate to apply fixed overhead to jobs. Now, let's analyze the variances for variable and fixed overhead.

## Variable Overhead Variances

Smart Touch uses a similar approach to analyze the variable overhead flexible budget variance as it did to analyze the direct materials and direct labor variances.

Let's review Exhibit 23-8 to determine why Smart Touch spent $1,000 more on variable overhead than it should have spent for 10,000 DVDs. To determine this, Smart Touch computes the variable overhead spending (price) and efficiency variances. Recall from Exhibit 23-8 the standard price for variable overhead is $2.00 per hour, and 4,000 hours were budgeted for 10,000 DVDs (.40 hours per DVD × 10,000 DVDs). But actual variable overhead cost was $9,000 (AP × AH), and it took 3,800 hours to make 10,000 DVDs.

### Variable Overhead Spending (Price) Variance

Using the formula, the variable overhead spending (price) variance was $1,400 unfavorable. The calculation is the same formula we used before—we just have to rearrange the equation as follows:

$$\begin{aligned}
\text{Variable Overhead Spending (Price) Variance} &= (AP - SP) \times AH \\
&\quad (AP \times AH) - (SP \times AH) \\[6pt]
&= (\$9,000) - (\$2.00 \times 3,800 \text{ hours}) \\
&= \$9,000 - \$7,600 \\
&= +\$1,400, \text{ or } \$1,400 \text{ U}
\end{aligned}$$

The $1,400 variable overhead spending (price) variance is *unfavorable* because Smart Touch actually spent $1,400 more than budgeted for variable overhead.

### Variable Overhead Efficiency Variance

Now let's see how efficiently Smart Touch used its variable overhead. Since variable overhead is applied based on direct labor hours used, this variance will also be favorable, as the direct labor efficiency variance was favorable. The *standard quantity of direct labor hours that workers should have used to make 10,000 DVDs* is .40 direct labor hours each, or 4,000 total direct labor hours.

The variable overhead efficiency variance is as follows:

Variable Overhead Efficiency Variance = (AH – SH) × SP

= (3,800 hours – 4,000 hours) × $2.00 per hour

= – 200 hours × $2.00

= –$400, or $400 F

The $400 variable overhead efficiency variance is *favorable* because laborers actually worked 200 *fewer* hours than the budget called for and variable overhead is applied based on direct labor hours.

### Summary of Variable Overhead Variances

Exhibit 23-11 summarizes how Smart Touch computes the variable overhead spending (price) and efficiency variances.

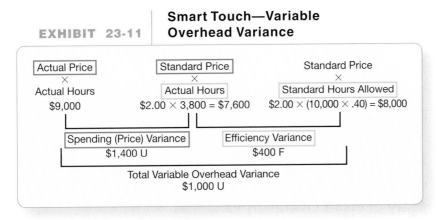

**EXHIBIT 23-11 | Smart Touch—Variable Overhead Variance**

The $1,000 unfavorable variable overhead variance indicates that variable overhead costs have increased more than expected. To manage Smart Touch's variable overhead costs, we need to get more insight:

- Smart Touch incurred $1,400 higher than anticipated actual variable overhead costs—for an unfavorable spending (price) variance.
- Workers made 10,000 DVDs in 3,800 hours instead of the budgeted 4,000 hours—for a favorable efficiency variance.

Management will want to investigate the variable overhead spending variance further to determine if the extra costs were controllable or uncontrollable.

## Fixed Overhead Variances

Smart Touch uses a similar approach to analyze the fixed overhead variances.

Let's review Exhibit 22-8 to determine why Smart Touch spent $300 more on fixed overhead than it budgeted. To determine this, Smart Touch computes the *fixed overhead spending* and *volume variances* in exactly the same way as it did for direct materials. Recall that the budgeted fixed overhead was $9,600. But actual fixed overhead cost was $12,300 (AP × AH) to make 10,000 DVDs.

### Fixed Overhead Spending Variance

The **fixed overhead spending variance** measures the difference between actual fixed overhead and budgeted fixed overhead to determine the controllable portion of total fixed overhead variance. Using the formula, the fixed overhead spending variance was $2,700 unfavorable. The calculation is the same formula we used before—we just have to rearrange the equation as follows:

Fixed Overhead Spending Variance = Actual fixed overhead − Budgeted fixed overhead
= $12,300 − $9,600
= +$2,700, or $2,700 U

The $2,700 fixed overhead spending variance is *unfavorable* because Smart Touch actually spent $2,700 more than budgeted for fixed overhead.

## Fixed Overhead Volume Variance

Now let's see how efficiently Smart Touch used its fixed overhead. The **fixed overhead volume variance** measures the difference between the budgeted fixed overhead and the amount of overhead that should have been applied to jobs based on the output. Since fixed overhead is applied at $3.00 per direct labor hour and Smart Touch budgeted to spend 4,000 hours to make 10,000 DVDs, this variance is favorable. The fixed overhead efficiency variance is as follows:

Fixed Overhead Volume Variance = Budgeted Fixed Overhead − Applied Fixed Overhead
= $9,600 − (4,000 hours × $3.00 per hour)
= $9,600 − $12,000
= −$2,400, or $2,400 F

The $2,400 fixed overhead volume variance is *favorable* because Smart Touch applied more overhead to jobs than the $9,600 budgeted fixed overhead amount.

## Summary of Fixed Overhead Variances

Exhibit 23-12 summarizes how Smart Touch computes the fixed overhead spending and volume variances.

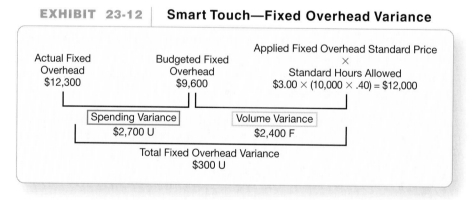

**EXHIBIT 23-12** | **Smart Touch—Fixed Overhead Variance**

The $300 unfavorable fixed overhead variance indicates that fixed overhead costs have increased more than expected. To manage Smart Touch's fixed overhead costs, we need to get more insight:

- Smart Touch incurred $2,700 higher than anticipated actual fixed overhead costs applied in actual allocations based on production—for an unfavorable spending variance.
- Workers made 10,000 DVDs, which would normally take 4,000 hours but actually only took 3,800 hours; thus, more overhead was applied to the job than was budgeted, which resulted in a $2,400 favorable volume variance. The volume variance can be misleading though because Smart Touch produced more than the static budget of 8,000 DVDs, but this was because workers were efficient.

Management will want to investigate the fixed overhead spending variance further to determine whether the extra costs were controllable or uncontrollable.

## Summary of Overhead Variances

Most companies compile cost information for the individual items of overhead, such as indirect materials, indirect labor, and utilities. Managers drill down by comparing actual to budgeted costs for each item. For example, Smart Touch's analysis might reveal that variable overhead costs were higher than expected because utility rates increased or because workers used more power than expected. Perhaps spending on fixed overhead increased because Smart Touch purchased new equipment and its depreciation increased.

# Standard Cost Accounting Systems

Next we'll cover standard cost journal entries and standard cost income statements.

**6** Record transactions at standard cost and prepare a standard cost income statement

## Journal Entries

We use Smart Touch's June transactions to demonstrate standard costing journal entries in a job costing context. Management needs to know about variances to address each problem. Therefore, Smart Touch records variances from standards as soon as possible. This means that Smart Touch records direct materials price variances when materials are purchased. It also means that Work in process inventory is debited (DVDs are recorded) at standard input quantities and standard prices. The entries for the month of June follow:

| 1. | Materials inventory (12,000 square feet AQ × $2.00 SP)    (A+) | 24,000 | |
|----|---|---|---|
| | Direct materials price variance    (CE+) | | 1,200 |
| | Accounts payable (12,000 AQ × $1.90 AP)    (L+) | | 22,800 |
| | *To record purchase of direct materials.* | | |

Entry 1 records the debit to Materials inventory, which is recorded at the *actual quantity* of vinyl purchases (12,000 square feet) at the *standard price* ($2 per square foot). In contrast, the credit to Accounts payable is for the *actual quantity* of vinyl purchased (12,000 square feet) at the *actual price* ($1.90 per square foot). Maintaining Materials inventory at the $2.00 *standard price* allows Smart Touch to record the direct materials price variance at the time of purchase. Recall that Smart Touch's direct materials price variance was $1,200 favorable. A favorable variance has a credit balance and is a contra expense. An unfavorable variance means more expense has been incurred than planned and would have a debit balance.

| 2. | Work in process inventory (10,000 square feet SQ × $2.00 SP)    (A+) | 20,000 | |
|----|---|---|---|
| | Direct materials efficiency variance    (E+) | 4,000 | |
| | Materials inventory (12,000 AQ × $2.00 SP)    (A−) | | 24,000 |
| | *To record use of direct materials.* | | |

In entry 2, Smart Touch debits Work in process inventory for the *standard cost* of the 10,000 square feet of direct materials that should have been used to make 10,000 DVDs. This maintains Work in process inventory at standard cost. Materials inventory is credited for the *actual quantity* of materials put into production (12,000 square feet) costed at the *standard price*.

Smart Touch's direct materials efficiency variance was $4,000 unfavorable. An unfavorable variance has a debit balance, which increases expense and decreases profits.

| 3. | | Manufacturing wages (3,800 AQ hours × $10.50 SP) (E+) | 39,900 | |
|---|---|---|---|---|
| | | Direct labor price variance (E+) | 1,900 | |
| | |    Wages payable (3,800 AQ × $11.00 AP) (L+) | | 41,800 |
| | | *To record direct labor costs incurred.* | | |

In entry 3, manufacturing wages is debited for the $10.50 *standard price* of 3,800 direct labor hours actually used. (The Manufacturing wages account contains both direct and indirect labor. Note entry 4 applies the amount of wages from the Manufacturing wages account to the Work in process inventory and Manufacturing overhead accounts for direct and indirect labor used.) Wages payable is credited for the *actual cost* (the *actual* hours worked at the *actual* wage rate) because this is the amount Smart Touch must pay the workers. The direct labor price variance is $1,900 unfavorable, a debit amount.

| 4. | | Work in process inventory (4,000 hours SQ × $10.50 SP) (A+) | 42,000 | |
|---|---|---|---|---|
| | |    Direct labor efficiency variance (CE+) | | 2,100 |
| | |    Manufacturing wages (3,800 AQ × $10.50 SP) (E−) | | 39,900 |
| | | *To allocate direct labor cost to production.* | | |

In entry 4, Smart Touch debits Work in process inventory for the standard cost per direct labor hour ($10.50) that should have been used for 10,000 DVDs (4,000 hours), like direct materials entry 2. Manufacturing wages is credited to close its prior debit balance for entry 3. The Direct labor efficiency variance is credited for the $2,100 favorable variance. This maintains Work in process inventory at standard cost.

| 5. | | Manufacturing overhead (actual cost) (E+) | 21,300 | |
|---|---|---|---|---|
| | |    Various accounts | | 21,300 |
| | | *To record actual overhead costs incurred.* | | |

Entry 5 records Smart Touch's actual overhead cost for June. $9,000 actual variable overhead plus $12,300 actual fixed overhead equals $21,300 actual Manufacturing overhead. Various accounts may include Accounts payable, Accumulated depreciation, or other related overhead accounts.

| 6. | | Work in process inventory (4,000 SQ hours × $5.00 SP) (A+) | 20,000 | |
|---|---|---|---|---|
| | |    Manufacturing overhead (E−) | | 20,000 |
| | | *To allocate overhead to production.* | | |

Entry 6 shows the overhead allocated to Work in process inventory computed as the standard overhead rate ($5.00 per hour) × standard quantity of the allocation base allowed for actual output (4,000 hours for 10,000 DVDs).

| 7. | | Finished goods inventory (A+) | 82,000 | |
|---|---|---|---|---|
| | |    Work in process inventory (A−) | | 82,000 |
| | | *To record completion of 10,000 DVDs ($20,000 of materials +* | | |
| | | *$42,000 of labor + $20,000 of manufacturing overhead),* | | |
| | | *all at standard cost.* | | |

Entry 7 transfers the standard cost of the 10,000 DVDs completed during June from Work in process inventory to Finished goods.

| 8. | Cost of goods sold     (E+) | 82,000 | |
|---|---|---|---|
| | Finished goods inventory     (A–) | | 82,000 |
| | *To record the cost of sales of 10,000 DVDs at standard cost.* | | |

Entry 8 transfers the cost of sales of the 10,000 DVDs completed at standard cost of $8.20 per DVD.

| 9. | Variable overhead spending (price) variance     (E+) | 1,400 | |
|---|---|---|---|
| | Fixed overhead spending variance     (E+) | 2,700 | |
| | Fixed overhead volume variance     (CE+) | | 2,400 |
| | Variable overhead efficiency variance     (CE+) | | 400 |
| | Manufacturing overhead     (E–) | | 1,300 |
| | *To record overhead variances and close the Manufacturing overhead account.* | | |

Entry 9 closes the Manufacturing overhead account and records the overhead variances.

Exhibit 23-13 shows the relevant Smart Touch accounts after posting these entries.

**EXHIBIT 23-13** | **Smart Touch's Flow of Costs in a Standard Costing System**

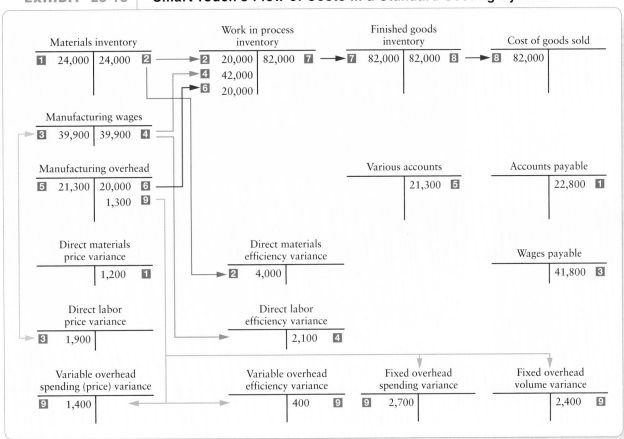

# Standard Cost Income Statement for Management

Smart Touch's top management needs to know about the company's cost variances. Exhibit 23-14 shows a standard cost income statement that highlights the variances for management.

The statement starts with sales revenue at standard and adds the favorable sales revenue variance of $1,000 (Exhibit 23-4) to yield actual sales revenue. Next, the statement shows the cost of goods sold at standard cost. Then the statement separately lists each manufacturing cost variance, followed by cost of goods sold at actual cost. At the end of the period, all the variance accounts are closed to zero out their balances. Operating income is thus closed to Income summary.

The income statement shows that the net effect of all the manufacturing cost variances is $3,900 unfavorable. Therefore, June's operating income is $3,900 lower than it would have been if all the actual manufacturing costs had been equal to their standard costs.

**EXHIBIT 23-14 | Standard Cost Income Statement**

**SMART TOUCH LEARNING, INC.**
**Standard Cost Income Statement**
**Month Ended June 30, 2014**

| | | | |
|---|---:|---:|---:|
| Sales revenue at standard (10,000 × $12) | | | $120,000 |
| Sales revenue variance | | | 1,000 |
| Sales revenue at actual | | | $121,000 |
| Cost of goods sold at standard cost | | $82,000 | |
| Manufacturing cost variances (parentheses denote a credit balance): | | | |
| Direct materials price variance | $(1,200) | | |
| Direct materials efficiency variance | 4,000 | | |
| Direct labor price variance | 1,900 | | |
| Direct labor efficiency variance | (2,100) | | |
| Variable overhead spending (price) variance | 1,400 | | |
| Variable overhead efficiency variance | (400) | | |
| Fixed overhead spending variance | 2,700 | | |
| Fixed overhead volume variance | (2,400) | | |
| Total manufacturing variance | | 3,900 | |
| Cost of goods sold at actual cost | | | 85,900 |
| Gross profit | | | $ 35,100 |
| Marketing and administrative expense* | | | 19,100 |
| Operating income | | | $ 16,000 |

*$12,400 + $6,700 from Exhibit 23-8, Panel A.

The Decision Guidelines on the next page summarize standard costing and variance analysis.

# Decision Guidelines 23-2

## STANDARD COSTS AND VARIANCE ANALYSIS

Now you have seen how managers use standard costs and variances to identify potential problems. Variances help managers see *why* actual costs differ from the budget. This is the first step in determining how to correct problems. Let's review how Smart Touch made some key decisions in setting up and using its standard cost system.

| Decision | Guidelines |
|---|---|
| • How do companies set standards? | • Historical performance data<br>• Engineering analysis/time-and-motion studies<br>• Continuous improvement standards<br>• Benchmarking |
| • How do companies compute a price variance for materials, labor, or variable overhead? | $$\text{Price variance} = \left( \begin{array}{c} \text{Actual price} \\ \text{per input unit} \end{array} - \begin{array}{c} \text{Standard price} \\ \text{per input unit} \end{array} \right) \times \begin{array}{c} \text{Actual quantity} \\ \text{of input} \end{array}$$ |
| • How do companies compute an efficiency variance for materials, labor, or variable overhead? | $$\text{Efficiency variance} = \left( \begin{array}{c} \text{Actual} \\ \text{quantity} \\ \text{of input} \end{array} - \begin{array}{c} \text{Standard} \\ \text{quantity of input} \\ \text{for actual output} \end{array} \right) \times \begin{array}{c} \text{Standard price} \\ \text{per input unit} \end{array}$$ |
| • Who is best able to explain a(n) | |
| • sales volume variance? | The Marketing Department |
| • sales revenue variance? | The Marketing Department |
| • direct material price variance? | The Purchasing Department |
| • direct material efficiency variance? | The Production Department |
| • direct labor price variance? | The Human Resources Department |
| • direct labor efficiency variance? | The Production Department |
| • overhead variance? | The Production Department |
| • How do companies compute fixed overhead variances? | $$\begin{array}{c} \text{Fixed overhead} \\ \text{spending} \\ \text{variance} \end{array} = \begin{array}{c} \text{Actual} \\ \text{fixed} \\ \text{overhead} \end{array} - \begin{array}{c} \text{Budgeted} \\ \text{fixed} \\ \text{overhead} \end{array}$$<br><br>$$\begin{array}{c} \text{Fixed overhead} \\ \text{volume} \\ \text{variance} \end{array} = \begin{array}{c} \text{Budgeted} \\ \text{fixed} \\ \text{overhead} \end{array} - \begin{array}{c} \text{Standard overhead} \\ \text{applied based} \\ \text{on actual output} \end{array}$$ |
| • How do companies record standard costs in the accounts? | • Materials inventory: Actual quantity at standard price<br>• Work in process inventory (and Finished goods inventory and Cost of goods sold): Standard quantity of inputs allowed for actual outputs, at standard price of inputs |
| • How do companies analyze cost variances? | • Debit balance → more expense (E+)<br>• Credit balance → less expense (CE+) |

# Summary Problem 23-2

Exhibit 23-8 indicates that Smart Touch sold 10,000 DVDs in June. Suppose Smart Touch had sold 7,000 DVDs instead of 10,000 and that *actual costs* were as follows:

| | |
|---|---|
| Direct materials (vinyl).............. | 7,400 square feet @ $2.00 per square foot |
| Direct labor................................ | 2,740 hours @ $10.00 per hour |
| Variable overhead..................... | $5,400 |
| Fixed overhead.......................... | $11,900 |

## Requirements

1. Given these new data, prepare an exhibit similar to Exhibit 23-8. Ignore marketing and administrative expense.
2. Compute price and efficiency variances for direct materials, direct labor, and variable overhead. Compute the spending and volume variances for fixed overhead.

# Solution

## Requirement 1

### PANEL A—Comparison of Actual Results with Flexible Budget for 7,000 DVDs

**SMART TOUCH LEARNING, INC.**
**Revised Data for Standard Costing Example**
Month Ended June 30, 2014

|  | Actual Results at Actual Prices | Flexible Budget for 7,000 DVDs | Flexible Budget Variance |
|---|---|---|---|
| Variable costs: |  |  |  |
|     Direct materials | $14,800 | $14,000 | $  800  U |
|     Direct labor | 27,400 | 29,400 | 2,000  F |
|     Variable overhead | 5,400 | 5,600 | 200  F |
|       Total variable costs | 47,600 | 49,000 | 1,400  F |
| Fixed costs: |  |  |  |
|     Fixed overhead | 11,900 | 9,600‡ | 2,300  U |
| Total costs | $59,500 | $58,600 | $  900  U |

‡Fixed overhead was budgeted at $9,600 per month.

### PANEL B—Computation of Flexible Budget for Direct Materials, Direct Labor, and Variable Overhead for 7,000 DVDs—Based on Standard Costs

|  | (1) Standard Quantity of Inputs Allowed for 7,000 DVDs | (2) Standard Price per Unit of Input | (3) (1) × (2) Flexible Budget for 7,000 DVDs |
|---|---|---|---|
| Direct materials | 1 square foot per DVD × 7,000 DVDs = 7,000 square feet | $  2.00 | $14,000 |
| Direct labor | .40 hours per DVD × 7,000 DVDs = 2,800 hours | $10.50 | 29,400 |
| Variable overhead | .40 hours per DVD × 7,000 DVDs = 2,800 hours | $  2.00 | 5,600 |

### PANEL C—Computation of Actual Costs for Direct Materials and Direct Labor for 7,000 DVDs

|  | (1) Actual Quantity of Inputs Used for 7,000 DVDs | (2) Actual Price per Unit of Input | (3) (1) × (2) Actual Cost for 7,000 DVDs |
|---|---|---|---|
| Direct materials | 7,400 square feet actually used | $2.00 actual cost/square foot | $14,800 |
| Direct labor | 2,740 hours actually used | $10.00 actual cost/hour | 27,400 |

**Requirement 2**

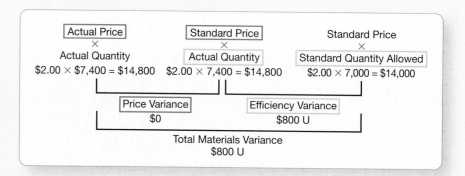

Actual Price × Actual Quantity
$2.00 × $7,400 = $14,800

Standard Price × Actual Quantity
$2.00 × 7,400 = $14,800

Standard Price × Standard Quantity Allowed
$2.00 × 7,000 = $14,000

Price Variance — $0

Efficiency Variance — $800 U

Total Materials Variance — $800 U

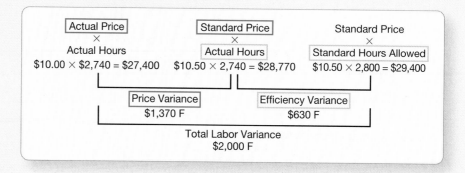

Actual Price × Actual Hours
$10.00 × $2,740 = $27,400

Standard Price × Actual Hours
$10.50 × 2,740 = $28,770

Standard Price × Standard Hours Allowed
$10.50 × 2,800 = $29,400

Price Variance — $1,370 F

Efficiency Variance — $630 F

Total Labor Variance — $2,000 F

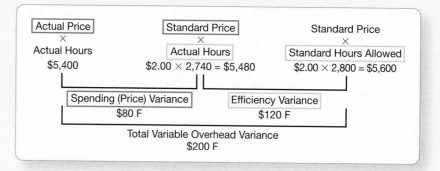

Actual Price × Actual Hours
$5,400

Standard Price × Actual Hours
$2.00 × 2,740 = $5,480

Standard Price × Standard Hours Allowed
$2.00 × 2,800 = $5,600

Spending (Price) Variance — $80 F

Efficiency Variance — $120 F

Total Variable Overhead Variance — $200 F

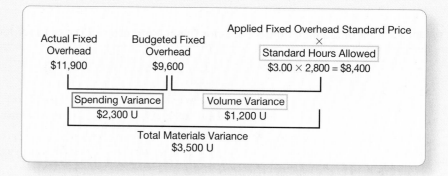

Actual Fixed Overhead
$11,900

Budgeted Fixed Overhead
$9,600

Applied Fixed Overhead Standard Price × Standard Hours Allowed
$3.00 × 2,800 = $8,400

Spending Variance — $2,300 U

Volume Variance — $1,200 U

Total Materials Variance — $3,500 U

# Review *Flexible Budgets and Standard Costs*

## ● Accounting Vocabulary

**Efficiency (Quantity) Variance (p. 1116)**
Measures whether the quantity of materials or labor used to make the actual number of units produced is within the standard allowed for that number of units produced. Computed as the difference in quantities (actual quantity of input used minus standard quantity of input allowed for the actual number of units produced) multiplied by the standard price per unit of the input.

**Fixed Overhead Spending Variance (p. 1123)**
Measures the difference between actual fixed overhead and budgeted fixed overhead to determine the controllable portion of total fixed overhead variance.

**Fixed Overhead Volume Variance (p. 1124)**
Measures the difference between the budgeted fixed overhead and the amount of overhead that should have been applied to jobs based on the output.

**Flexible Budget (p. 1107)**
A summarized budget that managers can easily compute for several different volume levels; separates variable costs from fixed costs.

**Flexible Budget Variance (p. 1108)**
The difference arising because the company had more or less revenue, or more or less cost, than expected for the *actual* level of units sold.

**Price (Rate) Variance (p. 1116)**
Measures how well the business keeps unit prices of material and labor inputs within standards. Computed as the difference in prices (actual price per unit minus standard price per unit) of an input multiplied by the actual quantity of the input.

**Sales Volume Variance (p. 1108)**
The difference arising only because the actual number of units sold differed from the number of units on which the static budget was based. Equals the difference between a static budget amount and a flexible budget amount.

**Standard Cost (p. 1113)**
A budget for a single unit.

**Static Budget (p. 1106)**
The budget prepared for only one level of sales volume. Also called the *master budget*.

**Variance (p. 1106)**
The difference between an actual amount and the budgeted amount. Labeled as favorable if it increases operating income and unfavorable if it decreases operating income.

## ● Destination: Student Success

### Student Success Tips

The following are hints on some common trouble areas for students in this chapter:

- Keep in mind that a static budget shows revenues and expenses at the expected output level for the period.

- Recall that a flexible budget shows revenues and expenses for multiple output levels.

- Remember that the income statement performance report compares actual results to flexible budget amounts to determine the flexible budget variance. The flexible budget is then compared to the static budget to determine the sales volume variance.

- Recall a price variance measures the difference in actual and standard price based on the actual amount used.

- Remember an efficiency variance measures the difference in the actual amount used and the standard amount based on the standard price.

- Keep in mind that overhead variances are measured separately for the variable and fixed portion of overhead.

- Remember that the journal entries in a standard cost system record WIP based on standard costs.

- Remember the differences in a standard costing income statement and the one you learned about in earlier chapters: 1) It shows all the variances individually on the statement. 2) Operating income is the same whether the company uses standard costing or not.

### Getting Help

If there's a learning objective from the chapter you aren't confident about, try using one or more of the following resources:

- Review Decision Guidelines 23-1 and 23-2 in the chapter.

- Review Summary Problem 23-1 in the chapter to reinforce your understanding of flexible budgets and the income statement performance report.

- Review Summary Problem 23-2 in the chapter to reinforce your understanding of variances.

- Practice additional exercises or problems at the end of Chapter 23 that cover the specific learning objective that is challenging you.

- Watch the white board videos for Chapter 23, located at myaccountinglab.com under the Chapter Resources button.

- Go to myaccountinglab.com and select the Study Plan button. Choose Chapter 23 and work the questions covering that specific learning objective until you've mastered it.

- Work the Chapter 23 pre/post tests in myaccountinglab.com.

- Consult the Check Figures for End of Chapter starters, exercises, and problems, located at myaccountinglab.com.

- Visit the learning resource center on your campus for tutoring.

# • Quick Check

Questions 1–4 rely on the following data. MajorNet Systems is a start-up company that makes connectors for high-speed Internet connections. The company has budgeted variable costs of $145 for each connector and fixed costs of $7,500 per month.

MajorNet's static budget predicted production and sales of 100 connectors in August, but the company actually produced and sold only 84 connectors at a total cost of $21,000.

1. MajorNet's total flexible budget cost for 84 connectors per month is
   a. $14,500.
   b. $12,180.
   c. $19,680.
   d. $21,000.

2. MajorNet's sales volume variance for total costs is
   a. $1,320 U.
   b. $1,320 F.
   c. $2,320 U.
   d. $2,320 F.

3. MajorNet's flexible budget variance for total costs is
   a. $1,320 U.
   b. $1,320 F.
   c. $2,320 U.
   d. $2,320 F.

4. MajorNet Systems' managers could set direct labor standards based on
   a. time-and-motion studies.
   b. continuous improvement.
   c. benchmarking.
   d. past actual performance.
   e. Items a, b, c, and d are all correct.

Questions 5–7 rely on the following data. MajorNet Systems has budgeted three hours of direct labor per connector, at a standard cost of $17 per hour. During August, technicians actually worked 189 hours completing 84 connectors. All 84 connectors actually produced were sold. MajorNet paid the technicians $17.80 per hour.

5. What is MajorNet's direct labor price variance for August?
   a. $67.20 U
   b. $151.20 U
   c. $201.60 U
   d. $919.80 U

6. What is MajorNet's direct labor efficiency variance for August?
   a. $919.80 F
   b. $1,071.00 F
   c. $1,121.40 F
   d. $3,364.20 F

7. The journal entry to record MajorNet's *use* of direct labor in August is which of the following?

   a. Manufacturing wages
       Direct labor efficiency variance
       Work in process inventory

   b. Work in process inventory
       Direct labor efficiency variance
       Manufacturing wages

   c. Work in process inventory
       Direct labor efficiency variance
       Manufacturing wages

   d. Manufacturing wages
       Direct labor efficiency variance
       Work in process inventory

Questions 8–10 rely on the following data. FrontGrade Systems allocates manufacturing overhead based on machine hours. Each connector should require 11 machine hours. According to the static budget, FrontGrade expected to incur the following:

> 1,100 machine hours per month (100 connectors × 11 machine hours per connector)
> $5,500 in variable manufacturing overhead costs
> $8,250 in fixed manufacturing overhead costs

During August, FrontGrade actually used 1,000 machine hours to make 110 connectors and spent $5,600 in variable manufacturing costs and $8,300 in fixed manufacturing overhead costs.

8. FrontGrade's predetermined standard *variable* manufacturing overhead rate is
   a. $5.00 per machine hour.
   b. $5.50 per machine hour.
   c. $7.50 per machine hour.
   d. $12.50 per machine hour.

9. Calculate the variable overhead spending variance for FrontGrade.
   a. $450 F
   b. $600 U
   c. $1,050 F
   d. $1,650 F

10. Calculate the variable overhead efficiency variance for FrontGrade.
   a. $450 F
   b. $600 U
   c. $1,050 F
   d. $1,650 F

Answers are given after Apply Your Knowledge (p. 1150).

# Assess Your Progress

## ● Short Exercises

**S23-1**    **❶ Matching terms [10 min]**
Consider the following terms:

a. Flexible Budget
b. Flexible Budget Variance
c. Sales Volume Variance
d. Static Budget
e. Variance

Consider the following definitions:

_____ 1. A summarized budget for several levels of volume that separates variable costs from fixed costs.

_____ 2. The budget prepared for only one level of sales volume.

_____ 3. The difference between an actual amount and the budget.

_____ 4. The difference arising because the company actually earned more or less revenue, or incurred more or less cost, than expected for the actual level of output.

_____ 5. The difference arising only because the number of units actually sold differs from the static budget units.

### Requirement
1. Match each term to the correct definition.

**S23-2** ① **Matching terms [10 min]**
Consider the following terms:

a. Benchmarking
b. Efficiency Variance
c. Fixed Overhead Spending Variance
d. Price Variance
e. Fixed Overhead Volume Variance
f. Standard Cost

Consider the following definitions:

_____ 1. Measures whether the quantity of materials or labor used to make the actual number of outputs is within the standard allowed for that number of outputs.

_____ 2. Using standards based on "best practice."

_____ 3. Measures how well the business keeps unit prices of material and labor inputs within standards.

_____ 4. A budget for a single unit.

_____ 5. Compares actual overhead spent to budgeted overhead costs.

_____ 6. Arises when budgeted overhead differs from applied overhead.

## Requirement

1. Match each term to the correct definition.

**S23-3** ① **Flexible budget preparation [10 min]**
Moje, Inc., manufactures travel locks. The budgeted selling price is $19 per lock, the variable cost is $8 per lock, and budgeted fixed costs are $15,000.

## Requirement

1. Prepare a flexible budget for output levels of 4,000 locks and 7,000 locks for the month ended April 30, 2012.

**S23-4** ② **Flexible budget variance [10–15 min]**
Consider the following partially completed income statement performance report for Gaje, Inc.

| GAJE, INC. | | | | |
|---|---|---|---|---|
| Income Statement Performance Report (partial) | | | | |
| Month Ended April 30, 2012 | | | | |
| | Actual Results at Actual Prices | Flexible Budget Variance | | Flexible Budget for Actual Number of Units Sold |
| Output units | 6,000 | | | 6,000 |
| Sales revenue | $ 90,000 | | | $ 78,000 |
| Variable expenses | 52,200 | | | 49,500 |
| Contribution margin | $ 37,800 | | | $ 28,500 |
| Fixed expenses | 16,200 | | | 15,300 |
| Operating income | $ 21,600 | | | $ 13,200 |

## Requirement

1. Complete the flexible budget variance analysis by filling in the blanks in the partial income statement performance report for 6,000 travel locks.

**S23-5**    ③ **Identifying the benefits of standard costs [5 min]**
Setting standards for a product may involve many employees of the company.

**Requirement**

1. Identify some of the employees who may be involved in setting the standard costs and describe what their role might be in setting those standards.

**S23-6**    ④ **Calculate materials variances [10–15 min]**
Johnson, Inc., is a manufacturer of lead crystal glasses. The standard materials quantity is 0.8 pound per glass at a price of $0.30 per pound. The actual results for the production of 6,900 glasses was 1.1 pounds per glass, at a price of $0.40 per pound.

**Requirement**

1. Calculate the materials price variance and the materials efficiency variance.

**S23-7**    ④ **Calculate labor variances [10–15 min]**
Johnson, Inc., manufactures lead crystal glasses. The standard direct labor time is 0.3 hour per glass, at a price of $13 per hour. The actual results for the production of 6,900 glasses were 0.2 hour per glass, at a price of $10 per hour.

**Requirement**

1. Calculate the labor price variance and the labor efficiency variance.

*Note: Short Exercises 23-6 and 23-7 should be completed before attempting Short Exercise 23-8.*

**S23-8**    ④ **Interpreting material and labor variances [5–10 min]**
Refer to your results from S23-6 and S23-7.

**Requirements**

1. For each variance, who in Johnson's organization is most likely responsible?
2. Interpret the direct materials and direct labor variances for Johnson's management.

*Note: Short Exercises 23-6 and 23-7 should be completed before attempting Short Exercise 23-9.*

**S23-9**    ⑤ **Standard overhead rates [5 min]**
Refer to the data from Johnson, Inc., in S23-6 and S23-7. The following information relates to the company's overhead costs:

| | |
|---|---|
| Static budget variable overhead | $ 9,000 |
| Static budget fixed overhead | $ 4,500 |
| Static budget direct labor hours | 1,800   hours |
| Static budget number of glasses | 6,000 |

Johnson allocates manufacturing overhead to production based on standard direct labor hours. Last month, Johnson reported the following actual results: actual variable overhead, $10,200; actual fixed overhead, $2,830.

**Requirement**

1. Compute the standard variable overhead rate and the standard fixed overhead rate.

*Note: Short Exercises 23-6, 23-7, and 23-9 should be completed before attempting Short Exercise 23-10.*

**S23-10**    ⑤ **Computing overhead variances [10–20 min]**
Refer to the Johnson data in S23-6, S23-7, and S23-9.

**Requirements**

1. Compute the variable and fixed overhead variances. Use Exhibits 23-11 and 23-12 as guides.
2. Explain why the variances are favorable or unfavorable.

*Note: Short Exercises 23-6, 23-7, and 23-10 should be completed before attempting Short Exercise 23-11.*

**S23-11** ❻ **Journalizing variances [15–25 min]**
Refer to your results from S23-6, S23-7, and S23-10.

### Requirement

1. Prepare the nine journal entries to record direct materials, labor, variable and fixed overhead, and the variances. Record the transfer to finished goods and COGS, assuming all production is sold. Last, record the entry to close the Manufacturing overhead account.

**S23-12** ❻ **Materials journal entries [5–10 min]**
The following materials variance analysis was performed for Brookman.

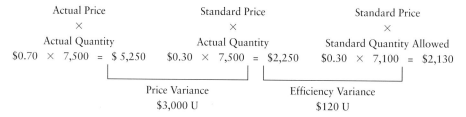

### Requirements

1. Record Brookman's direct materials journal entries.
2. Explain what management will do with this variance information.

**S23-13** ❻ **Labor journal entries [5–10 min]**
The following labor variance analysis was performed for Longman.

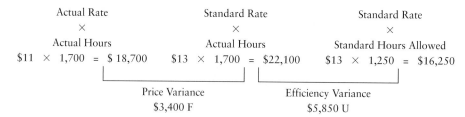

### Requirements

1. Record Longman's direct labor journal entries.
2. Explain what management will do with this variance information.

**S23-14** ❻ **Standard cost income statement [10–15 min]**
Consider the following information:

| | | | |
|---|---|---|---|
| Cost of goods sold | $367,000 | Direct labor efficiency variance | $18,000 F |
| Sales revenue | $550,000 | Variable overhead efficiency variance | $ 3,400 U |
| Direct materials price variance | $ 8,000 U | Fixed overhead volume variance | $12,000 F |
| Direct materials efficiency variance | $ 2,800 U | Marketing and administrative costs | $77,000 |
| Direct labor price variance | $ 42,000 U | Variable overhead spending variance | $ 700 F |
| Fixed overhead spending variance | $ 1,900 F | | |

### Requirement

1. Use the above information to prepare a standard cost income statement for Whitmer, using Exhibit 23-14 as a guide. Remember that unfavorable variances increase cost of goods sold.

# • Exercises

### E23-15  ❶ Preparing a flexible budget [10–15 min]

OfficePlus sells its main product, ergonomic mouse pads, for $12 each. Its variable cost is $5.20 per pad. Fixed costs are $205,000 per month for volumes up to 65,000 pads. Above 65,000 pads, monthly fixed costs are $280,000.

## Requirement

1. Prepare a monthly flexible budget for the product, showing sales revenue, variable costs, fixed costs, and operating income for volume levels of 45,000, 55,000, and 75,000 pads.

### E23-16  ❷ Preparing an income statement performance report [15–20 min]

Stenback Pro Company managers received the following incomplete performance report:

| | Actual Results at Actual Prices | Flexible Budget Variance | Flexible Budget for Actual Number of Units Sold | Sales Volume Variance | Static (Master) Budget |
|---|---|---|---|---|---|
| **STENBACK PRO COMPANY** | | | | | |
| **Income Statement Performance Report** | | | | | |
| **Year Ended July 31, 2012** | | | | | |
| Output units | 39,000 | —— | 39,000 | 3,000  F | —— |
| Sales revenue | $    218,000 | —— | $    218,000 | $    27,000  F | —— |
| Variable expenses | 84,000 | —— | 81,000 | 10,000  U | —— |
| Contribution margin | $    134,000 | —— | $    137,000 | $    17,000  F | —— |
| Fixed expenses | 108,000 | —— | 101,000 | 0 | —— |
| Operating income | $    26,000 | —— | $    36,000 | $    17,000  F | —— |

## Requirement

1. Complete the performance report. Identify the employee group that may deserve praise and the group that may be subject to criticism. Give your reasoning.

### E23-17  ❷ Preparing an income statement performance report [20–25 min]

Top managers of Kyler Industries predicted 2012 sales of 14,800 units of its product at a unit price of $8.50. Actual sales for the year were 14,600 units at $10.50 each. Variable costs were budgeted at $2.20 per unit, and actual variable costs were $2.30 per unit. Actual fixed costs of $41,000 exceeded budgeted fixed costs by $4,500.

## Requirement

1. Prepare Kyler's income statement performance report. What variance contributed most to the year's favorable results? What caused this variance?

### E23-18  ❸ ❹ Defining the benefits of setting cost standards, and calculating materials and labor variances [10–15 min]

Premium, Inc., produced 1,000 units of the company's product in 2012. The standard quantity of materials was three yards of cloth per unit at a standard price of $1.05 per *SP* yard. The accounting records showed that 2,600 yards of cloth were used and the company paid $1.10 per yard. Standard time was two direct labor hours per unit at a standard rate of $9.75 per direct labor hour. Employees worked 1,400 hours and were paid $9.25 per hour.

## Requirements

1. What are the benefits of setting cost standards?
2. Calculate the materials price variance and the materials efficiency variance, as well as the labor price and efficiency variances.

**E23-19** ➍ Calculating materials and labor variances [20–30 min]

Great Fender, which uses a standard cost accounting system, manufactured 20,000 boat fenders during the year, using 144,000 feet of extruded vinyl purchased at $1.05 per square foot. Production required 420 direct labor hours that cost $13.50 per hour. The materials standard was seven feet of vinyl per fender, at a standard cost of $1.10 per square foot. The labor standard was 0.025 direct labor hour per fender, at a standard price of $12.50 per hour.

**Requirement**

1. Compute the price and efficiency variances for direct materials and direct labor. Does the pattern of variances suggest Great Fender's managers have been making trade-offs? Explain.

*Note: Exercise 23-19 should be completed before attempting Exercise 23-20.*

**E23-20** ➎ Computing overhead variances [20–30 min]

Review the data from Great Fender given in E23-19. Consider the following additional information:

| | |
|---|---|
| Static budget variable overhead | $ 5,500 |
| Static budget fixed overhead | $22,000 |
| Static budget direct labor hours | 550 hours |
| Static budget number of units | 22,000 |

Great Fender allocates manufacturing overhead to production based on standard direct labor hours. Great Fender reported the following actual results for 2012: actual variable overhead, $4,950; actual fixed overhead, $23,000.

**Requirements**

1. Compute the variable and fixed overhead variances. Use Exhibits 23-11 and 23-12 as guides.
2. Explain why the variances are favorable or unfavorable.

*Note: Exercise 23-18 should be completed before attempting Exercise 23-21.*

**E23-21** ➎ Calculating overhead variances [10–15 min]

Review the data from Premium, Inc., given in Exercise 23-18. Consider the following additional information:

| | |
|---|---|
| Static budget variable overhead | $1,600 |
| Static budget fixed overhead | $3,200 |
| Static budget direct labor hours | 1,600 hours |
| Static budget number of units | 800 |

Premium allocates manufacturing overhead to production based on standard direct labor hours. Premium reported the following actual results for 2012: actual variable overhead, $1,900; actual fixed overhead, $3,300.

**Requirements**

1. Compute the variable and fixed overhead variances. Use Exhibits 23-11 and 23-12 as guides.
2. Explain why the variances are favorable or unfavorable.

**E23-22**  **6**  **Preparing a standard cost income statement [15 min]**

The May 2012 revenue and cost information for Houston Outfitters, Inc., follows:

| | |
|---|---|
| Sales revenue | $ 540,000 |
| Cost of goods sold (standard) | 341,000 |
| Direct materials price variance | 1,100  F |
| Direct materials efficiency variance | 6,100  F |
| Direct labor price variance | 4,200  U |
| Direct labor efficiency variance | 2,400  F |
| Variable overhead spending variance | 3,300  U |
| Fixed overhead volume variance | 8,100  F |
| Fixed overhead spending variance | 1,400  U |
| Variable overhead efficiency variance | 1,400  U |

## Requirement

1. Prepare a standard cost income statement for management through gross profit. Report all standard cost variances for management's use. Has management done a good or poor job of controlling costs? Explain.

*Note: Exercises 23-18 and 23-21 should be completed before attempting Exercise 23-23.*

**E23-23**  **6**  **Preparing journal entries [20–30 min]**

Review the results from E23-18 and E23-21.

## Requirement

1. Record the journal entries to record materials, labor, variable overhead, and fixed overhead. Record the journal entries to record the movement to finished goods and sale of all production for the year. Close out the manufacturing overhead account.

*Note: Exercise 23-19 and 23-20 should be completed before attempting Exercise 23-24.*

**E23-24**  **6**  **Preparing journal entries [20–30 min]**

Review the results from E23-19 and E23-20.

## Requirement

1. Record the journal entries to record materials, labor, variable overhead, and fixed overhead. Record the journal entries to record the movement to finished goods and sale of all production for the year. Close out the manufacturing overhead account.

*Note: Exercises 23-19, 23-20, and 23-24 should be completed before attempting Exercise 23-25.*

**E23-25**  **6**  **Preparing a standard cost income statement [15–20 min]**

Review your results from E23-19, E23-20, and E23-24. Assume each fender sold for $60 and total marketing and administrative costs were $400,000.

## Requirement

1. Prepare a standard cost income statement for 2012 for Great Fender.

## • Problems (Group A)

**P23-26A** ➊➌➍➎ **Preparing a flexible budget and computing standard cost variances [60–75 min]**

Preston Recliners manufactures leather recliners and uses flexible budgeting and a standard cost system. Preston allocates overhead based on yards of direct materials. The company's performance report includes the following selected data:

| | Static Budget (1,000 recliners) | Actual Results (980 recliners) |
|---|---|---|
| Sales  (1,000 recliners × $ 495) | $    495,000 | |
|       (980 recliners × $ 475) | | $    465,500 |
| Variable manufacturing costs: | | |
| Direct materials    (6,000 yds @ $8.80/yard) | 52,800 | |
|                     (6,150 yds @ $8.60/yard) | | 52,890 |
| Direct labor    (10,000 hrs @ $9.20/hour) | 92,000 | |
|                 (9,600 hrs @ $9.30/hour) | | 89,280 |
| Variable overhead    (6,000 yds @ $5.00/yard) | 30,000 | |
|                      (6,150 yds @ $6.40/yard) | | 39,360 |
| Fixed manufacturing costs: | | |
| Fixed overhead | 60,000 | 62,000 |
| Total cost of goods sold | $    234,800 | $    243,530 |
| Gross profit | $    260,200 | $    221,970 |

### Requirements

1. Prepare a flexible budget based on the actual number of recliners sold.

2. Compute the price variance and the efficiency variance for direct materials and for direct labor. For manufacturing overhead, compute the variable overhead spending, variable overhead efficiency, fixed overhead spending, and fixed overhead volume variances.

3. Have Preston's managers done a good job or a poor job controlling materials, labor, and overhead costs? Why?

4. Describe how Preston's managers can benefit from the standard costing system.

**P23-27A** ➋ **Preparing an income statement performance report [30 min]**

AllTalk Technologies manufactures capacitors for cellular base stations and other communications applications. The company's January 2012 flexible budget income statement shows output levels of 6,500, 8,000, and 10,000 units. The static budget was based on expected sales of 8,000 units.

| | Per Unit | By Units (Capacitors) | | |
|---|---|---|---|---|
| | | 6,500 | 8,000 | 10,000 |
| Sales revenue | $24 | $    156,000 | $    192,000 | $    240,000 |
| Variable expenses | $10 | 65,000 | 80,000 | 100,000 |
| Contribution margin | | $    91,000 | $    112,000 | $    140,000 |
| Fixed expenses | | 53,000 | 53,000 | 53,000 |
| Operating income | | $    38,000 | $    59,000 | $    87,000 |

**ALLTALK TECHNOLOGIES**
**Flexible Budget Income Statement**
**Month Ended January 31, 2012**

The company sold 10,000 units during January, and its actual operating income was as follows:

| ALLTALK TECHNOLOGIES | |
| --- | --- |
| Income Statement | |
| Month Ended January 31, 2012 | |
| Sales revenue | $ 246,000 |
| Variable expenses | 104,500 |
| Contribution margin | $ 141,500 |
| Fixed expenses | 54,000 |
| Operating income | $ 87,500 |

## Requirements

1. Prepare an income statement performance report for January.
2. What was the effect on AllTalk's operating income of selling 2,000 units more than the static budget level of sales?
3. What is AllTalk's static budget variance? Explain why the income statement performance report provides more useful information to AllTalk's managers than the simple static budget variance. What insights can AllTalk's managers draw from this performance report?

**P23-28A** ④ ⑤ ⑥ **Computing and journalizing standard cost variances [45 min]**
Java manufactures coffee mugs that it sells to other companies for customizing with their own logos. Java prepares flexible budgets and uses a standard cost system to control manufacturing costs. The standard unit cost of a coffee mug is based on static budget volume of 60,200 coffee mugs per month:

| | | |
| --- | --- | --- |
| Direct materials (0.2 lbs @ $0.25 per lb) | | $ 0.05 |
| Direct labor (3 minutes @ $0.12 per minute) | | 0.36 |
| Manufacturing overhead: | | |
|     Variable (3 minutes @ $0.05 per minute) | $ 0.15 | |
|     Fixed (3 minutes @ $0.14 per minute) | 0.42 | 0.57 |
| Total cost per coffee mug | | $ 0.98 |

Actual cost and production information for July 2012 follow:

a. Actual production and sales were 62,900 coffee mugs.
b. Actual direct materials usage was 10,000 lbs., at an actual price of $0.17 per lb.
c. Actual direct labor usage was 202,000 minutes at a total cost of $30,300.
d. Actual overhead cost was $10,000 variable and $30,500 fixed.
e. Marketing and administrative costs were $115,000.

## Requirements

1. Compute the price and efficiency variances for direct materials and direct labor.
2. Journalize the usage of direct materials and the assignment of direct labor, including the related variances.
3. For manufacturing overhead, compute the variable overhead spending and efficiency variances and the fixed overhead spending and volume variances.
4. Journalize the actual manufacturing overhead and the applied manufacturing overhead. Journalize the movement of all production from WIP. Journalize the closing of the manufacturing overhead account.
5. Java intentionally hired more-skilled workers during July. How did this decision affect the cost variances? Overall, was the decision wise?

*Note: Problem 23-28A should be completed before attempting Problem 23-29A.*

**P23-29A** ⑥ **Prepare a standard costing income statement [20 min]**
Review your results from P23-28A. Java's sales price per mug is $3.

## Requirement

1. Prepare the standard costing income statement for July 2012.

**P23-30A** ④⑤⑥ **Computing standard cost variances and reporting to management [45–60 min]**
HearSmart manufactures headphone cases. During September 2012, the company produced and sold 107,000 cases and recorded the following cost data:

Standard Cost Information:

|  | Quantity | | Price | |
| --- | --- | --- | --- | --- |
| Direct materials | 2 | parts | $ 0.16 | per part |
| Direct labor | 0.02 | hours | $ 8.00 | per hour |
| Variable manufacturing overhead | 0.02 | hours | $ 9.00 | per hour |

Fixed manufacturing overhead ($32,980 for static budget volume of 97,000 units and 1,940 hours, or $17 per hour)

Actual Information:

Direct materials (210,000 parts @ $0.21 per part = $44,100)
Direct labor (1,640 hours @ $8.15 per hour = $13,366)
Variable manufacturing overhead $8,000
Fixed manufacturing overhead $30,000

## Requirements

1. Compute the price and efficiency variances for direct materials and direct labor.
2. For manufacturing overhead, compute the variable overhead spending and efficiency variances and the fixed overhead spending and volume variances.
3. HearSmart's management used better quality materials during September. Discuss the trade-off between the two direct material variances.

## ● Problems (Group B)

**P23-31B** ❶ ❸ ❹ ❺ **Preparing a flexible budget and computing standard cost**
**variances [60–75 min]**

Relaxing Recliners manufactures leather recliners and uses flexible budgeting and a standard cost system. Relaxing allocates overhead based on yards of direct materials. The company's performance report includes the following selected data:

| | Static Budget (975 recliners) | Actual Results (955 recliners) |
|---|---|---|
| Sales  (975 recliners × $505) | $      492,375 | |
| (955 recliners × $485) | | $      463,175 |
| Variable manufacturing costs: | | |
| Direct materials     (5,850 yds @ $8.90/yard) | 52,065 | |
| (6,000 yds @ $8.70/yard) | | 52,200 |
| Direct labor     (9,750 hrs @ $9.00/hour) | 87,750 | |
| (9,350 hrs @ $9.10/hour) | | 85,085 |
| Variable overhead  (5,850 yds @ $5.30/yard) | 31,005 | |
| (6,000 yds @ $6.70/yard) | | 40,200 |
| Fixed manufacturing costs: | | |
| Fixed overhead | 60,255 | 62,255 |
| Total cost of goods sold | $      231,075 | $      239,740 |
| Gross profit | $      261,300 | $      223,435 |

### Requirements

1.  Prepare a flexible budget based on the actual number of recliners sold.

2.  Compute the price variance and the efficiency variance for direct materials and for direct labor. For manufacturing overhead, compute the variable overhead spending, variable overhead efficiency, fixed overhead spending, and fixed overhead volume variances.

3.  Have Relaxing's managers done a good job or a poor job controlling materials, labor, and overhead costs? Why?

4.  Describe how Relaxing's managers can benefit from the standard costing system.

**P23-32B** ❷ **Preparing an income statement performance report [30 min]**

Network Technologies manufactures capacitors for cellular base stations and other communication applications. The company's July 2012 flexible budget income statement shows output levels of 7,000, 8,500, and 10,500 units. The static budget was based on expected sales of 8,500 units.

| NETWORK TECHNOLOGIES Flexible Budget Income Statement Month Ended July 31, 2012 | | | | |
|---|---|---|---|---|
| | Per Unit | By Units (Capacitors) | | |
| | | 7,000 | 8,500 | 10,500 |
| Sales revenue | $25 | $   175,000 | $   212,500 | $   262,500 |
| Variable expenses | $13 | 91,000 | 110,500 | 136,500 |
| Contribution margin | | $    84,000 | $   102,000 | $   126,000 |
| Fixed expenses | | 56,000 | 56,000 | 56,000 |
| Operating income | | $    28,000 | $    46,000 | $    70,000 |

The company sold 10,500 units during July, and its actual operating income was as follows:

| NETWORK TECHNOLOGIES Income Statement Month Ended July 31, 2012 | |
| --- | --- |
| Sales revenue | $ 269,500 |
| Variable expenses | 141,500 |
| Contribution margin | $ 128,000 |
| Fixed expenses | 57,000 |
| Operating income | $ 71,000 |

## Requirements

1. Prepare an income statement performance report for July 2012.
2. What was the effect on Network's operating income of selling 2,000 units more than the static budget level of sales?
3. What is Network's static budget variance? Explain why the income statement performance report provides more useful information to Network's managers than the simple static budget variance. What insights can Network's managers draw from this performance report?

**P23-33B** ④⑤⑥ **Computing and journalizing standard cost variances [45 min]**
McKnight manufactures coffee mugs that it sells to other companies for customizing with their own logos. McKnight prepares flexible budgets and uses a standard cost system to control manufacturing costs. The standard unit cost of a coffee mug is based on static budget volume of 59,800 coffee mugs per month:

| | | |
| --- | --- | --- |
| Direct materials (0.2 lbs @ $0.25 per lb) | | $ 0.05 |
| Direct labor (3 minutes @ $0.11 per minute) | | 0.33 |
| Manufacturing overhead: | | |
| Variable (3 minutes @ $0.06 per minute) | $ 0.18 | |
| Fixed (3 minutes @ $0.15 per minute) | 0.45 | 0.63 |
| Total cost per coffee mug | | $ 1.01 |

Actual cost and production information for July 2012 follow:

a. Actual production and sales were 62,500 coffee mugs.
b. Actual direct materials usage was 10,000 lbs., at an actual price of $0.17 per lb.
c. Actual direct labor usage of 198,000 minutes at a total cost of $25,740.
d. Actual overhead cost was $8,500 variable and $32,100 fixed.
e. Marketing and administrative costs were $110,000.

## Requirements

1. Compute the price and efficiency variances for direct materials and direct labor.
2. Journalize the usage of direct materials and the assignment of direct labor, including the related variances.
3. For manufacturing overhead, compute the variable overhead spending and efficiency variances and the fixed overhead spending and volume variances.
4. Journalize the actual manufacturing overhead and the applied manufacturing overhead. Journalize the movement of all production from WIP. Journalize the closing of the manufacturing overhead account.
5. McKnight intentionally hired more-skilled workers during July. How did this decision affect the cost variances? Overall, was the decision wise?

*Note: Problem 23-33B should be completed before attempting Problem 23-34B.*

**P23-34B** ❻ **Prepare a standard costing income statement [20 min]**
Review your results from P23-33B. McKnight's sales price per mug is $5.

## Requirement

1. Prepare the standard costing income statement for July 2012.

**P23-35B** ❹❺❻ **Computing standard cost variances and reporting to management [45–60 min]**
SoundSmart manufactures headphone cases. During September 2012, the company produced 108,000 cases and recorded the following cost data:

### Standard Cost Information:

| | Quantity | Price |
|---|---|---|
| Direct materials | 2 parts | $ 0.16 per part |
| Direct labor | 0.02 hours | $ 7.00 per hour |
| Variable manufacturing overhead | 0.02 hours | $11.00 per hour |
| Fixed manufacturing overhead ($29,400 for static budget volume of 98,000 units and 1,960 hours, or $15 per hour) | | |

### Actual Information:

Direct materials (193,000 parts @ $0.21 per part = $40,530)
Direct labor (1,760 hours @ $7.15 per hour = $12,584)
Variable manufacturing overhead $12,000
Fixed manufacturing overhead, $30,000

## Requirements

1. Compute the price and efficiency variances for direct materials and direct labor.
2. For manufacturing overhead, compute the variable overhead spending and efficiency variances and the fixed overhead spending and volume variances.
3. SoundSmart's management used better quality materials during September. Discuss the trade-off between the two direct material variances.

## ● Continuing Exercise

**E23-36** ❹❻ **Calculating labor variances and journalizing labor transactions [15 min]** *MyAccountingLab*
This exercise continues the Lawlor Lawn Service, Inc., situation from Exercise 22-38 of Chapter 22. Lawlor's budgeted static production volume for the month was 440 lawns. The standard direct labor cost was $15.00 per hour and two hours standard per lawn.
Lawlor actually mowed 500 lawns in June. Actual labor costs were $20.00 per hour, and 900 hours were worked during June.

## Requirements

1. Compute the direct labor price and efficiency variances.
2. Journalize the transactions to record the incurrence and usage of direct labor in June for Lawlor.
3. Analyze the labor variances for Lawlor.

## ● Continuing Problem

*MyAccountingLab* ▌ **P23-37** ❹❻ Calculating materials and labor variances and preparing journal entries [20–25 min]

This problem continues the Draper Consulting, Inc., situation from Problem 22-39 of Chapter 22. Assume Draper has created a standard cost card for each job. Standard direct materials include 14 software packages at a cost of $900 per package. Standard direct labor costs per job include 90 hours at $120 per hour. Draper plans on completing 12 jobs during October.

Actual direct materials costs for October included 90 software packages at a total cost of $81,450. Actual direct labor costs included 100 hours per job at an average rate of $125 per hour. Draper completed all 12 jobs in October.

### Requirements

1. Calculate direct materials price and efficiency variances.
2. Calculate direct labor price and efficiency variances.
3. Prepare journal entries to record the use of both materials and labor for October for the company.

# Apply Your Knowledge

## ● Decision Cases

**Decision Case 23-1** Movies Galore distributes DVDs to movie retailers, including dot.coms. Movies Galore's top management meets monthly to evaluate the company's performance. Controller Allen Walsh prepared the following performance report for the meeting:

| MOVIES GALORE Income Statement Performance Report Month Ended July 31, 2010 | | | |
|---|---|---|---|
| | **Actual Results** | **Static Budget** | **Variance** |
| Sales revenue | $1,640,000 | $1,960,000 | $320,000 U |
| Variable costs: | | | |
| Cost of goods sold | 775,000 | 980,000 | 205,000 F |
| Sales commisions | 77,000 | 107,800 | 30,800 F |
| Shipping cost | 43,000 | 53,900 | 10,900 F |
| Total variable costs | $ 895,000 | $1,141,700 | $246,700 F |
| Contribution margin | 745,000 | 818,300 | 73,300 U |
| Fixed costs: | | | |
| Salary cost | 311,000 | 300,500 | 10,500 U |
| Depreciation cost | 209,000 | 214,000 | 5,000 F |
| Rent cost | 129,000 | 108,250 | 20,750 U |
| Advertising cost | 81,000 | 68,500 | 12,500 U |
| Total fixed costs | $ 730,000 | $ 691,250 | $ 38,750 U |
| Operating income | $ 15,000 | $ 127,050 | $112,050 U |

Walsh also revealed that the actual sale price of $20 per movie was equal to the budgeted sale price and that there were no changes in inventories for the month.

Management is disappointed by the operating income results. CEO Jilinda Robinson exclaims, "How can actual operating income be roughly 12% of the static budget amount when there are so many favorable variances?"

## Requirements

1.  Prepare a more informative performance report. Be sure to include a flexible budget for the actual number of DVDs bought and sold.
2.  As a member of Movies Galore's management team, which variances would you want investigated? Why?
3.  Robinson believes that many consumers are postponing purchases of new movies until after the introduction of a new format for recordable DVD players. In light of this information, how would you rate the company's performance?

**Decision Case 23-2** Suppose you manage the local Scoopy's ice cream parlor. In addition to selling ice-cream cones, you make large batches of a few flavors of milk shakes to sell throughout the day. Your parlor is chosen to test the company's "Made-for-You" system. This new system enables patrons to customize their milk shakes by choosing different flavors.

Customers like the new system and your staff appears to be adapting, but you wonder whether this new made-to-order system is as efficient as the old system in which you just made a few large batches. Efficiency is a special concern because your performance is evaluated in part on the restaurant's efficient use of materials and labor. Your superiors consider efficiency variances greater than 5% to be unacceptable.

You decide to look at your sales for a typical day. You find that the parlor used 390 pounds of ice cream and 72 hours of direct labor to produce and sell 2,000 shakes. The standard quantity allowed for a shake is 0.2 pound of ice cream and 0.03 hour of direct labor. The standard prices are $1.50 per pound for ice cream and $8 an hour for labor.

## Requirements

1.  Compute the efficiency variances for direct labor and direct materials.
2.  Provide likely explanations for the variances. Do you have reason to be concerned about your performance evaluation? Explain.
3.  Write a memo to Scoopy's national office explaining your concern and suggesting a remedy.

## ● Ethical Issues

Rita Lane is the accountant for Outdoor Living, a manufacturer of outdoor furniture that is sold through specialty stores and Internet companies. Lane is responsible for reviewing the standard costs. While reviewing the standards for the coming year, two ethical issues arise.

**Ethical Issue 23-1** Lane has been approached by Casey Henderson, a former colleague who worked with Lane when they were both employed by a public accounting firm. Henderson has recently started his own firm, Henderson Benchmarking Associates, which collects and sells data on industry benchmarks. He offers to provide Lane with benchmarks for the outdoor furniture industry free of charge if she will provide him with the last three years of Outdoor Living's standard and actual costs. Henderson explains that this is how he obtains most of his firm's benchmarking data. Lane always has a difficult time with the standard-setting process and believes that the benchmark data would be very useful.

**Ethical Issue 23-2** Outdoor Living's management is starting a continuous improvement policy that requires a 10% reduction in standard costs each year for the next three years. Dan Jacobs, manufacturing foreman of the Teak furniture line, asks Lane to set loose standard costs this year before the continuous improvement policy is implemented. Jacobs argues that there is no other way to meet the tightening standards while maintaining the high quality of the Teak line.

## Requirements

1.  Use the IMA's ethical guidelines (https://www.imanet.org/PDFs/Statement%20of%20 Ethics_web.pdf) to identify the ethical dilemma in each situation.
2.  Identify the relevant factors in each situation and suggest what Lane should recommend to the controller.

## ● Fraud Case 23-1

Aja could tell that this "patron" was not her store's usual type. She could see he did not care about fashion, and the customers that came to her shop in the Jacksonville mall were all tuned in to the latest styles. He came up to the register and took two pairs of jeans and an expensive sweater out of a bag to return. He didn't have a receipt. Aja looked at the garments. They weren't even close to his size. She had not seen him before, but she knew there were shoplifters who had been stealing from her company's stores throughout the state. They grabbed clothing from one location and returned it to another. He knew—and she knew—that her store had a loose return policy. Receipts were not required and cash was given. She knew it would be pointless to call security; there was no proof. She remained courteous and professional. Although his returns would not impact her own performance stats, she couldn't help feeling angry. A month later when the company changed its policy, Aja was relieved.

### Requirements

1. What factors does a company consider when it decides on a policy for returns?
2. How is theft of this type handled in the accounting system?

## ● Team Project 23-1

Lynx, Corp., manufactures windows and doors. Lynx has been using a standard cost system that bases price and quantity standards on Lynx's historical long-run average performance. Suppose Lynx's controller has engaged your team of management consultants to advise him or her whether Lynx should use some basis other than historical performance for setting standards.

### Requirements

1. List the types of variances you recommend that Lynx compute (for example, direct materials price variance for glass). For each variance, what specific standards would Lynx need to develop? In addition to cost standards, do you recommend that Lynx develop any non-financial standards?
2. There are many approaches to setting standards other than simply using long-run average historical prices and quantities.
   a. List three alternative approaches that Lynx could use to set standards, and explain how Lynx could implement each alternative.
   b. Evaluate each alternative method of setting standards, including the pros and cons of each method.
   c. Write a memo to Lynx's controller detailing your recommendations. First, should Lynx retain its historical data-based standard cost approach? If not, which of the alternative approaches should it adopt?

## ● Communication Activity 23-1

In 75 words or fewer, explain what a price variance is and describe its potential causes.

---

### Quick Check Answers

1. *c* 2. *d* 3. *a* 4. *e* 5. *b* 6. *b* 7. *b* 8. *a* 9. *b* 10. *c*

**For online homework, exercises, and problems that provide you immediate feedback, please visit myaccountinglab.com.**

# 24 Performance Evaluation and the Balanced Scorecard

Shift Your Focus   Product Costing   Cost Allocation

Cost-Volume-Profit   Relevant Information   Capital Budgeting

Budgeting   Cost Control   Performance Measures

## Learning Objectives

1 Explain why and how companies decentralize

2 Explain why companies use performance evaluation systems

3 Describe the balanced scorecard and identify key performance indicators for each perspective

4 Use performance reports to evaluate cost, revenue, and profit centers

5 Use ROI, RI, and EVA to evaluate investment centers

Our lives need balance. Even while we are students and our main focus is on our studies, we still need balance. Working accounting problems keeps our minds sharp, but we also need to take care of our physical well-being by eating properly, exercising, and getting enough sleep. And we need to take care of our emotional well-being by cultivating friendships and taking time to relax. An intellectual goal may be to earn an A in accounting, a physical goal may be to work out at the gym three times a week, and an emotional goal may be to take Friday nights off to spend time with friends. It is the combination of goals that keeps our lives in balance.

Many experts recommend writing down goals and posting them where we can see them every day, such as on a bulletin board. Keeping our goals in sight helps us remember and work toward achieving them.

Businesses also have goals they must communicate to their employees. Goals motivate employees to make decisions that are in the best interest of the company. Businesses often use a system—such as the *balanced scorecard*—for communicating the company's strategy to employees and for measuring how well they are achieving the goals. Communicating goals becomes more challenging as companies grow and decentralize decision making.

In this chapter, you'll learn about key performance indicators and the balanced scorecard. Later in the chapter we'll revisit Smart Touch Learning, but first we'll look at the advantages and disadvantages of decentralization.

# Decentralized Operations

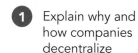

Explain why and how companies decentralize

In a small company, the owner or top manager often makes all planning and operating decisions. Small companies are most often considered to be **centralized companies** because centralizing decision making is easier due to the smaller scope of their operations. However, when a company grows, it is impossible for a single person to manage the entire organization's daily operations. Therefore, most companies decentralize as they grow. These are called **decentralized companies.**

Companies decentralize by splitting their operations into different divisions or operating units. Top management delegates decision-making responsibility to the unit managers. Top management determines the type of decentralization that best suits the company's strategy. For example, decentralization may be based on geographic area, product line, customer base, business function, or some other business characteristic. **Citizen's Bank** segments its operations by state (different geographic areas). **Sherwin-Williams** segments by customer base (commercial and consumer paint divisions). **PepsiCo** segments by brands (**Pepsi, Frito-Lay, Quaker, Gatorade,** and **Tropicana**). **UPS** segments first by function (domestic packaging, international packaging, and nonpackaging services), then by geographic area. Smart Touch thinks it will segment by product line (DVDs and Web-based learning).

## Advantages of Decentralization

What advantages does decentralization offer large companies? Let's take a look.

### Frees Top Management Time

By delegating responsibility for daily operations to unit managers, top management can concentrate on long-term strategic planning and higher-level decisions that affect the entire company. It also naturally places the decision makers (top management) closer to the source of the decisions.

### Supports Use of Expert Knowledge

Decentralization allows top management to hire the expertise each business unit needs to excel in its own specific operations. For example, decentralizing by state allows **Citizens Bank** to hire managers with specialized knowledge of the banking laws in each state. Such specialized knowledge can help unit managers make better decisions than could the company's top managers about product and business improvements within the business unit (state).

### Improves Customer Relations

Unit managers focus on just one segment of the company. Therefore, they can maintain closer contact with important customers than can upper management. Thus, decentralization often leads to improved customer relations and quicker customer response time.

### Provides Training

Decentralization also provides unit managers with training and experience necessary to become effective top managers. For example, companies often choose CEOs based on their past performance as division managers.

### Improves Motivation and Retention

Empowering unit managers to make decisions increases managers' motivation and retention. This improves job performance and satisfaction.

## Disadvantages of Decentralization

Despite its advantages, decentralization can also cause potential problems, including those outlined here.

### Duplication of Costs

Decentralization may cause the company to duplicate certain costs or assets. For example, each business unit may hire its own payroll department and purchase its own payroll software. Companies can often avoid such duplications by providing centralized services. For example, **Doubletree Hotels** segments its business by property, yet each property shares one centralized reservations office and one centralized Web site.

### Problems Achieving Goal Congruence

**Goal congruence** occurs when unit managers' goals align with top management's goals. Decentralized companies often struggle to achieve goal congruence. Unit managers may not fully understand the "big picture" of the company. They may make decisions that are good for their division but could harm another division or the rest of the company. For example, the purchasing department may buy cheaper components to decrease product cost. However, cheaper components may hurt the product line's quality, and the company's brand, *as a whole*, may suffer. Later in this chapter, we will see how managerial accountants can design performance evaluation systems that encourage goal congruence.

Although we've discussed some disadvantages of decentralization, it's important to note that the advantages of decentralization usually outweigh the disadvantages.

## Responsibility Centers

Decentralized companies delegate responsibility for specific decisions to each subunit, creating responsibility centers. Recall from Chapter 22 that a *responsibility center* is a part or subunit of an organization whose manager is accountable for specific activities. Exhibit 24-1 reviews the four most common types of responsibility centers.

> **Key Takeaway**
>
> As companies grow, they often decentralize by geographic area, product line, customer base, business function, or some other characteristic. Decentralization frees top management's time by delegating decision making, supports the use of expert knowledge, improves customer relations, provides training for managers, and improves employee motivation and retention. Disadvantages of decentralization include possible cost duplications and difficulty achieving goal congruence among decentralized divisions.

**EXHIBIT 24-1** | **The Four Most Common Types of Responsibility Centers**

| Responsibility Center | Manager is responsible for... | Examples |
|---|---|---|
| Cost center | Controlling costs | Production line at Dell Computer; legal department and accounting departments at Nike |
| Revenue center | Generating sales revenue | Midwest sales region at Pace Foods; central reservation office at Delta |
| Profit center | Producing profit through generating sales and controlling costs | Product line at Anheuser-Busch; individual Home Depot stores |
| Investment center | Producing profit and managing the division's invested capital | Company divisions, such as Walt Disney World Resorts and Toon Disney |

# Performance Measurement

 Explain why companies use performance evaluation systems

Once a company decentralizes operations, top management is no longer involved in running the subunits' day-to-day operations. Performance evaluation systems provide top management with a framework for maintaining control over the entire organization.

## Goals of Performance Evaluation Systems

When companies decentralize, top management needs a system to communicate its goals to subunit managers. Additionally, top management needs to determine whether the decisions being made at the subunit level are effectively meeting company goals. Let's look at the primary goals of performance evaluation systems.

### Promoting Goal Congruence and Coordination

As previously mentioned, decentralization increases the difficulty of achieving goal congruence. Unit managers may not always make decisions consistent with the overall goals of the organization. A company will be able to achieve its goals only if each unit moves, in a synchronized fashion, toward the overall company goals. The performance measurement system should provide incentives for coordinating the subunits' activities and direct them toward achieving the overall company goals.

### Communicating Expectations

To make decisions that are consistent with the company's goals, unit managers must know the goals and the specific part their unit plays in attaining those goals. The performance measurement system should spell out the unit's most critical objectives. Without a clear picture of what management expects, unit managers have little to guide their daily operating decisions.

### Motivating Unit Managers

Unit managers are usually motivated to make decisions that will help to achieve top management's expectations. For additional motivation, upper management may offer bonuses to unit managers who meet or exceed performance targets. Top management must exercise extreme care in setting performance targets, however. For example, managers measured solely by their ability to control costs may take whatever actions are necessary to achieve that goal, including sacrificing quality or customer service. But such actions would *not* be in the best interests of the firm as a whole. Therefore, upper management must consider the ramifications of the performance targets it sets for unit managers.

### Providing Feedback

As noted previously, in decentralized companies, top management is not involved in the day-to-day operations of each subunit. Performance evaluation systems provide upper management with the feedback it needs to maintain control over the entire organization, even though it has delegated responsibility and decision-making authority to unit managers. If targets are not met at the unit level, upper management will take corrective actions, ranging from modifying unit goals (if the targets were unrealistic) to replacing the unit manager (if the targets were achievable, but the manager failed to reach them).

### Benchmarking

Performance evaluation results are often used for benchmarking, which is the practice of comparing the company's achievements against the best practices in the industry. Comparing results against industry benchmarks is often more revealing than comparing results against budgets. To survive, a company must keep up with its competitors. Benchmarking helps the company determine whether it is performing at least as well as its competitors.

## Stop & Think...

Do companies only benchmark subunit performance against competitors and industry standards?

**Answer:** No. Companies also benchmark performance against the subunit's past performance. Historical trend data (measuring performance over time) helps managers assess whether their decisions are improving, having no effect, or adversely affecting subunit performance. Some companies also benchmark performance against other subunits with similar characteristics.

## Limitations of Financial Performance Measurement

In the past, performance measurement revolved almost entirely around *financial* performance. For example, until 1995, 95% of **UPS**'s performance measures were financial. On the one hand, this focus makes sense because the ultimate goal of a company is to generate profit. On the other hand, *current* financial performance tends to reveal the results of *past* actions rather than indicate *future* performance. For this reason, financial measures tend to be **lag indicators** (after the fact) rather than **lead indicators** (future predictors). Management needs to know the results of past decisions, but it also needs to know how current decisions may affect the future. To adequately assess the company, managers need both lead indicators and lag indicators.

Another limitation of financial performance measures is that they tend to focus on the company's short-term achievements rather than on long-term performance. Why is this the case? Because financial statements are prepared on a monthly, quarterly, or annual basis. To remain competitive, top management needs clear signals that assess and predict the company's performance over longer periods of time.

> **Key Takeaway**
>
> Performance evaluation systems provide top management with a framework for maintaining control over the entire organization once it is decentralized. Such systems should help management promote goal congruence, provide a tool for communications, motivate unit managers, provide feedback, and allow for benchmarking. These measures should not revolve around just financial performance measures, however.

# The Balanced Scorecard

In the early 1990s, Robert Kaplan and David Norton introduced the **balanced scorecard**.[1] The balanced scorecard recognizes that management must consider *both* financial performance measures (which tend to measure the results of actions already taken—lag indicators) and operational performance measures (which tend to drive future performance—lead indicators) when judging the performance of a company and its subunits. These measures should be linked with the company's goals and its strategy for achieving those goals. The balanced scorecard represents a major shift in corporate performance measurement. Rather than treating financial indicators as the sole measure of performance, companies recognize that they are only one measure among a broader set. Keeping score of operating measures *and* traditional financial measures gives management a "balanced" view of the organization.

**3**   Describe the balanced scorecard and identify key performance indicators for each perspective

---

[1]Robert Kaplan and David Norton, "The Balanced Scorecard—Measures That Drive Performance," *Harvard Business Review on Measuring Corporate Performance*, Boston, 1991, pp. 123–145; Robert Kaplan and David Norton, *Translating Strategy into Action: The Balanced Scorecard*, Boston, Harvard Business School Press, 1996.

Kaplan and Norton use the analogy of an airplane pilot to illustrate the necessity for a balanced scorecard approach to performance evaluation. The pilot of an airplane cannot rely on only one factor, such as wind speed, to fly a plane. Rather, the pilot must consider other critical factors, such as altitude, direction, and fuel level. Likewise, management cannot rely on only financial measures to guide the company. Management needs to consider other critical factors, such as customer satisfaction, operational efficiency, and employee excellence. Similar to the way a pilot uses cockpit instruments to measure critical factors, management uses *key performance indicators*—such as customer satisfaction ratings and revenue growth—to measure critical factors that affect the success of the company. As shown in Exhibit 24-2, **key performance indicators (KPIs)** are summary performance measures that help managers assess whether the company is achieving its goals.

EXHIBIT 24-2 | **Linking Company Goals to Key Performance Indicators (KPIs)**

# Four Perspectives of the Balanced Scorecard

The balanced scorecard views the company from four different perspectives, each of which evaluates a specific aspect of organizational performance:

1. Financial perspective
2. Customer perspective
3. Internal business perspective
4. Learning and growth perspective

Exhibit 24-3 on the following page illustrates how the company's strategy affects, and, in turn, is affected by all four perspectives. Additionally, it shows the cause-and-effect relationship linking the four perspectives.

Companies that adopt the balanced scorecard usually have specific goals they wish to achieve within each of the four perspectives. Once management clearly identifies the goals, it develops KPIs that will assess how well the goals are being achieved. That is, they measure actual results of KPIs against goal KPIs. The difference is the variance. If an individual KPI variance is positive, the company exceeded its goal. If an individual KPI variance is negative, the company did not meet the goal. This allows management to focus attention on the most critical elements and prevent information overload. Management should take care to use only a few KPIs for each perspective. Let's look at each of the perspectives and discuss the links among them.

**EXHIBIT 24-3** | **The Four Perspectives of the Balanced Scorecard**

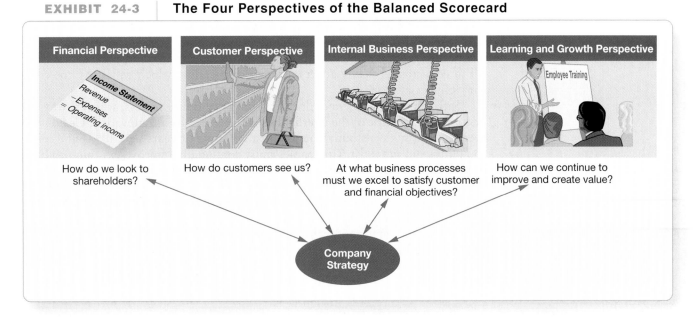

## Financial Perspective

This perspective helps managers answer the question, "How do we look to shareholders?" The ultimate goal of companies is to generate income for their owners. Therefore, company strategy revolves around increasing the company's profits through increasing revenue growth and productivity. Companies grow revenue by introducing new products, gaining new customers, and increasing sales to existing customers. Companies increase productivity through reducing costs and using the company's assets more efficiently. Managers may implement seemingly sensible strategies and initiatives, but the test of their judgment is whether these decisions increase company profits. The financial perspective focuses management's attention on KPIs that assess financial objectives, such as revenue growth and cost cutting. Some commonly used financial perspective KPIs include *sales revenue growth, gross margin growth*, and *return on investment*. The latter portion of this chapter discusses in detail the most commonly used financial perspective KPIs.

## Customer Perspective

This perspective helps managers evaluate the question, "How do customers see us?" Customer satisfaction is a top priority for long-term company success. If customers are not happy, they will not come back. Therefore, customer satisfaction is critical to achieving the company's financial goals outlined in the financial perspective of the balanced scorecard. Customers are typically concerned with four specific product or service attributes: (1) the product's price, (2) the product's quality, (3) the service quality at the time of sale, and (4) the product's delivery time (the shorter the better). Since each of these attributes is critical to making the customer happy, most companies have specific objectives for each of these attributes.

Businesses commonly use customer perspective KPIs, such as *customer satisfaction ratings*, to assess how they are performing on these attributes. No doubt you have filled out a customer satisfaction survey. Because customer satisfaction is crucial, customer satisfaction ratings often determine the extent to which bonuses are granted to restaurant managers. For example, if customer satisfaction ratings are greater than average, the KPI will be positive. If customer satisfaction ratings are lower than average, management will want to devise measures to improve customer satisfaction. Other typical customer perspective KPIs include *percentage of market share, increase in the number of customers, number of repeat customers*, and *rate of on-time deliveries*.

## Internal Business Perspective

This perspective helps managers address the question, "At what business processes must we excel to satisfy customer and financial objectives?" The answer to this question incorporates three factors: innovation, operations, and post-sales service. All three factors critically affect customer satisfaction, which will affect the company's financial success.

Satisfying customers once does not guarantee future success, which is why the first important factor of the internal business perspective is innovation. Customers' needs and wants constantly change. Just a couple of years ago, iPads and mini-computers did not exist. Companies must continually improve existing products (such as adding more applications to cell phones) and develop new products (such as the iPad) to succeed in the future. Companies commonly assess innovation using internal business perspective KPIs, such as the *number of new products developed* or *new-product development time*.

The second important factor of the internal business perspective is operations. Lean and effective internal operations allow the company to meet customers' needs and expectations. For example, the time it takes to manufacture a product (*manufacturing cycle time*) affects the company's ability to deliver quickly to meet a customer's demand. Production efficiency (*number of units produced per hour*) and product quality (*defect rate*) also affect the price charged to the customer. To remain competitive, companies must be at least as good as the industry leader at those internal operations that are essential to their business.

The third factor of the internal business perspective is post-sales service. How well does the company service customers after the sale? Claims of excellent post-sales service help to generate more sales. Management assesses post-sales service through the following typical internal business perspective KPIs: *number of warranty claims received*, *average repair time*, and *average wait time on the phone for a customer service representative*. So, for example, if the number of warranty claims is greater than the number of expected (or acceptable) warranty claims, the KPI will be negative. Management will want to devise measures to improve the quality of its products so it can reduce the number of warranty claims. If the number of warranty claims is less than the number of expected (or acceptable) warranty claims, that will be a positive KPI.

## Learning and Growth Perspective

This perspective helps managers assess the question, "How can we continue to improve and create value?" The learning and growth perspective focuses on three factors: (1) employee capabilities, (2) information system capabilities, and (3) the company's "climate for action." The learning and growth perspective lays the foundation needed to improve internal business operations, sustain customer satisfaction, and generate financial success. Without skilled employees, updated technology, and a positive corporate culture, the company will not be able to meet the objectives of the other perspectives.

Let's consider each of these factors. First, because most routine work is automated, employees are freed up to be critical and creative thinkers who, therefore, can help achieve the company's goals. The learning and growth perspective measures employees' skills, knowledge, motivation, and empowerment. Learning and growth perspective KPIs typically include *hours of employee training, employee satisfaction, employee turnover*, and *number of employee suggestions implemented*. Second, employees need timely and accurate information on customers, internal processes, and finances; therefore, other KPIs measure the maintenance and improvement of the company's information system. For example, KPIs might include the *percentage of employees having online access to information about customers*, and the *percentage of processes with real-time feedback on quality, cycle time, and cost*. Finally, management must create a corporate culture that supports and encourages communication, change, and growth. For example, a

**Connect To: Business**

The balanced scorecard is one performance tool a company may use to not only measure how well the company is meeting its strategic goals, but also to identify areas where the company may improve overall performance. Continuous improvement is the goal. Each area in which the company makes improvements to efficiency and effectiveness, no matter how small, improves KPIs. This often translates into leaner, more efficient and more profitable companies.

company may use the balanced scorecard to communicate strategy to every employee and to show each employee how his or her daily work contributed to company success. So, for example, managers might review the employee turnover KPI to determine whether the company is attracting and retaining skilled employees. If the data show the employee turnover rate is greater than the expected employee turnover rate, the KPI would be negative. Management will want to devise measures to identify the reasons for the increase in employee turnover and devise measures to increase employee retention. If the employee turnover rate is less than the expected employee turnover rate, that would be a positive KPI.

So far, we have looked at why companies decentralize, why they need to measure subunit performance, and how the balanced scorecard can help. In the second half of the chapter, we will focus on how companies measure the financial perspective of the balanced scorecard.

The Decision Guidelines and Summary Problem on the next pages ask you to put these concepts to use.

**Key Takeaway**

The balanced scorecard focuses performance measurement on progress toward the company's goals in each of the four perspectives. In designing the scorecard, managers start with the company's goals and its strategy for achieving those goals and then identify the *most* important measures of performance that will predict long-term success. Some of these measures are lead indicators, while others are lag indicators. Managers must consider the linkages between strategy and operations and how those operations will affect finances now and in the future.

# Decision Guidelines 24-1

As Smart Touch expanded its business operations, it had to make the following types of decisions when it decentralized and developed its balanced scorecard for performance evaluation.

| Decision | Guidelines |
|---|---|
| • On what basis should the company be decentralized? | The manner of decentralization should fit the company's strategy. Many companies decentralize based on geographic region, product line, business function, or customer type. |
| • Will decentralization have any negative impact on the company? | Decentralization usually provides many benefits; however, decentralization also has potential drawbacks:<br>• Subunits may duplicate costs or assets.<br>• Subunit managers may not make decisions that are favorable to the entire company. |
| • How can responsibility accounting be incorporated at decentralized companies? | Subunit managers are given responsibility for specific activities and are only held accountable for the results of those activities. Subunits generally fall into one of the following four categories according to their responsibilities:<br>1. Cost centers—responsible for controlling costs<br>2. Revenue centers—responsible for generating revenue<br>3. Profit centers—responsible for controlling costs and generating revenue<br>4. Investment centers—responsible for controlling costs, generating revenue, and efficiently managing the division's invested capital (assets) |
| • Is a performance evaluation system necessary? | While not mandatory, most companies will reap many benefits from implementing a well-designed performance evaluation system. Such systems promote goal congruence, communicate expectations, motivate managers, provide feedback, and enable benchmarking. |
| • Should the performance evaluation system include lag or lead measures? | Better performance evaluation systems include *both* lag and lead measures. Lag measures indicate the results of past actions, while lead measures try to predict future performance. |
| • What are the four balanced scorecard perspectives? | 1. Financial perspective<br>2. Customer perspective<br>3. Internal business perspective<br>4. Learning and growth perspective |
| • Must all four perspectives be included in the company's balanced scorecard? | Every company's balanced scorecard will be unique to its business and strategy. Because each of the four perspectives is causally linked, most companies will benefit from developing performance measures for each of the four perspectives. |

# Summary Problem 24-1

The balanced scorecard gives performance perspective from four different viewpoints.

**Requirements**

1. Each of the following describes a key performance indicator. Determine which of the balanced scorecard perspectives is being addressed (financial, customer, internal business, or learning and growth):
    a. Employee turnover
    b. Earnings per share
    c. Percentage of on-time deliveries
    d. Revenue growth rate
    e. Percentage of defects discovered during manufacturing
    f. Number of warranty claims
    g. New product development time
    h. Number of repeat customers
    i. Number of employee suggestions implemented

2. Read the following company initiatives and determine which of the balanced scorecard perspectives is being addressed (financial, customer, internal business, learning and growth):
    a. Purchasing efficient production equipment
    b. Providing employee training
    c. Updating retail store lighting
    d. Paying quarterly dividends to stockholders
    e. Updating the company's information system

## Solution

**Requirement 1**
    a. Learning and growth
    b. Financial
    c. Customer
    d. Financial
    e. Internal business
    f. Internal business
    g. Internal business
    h. Customer
    i. Learning and growth

**Requirement 2**
    a. Internal business
    b. Learning and growth
    c. Customer
    d. Financial
    e. Learning and growth

# Measuring the Financial Performance of Cost, Revenue, and Profit Centers

**④ Use performance reports to evaluate cost, revenue, and profit centers**

In this half of the chapter, we will take a more detailed look at how companies measure the financial perspective of the balanced scorecard for different subunits of the company. We will focus now on the financial performance measurement of each type of responsibility center.

Responsibility accounting performance reports capture the financial performance of cost, revenue, and profit centers. Recall from Chapter 22 that responsibility accounting performance reports compare *actual* results with *budgeted* amounts and display a variance, or difference, between the two amounts. Because *cost centers* are only responsible for controlling costs, their performance reports only include information on actual traceable costs versus budgeted *costs*. Likewise, performance reports for *revenue centers* only contain actual revenue versus budgeted *revenue*. However, *profit centers* are responsible for both controlling costs and generating revenue. Therefore, their performance reports contain actual and budgeted information on both their *revenues and costs*.

Cost center performance reports typically focus on the *flexible budget variance*—the difference between actual results and the flexible budget (as described in Chapter 23). Exhibit 24-4 shows an example of a cost center performance report for a regional payroll processing department of Smart Touch. Because the payroll processing department only incurs expenses and does not generate revenue, it is classified as a cost center.

**EXHIBIT 24-4** | **Example of a Cost Center Performance Report**

### SMART TOUCH LEARNING, INC.
#### Payroll Processing Department Performance Report
#### July 2014

| | Actual | Flexible Budget | Flexible Budget Variance (U or F) | % Variance* (U or F) |
|---|---|---|---|---|
| Salary and wages | $18,500 | $18,000 | $ 500 U | 2.8% U |
| Payroll benefits | 6,100 | 5,000 | 1,100 U | 22.0% U |
| Equipment depreciation | 3,000 | 3,000 | 0 | 0% |
| Supplies | 1,850 | 2,000 | 150 F | 7.5% F |
| Other expenses | 1,900 | 2,000 | 100 F | 5.0% F |
| Total expenses | $31,350 | $30,000 | $1,350 U | 4.5% U |

*% Variance = Flexible budget variance/flexible budget

Managers use *management by exception* to determine which variances in the performance report are worth investigating. **Management by exception** directs management's attention to important differences between actual and budgeted amounts. For example, management may only investigate variances that exceed a certain dollar amount (i.e., over $1,000) or a certain percentage of the budgeted figure (i.e., over 10%). Smaller variances signal that operations are close to target and do not require management's immediate attention. Consider the cost center performance report illustrated in Exhibit 24-4. Management might only investigate payroll benefits because the variance exceeds both $1,000 and 10%. Companies that use standard costs can compute price and efficiency variances, as described in Chapter 23, to better understand why significant flexible budget variances occurred.

Revenue center performance reports often highlight both the flexible budget variance and the sales volume variance. The performance report for the specialty

DVD department of Smart Touch might look similar to Exhibit 24-5, with detailed sales volume and revenue shown for each brand and type of DVD sold. (For simplicity, the exhibit shows volume and revenue for only one item.) The cash register barcoding system provides management with the sales volume and sales revenue generated by individual products.

| EXHIBIT 24-5 | **Example of a Revenue Center Performance Report** |
|---|---|

**SMART TOUCH LEARNING, INC.**
**Specialty DVD Department Performance Report**
**July 2014**

| Sales revenue | Actual Sales | Flexible Budget Variance | Flexible Budget | Sales Volume Variance | Static (Master) Budget |
|---|---|---|---|---|---|
| Number of Specialty DVDs | 2,480 | –0– | 2,480 | 155 F | 2,325 |
| Specialty DVDs | $40,920 | $3,720 U | $44,640 | $2,790 F | $41,850 |

Recall from Chapter 23 that the sales volume variance is due strictly to volume differences—selling more or fewer units (DVDs) than originally planned. The flexible budget variance, however, is due strictly to differences in the sales price—selling units for a higher or lower price than originally planned. Both the sales volume variance and the flexible budget variance help revenue center managers understand why they have exceeded or fallen short of budgeted revenue.

Managers of profit centers are responsible for both generating revenue and controlling costs so their performance reports include both revenues and expenses. Exhibit 24-6 shows an example of a profit center performance report for the DVD department.

| EXHIBIT 24-6 | **Example of a Profit Center Performance Report** |
|---|---|

**SMART TOUCH LEARNING, INC.**
**DVD—Performance Report**
**July 2014**

| | Actual | Flexible Budget | Flexible Budget Variance | % Variance (U or F) |
|---|---|---|---|---|
| Sales revenue | $5,243,600 | $5,000,000 | $243,600 F | 4.9% F |
| Variable expenses | 4,183,500 | 4,000,000 | 183,500 U | 4.6% U |
| Contribution margin | 1,060,100 | 1,000,000 | 60,100 F | 6.0% F |
| Traceable fixed expenses | 84,300 | 75,000 | 9,300 U | 12.4% U |
| Divisional segment margin | $ 975,800 | $ 925,000 | $ 50,800 F | 5.5% F |

Notice how this profit center performance report contains a line called "Traceable fixed expenses." Recall that one drawback of decentralization is that subunits may duplicate costs or assets. Many companies avoid this problem by providing centralized service departments where several subunits, such as profit centers, share assets or costs. For example, the payroll processing cost center shown in Exhibit 24-4 serves all of Smart Touch. In addition to centralized payroll departments, companies often provide centralized human resource departments, legal departments, and information systems.

When subunits share centralized services, should those services be "free" to the subunits? If they are free, the subunit's performance report will *not* include any charge for using those services. However, if they are not free, the performance report will show a charge for the traceable portion of those expenses, as you see in Exhibit 24-6. Most companies charge subunits for their use of centralized services because the subunit would incur a cost to buy those services on its own. For example, if Smart Touch did not operate a centralized payroll department, the DVD department would have to hire its own payroll department personnel and purchase computers, payroll software, and supplies necessary to process the department's payroll. As an alternative, it could outsource payroll to a company, such as **Paychex** or **ADP**. In either event, the department would incur a cost for processing payroll. It only seems fair that the department is charged for using the centralized payroll processing department. Notice we have excluded common fixed expenses not traceable to the DVD division.

Regardless of the type of responsibility center, performance reports should focus on information, not blame. Analyzing budget variances helps managers understand the underlying *reasons* for the unit's performance. Once management understands these reasons, it may be able to take corrective actions. But some variances are uncontrollable. For example, the 2010 **BP** oil spill in the Gulf of Mexico has caused damage to many businesses along the coast, as well as environmental damage to the wetlands and wildlife. Consequently, the price of seafood from the Gulf of Mexico increased because of the decreased supply. These price increases resulted in unfavorable cost variances for many restaurants and seafood retailers. Managers should not be held accountable for conditions they cannot control. Responsibility accounting can help management identify the causes of variances, thereby allowing them to determine what was controllable and what was not.

We have just looked at the detailed financial information presented in responsibility accounting performance reports. In addition to these *detailed* reports, upper management often uses *summary* measures—financial KPIs—to assess the financial performance of cost, revenue, and profit centers. Examples include the *cost per unit of output* (for cost centers), *revenue growth* (for revenue centers), and *gross margin growth* (for profit centers). KPIs such as these are used to address the financial perspective of the balanced scorecard for cost, revenue, and profit centers. In the next section, we will look at the most commonly used KPIs for investment centers.

## Stop & Think...

We have just seen that companies like Smart Touch use responsibility accounting performance reports to evaluate the financial performance of cost (payroll processing), revenue (specialty DVDs), and profit centers (DVD division). Are these types of responsibility reports sufficient for evaluating the financial performance of investment centers? Why or why not?

**Answer:** Investment centers are responsible not only for generating revenue and controlling costs, but also for efficiently managing the subunits' invested capital. The performance reports we have just seen address how well the subunits control costs and generate revenue, but they do not address how well the subunits manage their assets. Therefore, these performance reports will be helpful but not sufficient for evaluating investment center performance.

# Measuring the Financial Performance of Investment Centers

 **5** Use ROI, RI, and EVA to evaluate investment centers

Investment centers are typically large divisions of a company, such as the media division of **Amazon.com** or of Smart Touch. The duties of an investment center manager are similar to those of a CEO. The CEO is responsible for maximizing income, in relation to the company's invested capital, by using company assets efficiently.

Likewise, investment center managers are responsible not only for generating profit, but also for making the best use of the investment center's assets.

How does an investment center manager influence the use of the division's assets? An investment center manager has the authority to open new stores or close old stores. The manager may also decide how much inventory to hold, what types of investments to make, how aggressively to collect accounts receivable, and whether to invest in new equipment. In other words, the manager has decision-making responsibility over all of the division's assets.

Companies cannot evaluate investment centers the way they evaluate profit centers, based only on operating income. Why? Because operating income does not indicate how *efficiently* the division is using its assets. The financial evaluation of investment centers must measure two factors: (1) how much operating income the division is generating and (2) how efficiently the division is using its assets.

Consider Smart Touch. In addition to its DVD Division, it also has an online e-learning Division. Operating income, average total assets, and sales for the two divisions for July follow:

| Smart Touch | e-learning | DVD |
|---|---|---|
| Operating income | $ 450,000 | $ 975,800 |
| Average total assets | 2,500,000 | 6,500,000 |
| Sales | 7,500,000 | 5,243,600 |

Based on operating income alone, the DVD Division (with operating income of $975,800) appears to be more profitable than the e-learning Division (with operating income of $450,000). However, this comparison is misleading because it does not consider the assets invested in each division. The DVD Division has more assets than does the e-learning Division.

To adequately evaluate an investment center's financial performance, companies need summary performance measures—or KPIs—that include *both* the division's operating income *and* its assets (see Exhibit 24-7). In the next sections, we discuss three commonly used performance measures: return on investment (ROI), residual income (RI), and economic value added (EVA). All three measures incorporate both the division's assets and its operating income. For simplicity, we will leave the word *divisional* out of the equations. However, keep in mind that all of the equations use divisional data when evaluating a division's performance. Also, we will round each ratio to the nearest percentage.

**EXHIBIT 24-7** | **KPIs for Investment Centers**

# Return on Investment (ROI)

**Return on investment (ROI)** is one of the most commonly used KPIs for evaluating an investment center's financial performance. Companies typically define ROI as follows:

$$\text{ROI} = \frac{\text{Operating income}}{\text{Average total assets}}$$

ROI measures the amount of operating income an investment center earns relative to the amount of its average total assets. **The ROI formula focuses on the amount of operating income earned before other revenue/expense items (such as interest expense) by utilizing the average total assets employed for the year (denominator).** Each division's ROI is calculated as follows:

$$\text{e-learning Division's ROI} = \frac{\$450,000}{\$2,500,000} = 0.18, \text{ or } 18\%$$

$$\text{DVD Division's ROI} = \frac{\$975,800}{\$6,500,000} = 0.15, \text{ or } 15\%$$

Although the DVD Division has a higher operating income than the e-learning Division, the DVD Division is actually *less* profitable than the e-learning Division when we consider that the DVD Division requires more average total assets to generate its operating income.

If you had $1,000 to invest, would you rather invest it in the DVD Division or the e-learning Division? The DVD Division earns operating income of $0.15 on every $1.00 of average total assets, but the e-learning Division earns $0.18 on every $1.00 of average total assets. When top management decides how to invest excess funds, it often considers each division's ROI. A division with a higher ROI is more likely to receive extra funds because it has a history of providing a higher return.

In addition to comparing ROI across divisions, management also compares a division's ROI across time to determine whether the division is becoming more or less profitable in relation to its average total assets. Additionally, management often benchmarks divisional ROI with other companies in the same industry to determine how each division is performing compared to its competitors.

To determine what is driving a division's ROI, management often restates the ROI equation in its expanded form. Notice that Sales is incorporated in the denominator of the first term, and in the numerator of the second term. When the two terms are multiplied together, Sales cancels out, leaving the original ROI formula.

$$\text{ROI} = \frac{\text{Operating income}}{\text{Sales}} \times \frac{\text{Sales}}{\text{Average total assets}} = \frac{\text{Operating income}}{\text{Average total assets}}$$

Why do managers rewrite the ROI formula this way? Because it helps them better understand how they can improve their ROI. The first term in the expanded equation is called the **profit margin**:

$$\text{Profit margin} = \frac{\text{Operating income}}{\text{Sales}}$$

The profit margin shows how much operating income the division earns on every $1.00 of sales, so this term focuses on profitability. Each division's profit margin is calculated as follows:

$$\text{e-learning Division's profit margin} = \frac{\$450,000}{\$7,500,000} = 0.06, \text{ or } 6\%$$

$$\text{DVD Division's profit margin} = \frac{\$975,800}{\$5,243,600} = 0.186, \text{ or } 19\%$$

The e-learning Division has a profit margin of 6%, meaning that it earns operating income of $0.06 on every $1.00 of sales. The DVD Division, however, is much more profitable with a profit margin of 19%, earning $0.19 on every $1.00 of sales.

**Asset turnover** is the second term of the expanded ROI equation:

$$\text{Asset turnover} = \frac{\text{Sales}}{\text{Average total assets}}$$

Asset turnover shows how efficiently a division uses its average total assets to generate sales. Rather than focusing on profitability, asset turnover focuses on efficiency. Each division's asset turnover is calculated as follows:

$$\text{e-learning Division's asset turnover} = \frac{\$7,500,000}{\$2,500,000} = 3$$

$$\text{DVD Division's asset turnover} = \frac{\$5,243,600}{\$6,500,000} = 0.81$$

The e-learning Division has an asset turnover of 3. This means that the e-learning Division generates $3.00 of sales with every $1.00 of average total assets. The DVD Division's asset turnover is only 0.81. The DVD Division generates only $0.81 of sales with every $1.00 of average total assets. The e-learning Division uses its average total assets much more efficiently in generating sales than the DVD Division.

Putting the two terms back together in the expanded ROI equation gets the following:

|  | Profit margin | × | Asset turnover | = ROI |
|---|---|---|---|---|
| e-learning Division: | 6% | × | 3 | = 0.18 or 18% |
| DVD Division: | 19% | × | 0.81 | = 0.15 or 15% |

As you can see, the expanded ROI equation gives management more insight into the division's ROI. Management can now see that the DVD Division is more profitable on its sales (profit margin of 19%) than the e-learning Division (profit margin of 6%), but the e-learning Division is doing a better job of generating sales with its average total assets (asset turnover of 3) than the DVD Division (asset turnover of 0.81). Consequently, the e-learning Division has a higher ROI of 18%.

If managers are not satisfied with their division's asset turnover rate, how can they improve it? They might try to eliminate nonproductive assets, for example, by being more aggressive in collecting accounts receivables or by decreasing inventory levels. They might decide to change retail-store layout to increase sales.

What if management is not satisfied with the current profit margin? To increase the profit margin, management must increase the operating income earned on every dollar of sales. Management may cut product costs or selling and administrative costs, but it needs to be careful when trimming costs. Cutting costs in the short term can hurt long-term ROI. For example, sacrificing quality or cutting back on research and development could decrease costs in the short run but may hurt long-term sales. The balanced scorecard helps management carefully consider the consequences of cost-cutting measures before acting on them.

ROI has one major drawback. Evaluating division managers based solely on ROI gives them an incentive to adopt *only* projects that will maintain or increase their current ROI. Say that top management has set a company-wide target ROI of 16%. Both divisions are considering investing in in-store video display equipment that shows customers how to use featured products. This equipment will increase sales because customers are more likely to buy the products when they see these infomercials. The equipment would cost each division $100,000 and is expected to provide each division with $17,000 of annual operating income. The *equipment's* ROI is as follows:

$$\text{Equipment ROI} = \frac{\$17,000}{\$100,000} = 17\%$$

Upper management would want the divisions to invest in this equipment since the equipment will provide a 17% ROI, which is higher than the 16% target rate. But what will the managers of the divisions do? Because the DVD Division currently has an ROI of 15%, the new equipment (with its 17% ROI) will *increase* the division's *overall* ROI. Therefore, the DVD Division manager will buy the equipment. However, the e-learning Division currently has an ROI of 18%. If the e-learning Division invests in the equipment, its *overall* ROI will *decrease*. Therefore, the manager of the e-learning Division will probably turn down the investment. In this case, goal congruence is *not* achieved—only one division will invest in equipment. Yet top management wants both divisions to invest in the equipment because the equipment return exceeds the 16% target ROI. Next, we discuss a performance measure that overcomes this problem with ROI.

## Residual Income (RI)

**Residual income (RI)** is another commonly used KPI for evaluating an investment center's financial performance. Similar to ROI, RI considers both the division's operating income and its average total assets. RI measures the division's profitability and the efficiency with which the division uses its average total assets. RI also incorporates another piece of information: top management's target rate of return (ROI) (such as the 16% target return in the previous example). The target rate of return is the minimum acceptable rate of return that top management expects a division to earn with its average total assets. You will learn how to calculate target rate of return in your finance class. For now, we provide the target rate of return for you.

RI compares the division's actual operating income with the minimum operating income expected by top management *given the size of the division's average total assets.* **RI is the "extra" operating income above the minimum operating income.** A positive RI means that the division's operating income exceeds top management's target rate of return. A negative RI means the division is not meeting the target rate of return. Let's look at the RI equation and then calculate the RI for both divisions using the 16% target rate of return from the previous example.

$$\text{RI} = \text{Operating income} - \text{Minimum acceptable operating income}$$

In this equation, the minimum acceptable operating income is defined as top management's target rate of return multiplied by the division's average total assets. Therefore,

$$\text{RI} = \text{Operating income} - (\text{Target rate of return} \times \text{Average total assets})$$

$$\begin{aligned} \text{e-learning Division RI} &= \$450,000 - (16\% \times \$2,500,000) \\ &= \$450,000 - \$400,000 \\ &= \$50,000 \end{aligned}$$

The positive RI indicates that the e-learning Division exceeded top management's 16% target rate of return expectations. The RI calculation also confirms what we learned about the e-learning Division's ROI. Recall that the e-learning Division's ROI was 18%, which is higher than the target rate of return of 16%.

Now let's calculate the RI for the DVD Division:

$$\begin{aligned} \text{DVD Division RI} &= \$975,800 - (16\% \times \$6,500,000) \\ &= \$975,800 - \$1,040,000 \\ &= \$(64,200) \end{aligned}$$

The DVD Division's RI is negative. This means that the DVD Division did not use its average total assets as effectively as top management expected. Recall that the DVD Division's ROI of 15% fell short of the target rate of return of 16%.

Why would a company prefer to use RI over ROI for performance evaluation? The answer is that RI is more likely to lead to goal congruence than ROI. Consider the video display equipment that both divisions could buy. In both divisions, the equipment is expected to generate a 17% return. If the divisions are evaluated based on ROI, we learned that the DVD Division will buy the equipment because it will increase the division's ROI. The e-learning Division, on the other hand, will probably not buy the equipment because it will lower the division's ROI.

However, if management evaluates divisions based on RI rather than ROI, what will the divisions do? The answer depends on whether the project yields a positive or negative RI. Recall that the equipment would cost each division $100,000, but will provide $17,000 of operating income each year. The RI provided by *just* the equipment would be as follows:

$$\begin{aligned} \text{Equipment RI} &= \$17,000 - (\$100,000 \times 16\%) \\ &= \$17,000 - \$16,000 \\ &= \$1,000 \end{aligned}$$

If purchased, this equipment will *improve* each division's current RI by $1,000 each year. As a result, both divisions will be motivated to invest in the equipment. Goal congruence is achieved because both divisions will take the action that top management desires. That is, both divisions will invest in the equipment.

Another benefit of RI is that management may set different target returns for different divisions. For example, management might require a higher target rate of return from a division operating in a riskier business environment. If the DVD industry were riskier than the e-learning industry, top management might decide to set a higher target rate of return—perhaps 17%—for the DVD Division.

## Economic Value Added (EVA)

**Economic value added (EVA)** is a special type of RI calculation. Unlike the RI calculation we have just discussed, EVA looks at a division's RI through the eyes of the company's primary stakeholders: its investors (stockholders) and long-term creditors (such as bondholders). Since these stakeholders provide the company's capital, management often wishes to evaluate how efficiently a division is using its assets from these two stakeholders' viewpoints. EVA calculates RI for these stakeholders by specifically considering the following:

1. The after-tax operating income available to these stakeholders

2. The assets used to generate after-tax operating income for these stakeholders

3. The minimum rate of return required by these stakeholders (referred to as the **weighted average cost of capital**, or **WACC**)

Let's compare the EVA equation with the RI equation and then examine the differences in more detail:

RI = Operating income      − (Average total assets        × Target rate of return)

EVA = After-tax operating income − [(Average total assets − Current liabilities) × WACC%]

Both equations calculate whether any operating income was created by the division above and beyond expectations. They do this by comparing actual operating income with the minimum acceptable operating income. But note the differences in the EVA calculation:

1. The EVA calculation uses *after-tax operating income*, which is the operating income left over after subtracting income taxes. Why? Because the portion of operating income paid to the government is not available to investors (stockholders) and long-term creditors.

2. *Average total assets are reduced by current liabilities.* Why? Because funds owed to short-term creditors, such as suppliers (accounts payable) and employees (salary payable), will be paid in the immediate future and will not be available for generating operating income in the long run. The division is not expected to earn a return for investors (stockholders) and long-term creditors on those funds that will soon be paid out to short-term creditors.

3. The *WACC replaces management's target rate of return.* Since EVA focuses on investors (stockholders) and long-term creditors, it is *their* expected rate of return that should be used, not management's expected rate of return. The WACC, which represents the minimum rate of return expected by *investors (stockholders) and long-term creditors*, is the company's cost of raising capital from both groups of stakeholders. The riskier the business, the higher the WACC. The less risky the business, the lower the WACC. Management's target rate of return must at LEAST be equal to the cost of the capital (WACC) that the business is incurring to break even.

In summary, EVA incorporates all the elements of RI from the perspective of investors (stockholders) and long-term creditors. The goal for the company is positive EVA; therefore, after-tax operating income should be greater than the cost of the capital being employed [(Average total assets − current liabilities) × WACC%]. Now that we have walked through the equation's components, let's calculate EVA for the e-learning and DVD Divisions discussed earlier. We will need the following additional information:

| | |
|---|---|
| Effective income tax rate | 30% |
| WACC | 13% |
| e-learning Division's current liabilities | $150,000 |
| DVD Division's current liabilities | $250,000 |

The 30% effective income tax rate means that the government takes 30% of the company's operating income, leaving only 70% to the company's stakeholders. Therefore, we calculate *after-tax operating income* by multiplying the division's operating income by 70% (100% − effective income tax rate of 30%).

EVA = After-tax operating income − [(Average total assets − Current liabilities) × WACC%]

e-learning Division EVA = ($450,000 × 70%) − [($2,500,000 − $150,000) × 13%]
= $315,000 − ($2,350,000 × 13%)
= $315,000 − $305,500
= $9,500

DVD Division EVA = ($975,800 × 70%) − [($6,500,000 − 250,000) × 13%]
= $683,060 − ($6,250,000 × 13%)
= $683,060 − $812,500
= $(129,440)

These EVA calculations show that the e-learning Division has generated after-tax operating income in excess of expectations for its investors (stockholders) and long-term creditors, whereas the DVD Division has not.

Many firms, such as **Coca-Cola**, **Amazon.com**, and **J.C. Penney**, measure the financial performance of their investment centers using EVA. EVA promotes goal congruence, just as RI does. Additionally, EVA looks at the after-tax operating income generated by the division in excess of expectations, solely from the perspective of investors (stockholders) and long-term creditors. Therefore, EVA specifically addresses the financial perspective of the balanced scorecard that asks, "How do we look to stakeholders?"

Exhibit 24-8 summarizes the three KPIs commonly used to evaluate an investment center's financial performance, and some of their advantages.

**EXHIBIT 24-8** | **Three Investment Center KPIs: A Summary**

| Equation | $\text{ROI} = \dfrac{\text{Operating income}}{\text{Sales}} \times \dfrac{\text{Sales}}{\text{Average total assets}} = \dfrac{\text{Operating income}}{\text{Average total assets}}$ |
|---|---|
| Advantages | • The expanded equation provides management with additional information on profitability and efficiency<br>• Management can compare ROI across divisions and with other companies<br>• ROI is useful for resource allocation |
| Equation | $\text{RI} = \text{Operating income} - (\text{Average total assets} \times \text{Target rate of return})$ |
| Advantages | • Promotes goal congruence better than ROI<br>• Incorporates management's minimum required rate of return<br>• Management can use different target rates of return for divisions with different levels of risk |
| Equation | $\text{EVA} = \text{After-tax operating income} - [(\text{Average total assets} - \text{Current liabilities}) \times \text{WACC\%}]$ |
| Advantages | • Considers after-tax operating income generated for investors (stockholders) and long-term creditors in excess of their expectations<br>• Positive EVA clearly illustrates a positive return above the cost of capital (WACC)<br>• Promotes goal congruence |

## Limitations of Financial Performance Measures

We have just finished looking at three KPIs (ROI, RI, and EVA) commonly used to evaluate the financial performance of investment centers. As discussed in the following sections, all of these measures have drawbacks that management should keep in mind when evaluating the financial performance of investment centers.

### Measurement Issues

The ROI, RI, and EVA calculations appear to be very straightforward; however, management must make some decisions before these calculations can be made. For example, all three equations use the term *average total assets*. Recall that total assets is a balance sheet figure, which means that it is a snapshot at any given point in time. Because the total assets figure will be *different* at the beginning of the period and at the end of the period, most companies choose to use a simple average of the two figures in their ROI, RI, and EVA calculations.

Management must also decide if it really wants to include *all* assets in the average total asset figure. Many firms, such as **Walmart**, are continually buying land on which to build future retail outlets. Until those stores are built and opened, the land (including any construction in progress) is a nonproductive asset, which is not adding to the company's operating income. Including nonproductive assets in the average total asset figure will naturally drive down the ROI, RI, and EVA figures. Therefore, some firms will not include nonproductive assets in these calculations.

Another asset measurement issue is whether to use the gross book value of assets (the historical cost of the assets), or the net book value of assets (historical cost less accumulated depreciation). Many firms will use the net book value of assets because the figure is consistent with and easily pulled from the balance sheet. Because depreciation expense factors into the firm's operating income, the net book value concept is also consistent with the measurement of operating income. However, using the net book value of assets has a definite drawback. Over time, the net book value of assets decreases because accumulated depreciation continues to grow until the assets are fully depreciated. Therefore, ROI, RI, and EVA get *larger* over time *simply because of depreciation* rather than from actual improvements in operations. In addition, the rate of this depreciation effect will depend on the depreciation method used.

In general, calculating ROI based on the net book value of assets gives managers incentive to continue using old, outdated equipment because its low net book value results in a higher ROI. However, top management may want the division to invest in new technology to create operational efficiency (internal business perspective of the balanced scorecard) or to enhance its information systems (learning and growth perspective). The long-term effects of using outdated equipment may be devastating, as competitors use new technology to produce and sell at lower cost. Therefore, to create *goal congruence*, some firms prefer calculating ROI based on the gross book value of assets. The same general rule holds true for RI and EVA calculations—All else being equal, using net book value will increase RI and EVA over time.

## Short-Term Focus

One serious drawback of financial performance measures is their short-term focus. Companies usually prepare performance reports and calculate ROI, RI, and EVA figures over a one-year time frame or less. If upper management uses a short time frame, division managers have an incentive to take actions that will lead to an immediate increase in these measures, even if such actions may not be in the company's long-term interest (such as cutting back on R&D or advertising). On the other hand, some potentially positive actions considered by subunit managers may take longer than one year to generate income at the targeted level. Many product life cycles start slow, even incurring losses in the early stages, before generating profit. If managers are measured on short-term financial performance only, they may not introduce new products because they are not willing to wait several years for the positive effect to show up in their financial performance measures.

As a potential remedy, management can measure financial performance using a longer time horizon, such as three to five years. Extending the time frame gives subunit managers the incentive to think long term rather than short term and make decisions that will positively impact the company over the next several years.

The limitations of financial performance measures confirm the importance of the balanced scorecard. The deficiencies of financial measures can be overcome by taking a broader view of performance—including KPIs from all four balanced scorecard perspectives rather than concentrating on only the financial measures.

Next, take some time to review the Decision Guidelines and Summary Problem on the next pages.

---

**Key Takeaway**

To evaluate an investment center's financial performance, companies need summary performance measures—or KPIs—that include both the division's operating income and its assets. Commonly used KPIs for evaluating an investment center's financial performance are return on investment (ROI), residual income (RI), and economic value added (EVA). Each of these financial KPIs must be considered in conjunction with KPIs that come from all four of the balanced scorecard perspectives.

# Decision Guidelines 24-2

When managers at Smart Touch developed the financial perspective of their balanced scorecard, they had to make decisions such as the examples that follow.

| Decision | Guidelines |
|---|---|
| • How should the financial section of the balanced scorecard be measured for cost, revenue, and profit centers? | Responsibility accounting performance reports measure the financial performance of cost, revenue, and profit centers. These reports typically highlight the variances between budgeted and actual performance. |
| • How should the financial section of the balanced scorecard be measured for investment centers? | Investment centers require measures that take into account the division's operating income *and* the division's assets. Typical measures include the following:<br>• Return on investment (ROI)<br>• Residual income (RI)<br>• Economic value added (EVA) |
| • How is ROI computed and interpreted? | $$\text{ROI} = \text{Operating income} \div \text{Average total assets}$$<br>ROI measures the amount of operating income earned by a division relative to the size of its average total assets—the higher, the better. |
| • Can managers learn more by writing the ROI formula in its expanded form? | In its expanded form, ROI is written as follows:<br>$$\text{ROI} = \text{Profit margin} \times \text{Asset turnover}$$<br>where,<br>$$\text{Profit margin} = \text{Operating income} \div \text{Sales}$$<br>$$\text{Asset turnover} = \text{Sales} \div \text{Average total assets}$$<br>Profit margin focuses on profitability (the amount of operating income earned on every dollar of sales), while asset turnover focuses on efficiency (the amount of sales generated with every dollar of average total assets). |
| • How is RI computed and interpreted? | $$\text{RI} = \text{Operating income} - \left( \text{Target rate of return} \times \text{Average total assets} \right)$$<br>If RI is positive, the division is earning operating income at a rate that exceeds management's minimum expectations. |
| • How does EVA differ from RI? | EVA is a special type of RI calculation that focuses on the after-tax operating income (in excess of expectations) created by the division for two specific stakeholders: investors (stockholders) and long-term creditors. |
| • When calculating ROI, RI, or EVA, are there any measurement issues of concern? | If the net book value of assets is used to measure average total assets, ROI, RI, and EVA will "artificially" rise over time due to the depreciation of the assets. Using gross book value to measure average total assets eliminates this measurement issue.<br>Many firms use the average balance of total assets, rather than the beginning or ending balance of assets, when they calculate ROI, RI, and EVA. |

# Summary Problem 24-2

Assume Smart Touch expects each division to earn a 16% target rate of return. Smart Touch's weighted average cost of capital (WACC) is 13% and its effective income tax rate is 30%. Assume the company's original CD Division (an investment center) had the following results last year:

| | |
|---|---:|
| Operating income................................................ | $ 1,450,000,000 |
| Average total assets ............................................ | 16,100,000,000 |
| Current liabilities ............................................... | 3,600,000,000 |
| Sales.................................................................... | 26,500,000,000 |

## Requirements

1. Compute the CD Division's profit margin, asset turnover, and ROI. Round your results to three decimal places. Interpret the results in relation to the e-learning and DVD Divisions discussed in the chapter.
2. Compute and interpret the CD Division's RI.
3. Compute the CD Division's EVA. What does this tell you?
4. What can you conclude based on all three financial performance KPIs?

## Solution

### Requirement 1

| ROI = | Profit margin | $\times$ | Asset turnover |
|---|---|---|---|
| = | (Operating income $\div$ Sales) | $\times$ | (Sales $\div$ Average total assets) |
| = ($1,450,000,000 $\div$ $26,500,000,000$) $\times$ ($26,500,000,000 $\div$ $16,100,000,000$) | | | |
| = | 0.055 | $\times$ | 1.646 |
| = | 0.091 | | |

The original CD Division is far from meeting top management's expectations. Its ROI is only 9.1%. The profit margin of 5.5% is slightly lower than the e-learning Division and significantly lower than both divisions (6% for e-learning and 19% for the DVD Division). The asset turnover (1.646) is much lower than the e-learning Division (3 asset turnover) but much higher than the DVD Division asset turnover of 0.81. This means that the original CD Division is not generating sales from its average total assets as efficiently as the e-learning Division but is more efficient than the DVD Division. Division management needs to consider ways to increase the efficiency with which it uses divisional average total assets.

### Requirement 2

| RI = Operating income – (Target rate of return $\times$ Average total assets) | |
|---|---|
| = $ 1,450,000,000 – | (16% $\times$ $16,100,000,000) |
| = $ 1,450,000,000 – | $2,576,000,000 |
| = $(1,126,000,000) | |

The negative RI confirms the ROI results: The division is not meeting management's target rate of return.

## Requirement 3

$$\begin{aligned}
\text{EVA} &= \text{After-tax operating income} - [(\text{Average total assets} - \text{Current liabilities}) \times \text{WACC\%}] \\
&= (\$1,450,000,000 \times 70\%) - [(\$16,100,000,000 - \$3,600,000,000) \times 13\%] \\
&= \$1,015,000,000 \quad - \quad (\$12,500,000,000) \times 13\%) \\
&= \$1,015,000,000 \quad - \quad \$1,625,000,000 \\
&= \$(610,000,000)
\end{aligned}$$

The negative EVA means that the division is not generating after-tax operating income for investors (stockholders) and long-term creditors at the rate desired by these stakeholders.

## Requirement 4

All three investment center financial performance KPIs (ROI, RI, and EVA) point to the same conclusion: The original CD Division is not meeting financial expectations. Either top management and stakeholders' expectations are unrealistic or the division is not *currently* performing up to par. Recall, however, that financial performance measures tend to be lag indicators—measuring the results of decisions made in the past. The division's managers may currently be implementing new initiatives to improve the division's future profitability. Lead indicators should be used to project whether such initiatives are pointing the company in the right direction.

# Review *Performance Evaluation and the Balanced Scorecard*

## ● Accounting Vocabulary

**Asset Turnover (p. 1167)**
The amount of sales revenue generated for every dollar of average total assets; a component of the ROI calculation, computed as sales divided by average total assets.

**Balanced Scorecard (p. 1155)**
Recognition that management must consider both financial performance measures and operational performance measures when judging the performance of a company and its subunits.

**Centralized Companies (p. 1152)**
Companies in which all major planning and operating decisions are made by top management.

**Decentralized Companies (p. 1152)**
Companies that are segmented into different divisions or operating units; unit managers make planning and operating decisions for their unit.

**Economic Value Added (EVA) (p. 1169)**
A residual income measure calculating the amount of after-tax operating income generated by the company or its divisions in excess of stockholders' and long-term creditors' expectations.

**Goal Congruence (p. 1153)**
Aligning the goals of unit managers with the goals of top management.

**Key Performance Indicator(s) (KPIs) (p. 1156)**
Summary performance measures that help managers assess whether the company is achieving its goals.

**Lag Indicators (p. 1155)**
Performance measures that indicate past performance.

**Lead Indicators (p. 1155)**
Performance measures that forecast future performance.

**Management by Exception (p. 1162)**
Directs management's attention to important differences between actual and budgeted amounts.

**Profit Margin (p. 1166)**
The amount of operating income earned on every dollar of sales; a component of the ROI calculation, computed as operating income divided by sales.

**Residual Income (RI) (p. 1168)**
A measure of profitability and efficiency, computed as the excess of actual operating income over a specified minimum acceptable operating income.

**Return on Investment (ROI) (p. 1166)**
A measure of profitability and efficiency, computed as operating income divided by average total assets.

**Weighted Average Cost of Capital (WACC) (p. 1169)**
The company's cost of capital; the minimum rate of return expected by stockholders and long-term creditors.

## ● Destination: Student Success

### Student Success Tips

The following are hints on some common trouble areas for students in this chapter:

- Recall that companies decentralize as they grow.

- Keep in mind the advantages and disadvantages of decentralization.

- Remember that performance measurement systems are in place to help management communicate and evaluate goals to the various subunits in the company.

- Keep in mind the four perspectives of the balanced scorecard: financial, customer, internal business, and learning and growth perspective.

- Recall that the performance reports highlight variances between the budget plan and actual results. These variances signal to managers where to focus their time.

- Keep in mind that ROI, RI, and EVA are all financial performance measurement KPIs. Review Exhibit 24-8 for the formulas and advantages of each.

### Getting Help

If there's a learning objective from the chapter you aren't confident about, try using one or more of the following resources:

- Review Decision Guidelines 24-1 and 24-2 in the chapter.

- Review Summary Problem 24-1 in the chapter to reinforce your understanding of the four perspectives of the balanced scorecard.

- Review Summary Problem 24-2 in the chapter to reinforce your understanding of ROI, RI, and EVA.

- Practice additional exercises or problems at the end of Chapter 24 that cover the specific learning objective that is challenging you.

- Watch the white board videos for Chapter 24, located at myaccountinglab.com under the Chapter Resources button.

- Go to myaccountinglab.com and select the Study Plan button. Choose Chapter 24 and work the questions covering that specific learning objective until you've mastered it.

- Work the Chapter 24 pre/post tests in myaccountinglab.com.

- Visit the learning resource center on your campus for tutoring.

## • Quick Check

1. Which is *not* one of the potential advantages of decentralization?

   a. Improves motivation and retention    c. Improves customer relations

   b. Supports use of expert knowledge    d. Increases goal congruence

2. The **Quaker Foods** division of **PepsiCo** is most likely treated as a(n)

   a. revenue center.            c. investment center.

   b. cost center.             d. profit center.

3. Decentralization is often based on all the following except

   a. revenue size.           c. business function.

   b. geographic region.       d. product line.

4. Which of the following is NOT a goal of performance evaluation systems?

   a. Promoting goal congruence and coordination

   b. Communicating expectations

   c. Providing feedback

   d. Reprimanding unit managers

5. Which of the following balanced scorecard perspectives essentially asks, "Can we continue to improve and create value?"

   a. Customer           c. Financial

   b. Learning and growth      d. Internal business

The following data applies to questions 6 through 9. Assume the Residential Division of Kipper Faucets had the following results last year:

| | | | |
|---|---:|---|---:|
| Sales................... $ | 4,160,000 | Management's target rate of return .......... | 18% |
| Operating income.......... | 1,040,000 | WACC................................ | 15% |
| Average total assets ........ | 5,200,000 | | |
| Current liabilities .......... | 200,000 | | |

6. What is the division's profit margin?

   a. 400%           c. 25%

   b. 20%           d. 80%

7. What is the division's asset turnover?

   a. 0.20           c. 1.25

   b. 0.80           d. 0.25

8. What is the division's ROI?

   a. 20%           c. 500%

   b. 25%           d. 80%

9. What is the division's RI?

   a. $(140,000)       c. $140,000

   b. $104,000        d. $(104,000)

10. The performance evaluation of a cost center is typically based on its

    a. sales volume variance.      c. static budget variance.

    b. ROI.                d. flexible budget variance.

Answers are given after Apply Your Knowledge (p. 1190).

**Experience the Power of Practice!**

As denoted by the logo, all of these questions, as well as additional practice materials, can be found in

**MyAccountingLab**.

Please visit myaccountinglab.com

# Assess Your Progress

## ● Short Exercises

*MyAccountingLab* **S24-1** ❶ **Explaining why and how companies decentralize [5 min]**
Decentralization divides company operations into various reporting units. Most decentralized subunits can be described as one of four different types of responsibility centers.

### Requirements

1. Explain why companies decentralize. Describe some typical methods of decentralization.
2. List the four most common types of responsibility centers and describe their responsibilities.

**S24-2** ❶ **Explaining why and how companies decentralize [5 min]**
Each of the following managers has been given certain decision-making authority:

      **a.** Manager of Holiday Inn's Central Reservation Office
      **b.** Managers of various corporate-owned Holiday Inn locations
      **c.** Manager of the Holiday Inn Corporate Division
      **d.** Manager of the Housekeeping Department at a Holiday Inn
      **e.** Manager of the Holiday Inn Express Corporate Division
      **f.** Manager of the complimentary breakfast buffet at a Holiday Inn Express

### Requirement

1. Classify each of the managers according to the type of responsibility center they manage.

**S24-3** ❷ **Explaining why companies use performance evaluation systems [5 min]**
Well-designed performance evaluation systems accomplish many goals. Consider the following actions:

**a.** Comparing targets to actual results
**b.** Providing subunit managers with performance targets
**c.** Comparing actual results with industry standards
**d.** Providing bonuses to subunit managers who achieve performance targets
**e.** Aligning subunit performance targets with company strategy
**f.** Comparing actual results to the results of competitors
**g.** Taking corrective actions
**h.** Using the adage, "you get what you measure," when designing the performance evaluation system

### Requirement

1. State which goal is being achieved by the action.

**S24-4** ❸ **Describing the balanced scorecard and identifying key performance indicators for each perspective [5–10 min]**

Consider the following key performance indicators:

a. Number of employee suggestions implemented
b. Revenue growth
c. Number of on-time deliveries
d. Percentage of sales force with access to real-time inventory levels
e. Customer satisfaction ratings
f. Number of defects found during manufacturing
g. Number of warranty claims
h. ROI
i. Variable cost per unit
j. Percentage of market share
k. Number of hours of employee training
l. Number of new products developed
m. Yield rate (number of units produced per hour)
n. Average repair time
o. Employee satisfaction
p. Number of repeat customers

**Requirement**

1. Classify each of the preceding key performance indicators according to the balanced scorecard perspective it addresses. Choose from financial perspective, customer perspective, internal business perspective, or learning and growth perspective.

**S24-5** ❹ **Using performance reports to evaluate cost, revenue, and profit centers [5 min]**

Management by exception is a term often used in performance evaluation.

**Requirement**

1. Describe management by exception and how it is used in the evaluation of cost, revenue, and profit centers.

**S24-6** ❺ **Using ROI, RI, and EVA to evaluate investment centers [5–10 min]**

Consider the following data:

|  | Domestic | International |
| --- | --- | --- |
| Operating income . . . . . . . . | $ 7,000,000 | $ 8,000,000 |
| Average total assets . . . . . . | 23,000,000 | 31,000,000 |

**Requirement**

1. Which of the corporate divisions is more profitable? Explain.

**S24-7**   **⑤**   **Using ROI, RI, and EVA to evaluate investment centers [5–10 min]**

Extreme Sports Company makes snowboards, downhill skis, cross-country skis, skateboards, surfboards, and in-line skates. The company has found it beneficial to split operations into two divisions based on the climate required for the sport: Snow sports and Non-snow sports. The following divisional information is available for the past year:

|  | Sales | Operating Income | Average Total Assets | Current Liabilities | ROI |
|---|---|---|---|---|---|
| Snow sports | $ 5,500,000 | $ 935,000 | $ 4,500,000 | $ 420,000 | 20.8% |
| Non-snow sports | 8,400,000 | 1,428,000 | 6,700,000 | 695,000 | 21.3% |

Extreme's management has specified a 16% target rate of return. The company's weighted average cost of capital (WACC) is 10% and its effective tax rate is 38%.

### Requirement

1. Calculate each division's profit margin. Interpret your results.

*Note: Short Exercise 24-7 should be completed before attempting Short Exercise 24-8.*

**S24-8**   **⑤**   **Using ROI, RI, and EVA to evaluate investment centers [10 min]**

Refer to the information in S24-7.

### Requirements

1. Compute each division's asset turnover (round to two decimal places). Interpret your results.
2. Use your answers to Requirement 1, along with the profit margin, to recalculate ROI using the expanded formula. Do your answers agree with the basic ROI in S24-7?

*Note: Short Exercise 24-7 should be completed before attempting Short Exercise 24-9.*

**S24-9**   **⑤**   **Using ROI, RI, and EVA to evaluate investment centers [5–10 min]**

Refer to the information in S24-7.

### Requirement

1. Compute each division's RI. Interpret your results. Are your results consistent with each division's ROI?

*Note: Short Exercise 24-7 should be completed before attempting Short Exercise 24-10.*

**S24-10**   **⑤**   **Using ROI, RI, and EVA to evaluate investment centers [10–15 min]**

Refer to the information in S24-7.

### Requirement

1. Compute each division's EVA. Interpret your results.

## ● Exercises

MyAccountingLab   **E24-11**   **❶**   **Identifying responsibility centers after decentralization [10 min]**

Grandpa Joe's Cookie Company sells homemade cookies made with organic ingredients. His sales are strictly Web based. The business is taking off more than Grandpa Joe ever expected, with orders coming from across the country from both consumers and corporate event planners. Grandpa decides to decentralize and hires a full-time baker who will manage production and product cost and a Web designer/sales manager who will focus on increasing sales through the Web site. Grandpa Joe can no longer handle the business on his own, so he hires a business manager to work with the other employees to ensure the company is best utilizing its assets to produce profit. Grandpa will then have time to focus on new product development.

### Requirement

1. Now that Grandpa Joe's Cookie Company has decentralized, identify the type of responsibility center that each manager is managing.

**E24-12** ❷ **Explaining why companies use performance evaluation systems [5–10 min]**
Financial performance is measured in many ways.

## Requirements

1. Explain the difference between lag and lead indicators.

2. The following is a list of financial measures. Indicate whether each is a lag or a lead indicator:

   a. Income statement shows net income of $100,000.
   b. Listing of next week's orders of $50,000.
   c. Trend showing that average hits on the redesigned Web site are increasing at 5% per week.
   d. Price sheet from vendor reflecting that cost per pound of sugar for next month is $2.
   e. Contract signed last month with large retail store that guarantees a minimum shelf space for Grandpa's Overloaded Chocolate Cookies for the next year.

**E24-13** ❷ **Explaining why companies use performance evaluation systems [10 min]**
Well-designed performance evaluation systems accomplish many goals.

## Requirement

1. Describe the potential benefits performance evaluation systems offer.

**E24-14** ❸ **Describing the balanced scorecard and identifying key performance indicators for each perspective [10–15 min]**
Consider the following key performance indicators:

   a. Number of customer complaints
   b. Number of information system upgrades completed
   c. EVA
   d. New product development time
   e. Employee turnover rate
   f. Percentage of products with online help manuals
   g. Customer retention
   h. Percentage of compensation based on performance
   i. Percentage of orders filled each week
   j. Gross margin growth
   k. Number of new patents
   l. Employee satisfaction ratings
   m. Manufacturing cycle time (average length of production process)
   n. Earnings growth
   o. Average machine setup time
   p. Number of new customers
   q. Employee promotion rate
   r. Cash flow from operations
   s. Customer satisfaction ratings
   t. Machine downtime
   u. Finished products per day per employee
   v. Percentage of employees with access to upgraded system
   w. Wait time per order prior to start of production

## Requirement

1. Classify each indicator according to the balanced scorecard perspective it addresses. Choose from the financial perspective, customer perspective, internal business perspective, or the learning and growth perspective.

**E24-15**   **4** **Using performance reports to evaluate cost, revenue, and profit centers [10–15 min]**

One subunit of Mountain Sports Company had the following financial results last month:

| Mountain—Subunit X | Actual | Flexible Budget | Flexible Budget Variance (U or F) | % Variance (U or F) |
|---|---|---|---|---|
| Direct materials | $  28,500 | $  26,400 | | |
| Direct labor | 13,400 | 14,100 | | |
| Indirect labor | 26,200 | 22,700 | | |
| Utilities | 12,100 | 11,100 | | |
| Depreciation | 26,000 | 26,000 | | |
| Repairs and maintenance | 4,000 | 4,900 | | |
| Total | $ 110,200 | $ 105,200 | $ | |

### Requirements

1.  Complete the performance evaluation report for this subunit. Enter the variance percent as a percentage rounded to two decimal places.
2.  Based on the data presented, what type of responsibility center is this subunit?
3.  Which items should be investigated if part of management's decision criteria is to investigate all variances exceeding $2,500 or 10%?
4.  Should only unfavorable variances be investigated? Explain.

**E24-16**   **4** **Using performance reports to evaluate cost, revenue, and profit centers [15–20 min]**

The accountant for a subunit of Mountain Sports Company went on vacation before completing the subunit's monthly performance report. This is as far as she got:

| Mountain—Subunit X Revenue by Product | Actual Results at Actual Prices | Flexible Budget Variance | Flexible Budget for Actual Number of Units Sold | Sales Volume Variance | Static (Master) Budget |
|---|---|---|---|---|---|
| Downhill—RI | $  326,000 | | | $ 19,000 F | $  301,000 |
| Downhill—RII | 154,000 | | $ 164,000 | | 148,000 |
| Cross—EXI | 280,000 | $ 1,000 U | 281,000 | | 297,000 |
| Cross—EXII | 254,000 | | 249,000 | 16,500 U | 265,500 |
| Snow—LXI | 424,000 | 2,000 F | | | 402,000 |
| Total | $ 1,438,000 | $ | $ | $ | $ 1,413,500 |

### Requirements

1.  Complete the performance evaluation report for this subunit.
2.  Based on the data presented, what type of responsibility center is this subunit?
3.  Which items should be investigated if part of management's decision criteria is to investigate all variances exceeding $10,000?

**E24-17**  ⑤  **Using ROI, RI, and EVA to evaluate investment centers [10–15 min]**

Zooms, a national manufacturer of lawn-mowing and snow-blowing equipment, segments its business according to customer type: professional and residential. The following divisional information was available for the past year:

|  | Sales | Operating Income | Average Total Assets | Current Liabilities |
|---|---|---|---|---|
| Residential | $ 520,000 | $ 64,320 | $ 192,000 | $ 62,000 |
| Professional | 1,020,000 | 158,760 | 392,000 | 143,000 |

Management has a 26% target rate of return for each division. Zooms' weighted average cost of capital is 13% and its effective tax rate is 27%.

**Requirements**

1. Calculate each division's ROI. Round all of your answers to four decimal places.
2. Calculate each division's profit margin. Interpret your results.
3. Calculate each division's asset turnover. Interpret your results.
4. Use the expanded ROI formula to confirm your results from Requirement 1. What can you conclude?

*Note: Exercise 24-17 should be completed before attempting Exercise 24-18.*

**E24-18**  ⑤  **Using ROI, RI, and EVA to evaluate investment centers [10–15 min]**

Refer to the data in E24-17.

**Requirements**

1. Calculate each division's RI. Interpret your results.
2. Calculate each division's EVA. Interpret your results.

● Problems **(Group A)**

**P24-19A**  ① ② ③ ④  **Explaining why and how companies decentralize and why they use performance evaluation systems [30–45 min]**     *MyAccountingLab*

One subunit of Boxing Sports Company had the following financial results last month:

| Subunit X | Flexible Budget for Actual Number of Units Sold | Actual Results at Actual Prices | Flexible Budget Variance (U or F) | % Variance (U or F) |
|---|---|---|---|---|
| Sales | $ 453,000 | $ 479,000 | | |
| Variable expenses | 250,000 | 260,000 | | |
| Contribution margin | $ 203,000 | $ 219,000 | | |
| Fixed expenses | 52,000 | 56,000 | | |
| Operating income before traceable service department charges | $ 151,000 | $ 163,000 | | |
| Traceable fixed expenses | 33,000 | 38,000 | | |
| Divisional segment margin | $ 118,000 | $ 125,000 | $ | |

**Requirements**

1. Complete the performance evaluation report for this subunit (round to two decimal places).
2. Based on the data presented and your knowledge of the company, what type of responsibility center is this subunit?

3. Which items should be investigated if part of management's decision criteria is to investigate all variances equal to or exceeding $5,000 *and* exceeding 10% (both criteria must be met)?

4. Should only unfavorable variances be investigated? Explain.

5. Is it possible that the variances are due to a higher-than-expected sales volume? Explain.

6. Will management place equal weight on each of the $5,000 variances? Explain.

7. Which balanced scorecard perspective is being addressed through this performance report? In your opinion, is this performance report a lead or a lag indicator? Explain.

8. List one key performance indicator for the three other balanced scorecard perspectives. Make sure to indicate which perspective is being addressed by the indicators you list. Are they lead or lag indicators? Explain.

**P24-20A** ⑤ **Using ROI, RI, and EVA to evaluate investment centers [30–45 min]**
Consider the following condensed financial statements of Money Freedom, Inc. The company's target rate of return is 10% and its WACC is 7%:

| MONEY FREEDOM, INC. Comparative Balance Sheet As of December 31, 2012 and 2011 | | |
|---|---|---|
| **Assets** | **2012** | **2011** |
| Cash | $ 77,000 | $ 66,000 |
| Account receivable | 62,500 | 28,400 |
| Supplies | 500 | 600 |
| Property, plant, and equipment, net | 300,000 | 200,000 |
| Patents, net | 160,000 | 105,000 |
| Total assets | $ 600,000 | $ 400,000 |
| **Liabilities and Stockholders' Equity** | | |
| Accounts payable | $ 32,000 | $ 34,000 |
| Short-term notes payable | 146,000 | 48,000 |
| Long-term notes payable | 200,000 | 130,000 |
| Common stock, no par | 200,000 | 167,500 |
| Retained earnings | 22,000 | 20,500 |
| Total liabilities and stockholders' equity | $ 600,000 | $ 400,000 |

| MONEY FREEDOM, INC. Income Statement For the Year Ended December 31, 2012 | |
|---|---|
| Sales revenue | $5,000,000 |
| COGS | 2,900,000 |
| Gross profit | $2,100,000 |
| Operating expenses | 1,900,000 |
| Operating income | $ 200,000 |
| Other: Interest expense | (20,000) |
| Income before income tax expense | $ 180,000 |
| Income tax expense | (63,000) |
| Net income | $ 117,000 |

## Requirements

1. Calculate the company's profit margin. Interpret your results.

2. Calculate the company's asset turnover. Interpret your results.

3. Use the expanded ROI formula to confirm your results from Requirement 1. Interpret your results.

4. Calculate the company's RI. Interpret your results.

5. Calculate the company's EVA. Interpret your results.

**P24-21A  ⑤  Using ROI, RI, and EVA to evaluate investment centers [30–45 min]**

San Diego Paints is a national paint manufacturer and retailer. The company is segmented into five divisions: Paint stores (branded retail locations), Consumer (paint
sold through stores like **Sears** and **Lowe's**), Automotive (sales to auto manufacturers),
International, and Administration. The following is selected divisional information
for its two largest divisions: Paint stores and Consumer.

| | Sales | Operating Income | Average Total Assets | Current Liabilities |
|---|---|---|---|---|
| Paint stores | $ 3,960,000 | $    476,000 | $ 1,400,000 | $    340,000 |
| Consumer | 1,275,000 | 188,000 | 1,580,000 | 600,000 |

Management has specified a 19% target rate of return. The company's weighted
average cost of capital is 15%. The company's effective tax rate is 36%.

**Requirements**

1. Calculate each division's profit margin. Interpret your results.

2. Calculate each division's asset turnover. Interpret your results.

3. Use the expanded ROI formula to confirm your results from Requirement 1.
   Interpret your results.

4. Calculate each division's RI. Interpret your results and offer a recommendation
   for any division with negative RI.

5. Calculate each division's EVA. Interpret your results.

6. Describe some of the factors that management considers when setting its minimum target rate of return.

## ● Problems (Group B)

**P24-22B  ① ② ③ ④  Explaining why and how companies decentralize and why they**      *MyAccountingLab*
**use performance evaluation systems [30–45 min]**

One subunit of Freeway Sports Company had the following financial results last month:

| Subunit X | Flexible Budget for Actual Number of Units Sold | Actual Results at Actual Prices | Flexible Budget Variance (U or F) | % Variance (U or F) |
|---|---|---|---|---|
| Sales | $ 450,000 | $ 478,000 | | |
| Variable expenses | 253,000 | 263,000 | | |
| Contribution margin | $ 197,000 | $ 215,000 | | |
| Fixed expenses | 50,000 | 55,000 | | |
| Operating income before traceable service department charges | $ 147,000 | $ 160,000 | | |
| Traceable fixed expenses | 30,000 | 40,000 | | |
| Divisional segment margin | $ 117,000 | $ 120,000 | $ | |

**Requirements**

1. Complete the performance evaluation report for this subunit (round to two decimal places).

2. Based on the data presented and your knowledge of the company, what type of
   responsibility center is this subunit?

3. Which items should be investigated if part of management's decision criteria is to investigate all variances equal to or exceeding $10,000 *and* exceeding 10% (both criteria must be met)?

4. Should only unfavorable variances be investigated? Explain.

5. Is it possible that the variances are due to a higher-than-expected sales volume? Explain.

6. Will management place equal weight on each of the $10,000 variances? Explain.

7. Which balanced scorecard perspective is being addressed through this performance report? In your opinion, is this performance report a lead or a lag indicator? Explain.

8. List one key performance indicator for the three other balanced scorecard perspectives. Make sure to indicate which perspective is being addressed by the indicators you list. Are they lead or lag indicators? Explain.

**P24-23B** ⑤ **Using ROI, RI, and EVA to evaluate investment centers [30–45 min]**
Consider the following condensed financial statements of Secure Life, Inc. The company's target rate of return is 12% and its WACC is 9%:

| **SECURE LIFE, INC.** | | |
|---|---|---|
| **Comparative Balance Sheet** | | |
| **As of December 31, 2013 and 2012** | | |
| Assets | 2013 | 2012 |
| Cash | $ 82,000 | $ 50,000 |
| Accounts receivable | 54,000 | 20,500 |
| Supplies | 1,000 | 500 |
| Property, plant, and equipment, net | 275,000 | 180,000 |
| Patents, net | 138,000 | 99,000 |
| Total assets | $550,000 | $350,000 |
| **Liabilities and Stockholders' Equity** | | |
| Accounts payable | $ 40,000 | $ 32,000 |
| Short-term notes payable | 135,000 | 45,000 |
| Long-term notes payable | 170,000 | 125,000 |
| Common stock, no par | 150,000 | 130,000 |
| Retained earnings | 55,000 | 18,000 |
| Total liabilities and stockholders' equity | $550,000 | $350,000 |

| **SECURE LIFE, INC.** | |
|---|---|
| **Income Statement** | |
| **For the Year Ended December 31, 2013** | |
| Sales revenue | $6,750,000 |
| COGS | 3,200,000 |
| Gross profit | $3,550,000 |
| Operating expenses | 1,525,000 |
| Operating income | $2,025,000 |
| Other: Interest expense | (17,000) |
| Income before income tax expense | $2,008,000 |
| Income tax expense | (702,800) |
| Net income | $1,305,200 |

## Requirements

1. Calculate the company's profit margin. Interpret your results.
2. Calculate the company's asset turnover. Interpret your results.
3. Use the expanded ROI formula to confirm your results from Requirement 1. Interpret your results.
4. Calculate the company's RI. Interpret your results.
5. Calculate the company's EVA. Interpret your results.

**P24-24B** ⑤ **Using ROI, RI, and EVA to evaluate investment centers [30–45 min]**

Bear Paints is a national paint manufacturer and retailer. The company is segmented into five divisions: Paint stores (branded retail locations), Consumer (paint sold through stores like **Sears** and **Lowe's**), Automotive (sales to auto manufacturers), International, and Administration. The following is selected divisional information for its two largest divisions: Paint stores and Consumer:

|  | Sales | Operating Income | Average Total Assets | Current Liabilities |
|---|---|---|---|---|
| Paint stores | $ 3,940,000 | $    477,000 | $ 1,410,000 | $    343,000 |
| Consumer | 1,310,000 | 185,000 | 1,575,000 | 605,000 |

Management has specified a 21% target rate of return. The company's weighted average cost of capital is 14%. The company's effective tax rate is 34%.

## Requirements

1. Calculate each division's profit margin. Interpret your results.
2. Calculate each division's asset turnover. Interpret your results.
3. Use the expanded ROI formula to confirm your results from Requirement 1. Interpret your results.
4. Calculate each division's RI. Interpret your results and offer a recommendation for any division with negative RI.
5. Calculate each division's EVA. Interpret your results.
6. Describe some of the factors that management considers when setting its minimum target rate of return.

# • Continuing Exercise

**MyAccountingLab** **E24-25** ⑤ **Calculating profit margin for an investment center [10–15 min]**
This exercise continues the Lawlor Lawn Service, Inc., situation from Exercise 23-38 of Chapter 23. Lawlor Lawn Service experienced sales of $500,000 and operating income of $65,000 for 2013. Total assets were $250,000 and total liabilities were $25,000 at the end of 2013. Lawlor's target rate of return is 16% and WACC is 12%. Its 2013 tax rate was 32%.

### Requirement

1. Calculate Lawlor's profit margin for 2013.

# • Continuing Problem

**MyAccountingLab** **P24-26** ⑤ **Using ROI, RI, and EVA to evaluate investment centers [10–15 min]**
This problem continues the Draper Consulting, Inc., situation from Problem 23-39 of Chapter 23. Draper Consulting reported 2013 sales of $3,750,000 and operating income of $210,000. Average total assets during 2013 were $600,000 and total liabilities at the end of 2013 were $180,000. Draper's target rate of return is 14% and WACC is 7%. Its 2013 tax rate was 36%.

### Requirement

1. Calculate Draper's profit margin, asset turnover, and EVA for 2013.

# Apply Your Knowledge

# • Decision Case 24-1

**Colgate-Palmolive** operates two product segments. Using the company Web site, locate segment information for the company's latest published annual report. (*Hint*: Go to the company Web site and look under "for investors." From there, find the information on the "10-K." Within the 10-K, find the Financial Statements and Supplemental Data and look for one of the notes to the financial statements that provides Segment Information.)

### Requirements

1. What are the two product segments? Gather data about each segment's net sales, operating income, and identifiable assets.
2. Calculate ROI for each segment.
3. Which segment has the highest ROI? Explain why.
4. If you were on the top management team and could allocate extra funds to only one division, which division would you choose? Why?

## ● Ethical Issue 24-1

Dixie Irwin is the department manager for Religious Books, a manufacturer of religious books that are sold through Internet companies. Irwin's bonus is based on reducing production costs.

### Requirement

1. Irwin has identified a supplier, Cheap Paper, that can provide paper products at a 10% cost reduction. The paper quality is not the same as that of the current paper used in production. If Irwin uses the supplier, he will certainly achieve his personal bonus goals; however, other company goals may be in jeopardy. Identify the key performance issues at risk and recommend a plan of action for Irwin.

## ● Fraud Case 24-1

Everybody knew Ed McAlister was a brilliant businessman. He had taken a small garbage collection company in Kentucky and built it up to be one of the largest and most profitable waste management companies in the Midwest. But when he was convicted of a massive financial fraud, what surprised everyone was how crude and simple the scheme was. To keep the earnings up and the stock prices soaring, he and his cronies came up with an almost foolishly simple scheme: First, they doubled the useful lives of the dumpsters. That allowed them to cut depreciation expense in half. The following year, they simply increased the estimated salvage value of the dumpsters, allowing them to further reduce depreciation expense. With thousands of dumpsters spread over 14 states, these simple adjustments gave the company an enormous boost to the bottom line. When it all came tumbling down, McAlister had to sell everything he owned to pay for his legal costs and was left with nothing.

### Requirements

1. If an asset has either too long a useful life or too high an estimated salvage value, what happens, from an accounting perspective, when that asset is worn out and has to be disposed of?

2. Do the rules of GAAP (generally accepted accounting principles) mandate specific lives for different types of assets? What is the role of the outside auditor in evaluating the reasonableness of depreciation lives and salvage values?

## ● Team Project 24-1

Each group should identify one public company's product that it wishes to evaluate. The team should gather all the information it can about the product.

### Requirement

1. Develop a list of key performance indicators for the product.

# • Communication Activity 24-1

In 150 words or fewer, list each of the four perspectives of the balanced scorecard. Give an example of one KPI from each of the perspectives and explain what measure the KPI provides for a retailing business.

---

## Quick Check Answers

1. *d* 2. *c* 3. *a* 4. *d* 5. *b* 6. *c* 7. *b* 8. *a* 9. *b* 10. *d*

**For online homework, exercises, and problems that provide you immediate feedback, please visit myaccountinglab.com.**

2 0 0 9

# amazon.com®

P A R T I A L
A N N U A L   R E P O R T

http://media.corporate-ir.net/media_files/irol/97/97664/2007AR.pdf

### Report of Ernst & Young LLP, Independent Registered Public Accounting Firm

The Board of Directors and Stockholders
Amazon.com, Inc.

We have audited the accompanying consolidated balance sheets of Amazon.com, Inc. as of December 31, 2009 and 2008, and the related consolidated statements of operations, stockholders' equity, and cash flows for each of the three years in the period ended December 31, 2009. These financial statements are the responsibility of the Company's management. Our responsibility is to express an opinion on these financial statements based on our audits.

We conducted our audits in accordance with the standards of the Public Company Accounting Oversight Board (United States). Those standards require that we plan and perform the audit to obtain reasonable assurance about whether the financial statements are free of material misstatement. An audit includes examining, on a test basis, evidence supporting the amounts and disclosures in the financial statements. An audit also includes assessing the accounting principles used and significant estimates made by management, as well as evaluating the overall financial statement presentation. We believe that our audits provide a reasonable basis for our opinion.

In our opinion, the financial statements referred to above present fairly, in all material respects, the consolidated financial position of Amazon.com, Inc. at December 31, 2009 and 2008, and the consolidated results of its operations and its cash flows for each of the three years in the period ended December 31, 2009, in conformity with U.S. generally accepted accounting principles.

As discussed in Note 1 to the consolidated financial statements, the Company adopted FASB No. 141(R) *Business Combinations*, codified in ASC 805, *Business Combinations*, effective January 1, 2009.

We also have audited, in accordance with the standards of the Public Company Accounting Oversight Board (United States), Amazon.com, Inc.'s internal control over financial reporting as of December 31, 2009, based on criteria established in Internal Control—Integrated Framework issued by the Committee of Sponsoring Organizations of the Treadway Commission and our report dated January 28, 2010 expressed an unqualified opinion thereon.

/s/ Ernst & Young LLP

Seattle, Washington
January 28, 2010

37

## AMAZON.COM, INC.

### CONSOLIDATED STATEMENTS OF CASH FLOWS
(in millions)

|  | Year Ended December 31, | | |
|---|---|---|---|
|  | 2009 | 2008 | 2007 |
| CASH AND CASH EQUIVALENTS, BEGINNING OF PERIOD | $ 2,769 | $ 2,539 | $1,022 |
| OPERATING ACTIVITIES: | | | |
| Net income | 902 | 645 | 476 |
| Adjustments to reconcile net income to net cash from operating activities: | | | |
| Depreciation of fixed assets, including internal-use software and website development, and other amortization | 378 | 287 | 246 |
| Stock-based compensation | 341 | 275 | 185 |
| Other operating expense (income), net | 103 | (24) | 9 |
| Losses (gains) on sales of marketable securities, net | (4) | (2) | 1 |
| Other expense (income), net | (15) | (34) | 12 |
| Deferred income taxes | 81 | (5) | (99) |
| Excess tax benefits from stock-based compensation | (105) | (159) | (257) |
| Changes in operating assets and liabilities: | | | |
| Inventories | (531) | (232) | (303) |
| Accounts receivable, net and other | (481) | (218) | (255) |
| Accounts payable | 1,859 | 812 | 928 |
| Accrued expenses and other | 300 | 247 | 429 |
| Additions to unearned revenue | 1,054 | 449 | 244 |
| Amortization of previously unearned revenue | (589) | (344) | (211) |
| Net cash provided by (used in) operating activities | 3,293 | 1,697 | 1,405 |
| INVESTING ACTIVITIES: | | | |
| Purchases of fixed assets, including internal-use software and website development | (373) | (333) | (224) |
| Acquisitions, net of cash acquired, and other | (40) | (494) | (75) |
| Sales and maturities of marketable securities and other investments | 1,966 | 1,305 | 1,271 |
| Purchases of marketable securities and other investments | (3,890) | (1,677) | (930) |
| Net cash provided by (used in) investing activities | (2,337) | (1,199) | 42 |
| FINANCING ACTIVITIES: | | | |
| Excess tax benefits from stock-based compensation | 105 | 159 | 257 |
| Common stock repurchased | | (100) | (248) |
| Proceeds from long-term debt and other | 87 | 98 | 115 |
| Repayments of long-term debt and capital lease obligations | (472) | (355) | (74) |
| Net cash provided by (used in) financing activities | (280) | (198) | 50 |
| Foreign-currency effect on cash and cash equivalents | (1) | (70) | 20 |
| Net increase in cash and cash equivalents | 675 | 230 | 1,517 |
| CASH AND CASH EQUIVALENTS, END OF PERIOD | $ 3,444 | $ 2,769 | $2,539 |
| SUPPLEMENTAL CASH FLOW INFORMATION: | | | |
| Cash paid for interest | $ 32 | $ 64 | $ 67 |
| Cash paid for income taxes | 48 | 53 | 24 |
| Fixed assets acquired under capital leases and other financing arrangements | 147 | 148 | 74 |
| Fixed assets acquired under build-to-suit leases | 188 | 72 | 15 |
| Conversion of debt | — | 605 | 1 |

See accompanying notes to consolidated financial statements.

38

# AMAZON.COM, INC.

## CONSOLIDATED STATEMENTS OF OPERATIONS
### (in millions, except per share data)

| | Year Ended December 31, | | |
| --- | --- | --- | --- |
| | 2009 | 2008 | 2007 |
| Net sales | $24,509 | $19,166 | $14,835 |
| Cost of sales | 18,978 | 14,896 | 11,482 |
| Gross profit | 5,531 | 4,270 | 3,353 |
| Operating expenses (1): | | | |
| Fulfillment | 2,052 | 1,658 | 1,292 |
| Marketing | 680 | 482 | 344 |
| Technology and content | 1,240 | 1,033 | 818 |
| General and administrative | 328 | 279 | 235 |
| Other operating expense (income), net | 102 | (24) | 9 |
| Total operating expenses | 4,402 | 3,428 | 2,698 |
| Income from operations | 1,129 | 842 | 655 |
| Interest income | 37 | 83 | 90 |
| Interest expense | (34) | (71) | (77) |
| Other income (expense), net | 29 | 47 | (8) |
| Total non-operating income (expense) | 32 | 59 | 5 |
| Income before income taxes | 1,161 | 901 | 660 |
| Provision for income taxes | (253) | (247) | (184) |
| Equity-method investment activity, net of tax | (6) | (9) | — |
| Net income | $ 902 | $ 645 | $ 476 |
| Basic earnings per share | $ 2.08 | $ 1.52 | $ 1.15 |
| Diluted earnings per share | $ 2.04 | $ 1.49 | $ 1.12 |
| Weighted average shares used in computation of earnings per share: | | | |
| Basic | 433 | 423 | 413 |
| Diluted | 442 | 432 | 424 |

(1) Includes stock-based compensation as follows:

| | | | |
| --- | --- | --- | --- |
| Fulfillment | $ 79 | $ 61 | $ 39 |
| Marketing | 20 | 13 | 8 |
| Technology and content | 182 | 151 | 103 |
| General and administrative | 60 | 50 | 35 |

See accompanying notes to consolidated financial statements.

39

## AMAZON.COM, INC.

### CONSOLIDATED BALANCE SHEETS
**(in millions, except per share data)**

| | December 31, | |
|---|---|---|
| | **2009** | **2008** |
| **ASSETS** | | |
| Current assets: | | |
| Cash and cash equivalents | $ 3,444 | $2,769 |
| Marketable securities | 2,922 | 958 |
| Inventories | 2,171 | 1,399 |
| Accounts receivable, net and other | 988 | 827 |
| Deferred tax assets | 272 | 204 |
| Total current assets | 9,797 | 6,157 |
| Fixed assets, net | 1,290 | 854 |
| Deferred tax assets | 18 | 145 |
| Goodwill | 1,234 | 438 |
| Other assets | 1,474 | 720 |
| Total assets | $13,813 | $8,314 |
| **LIABILITIES AND STOCKHOLDERS' EQUITY** | | |
| Current liabilities: | | |
| Accounts payable | $ 5,605 | $3,594 |
| Accrued expenses and other | 1,759 | 1,152 |
| Total current liabilities | 7,364 | 4,746 |
| Long-term debt | 109 | 409 |
| Other long-term liabilities | 1,083 | 487 |
| Commitments and contingencies | | |
| Stockholders' equity: | | |
| Preferred stock, $0.01 par value: | | |
| Authorized shares—500 | — | — |
| Issued and outstanding shares—none | | |
| Common stock, $0.01 par value: | | |
| Authorized shares—5,000 | | |
| Issued shares—461 and 445 | — | — |
| Outstanding shares—444 and 428 | 5 | 4 |
| Treasury stock, at cost | (600) | (600) |
| Additional paid-in capital | 5,736 | 4,121 |
| Accumulated other comprehensive income (loss) | (56) | (123) |
| Retained earnings (accumulated deficit) | 172 | (730) |
| Total stockholders' equity | 5,257 | 2,672 |
| Total liabilities and stockholders' equity | $13,813 | $8,314 |

See accompanying notes to consolidated financial statements.

40

## AMAZON.COM, INC.
## CONSOLIDATED STATEMENTS OF STOCKHOLDERS' EQUITY
### (in millions)

| | Common Stock Shares | Common Stock Amount | Treasury Stock | Additional Paid-In Capital | Accumulated Other Comprehensive Income (Loss) | Retained Earnings (Accumulated Deficit) | Total Stockholders' Equity |
|---|---|---|---|---|---|---|---|
| Balance at December 31, 2006 | 414 | $ 4 | $(252) | $2,517 | $ (1) | $(1,837) | $ 431 |
| Net income | — | — | — | — | — | 476 | 476 |
| Foreign currency translation losses, net of tax | — | — | — | — | (3) | — | (3) |
| Change in unrealized losses on available-for-sale securities, net of tax | — | — | — | — | 8 | — | 8 |
| Amortization of unrealized loss on terminated Euro Currency Swap, net of tax | — | — | — | — | 1 | — | 1 |
| Comprehensive income | | | | | | | 482 |
| Change in accounting principle | — | — | — | 2 | — | (14) | (12) |
| Unrecognized excess tax benefits from stock-based compensation | — | — | — | 4 | — | — | 4 |
| Exercise of common stock options and conversion of debt | 8 | — | — | 92 | — | — | 92 |
| Repurchase of common stock | (6) | — | (248) | — | — | — | (248) |
| Excess tax benefits from stock-based compensation | — | — | — | 257 | — | — | 257 |
| Stock-based compensation and issuance of employee benefit plan stock | — | — | — | 191 | — | — | 191 |
| Balance at December 31, 2007 | 416 | 4 | (500) | 3,063 | 5 | (1,375) | 1,197 |
| Net income | — | — | — | — | — | 645 | 645 |
| Foreign currency translation losses, net of tax | — | — | — | — | (127) | — | (127) |
| Change in unrealized losses on available-for-sale securities, net of tax | — | — | — | — | (1) | — | (1) |
| Comprehensive income | | | | | | | 517 |
| Unrecognized excess tax benefits from stock-based compensation | — | — | — | (8) | — | — | (8) |
| Exercise of common stock options and conversion of debt | 14 | — | — | 624 | — | — | 624 |
| Repurchase of common stock | (2) | — | (100) | — | — | — | (100) |
| Excess tax benefits from stock-based compensation | — | — | — | 154 | — | — | 154 |
| Stock-based compensation and issuance of employee benefit plan stock | — | — | — | 288 | — | — | 288 |
| Balance at December 31, 2008 | 428 | 4 | (600) | 4,121 | (123) | (730) | 2,672 |
| Net income | — | — | — | — | — | 902 | 902 |
| Foreign currency translation gains net of tax | — | — | — | — | 62 | — | 62 |
| Change in unrealized gains on available-for-sale securities, net of tax | — | — | — | — | 4 | — | 4 |
| Amortization of unrealized loss on terminated Euro Currency Swap, net of tax | — | — | — | — | 1 | — | 1 |
| Comprehensive income | | | | | | | 969 |
| Exercise of common stock options | 7 | — | — | 19 | — | — | 19 |
| Issuance of common stock for acquisition activity | 9 | 1 | — | 1,144 | — | — | 1,145 |
| Excess tax benefits from stock-based compensation | — | — | — | 103 | — | — | 103 |
| Stock-based compensation and issuance of employee benefit plan stock | — | — | — | 349 | — | — | 349 |
| Balance at December 31, 2009 | 444 | $ 5 | $(600) | $5,736 | $ (56) | $ 172 | $5,257 |

See accompanying notes to consolidated financial statements.

41

# AMAZON.COM, INC.

## NOTES TO CONSOLIDATED FINANCIAL STATEMENTS

### Note 1—DESCRIPTION OF BUSINESS AND ACCOUNTING POLICIES

*Description of Business*

Amazon.com opened its virtual doors on the World Wide Web in July 1995 and offers Earth's Biggest Selection. We seek to be Earth's most customer-centric company for three primary customer sets: consumers, sellers, and developers. We serve consumers through our retail websites and focus on selection, price, and convenience. We also manufacture and sell the Kindle e-reader. We offer programs that enable sellers to sell their products on our websites and their own branded websites and to fulfill orders through us. We serve developers through Amazon Web Services, which provides access to technology infrastructure that developers can use to enable virtually any type of business. In addition, we generate revenue through co-branded credit card agreements and other marketing and promotional services, such as online advertising.

We have organized our operations into two principal segments: North America and International. See "Note 11—Segment Information."

*Principles of Consolidation*

The consolidated financial statements include the accounts of the Company, its wholly-owned subsidiaries, and those entities in which we have a variable interest and are the primary beneficiary. Intercompany balances and transactions have been eliminated.

*Use of Estimates*

The preparation of financial statements in conformity with U.S. GAAP requires estimates and assumptions that affect the reported amounts of assets and liabilities, revenues and expenses, and related disclosures of contingent liabilities in the consolidated financial statements and accompanying notes. Estimates are used for, but not limited to, valuation of investments, collectability of receivables, sales returns, incentive discount offers, valuation of inventory, depreciable lives of fixed assets and internally-developed software, valuation of acquired intangibles and goodwill, income taxes, stock-based compensation, and contingencies. Actual results could differ materially from those estimates.

*Subsequent Events*

We have evaluated subsequent events and transactions for potential recognition or disclosure in the financial statements through January 28, 2010, the day the financial statements were issued.

*Earnings per Share*

Basic earnings per share is calculated using our weighted-average outstanding common shares. Diluted earnings per share is calculated using our weighted-average outstanding common shares including the dilutive effect of stock awards as determined under the treasury stock method.

42

## AMAZON.COM, INC.

### NOTES TO CONSOLIDATED FINANCIAL STATEMENTS—(Continued)

The following table shows the calculation of diluted shares (in millions):

| | Year Ended December 31, | | |
|---|---|---|---|
| | 2009 | 2008 | 2007 |
| Shares used in computation of basic earnings per share | 433 | 423 | 413 |
| Total dilutive effect of outstanding stock awards (1) | 9 | 9 | 11 |
| Shares used in computation of diluted earnings per share | 442 | 432 | 424 |

(1)  Calculated using the treasury stock method, which assumes proceeds are used to reduce the dilutive effect of outstanding stock awards. Assumed proceeds include the unrecognized deferred compensation of stock awards, and assumed tax proceeds from excess stock-based compensation deductions.

### Treasury Stock

We account for treasury stock under the cost method and include treasury stock as a component of stockholders' equity.

### Cash and Cash Equivalents

We classify all highly liquid instruments, including money market funds that comply with Rule 2a-7 of the Investment Company Act of 1940, with an original maturity of three months or less at the time of purchase as cash equivalents.

### Inventories

Inventories, consisting of products available for sale, are accounted for using primarily the FIFO method, and are valued at the lower of cost or market value. This valuation requires us to make judgments, based on currently-available information, about the likely method of disposition, such as through sales to individual customers, returns to product vendors, or liquidations, and expected recoverable values of each disposition category.

We provide fulfillment-related services in connection with certain of our sellers' programs. The third party seller maintains ownership of their inventory, regardless of whether fulfillment is provided by us or the third party seller, and therefore these products are not included in our inventories.

### Accounts Receivable, Net, and Other

Included in "Accounts receivable, net, and other" on our consolidated balance sheets are amounts primarily related to vendor and customer receivables. At December 31, 2009 and 2008, vendor receivables, net, were $495 million and $400 million, and customer receivables, net, were $341 million and $311 million.

### Allowance for Doubtful Accounts

We estimate losses on receivables based on known troubled accounts and historical experience of losses incurred. The allowance for doubtful customer and vendor receivables was $72 million and $81 million at December 31, 2009 and 2008.

43

## AMAZON.COM, INC.

## NOTES TO CONSOLIDATED FINANCIAL STATEMENTS—(Continued)

*Internal-use Software and Website Development*

Costs incurred to develop software for internal use and our websites are capitalized and amortized over the estimated useful life of the software. Costs related to design or maintenance of internal-use software and website development are expensed as incurred. For the years ended 2009, 2008, and 2007, we capitalized $187 million (including $35 million of stock-based compensation), $187 million (including $27 million of stock-based compensation), and $129 million (including $21 million of stock-based compensation) of costs associated with internal-use software and website development. Amortization of previously capitalized amounts was $172 million, $143 million, and $116 million for 2009, 2008, and 2007.

*Depreciation of Fixed Assets*

Fixed assets include assets such as furniture and fixtures, heavy equipment, technology infrastructure, internal-use software and website development. Depreciation is recorded on a straight-line basis over the estimated useful lives of the assets (generally two years for assets such as internal-use software, three years for our technology infrastructure, five years for furniture and fixtures, and ten years for heavy equipment). Depreciation expense is generally classified within the corresponding operating expense categories on our consolidated statements of operations.

*Leases and Asset Retirement Obligations*

We categorize leases at their inception as either operating or capital leases. On certain of our lease agreements, we may receive rent holidays and other incentives. We recognize lease costs on a straight-line basis without regard to deferred payment terms, such as rent holidays that defer the commencement date of required payments. Additionally, incentives we receive are treated as a reduction of our costs over the term of the agreement. Leasehold improvements are capitalized at cost and amortized over the lesser of their expected useful life or the life of the lease, excluding renewal periods. We establish assets and liabilities for the estimated construction costs incurred under build-to-suit lease arrangements to the extent we are involved in the construction of structural improvements or take some level of construction risk prior to commencement of a lease.

We establish assets and liabilities for the present value of estimated future costs to return certain of our leased facilities to their original condition. Such assets are depreciated over the lease period into operating expense, and the recorded liabilities are accreted to the future value of the estimated restoration costs.

*Goodwill*

We evaluate goodwill for impairment annually and when an event occurs or circumstances change that indicate that the carrying value may not be recoverable. We test goodwill for impairment by first comparing the book value of net assets to the fair value of the reporting units. If the fair value is determined to be less than the book value, a second step is performed to compute the amount of impairment as the difference between the estimated fair value of goodwill and the carrying value. We estimate the fair value of the reporting units using discounted cash flows. Forecasts of future cash flow are based on our best estimate of future net sales and operating expenses, based primarily on estimated category expansion, pricing, market segment penetration and general economic conditions.

We conduct our annual impairment test as of October 1 of each year, and have determined there to be no impairment for any of the periods presented. There were no events or circumstances from the date of our assessment through December 31, 2009 that would impact this conclusion.

44

## AMAZON.COM, INC.

## NOTES TO CONSOLIDATED FINANCIAL STATEMENTS—(Continued)

See "Note 4—Acquisitions, Goodwill, and Acquired Intangible Assets."

*Other Assets*

Included in "Other assets" on our consolidated balance sheets are amounts primarily related to marketable securities restricted for longer than one year, the majority of which are attributable to collateralization of bank guarantees and debt related to our international operations; acquired intangible assets, net of amortization; deferred costs; certain equity investments; and intellectual property rights, net of amortization.

*Investments*

We generally invest our excess cash in investment grade short to intermediate term fixed income securities and AAA-rated money market funds. Such investments are included in "Cash and cash equivalents," or "Marketable securities" on the accompanying consolidated balance sheets, classified as available-for-sale, and reported at fair value with unrealized gains and losses included in "Accumulated other comprehensive income (loss)."

Equity investments are accounted for using the equity method of accounting if the investment gives us the ability to exercise significant influence, but not control, over an investee. The total of these investments in equity-method investees, including identifiable intangible assets, deferred tax liabilities and goodwill, is classified on our consolidated balance sheets as "Other assets." Our share of the investees' earnings or losses and amortization of the related intangible assets, if any, is classified as "Equity-method investment activity, net of tax" on our consolidated statements of operations.

Equity investments without readily determinable fair values for which we do not have the ability to exercise significant influence are accounted for using the cost method of accounting. Under the cost method, investments are carried at cost and are adjusted only for other-than-temporary declines in fair value, distributions of earnings, and additional investments.

Equity investments that have readily determinable fair values are classified as available-for-sale and are recorded at fair value with unrealized gains and losses, net of tax, included in "Accumulated other comprehensive loss."

We periodically evaluate whether declines in fair values of our investments below their cost are other-than-temporary. This evaluation consists of several qualitative and quantitative factors regarding the severity and duration of the unrealized loss as well as our ability and intent to hold the investment until a forecasted recovery occurs. Additionally, we assess whether it is more likely than not we will be required to sell any investment before recovery of its amortized cost basis. Factors considered include quoted market prices; recent financial results and operating trends; other publicly available information; implied values from any recent transactions or offers of investee securities; other conditions that may affect the value of our investments; duration and severity of the decline in value; and our strategy and intentions for holding the investment.

*Long-Lived Assets*

Long-lived assets, other than goodwill, are reviewed for impairment whenever events or changes in circumstances indicate that the carrying amount of the assets might not be recoverable. Conditions that would necessitate an impairment assessment include a significant decline in the observable market value of an asset, a significant change in the extent or manner in which an asset is used, or any other significant adverse change that would indicate that the carrying amount of an asset or group of assets may not be recoverable.

45

**AMAZON.COM, INC.**

**NOTES TO CONSOLIDATED FINANCIAL STATEMENTS—(Continued)**

For long-lived assets used in operations, impairment losses are only recorded if the asset's carrying amount is not recoverable through its undiscounted, probability-weighted future cash flows. We measure the impairment loss based on the difference between the carrying amount and estimated fair value.

Long-lived assets are considered held for sale when certain criteria are met, including when management has committed to a plan to sell the asset, the asset is available for sale in its immediate condition, and the sale is probable within one year of the reporting date. Assets held for sale are reported at the lower of cost or fair value less costs to sell. Assets held for sale were not significant at December 31, 2009 or 2008.

*Accrued Expenses and Other*

Included in "Accrued expenses and other" at December 31, 2009 and 2008 were liabilities of $347 million and $270 million for unredeemed gift certificates. We reduce the liability for a gift certificate when it is applied to an order. If a gift certificate is not redeemed, we recognize revenue when it expires or, for a certificate without an expiration date, when the likelihood of its redemption becomes remote, generally two years from date of issuance.

*Unearned Revenue*

Unearned revenue is recorded when payments are received in advance of performing our service obligations and is recognized over the service period. Current unearned revenue is included in "Accrued expenses and other" and non-current unearned revenue is included in "Other long-term liabilities" on our consolidated balance sheets. Current unearned revenue was $511 million and $191 million at December 31, 2009 and 2008. Non-current unearned revenue was $201 million and $46 million at December 31, 2009 and 2008.

*Income Taxes*

Income tax expense includes U.S. and international income taxes. Except as required under U.S. tax law, we do not provide for U.S. taxes on our undistributed earnings of foreign subsidiaries that have not been previously taxed since we intend to invest such undistributed earnings indefinitely outside of the U.S. Undistributed earnings of foreign subsidiaries that are indefinitely invested outside of the U.S were $912 million at December 31, 2009. Determination of the unrecognized deferred tax liability that would be incurred if such amounts were repatriated is not practicable.

Deferred income tax balances reflect the effects of temporary differences between the carrying amounts of assets and liabilities and their tax bases and are stated at enacted tax rates expected to be in effect when taxes are actually paid or recovered.

Deferred tax assets are evaluated for future realization and reduced by a valuation allowance to the extent we believe a portion will not be realized. We consider many factors when assessing the likelihood of future realization of our deferred tax assets, including our recent cumulative earnings experience and expectations of future taxable income and capital gains by taxing jurisdiction, the carry-forward periods available to us for tax reporting purposes, and other relevant factors. We allocate our valuation allowance to current and long-term deferred tax assets on a pro-rata basis.

We utilize a two-step approach to recognizing and measuring uncertain tax positions (tax contingencies). The first step is to evaluate the tax position for recognition by determining if the weight of available evidence indicates it is more likely than not that the position will be sustained on audit, including resolution of related

46

**AMAZON.COM, INC.**

**NOTES TO CONSOLIDATED FINANCIAL STATEMENTS—(Continued)**

appeals or litigation processes. The second step is to measure the tax benefit as the largest amount which is more than 50% likely of being realized upon ultimate settlement. We consider many factors when evaluating and estimating our tax positions and tax benefits, which may require periodic adjustments and which may not accurately forecast actual outcomes. We include interest and penalties related to our tax contingencies in income tax expense.

*Fair Value of Financial Instruments*

Fair value is defined as the price that would be received to sell an asset or paid to transfer a liability in an orderly transaction between market participants at the measurement date. To increase the comparability of fair value measures, the following hierarchy prioritizes the inputs to valuation methodologies used to measure fair value:

**Level 1**—Valuations based on quoted prices for identical assets and liabilities in active markets.

**Level 2**—Valuations based on observable inputs other than quoted prices included in Level 1, such as quoted prices for similar assets and liabilities in active markets, quoted prices for identical or similar assets and liabilities in markets that are not active, or other inputs that are observable or can be corroborated by observable market data.

**Level 3**—Valuations based on unobservable inputs reflecting our own assumptions, consistent with reasonably available assumptions made by other market participants. These valuations require significant judgment.

We measure the fair value of money market funds based on quoted prices in active markets for identical assets or liabilities. All other financial instruments were valued based on quoted market prices of similar instruments and other significant inputs derived from or corroborated by observable market data.

*Revenue*

We recognize revenue from product sales or services rendered when the following four revenue recognition criteria are met: persuasive evidence of an arrangement exists, delivery has occurred or services have been rendered, the selling price is fixed or determinable, and collectability is reasonably assured. Revenue arrangements with multiple deliverables are divided into separate units of accounting if the deliverables in the arrangement meet the following criteria: there is standalone value to the delivered item; there is objective and reliable evidence of the fair value of the undelivered items; and delivery of any undelivered item is probable.

We evaluate whether it is appropriate to record the gross amount of product sales and related costs or the net amount earned as commissions. Generally, when we are primarily obligated in a transaction, are subject to inventory risk, have latitude in establishing prices and selecting suppliers, or have several but not all of these indicators, revenue is recorded gross. If we are not primarily obligated and amounts earned are determined using a fixed percentage, a fixed-payment schedule, or a combination of the two, we generally record the net amounts as commissions earned.

Product sales and shipping revenues, net of promotional discounts, rebates, and return allowances, are recorded when the products are shipped and title passes to customers. Retail sales to customers are made pursuant to a sales contract that provides for transfer of both title and risk of loss upon our delivery to the carrier. Return allowances, which reduce product revenue, are estimated using historical experience. Revenue from product sales and services rendered is recorded net of sales and consumption taxes. Amounts received in advance for subscription services, including amounts received for Amazon Prime and other membership programs, are

47

AMAZON.COM, INC.

**NOTES TO CONSOLIDATED FINANCIAL STATEMENTS—(Continued)**

deferred and recognized as revenue over the subscription term. For our products with multiple elements, where objective and reliable evidence of fair value for the undelivered elements cannot be established, we recognize the revenue and related cost over the expected life of the product.

We periodically provide incentive offers to our customers to encourage purchases. Such offers include current discount offers, such as percentage discounts off current purchases, inducement offers, such as offers for future discounts subject to a minimum current purchase, and other similar offers. Current discount offers, when accepted by our customers, are treated as a reduction to the purchase price of the related transaction, while inducement offers, when accepted by our customers, are treated as a reduction to purchase price based on estimated future redemption rates. Redemption rates are estimated using our historical experience for similar inducement offers. Current discount offers and inducement offers are presented as a net amount in "Net sales."

Commissions and per-unit fees received from sellers and similar amounts earned through other seller sites are recognized when the item is sold by seller and our collectability is reasonably assured. We record an allowance for estimated refunds on such commissions using historical experience.

*Shipping Activities*

Outbound shipping charges to customers are included in "Net sales" and were $924 million, $835 million, and $740 million for 2009, 2008, and 2007. Outbound shipping-related costs are included in "Cost of sales" and totaled $1.8 billion, $1.5 billion, and $1.2 billion for 2009, 2008, and 2007. The net cost to us of shipping activities was $849 million, $630 million, and $434 million for 2009, 2008 and 2007.

*Cost of Sales*

Cost of sales consists of the purchase price of consumer products and content sold by us, inbound and outbound shipping charges, packaging supplies, and costs incurred in operating and staffing our fulfillment and customer service centers on behalf of other businesses. Shipping charges to receive products from our suppliers are included in our inventory, and recognized as "Cost of sales" upon sale of products to our customers. Payment processing and related transaction costs, including those associated with seller transactions, are classified in "Fulfillment" on our consolidated statements of operations.

*Vendor Agreements*

We have agreements to receive cash consideration from certain of our vendors, including rebates and cooperative marketing reimbursements. We generally consider amounts received from our vendors as a reduction of the prices we pay for their products and, therefore, we record such amounts as either a reduction of "Cost of sales" on our consolidated statements of operations, or, if the product inventory is still on hand, as a reduction of the carrying value of inventory. Vendor rebates are typically dependent upon reaching minimum purchase thresholds. We evaluate the likelihood of reaching purchase thresholds using past experience and current year forecasts. When volume rebates can be reasonably estimated, we record a portion of the rebate as we make progress towards the purchase threshold.

When we receive direct reimbursements for costs incurred by us in advertising the vendor's product or service, the amount we receive is recorded as an offset to "Marketing" on our consolidated statements of operations.

48

*Fulfillment*

Fulfillment costs represent those costs incurred in operating and staffing our fulfillment and customer service centers, including costs attributable to buying, receiving, inspecting, and warehousing inventories; picking, packaging, and preparing customer orders for shipment; payment processing and related transaction costs, including costs associated with our guarantee for certain seller transactions; and responding to inquiries from customers. Fulfillment costs also include amounts paid to third parties that assist us in fulfillment and customer service operations. Certain of our fulfillment-related costs that are incurred on behalf of other businesses are classified as cost of sales rather than fulfillment.

*Marketing*

Marketing costs consist primarily of online advertising, including through our Associates program, sponsored search, portal advertising, and other initiatives. We pay commissions to participants in our Associates program when their customer referrals result in product sales and classify such costs as "Marketing" on our consolidated statements of operations. We also participate in cooperative advertising arrangements with certain of our vendors, and other third parties.

Marketing expenses also consist of public relations expenditures; payroll and related expenses for personnel engaged in marketing, business development, and selling activities; and to a lesser extent, traditional advertising.

Advertising and other promotional costs, which consist primarily of online advertising, are expensed as incurred, and were $593 million, $420 million, and $306 million, in 2009, 2008, and 2007. Prepaid advertising costs were not significant at December 31, 2009 and 2008.

*Technology and Content*

Technology and content expenses consist principally of payroll and related expenses for employees involved in, application development, category expansion, editorial content, buying, merchandising selection, and systems support, as well as costs associated with the compute, storage and telecommunications infrastructure used internally and supporting Amazon Web Services.

Technology and content costs are expensed as incurred, except for certain costs relating to the development of internal-use software and website development, including software used to upgrade and enhance our websites and processes supporting our business, which are capitalized and amortized over two years.

*General and Administrative*

General and administrative expenses consist of payroll and related expenses for employees involved in general corporate functions, including accounting, finance, tax, legal, and human relations, among others; costs associated with use by these functions of facilities and equipment, such as depreciation expense and rent; professional fees and litigation costs; and other general corporate costs.

*Stock-Based Compensation*

Compensation cost for all stock-based awards is measured at fair value on date of grant and recognized over the service period for awards expected to vest. The fair value of restricted stock units is determined based on the number of shares granted and the quoted price of our common stock. Such value is recognized as expense over the service period, net of estimated forfeitures, using the accelerated method. The estimation of stock awards that

49

will ultimately vest requires judgment, and to the extent actual results or updated estimates differ from our current estimates, such amounts will be recorded as a cumulative adjustment in the period estimates are revised. We consider many factors when estimating expected forfeitures, including types of awards, employee class, and historical experience.

### Other Income (Expense), Net

Other income (expense), net, consists primarily of gains and losses on sales of marketable securities, foreign currency transaction gains and losses, and other losses.

### Foreign Currency

We have internationally-focused websites for the United Kingdom, Germany, France, Japan, Canada, and China. Net sales generated from internationally-focused websites, as well as most of the related expenses directly incurred from those operations, are denominated in the functional currencies of the resident countries. The functional currency of our subsidiaries that either operate or support these international websites is the same as the local currency. Assets and liabilities of these subsidiaries are translated into U.S. Dollars at period-end exchange rates, and revenues and expenses are translated at average rates prevailing throughout the period. Translation adjustments are included in "Accumulated other comprehensive income (loss)," a separate component of stockholders' equity, and in the "Foreign currency effect on cash and cash equivalents," on our consolidated statements of cash flows. Transaction gains and losses arising from transactions denominated in a currency other than the functional currency of the entity involved are included in "Other income (expense), net" on our consolidated statements of operations.

Gains and losses arising from intercompany foreign currency transactions are included in net income. In connection with the remeasurement of intercompany balances, we recorded gains of $5 million, $23 million and $32 million in 2009, 2008 and 2007.

### Recent Accounting Pronouncements

In December 2007, the Financial Accounting Standards Board ("FASB") issued Statements of Financial Accounting Standards ("SFAS") No. 141 (R), *Business Combinations*, codified as Accounting Standards Codification ("ASC") 805, *Business Combinations,* and SFAS No. 160, *Noncontrolling Interests in Consolidated Financial Statements*, codified as ASC 810, *Consolidations.* SFAS No. 141 (R) requires an acquirer to measure the identifiable assets acquired, the liabilities assumed, and any noncontrolling interest in the acquired entity at their fair values on the acquisition date, with goodwill being the excess value over the net identifiable assets acquired. SFAS No. 160 clarifies that a noncontrolling interest in a subsidiary should be reported as equity in the consolidated financial statements. The calculation of earnings per share will continue to be based on income amounts attributable to the parent. SFAS No. 141 (R) impacted acquisitions closed on or after January 1, 2009. Adoption did not have a material impact on our consolidated financial statements on the date of adoption.

In December 2009, the FASB issued Accounting Standards Update ("ASU") 2009-17, which codifies SFAS No. 167, *Amendments to FASB Interpretation No. 46(R)* issued in June 2009. ASU 2009-17 requires a qualitative approach to identifying a controlling financial interest in a variable interest entity ("VIE"), and requires ongoing assessment of whether an entity is a VIE and whether an interest in a VIE makes the holder the primary beneficiary of the VIE. ASU 2009-17 is effective for annual reporting periods beginning after November 15, 2009. We do not expect the adoption of ASU 2009-17 to have a material impact on our consolidated financial statements.

50

**AMAZON.COM, INC.**

**NOTES TO CONSOLIDATED FINANCIAL STATEMENTS—(Continued)**

In October 2009, the FASB issued ASU 2009-13, which amends ASC Topic 605, *Revenue Recognition.* Under this standard, management is no longer required to obtain vendor-specific objective evidence or third party evidence of fair value for each deliverable in an arrangement with multiple elements, and where evidence is not available we may now estimate the proportion of the selling price attributable to each deliverable. We have chosen to prospectively adopt this standard as of January 1, 2010.

Sales of our Kindle e-reader are considered arrangements with multiple elements which include the device, wireless access and delivery and software upgrades. The revenue related to the device, which is the substantial portion of the total sale price, and related costs will be recognized at time of delivery. Revenue for the wireless access and delivery and software upgrades will continue to be amortized over the life of the device, which remains estimated at two years.

We cannot reasonably estimate the effect of adopting this standard on future financial periods as the impact will vary based on actual volume of activity under these types of revenue arrangements.

For arrangements entered into prior to the adoption of the new accounting standard and for which revenue had been previously deferred, we will recognize $508 million throughout 2010 and 2011.

In January 2010, the FASB issued ASU 2010-6, *Improving Disclosures About Fair Value Measurements,* which requires reporting entities to make new disclosures about recurring or nonrecurring fair-value measurements including significant transfers into and out of Level 1 and Level 2 fair-value measurements and information on purchases, sales, issuances, and settlements on a gross basis in the reconciliation of Level 3 fair- value measurements. ASU 2010-6 is effective for annual reporting periods beginning after December 15, 2009, except for Level 3 reconciliation disclosures which are effective for annual periods beginning after December 15, 2010. We do not expect the adoption of ASU 2010-6 to have a material impact on our consolidated financial statements.

## Note 2—CASH, CASH EQUIVALENTS, AND MARKETABLE SECURITIES

As of December 31, 2009 and 2008 our cash, cash equivalents, and marketable securities primarily consisted of cash, government and government agency securities, AAA-rated money market funds and other investment grade securities. Such amounts are recorded at fair value. The following table summarizes, by major security type, our cash, cash equivalents and marketable securities (in millions):

| | December 31, 2009 | | | |
| --- | --- | --- | --- | --- |
| | Cost or Amortized Cost | Gross Unrealized Gains | Gross Unrealized Losses | Total Estimated Fair Value |
| Cash | $ 391 | $— | $— | $ 391 |
| Money market funds | 2,750 | — | — | 2,750 |
| Foreign government and agency securities | 1,992 | 7 | — | 1,999 |
| Corporate debt securities (1) | 206 | 5 | — | 211 |
| U.S. government and agency securities | 1,268 | 5 | (5) | 1,268 |
| Asset-backed securities | 44 | 2 | — | 46 |
| Other fixed income securities | 6 | — | — | 6 |
| Equity securities | 2 | — | (1) | 1 |
| | $6,659 | $ 19 | $ (6) | $6,672 |
| Less: Long-term marketable securities (2) | | | | (306) |
| Total cash, cash equivalents, and marketable securities | | | | $6,366 |

51

AMAZON.COM, INC.

NOTES TO CONSOLIDATED FINANCIAL STATEMENTS—(Continued)

| | December 31, 2008 | | | |
|---|---|---|---|---|
| | Cost or Amortized Cost | Gross Unrealized Gains | Gross Unrealized Losses | Total Estimated Fair Value |
| Cash | $ 355 | $— | $— | $ 355 |
| Money market funds | 1,682 | — | — | 1,682 |
| Foreign government and agency securities | 1,120 | 8 | — | 1,128 |
| Corporate debt securities (1) | 194 | 2 | (2) | 194 |
| U.S. government and agency securities | 589 | 5 | — | 594 |
| Asset-backed securities | 62 | — | (4) | 58 |
| Other fixed income securities | 23 | — | — | 23 |
| Equity securities | 2 | — | (1) | 1 |
| | $4,027 | $ 15 | $ (7) | $4,035 |
| Less: Long-term marketable securities (2) | | | | (308) |
| Total cash, cash equivalents, and marketable securities | | | | $3,727 |

(1) Corporate debt securities include investments in financial, insurance, and corporate institutions. No single issuer represents a significant portion of the total corporate debt securities portfolio.

(2) We are required to pledge or otherwise restrict a portion of our marketable securities as collateral for standby letters of credit, guarantees, debt, and real estate lease agreements. We classify cash and marketable securities with use restrictions of twelve months or longer as non-current "Other assets" on our consolidated balance sheets. See "Note 7—Commitments and Contingencies."

The following table summarizes gross gains and gross losses realized on sales of available-for-sale marketable securities (in millions):

| | Year Ended December 31, | | |
|---|---|---|---|
| | 2009 | 2008 | 2007 |
| Realized gains | $ 4 | $9 | $2 |
| Realized losses | — | 7 | 3 |

The following table summarizes contractual maturities of our cash equivalent and marketable fixed-income securities as of December 31, 2009 (in millions):

| | Amortized Cost | Estimated Fair Value |
|---|---|---|
| Due within one year | $4,908 | $4,909 |
| Due after one year through five years | 1,358 | 1,371 |
| | $6,266 | $6,280 |

52

# AMAZON.COM, INC.

## NOTES TO CONSOLIDATED FINANCIAL STATEMENTS—(Continued)

The following table summarizes, by major security type, our assets that are measured at fair value on a recurring basis and are categorized using the fair value hierarchy (in millions):

| | | December 31, 2009 | | | |
|---|---|---|---|---|---|
| | Cash | Level 1 Estimated Fair Value | Level 2 Estimated Fair Value | Level 3 Estimated Fair Value | Total Estimated Fair Value |
| Cash | $391 | $  — | $  — | $— | $  391 |
| Money market funds | — | 2,750 | — | — | 2,750 |
| Foreign government and agency securities | — | — | 1,999 | — | 1,999 |
| Corporate debt securities | — | — | 211 | — | 211 |
| U.S. government and agency securities | — | — | 1,268 | — | 1,268 |
| Asset-backed securities | — | — | 46 | — | 46 |
| Other fixed income securities | — | — | 6 | — | 6 |
| Equity securities | — | 1 | — | — | 1 |
| | $391 | $2,751 | $3,530 | $— | $6,672 |

| | | December 31, 2008 | | | |
|---|---|---|---|---|---|
| | Cash | Level 1 Estimated Fair Value | Level 2 Estimated Fair Value | Level 3 Estimated Fair Value | Total Estimated Fair Value |
| Cash | $355 | $  — | $  — | $— | $  355 |
| Money market funds | — | 1,682 | — | — | 1,682 |
| Foreign government and agency securities | — | — | 1,128 | — | 1,128 |
| Corporate debt securities | — | — | 194 | — | 194 |
| U.S. government and agency securities | — | — | 594 | — | 594 |
| Asset-backed securities | — | — | 58 | — | 58 |
| Other fixed income securities | — | — | 23 | — | 23 |
| Equity securities | — | 1 | — | — | 1 |
| | $355 | $1,683 | $1,997 | $— | $4,035 |

53

## Note 3—FIXED ASSETS

Fixed assets, at cost, consisted of the following (in millions):

| | December 31, | |
| --- | --- | --- |
| | 2009 | 2008 |
| **Gross Fixed Assets:** | | |
| Fulfillment and customer service | $ 551 | $ 564 |
| Technology infrastructure | 551 | 348 |
| Internal-use software, content, and website development | 398 | 331 |
| Construction in progress (1) | 278 | 87 |
| Other corporate assets | 137 | 79 |
| Gross fixed assets | 1,915 | 1,409 |
| **Accumulated Depreciation:** | | |
| Fulfillment and customer service | 202 | 254 |
| Technology infrastructure | 178 | 82 |
| Internal-use software, content, and website development | 207 | 159 |
| Other corporate assets | 38 | 60 |
| Total accumulated depreciation | 625 | 555 |
| Total fixed assets, net | $1,290 | $ 854 |

(1) We capitalize construction in progress and record a corresponding long-term liability for certain lease agreements, including our Seattle, Washington corporate office space subject to leases scheduled to begin upon completion of development between 2010 and 2013. See "Note 6—Other Long-Term Liabilities" and "Note 7—Commitments and Contingencies" for further discussion.

Depreciation expense on fixed assets was $384 million, $311 million, and $258 million, which includes amortization of fixed assets acquired under capital lease obligations of $88 million, $50 million, and $40 million for 2009, 2008, and 2007. Gross assets remaining under capital leases were $430 million and $304 million at December 31, 2009 and 2008. Accumulated depreciation associated with capital leases was $184 million and $116 million at December 31, 2009 and 2008.

## Note 4—ACQUISITIONS, GOODWILL, AND ACQUIRED INTANGIBLE ASSETS

*2009 Acquisition Activity*

On November 1, 2009, we acquired 100% of the outstanding equity of Zappos.com, Inc. ("Zappos"), in exchange for shares of our common stock, to expand our presence in softline retail categories, such as shoes and apparel.

The fair value of Zappos' stock options assumed was determined using the Black-Scholes model. The following table summarizes the consideration paid for Zappos (in millions):

| | |
| --- | --- |
| Stock issued | $1,079 |
| Assumed stock options, net | 55 |
| | $1,134 |

The purchase price was allocated to the tangible assets and intangible assets acquired and liabilities assumed based on their estimated fair values on the acquisition date, with the remaining unallocated purchase price recorded as goodwill. The fair value assigned to identifiable intangible assets acquired has been determined primarily by using the income approach. Purchased identifiable intangible assets are amortized on a straight-line and accelerated basis over their respective useful lives.

The following summarizes the allocation of the Zappos purchase price (in millions):

| | |
|---|---:|
| Goodwill | $ 778 |
| Other net assets acquired | 83 |
| Deferred tax liabilities net | (167) |
| Intangible assets (1): | |
| Marketing-related | 223 |
| Contract-based | 103 |
| Customer-related | 114 |
| | $1,134 |

(1)  Acquired intangible assets have estimated useful lives of between 1 and 10 years.

Zappos' financial results have been included in our consolidated statements of income as of November 1, 2009. The following pro forma financial information presents the results as if the Zappos acquisition had occurred at the beginning of each year presented (in millions):

| | Year Ended December 31, | |
|---|---:|---:|
| | 2009 | 2008 |
| Net sales | $25,064 | $19,801 |
| Net income | 853 | 606 |

We acquired certain additional companies during 2009 for an aggregate purchase price of $26 million, resulting in goodwill of $16 million and acquired intangible assets of $5 million. The results of operations of each of the businesses acquired have been included in our consolidated results from each transactions closing date forward. The effect of these acquisitions on consolidated net sales and operating income during 2009 was not significant.

*2008 and 2007 Acquisition Activity*

We acquired certain companies during 2008 for an aggregate purchase price of $432 million, resulting in goodwill of $210 million and acquired intangible assets of $162 million.

We acquired certain companies during 2007 for an aggregate purchase price of $33 million, resulting in goodwill of $21 million and acquired intangible assets of $18 million. We also made principal payments of $13 million on acquired debt in connection with one of these acquisitions.

The results of operations of each of the businesses acquired in 2008 and 2007 have been included in our consolidated results from each transaction closing date forward. The effect of these acquisitions on consolidated net sales and operating income during 2008 and 2007 was not significant.

55

**AMAZON.COM, INC.**

**NOTES TO CONSOLIDATED FINANCIAL STATEMENTS—(Continued)**

*Goodwill*

The following summarizes our goodwill activity in 2009 (in millions):

| | |
|---|---|
| Goodwill—January 1, 2009 | $ 438 |
| New acquisitions | 794 |
| Other adjustments (1) | 2 |
| Goodwill—December 31, 2009 | $1,234 |

(1) Primarily includes changes in foreign exchange for goodwill in our International segment.

At December 31, 2009 and December 31, 2008, approximately 9% and 22% of our acquired goodwill related to our International segment.

*Intangible Assets*

Acquired intangible assets, included within "Other assets" on our consolidated balance sheets, consist of the following:

| | December 31, | | | | | | |
|---|---|---|---|---|---|---|---|
| | 2009 | | | | 2008 | | |
| | Weighted Average Life Remaining | Acquired Intangibles, Gross (1) | Accumulated Amortization (1) | Acquired Intangibles, Net | Acquired Intangibles, Gross (1) | Accumulated Amortization (1) | Acquired Intangibles, Net |
| | | | | (in millions) | | | |
| Marketing-related | 9.5 | $249 | $(11) | $238 | $ 23 | $ (4) | $ 19 |
| Contract-based | 3 | 166 | (20) | 146 | 62 | (8) | 54 |
| Technology and content | 3.1 | 15 | (7) | 8 | 10 | (5) | 5 |
| Customer-related | 4.8 | 215 | (40) | 175 | 97 | (15) | 82 |
| Acquired intangibles (2) | 7.3 | $645 | $(78) | $567 | $192 | $(32) | $160 |

(1) Excludes the original cost and accumulated amortization of fully-amortized intangibles.
(2) Intangible assets have estimated useful lives of between 1 and 13 years.

Amortization expense for acquired intangibles was $48 million, $29 million, and $13 million in 2009, 2008, and 2007. Expected future amortization expense of acquired intangible assets as of December 31, 2009 is as follows (in millions):

| Year Ended December 31, | |
|---|---|
| 2010 | $100 |
| 2011 | 90 |
| 2012 | 74 |
| 2013 | 69 |
| 2014 | 58 |
| Thereafter | 176 |
| | $567 |

56

### Note 5—LONG-TERM DEBT

Our long-term debt is summarized as follows:

| | December 31, | |
|---|---|---|
| | 2009 | 2008 |
| | (in millions) | |
| 6.875% PEACS | $— | $335 |
| Other long-term debt | 131 | 133 |
| | 131 | 468 |
| Less current portion of long-term debt | (22) | (59) |
| | $109 | $409 |

In February 2008 our Board of Directors authorized a debt repurchase program, replacing our previous debt repurchase authorization in its entirety, and pursuant to which we redeemed for cash the remaining €240 million ($319 million based on the Euro to U.S. Dollar exchange rate on the date of redemption) in principal of our 6.875% PEACS in 2009, and we redeemed the remaining principal amount of $899 million of our outstanding 4.75% Convertible Subordinated Notes in 2008.

Other long-term debt relates to amounts borrowed to fund certain international operations.

### Note 6—OTHER LONG-TERM LIABILITIES

Our other long-term liabilities are summarized as follows:

| | December 31, | |
|---|---|---|
| | 2009 | 2008 |
| | (in millions) | |
| Tax contingencies | $ 202 | $144 |
| Long-term capital lease obligations | 143 | 124 |
| Construction liability | 278 | 87 |
| Other | 460 | 132 |
| | $1,083 | $487 |

*Tax Contingencies*

As of December 31, 2009 and 2008, we have provided tax reserves for tax contingencies, inclusive of accrued interest and penalties, of approximately $202 million and $144 million for U.S. and foreign income taxes. These contingencies primarily relate to transfer pricing, state income taxes, and research and development credits. See "Note 10—Income Taxes" for discussion of tax contingencies.

57

*Capital Leases*

Certain of our equipment fixed assets, primarily related to technology infrastructure, have been acquired under capital leases. Long-term capital lease obligations are as follows:

|  | December 31, 2009 |
| --- | --- |
|  | (in millions) |
| Gross capital lease obligations | $ 276 |
| Less imputed interest | (14) |
| Present value of net minimum lease payments | 262 |
| Less current portion | (119) |
| Total long-term capital lease obligations | $ 143 |

*Construction Liabilities*

We capitalize construction in progress and record a corresponding long-term liability for certain lease agreements, including our Seattle, Washington corporate office space subject to leases scheduled to begin upon completion of development between 2010 and 2013.

For build-to-suit lease arrangements where we are involved in the construction of structural improvements prior to the commencement of the lease or take some level of construction risk, we are considered the owner of the assets during the construction period. Accordingly, as the landlord incurs the construction project costs, the assets and corresponding financial obligation are recorded in "Fixed assets, net" and "Other long-term liabilities" on our consolidated balance sheet. Once the construction is completed, if the lease meets certain "sale-leaseback" criteria, we will remove the asset and related financial obligation from the balance sheet and treat the building lease as an operating lease. If upon completion of construction, the project does not meet the "sale-leaseback" criteria, the leased property will be treated as a capital lease for financial reporting purposes.

The remainder of our other long-term liabilities primarily include deferred tax liabilities, unearned revenue, asset retirement obligations, and deferred rental liabilities.

## Note 7—COMMITMENTS AND CONTINGENCIES

*Commitments*

We lease office, fulfillment center, and data center facilities and fixed assets under non-cancelable operating and capital leases. Rental expense under operating lease agreements was $171 million, $158 million, and $141 million for 2009, 2008, and 2007.

In December 2007, we entered into a series of leases and other agreements for the lease of corporate office space to be developed in Seattle, Washington with initial terms of up to 16 years commencing on completion of development between 2010 and 2013, with options to extend for two five-year periods. We expect to occupy approximately 1.7 million square feet of office space. We also have an option to lease up to an additional approximately 500,000 square feet at rates based on fair market values at the time the option is exercised, subject to certain conditions. In addition, if interest rates exceed a certain threshold, we have the option to provide financing for some of the buildings.

**AMAZON.COM, INC.**

**NOTES TO CONSOLIDATED FINANCIAL STATEMENTS—(Continued)**

The following summarizes our principal contractual commitments, excluding open orders for inventory purchases that support normal operations, as of December 31, 2009:

| | Year Ended December 31, | | | | | Thereafter | Total |
|---|---|---|---|---|---|---|---|
| | 2010 | 2011 | 2012 | 2013 | 2014 | | |
| | | | (in millions) | | | | |
| Operating and capital commitments: | | | | | | | |
| Debt principal and interest ................... | $ 31 | $ 47 | $ 36 | $ 36 | $— | $ — | $ 150 |
| Capital leases, including interest ............. | 130 | 95 | 44 | 8 | 3 | — | 280 |
| Operating leases .......................... | 162 | 146 | 130 | 122 | 115 | 317 | 992 |
| Other commitments (1)(2) .................. | 187 | 101 | 93 | 89 | 88 | 1,181 | 1,739 |
| Total commitments ................... | $510 | $389 | $303 | $255 | $206 | $1,498 | $3,161 |

(1) Includes the estimated timing and amounts of payments for rent, operating expenses, and tenant improvements associated with approximately 1.7 million square feet of corporate office space. The amount of space available and our financial and other obligations under the lease agreements are affected by various factors, including government approvals and permits, interest rates, development costs and other expenses and our exercise of certain rights under the lease agreements.

(2) Excludes $181 million of tax contingencies for which we cannot make a reasonably reliable estimate of the amount and period of payment, if any.

*Pledged Securities*

We have pledged or otherwise restricted a portion of our cash and marketable securities as collateral for standby letters of credit, guarantees, debt, and real estate leases. We classify cash and marketable securities with use restrictions of twelve months or longer as non-current "Other assets" on our consolidated balance sheets. The amount required to be pledged for certain real estate lease agreements changes over the life of our leases based on our credit rating and changes in our market capitalization. Information about collateral required to be pledged under these agreements is as follows:

| | Standby and Trade Letters of Credit and Guarantees | Debt (1) | Real Estate Leases (2) | Total |
|---|---|---|---|---|
| | | (in millions) | | |
| Balance at December 31, 2008 ........................ | $138 | $160 | $10 | $308 |
| Net change in collateral pledged ....................... | 4 | (3) | (6) | (5) |
| Balance at December 31, 2009 ........................ | $142 | $157 | $ 4 | $303 |

(1) Represents collateral for certain debt related to our international operations.

(2) At December 31, 2009, our market capitalization was $59.8 billion. The required amount of collateral to be pledged will increase by $1.5 million if our market capitalization is equal to or below $40 billion, an additional $5 million if our market capitalization is equal to or below $18 billion, and an additional $6 million if our market capitalization is equal to or below $13 billion.

*Legal Proceedings*

The Company is involved from time to time in claims, proceedings and litigation, including the following:

In June 2001, Audible, Inc., our subsidiary acquired in March 2008, was named as a defendant in a securities class-action filed in United States District Court for the Southern District of New York related to its

59

## AMAZON.COM, INC.

### NOTES TO CONSOLIDATED FINANCIAL STATEMENTS—(Continued)

initial public offering in July 1999. The lawsuit also named certain of the offering's underwriters, as well as Audible's officers and directors as defendants. Approximately 300 other issuers and their underwriters have had similar suits filed against them, all of which are included in a single coordinated proceeding in the Southern District of New York. The complaints allege that the prospectus and the registration statement for Audible's offering failed to disclose that the underwriters allegedly solicited and received "excessive" commissions from investors and that some investors allegedly agreed with the underwriters to buy additional shares in the aftermarket in order to inflate the price of Audible's stock. Audible and its officers and directors were named in the suits pursuant to Section 11 of the Securities Act of 1933, Section 10(b) of the Securities Exchange Act of 1934, and other related provisions. The complaints seek unspecified damages, attorney and expert fees, and other unspecified litigation costs. In March 2009, all parties, including Audible, reached a settlement of these class actions that would resolve this dispute entirely with no payment required from Audible. The settlement was approved by the Court in October 2009, and that settlement is currently under appeal to the Court of Appeals for the Second Circuit.

Beginning in March 2003, we were served with complaints filed in several different states, including Illinois, by a private litigant, Beeler, Schad & Diamond, P.C., purportedly on behalf of the state governments under various state False Claims Acts. The complaints allege that we (along with other companies with which we have commercial agreements) wrongfully failed to collect and remit sales and use taxes for sales of personal property to customers in those states and knowingly created records and statements falsely stating we were not required to collect or remit such taxes. In December 2006, we learned that one additional complaint was filed in the state of Illinois by a different private litigant, Matthew T. Hurst, alleging similar violations of the Illinois state law. All of the complaints seek injunctive relief, unpaid taxes, interest, attorneys' fees, civil penalties of up to $10,000 per violation, and treble or punitive damages under the various state False Claims Acts. It is possible that we have been or will be named in similar cases in other states as well. We dispute the allegations of wrongdoing in these complaints and intend to vigorously defend ourselves in these matters.

In December 2005, Registrar Systems LLC filed a complaint against us and Target Corporation for patent infringement in the United States District Court for the District of Colorado. The complaint alleges that our website technology, including the method by which Amazon.com enables customers to use Amazon.com account information on websites that Amazon.com operates for third parties, such as Target.com, infringes two patents obtained by Registrar Systems purporting to cover methods and apparatuses for a "World Wide Web Registration Information Processing System" (U.S. Patent Nos. 5,790,785 and 6,823,327) and seeks injunctive relief, monetary damages in an amount no less than a reasonable royalty, prejudgment interest, costs, and attorneys' fees. In September 2006, the Court entered an order staying the lawsuit pending the outcome of the Patent and Trademark Office's re-examination of the patents in suit. We dispute the allegations of wrongdoing in this complaint and intend to vigorously defend ourselves in this matter.

In August 2006, Cordance Corporation filed a complaint against us for patent infringement in the United States District Court for the District of Delaware. The complaint alleges that our website technology, including our 1-Click ordering system, infringes a patent obtained by Cordance purporting to cover an "Object-Based Online Transaction Infrastructure" (U.S. Patent No. 6,757,710) and seeks injunctive relief, monetary damages in an amount no less than a reasonable royalty, treble damages for alleged willful infringement, prejudgment interest, costs, and attorneys' fees. In response, we asserted a declaratory judgment counterclaim in the same action alleging that a service that Cordance has advertised its intent to launch infringes a patent owned by us entitled "Networked Personal Contact Manager" (U.S. Patent No. 6,269,369). In August 2009, the case was tried and the jury ruled that Amazon was not liable on Cordance's claims. An appeal is expected.

In October 2007, Digital Reg of Texas, LLC filed a complaint against our subsidiary, Audible, Inc., and several other defendants in the United States District Court for the Eastern District of Texas. The complaint

60

alleges that Audible's digital rights management technology infringes a patent obtained by Digital Reg purporting to cover a system for "Regulating Access to Digital Content" (U.S. Patent No. 6,389,541) and seeks injunctive relief, monetary damages, enhanced damages for alleged willful infringement, prejudgment and post-judgment interest, costs and attorneys' fees. In November 2009, we obtained a license to the patent in suit and were dismissed from the lawsuit with prejudice.

In January 2009, we learned that the United States Postal Service, including the Postal Service Office of Inspector General, is investigating our compliance with Postal Service rules, and we are cooperating.

In March 2009, Discovery Communications, Inc. filed a complaint against us for patent infringement in the United States District Court for the District of Delaware. The complaint alleges that our Kindle and Kindle 2 wireless reading devices infringe a patent owned by Discovery purporting to cover an "Electronic Book Security and Copyright Protection System" (U.S. Patent No. 7,298,851) and seeks monetary damages, a continuing royalty sufficient to compensate Discovery for any future infringement, treble damages, costs and attorneys fees. In May 2009, we filed counterclaims and an additional lawsuit in the United States District Court for the Western District of Washington against Discovery alleging infringement of several patents owned by Amazon and requesting a declaration that several Discovery patents, including the one listed above, are invalid and unenforceable. We dispute the allegations of wrongdoing and intend to vigorously defend ourselves in this matter.

In March 2009, the Tobin Family Education and Health Foundation filed a complaint against us for patent infringement in the United States District Court for the Middle District of Florida. The complaint alleges, among other things, that the technology underlying the Amazon Associates program infringes a patent owned by Tobin purporting to cover a "Method and System for Customizing Marketing Services on Networks Communication with Hypertext Tagging Conventions" (U.S. Patent No. 7,505,913) and seeks injunctive relief, monetary damages, costs and attorneys fees. We dispute the allegations of wrongdoing and intend to vigorously defend ourselves in this matter.

In April 2009, Parallel Networks, LLC filed a complaint against us for patent infringement in the United States District Court for the Eastern District of Texas. The complaint alleges, among other things, that our website technology infringes a patent owned by Parallel Networks purporting to cover a "Method And Apparatus For Client-Server Communication Using a Limited Capability Client Over A Low-Speed Communications Link" (U.S. Patent No. 6,446,111) and seeks injunctive relief, monetary damages, costs and attorneys fees. We dispute the allegations of wrongdoing and intend to vigorously defend ourselves in this matter.

In May 2009, Big Baboon, Inc. filed a complaint against us for patent infringement in the United States District Court for the Central District of California. The complaint alleges, among other things, that our third-party selling and payments technology infringes a patent owned by Big Baboon, Inc. purporting to cover an "Integrated Business-to-Business Web Commerce and Business Automation System" (U.S. Patent No. 6,115,690) and seeks injunctive relief, monetary damages, treble damages, costs and attorneys fees. We dispute the allegations of wrongdoing and intend to vigorously defend ourselves in this matter.

In June 2009, Bedrock Computer Technologies LLC filed a complaint against us for patent infringement in the United States District Court for the Eastern District of Texas. The complaint alleges, among other things, that our website technology infringes a patent owned by Bedrock purporting to cover a "Method And Apparatus For Information Storage and Retrieval Using a Hashing Technique with External Chaining and On-the-Fly Removal of Expired Data" (U.S. Patent Nos. 5,893,120) and seeks injunctive relief, monetary damages, enhanced damages, a compulsory future royalty, costs and attorneys fees. We dispute the allegations of wrongdoing and intend to vigorously defend ourselves in this matter.

In September 2009, SpeedTrack, Inc. filed a complaint against us for patent infringement in the United States District Court for the Northern District of California. The complaint alleges, among other things, that our website technology infringes a patent owned by SpeedTrack purporting to cover a "Method For Accessing Computer Files and Data, Using Linked Categories Assigned to Each Data File Record on Entry of the Data File Record" (U.S. Patent Nos. 5,544,360) and seeks injunctive relief, monetary damages, enhanced damages, costs and attorneys fees. In November 2009, the Court entered an order staying the lawsuit pending the outcome of the Patent and Trademark Office's re-examination of the patent in suit and the resolution of similar litigation against another party. We dispute the allegations of wrongdoing and intend to vigorously defend ourselves in this matter.

In September 2009, Alcatel-Lucent USA Inc. filed a complaint against us for patent infringement in the United States District Court for the Eastern District of Texas. The complaint alleges that our website technology and digital content distribution systems infringe six of Alcatel-Lucent's patents and seeks injunctive relief, monetary damages, a continuing royalty sufficient to compensate Alcatel-Lucent for any future infringement, treble damages, costs and attorneys fees. In January 2010, we filed counterclaims against Alcatel-Lucent alleging infringement of a patent owned by Amazon and that the patents asserted by Alcatel-Lucent are invalid and unenforceable. We dispute the allegations of wrongdoing and intend to vigorously defend ourselves in this matter.

In October 2009, Eolas Technologies Incorporated filed a complaint against us for patent infringement in the United States District Court for the Eastern District of Texas. The complaint alleges, among other things, that our website technology infringes two patents owned by Eolas purporting to cover "Distributed Hypermedia Method for Automatically Invoking External Application Providing Interaction and Display of Embedded Objects within a Hypermedia Document" (U.S. Patent No. 5,838,906) and "Distributed Hypermedia Method and System for Automatically Invoking External Application Providing Interaction and Display of Embedded Objects within a Hypermedia Document" (U.S. Patent No. 7,599,985) and seeks injunctive relief, monetary damages, costs and attorneys fees. We dispute the allegations of wrongdoing and intend to vigorously defend ourselves in this matter.

In October 2009, Leon Stambler filed a complaint against us for patent infringement in the United States District Court for the Eastern District of Texas. The complaint alleges, among other things, that our use of secure online payments systems and services infringes two patents owned by Stambler purporting to cover a "Method for Securing Information Relevant to a Transaction" (U.S. Patent Nos. 5,793,302 and 5,974,148) and seeks monetary damages, costs and attorneys fees. We dispute the allegations of wrongdoing and intend to vigorously defend ourselves in this matter.

In December 2009, Nazomi Communications, Inc. filed a complaint against us for patent infringement in the United States District Court for the Eastern District of Texas. The complaint alleges, among other things, that the processor core in our Kindle 2 device infringes two patents owned by Nazomi purporting to cover "Java virtual machine hardware for RISC and CISC processors" and "Java hardware accelerator using microcode engine" (U.S. Patent Nos. 7,080,362 and 7,225,436) and seeks monetary damages, injunctive relief, costs and attorneys fees. We dispute the allegations of wrongdoing and intend to vigorously defend ourselves in this matter.

Depending on the amount and the timing, an unfavorable resolution of some or all of these matters could materially affect our business, results of operations, financial position, or cash flows.

See also "Note 10—Income Taxes."

*Inventory Suppliers*

During 2009, no vendor accounted for 10% or more of our inventory purchases. We generally do not have long-term contracts or arrangements with our vendors to guarantee the availability of merchandise, particular payment terms, or the extension of credit limits.

### Note 8—STOCKHOLDERS' EQUITY

*Preferred Stock*

We have authorized 500 million shares of $0.01 par value Preferred Stock. No preferred stock was outstanding for any period presented.

*Common Stock*

Common shares outstanding plus shares underlying outstanding stock awards totaled 461 million, 446 million, and 435 million at December 31, 2009, 2008 and 2007. These totals include all stock-based awards outstanding, without regard for estimated forfeitures, consisting of vested and unvested awards. Common shares outstanding increased in 2009 due primarily to issuance of stock to acquire Zappos and vesting of restricted stock units.

*Stock Repurchase Activity*

We did not repurchase any of our common stock in 2009. We repurchased 2.2 million shares of common stock for $100 million in 2008 under the $1 billion repurchase program authorized by our Board of Directors in February 2008. We repurchased 6.3 million shares of common stock for $248 million in 2007 under the $500 million repurchase program authorized by our Board of Directors in August 2006.

In January 2010, our Board of Directors authorized a program to repurchase up to $2 billion of our common stock which replaces the Board's prior authorization.

*Stock Award Plans*

Employees vest in restricted stock unit awards over the corresponding service term, generally between two and five years.

*Stock Award Activity*

We granted restricted stock units representing 6.0 million, 7.3 million, 7.6 million shares of common stock during 2009, 2008, and 2007 with a per share weighted average fair value of $79.24, $72.21, and $47.04.

**NOTES TO CONSOLIDATED FINANCIAL STATEMENTS—(Continued)**

The following summarizes our restricted stock unit activity (in millions):

|  | Number of Units |
|---|---|
| Outstanding at January 1, 2007 | 14.5 |
| Units granted | 7.6 |
| Units vested | (3.3) |
| Units forfeited | (2.5) |
| Outstanding at December 31, 2007 | 16.3 |
| Units granted | 7.3 |
| Units vested | (5.5) |
| Units forfeited | (1.4) |
| Outstanding at December 31, 2008 | 16.7 |
| Units granted | 6.0 |
| Units vested | (6.0) |
| Units forfeited | (1.0) |
| Outstanding at December 31, 2009 | 15.7 |

Scheduled vesting for outstanding restricted stock units at December 31, 2009 is as follows (in millions):

|  | Year Ended December 31, | | | | | | |
|---|---|---|---|---|---|---|---|
|  | 2010 | 2011 | 2012 | 2013 | 2014 | Thereafter | Total |
| Scheduled vesting—restricted stock units | 5.9 | 5.5 | 2.6 | 1.4 | 0.2 | 0.1 | 15.7 |

As of December 31, 2009, there was $415 million of net unrecognized compensation cost related to unvested stock-based compensation arrangements. This compensation is recognized on an accelerated basis resulting in approximately half of the compensation expected to be expensed in the next twelve months, and has a weighted average recognition period of 1.2 years.

During 2009 and 2008, the fair value of restricted stock units that vested was $551 million and $362 million.

As matching contributions under our 401(k) savings plan, we granted 0.1 million shares of common stock in both 2009 and 2008. Shares granted as matching contributions under our 401(k) plan are included in outstanding common stock when issued.

*Common Stock Available for Future Issuance*

At December 31, 2009, common stock available for future issuance to employees is 149 million shares.

### Note 9—OTHER COMPREHENSIVE INCOME (LOSS)

The components of other comprehensive income (loss) are as follows:

| | Year Ended December 31, | | |
|---|---|---|---|
| | **2009** | **2008** | **2007** |
| | (in millions) | | |
| Net income | $902 | $ 645 | $476 |
| Net change in unrealized gains/losses on available-for-sale securities: | | | |
| Unrealized gains (losses), net of tax of $(2), $0, and $(4) | 7 | — | 8 |
| Reclassification adjustment for losses (gains) included in net income, net of tax effect of $1, $1, and $0 | (3) | (1) | — |
| Net unrealized gains (losses) on available for sale securities | 4 | (1) | 8 |
| Foreign currency translation adjustment, net of tax effect of $0, $3, and $6 | 62 | (127) | (3) |
| Amortization of net unrealized losses on terminated Euro Currency Swap, net of tax effect of $0, $0, and $0 | 1 | — | 1 |
| Other comprehensive income (loss) | 67 | (128) | 6 |
| Comprehensive income | $969 | $ 517 | $482 |

Balances within accumulated other comprehensive income (loss) are as follows:

| | December 31, | |
|---|---|---|
| | **2009** | **2008** |
| | (in millions) | |
| Net unrealized losses on foreign currency translation, net of tax | $ (66) | $(128) |
| Net unrealized gains on available-for-sale securities, net of tax | 10 | 6 |
| Net unrealized losses on terminated Euro Currency Swap, net of tax | — | (1) |
| Total accumulated other comprehensive income (loss) | $ (56) | $(123) |

## AMAZON.COM, INC.

## NOTES TO CONSOLIDATED FINANCIAL STATEMENTS—(Continued)

### Note 10—INCOME TAXES

In 2009, 2008 and 2007 we recorded net tax provisions of $253 million, $247 million, and $184 million. A majority of this provision is non-cash. We have current tax benefits and net operating losses relating to excess stock-based compensation that are being utilized to reduce our U.S. taxable income. As such, cash taxes paid, net of refunds, were $48 million, $53 million, and $24 million for 2009, 2008, and 2007.

The components of the provision for income taxes, net are as follows:

|  | Year Ended December 31, | | |
| --- | --- | --- | --- |
|  | 2009 | 2008 | 2007 |
|  | (in millions) | | |
| Current taxes: | | | |
| U.S. and state | $149 | $227 | $ 275 |
| International | 23 | 25 | 8 |
| Current taxes | 172 | 252 | 283 |
| Deferred taxes: | | | |
| U.S. and state | 89 | 3 | (109) |
| International | (8) | (8) | 10 |
| Deferred taxes | 81 | (5) | (99) |
| Provision for income taxes, net | $253 | $247 | $ 184 |

U.S. and international components of income before income taxes are as follows:

|  | Year Ended December 31, | | |
| --- | --- | --- | --- |
|  | 2009 | 2008 | 2007 |
|  | (in millions) | | |
| U.S. | $ 529 | $436 | $360 |
| International (1) | 632 | 465 | 300 |
| Income before income taxes | $1,161 | $901 | $660 |

(1) Included in 2008 is the impact of the $53 million non-cash gain associated with the sale of our European DVD rental assets. This gain was taxed at rates substantially below the 35% U.S. federal statutory rate.

The items accounting for differences between income taxes computed at the federal statutory rate and the provision recorded for income taxes are as follows:

|  | Year Ended December 31, | | |
| --- | --- | --- | --- |
|  | 2009 | 2008 | 2007 |
| Federal statutory rate | 35.0% | 35.0% | 35.0% |
| Effect of: | | | |
| Impact of foreign tax differential | (16.9) | (13.8) | (11.7) |
| State taxes, net of federal benefits | 1.1 | 2.8 | 2.1 |
| Tax credits | (0.4) | (2.2) | (1.1) |
| Nondeductible stock-based compensation | 1.7 | 1.7 | 1.4 |
| Valuation allowance | 0.4 | 2.6 | (1.2) |
| Other, net | 1.0 | 1.3 | 3.4 |
| Total | 21.9% | 27.4% | 27.9% |

66

## NOTES TO CONSOLIDATED FINANCIAL STATEMENTS—(Continued)

The effective tax rate in 2009, 2008, and 2007 was lower than the 35% U.S. federal statutory rate primarily due to earnings of our subsidiaries outside of the U.S. in jurisdictions where our effective tax rate is lower than in the U.S. Included in the total tax provision as a discrete item during 2008 is the impact related to the $53 million noncash gain associated with the sale of our European DVD rental assets. This gain was taxed at rates substantially below the 35% U.S. federal statutory rate.

Deferred income tax assets and liabilities are as follows:

| | December 31, | |
| --- | --- | --- |
| | 2009 | 2008 |
| | (in millions) | |
| Deferred tax assets: | | |
| Net operating losses—stock-based compensation (1) | $ 120 | $ 120 |
| Net operating losses—other | 50 | 31 |
| Net operating losses—obtained through acquisitions (2) | 7 | 14 |
| Stock-based compensation | 118 | 73 |
| Assets held for investment | 125 | 152 |
| Revenue items | 58 | 53 |
| Expense items | 172 | 155 |
| Other items | 42 | 40 |
| Net tax credits (3) | 6 | 2 |
| Total gross deferred tax assets | 698 | 640 |
| Less valuation allowance (4) | (173) | (199) |
| Deferred tax assets, net of valuation allowance | 525 | 441 |
| Deferred tax liabilities: | | |
| Basis difference in intangible assets | (218) | (80) |
| Expense items | (168) | (12) |
| Deferred tax assets, net of valuation allowance and deferred tax liabilities | $ 139 | $ 349 |

(1) Excludes unrecognized federal net operating loss carryforward deferred tax assets of $40 million and $73 million at December 31, 2009 and 2008. The total gross deferred tax assets relating to our federal excess stock-based compensation net operating loss carryforwards at December 31, 2009 and 2008 were $160 million and $193 million (relating to approximately $456 million and $550 million of our federal net operating loss carryforwards). The majority of our net operating loss carryforwards begin to expire in 2021 and thereafter.

(2) The utilization of some of these net operating loss carryforwards is subject to an annual limitation under applicable provisions of the Internal Revenue Code.

(3) Presented net of fully reserved deferred tax assets associated with tax credits of $193 million and $130 million at December 31, 2009 and 2008. Total tax credits available to be claimed in future years are approximately $199 million and $171 million as of December 31, 2009 and 2008, and begin to expire in 2017.

(4) Relates primarily to deferred tax assets that would only be realizable upon the generation of future capital gains and net income in certain foreign taxing jurisdictions.

### Tax Contingencies

We are subject to income taxes in the U.S. and numerous foreign jurisdictions. Significant judgment is required in evaluating our tax positions and determining our provision for income taxes. During the ordinary

67

**AMAZON.COM, INC.**

**NOTES TO CONSOLIDATED FINANCIAL STATEMENTS—(Continued)**

course of business, there are many transactions and calculations for which the ultimate tax determination is uncertain. We establish reserves for tax-related uncertainties based on estimates of whether, and the extent to which, additional taxes will be due. These reserves are established when we believe that certain positions might be challenged despite our belief that our tax return positions are fully supportable. We adjust these reserves in light of changing facts and circumstances, such as the outcome of tax audits. The provision for income taxes includes the impact of reserve provisions and changes to reserves that are considered appropriate.

The reconciliation of our tax contingencies is as follows (in millions):

| | December 31, | |
|---|---|---|
| | **2009** | **2008** |
| | (in millions) | |
| Gross tax contingencies—January 1, 2009 | $166 | $112 |
| Gross increases to tax positions in prior periods | 15 | 39 |
| Gross decreases to tax positions in prior periods | — | (4) |
| Gross increases to current period tax positions | 1 | 22 |
| Audit settlements paid during 2008 | — | (3) |
| Foreign exchange gain (loss) on tax contingencies | (1) | — |
| Gross tax contingencies—December 31, 2009 (1) | $181 | $166 |

_____

(1) As of December 31, 2009, we had $181 million of tax contingencies of which $180 million, if fully recognized, would decrease our effective tax rate and increase additional paid-in capital by $1 million to reflect the tax benefits of excess stock-based compensation deductions.

Due to the nature of our business operations we expect the total amount of tax contingencies for prior period tax positions will grow in 2010 in comparable amounts to 2009. We do not believe it is reasonably possible that the total amount of unrecognized tax benefits will significantly decrease in 2010. The increase to current period tax positions in 2008 resulted primarily from acquisition-related activity and new regulations.

As of December 31, 2009 and 2008, we had accrued interest and penalties, net of federal income tax benefit, related to tax contingencies of $17 million and $14 million. Interest and penalties, net of federal income tax benefit, recognized for the year ended December 31, 2009 and 2008 was $3 million and $5 million.

We are under examination, or may be subject to examination, by the Internal Revenue Service ("IRS") for calendar years 2005 through 2009. Additionally, any net operating losses that were generated in prior years and utilized in 2005 through 2009 may also be subject to examination by the IRS. We are under examination, or may be subject to examination, in the following major jurisdictions for the years specified: Kentucky for 2005 through 2009, France for 2006 through 2009, Germany for 2003 through 2009, Luxembourg for 2004 through 2009, and the United Kingdom for 2003 through 2009. In addition, in 2007, Japanese tax authorities assessed income tax, including penalties and interest, of approximately $120 million against one of our U.S. subsidiaries for the years 2003 through 2005. We believe that these claims are without merit and are disputing the assessment. Further proceedings on the assessment have been stayed during negotiations between U.S. and Japanese authorities over the double taxation issues the assessment raises, and we have provided bank guarantees to suspend enforcement of the assessment. We also may be subject to income tax examination by Japanese tax authorities for 2006 through 2009.

68

# AMAZON.COM, INC.

## NOTES TO CONSOLIDATED FINANCIAL STATEMENTS—(Continued)

### Note 11—SEGMENT INFORMATION

We have organized our operations into two principal segments: North America and International. We present our segment information along the same lines that our chief executive reviews our operating results in assessing performance and allocating resources.

We allocate to segment results the operating expenses "Fulfillment," "Marketing," "Technology and content," and "General and administrative," but exclude from our allocations the portions of these expense lines attributable to stock-based compensation. We do not allocate the line item "Other operating expense (income), net" to our segment operating results. A significant majority of our costs for "Technology and content" are incurred in the United States and most of these costs are allocated to our North America segment. There are no internal revenue transactions between our reporting segments.

*North America*

The North America segment consists of amounts earned from retail sales of consumer products (including from sellers) and subscriptions through North America-focused websites such as *www.amazon.com* and *www.amazon.ca*. This segment includes export sales from *www.amazon.com* and *www.amazon.ca*.

*International*

The International segment consists of amounts earned from retail sales of consumer products (including from sellers) and subscriptions through internationally focused websites such as *www.amazon.co.uk*, *www.amazon.de*, *www.amazon.co.jp*, *www.amazon.fr*, and *www.amazon.cn*. This segment includes export sales from these internationally based sites (including export sales from these sites to customers in the U.S. and Canada), but excludes export sales from *www.amazon.com* and *www.amazon.ca*.

69

Information on reportable segments and reconciliation to consolidated net income is as follows:

| | Year Ended December 31, | | |
| | 2009 | 2008 | 2007 |
|---|---|---|---|
| | (in millions) | | |
| **North America** | | | |
| Net sales | $12,828 | $10,228 | $ 8,095 |
| Cost of sales | 9,538 | 7,733 | 6,064 |
| Gross profit | 3,290 | 2,495 | 2,031 |
| Direct segment operating expenses | 2,581 | 2,050 | 1,631 |
| Segment operating income | $ 709 | $ 445 | $ 400 |
| **International** | | | |
| Net sales | $11,681 | $ 8,938 | $ 6,740 |
| Cost of sales | 9,440 | 7,163 | 5,418 |
| Gross profit | 2,241 | 1,775 | 1,322 |
| Direct segment operating expenses | 1,378 | 1,127 | 873 |
| Segment operating income | $ 863 | $ 648 | $ 449 |
| **Consolidated** | | | |
| Net sales | $24,509 | $19,166 | $14,835 |
| Cost of sales | 18,978 | 14,896 | 11,482 |
| Gross profit | 5,531 | 4,270 | 3,353 |
| Direct segment operating expenses | 3,959 | 3,177 | 2,504 |
| Segment operating income | 1,572 | 1,093 | 849 |
| Stock-based compensation | (341) | (275) | (185) |
| Other operating expense, net | (102) | 24 | (9) |
| Income from operations | 1,129 | 842 | 655 |
| Total non-operating income (expense), net | 32 | 59 | 5 |
| Provision for income taxes | (253) | (247) | (184) |
| Equity-method investment activity, net of tax | (6) | (9) | — |
| Net income | $ 902 | $ 645 | $ 476 |

Net sales shipped to customers outside of the U.S. represented approximately half of net sales for 2009, 2008, and 2007. Net sales from *www.amazon.de*, *www.amazon.co.jp*, and *www.amazon.co.uk* each represented 13% to 17% of consolidated net sales in 2009, 2008 and 2007.

Total assets, by segment, reconciled to consolidated amounts were (in millions):

| | December 31, | |
| | 2009 | 2008 |
|---|---|---|
| North America | $ 9,252 | $5,266 |
| International | 4,561 | 3,048 |
| Consolidated | $13,813 | $8,314 |

70

Fixed assets, net, by segment, reconciled to consolidated amounts were (in millions):

|  | December 31, | |
|  | 2009 | 2008 |
|---|---|---|
| North America | $1,059 | $666 |
| International | 231 | 188 |
| Consolidated | $1,290 | $854 |

Depreciation expense, by segment, is as follows (in millions):

|  | Year Ended December 31, | | |
|  | 2009 | 2008 | 2007 |
|---|---|---|---|
| North America | $327 | $262 | $212 |
| International | 57 | 49 | 46 |
| Consolidated | $384 | $311 | $258 |

## Note 12—QUARTERLY RESULTS (UNAUDITED)

The following tables contain selected unaudited statement of operations information for each quarter of 2009 and 2008. The following information reflects all normal recurring adjustments necessary for a fair presentation of the information for the periods presented. The operating results for any quarter are not necessarily indicative of results for any future period. Our business is affected by seasonality, which historically has resulted in higher sales volume during our fourth quarter.

Unaudited quarterly results are as follows (in millions, except per share data):

|  | Year Ended December 31, 2009 (1) | | | |
|  | Fourth Quarter | Third Quarter | Second Quarter | First Quarter |
|---|---|---|---|---|
| Net sales | $9,519 | $5,449 | $4,651 | $4,889 |
| Gross profit | 1,976 | 1,273 | 1,133 | 1,148 |
| Income before income taxes | 471 | 262 | 179 | 248 |
| Provision for income taxes | 85 | 60 | 39 | 69 |
| Net income | 384 | 199 | 142 | 177 |
| Basic earnings per share | $ 0.87 | $ 0.46 | $ 0.33 | $ 0.41 |
| Diluted earnings per share | $ 0.85 | $ 0.45 | $ 0.32 | $ 0.41 |
| Shares used in computation of earnings per share: | | | | |
| Basic | 440 | 432 | 431 | 429 |
| Diluted | 450 | 441 | 440 | 437 |

71

## AMAZON.COM, INC.

## NOTES TO CONSOLIDATED FINANCIAL STATEMENTS—(Continued)

|  | Year Ended December 31, 2008 (1) | | | |
| --- | --- | --- | --- | --- |
|  | Fourth Quarter | Third Quarter | Second Quarter | First Quarter |
| Net sales (2) | $6,704 | $4,264 | $4,063 | $4,135 |
| Gross profit | 1,348 | 999 | 967 | 956 |
| Income before income taxes | 302 | 182 | 208 | 207 |
| Provision for income taxes | 79 | 59 | 46 | 62 |
| Net income | 225 | 118 | 158 | 143 |
| Basic earnings per share | $ 0.52 | $ 0.28 | $ 0.38 | $ 0.34 |
| Diluted earnings per share | $ 0.52 | $ 0.27 | $ 0.37 | $ 0.34 |
| Shares used in computation of earnings per share: | | | | |
| Basic | 428 | 427 | 420 | 417 |
| Diluted | 436 | 436 | 430 | 426 |

(1)  The sum of quarterly amounts, including per share amounts, may not equal amounts reported for year-to-date periods. This is due to the effects of rounding and changes in the number of weighted-average shares outstanding for each period.

(2)  Our year-over-year revenue growth was 36% for the first three quarters of 2008. For Q4 2008, our quarterly revenue growth rates declined to 18%, driven primarily by decreased consumer demand following disruptions in the global financial markets and changes in foreign exchange rates (excluding the $320 million unfavorable impact from year-over-year changes in foreign exchange rates throughout the fourth quarter, net sales would have grown 24% compared with Q4 2007).

72

**Item 9.** *Changes in and Disagreements with Accountants On Accounting and Financial Disclosure*

None.

**Item 9A.** *Controls and Procedures*

*Evaluation of Disclosure Controls and Procedures*

We carried out an evaluation required by the 1934 Act, under the supervision and with the participation of our principal executive officer and principal financial officer, of the effectiveness of the design and operation of our disclosure controls and procedures, as defined in Rule 13a-15(e) of the 1934 Act, as of December 31, 2009. Based on this evaluation, our principal executive officer and principal financial officer concluded that, as of December 31, 2009, our disclosure controls and procedures were effective to provide reasonable assurance that information required to be disclosed by us in the reports that we file or submit under the 1934 Act is recorded, processed, summarized, and reported within the time periods specified in the SEC's rules and forms and to provide reasonable assurance that such information is accumulated and communicated to our management, including our principal executive officer and principal financial officer, as appropriate to allow timely decisions regarding required disclosures.

*Management's Report on Internal Control over Financial Reporting*

Management is responsible for establishing and maintaining adequate internal control over financial reporting, as defined in Rule 13a-15(f) of the 1934 Act. Management has assessed the effectiveness of our internal control over financial reporting as of December 31, 2009 based on criteria established in Internal Control—Integrated Framework issued by the Committee of Sponsoring Organizations of the Treadway Commission. As a result of this assessment, management concluded that, as of December 31, 2009, our internal control over financial reporting was effective in providing reasonable assurance regarding the reliability of financial reporting and the preparation of financial statements for external purposes in accordance with generally accepted accounting principles. Ernst & Young has independently assessed the effectiveness of our internal control over financial reporting and its report is included below.

*Changes in Internal Control Over Financial Reporting*

There were no changes in our internal control over financial reporting during the quarter ended December 31, 2009 that materially affected, or are reasonably likely to materially affect, our internal control over financial reporting.

*Limitations on Controls*

Our disclosure controls and procedures and internal control over financial reporting are designed to provide reasonable assurance of achieving their objectives as specified above. Management does not expect, however, that our disclosure controls and procedures or our internal control over financial reporting will prevent or detect all error and fraud. Any control system, no matter how well designed and operated, is based upon certain assumptions and can provide only reasonable, not absolute, assurance that its objectives will be met. Further, no evaluation of controls can provide absolute assurance that misstatements due to error or fraud will not occur or that all control issues and instances of fraud, if any, within the Company have been detected.

73

**Report of Ernst & Young LLP, Independent Registered Public Accounting Firm**

The Board of Directors and Stockholders
Amazon.com, Inc.

We have audited Amazon.com, Inc.'s internal control over financial reporting as of December 31, 2009, based on criteria established in Internal Control—Integrated Framework issued by the Committee of Sponsoring Organizations of the Treadway Commission (the COSO criteria). Amazon.com, Inc.'s management is responsible for maintaining effective internal control over financial reporting and for its assessment of the effectiveness of internal control over financial reporting included in the accompanying Management's Report on Internal Control over Financial Reporting. Our responsibility is to express an opinion on the Company's internal control over financial reporting based on our audit.

We conducted our audit in accordance with the standards of the Public Company Accounting Oversight Board (United States). Those standards require that we plan and perform the audit to obtain reasonable assurance about whether effective internal control over financial reporting was maintained in all material respects. Our audit included obtaining an understanding of internal control over financial reporting, assessing the risk that a material weakness exists, testing and evaluating the design and operating effectiveness of internal control based on the assessed risk, and performing such other procedures as we considered necessary in the circumstances. We believe that our audit provides a reasonable basis for our opinion.

A company's internal control over financial reporting is a process designed to provide reasonable assurance regarding the reliability of financial reporting and the preparation of financial statements for external purposes in accordance with generally accepted accounting principles. A company's internal control over financial reporting includes those policies and procedures that (1) pertain to the maintenance of records that, in reasonable detail, accurately and fairly reflect the transactions and dispositions of the assets of the company; (2) provide reasonable assurance that transactions are recorded as necessary to permit preparation of financial statements in accordance with generally accepted accounting principles, and that receipts and expenditures of the company are being made only in accordance with authorizations of management and directors of the company; and (3) provide reasonable assurance regarding prevention or timely detection of unauthorized acquisition, use, or disposition of the company's assets that could have a material effect on the financial statements.

Because of its inherent limitations, internal control over financial reporting may not prevent or detect misstatements. Also, projections of any evaluation of effectiveness to future periods are subject to the risk that controls may become inadequate because of changes in conditions, or that the degree of compliance with the policies or procedures may deteriorate.

In our opinion, Amazon.com, Inc. maintained, in all material respects, effective internal control over financial reporting as of December 31, 2009, based on the COSO criteria.

We have also audited, in accordance with the standards of the Public Company Accounting Oversight Board (United States), the consolidated balance sheets of Amazon.com, Inc. as of December 31, 2009 and 2008, and the related consolidated statements of operations, stockholders' equity, and cash flows for each of the three years in the period ended December 31, 2009 of Amazon.com, Inc. and our report dated January 28, 2010 expressed an unqualified opinion thereon.

/s/   Ernst & Young LLP

Seattle, Washington
January 28, 2010

**Item 9B.** *Other Information*

None.

## PART III

**Item 10.** *Directors, Executive Officers and Corporate Governance*

Information regarding our Executive Officers required by Item 10 of Part III is set forth in Item 1 of Part I "Business—Executive Officers and Directors." Information required by Item 10 of Part III regarding our Directors and any material changes to the process by which security holders may recommend nominees to the Board of Directors is included in our Proxy Statement relating to our 2010 Annual Meeting of Shareholders, and is incorporated herein by reference. Information relating to our Code of Business Conduct and Ethics and to compliance with Section 16(a) of the 1934 Act is set forth in our Proxy Statement relating to our 2010 Annual Meeting of Shareholders and is incorporated herein by reference. To the extent permissible under Nasdaq rules, we intend to disclose amendments to our Code of Business Conduct and Ethics, as well as waivers of the provisions thereof, on our investor relations website under the heading "Corporate Governance" at www.amazon.com/ir.

**Item 11.** *Executive Compensation*

Information required by Item 11 of Part III is included in our Proxy Statement relating to our 2010 Annual Meeting of Shareholders and is incorporated herein by reference.

**Item 12.** *Security Ownership of Certain Beneficial Owners and Management and Related Shareholder Matters*

Information required by Item 12 of Part III is included in our Proxy Statement relating to our 2010 Annual Meeting of Shareholders and is incorporated herein by reference.

**Item 13.** *Certain Relationships and Related Transactions*

Information required by Item 13 of Part III is included in our Proxy Statement relating to our 2010 Annual Meeting of Shareholders and is incorporated herein by reference.

**Item 14.** *Principal Accountant Fees and Services*

Information required by Item 14 of Part III is included in our Proxy Statement relating our 2010 Annual Meeting of Shareholders and is incorporated herein by reference.

## PART IV

**Item 15.** *Exhibits, Financial Statement Schedules*

(a) *List of Documents Filed as a Part of This Report:*

(1) *Index to Consolidated Financial Statements:*

Report of Ernst & Young LLP, Independent Registered Public Accounting Firm

Consolidated Statements of Cash Flows for each of the three years ended December 31, 2009

Consolidated Statements of Operations for each of the three years ended December 31, 2009

75

Consolidated Balance Sheets as of December 31, 2009 and 2008

Consolidated Statements of Stockholders' Equity for each of the three years ended December 31, 2009

Notes to Consolidated Financial Statements

Report of Ernst & Young LLP, Independent Registered Public Accounting Firm

(2) *Index to Exhibits*

See exhibits listed under the Exhibit Index below.

## SIGNATURES

Pursuant to the requirements of Section 13 or 15(d) of the Securities Exchange Act of 1934, the registrant has duly caused this Report to be signed on its behalf by the undersigned, thereunto duly authorized, as of January 28, 2010.

AMAZON.COM, INC.

By:         /S/   JEFFREY P. BEZOS

**Jeffrey P. Bezos**
**President, Chief Executive Officer**
**and Chairman of the Board**

Pursuant to the requirements of the Securities Exchange Act of 1934, this Report has been signed below by the following persons on behalf of the registrant and in the capacities indicated as of January 28, 2010.

| Signature | Title |
|---|---|
| /S/ JEFFREY P. BEZOS<br>**Jeffrey P. Bezos** | Chairman of the Board, President and Chief Executive Officer (Principal Executive Officer) |
| /S/ THOMAS J. SZKUTAK<br>**Thomas J. Szkutak** | Senior Vice President and Chief Financial Officer (Principal Financial Officer) |
| /S/ SHELLEY REYNOLDS<br>**Shelley Reynolds** | Vice President, Worldwide Controller (Principal Accounting Officer) |
| /S/ TOM A. ALBERG<br>**Tom A. Alberg** | Director |
| /S/ JOHN SEELY BROWN<br>**John Seely Brown** | Director |
| /S/ L. JOHN DOERR<br>**L. John Doerr** | Director |
| /S/ WILLIAM B. GORDON<br>**William B. Gordon** | Director |
| /S/ ALAIN MONIÉ<br>**Alain Monié** | Director |
| /S/ THOMAS O. RYDER<br>**Thomas O. Ryder** | Director |
| /S/ PATRICIA Q. STONESIFER<br>**Patricia Q. Stonesifer** | Director |

77

# Present Value Tables

**TABLE B-1** | **Present Value of $1**

Present Value

| Periods | 1% | 2% | 3% | 4% | 5% | 6% | 7% | 8% | 9% | 10% | 12% | 14% | 15% | 16% | 18% | 20% |
|---|---|---|---|---|---|---|---|---|---|---|---|---|---|---|---|---|
| 1 | 0.990 | 0.980 | 0.971 | 0.962 | 0.952 | 0.943 | 0.935 | 0.926 | 0.917 | 0.909 | 0.893 | 0.877 | 0.870 | 0.862 | 0.847 | 0.833 |
| 2 | 0.980 | 0.961 | 0.943 | 0.925 | 0.907 | 0.890 | 0.873 | 0.857 | 0.842 | 0.826 | 0.797 | 0.769 | 0.756 | 0.743 | 0.718 | 0.694 |
| 3 | 0.971 | 0.942 | 0.915 | 0.889 | 0.864 | 0.840 | 0.816 | 0.794 | 0.772 | 0.751 | 0.712 | 0.675 | 0.658 | 0.641 | 0.609 | 0.579 |
| 4 | 0.961 | 0.924 | 0.888 | 0.855 | 0.823 | 0.792 | 0.763 | 0.735 | 0.708 | 0.683 | 0.636 | 0.592 | 0.572 | 0.552 | 0.516 | 0.482 |
| 5 | 0.951 | 0.906 | 0.883 | 0.822 | 0.784 | 0.747 | 0.713 | 0.681 | 0.650 | 0.621 | 0.567 | 0.519 | 0.497 | 0.476 | 0.437 | 0.402 |
| 6 | 0.942 | 0.888 | 0.837 | 0.790 | 0.746 | 0.705 | 0.666 | 0.630 | 0.596 | 0.564 | 0.507 | 0.456 | 0.432 | 0.410 | 0.370 | 0.335 |
| 7 | 0.933 | 0.871 | 0.813 | 0.760 | 0.711 | 0.665 | 0.623 | 0.583 | 0.547 | 0.513 | 0.452 | 0.400 | 0.376 | 0.354 | 0.314 | 0.279 |
| 8 | 0.923 | 0.853 | 0.789 | 0.731 | 0.677 | 0.627 | 0.582 | 0.540 | 0.502 | 0.467 | 0.404 | 0.351 | 0.327 | 0.305 | 0.266 | 0.233 |
| 9 | 0.914 | 0.837 | 0.766 | 0.703 | 0.645 | 0.592 | 0.544 | 0.500 | 0.460 | 0.424 | 0.361 | 0.308 | 0.284 | 0.263 | 0.225 | 0.194 |
| 10 | 0.905 | 0.820 | 0.744 | 0.676 | 0.614 | 0.558 | 0.508 | 0.463 | 0.422 | 0.386 | 0.322 | 0.270 | 0.247 | 0.227 | 0.191 | 0.162 |
| 11 | 0.896 | 0.804 | 0.722 | 0.650 | 0.585 | 0.527 | 0.475 | 0.429 | 0.388 | 0.350 | 0.287 | 0.237 | 0.215 | 0.195 | 0.162 | 0.135 |
| 12 | 0.887 | 0.788 | 0.701 | 0.625 | 0.557 | 0.497 | 0.444 | 0.397 | 0.356 | 0.319 | 0.257 | 0.208 | 0.187 | 0.168 | 0.137 | 0.112 |
| 13 | 0.879 | 0.773 | 0.681 | 0.601 | 0.530 | 0.469 | 0.415 | 0.368 | 0.326 | 0.290 | 0.229 | 0.182 | 0.163 | 0.145 | 0.116 | 0.093 |
| 14 | 0.870 | 0.758 | 0.661 | 0.577 | 0.505 | 0.442 | 0.388 | 0.340 | 0.299 | 0.263 | 0.205 | 0.160 | 0.141 | 0.125 | 0.099 | 0.078 |
| 15 | 0.861 | 0.743 | 0.642 | 0.555 | 0.481 | 0.417 | 0.362 | 0.315 | 0.275 | 0.239 | 0.183 | 0.140 | 0.123 | 0.108 | 0.084 | 0.065 |
| 16 | 0.853 | 0.728 | 0.623 | 0.534 | 0.458 | 0.394 | 0.339 | 0.292 | 0.252 | 0.218 | 0.163 | 0.123 | 0.107 | 0.093 | 0.071 | 0.054 |
| 17 | 0.844 | 0.714 | 0.605 | 0.513 | 0.436 | 0.371 | 0.317 | 0.270 | 0.231 | 0.198 | 0.146 | 0.108 | 0.093 | 0.080 | 0.060 | 0.045 |
| 18 | 0.836 | 0.700 | 0.587 | 0.494 | 0.416 | 0.350 | 0.296 | 0.250 | 0.212 | 0.180 | 0.130 | 0.095 | 0.081 | 0.069 | 0.051 | 0.038 |
| 19 | 0.828 | 0.686 | 0.570 | 0.475 | 0.396 | 0.331 | 0.277 | 0.232 | 0.194 | 0.164 | 0.116 | 0.083 | 0.070 | 0.060 | 0.043 | 0.031 |
| 20 | 0.820 | 0.673 | 0.554 | 0.456 | 0.377 | 0.312 | 0.258 | 0.215 | 0.178 | 0.149 | 0.104 | 0.073 | 0.061 | 0.051 | 0.037 | 0.026 |
| 21 | 0.811 | 0.660 | 0.538 | 0.439 | 0.359 | 0.294 | 0.242 | 0.199 | 0.164 | 0.135 | 0.093 | 0.064 | 0.053 | 0.044 | 0.031 | 0.022 |
| 22 | 0.803 | 0.647 | 0.522 | 0.422 | 0.342 | 0.278 | 0.226 | 0.184 | 0.150 | 0.123 | 0.083 | 0.056 | 0.046 | 0.038 | 0.026 | 0.018 |
| 23 | 0.795 | 0.634 | 0.507 | 0.406 | 0.326 | 0.262 | 0.211 | 0.170 | 0.138 | 0.112 | 0.074 | 0.049 | 0.040 | 0.033 | 0.022 | 0.015 |
| 24 | 0.788 | 0.622 | 0.492 | 0.390 | 0.310 | 0.247 | 0.197 | 0.158 | 0.126 | 0.102 | 0.066 | 0.043 | 0.035 | 0.028 | 0.019 | 0.013 |
| 25 | 0.780 | 0.610 | 0.478 | 0.375 | 0.295 | 0.233 | 0.184 | 0.146 | 0.116 | 0.092 | 0.059 | 0.038 | 0.030 | 0.024 | 0.016 | 0.010 |
| 26 | 0.772 | 0.598 | 0.464 | 0.361 | 0.281 | 0.220 | 0.172 | 0.135 | 0.106 | 0.084 | 0.053 | 0.033 | 0.026 | 0.021 | 0.014 | 0.009 |
| 27 | 0.764 | 0.586 | 0.450 | 0.347 | 0.268 | 0.207 | 0.161 | 0.125 | 0.098 | 0.076 | 0.047 | 0.029 | 0.023 | 0.018 | 0.011 | 0.007 |
| 28 | 0.757 | 0.574 | 0.437 | 0.333 | 0.255 | 0.196 | 0.150 | 0.116 | 0.090 | 0.069 | 0.042 | 0.026 | 0.020 | 0.016 | 0.010 | 0.006 |
| 29 | 0.749 | 0.563 | 0.424 | 0.321 | 0.243 | 0.185 | 0.141 | 0.107 | 0.082 | 0.063 | 0.037 | 0.022 | 0.017 | 0.014 | 0.008 | 0.005 |
| 30 | 0.742 | 0.552 | 0.412 | 0.308 | 0.231 | 0.174 | 0.131 | 0.099 | 0.075 | 0.057 | 0.033 | 0.020 | 0.015 | 0.012 | 0.007 | 0.004 |
| 40 | 0.672 | 0.453 | 0.307 | 0.208 | 0.142 | 0.097 | 0.067 | 0.046 | 0.032 | 0.022 | 0.011 | 0.005 | 0.004 | 0.003 | 0.001 | 0.001 |
| 50 | 0.608 | 0.372 | 0.228 | 0.141 | 0.087 | 0.054 | 0.034 | 0.021 | 0.013 | 0.009 | 0.003 | 0.001 | 0.001 | 0.001 | | |

**TABLE B-2** | **Present Value of Annuity of $1**

Present Value

| Periods | 1% | 2% | 3% | 4% | 5% | 6% | 7% | 8% | 9% | 10% | 12% | 14% | 15% | 16% | 18% | 20% |
|---|---|---|---|---|---|---|---|---|---|---|---|---|---|---|---|---|
| 1 | 0.990 | 0.980 | 0.971 | 0.962 | 0.952 | 0.943 | 0.935 | 0.926 | 0.917 | 0.909 | 0.893 | 0.877 | 0.870 | 0.862 | 0.847 | 0.833 |
| 2 | 1.970 | 1.942 | 1.913 | 1.886 | 1.859 | 1.833 | 1.808 | 1.783 | 1.759 | 1.736 | 1.690 | 1.647 | 1.626 | 1.605 | 1.566 | 1.528 |
| 3 | 2.941 | 2.884 | 2.829 | 2.775 | 2.723 | 2.673 | 2.624 | 2.577 | 2.531 | 2.487 | 2.402 | 2.322 | 2.283 | 2.246 | 2.174 | 2.106 |
| 4 | 3.902 | 3.808 | 3.717 | 3.630 | 3.546 | 3.465 | 3.387 | 3.312 | 3.240 | 3.170 | 3.037 | 2.914 | 2.855 | 2.798 | 2.690 | 2.589 |
| 5 | 4.853 | 4.713 | 4.580 | 4.452 | 4.329 | 4.212 | 4.100 | 3.993 | 3.890 | 3.791 | 3.605 | 3.433 | 3.352 | 3.274 | 3.127 | 2.991 |
| 6 | 5.795 | 5.601 | 5.417 | 5.242 | 5.076 | 4.917 | 4.767 | 4.623 | 4.486 | 4.355 | 4.111 | 3.889 | 3.784 | 3.685 | 3.498 | 3.326 |
| 7 | 6.728 | 6.472 | 6.230 | 6.002 | 5.786 | 5.582 | 5.389 | 5.206 | 5.033 | 4.868 | 4.564 | 4.288 | 4.160 | 4.039 | 3.812 | 3.605 |
| 8 | 7.652 | 7.325 | 7.020 | 6.733 | 6.463 | 6.210 | 5.971 | 5.747 | 5.535 | 5.335 | 4.968 | 4.639 | 4.487 | 4.344 | 4.078 | 3.837 |
| 9 | 8.566 | 8.162 | 7.786 | 7.435 | 7.108 | 6.802 | 6.515 | 6.247 | 5.995 | 5.759 | 5.328 | 4.946 | 4.772 | 4.607 | 4.303 | 4.031 |
| 10 | 9.471 | 8.983 | 8.530 | 8.111 | 7.722 | 7.360 | 7.024 | 6.710 | 6.418 | 6.145 | 5.650 | 5.216 | 5.019 | 4.833 | 4.494 | 4.192 |
| 11 | 10.368 | 9.787 | 9.253 | 8.760 | 8.306 | 7.887 | 7.499 | 7.139 | 6.805 | 6.495 | 5.938 | 5.553 | 5.234 | 5.029 | 4.656 | 4.327 |
| 12 | 11.255 | 10.575 | 9.954 | 9.385 | 8.863 | 8.384 | 7.943 | 7.536 | 7.161 | 6.814 | 6.194 | 5.660 | 5.421 | 5.197 | 4.793 | 4.439 |
| 13 | 12.134 | 11.348 | 10.635 | 9.986 | 9.394 | 8.853 | 8.358 | 7.904 | 7.487 | 7.103 | 6.424 | 5.842 | 5.583 | 5.342 | 4.910 | 4.533 |
| 14 | 13.004 | 12.106 | 11.296 | 10.563 | 9.899 | 9.295 | 8.745 | 8.244 | 7.786 | 7.367 | 6.628 | 6.002 | 5.724 | 5.468 | 5.008 | 4.611 |
| 15 | 13.865 | 12.849 | 11.938 | 11.118 | 10.380 | 9.712 | 9.108 | 8.559 | 8.061 | 7.606 | 6.811 | 6.142 | 5.847 | 5.575 | 5.092 | 4.675 |
| 16 | 14.718 | 13.578 | 12.561 | 11.652 | 10.838 | 10.106 | 9.447 | 8.851 | 8.313 | 7.824 | 6.974 | 6.265 | 5.954 | 5.669 | 5.162 | 4.730 |
| 17 | 15.562 | 14.292 | 13.166 | 12.166 | 11.274 | 10.477 | 9.763 | 9.122 | 8.544 | 8.022 | 7.120 | 6.373 | 6.047 | 5.749 | 5.222 | 4.775 |
| 18 | 16.398 | 14.992 | 13.754 | 12.659 | 11.690 | 10.828 | 10.059 | 9.372 | 8.756 | 8.201 | 7.250 | 6.467 | 6.128 | 5.818 | 5.273 | 4.812 |
| 19 | 17.226 | 15.678 | 14.324 | 13.134 | 12.085 | 11.158 | 10.336 | 9.604 | 8.950 | 8.365 | 7.366 | 6.550 | 6.198 | 5.877 | 5.316 | 4.844 |
| 20 | 18.046 | 16.351 | 14.878 | 13.590 | 12.462 | 11.470 | 10.594 | 9.818 | 9.129 | 8.514 | 7.469 | 6.623 | 6.259 | 5.929 | 5.353 | 4.870 |
| 21 | 18.857 | 17.011 | 15.415 | 14.029 | 12.821 | 11.764 | 10.836 | 10.017 | 9.292 | 8.649 | 7.562 | 6.687 | 6.312 | 5.973 | 5.384 | 4.891 |
| 22 | 19.660 | 17.658 | 15.937 | 14.451 | 13.163 | 12.042 | 11.061 | 10.201 | 9.442 | 8.772 | 7.645 | 6.743 | 6.359 | 6.011 | 5.410 | 4.909 |
| 23 | 20.456 | 18.292 | 16.444 | 14.857 | 13.489 | 12.303 | 11.272 | 10.371 | 9.580 | 8.883 | 7.718 | 6.792 | 6.399 | 6.044 | 5.432 | 4.925 |
| 24 | 21.243 | 18.914 | 16.936 | 15.247 | 13.799 | 12.550 | 11.469 | 10.529 | 9.707 | 8.985 | 7.784 | 6.835 | 6.434 | 6.073 | 5.451 | 4.937 |
| 25 | 22.023 | 19.523 | 17.413 | 15.622 | 14.094 | 12.783 | 11.654 | 10.675 | 9.823 | 9.077 | 7.843 | 6.873 | 6.464 | 6.097 | 5.467 | 4.948 |
| 26 | 22.795 | 20.121 | 17.877 | 15.983 | 14.375 | 13.003 | 11.826 | 10.810 | 9.929 | 9.161 | 7.896 | 6.906 | 6.491 | 6.118 | 5.480 | 4.956 |
| 27 | 23.560 | 20.707 | 18.327 | 16.330 | 14.643 | 13.211 | 11.987 | 10.935 | 10.027 | 9.237 | 7.943 | 6.935 | 6.514 | 6.136 | 5.492 | 4.964 |
| 28 | 24.316 | 21.281 | 18.764 | 16.663 | 14.898 | 13.406 | 12.137 | 11.051 | 10.116 | 9.307 | 7.984 | 6.961 | 6.534 | 6.152 | 5.502 | 4.970 |
| 29 | 25.066 | 21.844 | 19.189 | 16.984 | 15.141 | 13.591 | 12.278 | 11.158 | 10.198 | 9.370 | 8.022 | 6.983 | 6.551 | 6.166 | 5.510 | 4.975 |
| 30 | 25.808 | 22.396 | 19.600 | 17.292 | 15.373 | 13.765 | 12.409 | 11.258 | 10.274 | 9.427 | 8.055 | 7.003 | 6.566 | 6.177 | 5.517 | 4.979 |
| 40 | 32.835 | 27.355 | 23.115 | 19.793 | 17.159 | 15.046 | 13.332 | 11.925 | 10.757 | 9.779 | 8.244 | 7.105 | 6.642 | 6.234 | 5.548 | 4.997 |
| 50 | 39.196 | 31.424 | 25.730 | 21.482 | 18.256 | 15.762 | 13.801 | 12.234 | 10.962 | 9.915 | 8.305 | 7.133 | 6.661 | 6.246 | 5.554 | 4.999 |

# Future Value Tables

**Future Value of $1**

Future Value

| Periods | 1% | 2% | 3% | 4% | 5% | 6% | 7% | 8% | 9% | 10% | 12% | 14% | 15% |
|---|---|---|---|---|---|---|---|---|---|---|---|---|---|
| 1 | 1.010 | 1.020 | 1.030 | 1.040 | 1.050 | 1.060 | 1.070 | 1.080 | 1.090 | 1.100 | 1.120 | 1.140 | 1.150 |
| 2 | 1.020 | 1.040 | 1.061 | 1.082 | 1.103 | 1.124 | 1.145 | 1.166 | 1.188 | 1.210 | 1.254 | 1.300 | 1.323 |
| 3 | 1.030 | 1.061 | 1.093 | 1.125 | 1.158 | 1.191 | 1.225 | 1.260 | 1.295 | 1.331 | 1.405 | 1.482 | 1.521 |
| 4 | 1.041 | 1.082 | 1.126 | 1.170 | 1.216 | 1.262 | 1.311 | 1.360 | 1.412 | 1.464 | 1.574 | 1.689 | 1.749 |
| 5 | 1.051 | 1.104 | 1.159 | 1.217 | 1.276 | 1.338 | 1.403 | 1.469 | 1.539 | 1.611 | 1.762 | 1.925 | 2.011 |
| 6 | 1.062 | 1.126 | 1.194 | 1.265 | 1.340 | 1.419 | 1.501 | 1.587 | 1.677 | 1.772 | 1.974 | 2.195 | 2.313 |
| 7 | 1.072 | 1.149 | 1.230 | 1.316 | 1.407 | 1.504 | 1.606 | 1.714 | 1.828 | 1.949 | 2.211 | 2.502 | 2.660 |
| 8 | 1.083 | 1.172 | 1.267 | 1.369 | 1.477 | 1.594 | 1.718 | 1.851 | 1.993 | 2.144 | 2.476 | 2.853 | 3.059 |
| 9 | 1.094 | 1.195 | 1.305 | 1.423 | 1.551 | 1.689 | 1.838 | 1.999 | 2.172 | 2.358 | 2.773 | 3.252 | 3.518 |
| 10 | 1.105 | 1.219 | 1.344 | 1.480 | 1.629 | 1.791 | 1.967 | 2.159 | 2.367 | 2.594 | 3.106 | 3.707 | 4.046 |
| 11 | 1.116 | 1.243 | 1.384 | 1.539 | 1.710 | 1.898 | 2.105 | 2.332 | 2.580 | 2.853 | 3.479 | 4.226 | 4.652 |
| 12 | 1.127 | 1.268 | 1.426 | 1.601 | 1.796 | 2.012 | 2.252 | 2.518 | 2.813 | 3.138 | 3.896 | 4.818 | 5.350 |
| 13 | 1.138 | 1.294 | 1.469 | 1.665 | 1.886 | 2.133 | 2.410 | 2.720 | 3.066 | 3.452 | 4.363 | 5.492 | 6.153 |
| 14 | 1.149 | 1.319 | 1.513 | 1.732 | 1.980 | 2.261 | 2.579 | 2.937 | 3.342 | 3.798 | 4.887 | 6.261 | 7.076 |
| 15 | 1.161 | 1.346 | 1.558 | 1.801 | 2.079 | 2.397 | 2.759 | 3.172 | 3.642 | 4.177 | 5.474 | 7.138 | 8.137 |
| 16 | 1.173 | 1.373 | 1.605 | 1.873 | 2.183 | 2.540 | 2.952 | 3.426 | 3.970 | 4.595 | 6.130 | 8.137 | 9.358 |
| 17 | 1.184 | 1.400 | 1.653 | 1.948 | 2.292 | 2.693 | 3.159 | 3.700 | 4.328 | 5.054 | 6.866 | 9.276 | 10.76 |
| 18 | 1.196 | 1.428 | 1.702 | 2.026 | 2.407 | 2.854 | 3.380 | 3.996 | 4.717 | 5.560 | 7.690 | 10.58 | 12.38 |
| 19 | 1.208 | 1.457 | 1.754 | 2.107 | 2.527 | 3.026 | 3.617 | 4.316 | 5.142 | 6.116 | 8.613 | 12.06 | 14.23 |
| 20 | 1.220 | 1.486 | 1.806 | 2.191 | 2.653 | 3.207 | 3.870 | 4.661 | 5.604 | 6.728 | 9.646 | 13.74 | 16.37 |
| 21 | 1.232 | 1.516 | 1.860 | 2.279 | 2.786 | 3.400 | 4.141 | 5.034 | 6.109 | 7.400 | 10.80 | 15.67 | 18.82 |
| 22 | 1.245 | 1.546 | 1.916 | 2.370 | 2.925 | 3.604 | 4.430 | 5.437 | 6.659 | 8.140 | 12.10 | 17.86 | 21.64 |
| 23 | 1.257 | 1.577 | 1.974 | 2.465 | 3.072 | 3.820 | 4.741 | 5.871 | 7.258 | 8.954 | 13.55 | 20.36 | 24.89 |
| 24 | 1.270 | 1.608 | 2.033 | 2.563 | 3.225 | 4.049 | 5.072 | 6.341 | 7.911 | 9.850 | 15.18 | 23.21 | 28.63 |
| 25 | 1.282 | 1.641 | 2.094 | 2.666 | 3.386 | 4.292 | 5.427 | 6.848 | 8.623 | 10.83 | 17.00 | 26.46 | 32.92 |
| 26 | 1.295 | 1.673 | 2.157 | 2.772 | 3.556 | 4.549 | 5.807 | 7.396 | 9.399 | 11.92 | 19.04 | 30.17 | 37.86 |
| 27 | 1.308 | 1.707 | 2.221 | 2.883 | 3.733 | 4.822 | 6.214 | 7.988 | 10.25 | 13.11 | 21.32 | 34.39 | 43.54 |
| 28 | 1.321 | 1.741 | 2.288 | 2.999 | 3.920 | 5.112 | 6.649 | 8.627 | 11.17 | 14.42 | 23.88 | 39.20 | 50.07 |
| 29 | 1.335 | 1.776 | 2.357 | 3.119 | 4.116 | 5.418 | 7.114 | 9.317 | 12.17 | 15.86 | 26.75 | 44.69 | 57.58 |
| 30 | 1.348 | 1.811 | 2.427 | 3.243 | 4.322 | 5.743 | 7.612 | 10.06 | 13.27 | 17.45 | 29.96 | 50.95 | 66.21 |
| 40 | 1.489 | 2.208 | 3.262 | 4.801 | 7.040 | 10.29 | 14.97 | 21.72 | 31.41 | 45.26 | 93.05 | 188.9 | 267.9 |
| 50 | 1.645 | 2.692 | 4.384 | 7.107 | 11.47 | 18.42 | 29.46 | 46.90 | 74.36 | 117.4 | 289.0 | 700.2 | 1,084 |

**TABLE B-4** | **Future Value of Annuity of $1**

Future Value

| Periods | 1% | 2% | 3% | 4% | 5% | 6% | 7% | 8% | 9% | 10% | 12% | 14% | 15% |
|---|---|---|---|---|---|---|---|---|---|---|---|---|---|
| 1 | 1.000 | 1.000 | 1.000 | 1.000 | 1.000 | 1.000 | 1.000 | 1.000 | 1.000 | 1.000 | 1.000 | 1.000 | 1.000 |
| 2 | 2.010 | 2.020 | 2.030 | 2.040 | 2.050 | 2.060 | 2.070 | 2.080 | 2.090 | 2.100 | 2.120 | 2.140 | 2.150 |
| 3 | 3.030 | 3.060 | 3.091 | 3.122 | 3.153 | 3.184 | 3.215 | 3.246 | 3.278 | 3.310 | 3.374 | 3.440 | 3.473 |
| 4 | 4.060 | 4.122 | 4.184 | 4.246 | 4.310 | 4.375 | 4.440 | 4.506 | 4.573 | 4.641 | 4.779 | 4.921 | 4.993 |
| 5 | 5.101 | 5.204 | 5.309 | 5.416 | 5.526 | 5.637 | 5.751 | 5.867 | 5.985 | 6.105 | 6.353 | 6.610 | 6.742 |
| 6 | 6.152 | 6.308 | 6.468 | 6.633 | 6.802 | 6.975 | 7.153 | 7.336 | 7.523 | 7.716 | 8.115 | 8.536 | 8.754 |
| 7 | 7.214 | 7.434 | 7.662 | 7.898 | 8.142 | 8.394 | 8.654 | 8.923 | 9.200 | 9.487 | 10.09 | 10.73 | 11.07 |
| 8 | 8.286 | 8.583 | 8.892 | 9.214 | 9.549 | 9.897 | 10.26 | 10.64 | 11.03 | 11.44 | 12.30 | 13.23 | 13.73 |
| 9 | 9.369 | 9.755 | 10.16 | 10.58 | 11.03 | 11.49 | 11.98 | 12.49 | 13.02 | 13.58 | 14.78 | 16.09 | 16.79 |
| 10 | 10.46 | 10.95 | 11.46 | 12.01 | 12.58 | 13.18 | 13.82 | 14.49 | 15.19 | 15.94 | 17.55 | 19.34 | 20.30 |
| 11 | 11.57 | 12.17 | 12.81 | 13.49 | 14.21 | 14.97 | 15.78 | 16.65 | 17.56 | 18.53 | 20.65 | 23.04 | 24.35 |
| 12 | 12.68 | 13.41 | 14.19 | 15.03 | 15.92 | 16.87 | 17.89 | 18.98 | 20.14 | 21.38 | 24.13 | 27.27 | 29.00 |
| 13 | 13.81 | 14.68 | 15.62 | 16.63 | 17.71 | 18.88 | 20.14 | 21.50 | 22.95 | 24.52 | 28.03 | 32.09 | 34.35 |
| 14 | 14.95 | 15.97 | 17.09 | 18.29 | 19.60 | 21.02 | 22.55 | 24.21 | 26.02 | 27.98 | 32.39 | 37.58 | 40.50 |
| 15 | 16.10 | 17.29 | 18.60 | 20.02 | 21.58 | 23.28 | 25.13 | 27.15 | 29.36 | 31.77 | 37.28 | 43.84 | 47.58 |
| 16 | 17.26 | 18.64 | 20.16 | 21.82 | 23.66 | 25.67 | 27.89 | 30.32 | 33.00 | 35.95 | 42.75 | 50.98 | 55.72 |
| 17 | 18.43 | 20.01 | 21.76 | 23.70 | 25.84 | 28.21 | 30.84 | 33.75 | 36.97 | 40.54 | 48.88 | 59.12 | 65.08 |
| 18 | 19.61 | 21.41 | 23.41 | 25.65 | 28.13 | 30.91 | 34.00 | 37.45 | 41.30 | 45.60 | 55.75 | 68.39 | 75.84 |
| 19 | 20.81 | 22.84 | 25.12 | 27.67 | 30.54 | 33.76 | 37.38 | 41.45 | 46.02 | 51.16 | 63.44 | 78.97 | 88.21 |
| 20 | 22.02 | 24.30 | 26.87 | 29.78 | 33.07 | 36.79 | 41.00 | 45.76 | 51.16 | 57.28 | 72.05 | 91.02 | 102.4 |
| 21 | 23.24 | 25.78 | 28.68 | 31.97 | 35.72 | 39.99 | 44.87 | 50.42 | 56.76 | 64.00 | 81.70 | 104.8 | 118.8 |
| 22 | 24.47 | 27.30 | 30.54 | 34.25 | 38.51 | 43.39 | 49.01 | 55.46 | 62.87 | 71.40 | 92.50 | 120.4 | 137.6 |
| 23 | 25.72 | 28.85 | 32.45 | 36.62 | 41.43 | 47.00 | 53.44 | 60.89 | 69.53 | 79.54 | 104.6 | 138.3 | 159.3 |
| 24 | 26.97 | 30.42 | 34.43 | 39.08 | 44.50 | 50.82 | 58.18 | 66.76 | 76.79 | 88.50 | 118.2 | 158.7 | 184.2 |
| 25 | 28.24 | 32.03 | 36.46 | 41.65 | 47.73 | 54.86 | 63.25 | 73.11 | 84.70 | 98.35 | 133.3 | 181.9 | 212.8 |
| 26 | 29.53 | 33.67 | 38.55 | 44.31 | 51.11 | 59.16 | 68.68 | 79.95 | 93.32 | 109.2 | 150.3 | 208.3 | 245.7 |
| 27 | 30.82 | 35.34 | 40.71 | 47.08 | 54.67 | 63.71 | 74.48 | 87.35 | 102.7 | 121.1 | 169.4 | 238.5 | 283.6 |
| 28 | 32.13 | 37.05 | 42.93 | 49.97 | 58.40 | 68.53 | 80.70 | 95.34 | 113.0 | 134.2 | 190.7 | 272.9 | 327.1 |
| 29 | 33.45 | 38.79 | 45.22 | 52.97 | 62.32 | 73.64 | 87.35 | 104.0 | 124.1 | 148.6 | 214.6 | 312.1 | 377.2 |
| 30 | 34.78 | 40.57 | 47.58 | 56.08 | 66.44 | 79.06 | 94.46 | 113.3 | 136.3 | 164.5 | 241.3 | 356.8 | 434.7 |
| 40 | 48.89 | 60.40 | 75.40 | 95.03 | 120.8 | 154.8 | 199.6 | 259.1 | 337.9 | 442.6 | 767.1 | 1,342 | 1,779 |
| 50 | 64.46 | 84.58 | 112.8 | 152.7 | 209.3 | 290.3 | 406.5 | 573.8 | 815.1 | 1,164 | 2,400 | 4,995 | 7,218 |

# Glindex
*A Combined Glossary/Subject Index*

## A

Accelerated Depreciation Method. A depreciation method that writes off more of the asset's cost near the start of its useful life than the straight-line method does. 462, 479

Account. The detailed record of all the changes that have occurred in a particular asset, liability, or owner's equity (stockholders' equity) during a period. The basic summary device of accounting. 63, 98
  normal balance of 72
  opening the 69

Account form 212

Account numbers 65

Account Payable. A liability backed by the general reputation and credit standing of the debtor. 15, 36

Account Receivable. The right to receive cash in the future from customers to whom the business has sold goods or for whom the business has performed services. 15, 36

Accounting, and the business environment 1
  accounting vocabulary 2, 36–37
  apply your knowledge
    communication activity 61
    decision cases 58–59
    ethical issues 59
    financial statement case 60
    fraud case 60
    team projects 60–61
  assess your progress
    exercises 39–46, 56
    practice set, 57
    problems 47–55, 56
  business organizations, types of 5–7
  concepts and principles 9–11
  destination: student success 37
  ethics in 5
  governing organizations 4–5
  major business decisions, guidelines for 25
  profession of 4–5
  quick check 38–39
  standards of professional conduct 5
  summary problem 26–27
  transactions in 13–18
    analysis (demo doc) 28–35
    evaluating, user perspective of 18–22
  users of accounting information 2–3

Accounting. The information system that measures business activities, processes that information into reports, and communicates the results to decision makers. 2, 36
  accrual vs. cash-basis 131–32
  financial 2
  managerial 3
  separating from operations 359

Accounting conservatism 313

Accounting Cycle. Process by which companies produce their financial statements for a specific period. 199, 228
  of merchandiser 276

Accounting cycle, completing 199
  accounting ratios 213–214

accounting vocabulary 228
accounting worksheet 200–202
adjusting entries, recording 204–207
apply your knowledge
  communication activity 253
  decision case 251
  ethical issue 251–252
  financial statement case 252
  fraud case 252
  team project 252–253
assess your progress
  exercises 230–238, 249
  practice set 250
  problems 239–249, 250
assets and liabilities, classifying 210–213
balance sheet
  classified 211–212
  forms 212–213
closing the accounts 207–209
decision guidelines 215
demo doc 220–227
destination: student success 228–229
financial statements, preparing 204
post-closing trial balance 210
quick check 229–230
summary problems 202–203, 216–219

Accounting data
  flow of 73

Accounting Equation. The basic tool of accounting, measuring the resources of the business and the claims to those resources: Assets = Liabilities + Equity. 11–13, 36, 63
  assets and liabilities 11
  owner's equity 12
  rules of debit and credit and 68, 71
  transaction analysis using (demo doc) 28–35

Accounting period 132–133

Accounting process
  decision guidelines 152

Accounting profession 4–5

Accounting ratios 213–214
  current ratio 214
  debt ratio 214

Accounting records
  accuracy of 356

Accounting worksheet 200–202

Accounts
  permanent 207
  reasons for adjusting 135–136
  temporary 207, 208

Accounts payable 64, 497

Accounts receivable 63

Accounts Receivable Turnover Ratio. A ratio that measures the number of times the company sells and collects the average receivables balance in a year. To compute accounts receivable turnover, divide net credit sales by average net accounts receivable. 425, 428, 736–737, 749

Accrual. The cash payment occurs after an expense is recorded or the cash is received after the revenue is earned. 136, 162

Accrual-Basis Accounting. Accounting that records revenues when earned and expenses when incurred. 131, 166, 1017
  vs. cash-basis accounting 131–32
  ethical issues in 151

Accrued Expense. An expense that the business has incurred but not yet paid. 136, 140–142, 166

Accrued expenses (accrued liabilities) 499

Accrued Liability. A liability for which the business knows the amount owed but the bill has not been paid. 64, 98

Accrued Revenue. A revenue that has been earned but for which the cash has not been collected yet. 142–143, 166

Accumulated Depreciation. The sum of all depreciation expense recorded to date for an asset. 139, 166

Acid-Test Ratio. Ratio of the sum of cash plus short-term investments plus net current receivables to total current liabilities. Tells whether the entity could pay all its current liabilities if they came due immediately. Also called the quick ratio. 424, 428, 734–735

Acquisitions
  computing 670–671

Activity-Based Costing (ABC). Focuses on activities as the fundamental cost objects. The costs of those activities become the building blocks for allocating the costs of products and services. 882, 902
  accounting vocabulary 902
  activity-based management, using ABC
    for decision making 886–890
    for cost cutting 887–890
    for pricing and product mix decisions 886–887
  apply your knowledge
    communication activity, 923
    decision cases 919–920
    ethical issue 920
    fraud case 920–921
    team project 921–922
  assess your progress
    exercises 904–913, 918
    problems 913–918, 919–920
  decision guidelines 891
  destination: student success 902
  developing system of 883
  refining cost systems 881–886
  quick check 903–904
  summary problems 892–893
  vs. traditional costing systems 883–886

Activity-Based Management (ABM). Using activity-based cost information to make decisions that increase profits while satisfying customers' needs. 886, 902
  cost cutting 887–890
  pricing and product mix decisions 886–887

Additional Paid-In Capital. The paid-in capital in excess of par plus other accounts combined for reporting on the

**Time (Period).** The period of time during which interest is computed. It extends from the original date of the note to the maturity date. Also called the note term or interest period. 419, 429

**Time record** 828

**Time Value of Money.** Recognition that money earns income over time. 538, 550, 565, 1021
  factors affecting 1021
  future/present value factors 1023
  future/present values: points along the time line 1022
  single sums and annuities, calculating future values using FV factors 1023–1024
  single sums and annuities, calculating present values using PV factors 1024–1025

**Time-and-a-half** 505

**Time-based competition** 776

**Time-Period Concept.** Ensures that information is reported at least annually. 134–135, 166

**Times-Interest-Earned Ratio.** Ratio of EBIT to interest expense. Measures the number of times that EBIT can cover (pay) interest expense. Also called the interest-coverage ratio. 738, 749

**Timing Difference.** Differences that arise between the balance on the bank statement and the balance on the books because of a time lag in recording transactions. 364, 382

**Tombstones** 585

**Total Fixed Costs.** Costs that do not change over wide changes in volume. 926, 946

**Total Quality Management (TQM).** A philosophy designed to integrate all organizational areas in order to provide customers with superior products and services, while meeting organizational goals throughout the value chain. 777, 794, 897

**Total Variable Costs.** Costs that change in total in direct proportion to changes in volume. 925, 946

**Traceable fixed costs.** Fixed costs that can be directly associated with an individual product, division, or business segment. A traceable fixed cost would disappear if the company discontinued making the product or discontinued operating the division or the segment. 1077, 1084
  assigning 1077

**Trade Names.** Assets that represent distinctive identifications of a product or service. Also called brand names. 474, 480

**Trade Receivables.** Amounts to be collected from customers from sales made on credit. Also called Accounts receivable. 405, 429

**Trademarks.** Assets that represent distinctive identifications of a product or service. 474, 480

**Trading on the Equity.** Earning more income on borrowed money than the related interest expense, thereby increasing the earnings for the owners of the business. Also called leverage. 740, 749

**Training** 1152

**Transaction.** An event that affects the financial position of a particular entity and can be measured and recorded reliably. 13, 37
  accounting for 13–18

**Transactions, and recording business**
  accounting vocabulary 98
  analyzing and recording
    debit/credit (demo docs) 89–97
    decision guidelines for 84
  apply your knowledge
    communication activity, 129
    decision cases 127–128
    ethical issue 128
    financial statement case 129
    fraud case 128
    team project 129
  assess your progress
    exercises 101–109, 125
    practice set 127
    problems 109–125, 126
  destination: student success 98
  dual effects of 67
  journalizing and posting 73–80
  quick check 99–100
  steps in recording process 69–72

**Transaction date** 81

**Transferability of ownership**
  of proprietorship 8

**Transferred-In Costs.** Costs that were incurred in a previous process and brought into a later process as part of the product's cost. 834, 868

**Transportation costs** 260–262, 304, 349
  recording, 304

**Transposition** 81

**Treasurer.** In a large company, the person in charge of writing checks. 359, 382

**Treasury Stock.** A corporation's own stock that it has previously issued and later reacquired. 629–631, 645
  basics of 629
  computing, on statement of cash flows 672–673
  decision guidelines for 634
  limits on purchases 632
  purchase of 629–630
  retirement of 631
  sale of 630–631

**Trend Analysis.** A form of horizontal analysis in which percentages are computed by selecting a base year as 100% and expressing amounts for following years as a percentage of the base amount. 726, 749

**Trial Balance.** A list of all the accounts with their balances at a point in time. 63, 80, 98
  adjusted 147–148
  balance sheet vs. 80
  error correction 81
  post-closing 210

  preparing from T-accounts 80–83
  summary problem 85–88
  unadjusted 135

**Trojan.** A malicious computer program that hides inside a legitimate program and works like a virus. 360, 382

**U**

**Unadjusted trial balance** 135

**Uncollectible Account Expense.** Cost to the seller of extending credit. Arises from the failure to collect from credit customers. Also called doubtful account expense or bad debt expense. 407, 429
  identifying and writing off, 411

**Underallocated (Manufacturing) Overhead.** Occurs when the manufacturing overhead allocated to Work in process inventory is less than the amount of manufacturing overhead costs actually incurred. 825, 827, 834

**Underwriter.** A firm, such as Morgan Stanley, that usually agrees to buy all the stock a company wants to issue if the firm cannot sell the stock to its clients. 585, 603

**Unearned Revenue.** A liability created when a business collects cash from customers in advance of doing work. Also called deferred revenue. 143–147, 166, 500

**Unemployment Compensation Tax.** Payroll tax paid by employers to the government, which uses the money to pay unemployment benefits to people who are out of work. 508, 515

**Unit costs** 779, 781, 814

**Unit managers**
  communication with 1154
  motivating 1154

**Unit product costs** 814
  calculating 789–790

**Units-of-Production (UOP) Depreciation Method.** Depreciation method by which a fixed amount of depreciation is assigned to each unit of output produced by an asset. 459, 461, 464, 480

**Untraceable fixed costs.** Fixed costs that cannot be directly associated with an individual product, division, or business segment. Also called common fixed costs. 1077, 1084

**V**

**Value Engineering.** Reevaluating activities to reduce costs while satisfying customer needs. 887, 902

**Value Chain.** Includes all activities that add value to a company's products and services. 777, 794

**Variable Costs.** Costs that increase or decrease in total in direct proportion to increases or decreases in the volume of activity. 925, 938, 946

**Variance.** The difference between an actual amount and the budgeted amount. Labeled as favorable if it increases operating

# Company Index